TRANSFORMATIONS

Women, Gender, and Psychology

THIRD EDITION

Mary Crawford

University of Connecticut

Mc
Graw
Hill
Education

TRANSFORMATIONS: WOMEN, GENDER, AND PSYCHOLOGY,
THIRD EDITION

Published by McGraw-Hill Education, 2 Penn Plaza, New York, NY 10121. Copyright © 2018 by McGraw-Hill
Education. All rights reserved. Printed in the United States of America. Previous editions © 2012 and 2006. No
part of this publication may be reproduced or distributed in any form or by any means, or stored in a database or
retrieval system, without the prior written consent of McGraw-Hill Education, including, but not limited to, in
any network or other electronic storage or transmission, or broadcast for distance learning.

Some ancillaries, including electronic and print components, may not be available to customers outside the
United States.

This book is printed on acid-free paper.

1 2 3 4 5 6 7 8 9 LCR 21 20 19 18 17

ISBN 978-0-078-02698-0
MHID 0-078-02698-9

Portfolio Manager: *Jamie Laferrera*
Product Developer: *Francesca King*
Marketing Manager: *Augustine Laferrera*
Content Project Manager: *Maria McGreal*
Buyer: *Sue Culbertson*
Design: *Lumina Datamatics*
Content Licensing Specialist: *Melisa Seegmiller*
Cover Image: ©Kirsten *Hinte / 123RF*
Compositor: *Lumina Datamatics*

All credits appearing on page or at the end of the book are considered to be an extension of the copyright page.

Library of Congress Cataloging-in-Publication Data

Cataloging-in-Publication Data has been requested from the Library of Congress.

The Internet addresses listed in the text were accurate at the time of publication. The inclusion of a website does
not indicate an endorsement by the authors or McGraw-Hill Education, and McGraw-Hill Education does not
guarantee the accuracy of the information presented at these sites.

mheducation.com/highered

In memory of my daughter
Mary Ellen Drummer
A feminist voice stilled too soon

∾

About the Author

∾

MARY CRAWFORD is Professor Emerita of Psychology and former director of the Women's Studies Program at the University of Connecticut. As a faculty member at West Chester University of Pennsylvania, she earned the Trustees' Award for Lifetime Achievement for her research and teaching on women and gender. She has also held the Jane W. Irwin Chair in Women's Studies at Hamilton College, served as distinguished Visiting Teacher/Scholar at the College of New Jersey, and directed the graduate program in Women's Studies at the University of South Carolina. Professor Crawford received her PhD in experimental psychology from the University of Delaware. She has served as a consulting editor for *Sex Roles*, an associate editor of *Feminism & Psychology,* and is a Fellow of both the American Psychological Association and the American Psychological Society. Mary Crawford has spoken and written about the psychology of women and gender for audiences as diverse as the British Psychological Society, *Ms.* Magazine, and the Oprah Winfrey Show. In addition to more than 120 publications on women and gender, she has written or edited 10 books including *Gender and Thought: Psychological Perspectives* (1989); *Talking Difference: On Gender and Language* (1995); *Gender Differences in Human Cognition* (1997); *Coming Into Her Own: Educational Success in Girls and Women* (1999); and *Innovative Methods for Feminist Psychological Research* (1999), which received the Distinguished Publication Award from the Association for Women in Psychology. As a Fulbright Senior Scholar, she lived and worked in Kathmandu, Nepal, where she collaborated with Nepali NGOs to develop interventions to reduce sex trafficking. Her book, *Sex Trafficking in South Asia: Telling Maya's Story* (2011), is both a memoir about the experience of doing research with women in Nepal and a feminist analysis of sex trafficking in South Asia.

Contents

∾

Chapter 9   Mothering   268

Preface

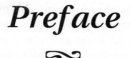

As I wrote this edition of *Transformations* during the latter half of 2016 and the first half of 2017, the larger social and political context was very much on my mind. While I summarized the latest research on such topics as women's leadership, backlash against competent women, sexual harassment, transgender identity, reproductive justice, and feminist activism, a presidential election campaign was being held. For the first time in American history, it pitted a male and a female candidate from the two major political parties against each other, and it was remarkably bitter and divisive.

During this time period, sexual assault and harassment were constantly in the news: Donald Trump was caught on tape bragging about grabbing women by the genitals, and retaliated with accusations about former president Bill Clinton; Fox News head Roger Ailes was forced to resign after a longtime culture of harassment at the network was revealed; and a pending sexual assault lawsuit against Bill Cosby repeatedly made headlines. A "bathroom bill" discriminating against trans people was on, off, and on again. State legislatures and the Trump administration moved to restrict women's reproductive rights in the U.S. and around the world. And this was just the United States. Globally, girls and women were being kidnapped and held as sex slaves by terrorist groups. Nearly two out of five female murder victims were killed by partners or former partners. Two-thirds of the world's illiterate people were female; and sex trafficking continued unabated.

As I joined the millions of people who marched in global protest on January 21, 2017, I thought: Whatever one's stance on political or social issues, gender is still a very important category. Gender *matters*—to each of us as an individual, as social beings, and as citizens.

Writing this book during a period of national ferment about gender issues was a powerful experience in the importance of feminist theory, research, scholarship, and activism for the 21st century. It is more important than ever to bring accurate information to students and to help them learn how to think critically and compassionately about women's lives. Empirical social science, interpretive analysis grounded in the lived experience of women, and critical thinking skills are tools for fighting sexism and misinformation. The research presented in this third edition of *Transformations* reflects my sincere effort to offer you the best of feminist psychological scholarship for your classroom.

I wrote this book originally to share my excitement about the psychology of women and gender. I chose *Transformations* for the title because this book explores many kinds of transformations. As I complete the third edition, the concept of transformation remains central to my thinking about this branch of psychology.

First, this book reflects the developmental transformations of a woman's life. Each person who is labeled female at birth progresses in turn from gender-innocent infant to gender-socialized child; from girl to woman; and from young woman to old woman. The process of developing a gender identity and a sexual identity are transformative. Think too of the transformation from sexual inexperience to sexual maturity and agency, and the shift in identity that happens as a young person goes from being a student to a working adult or an older person retires from paid work. Motherhood is another profound transformation of self, roles, and behavior. And, too often, girls and women victimized by gender-based violence are forced to transform themselves from victim to survivor. Being a woman is not a static condition, but rather a dynamic, ever-shifting social construction.

A second meaning of my title reflects the transformation within psychology that made this book, and others like it, possible. In the past, women were routinely omitted from psychology textbooks, research on women was scarce or negatively biased, and women themselves encountered resistance to becoming psychologists and engaging in research and practice. Today, the psychology of women and gender is a flourishing part of psychology. The perspectives of feminist psychology have changed research, practice, and theory in every area of psychology. Women now earn the majority of professional degrees in psychology, and most psychology departments offer courses in women and gender. These changes, which came about through feminist activism and struggle, have been astonishingly successful.

I've been teaching the psychology of women and gender since 1975 and writing about it for students since 1992. I'm gratified that the first two editions of *Transformations* were adopted by many instructors and became student favorites. After describing the book's distinguishing features and conceptual framework, I'll focus on what's new in this edition.

A Focus on Multiculturalism, Diversity, and Intersectionality

Throughout this book, U.S. women of color and women from other cultures are central in research and theory. This starts in Chapter 1, where Black feminist, transnational, and global feminist perspectives are introduced and gender is compared to other systems of social classification such as race and ethnicity. I define the concept of intersectionality in Chapter 1 and discuss its importance for feminist psychology, setting the stage for integrating intersectional research into topical chapters that follow. By introducing this key theoretical principle of feminist studies under a major heading, I signal its importance. In the chapters that follow, I apply intersectional analyses to such issues as micro-aggressions, minority stress, multiple oppressions, stereotype threat, sexual harassment, sex discrimination at work, and the effects of being privileged on some dimensions but not others.

The emphasis on systemic oppression continues in Chapter 2 with extended discussion of how systems of social classification are linked and mutually reinforcing. Chapter 4, The Meanings of Difference, focuses on the social dimensions that define difference and cause some groups to be evaluated as less worthy than others. Having set the theoretical framework for integrating intersectionality and a social constructionist perspective on difference, each chapter for the remainder of the book incorporates the experiences of women of diverse sexualities, ethnicities, social classes, (dis)abilities, nationalities, and ages.

Fortunately, there is an increasing amount of research being done with lesbian, gay, and transgender people; with women and men of color; with people who have disabilities; and with international populations. Integrating these dimensions of diversity throughout the book, I explore how they structure girls' and women's experiences including gender socialization, adult relationships, parenting, physical health, and psychological well-being.

Every chapter incorporates dimensions of diversity and explores the intersectionality of identities along these dimensions. Here are a few examples: studies of lesbian married couples (Chapter 8); ethnic diversity and sexual identities (Chapter 7); stereotypes of race/ethnicity and social class (Chapter 3); culture, ethnicity, and the expression of emotion (Chapter 4); the wage gap, workplace sex discrimination, and sexual harassment in relation to ethnicity and gender (Chapter 10); cross-cultural differences in aging and in attitudes toward the elderly (Chapter 11); sexual scripts across ethnic groups and cultures (Chapter 7); feminist therapy for diverse women (Chapter 13); disability and sexuality (Chapter 7); the diversity of women who mother, including ethnic minorities, teen mothers, trans parents, and lesbian mothers (Chapter 9); and the effects of ethnicity and social class on gender socialization (Chapter 6).

Cross-cultural perspectives are valuable for many reasons. First, they can help students learn that what seems natural, normal, and perhaps biologically ordained in their own culture is not universal. Second, they can foster critical thinking on women's status and rights as a global problem. Finally, girls and women whose voices were formerly silenced and whose presence was invisible are now seen and heard. Textbooks like this can play a part in transforming psychology from its formerly White, middle-class North American focus into a psychology of all people. For all these reasons, I am passionate about making sure this book reflects women in all their diversity.

Gender: A Social System Linked to Status and Power

Transformations presents a broad, comprehensive theoretical framework for understanding how the lives of all people, but particularly the lives of girls and women, are shaped by gender. Rather than conceiving gender as a collection of individual traits or attributes, this book presents gender as a *social system* that is used to categorize people and is linked to power and status.

The gender system is analyzed throughout the book at three levels: sociocultural, interpersonal, and individual. Because conceptualizing gender as a social system is important from the start, the second chapter of the book is devoted to gender, status, and power. This chapter explains the gender system and how it works at each of the three levels and demonstrates how they are linked.

As Chapter 2 explains, at the sociocultural level men have more institutional and public power, and therefore political, religious, and normative power is concentrated largely in the hands of men. Of course, all men are not equally privileged, nor are all women equally disadvantaged. The gender system interacts with systems based on race/ethnicity, social class, heterosexuality, and other dimensions of difference. An understanding of the gender system at this level provides a context for the other levels and reduces the tendency to think of gender as mere sex differences.

At the second level of the gender system, gender is created, performed, and perpetuated in social interaction—what social constructionists call *doing gender.* I explore this topic not just as the social display of differences, but also as the social enactment of status and power. Gender-linked behaviors such as interrupting and smiling, for example, reflect and perpetuate women's subordinate status.

The gender system operates at the individual level as women internalize their subordinate social status. Well-documented psychological phenomena such as denial of personal discrimination, lack of entitlement, and gendered psychological disorders such as depression can be related to internalized subordination. By conceptualizing gender as a social system operating at three levels, my goal is to provide students with an analytical tool for understanding how gender affects all our lives in both public and private domains.

Research Methods: Attention to Process

From the start, this book has been based on scientific knowledge about women and gender. As in previous editions, research *processes* get plenty of attention. I believe it is important to show students how scientific knowledge is acquired, to help them see the methods and processes by which researchers reach their conclusions. In Chapter 1, I explain that psychological researchers use a variety of quantitative and qualitative methods, and define several of the most commonly used, briefly discussing their strengths and limitations. This background prepares students for the more sophisticated discussions that follow in Chapters 1 and 4 about sources of sex bias in psychological research, the meaning of statistical significance (including what it does *not* mean), the role of values in psychological research, and feminist values in research.

The methodological emphasis is reinforced by another feature of this text: Research Focus boxes that zero in on a specific study showing its method, results, and importance. These boxes feature diverse methods including surveys, experiments, interviews, and case studies. In addition to these spotlighted studies, there are graphs and tables throughout the text that summarize the results of other studies. Also, when describing individual studies verbally, I report the methods and results of both classic and recent research in enough detail that students can see *how* the researcher reached her conclusions. At times, I point out the limitations of a study, counter its conclusions, or discuss ethical lapses in the conduct of the research. In all these ways, my intention is to help students understand how claims about gender should be based on evidence and reasoning, and to learn to think critically about the production of knowledge.

A Positive Focus on Social Change

One of the key features of this book is its positive message about social change. Studying the psychology of women and gender can be a rewarding experience for students. However, learning about sexism, discrimination, and the difficulty of changing the gender system can also be overwhelming. I have found that, even though most social science research focuses on problems, it is crucial to offer students a focus on solutions as well. In other words, it is important that students learn not only about problems created by the gender system, but also what is happening to solve them. Therefore, this book does more than focus on injustice and inequality. Every chapter ends with a section titled *Making a Difference* that focuses on social change. In keeping with the organizing theoretical framework of the book, social changes at the societal/cultural, interpersonal, and individual levels are presented and evaluated. Transforming psychology, and transforming the world, toward being more woman-friendly and gender-equal is an ongoing process. A central message of this book, and one that closes each chapter, is that every student can be a part of this transformation.

New in this Edition

Transformations 3e reflects the most current research and theory, with more than 600 *new* references since the previous edition. Here, I list highlights of new and updated topics.

Chapter 1: Paving the Way

- A new section on intersectionality
- An introduction to transnational feminism
- How the use of Internet samples is reducing sampling bias in research

Chapter 2: Gender, Status, and Power

- New research on "doing gender" in online communication
- Micro-aggressions: An intersectional perspective
- Backlash against agentic and ambitious women
- "Mansplaining," "manologues," and conversational dominance
- How to change sexist attitudes
- NEW BOX: Malala Yousafzai

Chapter 3: Images of Women

- Updated research on sexist/nonsexist language
- Latest research on media images
  - "post-feminist" ads
  - Latinas, African-American women
  - female athletes in the media
- An intersectional analysis of gender and ethnic stereotypes
- NEW BOX: The Bechdel Test (Does your Favorite Movie Pass This Handy Sexism Quiz?)

Chapter 4: The Meanings of Difference

- Increased emphasis on meta-analysis, both usefulness and critique of
  - concept of effect size, meaning of a small, medium, and large effect size
  - moderator variables
- The shrinking gender gap in math performance
- Intersectional approach to stereotype threat and stereotype boost
- Techniques for reducing or eliminating stereotype threat in vulnerable groups and equalizing opportunities for girls in math and science

Chapter 5: Sex, Gender, and Bodies

- Extensively updated—still the only textbook in the field to present a social constructionist perspective on the concept of binary sex
- The most recent research on chromosomal and hormonal variations such as XYY syndrome, Turner syndrome, CAH
- New psychiatric classification, terminology and research on intersex, transgender, fluid, genderqueer, agender, and nonbinary identities
  - DSM category of gender dysphoria: definition; diagnosis in children, adolescents and adults; critique
  - New evidence for genetic links in transgender reported and evaluated
  - Psychological outcomes of gender affirmation (formerly termed sex change) surgery
  - Psychological adjustment in transgender individuals
- Genetic influences on sexual orientation
- Prenatal hormone exposure (CAH) and women's sexual orientation
- Transphobia, genderism, hate crimes against trans people
- Updated information on third-sex categories in other cultures
- NEW BOXES:
  - Genderqueer pronouns: A New User's Guide
  - Research Focus: Life Experiences of Intersex People
  - Caster Semenya, Dutee Chand, and Gender Verification of Female Athletes

Chapter 6: Gendered Identities: Childhood and Adolescence

- Strategies for teaching children to think critically about the stereotypical messages in their storybooks and on TV
- How and why some girls sustain a deviation from prescribed femininity by being "tomboys" throughout middle childhood
- Early sexualization of girls
- Meta-analyses and cross-cultural comparisons of gender and physical and relational aggression
- Sexual objectification in adolescent girls
- Sexual harassment in middle school and high school
- How to help adolescent girls stay "in the body" and reduce self-objectification
- NEW BOXES:
  - Little Kids Scope Out the Hidden Messages in Their Storybooks—And Come Up with Some Bright Ideas for Gender Equality
  - The Gendered Toy Marketing Debate

Chapter 7: Sex, Love, and Romance

- Chapter has been extensively updated to focus on contemporary issues
- Ideals of heteronormative romance vs. hookup practices (booty call, friends with benefits ...)
- Gender differences and similarities in hookup experiences
- Early sexual initiation
- New research on the coming-out process for lesbian and bisexual women
- Sexual fluidity in women
- Intersections of ethnic and sexual identity
- New section on Internet dating
- Current research on sexual double standards
- Critique of abstinence-based sex education
- NEW BOXES:
  - Research Focus: Women's Masturbation: Experiences of Sexual Empowerment in a Primarily Sex-Positive Sample
  - Purity Balls and Virginity Pledges

Chapter 8: Commitments: Women and Close Relationships

- Changing patterns of heterosexual marriage
- The trend toward serial cohabitation and long-term singlehood among women
- Lesbian couples and lesbian marriages
- The psychological and economic consequences of divorce
- NEW BOXES:
  - Timeline/History of Marriage Equality for Gay/Lesbian Couples
  - Del Martin and Phyllis Lyon: A Marriage to Remember

Chapter 9: Mothering

- An inclusive, intersectional perspective that includes teen mothers, single mothers, LBTQ, African-American mothers, and the place of fathers in childbirth and parenting
- Persistence of pronatalism and the motherhood mystique
- Child free by choice
- Infertility
- Updated information on abortion and attempts to restrict access
- Ethical issues in surrogate parenthood
- Attitudes toward pregnant women
- Risk factors for postpartum depression
- Family-friendly social policy and workplaces
- NEW BOX:
  - MomsRising.org: Grassroots Advocacy for Women, Mothers, and Families

Chapter 10: Work and Achievement

- Updated research on women's unpaid work
  - Housework as real work, relational work, and the two-person career
- Occupational segregation, the glass ceiling
- Gender bias in hiring and promotion
- Tokenism: An intersectional analysis
- The importance of mentoring
- Expectancies, values, and career paths (Eccles' expectancy-values theory)
- Achieving work-life balance
- NEW BOX: Women in Startup Companies and Venture Capital

Chapter 11: The Second Half: Midlife and Aging

- Ageism in individualistic and collectivistic cultures
- Images of older women in the media
- Social impact of age stereotypes
- Current research on menopause and hormone replacement therapy
- Exercise and fitness in middle and later life
- Older women's sexuality: from the "cougar" to old age
- Lesbians in later life: visibility, sexuality, adjustment, couples, retirement
- Role changes of later life: becoming a grandmother, losing a life partner, retirement

Chapter 12: Violence against Women

- New Section, *Violence and Social Media,* covers revenge porn, disseminating text messages without consent, other forms of non-consensual pornography, and new legal protections against these offenses
- New section, *Stalking,* includes cyberstalking

- Updated research on rape, sexual assault, and prevention programs aimed at men
- NEW BOX: It's On Us: Intervening to reduce sexual assault on campuses

Chapter 13: Psychological Disorders, Therapy, and Women's Well-Being

- Continuing the focus of earlier editions, Feminist and social constructionist approach to psychological disorders puts psychological well-being in social and historical context
- Premenstrual Dysphoric Disorder (PMDD) in the DSM
- Objectification, ethnic group identification, and eating disorders
- PMDD as a culture-bound syndrome
- Pharmaceutical industry influence on DSM revisions
- NEW BOXES:
  - Judith Worrell: Pioneer in Feminist Therapy
  - Prozac, Sarafem, and the Rebranding of Psycho-Pharmaceutical Drugs

Chapter 14: Making a Difference: Toward a Better Future for Women

- Updated research on
- Ethnically diverse students' attitudes toward feminism
- Feminists' and nonfeminists' attitudes toward men
- Feminist attitudes and psychological well-being in women

Transformations 3e is readable, lively, and easy to follow. It's a student-friendly text, with a generous sprinkling of cartoons and photographs that brighten the pages. Finally, each chapter ends with "Exploring Further," which offers new research resources, websites, and information for activism.

Mc Graw Hill Education | connect®

The third edition of *Transformations: Women, Gender & Psychology*, is now available online with Connect, McGraw-Hill Education's integrated assignment and assessment platform. Connect also offers SmartBook for the new edition, which is the first adaptive reading experience proven to improve grades and help students study more effectively. All of the title's website and ancillary content is also available through Connect, including:

- A full Test Bank of multiple choice questions that test students on central concepts and ideas in each chapter.
- An Instructor's Manual for each chapter with full chapter outlines, sample test questions, and discussion topics.
- Lecture Slides for instructor use in class and downloadable RAP forms.

McGraw-Hill Connect® is a highly reliable, easy-to-use homework and learning management solution that utilizes learning science and award-winning adaptive tools to improve student results.

Homework and Adaptive Learning

- Connect's assignments help students contextualize what they've learned through application, so they can better understand the material and think critically.
- Connect will create a personalized study path customized to individual student needs through SmartBook®.
- SmartBook helps students study more efficiently by delivering an interactive reading experience through adaptive highlighting and review.

Over **7 billion questions** have been answered, making McGraw-Hill Education products more intelligent, reliable, and precise.

Connect's Impact on Retention Rates, Pass Rates, and Average Exam Scores

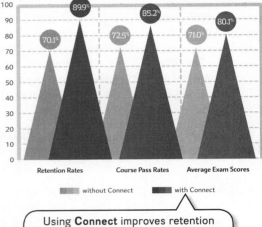

Using **Connect** improves retention rates by **19.8%**, passing rates by **12.7%**, and exam scores by **9.1%**.

73% of instructors who use **Connect** require it; instructor satisfaction **increases** by 28% when **Connect** is required.

Quality Content and Learning Resources

- Connect content is authored by the world's best subject matter experts, and is available to your class through a simple and intuitive interface.
- The Connect eBook makes it easy for students to access their reading material on smartphones and tablets. They can study on the go and don't need internet access to use the eBook as a reference, with full functionality.
- Multimedia content such as videos, simulations, and games drive student engagement and critical thinking skills.

©McGraw-Hill Education

Robust Analytics and Reporting

©Hero Images/Getty Images

- Connect Insight® generates easy-to-read reports on individual students, the class as a whole, and on specific assignments.

- The Connect Insight dashboard delivers data on performance, study behavior, and effort. Instructors can quickly identify students who struggle and focus on material that the class has yet to master.

- Connect automatically grades assignments and quizzes, providing easy-to-read reports on individual and class performance.

Impact on Final Course Grade Distribution

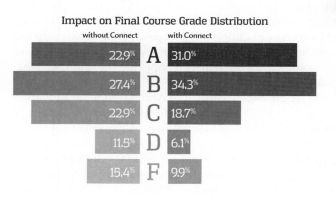

without Connect		with Connect
22.9%	A	31.0%
27.4%	B	34.3%
22.9%	C	18.7%
11.5%	D	6.1%
15.4%	F	9.9%

More students earn As and Bs when they use Connect.

Trusted Service and Support

- Connect integrates with your LMS to provide single sign-on and automatic syncing of grades. Integration with Blackboard®, D2L®, and Canvas also provides automatic syncing of the course calendar and assignment-level linking.

- Connect offers comprehensive service, support, and training throughout every phase of your implementation.

- If you're looking for some guidance on how to use Connect, or want to learn tips and tricks from super users, you can find tutorials as you work. Our Digital Faculty Consultants and Student Ambassadors offer insight into how to achieve the results you want with Connect.

www.mheducation.com/connect

Acknowledgments

Writing a textbook is a daunting task. I could not have done it without the support of family, friends, and colleagues.

Annie B. Fox, PhD, wrote chapter 12, on gender-based violence, and updated Chapter 13, Psychological Disorders, Therapy, and Women's Well-Being. Annie also conceived and wrote most of the lively text boxes that appear throughout the book. Thank you, Annie, for taking an increasing role in *Transformations 3e*, applying your classroom experience and psychological expertise to make it better than ever.

Chapter 13 was previously contributed by Britain Scott, who could not participate in this edition due to other commitments. Britain's expertise remains visible in the innovative social constructionist approach, historical sweep, and approachable style of Chapter 13. I thank Britain again for her many contributions to the first two editions.

Christy Starr, graduate student at University of California Santa Cruz, was a capable and hardworking research assistant for this edition and also contributed the section on sexualization of girls in Chapter 6. Thank you, Christy, for your dedication to the project, feminist ideals, and strong work ethic. Thanks to Dawn M. Brown, graduate student at University of Illinois at Champaign-Urbana, who offered guidance on gender identity terminology and pronoun use. Working with these strong and capable younger women gives me renewed hope that the feminist transformation of society will continue.

Thanks to Julia and David Apgar, Ben Chaffin, and Annie Duong for providing the photos of their dressed-up kids in Chapter 6, and to Alex Olson, a student at Normandale Community College in Minnesota, who helped me select the many new photographs that illustrate this edition.

I am grateful to the publishing pros at McGraw-Hill: Product Developer Francesca King, Portfolio Manager Jamie Laferrera, Content Licencing Specialist Melisa Seegmiller, and at **ansr**source, Developmental Editor Anne Sheroff, and Photo Researcher Jennifer Blankenship.

I would also like to thank the pre-publication reviewers for this edition who generously provided me with feedback: John M. Adams, University of Alabama; Grace Deason, University of Wisconsin—La Crosse; Alishia Huntoon, Oregon Institute of Technology; Jamie Franco-Zamudio, Spring Hill College; Jennifer Katz, SUNY Geneseo; Shannon Quintana, Miami Dade College; Christine Smith, University of Wisconsin-Green Bay; Megan L. Strain, University of Nebraska at Kearney; and Katherine Urquhart, University of Central Florida.

I thank, too, the friends and family who put up with the absent-mindedness and crankiness of a writer in the throes of a big project, especially my partner Roger Chaffin. Because Roger is an accomplished cognitive psychologist, our dialogues about my work are helpful and constructive. He is there with day-to-day encouragement and tech support. Most important, because he is committed to an egalitarian relationship, I enjoy a balanced life of work and family, full of love, laughter, music, and adventure. Thank you, Roger.

Mary Crawford

PART 1

Introduction

CHAPTER 1   PAVING THE WAY

Paving the Way

$\mathcal{T}$his book is called *Transformations*. I hope you find this title intriguing. I chose it because we are living in an era when opportunities for girls and women have changed dramatically, and psychology has played a part in those changes. Still, gender equality is a transformation that is not yet complete. Consider the current situation:

- Only 19 percent of the U.S. Congress and 12 percent of state governors are women.
- In the United States, women earn about 78 cents for every dollar earned by men. Worldwide, the difference is even greater—women earn only about 52 percent of what men earn.
- The United Nations estimates that 115 million women are missing from the global population—dead because, as females, they were unwanted.
- Women have been heads of state in 70 countries around the world, yet in others they lack basic human rights such as going to school.

Although some things have changed for the better, a worldwide wage gap, under-representation of women in positions of status and power, and significant problems of violence against girls and women persist. Gender, sexuality, and power are at the core of social controversies around the world.

Beginnings

We are living in an era in which nothing about women, sexuality, and gender seems certain. Entering this arena of change, psychology has developed research and theory about women and gender. This branch of psychology is usually called *feminist psychology*, the **psychology of women**, or the **psychology of gender** (Russo & Dumont, 1997). Those who use the term feminist psychology tend to emphasize theoretical connections to women's studies and social activism. Those who use psychology of women tend to focus on women's lives and experiences as the topics of study. Those who use psychology of gender tend to focus on the social and biological processes that create differences between women and men. This book includes all these perspectives and uses all three terms. There is a lot to learn about this exciting field.

How Did the Psychology of Women Get Started?

As the women's movement of the late 1960s made women and gender a central social concern, the field of psychology began to examine the bias that had characterized its knowledge about women. The more closely psychologists looked at the ways psychology had thought about women, the more problems they saw. They began to realize that women had been left out of many studies. Even worse, theories were constructed from a male-as-norm viewpoint, and women's behavior was explained as a deviation from the male standard. Often, stereotypes of women went unchallenged. Good psychological adjustment for women was defined in terms of fitting into traditional feminine norms—marrying, having babies, and *not* being too independent or ambitious.

When women behaved differently from men, the differences were likely to be attributed to their female biology instead of social influences (Marecek et al., 2002).

These problems were widespread. Psychologists began to realize that most psychological knowledge about women and gender was ***androcentric,*** or male-centered. They began to rethink psychological concepts and methods and to produce new research with women as the focus of study. Moreover, they began to study topics of importance to women and to develop ways of analyzing social relations between women and men. As a result, psychology developed new ways of thinking about women, expanded its research methods, and developed new approaches to therapy and counseling.

Women within psychology were an important force for change. Starting in the late 1960s, they published many books and articles showing how psychology was misrepresenting women and how it needed to change. One of the first was Naomi Weisstein (1968), who declared that the psychology of that era had nothing to say about what women are really like, what they need, and what they want because psychology did not know very much at all about women. Another was Phyllis Chesler, whose book *Women and Madness* (1972) claimed that psychology and psychiatry were used to control women.

The new feminist psychologists began to do research on topics that were previously ignored. The new field soon developed its own professional research journals focusing on the psychology of women or gender: for example, *Sex Roles,* which began publishing in 1975; *Psychology of Women Quarterly* (1976); *Women and Therapy* (1982); and *Feminism & Psychology* (1991). These journals were extremely important in providing outlets for research that might have seemed unorthodox, unimportant, or even trivial to the psychological establishment at the time. (I well remember my tenure interview, when a senior male faculty member on the committee looked up from my list of publications and said in genuine puzzlement, "But this isn't research, it's just a lot of stuff about women." Luckily, I had also done some research with white rats, which apparently sufficed to prove that I was a real scientist). The research topics explored in those new journals opened a vast new field of knowledge. In 2011, upon the 35th anniversary of the APA journal *Psychology of Women Quarterly,* the editors looked back at the 100 most influential articles that had been published in the journal since its inception, and found that they could be grouped into four general themes: feminist research methods; women and girls in social context, including gender roles and sexism; violence against women; and women's bodies and sexualities (Rutherford & Yoder, 2011). These areas are still important today and are key components of this book.

Teaching students about the psychology of women has been an important contribution of feminist psychology from the start. Before 1968, there were virtually no college courses in the psychology of women or gender. Today, undergraduate and graduate courses in women and gender studies are part of the standard course listings in many, if not most, psychology departments, and research on women, gender, and diversity is being integrated into the entire psychology curriculum, due to the efforts of professional groups such as APA's Committee on Women in Psychology (Chrisler et al., 2013). The androcentric psychology of the past has been replaced by a more encompassing perspective that includes the female half of the population and acknowledges all kinds of human diversity (Morris, 2010).

The psychology of women and gender is rich in theoretical perspectives and research evidence. Virtually every area of psychology has been affected by its theories and research (Marecek et al., 2002). This book is an invitation to explore the knowledge and participate in the ongoing debates of feminist psychology.

Psychology and the Women's Movement

The emergence of interest in women and gender took place in a social context marked by changing roles for women and the growth of a feminist social movement in the 1960s. Questioning psychology's representation of women was part of the general questioning of women's place that was led by women's liberation activists.

The First and Second Waves

The women's movement of the 1960s was not the first. A previous women's rights movement had reached its peak more than a hundred years earlier with the Seneca Falls Declaration of 1848, which rejected the doctrine of female inferiority then taught by academics and clergy (Harris, 1984). However, this *first wave* of the women's movement lost momentum in the 1920s, after women had won the vote, because women believed that voting would lead to political, social, and economic equality. Psychology's interest in sex differences and gender waned.

but it didn't

With the rebirth of the women's movement in the 1960s, researchers again became interested in the study of women and gender. Women psychologists and men who supported their goals also began to work toward improved status for women within the field of psychology. Feminist activism made a big difference for women of this era, who had been openly discriminated against. Psychologist Carolyn Sherif remembered it this way:

> To me, the atmosphere created by the women's movement was like breathing fresh air after years of gasping for breath. . . . I did not become a significantly better social psychologist between 1969 and 1972, but I surely was treated as a better social psychologist. (Sherif, 1983, p. 280)

Activists—mostly graduate students and newcomers to psychology—formed the Association for Women in Psychology (AWP) in 1969. At about the same time, others—mostly older, more established psychologists—lobbied the American Psychological Association (APA) to form a Division of the Psychology of Women. This Division 35 was officially approved in 1973. APA's Committee on Women in Psychology (CWP) also was founded in 1973. Women in psychology had been protesting unfair treatment for over a century, but it was not until the resurgence of the feminist movement that they engaged in collective action and made their voices heard. The CWP has continued to engage in feminist activism on behalf of women in psychology for over 40 years (Chrisler et al., 2013). Divisions on ethnic minority psychology (Division 45), gay/lesbian issues (Division 44), and the study of men and masculinity (Division 51) were established later, with the support of Division 35.

Progress in incorporating women also occurred among Canadian psychologists (Parlee, 1985) and the British Psychological Society, where there is now a Psychology of Women Section (Wilkinson, 1997a).

These organizational changes acknowledged the presence of diverse women in psychology and helped enhance their professional identity (Scarborough & Furumoto, 1987). And none too soon—women now earn 74 percent of PhDs awarded in psychology, and ethnic minorities earn 24 percent (American Psychological Association, 2014).

The Third Wave

AWP continues to thrive, holding annual conferences that welcome students. Division 35, now named the Society for the Psychology of Women, is one of the larger and more active divisions of APA. Feminist theory and activism continue to develop as younger women tackle some of the unfinished business of the first two waves, such as ensuring reproductive freedom, ending violence against girls and women, and integrating women into leadership positions.

Third-wave feminism developed in the 1990s as young women responded not only to the gains of second-wave feminism but also to its limitations. It is less connected to the psychological establishment than earlier feminist movements were. Some third-wave groups, such as the Riot grrrls, came out of the antiestablishment punk movement. Riot grrrl bands and zines of the 1990s often proclaimed the joys of women's sexuality, self-reliance, and empowerment. One example of third wave feminist activism is the SlutWalk movement, which originated in Canada in 2011 after a Toronto police officer advised women to "avoid dressing like sluts" in order not to be raped. SlutWalks have since taken place in many cities around the world, a strategy to show that the victims of sexual assault are not to blame, while reclaiming a word that has been used to shame women.

Third-wave groups emphasize social activism—women working collectively for social justice—just as their second-wave counterparts did before them. Though the issues and the voices have changed, third-wave feminism is clearly connected to its foremothers' visions (Baumgardner & Richards, 2000, 2005).

Voices from the Margins: A History

Until recently, the power to define and pursue knowledge has been largely in the hands of men. Men controlled the institutions of knowledge, and even when women acquired expertise, they did not always get the respect or status they deserved. History is full of stories about learned women whose work was attributed to their fathers, their brothers, their teachers, or "anonymous."

One illustration of how a woman could have outstanding expertise and yet be denied legitimacy is the story of Mary Calkins (1863–1930), who attended Harvard University during the latter part of the 19th century. Because Harvard was an all-male university, she was permitted to take courses only if she sat behind a curtain or got private tutoring. Despite completing an impressive PhD dissertation, she was denied a PhD from Harvard because she was a woman. Nevertheless, Calkins taught for many years at Wellesley College, established an experimental laboratory there, and made important contributions to psychology. She was the first woman president of both the American Psychological Association and the American Philosophical Association. In 1927, toward the end of her life, a group of distinguished male psychologists and philosophers, all Harvard degree holders, wrote to the president of Harvard requesting that Calkins be awarded the degree that she had earned. Their request was refused (Scarborough & Furumoto, 1987).

Although Mary Calkins triumphed personally, her life illustrates the way even outstanding women may be marginalized. For example, she taught for her entire career at a small women's college where she did not have doctoral students. Under these conditions, her theories and research projects did not receive the recognition and follow-up they deserved. Similar stories have been uncovered about other early feminist psychologists (Scarborough & Furumoto, 1987). If a woman scientist does not have the power to have her research and theories taken seriously and passed on to the next generation, she is being denied true equality.

By the early 1900s, women had begun to gain access to higher education in the United States and Europe. Some of the first scientifically trained women devoted their research efforts to challenging accepted wisdom about the extent and nature of sex differences. Helen Thompson Wooley conducted the first experimental laboratory study of sex differences in mental traits. In interpreting her results, she stressed the overall similarity of women's and men's performance. She also was openly critical of the antiwoman prejudices held by some male scientists, remarking daringly in a 1910 *Psychological Bulletin* article: "There is perhaps no field aspiring to be scientific where flagrant personal bias, logic martyred in the cause of supporting a prejudice, unfounded assertions, and even sentimental rot and drivel, have run riot to such an extent as here" (Wooley, 1910, p. 340).

The work of these pioneering women psychologists opened the way for research to replace unexamined assumptions about women's so-called natural limitations (Rosenberg, 1982). Determined to demonstrate women's capacity to contribute to modern science on an equal basis with men, they chose their research projects to challenge beliefs about women's limitations. In a sense, their research projects were dictated by other people's questions. Faced with the necessity of proving their very right to do research, these women labored to refute hypotheses that they did not find credible. Moreover, they worked in a social context that denied them opportunities because of their sex and forced them to make cruel choices between work and family relationships (Scarborough & Furumoto, 1987). Their story is one,

> in many ways, of failure—of women restricted by simple prejudice to the periphery of academe, who never had access to the professional chairs of the major universities, who never commanded the funds to direct large-scale research, who never trained the graduate students who might have spread their influence, and who, by the 1920s, no longer had the galvanizing support of a woman's movement to give political effect to their ideas (Rosenberg, 1982, p. xxi).

The efforts of women and minorities remained voices from the margins until relatively recently (see Box 1.1). The existence of AWP, Division 35, women's studies programs, and dozens of feminist journals guarantee that research on the psychology of women and gender will not fade away again as it did in the 1920s. Because the psychology of women developed in a social context of feminism, it is important to look closely at the relationship between the two.

BOX 1.1 ∾   Women and the APA

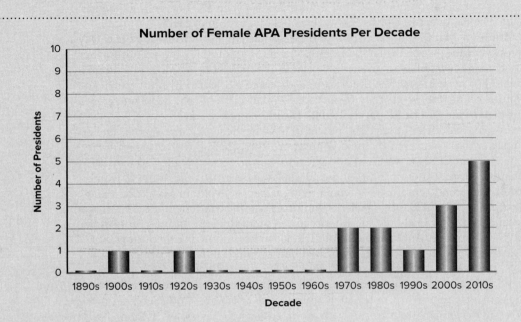

For most of the APA's 124-year history, women rarely served as president of the organization. Prior to 1970, only two women had been elected APA president. However, since the rise of the feminist movement beginning in the 1970's, the number of women elected president of APA has continued to grow. In fact, since 2010, the members of APA have elected five female presidents. Susan H. McDonald, a distinguished professor and director of the Institute for the Family in the Department of Psychiatry at the University of Rochester, served as President of APA for 2016–2017.

Source: http://www.apa.org/about/governance/president/past-presidents.aspx

Contributed by Annie B. Fox

What Is Feminism?

The writer Rebecca West noted in 1913: "I myself have never been able to find out precisely what feminism is: I only know that people call me a feminist whenever I express sentiments that differentiate me from a doormat" (quoted in Kramarae & Treichler, 1985, p. 160). Nearly 100 years later, third wave feminists Jennifer Baumgardner and Amy Richards (2000, p. 17) wrote, "For our generation, feminism is like fluoride. We scarcely notice that we have it—it's simply in the water." Along the way, there have been a lot of misconceptions. Exactly what is feminism and what does it mean to call oneself a feminist?

Feminism Has Many Meanings

Contemporary feminist theory has many variants. Each can be thought of as a different lens through which to view the experiences of women, and, like different lenses, each is useful for focusing on particular phenomena.

What are the most influential feminist theoretical perspectives? In the United States, they include liberal, radical, womanist (woman of color), and cultural feminism. Belief in these different branches of feminism has been defined, reliably measured, and shown to predict people's behavior (Henley et al., 1998). As feminism expands worldwide, there is a new emphasis on global feminism as well. Let's look briefly at each perspective.

Liberal feminism is familiar to most people because it relies on deeply held American beliefs about equality—an orientation that connects it to political liberalism. From this perspective, a feminist is a person who believes that women are entitled to full legal and social equality with men and who favors changes in laws, customs, and values to achieve the goal of equality. The liberal feminist perspective has fostered research on such topics as how people react to others when they violate gender norms (Chapter 2), how children are socialized to accept gender roles (Chapters 4 and 6), and sex discrimination in employment (Chapter 10). It emphasizes the similarities between males and females, maintaining that given equal environments and opportunities, males and females will behave similarly.

Radical feminism emphasizes male control and domination of women throughout history. This perspective views the control of women by men as the first and most fundamental form of oppression: women as a group are oppressed by men as a group. According to radical feminists, oppression on the basis of being a woman is one thing all women have in common. Radical feminist theory has fostered much research on violence against women (see Chapter 12). Some radical feminists have endorsed **separatism,** the idea that women can escape patriarchy only by creating their own woman-only communities. For example, the Michigan Womyn's Music Festival, an annual event for 40 years, was grounded in the radical tradition. Only women could attend, and many came year after year, treasuring this safe and empowering women's space (Browne, 2011). The festival ended in 2015, partly over dissent about whether transgender women should be included (Ring, 2015).

Woman-of-color feminism, or *womanism,* began with criticism of the White women's movement for excluding women of color; the word womanism was coined by African American writer Alice Walker. This type of feminism focuses on issues of importance to minority communities: poverty, racism, jobs, health care, and access to education. In general, womanists do not see men of color as their oppressors but as brothers who suffer the effects of racism just as women of color do; therefore, womanism is particularly inclusive of men and rejects the notion of separatism. People who adopt this feminist perspective emphasize the effects of racial stereotyping (Chapter 3) and prejudice (Chapters 2 and 10). They also point out the strengths and positive values of minority communities, such as the multigenerational support and closeness of African American families (Chapter 9).

Cultural feminism emphasizes differences between women and men. This perspective stresses that qualities characteristic of women have been devalued and should be honored and respected in society. It views some gender differences in values and social behaviors as either an essential part of womanhood or so deeply socialized that they are virtually universal and unlikely to change—for example, the tendency for women to be more nurturing and caring than men. Cultural feminism has been useful in understanding the importance of unpaid work contributed by women, such as caring for the young, the ill, and the elderly (Chapters 9–11).

Feminism is a worldwide social movement. *Global feminism* focuses on how prejudice and discrimination against women are related across cultures, and how they are connected to neocolonialism and global capitalism. Issues of special concern to global feminists include sweatshop labor, unequal access to health care and education, sex trafficking, and violence against girls and women in developing countries (Chapter 12). An important part of global feminism is the recognition that Western feminists do not have all the answers for women from other cultures. For example, in some societies women are strongly pressured to undergo genital cutting (Chapter 7) or required to veil their faces and bodies in public. Though Western women may criticize these practices, it is important to remember that Western society also restricts women's bodily freedom and integrity through practices like sexual harassment in public places and pressure to seek the perfect body through dieting and cosmetic surgery (Chapters 2, 3, and 11). All around the world, women bear a disproportionate burden of the inequalities caused by colonialism, global capitalism, and economic exploitation. Understanding gender oppression in conjunction with these other kinds of power imbalances is the work of *transnational feminism*, and it requires structural analysis as well as individual-level analysis (Else-Quest & Grabe, 2012; Grabe & Else-Quest, 2012).

The diversity of frameworks and values in feminist thought may seem confusing, but it is also healthy and productive. Different feminist perspectives can be used to develop and compare diverse viewpoints on women's experiences. This book draws on a variety of feminist perspectives, using each as a lens to help clarify particular topics, and sometimes comparing several feminist perspectives on an issue. However, within psychology, liberal feminism and cultural feminism have generated more debate and research than any other views. Therefore, Chapter 4 is devoted to contrasting liberal and cultural feminist perspectives on the question, "Just how different are women and men?"

Is There a Simple Definition?

Feminist perspectives share two important themes. First, feminism values women as important and worthwhile human beings. Second, feminism recognizes the need for social change if women are to lead secure and satisfying lives. Perhaps the simplest definition of a *feminist* is an individual who holds these basic beliefs: that women are valuable and that social change to benefit women is needed. The core social change that feminists advocate is an end to all forms of domination, those of men over women and those among women (Kimball, 1995). Therefore, perhaps the simplest definition of *feminism* is one proposed by Black feminist theorist bell hooks (1984): it is a movement to end sexism and sexist oppression. (The definition and implications of sexism are explored more fully in Chapter 2.) Broad definitions allow feminists to work for political and social change together, while recognizing that ideas about how to reach their goals may differ.

Can men be feminists? Certainly! Men can hold the values I've described as feminist: they can value women as worthwhile human beings and work for social change to reduce sexism and sex discrimination. Some men who share these values call themselves feminists. Others prefer the label **_profeminist,_** believing that this term acknowledges women's leadership of the feminist movement and expresses their understanding that women and men have different experiences of gender.

Feminist perspectives in general can be contrasted to **_conservatism_** (Henley et al., 1998). Social conservatives seek to keep gender arrangements as they have been in much of the past, with men holding more public power and status and women being more or less defined by their sexuality and their roles as wives and mothers. Conservatives often urge a return to what they consider the good old days when there were (apparently) no lesbian, gay, or transgendered people, good young women all got married and produced babies, abortion and divorce were out of the question, and the world of work and achievement was a man's world.

The conservative view has usually been justified on the grounds of biology or religion. The biological justification states that gender-related behaviors are determined by innate and unchangeable biological differences far more than by social conditions. Therefore, women should not try to do things that go against their nature. For example, if women are biologically destined to be more nurturing due to the fact that they are the sex that gives birth, it is unnatural and wrong for women to limit their childbearing or take on jobs that may interfere with their nurturing roles. The religious justification (often combined with the biological justification) is that a supreme being ordains female submission and subordination. For example, some religions teach that women must be obedient to their husbands; others forbid contraception, or grant only men the right to divorce. Some forbid women to be in positions of authority or spiritual power. Well into the 21st century, the Roman Catholic Church maintains that ordaining women as priests is a sin on a par with child sexual abuse (Vatican Angers Many, 2010). Just a few years earlier, the Southern Baptist Church urged a return to female submission as a solution to social problems such as child abuse and violence against women. In a perversion of conservative religious doctrine, the radical Islamists of ISIS use religion to justify the serial rape and sex slavery of women they hold captive (Callimachi, 2016).

Over the past 40 years, attitudes toward women have grown less conservative and more liberal in the United States (Donnelly et al., 2016). However, social conservatism is still a powerful political force, and more subtle forms of prejudice against women have emerged (see Chapter 2). The history of women in psychology teaches us that psychologists are not immune to such prejudice. The attitudes that permeate a culture also seep into scientific research. One important goal of feminist psychology is to challenge hidden biases in research and thus to foster better research on women and gender.

Methods and Values in Psychological Research

Psychology's Methods

Psychologists use a variety of research methods to answer their questions. The diversity of methods allows psychologists to tailor a method that is right for the question they seek to answer.

Most psychologists use **_quantitative methods:_** those that involve measuring behavior, averaging it over a group of people, and comparing groups with statistical tests. Ideally, quantitative methods allow for the use of random samples, so that the results can be *generalized,* or applied to more people than just the few who were studied.

Some quantitative methods, such as *surveys,* are largely descriptive: they report the beliefs, attitudes, or opinions of groups of people. A good example is the public opinion poll, where attitudes toward gay marriage or affirmative action are assessed. In the interests of efficiency, all participants are asked the same questions. Therefore, it is extremely important that the survey is designed to ask the right questions, and to provide meaningful answer options.

Correlational studies can determine whether two or more variables are related to each other, but they cannot determine whether that relationship is causal. For example, correlational research has demonstrated that, as more American women began to work outside the home over the past 40 years, the divorce rate rose. But it cannot answer the question of why women's work and the divorce rate rose together. Is it because working women are not good wives? Or because women who can support themselves are less likely to stay in bad marriages? Or perhaps it's because there has been a widespread shift away from traditional attitudes during the last 40 years, so that both divorce and women's working are more socially acceptable? Other kinds of research are needed to answer questions of causality on this topic—research that I'll describe in Chapters 8 and 10.

If a researcher is interested in change over time within the same individuals, she might use a *longitudinal design,* measuring variables at two or more points in time. An example would be to ask couples about their marital satisfaction both before and after the birth of their first child. Statistical techniques allow the researcher to see which variables at Time 1 predict behavior at Time 2. Another approach is to do *archival research,* where the researcher looks for relationships among variables in a preexisting set of data such as national test scores.

Many psychologists rely on *experiments,* in which one or more variables are systematically manipulated to determine whether there is a causal relationship among them. Experiments are often considered the gold standard of methods, because finding out whether a change in Variable A *causes* a change in Variable B is important to scientific understanding and theory building. Moreover, most experiments are done under carefully controlled laboratory conditions, which increases psychologists' confidence that they are measuring variables accurately.

Other psychological research methods are *qualitative:* they explore a topic in an open-ended way, without trying to systematically count or manipulate behaviors. *Interviews* (usually individual) and *focus groups* (usually groups of 3–12) are the qualitative methods most often used in psychology and women's studies (O' Shaughnessy & Krogman, 2012). Often, researchers summarize qualitative data by grouping participants' comments by theme; they may also quote the participants directly. Sometimes, participants' talk is analyzed using one of a variety of approaches grouped under the term *discourse analysis.* Other examples of qualitative research are the *case study* (an in-depth study of a single individual) and the *ethnography,* in which the researcher works within a community and tries to learn its customs and beliefs. Qualitative methods provide an intimate look at participants' thoughts and feelings. However, because they generally use small, nonrandom samples and non-numerical measures, qualitative studies are not easily generalized to larger populations.

I've used most of these quantitative and qualitative methods myself, as I've studied women and gender over the course of my career. What I've learned by doing research is that each method has its strengths and weaknesses. As I describe research (my own and others') for you throughout this book, I will tell you what method was used, and I will remind you from time to time that the results of scientific research are always limited and subject to interpretation.

Scientific research is often represented to students as a purely objective process in which a neutral, disinterested scientist investigates and reveals the secrets of nature. However, psychology has sometimes been anything but neutral in explaining the behavior of women. Feminist psychologists have identified specific methodological flaws in traditional research on women.

Toward Gender-Fair Research

Let's look briefly at the research process. The researcher starts by generating a question to be answered by gathering information systematically. The question may originate in a theory, a personal experience, or an observation, or it may be raised by previous research. The next step is to develop a systematic strategy for answering the question—often called *designing the research.* In the design stage, a method is selected, such as experiment, survey, or case study. Research participants are chosen, materials such as questionnaires or laboratory setups are devised, and ways to measure the behaviors in question are decided on.

Next, the data are collected and analyzed so that patterns of results become clear. Because most psychologists rely on quantitative methods, statistical techniques are usually used for this task. The researcher then interprets the meaning of his or her results and draws conclusions from them. If reviewers and journal editors judge the research to be well conducted and important, the results are published in a scientific journal where they can influence future research and theory. Some research makes its way from journals into textbooks, influencing teachers and students as well as other researchers. Some even gets reported in the mass media, opening the possibility that it may influence millions of readers' and viewers' beliefs.

Biases can enter into the research process at any stage. In describing a few common types of bias at each stage, I will focus on gender-related examples. However, the principles of gender-fair research also apply to eliminating biases related to such characteristics as race/ethnicity, social class, or sexual orientation (Denmark et al., 1988).

Question Formulation

The process of creating research questions is perhaps the most neglected and understudied part of the scientific enterprise. Unexamined personal biases and androcentric theories may lead to biased research questions. Gender stereotypes related to the topic can bias the question and therefore the outcome of the study.

For example, in the past, many studies of leadership defined it in terms of dominance, aggression, and other stereotypically male attributes. It is only recently that psychologists have developed more inclusive definitions of leadership that include the ability to negotiate, to be considerate of others, and to help others resolve conflicts without confrontation—the "people skills" that make leaders more effective. Another example of bias in question formulation is found in the large amount of past research on mothers who worked outside the home. Much of it focused on the question of whether the mothers' work endangered their children's psychological welfare. There was much less research on whether fathers' work endangered their children's welfare or on whether mothers' employment might benefit mothers or children.

Designing Research

In the design phase of research, one important aspect is deciding how to measure the behaviors under study. If the measures are biased, the results will be, too. An extreme example of a biased measure comes from a survey study of women's sexuality. Participants were asked to describe their roles in sexual intercourse by choosing one of the following responses: passive, responsive, resistant, aggressive, deviant, or other. The outcome of this research might have been very different if women had also been allowed to choose from alternatives such as active, initiating, playful, and joyous (Bart, 1971; Wallston & Grady, 1985).

Choice of research participants is subject to many possible biases. Since the 1940s psychology has come to rely more and more on college student samples, creating biases of age, social class, and developmental stage (Sears, 1986). And the college students who participate in psychological research are not even representative of all American college students, because they are likely to be drawn mostly from introductory psychology courses, and because research is done mainly at universities and elite colleges, not at community colleges and less selective ones. The psych department subject pool may be a handy way for researchers to fill their quota, but it is far from representative of humanity!

Another important bias in choosing participants is that, for most of psychology's history, males were more likely to be studied than females, and male-only studies were considered representative of people in general. In contrast, when researchers used an all-female sample, they were more likely to state it in the article's title, to discuss their reasons for studying women, and to point out that their results could not be generalized to men (Ader & Johnson, 1994). It seems that psychologists felt it was important to indicate the limitations of an all-female sample, but they saw nothing remarkable about an all-male sample—males were the norm.

Other types of sampling bias still persist. Research on ethnic minority people of both sexes is scarce except when they are seen as creating social problems (Reid & Kelly, 1994). There has been abundant research on teen pregnancy among African American women, for example, but little research on their leadership, creativity, or coping skills for dealing with racism. Poor and working-class women, too, were virtually ignored (Bing & Reid, 1996; Reid, 1993). And women who happen not to be heterosexual will have trouble finding people like themselves in psychological research. Reviews of all psychological studies published from 1975 to 2009 have shown that nonheterosexual people were included in less than 1 percent of research, and lesbians and bisexual women were significantly less likely to be studied than gay and bisexual men (Lee & Crawford, 2007, 2012).

Many well-known psychologists, both female and male, have pointed out that psychology, supposedly the science of human behavior, is more accurately described as the science of the behavior of college sophomores, and straight White male college sophomores at that. Fortunately, many of the sampling biases I've described are declining. For example, the proportion of studies that include only men has been decreasing since the 1970s (Gannon et al., 1992), and the proportion of psychological research with low-income and working-class women has increased significantly in the past decade (Reid, 2011). The availability of Internet samples has broadened psychology's base beyond college students, too.

Analyzing Data: A Focus on Differences

Psychologists have come to rely on quantitative methods, and therefore they almost always use statistical tests in data analysis. Over the past 35 years, both the number of articles using statistics and the number of statistical tests per article have increased. Statistics can be a useful tool, but they also can lead to conceptual difficulties in research on sex and gender.

Statistical models lead to a focus on differences rather than similarities. The logic of statistical analysis involves comparing two groups to see if the average difference between them is statistically significant. Unfortunately, it is not easy to make meaningful statements about similarities using statistical reasoning.

It is also unfortunate that statisticians chose the term *significant* to describe the outcome of a set of mathematical operations. As used by most people the word means important, but as used by statisticians it means only that the obtained difference between two groups is unlikely to be due to mere chance. A statistically significant difference does not necessarily have any practical or social significance (Favreau, 1997). The meaning and interpretation of difference will be discussed in more detail in Chapter 4.

Interpreting and Publishing Research Results

Psychology's focus on group differences affects the ways that results are interpreted and conveyed to others. One type of interpretation bias—termed *overgeneralization*—occurs when gender differences in performing a specific task are interpreted as evidence of a more general difference, perhaps even one that is considered permanent and unchangeable. For example, because samples of highly gifted junior-high boys score higher on SAT math tests than similar samples of girls, some psychologists have argued that males in general have a biological superiority in math ability.

Another kind of interpretation bias occurs when the performance style more typical of girls or women is given a negative label. For example, girls get better grades in school in virtually every subject, but this is not usually interpreted as evidence that they are superior in intelligence. Instead, girls' academic achievement may be discounted; they are sometimes said to get good grades by being nice or compliant.

Overgeneralizing and other interpretation biases encourage us to think of men and women as two totally separate categories. But it is simply not true that "men are from Mars, women from Venus." On many traits and behaviors, men and women are far more alike than different. Even when a statistically significant difference is found, there is always considerable overlap between the two groups (see Chapter 4).

Problems of interpretation are compounded by publication biases. Because of reliance on the logic of statistical analysis, studies that report differences between women and men are more likely to be published than those that report similarities. Moreover, the editorial boards of most journals still are predominately made up of White men, who may perhaps see topics relevant to women and ethnic minorities as less important than topics relevant to people more like themselves (Denmark et al., 1988). Until feminist psychology was formed, there was very little psychological research on pregnancy and mothering, women's leadership, violence against women, or gender issues in therapy.

Bias continues after publication. The media notice some findings, but others are overlooked. Television and the popular press often actively publicize the latest discoveries about gender differences. Of course, some of these differences may not be very important, and others may not hold up in future research, but the public is less likely to hear about that, because gender similarities are not news.

In summary, research is a human activity, and the biases held by those who do research can affect any stage of the process. As more diverse people become psychologists, they are bringing new values, beliefs, and research questions. They also may question and challenge the biases in others' research. Feminist psychologists have led the way by demonstrating that gender bias exists in psychological research and showing how it can be reduced.

Gender-fair research is not value-free; that is, gender-fair research practices do not eliminate value judgments from the research process. Androcentric research is based on the value judgment that men and their concerns are more important and worthy of study than women and their concerns. In contrast, gender-fair research is based on the value judgment that women and men and their concerns are of equal worth and importance (Eichler, 1988).

Feminist Values in Research

Although feminist psychologists have been critical of psychology, they remain committed to it, expressing feminist values in their work (Grossman et al., 1997). What are some of these values?

Empirical Research Is a Worthwhile Activity

Although feminist psychologists recognize that science is far from perfect, they value its methods. Scientific methods are the most systematic way yet devised to answer questions about the natural and social world. Rather than abandon those methods or endlessly debate whether there is one perfect feminist way to do research, they go about their work using a rich variety of methods, theories, and approaches (Kimmel & Crawford, 2000; Rutherford, 2011).

Research Methods Should Be Critically Examined

Feminist theorists have pointed out that methods are not neutral tools; the choice of method always shapes and constrains what can be found (Kimmel & Crawford, 2000). For example, which is the better way to study female sexuality— by measuring physiological changes during arousal and orgasm or by interviewing women about their subjective experiences of arousal and orgasm? The two methods might produce very different discoveries about female sexuality (Tiefer, 1989).

Traditionally, experimentation has been the most respected psychological method. However, experimental methods have been criticized for at least two reasons. First, in an experiment, the researcher creates an artificial environment and manipulates the experience of the participants. Because of this artificiality, behavior in the laboratory may not be representative of behavior in other situations (Sherif, 1979). Second, experiments are inherently hierarchical, with "the powerful, all-knowing researchers instructing, observing, recording, and sometimes deceiving the subjects" (Peplau & Conrad, 1989). The inequality of the experimental situation may be particularly acute when the researcher is male and the person being studied is female (McHugh et al., 1986).

On the other hand, many important advances in understanding women and gender have come about because of experimental results. For example, experimental research has helped us understand gender stereotypes and their impact (see Chapter 3). Just as any research method can be used in biased ways, any method can be used toward the goal of understanding women and gender (Rutherford, 2011). When a variety of methods are used, results based on different approaches can be compared with each other, and a richer and more complete picture of women's lives will emerge.

Both Women and Men Can Conduct Feminist Research

Most feminist researchers in psychology are women. The membership of APA's Division 35 is more than 90 percent female, and women have been leaders in developing new theories and conducting new research about women and gender ever since the first women earned their PhDs in psychology. However, it is important not to equate female with feminist and male with nonfeminist. Women who are psychologists work in every area from physiological to clinical psychology. Women psychologists may or may not personally identify as feminists, and even when they do, they may not bring a feminist perspective to their research. Also, male psychologists can identify as feminist. Men can and do conduct research on women and gender, and many conduct research on masculinity, men's lives, and male gender roles. Of course, all psychologists—male and female, feminist and nonfeminist—should, at a minimum, try to conduct their research in gender-fair ways and work to eliminate gender bias from their professional practices and behaviors.

Science Can Never Be Fully Objective or Value-Neutral

Science is done by human beings, all of whom bring their own perspectives to their work, based on their personal backgrounds. Because the perspectives of dominant groups in a society are normative, they are not always recognized as being infused with dominant group values. When others—women and minorities, for example—question the assumptions of the dominant group, the underlying values are made more visible.

One of the most important insights of feminism is that research and the creation of knowledge do not occur in a social vacuum. Rather, each research project or theory is situated in a particular period in history and a particular social context. The psychology of women and gender is not unique in being affected by social currents such as feminism, conservatism, and liberalism. All of psychology is affected. Moreover, psychology in turn affects social issues and social policy through providing ways to interpret human behavior. Because psychology is a cultural institution, doing psychological research is inevitably a political act (Crawford & Marecek, 1989).

Although the effects of values on the scientific process are inevitable, they need not be negative for women. Like many other feminist psychologists, I believe that psychology should admit its values and acknowledge that they are part of the research process (Crawford & Marecek, 1989). Opening our values to scrutiny can only strengthen our research. An awareness of the politics of science can help feminist psychologists use science to foster social change and improve women's lives (Peplau & Conrad, 1989).

Social, Historical, and Political Forces Shape Human Behavior

Because feminists believe that gender equality is possible, although it has not yet been achieved, they are sensitive to the ways that social contexts and forces shape people's behavior and limit human potential. Feminist psychologists try to understand not only the effects of gender, but also the effects of other systems of social classification such as race, social class, and sexuality. They try to clarify the ways that sociocultural forces, as well as biological and psychological ones, affect behavior.

Feminist psychologists respect the diversity of women and recognize that it is important to study varied groups. For example, White U.S. women generally have lower self-esteem than men, but this is not true of African American women. Such differences can show how women's psychology is affected by their social and cultural backgrounds, not just their biology.

Intersectionality

Women are not all alike, and we shouldn't assume that all women have a lot in common simply because they are women. For example, a woman who is wealthy and privileged might have more in common with wealthy and privileged men than with a woman who has been poor all her life. An African American or Latina woman shares more with African American or Latino men when it comes to the lived experience of racism than she does with White women. Lesbians share what it's like to be in a sexual minority with gay men, bisexuals, and transgender people, not with heterosexual women. Women of color and white women may both encounter sexism, but in different ways. Age and disability can be dimensions of discrimination for both women and men. All these examples illustrate the concept of *intersectionality:* each individual is a member of many social groups, and membership in all these groups has consequences for individual identity and social position. The most important groups in the eyes of society are gender, race, class, and sexuality.

Intersectionality is a key theoretical principle in feminist studies, a contribution of Black feminist theorists who observed that women of color often experience simultaneous discrimination on the basis of gender and race (Cole, 2009).

Acknowledging the intersection of social identities allows researchers to understand multiple oppressions—and also the effects of being relatively privileged on some dimensions but not on others.

Intersectionality is an important theoretical principle for psychological research. Feminist psychologist Elizabeth Cole (2009) has proposed that taking intersectionality seriously prompts us to ask three questions about our research designs:

- *Who is included in a category?* The category "female" includes women of different social classes, ethnicities, sexualities, and age groups. Asking who is included in a category can encourage researchers to represent those who have been overlooked in past research and prevent misconceptions about members of minority groups.
- *What role does inequality play?* Social categories such as gender, race, class and sexuality are not mere differences; they are also dimensions of power and status. Membership in these categories places individuals in positions of relative advantage/disadvantage to each other, and can affect their perceptions and their life experiences, even their health and their exposure to violence. Gender, power, and status, and their links to prejudice and discrimination on other dimensions of social identity, are explored in Chapter 2.
- *Where are there similarities?* Even groups that may seem fundamentally different may have common ground that can be discovered if researchers look at their behavior and experience, instead of thinking of them as mere categories.

Psychology's long history of androcentric bias and omitting diverse people from its knowledge base is changing at last. This broadens the way to understanding how individuals' intersecting identities and the life experiences that they lead to are related to larger social structures and systematic oppression (Rosenthal, 2016). Throughout this book, I take an intersectionalist perspective on women's lives, including gender stereotypes, physical and psychological gender differences, gender socialization, relationships, sexuality, parenting, work, physical health, aging, and psychological well-being.

About This Book

This book draws on the work of hundreds of psychologists, both women and men, who have contributed to the ongoing process of transforming psychology. It also draws on the work of feminist theorists and researchers in other disciplines, including philosophy, history, anthropology, sociology, political science, and cultural studies. This book, then, provides both a critique of androcentric knowledge about women and an introduction to the groundbreaking research that has emerged from feminist psychology.

As you read the chapters that follow, you will see that certain threads run through them. Three of these threads in particular are important to highlight at the start. First, _women have not yet achieved full equality with men._ There are persistent differences in power and social standing that shape women's lives. In many cultures and time periods, women have been treated as second-class citizens. Some of the inequalities are glaring—such as denying women the right to vote, own property, use public spaces, or make decisions about our own bodies. Other inequalities are more subtle—such as being subjected to everyday sexist hassles or being paid less at work. Everywhere, power differences are implicated in the shocking worldwide prevalence of violence against girls and women. Gender, power, and social status are so important that they are the focus of Chapter 2. The causes and effects of various kinds of violence against girls and women are highlighted in Chapter 12.

A second thread that runs throughout this book concerns *differences and similarities.* Women and men are not complete opposites of each other. Rather, there is a great deal of overlap in the psychology of women and men. Gender differences are important, but we should also think about gender similarities. When gender differences do occur, we should ask where they come from and how they connect to differences in power and social position.

A third thread that runs throughout this book is that *psychology can contribute to social change.* Traditionally, psychologists have focused on changing individuals. They have developed techniques to change attitudes, increase insight and self-understanding, teach new behavioral skills, and reduce or eliminate self-defeating thinking and behaviors. They have applied these techniques in a variety of educational and therapeutic settings. In this book there are many examples of how feminist psychology has adapted and used these techniques.

However, research on women and gender indicates that there are limits to the power of individual change. Many of the problems that confront women are the result of social structures and practices that put women at a disadvantage and interfere with their living happy, productive lives. Social-structural problems cannot be solved solely through individual changes in attitudes and behavior; rather, the social institutions that permit the devaluation and victimization of women must also be changed. Therefore, throughout this book I discuss the implications of psychological research for changing institutions such as traditional marriage, language use, child rearing, the workplace, and the media. Every chapter ends with a section called *Making a Difference,* which showcases how individuals and groups are changing society toward a more feminist ideal.

A Personal Reflection

Because I believe that personal values shape how a researcher approaches his or her topic, I would like to share with you a little about myself and the experiences and values that shaped the writing of this book.

I started out as a psychologist in the field of learning theory. I was taught that to be a good scientist I must separate my personal or social concerns from my scientific problem solving. My dissertation was an analysis of species-specific reactions in rats and their effects on classical and operant conditioning. I enjoyed doing research. It was exciting to learn how to design a good study, do statistical tests, and write an article for publication. Learning theory is one of the oldest branches of psychology; methods and theories were highly developed, and I could learn how to do it all from well-established experts. My mentor and dissertation advisor was a good scientist and a kind man who treated me with respect. He understood that as a single mom with two young children I was juggling a lot of competing demands, and he encouraged me to become the best researcher I could.

However, soon after I completed my PhD research, my feelings about being a psychologist began to change. More and more, my research seemed like a series of intellectual puzzles that had no connection to the rest of my life. In the lab, I studied abstract theories of conditioning, accepting the assumption that the principles were similar for rats and humans. In the "real world," I became involved in feminist activism and began to see things I had never noticed before. I saw sex discrimination in my university and knew women who struggled to hold their families together in poverty. Trying to build a new egalitarian marriage and bring up my children in nonsexist ways made me much more aware of social pressures to conform to traditional gender roles. I began to ask myself why I was doing a kind of psychology that had so little to say about the world as I knew it. I turned to the study of women and gender in order to make my personal and intellectual life congruent and to begin using my skills as a psychologist on behalf of social change.

Today, I still value my early research for teaching me how to go about scientific inquiry systematically and responsibly, but I have changed my views about what the important questions in psychology are and which theoretical frameworks have the most potential. I chose to develop a new specialization, the study of women and gender, and I have been doing research in this area ever since. I write this book in the hope that it will contribute in some small way to the creation of a transformed psychology, by introducing the psychology of women to the next generation of students (and future psychologists).

I have taught the psychology of women to graduate and undergraduate students for 35 years. My students have differed in their racial and ethnic backgrounds, age, life experience, and sexualities. Their personal beliefs and values about feminism, women, and gender varied a great deal. In short, my students have been a diverse group of people. I have welcomed that diversity, and in this book I try to reflect what I have learned from it. Whatever your own background, I welcome you, my newest student, to the study of women and gender. I hope that it will make a difference for you.

I anticipate that you, like many of my students before you, will experience growth in at least some of the following areas as a result of your studies:

- *Critical thinking skills.* By studying the psychology of women, you can learn to evaluate psychological research critically and become a more astute, perceptive observer of human behavior.
- *Empathy for women.* You may come to appreciate the experiences and viewpoints of your mother, your sisters, and your women friends better. In addition, women students may experience a heightened sense of connection with women as a group.
- *The ability to see the intersectionality of women's social positions and identities.* The psychology of women is closely linked to their place in society and culture.
- *Knowledge and understanding about social inequities.* The focus is on the gender system, sexism, and sex discrimination. However, gender always interacts with other systems of domination such as racism and heterosexism.
- *A commitment to work toward social change.* Psychological research and knowledge only matters when it is used.

Many of my past students have told me that their first course in women and gender raised as many questions as it answered, and was at times challenging, even upsetting. From these students I learned that I cannot promise my future students any easy answers. Acquiring knowledge is an ongoing process, for professional researchers as well as for college students. I invite you to join me in that journey.

Exploring Further

∽

Special Section: Intersectionality Research and Feminist Psychology. Psychology of Women Quarterly, 2016, 40, 155–183.
   This is an advanced discussion among top researchers about how to integrate intersectionality into research methods and practices. In their conversation you can observe the ongoing work of feminist psychologists to bring about a more inclusive psychology by developing intersectionality theory.

Rutherford, A., Marecek, J., & Sheese, K. (2012). Psychology of women and gender. In D. K. Freedheim & I. B. Weiner (Eds.), Handbook of Psychology, Volume 1: History of Psychology, Second edition (pp. 279–301). New York: Wiley.
   An overview of the development of feminist psychology and its effects on psychology as a science and a profession dedicated to helping people.

Cobble, Dorothy S., Gordon, Linda, & Henry, Astrid. (2014). Feminism Unfinished: A Short, Surprising History of American Women's Movements. New York: Norton.
   Feminism has utterly changed our world in the nearly 100 years since women won the vote, say the smart and lively historians who wrote this book. Its influence has been so widespread that it has blended into the culture and been insufficiently analyzed. Their aim is to remedy that. The result is a history book that's hard to put down.

Feminist Voices in Psychology. http://www.feministvoices.com
   A multimedia Internet archive featuring the women of psychology's past and the diverse voices of contemporary feminist psychologists. In interviews available on the site, feminist pioneers talk about their challenge to mainstream psychology and experts in feminist psychology talk about ongoing challenges and future directions for women and feminism in psychology.

Text Credits

∽

PART 2

Gender in Social Context

CHAPTER 2

Gender, Status, and Power

∽

There are only two kinds of women: goddesses and doormats.

—Artist Pablo Picasso

"I—excuse the expression—she's the stereotypical bitch, you know what I mean?"

*—TV host Glenn Beck, about then-Presidential candidate
Hillary Clinton (Biedlingmaier, 2007).*

If combat means living in a ditch, females have biological problems staying in a ditch for 30 days because they get infections and they don't have upper body strength. . . . On the other hand, men are basically little piglets. You drop them in the ditch, they roll around in it.

*—Former Speaker of the U.S. House of Representatives,
Newt Gingrich, on women in the military*

I think everyone has to work at being a man or a woman. Transgendered people are probably more aware of doing the work, that's all.

—Transgender activist Kate Bornstein

As far as I'm concerned, being any gender at all is a drag.

—Rock musician Patti Smith

*T*hese speakers have very clear opinions about men, women, and gender. Yet their words reflect contradictory notions about the meanings of these concepts. Gingrich believes that women have biological limitations that make them unfit for military duty, although men's "piglet" qualities do not seem to be a problem. But Glenn Beck and Pablo Picasso—men of power and influence—do not hesitate to talk of women in negative and stereotypical ways. In contrast, Patti Smith and Kate Bornstein view sex and gender almost as a choice, like a costume that one can choose to wear—or not.

Sorting out the multiple and conflicting meanings of biological sex, femininity, masculinity, and the social roles related to them has not been an easy task for psychologists. In this chapter we separate sex from gender and look at how gender is related to status and power.

What Is Gender?

Researchers who study the psychology of women distinguish between the concepts of sex and gender, a distinction that was first made in the late 1970s (Unger, 1979). *Sex* was defined as biological differences in genetic composition and reproductive anatomy and function. Human infants are labeled as one sex or the other, female or male, at birth, based on the appearance of their genitals. It sounds like a simple and straightforward matter, though in fact it can be surprisingly complex (see Chapter 5).

Gender, in contrast to sex, was originally defined as the characteristics and traits each society considers appropriate for males and females, the traits that make up masculinity and femininity (Unger, 1979). All known societies recognize biological sex and use it as the basis for social distinctions. In our own society, the process of creating gendered human beings starts at birth. When a baby is born, the presence of a vagina or penis represents sex—but the pink or blue blanket that soon enfolds the baby represents gender. The blanket serves as a cue that this infant is to be treated as a boy or girl, not as a generic human being, from the start.

According to these definitions, sex is to gender as nature is to nurture. That is, sex pertains to what is biological or natural, while gender pertains to what is learned or cultural. The sex/gender distinction was important because it enabled psychologists to separate conceptually the social aspects of gender from the biology of sex, and opened the ways to scientific study of such topics as how children are socialized to conform to their society's gender expectations. Distinguishing sex from gender was an important step in recognizing that biology is not destiny—that many of the apparent differences between women and men might be societally imposed rather than natural or inevitable.

However, the sex/gender distinction made at that time was soon seen to be limited. First, it sets up sex and gender as a nature/nurture dichotomy. Most psychologists now acknowledge that nature and nurture are so intertwined in human psychology that it is often impossible to determine the exact contribution of each. Another problem is that viewing gender as a set of stable, socialized traits does not capture the dynamic, interactive ways that people act out their own gender roles and respond to others according to their gender (Deaux & Major, 1987; Crawford, 1995). The trait view of gender also fails to recognize that gender is a culturally shared system through which societies organize relations between males and females (Bem, 1993), or that it marks social power and status (Henley, 1977; Crawford, 1995). A broader concept of gender was needed.

In this book, I take a dynamic approach, defining *gender* as *a classification system that influences access to power and resources and shapes the relations among women and men.* All known human societies make social distinctions based on gender.

Gender distinctions occur at many levels in society. Their influence is so pervasive that, like fish in water, we may be unaware that they surround us. Gender-related processes influence behavior, thoughts, and feelings in individuals; they affect interactions among individuals; and they help determine the structure of social institutions. The processes by which differences are created and power is allocated can be understood by considering how gender is played out at three levels: societal, interpersonal, and individual. In this chapter I describe how gender distinctions are created and maintained at these three levels, and how the levels are linked. Throughout the book, I will return to these levels of analysis to help illuminate how gender works.

Gender Shapes Societies and Cultures

Most societies are *hierarchical*—they have one or more dominant groups and other subordinate groups. The dominant group has more of whatever that society values, whether it be cattle, land, the opportunity to get a good education, or high-paying jobs. In other words, the dominant group has more *power*—defined as the ability to control the outcomes of others by providing or withholding resources—and higher *status*—defined as social standing that elicits respect (Keltner et al., 2003). Societies organize hierarchies on the basis of a variety of arbitrary distinctions—tribe, caste, skin color, religion—and these vary from one society to another. Gender, however, is used universally. To a greater or lesser degree, most modern societies are *patriarchal*, a word that literally means "ruled by the fathers." Patriarchal social systems allocate more power and higher status to men.

Gender and Power

The power conferred by gender is pervasive and multidimensional. For example:

- By and large, men make the laws that everyone must obey. According to the United Nations, in the year 2015 women accounted for only about 22% of members of national parliaments and congresses worldwide.
- Organized religion is a powerful influence in maintaining patriarchy. The Jewish, Islamic, and Christian traditions all view the deity as masculine, prescribe subservient or limited roles for women, and restrict women's participation and influence within the religious establishment. Cross-culturally, greater religiosity is linked with hostility toward women and opposition to gender equality (Harville & Rienzi, 2000; Taşdemir & Sakallı-Uğurlu, 2010).
- Men have more control over public discourse. For example, 78% of TV's foreign policy analysts and reporters are male, as are 74% of the guests on important talk shows like *Face the Nation* and *Meet the Press*. 86% of TV show episodes are directed by men (Women's Media Center, 2015). This exclusion of diverse women from positions of power in commentary and entertainment leaves plenty of room for the stereotypical and demeaning images of women that are prevalent in the mass media (see Chapter 3).
- According to the United Nations, men have more wealth and more leisure time in virtually every society. Much of the work women do is unpaid (child care, subsistence farming, and housework). When they work for pay, women earn less than men for similar or equivalent tasks (see Chapter 10). Therefore, women have less wealth despite working longer hours than men.
- Women have less access to education than men do. In developing countries, more boys are sent to school, while girls are kept at home to care for younger siblings and do housework. Worldwide, literacy rates are lower for women (UNESCO, 2016). In developed countries, where girls and women have access to education, studies show that boys get more attention from teachers and are more often allowed to dominate class time (Beaman et al., 2006; Fisher, 2014).

Gender inequality is global. Each year, the World Economic Forum compiles a Global Gender Gap Index that compares women and men in 145 countries on four important indicators: health and survival, educational attainment, economic participation and opportunity, and political empowerment (World Economic Forum, 2015). The Global Gender Gap Index measures how well off women are compared to the men in their own country. As of 2015, no country in the world had achieved complete equality on this index. (The United States ranks 28th). The good news is that a few, most notably the Nordic countries, come close, and that there is a global trend toward increasing equality over time. However, the global gender equality gap reminds us that gender is a universal marker not just of femininity and masculinity but of social status and power.

Justifying Gender Inequality

Not only do dominant groups have more power, they use a variety of tactics to hold on to their power and maintain inequity among groups (Sidanius & Pratto, 1999). *Legitimizing myths* are attitudes, values, and beliefs that serve to justify hierarchical social practices. Many of the legitimizing myths of patriarchy emphasize that women are fundamentally different from men. They may be seen as evil and treacherous (in need of control), or incompetent (in need of restriction for their own good). They may be regarded as helpless, overemotional, and fragile (in need of protection), or pure and self-sacrificing (to be put on a pedestal). Such myths are deeply embedded in culture. For example, the archetype of women as evil and treacherous recurs in religion (witch hunts, Eve), fairy tales (wicked stepmothers), personality stereotypes (women are seen as gossipy, catty), and myths about rape (the belief that women frequently make false accusations in order to trap men). Legitimizing myths are often so widely accepted that they seem to be undeniably true.

Prejudice is a negative attitude or feeling toward a person because of his or her membership in a particular social group. The negative attitudes and feelings could include disdain, hatred, or simply feeling uncomfortable around members of the devalued group. Prejudice often includes the belief that it is acceptable or right to treat others unequally. Prejudice on the basis of sex or gender is termed *sexism*. For example, the belief that it is more important to give boys than girls a good education is sexist. However, sexism is often more subtle and complicated than in this example; we return to sexist prejudice later in this chapter. A related prejudice is *heterosexism*, or negative attitudes and beliefs about lesbian, gay, transgendered, and bisexual people.

Discrimination involves treating people unfairly because of their membership in a particular group. A teacher who pays more attention to the boys in class or a committee that preferentially awards scholarships to male students is engaging in *sex discrimination.* Many studies have found that sex discrimination is common, for example, in hiring and promotion on the job (Crosby et al., 2003).

A widespread and systematic pattern of prejudice and discrimination is sometimes termed *oppression*. For example, from 1996 to 2002, the Taliban government oppressed women and girls in Afghanistan by denying them basic human rights such as health care, education, freedom of movement, and a voice in public affairs (Brodsky, 2003). A shocking example of oppression—and an inspiring story of resistance—is the life of Malala Yousafzai, a Pakistani advocate for girls' education and the youngest person ever awarded the Nobel Peace Prize (see Box 2.1).

Box 2.1 ～ Malala Yousafzai

Malala Yousafzai was born in 1997 in Mingora, Pakistan. Malala's father is an anti-Taliban activist and outspoken advocate against the Taliban's restriction on girls' education. When the Taliban banned girls from receiving an education and demanded that schools close down, Malala began to speak out. When she was just 11 years old, she gave a speech entitled, "How dare the Taliban take away my basic right to an education?" In 2009, she began blogging anonymously for the BBC about her life under Taliban rule and her views about girls' right to an education. Through her speeches and her blog, Malala became a very vocal advocate for girls' and women's right to an education, even earning a nomination for the International Children's Peace Prize in 2011.

But her activism was not without consequences, as Malala became a target of the Taliban. Taliban leaders called for her death, and on October 9, 2012, Malala was shot in the head on the bus she was riding home from school. Malala survived the attack, and was eventually flown to Birmingham, England to receive care. After multiple surgeries to repair the damage to her face and neck, she was able to start attending school in Birmingham.

She was nominated for a Nobel Peace Prize in 2013, and became the youngest person to receive the award in 2014 at age 17. In 2013 she also released a book entitled, *"I Am Malala: The Girl Who Stood Up for Education and Was Shot by the Taliban."* Today, Malala continues to fight for the rights of girls and women. With her father, she started the Malala Fund in order to bring increased awareness to the importance of educating girls and women, and to empower others to demand change. On her 18th birthday in 2015, she opened a school for Syrian refugees in Lebanon, which plans to educate 200 girls age 14–18.

©Splash News/Newscom

Sources: http://www.malala.org; http://www.biography.com/people/malala-yousafzai-21362253

Contributed by Annie B. Fox

Gender Shapes Social Interactions

Gender affects interactions among people in everyday life. Here we look at how people notice gender and how status and power are conveyed through gender cues.

Think of the last time you bought coffee or a snack. Quickly, try to describe the person who waited on you by listing that person's most important characteristics. Try to give the best "eyewitness testimony" you can.

What characteristics did you list first? People were asked to do a similar task—describe the person who had just sold them a subway token—in a study meant to show that gender is an important category in interpersonal interaction (Grady, 1977). Gender was indeed important. Participants *always* mentioned that the token seller was a woman; in fact, it was the first or second characteristic listed by every single participant. In this case, the token seller happened to be not only female but also African American. Statistically, mentioning ethnicity first would provide more information—"female" rules out only half the U.S. population, while "African American" rules out about 85%. But people do not categorize along statistical lines. Some categories are more salient or noticeable than others—and gender is one of the most salient of all. Many other studies have shown that people overrely on gender as a cognitive category. For example, when research participants watch a video of a discussion group, and later mistakenly mix people up in trying to remember who said or did what, they are more likely to confuse two people of the same gender than two of the same age, ethnic group, or even the same name (Fiske et al., 1991).

Gender is so important that when gender cues are ambiguous, people engage in cognitive puzzle solving to figure out the "correct" gender.

In real life, the cues are usually clear; when they're not, it makes us uneasy (see Figure 2.1). We need to be clear about others' gender when we interact with them, because gender is one of the most important social characteristics we use to classify and evaluate other people.

Constructing Gender through Female Bodies

Because gender is so important in interaction, people strive to make it apparent at first glance. That is, femininity and masculinity are expressed through clothing, hairstyle, body exposure, and so on. But the burden of gender construction is not equally borne by male and female bodies. By far, the majority of gender construction in contemporary industrialized cultures takes place through women's appearance.

Consider a hypothetical scenario: Suppose a group of women and men were banished to the wilderness for several months with no mirrors, razors, grooming products, or labor-saving devices (and no reality-television crew lurking in the trees). Would the group come back to our civilization looking more "feminine" or more "masculine"? Well, let's see, they'd be hairier, dirtier, stronger smelling, more muscular . . . doesn't sound much like our culture's idea of femininity. To us, more physically natural means more masculine; more groomed, scented, modified, and adorned means more feminine. Think of the many grooming options women are exhorted to

©Lars A. Niki

FIGURE 2.1   Gender as performance. A feminine appearance is the result of time, money, and effort.

use every day for creating a feminine appearance from head to toe: coloring, straightening, curling, and styling hair; painting eyelashes, brows, and eyelids; coating facial skin with makeup; reddening the lips; applying lotions and creams to smooth the skin and prevent wrinkles; tanning the body; removing hair from underarms, legs, and genital area; painting finger- and toenails—the list can be extended indefinitely, as new beauty products are invented to remedy (socially invented) deficiencies of femininity.

Clothing and accessories also communicate femininity. Jeans are gender-neutral, but if they are supertight they are feminine. Plain tie shoes are gender-neutral, but add a high heel and they are feminine. T-shirts are gender-neutral, but with a deeply scooped neck and cap sleeves, they are feminine. Skirts and dresses are feminine. Anything with bows or lace is feminine. Hair ornaments are strictly for the girls. In contrast, our culture no longer designates any clothing or accessories as clear signals of masculinity, except, perhaps, the jock strap.

Both femininity and masculinity are performances to some extent, but a feminine appearance is more of a put-on than a masculine appearance (see Figure 2.2). In the process of assuming a feminine persona, a woman's body becomes more than her means of interaction with the material world; it becomes a visible marker serving to maintain socially constructed gender differences and gender roles. Of course, males and females naturally look different; being able to distinguish between the sexes is important to heterosexual reproduction, and secondary sex characteristics like breasts and beards help us to do so. But a natural need to make

©mimagephotography/Shutterstock RF

FIGURE 2.2

distinctions does not necessitate that the bulk of differentiation must take place through female appearance. That *women's* bodies primarily serve as the canvas on which we paint gender may have to do with power.

Gender as a Presentation of Self

Appearance is not the only way we strive to present ourselves as gendered beings. We turn now to exploring how people perform the gender that is assigned to them.

Imagine that you are deciding what to wear for a job interview. You want the job and expect that the interviewer will be an important man. Now imagine that you find out that the interviewer has very traditional—even sexist—attitudes toward women. When college women were put in this situation as research participants, they changed their interaction style according to their expectations about the interviewer. When they expected to meet a sexist man, they wore more makeup and accessories than when they expected to meet a nonsexist man. Although the interviewer knew nothing about their expectations and behaved similarly to all, the women also made less eye contact with the "sexist" man and gave more conventional responses to his questions about their plans for marriage and children (von Baeyer et al., 1981). This is an example of *self-presentation*, or acting out a self in response to the expectations of others.

Both women and men tailor their self-presentation to the audience. In a classic study, female college students were given a description of a male student who was either desirable or undesirable as a potential date and who was characterized as having traditional or more modern values. When the women thought they would have the opportunity to meet the man, they changed their descriptions of themselves to fit the man's traditional or modern values—but only if he was attractive (Zanna & Pack, 1975). A later study showed that male students do exactly the same thing when they think they will have a chance to meet an attractive woman (Morier & Seroy, 1994).

Self-presentation is a strategic choice. In the age of chat rooms, Facebook, Twitter, and Instagram, creating and maintaining a feminine or masculine self-presentation is different from old-fashioned face-to-face communication. When you create a personal website or Facebook profile, you have to list or describe characteristics that would have been evident in person. This gives you the opportunity to be selective about what aspects of yourself you want to present.

One group of researchers explored gendered selves online by analyzing 1000 messages sent by heterosexual teens (ages 17–19) in chat rooms (Kapidzic & Herring, 2011). Their results showed that teen girls tended to present themselves as emotional, friendly, good listeners, sexually available, and eager to please males while the teen boys presented themselves as more assertive, manipulative, initiating, and visually dominant.

The online gendered self must be managed, because it can be very public. For example, young women may want to get drunk and have fun but also still be regarded as respectable and feminine, creating dilemmas of self-presentation (Hutton et al., 2016). In a qualitative study of young women's drinking practices and uses of Facebook, focus group discussions with groups of New Zealand women friends aged 18–25 years revealed that they experienced significant tensions in expressing their "drunken femininities" both in public and online. For example, they posted Facebook pictures showing themselves partying and intoxicated, but they "airbrushed" or edited the photos to minimize the appearance of intoxication.

It's not just young people—adults, too, are faced with dilemmas of self-representation in the digital age. In an interview study of users of online dating sites, both the women and men (who ranged in age from 18 to 47) admitted to creating a more desirable self in their profiles (Ellison et al., 2011). One man, who said that he had quite a "tummy," still listed his body type as "athletic," because, he said, he did have muscles, they just happened to be covered up by his tummy. A woman's profile said that she went to the gym 2–3 times a week, though she did not actually have a gym membership. She explained that as soon as she got a better job, and had the money, she intended to get a membership. Many participants said they thought a certain amount of "fibbing" was acceptable and expected it from others: a woman takes a few years off her age, a man adds an inch or two to his height, and anyone can shed a few pounds in a profile.

Self-presentation strategies make sense because they may have a positive influence on others. Clearly, people's behavior influences how others respond to them. People's actions may even produce the very behaviors they expect from others. This is illustrated by a classic study that involved deceiving people about their interaction partner. Pairs of college women and men had telephone conversations. Unbeknownst to the women, the men had been provided with photographs of random women, some attractive and some unattractive. Thus, each man thought he was conversing with either an attractive or an unattractive woman, but the actual person he talked to was not the one in the photo he saw. Next, independent judges listened to the women's part of the conversation and rated each woman on her personality. Women who had been labeled as attractive were rated as friendlier, more sociable, and more likable than those who had been labeled as unattractive. What was happening here? Apparently, the men treated the women differently in subtle ways, so that the conversation brought out the best in those who were treated like attractive women (Snyder et al., 1977). This kind of influence is most likely to occur when people are relying on minimal information about another person—such as initial encounters (Valentine et al., 2001).

These studies show that gender can become a *self-fulfilling prophecy*. In other words, expectations can make the expected events come true. The earliest studies on self-fulfilling prophecies showed that they can have powerful and lasting effects. When a teacher was led to believe that a particular child was gifted, the child's IQ score went up, even though that child had been randomly selected (Rosenthal & Jacobson, 1968). Apparently, the teachers' beliefs led them to unwittingly treat the "gifted" children in ways that fostered their intellectual growth. One area where gender-linked self-fulfilling prophecies potentially can harm women is the job interview. Usually, the applicant and the interviewer are strangers, so they have a minimum background knowledge of each other as individuals. If the interviewer holds stereotypical negative beliefs about women's competence as leaders and managers in the workplace, will these beliefs affect the applicant's interview performance and the hiring decision? In a mock-interview experiment, male university students were assigned the role of interviewer and female students the role of applicant for a job as regional marketing manager for a convenience store chain (Latu et al, 2015). First, in what they thought was a different study, their gender stereotypical beliefs and sexist attitudes were measured. After the interview, each interviewer and applicant evaluated the performance of the applicant independently of each other. Not surprisingly, the more a male interviewer associated women with incompetence and men with competence, the less hirable he evaluated the female applicant. But a self-fulfilling prophecy also occurred: the less hirable the male interviewer evaluated the female applicant, the less hirable she evaluated herself following the interview, and the lower her actual performance was rated by independent observers. Somehow, during the social interaction of the interview, the male interviewer's negative stereotypical expectations were conveyed to the applicant, affecting her performance.

"Doing Gender"

With these dynamic processes in mind, gender can be viewed as a social performance: like actors in a play, people enact "man" or "woman." With themselves and others as the audience, they actively create and construct their gender. From this perspective, gender is not something people *have*, like brown eyes or curly hair, but something that people *do* (West & Zimmerman, 1987). In this ongoing performance, "being a woman" is created by social consensus:

> There is no such thing as "being a woman" outside the various practices that define womanhood for my culture—practices ranging from the sort of work I do to my sexual preferences to the clothes I wear to the way I use language. (Cameron, 1996, p. 46)

The performance of gender is sometimes deliberate. Have you ever seen the TV and print ads for 900 lines that promise conversations with "Hot babes!" and "Sexy, horny women!"? One researcher interviewed a group of phone sex workers employed on these lines (Hall, 1995). The sex workers reported that they consciously strove to create themselves as the fantasy women that their clients desired. Because phone sex does not provide visual cues, the sex workers created the sexy "babes" of porn fantasy entirely through their language. As sellers of a commodity, the workers were aware of what kind of women's language is marketable as sexy: feminine or flowery words, suggestive comments, and a dynamic intonation pattern (breathy, excited, varied in pitch, lilting).

This study illustrates that people cooperate in producing gender (Marecek et al., 2004). To the male callers, the fantasy woman constructed entirely through language was presumably satisfying. Callers paid well for the service, and many requested the same worker on repeat calls. The sex workers reported that they liked their jobs because they earned good money and had low overhead (they did not need expensive clothing and they could work from home). One even said that she often washed the dishes while talking to a caller. Strikingly, one of the most successful phone sex workers was a man who impersonated a woman. Clearly, this man was adept at performing femininity.

Of course, gender performances are not limited to femininity. Indeed, femininity has meaning only in contrast to masculinity. The gender system requires that men "do" being a man as much as women "do" being a woman. In a study of male college students' conversation while watching a basketball game on TV, the students bragged about their sexual exploits with women and gossiped about other men, especially those they did not like, whom they denigrated as "gay," "artsy-fartsy fags," and "homos." In their talk, these young men displayed their heterosexuality and distanced themselves from other men who were supposedly less masculine. This kind of talk "is not only *about* masculinity, it is a sustained performance *of* masculinity" (Cameron, 1997, p. 59).

Constructing Gender in Interaction

It is important to remember that, outside the realm of appearance, doing gender usually takes place without reflection or conscious awareness. Unlike phone sex workers, most people are not *consciously* striving to produce a gendered persona when they interact with others. Instead, like the women who shaped their own behavior to meet what they thought were the expectations of an interviewer, or the men who disparaged "fags" in the studies described earlier, most people do gender without thinking consciously about the process. And they do it even though, if asked, they would say they believe in gender equality (Rashotte & Webster, 2005). Women's second-class status is created and maintained as people do gender in everyday social interaction. Let's look at how this can happen.

Talking Down, Ordering Around, and Silencing

Members of subordinate groups may be treated disrespectfully in everyday conversation. Dominant group members may use particular ways of talking or kinds of talk to assert and maintain their status, especially when the person they are talking to wants to be seen as an equal (Ruscher, 2001).

The most basic kind of conversational disrespect is not allowing the other person to be heard at all by interrupting, controlling the topic, and taking up most of the talk time. A great deal of research shows that men use these tactics in conversation with women more than they do with other men and more than women do with each other. For example, a classic study in which researchers listened in on same- and mixed-sex conversations in public places showed that 96% of interruptions in male-female conversations were by male speakers. In same-sex pairs, interruptions were about equally divided between the two speakers (Zimmerman & West, 1975). Of course, not all interruptions are hostile. Sometimes, a listener jumps in and interrupts out of interest and enthusiasm. These sorts of interruptions are relatively gender-neutral. However, men do more *intrusive interruptions*—the kind that are active attempts to end the other speaker's turn and take over the conversation. Moreover, men make a larger proportion of intrusive interruptions in unstructured and naturalistic settings than in the lab—settings that more closely resemble everyday interaction (Anderson & Leaper, 1998).

If a woman does interrupt another speaker, she risks social disapproval—especially if she interrupts a man. When college students heard audiotapes of (carefully matched) same- and mixed-sex interactions, they gave the lowest ratings to a woman who interrupted a man. Both male and female participants saw her as more rude and disrespectful than interrupters in the other pairs. Their judgments reflect the view that men *should* have higher status in conversation. When a woman interrupts a man, she is doing more than just breaking a politeness rule; she is violating the social order that gives more respect to men (LaFrance, 1992; Youngquist, 2008).

The double standard extends to politeness too, at least if you ask Donald Trump. One researcher used the method of discourse analysis to analyze an episode of *The Apprentice* (Sung, 2012). During the episode, one woman mildly criticized another woman. Trump—whose behavior throughout the series was a caricature of aggressive masculinity—repeatedly referred to this remark as very rude, saying that she treated the other woman like a dog, treated her terribly, and that her behavior was repulsive. He seemed not to be comparing it to his own near-constant use of interrupting, attacking, insulting, criticizing, and dominating talk, but instead to a belief that women should always be utterly polite, even in the competitive and hyper-masculine atmosphere of the (reality TV) boardroom.

Despite widespread beliefs that women are more talkative, men have been shown to take more than a fair share of talk time in a variety of settings including classrooms, business meetings, and informal conversations (Crawford, 1995). In a review of 63 studies done over a 40-year period, 34 studies showed men talking more than women and only 2 showed women talking more than men (the others showed no differences or had mixed results) (James & Drakich, 1993). The differences were most apparent in task-oriented situations, such as committee meetings, classrooms, and problem-solving groups. These results suggest that context does make a difference: men dominate talk more in contexts where there is more at stake in terms of asserting one's status and getting one's own way.

Conversational dominance can be more subtle than just taking up most of the talk time. For example, imagine that you are teaching someone how to do the wash. Would you be more likely to use direct commands ("Put the whites in one pile") or suggestions ("It's probably best to separate the whites and the colors")? The use of imperative (command) verbs can be a way of talking down, which implies that the learner is not very competent. In an interesting study of gender, status, and language, college students learned how to do the Heimlich maneuver by watching a slide show (Duval & Ruscher, 1994). This task was chosen because it was gender neutral and unfamiliar to most students. After watching the slide show, participants were asked to explain the Heimlich maneuver to either a male or female participant who had not seen the slides. The researchers predicted that men would use more direct orders in explaining the technique to women than to other men, because they would presume that women held lower status and less knowledge than themselves. As predicted, men used more imperative verbs when teaching a woman than were used in any of the other teacher-learner pairs.

Being stuck in a conversation with a guy who does almost all the talking is no fun. Having someone explain things to you that you understand perfectly well is pretty tedious, too.

They happen often enough that they've generated two new words for the English language: *manologue* and *mansplaining*! Actually, it's unfair to use these terms, because they stereotype men; certainly not all men are guilty of these forms of conversational dominance, and women can be insensitive and domineering in conversation, too. However it is fair to say that conversational dominance is linked to gender, and that being talked down and ordered around can create a self-fulfilling prophecy. After a while, the person on the receiving end, who is treated as though they are unimportant and incompetent, may start to feel that way.

Nonverbal Messages

Tara and Tom are assistant managers at separate branches of a local business. They meet for lunch to talk about ideas for increasing profits. When Tom talks, Tara keeps her eyes on his face and smiles a lot. When Tara talks, Tom gazes out the window. When he wants to jot something down, he borrows Tara's pen without asking. While they talk, Tom leans away from Tara and pulls the papers on the table between them closer to him. When they get up to leave, Tara looks closely at Tom's face to assess whether he has found the meeting useful. Tom touches Tara lightly on the shoulder.

As this example shows, not all communication relies on words. Here we consider how gendered patterns of nonverbal communication convey status and power in North American society. Although Tara and Tom are ostensibly meeting as equal colleagues, their nonverbal communication patterns convey a clear message about who is more powerful and important.

High-status people have more nonverbal privileges and fewer nonverbal obligations. They can take up more space, invade the space of others, and touch them and
their possessions. They are less obligated to show their interest and involvement in
others' talk. Pioneering research by psychologist Nancy Henley led her to propose
the theory that when women and men interact, the nonverbal behavior of men is
like that of high-status, dominant individuals, and the nonverbal behavior of
women is like that of lower-status, submissive individuals (Henley, 1973, 1977).
(See Figure 2.3.) This nonverbal dominance not only reflects status differentials, it
performs—and thus perpetuates—them. With Henley's theory in mind, let's look
at each of the differences shown by Tom and Tara.

Many studies have found that women smile much more than men do in interaction (Hall, 2006; LaFrance et al., 2003). Smiling is a socially positive activity that
conveys emotional expressiveness and shows interest and involvement, but are all
those smiles genuine? High- and low-status people may give (and get) different
kinds of smiles. When people are interacting with equal- or lower-status others,
their smiles are likely to be consistent with the emotions they report. However,
when they are interacting with higher-status others, their smiles are less related to
their actual positive emotions (Hecht & LaFrance, 1998). In other words, when
high-status people smile at others, it is because they are feeling good; when low-
status people smile it may be because they feel a need to please their interaction
partner. High-status people probably should not assume that their subordinates are
overjoyed or even interested just because they are smiling. Women, like low-status

©JGI Media Bakery RF

**FIGURE 2.3   Cues to status in interaction include patterns of smiling, posture, gesture,
eye contact, talking, and listening.**

people, seem to feel an obligation to smile (LaFrance, 2001). If a woman violates that obligation, she may be admonished to "Cheer up" or asked "What's the matter with you?"

The patterns of looking and speaking used by Tom and Tara also reflect status differences. Looking at conversational partners when they are speaking communicates respect and interest. The more power and status a person has, the less they need to offer this kind of respect. High-status people look at their subordinates while speaking to them, but tend to look away when it's the subordinate's turn to talk—a pattern termed *visual dominance.* In a study of interaction in mixed-sex pairs, visual dominance was about equal in women and men who had more expertise on the topic than their conversational partners. However, when their expertise was the same as their partner's, men showed more visual dominance than women. In other words, when participants lacked any other cues to status, they relied on gender, and enacted the men's dominance in eye contact (Dovidio et al., 1988).

When Tom leaned away from Tara and pulled the papers closer to himself, he was echoing a gendered pattern of distancing behavior documented in research. In one study, college students in same- and mixed-gender pairs were given 10 minutes to build a domino tower (Lott, 1987). When working with a woman, men more often turned their faces or bodies away and put the dominoes closer to themselves than when they worked with another man. (Women treated men and other women alike.) This kind of microdiscrimination reflects and reinforces men's higher status.

Probably the most ambiguous nonverbal behavior between Tom and Tara was Tom's parting touch. Did it communicate friendship? Sexual interest? Or "Don't forget that I'm in charge here"? Like many other nonverbal behaviors, touch can communicate either intimacy or dominance. Whether A is "caressing" or "pawing" B, being affectionate or invasive, can be hard to determine (Ruscher, 2001). (See Figure 2.4.) Henley suggests that intimacy behaviors can be distinguished from dominance behaviors by whether the recipient welcomes the touch and whether she can comfortably reciprocate it. Men, because of their higher status, are allowed to initiate more touch with women, particularly in public interaction.

In a creative field study, college student researchers were trained to unobtrusively observe professors interacting at professional conventions (Hall, 1996). The researchers did not just determine whether men touched women more than vice versa. They coded the kinds of touch that were used: brief "spot" touches or more personal pats and hugs; what body parts were touched (hand, arm, shoulder); and the apparent function (greeting, affection, control). Also, they independently assessed each professor's status based on number of publications, the prestige of the professor's university, and related measures. There was strong evidence that lower- and higher-status people initiated different kinds of touch. Lower-status people initiated more handshakes, but higher-status people more often touched others' arm or shoulder. It seemed that high-status people were *displaying* status through using more intrusive arm-and-shoulder touch, while lower-status people were trying to *gain* status by politely offering to shake hands. Gender was important, too. When the male and female professor in a pair had equal status, men initiated more

FIGURE 2.4   Touch can be an ambiguous cue. In this office interaction, is it meant to be friendly, helpful, or sexually intrusive?

touching. In other words, gender itself served as a cue to status when all else was equal, and women were treated like lower-status others.

Gender differences in nonverbal behavior are not due entirely to power and status. Nonverbal behavior has many functions and varies considerably according to age, ethnicity, and culture. Nonverbal behavior may also be related to physical size differences. Clearly, though, one function of nonverbal cues is to signal the unequal status of women and men.

Hassles, Stressors, and Microagressions

If women are indeed treated as a subordinate group, we would expect that they would often experience "hassles" that are related to second-class status. Research confirms that these hassles are a part of life for women. When college women and men were asked to keep diaries of sexist incidents and their impact in a series of studies, the women reported an average of one to two such incidents each week, whereas men reported only about one every two weeks (Swim et al., 2001). Here are a few examples of the experiences reported by women:

Gender role stereotyping: "You're a woman, so fold my laundry."

Demeaning remarks: "I was hanging out with some friends when one guy in the apartment said, "Yo bitch, get me some beer!"

Sexual objectification: Walking home from a party, a woman encountered three men. One complimented her on the belt she was wearing, and another said, "Forget the belt, look at her rack."

Living with everyday sexism has a negative effect on the well-being of both women and men. In these studies, participants who experienced more sexist hassles reported higher anger, anxiety, and depression, along with lower self-esteem and reduced comfort in social situations. Because women experience significantly more sexist hassles overall than men, the impact on them is greater.

Studies using more diverse samples show similar results. When researchers used a detailed survey to measure women's experiences of sexism within the past year and also over a lifetime, they found that such experiences are almost universal—99% of the women had experienced a sexist event at least once, and 97% within the past year (Klonoff & Landrine, 1995). The most common experiences included being subjected to sexist jokes (94%), being treated with a lack of respect (83%), being called sexist names, and being sexually harassed (82% for each). A majority of the women surveyed (56%) said that they had been hit, pushed, or physically threatened because of being a woman. (See Table 2.1.)

The sample of more than 600 women in this study was ethnically and economically diverse. Women of color and White women reported experiencing similar kinds of sexist events; however, women of color reported more sexist experiences overall. Like the college students in the diary studies, these women also experienced psychological costs. The number of sexist experiences reported was related to the overall number of psychological and physical symptoms reported and to specific problems such as depression, premenstrual symptoms, and obsessive-compulsive behaviors. In fact, sexism statistically predicted psychological and physical problems better than other measures of stressful life events alone (Landrine et al., 1995). The impact of sexist hassles is also clear in a study of military personnel (Murdoch et al., 2007). More women than men (80% versus 45%) reported having experienced such stressors as sexual harassment or challenges about their sexual identity. Both male and female personnel who reported more stressor experiences had poorer social and work functioning, more physical problems, and more symptoms of posttraumatic stress disorder, depression, and anxiety.

Recent research has shown that heterosexist hassles have negative effects on lesbian, gay, and bisexual (LGB) individuals. When asked to keep daily diaries, a sample of LGB people reported that experiencing heterosexist hassles led to increased anger and anxiety. Moreover, these experiences caused the LGB participants to lower their own acceptance of themselves as LGBs, and negatively influenced their perceptions of other lesbians, gays, and bisexuals (Swim et al., 2009). Moreover, a focus group study of bisexual women revealed that they experienced subtler forms of disrespect including indirect hostility, pressures to change, and denial/dismissal of their sexuality. One woman in this study said that being bisexual meant "negotiating life as if there are landmines out there" (Bostwick & Hequembourg, 2014, p. 493).

These subtle insults are *micro-aggressions:* brief verbal or behavioral indignities that communicate hostile or derogatory attitudes toward a person because of their identity as part of a devalued group (Nadal et al., 2015). These slights and insults may or may not be intentional, but they can be harmful nevertheless. Members of ethnic and racial minority groups, as well as women, are exposed to

TABLE 2.1   Women's Experiences of Sexism. Percentages are those women who said they had experienced each type of incident *because of being a woman.*

Item	Percent Who Experienced It within Lifetime	Percent Who Experienced It within Past Year
Treated unfairly by teachers/professors	53	25
your employer, boss, or supervisors	60	32
your coworkers, fellow students, or colleagues	58	37
people in service jobs (store clerks, servers, bartenders, bank tellers, mechanics)	77	62
strangers	73	59
people in helping jobs (doctors, nurses, psychiatrists, case workers, dentists, school counselors, therapists, pediatricians, school principals, gynecologists)	59	40
your boyfriend, husband, or other important man in your life	75	50
Denied a raise, promotion, tenure, good assignment, job, or other such thing at work that you deserved	40	18
People have made inappropriate or unwanted sexual advances to you	82	55
People failed to show you respect	83	62
Been really angry about something sexist that was done to you	76	52
Forced to take drastic steps (filing a grievance/lawsuit, quitting your job, moving away) to deal with a sexist incident	19	9
Been called a sexist name like bitch, cunt, chick, or other names	82	54
Gotten into an argument or a fight about something sexist that was done or said to you or somebody else	66	44
Been made fun of, picked on, pushed, shoved, hit, or threatened with harm	56	29
Heard people making sexist jokes or degrading sexual jokes	94	84

Source: Adapted from Klonoff, E. A., & Landrine, H. (1995). The schedule of sexist events: A measure of lifetime and recent sexist discrimination in women's lives. *Psychology of Women Quarterly, 19,* 439–472. Percentages have been rounded to the nearest whole number.

micro-aggressions (Nadal et al., 2014). Other recent studies have focused on people with disabilities and members of minority religious groups (Nadal et al., 2015).

Most research on micro-aggression has focused on single identities. But as we learned in Chapter 1, the intersection of multiple identities is very important. One group of researchers recently re-analyzed the data from six previous qualitative studies of micro-aggressions whose participants were male, female, transgender, Muslim, African-American, lesbian, gay, bisexual, and Arab American, looking for intersecting domains such as race and gender, race and religion, gender and religion, and gender and sexual identity. The results showed several themes related to intersections of identities. For example, one theme was that women of color were sometimes treated as exotic and different from other women; another was gender-based stereotypes for lesbians and gay men (e.g., all gay men are into fashion) (Nadal et al., 2015). Because each of the original studies had focused on only one group they had missed these intersections of micro-aggressions in their data analyses.

The differential impact of hassles, stressors, and micro-aggressions on people with multiple marginalized identities points up the importance of the principle of intersectionality introduced in Chapter 1. Women whose identities are linked not only to their gender status but to their marginalized status as women of color or lesbian/bisexual women experience more of these negative events. Clearly, being treated like a second-class citizen in everyday interactions is a major source of stress, and research has linked these events to decreased psychological and physical health and well-being. When disrespect comes your way because you are a woman, or a person of color, or gay—or all of the above—it is inherently degrading, and very personal. It is an attack on an essential part of who you are, and one that you cannot change (Klonoff & Landrine, 1995).

Backlash and Double Binds

Why do women (and members of other subordinated groups) put up with unequal treatment? Why don't they just start acting like members of the dominant group? Surely, women can tell sexist jokes, order men around, interrupt them, and call them names. Aside from the fact that this kind of equality would create a pretty unpleasant society to live in, there are other reasons.

Dominant behaviors are strongly associated with men. In one study, college students and other young adults were shown a list of dominant and submissive social behaviors and asked to rate how often a typical man or woman would behave that way. The participants reported that dominant acts (setting goals for a group, refusing to back down in an argument) were more likely to be done by a man, and submissive acts (accepting verbal abuse, not complaining when overcharged at the store) were more likely to be done by a woman (McCreary & Rhodes, 2001). Because dominant behaviors are linked in people's belief systems with men, they may be less effective when used by women.

Backlash is a negative reaction against women whose behavior violates gender norms. Many studies from the 1980s to the present show that women who take on leadership roles, or act assertive or dominant, are judged as more hostile, less socially

skilled or just not as likable as men who behave in the same way (Amanatullah &
Tinsley, 2013). It's easy to find examples of harsh judgments of women's ambition
and ability. For example, one study examined newspaper coverage in the first five
days after Julia Gillard became the first female Prime Minister of Australia in 2010
(Hall & Donaghue, 2013). Gillard's ambition was presented as both ruthless (she
"took up the knife and planted it in his back") and gender deviant ("anyone expecting
Parliament to be a softer, gentler place because a woman is in charge is likely to be
disappointed").

Let's look at laboratory studies that illustrate the backlash effect. In one series
of experiments, college students saw vignettes or videos showing women or men
negotiating a job offer for themselves or for another person and were asked to evaluate the negotiator. When the negotiator was a woman who acted assertively on her
own behalf there was a backlash. People thought she was arrogant, self-entitled,
and dominant and they said they would not want to work with her. Only when she
negotiated on behalf of another person and not for herself was she perceived positively. Assertive men were perceived positively whether they negotiated for themselves or for another person (Amanatullah & Tinsley, 2013). In another study,
participants rated a talkative female CEO in a vignette as significantly less competent and less suitable for leadership than a male CEO who talked exactly the same
amount (Brescoll, 2011). All participants in this study were adults with workplace
experience. It seems they had learned in the real world that women are not supposed to show their power by speaking up.

Backlash against assertive women creates a *double bind:* a "damned if you do,
damned if you don't" situation. Women who act assertively may be seen as competent but not likable; those who act in a more stereotypically feminine way may
be perceived as likable but not competent. Double binds create no-win
situations.

Let's take the example of communication style. In American society, speaking
up for oneself, expressing opinions, and being assertive about one's rights are
valued—so much so that assertiveness training workshops are a popular type of
psychological self-improvement. Many of these workshops are aimed specifically at
women. However, when women adopt this assertive style, they may be judged differently than men who speak the same way. In one early study, college students and
older adults were asked to read scenarios in which a male or female speaker
behaved assertively but respectfully (for example, politely asking a supervisor not to
call him/her "kiddo" in front of clients). Participants, especially those who were
older and male, judged assertive women as equally competent but less likable than
assertive men (Crawford, 1988). The double bind is obvious: women, but not men,
have to choose between being unassertive (and letting others dominate them) and
being assertive (and risking being disliked). The double bind of competence versus
likability persists for women. A recent meta-analysis of 71 studies concluded that
"Dominant women (compared with dominant men) may have difficulty getting
hired or securing votes, and this is because they are seen as less likable, not because
they are seen as less competent" (Williams & Tiedens, 2016, p. 179). In the United
States, where women still are a small minority in elected political offices, the effects
of backlash are very real.

Other studies also show that so-called masculine speech is less effective for women than for men. Male raters viewed women who spoke in a competent, assertive style as less likable, less influential, and more threatening than men who used the same style—unless they went out of their way to appear warm and friendly (Carli, 2001). This double standard hinders female politicians. When Hillary Clinton raised her voice while competing against Bernie Sanders in the 2016 Democratic primary race, opponents attacked her. One said, "Has nobody told her that the microphone works?" and another suggested that she "get off this screaming stuff." Meanwhile, her supporters pointed out, Bernie Sanders almost always "bellows at the top of his lungs" (Milbank, 2016). When Sanders or other male politicians yell it shows their dedication to the cause, but when Clinton or other women politicians yell it comes across as strident and shrill.

Women face double binds not only with their voice but with their appearance. In the 80s, women who wanted positions of power and influence were told to dress in power suits: padded shoulders, navy blue or gray, conservative cut, but with a feminine touch of a bow at the neckline. In 2016, a New York Times fashion supplement advised women that they can now wear thigh-high slit skirts, navel-baring bra tops, lace slip dresses, leather, ruffles, and sequins to the office—"the new power dressing" (Prickett, 2016). Either way, what this advice tells us is that women are still judged by their appearance to a greater extent than men are, and still have to walk that line between likability and competence. For men there is no dilemma. A suit and tie suffices for a professional occupation, khakis and button-down shirt works for a tech occupation. Nobody questions your competence or likability according to what you wear, within reasonable bounds. Can we even imagine a men's magazine advising them to dress for power by unbuttoning their shirts to the waist at the office?

The double bind of appearance creates practical dilemmas for women as they try to negotiate how much they should focus on looking sexy and attractive. There are no simple answers to these dilemmas. In one experiment, evaluations of sexily dressed women were different depending on whether they had high-status or low-status jobs. Participants evaluated a videotaped female target whose physical attractiveness was held constant, but who was dressed in sexy or businesslike attire and allegedly either a manager or a receptionist. Participants were more negative toward the sexily attired manager and rated her as less competent than the neutrally attired manager. In contrast, the dress style of the receptionist had no effect on their judgments of her likeability or competence. These findings suggest that a sexy self-presentation harms women in high-, but not low-, status jobs (Glick et al., 2005).

The Gender Management Game

Gender is an asset for men because masculinity is linked with perceptions of dominance, competence, and normative behavior. Gender is a liability for women because these dominant and masterful characteristics are still not equally valued in women, and the characteristics that *are* valued—a tentative, soft speech style, feminine attractiveness—are not always associated with competence. The ever-present possibility of being devalued, disliked, or discounted for behaving in ways that are acceptable for men means that women must adopt ***gender management*** *strategies:* ways of behaving that are aimed at softening a woman's impact, reassuring others that she is not threatening, and displaying niceness as well as (not too much) competence. It isn't easy; behaviors that make a woman appear more competent (like speaking up about her own ability) also may make her appear less likable (Rudman & Glick, 1999).

Gender management strategies have been shown in laboratory studies. In one, participants faced a hypothetical situation in which they were the lowest- or highest-power person in a problem-solving group at work (Brescoll, 2011). High-power women, but not men, said they would talk less in the group, so that they wouldn't be disliked. The same researcher also looked at a real-world situation of power deployment: the amount of time U.S. senators spent talking on the Senate floor. Using independent measures of the actual power of each senator (positions on important committees, getting legislation passed, etc.) the researcher correlated C-SPAN footage of talk time with power for each male and female senator. For male senators, there was a direct and positive relationship: the more power the more talk. For female senators, there was no relationship. Although this study was correlational and could not show causation, given all the other research on double binds for women, the researcher's best guess was that even powerful female senators fear backlash if they talk "too much."

What happens to women who do not play the gender management game? An example is the case of Ann Hopkins, who was denied a partnership in a major corporation despite the fact that she had contributed more billable hours and brought in more earnings than any of the 87 male employees proposed for partner—$25 million in revenue (Fiske et al., 1991). The reason? Hopkins was told that she lacked interpersonal skills, ought to go to "charm school," wear makeup and jewelry, have her hair styled, and dress in more feminine clothes. Hopkins sued, and a group of eminent psychologists served as expert witnesses on her behalf when the case (*Hopkins v. Price Waterhouse*) went to the U.S. Supreme Court. Fortunately, the Court was not fooled by the excuses given for denying Hopkins her promotion. Ruling in her favor, they specifically pointed out the double bind she had been placed in:

> An employer who objects to aggressiveness in women but whose positions require this trait places women in an intolerable Catch-22: out of a job if they behave aggressively and out of a job if they don't. (as cited in Fiske et al., 1991)

Gender Shapes Individuals

To a greater or lesser extent, women and men come to accept gender distinctions visible at the social structural level and enacted at the interpersonal level as part of the self-concept. This process is called *gender typing.* As individuals become *gender-typed,* they ascribe to themselves the traits, behaviors, and roles normative for people of their sex in their culture. Gender typing is an important part of identity for most people, and the topic has generated a great deal of psychological research. In Chapter 6, we will look in detail at the gender-typing process during childhood and adolescence. Here, in keeping with the theme of power and status, I focus on how women's subordinate status becomes internalized.

People accept much more than the traits designated as masculine or feminine in their culture. They also internalize the ideologies that support the gender system. These ideologies become consensual—they are shared by members of dominant and subordinate groups alike (Sidanius & Pratto, 1999). In other words, members of both the dominant and subordinate groups come to believe the legitimizing myths of the dominant group, and develop attitudes that serve to justify its dominance. When members of subordinate groups accept the myths that justify their inequality, the dominant group usually does not need to control them through force or other harsh methods. Instead, subordinates usually control themselves.

Justifying Inequality

Strangve as it may seem, "oppression is very much a cooperative game" (Sidanius & Pratto, 1999, p. 43). Let's look at beliefs and attitudes held by both women and men that justify and sustain inequality.

Denial of Personal Discrimination

The American legal system is based on the idea of fairness: If you believe you have been wronged or discriminated against, you have the right to seek justice. Unfortunately, a large research literature in social psychology shows that victims of injustice often do not recognize that they are being treated unfairly.

It's not that people are blind to discrimination at the group level. If you ask Latino/as about racial discrimination in the United States, or ask women about sex discrimination, or ask gay and lesbian people about heterosexist discrimination, they are very likely to acknowledge that such discrimination does happen. However, when asked if they have ever *personally* been discriminated against, they are much less likely to acknowledge that it has happened to them. This discrepancy is termed ***denial of personal discrimination*** (Crosby et al., 2003).

Denial of personal discrimination is pervasive. It has been documented in women, ethnic and linguistic minorities in Canada, as well as women, gay and lesbian people, and African Americans in the United States (Crosby et al., 2003). In the first, now-classic, study (Crosby, 1982), a large sample of employed women and men in the northeastern United States were asked in detail about their perceptions of the position of working women and about their satisfaction with their own working position. The researcher was surprised to find that, although the employed women were, by objective measures, victims of salary discrimination, they weren't any less happy about their treatment at work than the men were. They did acknowledge the disadvantages faced by working women in general, but, "It seemed as if each woman saw herself as the one lucky exception to the general rule of sex discrimination" (Crosby et al., 2003, p. 104). Of course it is logically impossible for a group to be subject to discrimination and for every individual in that group to be exempt from it!

Denial of personal discrimination is probably related to the need to believe in a just world, where each person gets what he or she deserves (Crosby et al., 2003). It may also be related to shifting standards of evaluation—people may evaluate a salary of X dollars a week as merely adequate for a man but very good for a woman, instead of comparing them equally (Biernat & Kobrynowicz, 1999). And denial of personal discrimination is related to belief in the legitimizing myths of the dominant group. In other words, the more one accepts ideologies that justify the status quo of power and status, the less one perceives discrimination. This was tested in a study comparing high-status groups (European Americans and men) with low-status groups (African Americans, Latino/a Americans, and women). The more that members of low-status groups accepted the belief that America is an open society where anyone can get ahead if they just work hard enough, the less likely they were to report that they had experienced discrimination. Next, the researchers rigged a laboratory situation in which women experienced rejection by a man (not being offered a desirable job in the experiment) or men experienced the same rejection from a woman. The more a woman believed in the myth of the open society, the less likely she was to believe that her rejection was due to discrimination. In contrast, the more a man believed in the myth, the more likely he was to believe he'd been discriminated against. Thus, believing in upward mobility—the ideology of the dominant group—affects how people interpret whether they have experienced discrimination (Major et al., 2002).

Denial of personal discrimination has important social consequences. When members of subordinated groups do not have a sense of personal injustice, they may be slow to take action against their own disadvantaged situation. If you don't know that you've been wronged you are unlikely to protest; if no one recognizes personal discrimination it's hard to start correcting it.

How Much Is Your Work Worth? Gender and Entitlement

> You are an employee in an assisted living facility for older adults. Your supervisor is considering offering the residents help with shopping and asks you to generate some ideas on whether it would be a good idea to encourage online shopping. Because it's an extra project, the supervisor asks you to suggest how much you think you should be paid for the task of writing down your thoughts on this issue.

In an experiment where the situation was similar to our example (Jost, 1997), the women who participated paid themselves 18% less and rated their ideas as less original than did the men, despite the fact that independent judges (who did not know the gender of the authors) rated the men's and women's work as equally good. Research studies have repeatedly shown that when women and men are asked to specify an appropriate pay rate for their work, women say their work is worth less than men do (Steil et al., 2001). They seem not to feel entitled to equality.

Women often justify the lower pay they give themselves by believing that their work is not as good as others' work, but even when they recognize that the quality of their work is equal, they still may pay themselves less (Major, 1994). Like denial of personal discrimination, this is a pervasive phenomenon that deters women from taking action or protesting against their subordinate status. Like denial, it may reflect internalization of the values of the dominant group.

One reason women may not feel entitled to equal pay is that they compare themselves to other women who are also underpaid (Davison, 2014). Another reason is that they base their idea of fair pay on previous experience, in which they actually were underpaid. In one study, college students were asked about their expectations of earnings in the future. The women tended to believe that they deserved less than did the men. However, this gender difference in entitlement was accounted for by differences in the actual earnings from the students' most recent summer jobs, where the women had earned less than the men on average (Desmarais & Curtis, 1997). Gender differences in entitlement also reflect other kinds of status inequalities. When researchers experimentally raised women's status (by telling participants that women were particularly good at the task), the gender difference disappeared—high-status women paid themselves as much as men did (Hogue & Yoder, 2003).

Whatever the underlying reasons for denial of personal discrimination and gender differences in entitlement (and there may be several), these lines of research suggest that those who are treated like second-class citizens learn to accept inequality as the norm. These beliefs and attitudes, shaped by differential opportunities and maintained in social interaction, are the products of the gender system.

Sexist Attitudes

Sexist prejudice is not just a matter of men disliking women. Sexist attitudes are more complicated than that. Both women and men agree that women are generally nicer and more pleasant than men (Eagly & Mladinic, 1993). Moreover, attitudes toward women have changed in a positive direction over past decades. However, sexism persists. Today's sexism is likely to be more subtle and conflicted than the sexism of the past.

Contemporary sexism aimed at women is likely to be ***ambivalent:*** it involves both hostility and benevolence toward women (Glick & Fiske, 1996). ***Hostile sexism*** involves the beliefs that women are inferior and that they are threatening to take over men's rightful (dominant) place. People who score high on hostile sexism agree with statements like these:

- Women seek to gain power by getting control over men.
- Most women interpret innocent remarks or acts as being sexist.

Benevolent sexism emphasizes that women are special beings to be cherished and protected, as measured by items such as these:

- A good woman should be set on a pedestal by her man.
- Many women have a quality of purity that few men possess.

If benevolent sexism reflects a positive view that women should be cherished and protected by men, why is it a problem? Although benevolent sexism seems less harmful than hostile sexism, it has several insidious dangers. It exaggerates the differences between women and men (see Chapter 4). It may lead women to accept rules and regulations about where they can go and what they can do because "it's for your own good" (Moya et al., 2007). It may impair women's performance on cognitive tasks by causing them to doubt their ability (Dardenne et al., 2007). Moreover, people who are pure, innocent, fragile, and worthy of protection are not likely to be thought of as capable leaders. Being put on a pedestal may offer some compensation for the patriarchal status quo. However, life on a pedestal can be quite confining.

Men who endorse both kinds of sexism—termed *ambivalent sexists*—have polarized images of women. For example, they acknowledge that "career women" are intelligent and hardworking, but they also believe that they are aggressive, selfish, and cold. The women they feel the most positive about are those in roles that serve men's needs, such as homemakers and "sexy babes" (Glick et al., 1997). Women who endorse benevolent sexism are likely to score high in a personality trait called *psychological entitlement,* a pervasive sense of deserving special treatment (Grubbs et al., 2014; Hammond et al., 2014). Ambivalent sexism is hard to change because benevolence is often not recognized as a form of prejudice by either women or men (Baretto & Ellmers, 2005). Thus, a sexist man can easily deny his prejudice. ("But I *love* women; I think they're wonderful and deserve to be treasured!") This paternalism may hinder him and others from recognizing the more hostile aspect of his sexism (". . . as long as they stay in their place"). And the protectionism of benevolent sexism might make some women feel like princesses.

Ambivalent sexism has been measured in more than 15,000 people in 19 nations (though the samples were heavily weighted toward college students) (Glick et al., 2000). Both hostile and benevolent sexism were found to be quite common. In every country studied, men endorsed hostile sexism more than women did, although the gender differences were much larger in some countries (South Africa, Italy) than in others (England, the Netherlands). Surprisingly, though, women endorsed benevolent sexism as much as men did in about half the countries studied—and in four countries (Cuba, Nigeria, South Africa, and Botswana)—women scored higher than men did. Patterns of correlations showed that the more sexist a nation's men were, the more women of that nation endorsed benevolent sexism.

Moreover, the differences among countries in this study were systematically related to women's status and power within each society. Using measures of gender inequality developed by the United Nations that assessed such factors as women's proportion of seats in parliament, earned income, literacy rates, and life expectancy, the research team found that the more that men in a given country endorsed sexist beliefs, the lower the status of women in that country.

Benevolent sexism is correlated with hostile sexism, and the two sustain patriarchy in complementary ways. Benevolent sexism rewards those women who accept conventional gender norms and power relations. Thus, women tend to endorse benevolent sexist beliefs when they think that the men around them do (Sibley et al., 2009). Hostile sexism punishes women who challenge the status quo. For example, when a sample of English college men read a scenario about an acquaintance rape, those who scored higher in hostile sexism were more likely to think that the victim's resistance was not sincere, and to say they might behave the same way as the rapist in the same situation (Masser et al., 2006). In societies where a great many men are hostile sexists, women may cope by believing that if they behave according to the societal rules for good women, they will be protected. "The irony is that women are forced to seek protection from the very group that threatens them, and the greater the threat, the stronger the incentive to accept benevolent sexism's protective ideology" (Glick & Fiske, 2001, p. 113).

Sexist attitudes such as these portray women as *either* competent and autonomous *or* likable and worthy, and they are one source of many double binds like those described earlier. Both hostile and benevolent sexism help perpetuate the higher status and social power of men.

Sexism is related to prejudice against other lower-status groups. *Social dominance orientation (SDO)* is a general measure of how much an individual supports the domination of supposedly inferior groups by superior groups (Sidanius & Pratto, 1999). SDO is relevant to many dimensions of discrimination, including race, religion, sexuality, gender, and nationality. People who are high in SDO tend to agree with statements like these:

- This country would be better off if inferior groups stayed in their place.
- To get ahead in life, it is sometimes necessary to step on other groups of people.

People who are high in SDO tend to show racial and ethnic prejudice, sexism, heterosexism, acceptance of rape myths, political conservatism, and right-wing authoritarianism (Christopher & Mull, 2006; Christopher et al., 2013). They tend to support social policies that favor high-status groups and oppose policies that would give more power to lower-status groups. Thus, they are likely to support more spending on prisons and the military, and oppose women's rights, gay and lesbian rights, universal health care, antipoverty programs, and affirmative action. Men and women have been measured on SDO in 45 samples totaling over 19,000 participants in 10 countries. In 39 of these samples, men scored significantly higher on SDO than did women, and in 6, they scored about the same; there was not a single sample in which women scored higher than men (Sidanius & Pratto, 1999).

Linking the Levels of Gender: A Summary

Gender has a complex structure of meanings. Feminists initially distinguished it from sex by defining it as the traits and roles considered appropriate for males and females. With this definition, they emphasized that gender is a socialized part of self and identity. Today, the understanding of gender is much broader. We have learned that gender can be conceptualized as:

- A universal system of social classification that accords greater power and status to men
- A dynamic process of performing what it means to be female or male
- An aspect of individual identity and attitudes

When focusing on gender as a social system, we emphasized societal power structures that support patriarchy. When focusing on gender as a self-presentation and a performance, we emphasized the many small, almost invisible ways that people present themselves as gendered beings and conform to others' gender-based expectations, emphasizing that for women, doing gender also means doing subordination. The performance of gender is usually not a conscious, self-aware choice;

rather it is a more or less automatic response to social pressures. When focusing on gender as a socialized aspect of individuals, we saw that both women and men who live in a context of gender hierarchy may come to accept beliefs and attitudes that justify and maintain gender inequality (and often other forms of inequality as well, such as racism and heterosexism). In other words, the patriarchal ideology of gender "gets in your head," becoming part of an individual's identity and world view. The three levels of the gender system are linked, reinforcing each other.

There is one important aspect of gender that characterizes all these levels: power. Patriarchy is a system that accords more power and higher social status to men. Gender is expressed differently in different societies, and the degree of women's subordination varies across time and place, but there are no known cultures where women have more social and political advantages than men.

Throughout this chapter I have described social scientists' efforts to understand the gender system through various types of systematic research. Before closing, let's take one more look at the gender system, this time through one woman's eyes.

Shukria's Story

Shukria, a nurse anesthesiologist in a busy hospital in Kabul, Afghanistan, may know a little more about the gender system than most of us. She's a thirty-something, married mother of three, but until a month before her wedding, Shukria was Shukur, and Shukur was a boy.

In Afghanistan, sons are so precious that when a family has none or few, a girl may be raised as a boy, a largely secretive custom called *bacha posh* (Nordberg, 2014). Her parents and a few close family members know her real sex, of course. But in the outside world—school, mosque, and shops—she is a son, with all the status that provides to the individual and the family. For the girl, it's an honor. She has freedom of movement, educational opportunity, and status that other girls are denied—until just before puberty, when she's forced to become a girl again. Unlike "his" five sisters, Shukur did not have to do household chores such as cooking and cleaning. He and his one brother got to eat first, speak up, and play outdoors. Shukur was strong, and smart, and managed to convince the family to let him train as a nurse. Soon, his earnings at the hospital were reason enough to let him keep his male identity into his late teens. But then the Taliban arrived, and the masquerade became too dangerous. Shukur's parents announced that a husband had been arranged and provided her with women's clothing. At the engagement party, she met her future husband and began to dress as a woman for the first time in her life.

As a bride, Shukria had to learn how to do gender as a woman and unlearn her manly ways. Being raised as a boy did not change her sexuality, and she adjusted well to marital sex and motherhood. But her voice was too loud and too deep. She didn't know how to sit properly, with her legs folded under. She was used to walking fast, with her head up, swinging her arms, or standing with legs apart and hands in pockets, wearing jeans and a leather jacket. Now, she could hardly see where she was going through the tiny screen of her burka. Other women had to constantly remind her how to walk with her head bent submissively, not taking up much space. She had no idea how to cook or clean or mend her husband's clothes, things that are supposed to come naturally to women. Her hair was a mess, she hated the smell of perfume, and she simply did not know how to talk about the things the other wives were interested in. At first, the hardest thing was realizing that she couldn't leave the house. She would walk out the door just like a man, and have to be brought back and scolded. Fifteen years after the switch, Shukria feels that masculinity was her first language, and, although she always knew she was female, she had to change everything about herself to conform to her society's definition of a woman.

Shukria lives in one of the world's most extreme patriarchal societies. Women are still regarded as the property of men, divorce is almost impossible for a woman to obtain, and domestic violence is normative—all examples of how the gender system restricts women at the structural level. At the interactional level, Shukria has vividly experienced how differently women and men present the self in posture and speech as submissive or dominant, and how appearance norms enforce gender hierarchy. At the individual level, Shukria feels that she still has to work very hard at being a woman and that she may never entirely succeed. However, she does not feel sorry for herself. Instead, she believes that, inside, she has the soul of a brave man.

You may be thinking that gender could have such pervasive influence on a person's life only in a highly patriarchal society. But I invite you to consider how your life would be different if you woke up tomorrow morning and found that you had changed gender.

Making a Difference

Women's movements around the world and across time have been made up of women and men working to secure equal human rights for all. The first wave of feminist activists included the suffragists who achieved the vote for women in the early 1900s. The second wave, whose activism began in the 1960s, worked on reproductive rights, workplace equality, sexism in the media, and an end to violence against women. Many younger women identify as third-wave feminists who are defining their own goals for the next round of social change.

Transforming Ourselves

What can be done to change internalized sexist beliefs and attitudes? In the 1970s, second wave feminists developed consciousness raising (C–R) groups, in which women met informally to talk about their lives as women. Women who took part in these groups began to see that their problems were not just individual deficiencies but were related to society's devaluation of women. C–R groups encouraged social action, leading to such activities as opening shelters for battered women and protesting against sexist advertising. As women made some social progress in the 1970s and 1980s, these groups disappeared (Kahn and Yoder, 1989). However, in their day they led to positive changes for the women in them, including greater awareness of sexism and injustice, and improved self-image and self-acceptance (Kravetz, 1980). Today, women (and men) are more likely to find a pro-feminist community online. (Check out the community forum at *feministing.com*, an open

site where people can post blogs, rants, raves, and opinion pieces). Feminist counseling and therapy, discussed in Chapter 13, also can empower women, men, and
couples of all sexualities who want to make changes in their lives.

Education is another powerful tool for reducing sexism. When people learn to
think critically about the gender system they may become more aware of sexism and
may even change their sexist attitudes. Raising awareness about male privilege is
another starting place. Both male and female students increased their understanding
of the advantages and privileges accorded men in our society after watching a video in
which men discussed topics such as the lower risk of sexual assault, the freedom from
constant worry about looks and appearance, the wage gap, and so on, compared to a
control group that read these facts in a handout (Case et al., 2014). However, the students' scores on hostile and benevolent sexism did not change; these underlying attitudes are harder to budge. Courses in women and gender studies can help. In one
study, taking a single women's studies course led to a decrease in the passive acceptance of sexism, an increase in commitment to feminism, and plans for social activism
in women students (Bargad & Hyde, 1991). Courses in women and gender studies can
change attitudes for both women and men (Steiger, 1981), but very few men take such
courses unless they are part of a diversity or multicultural requirement.

Transforming Interpersonal Relations

As this chapter has shown, gender inequity is reproduced in everyday interactions
with others, often outside our awareness. Even the most well-meaning people can
respond to others in sexist ways, and sexist patterns of interaction lead to self-fulfilling
prophecies. These social processes are largely invisible and taken for granted.

Doing gender can be disrupted when people become more aware of how the
gender system operates. One important strategy for change is to pay attention to how
we often respond to others as members of a category (see Chapter 3). Knowing how
power and attractiveness create double binds for women can help change the categorization processes that create sex discrimination. More and more women are seeking
positions of power and leadership in business, education, and public service. If each
of us tries to remain aware of how women are judged with double binds of competence and likability and double standards of behavior compared to men, perhaps we
will be less likely to make those flawed judgments and more likely to judge on an
equal basis. Journalist Frank Bruni (2016) reminded the public of these double standards during the 2016 presidential race by asking us to imagine the candidacy of a
"rich, brash real estate magnate and reality TV star named Donna Trump." Donna
has been married three times, brags about her wealth and sexual prowess, makes
sexist and vulgar comments about men and racist comments about minorities and
immigrants. How well do you think The Donna would do in the polls?

When awareness of sexism is raised, small acts of resistance can follow. Writer
Gloria Steinem called this kind of resistance "outrageous acts and everyday rebellions" (Steinem, 1983). For example, everyday ways of doing gender are disrupted
when people refuse to be cooperative or silent in the face of sexism. It isn't easy to
speak up when you hear a sexist remark. However, research has shown that it can
be effective. Confronting prejudice is most likely to change attitudes when the

confrontation is nonthreatening in tone and when it comes from someone who is not a member of the target group (Monteith & Czopp, 2003). In other words, White people who speak out against racism, men who speak out against sexism, and straight people who speak out against heterosexism may be particularly likely to be heard—especially if they do it with respect and tact.

As another kind of "everyday rebellion," you might try disrupting gender norms. (What happens when a woman holds the door open for a man, or pays the bar tab for both?) One feminist proposed a "smile boycott": for an entire day, try smiling only when you are genuinely pleased, and keep a journal about your own and others' reactions. Do you think the results would be different for men and women who decline to smile?

Transforming the Structures of Inequality

Transforming gender at the social structural level is linked with the individual and interactional transformations just described. When people are empowered as individuals, they can speak out against injustice, and they can begin to change the institutions, laws, customs, and norms that harm girls and women. The effect is reciprocal, as speaking out leads to increased feelings of self-efficacy and empowerment.

Social change is not easy. It demands the power of collective action—working together for social change. Many of the great social movements in history, such as the anti-apartheid movement in South Africa, have been led by members of subordinated groups (Lee et al., 2011). The history of the women's movement is a history of collective action by women and men on behalf of equality for women.

What factors influence women today to engage in collective action? A series of studies with women (some with college students, others with web-based samples of older adults) showed that exposure to hostile sexism increased participants' desire to do something about sexism (Becker & Wright, 2011). However, exposure to benevolent sexism decreased their desire for social change. For example, in one study participants first read statements about hostile or benevolent sexism and then were offered the opportunity to distribute flyers on gender equality at their university or to sign a petition demanding the hiring of more women professors. Those who had experienced hostile sexism were more likely to participate in these forms of collective action; those who had experienced benevolent sexism were less likely. The ideology of benevolent sexism increased their perception that the gender system is fair and that there were personal advantages to them in being women. The researchers termed this "the dark side of chivalry"—the dominant group uses "sweet persuasion" to maintain a position of power. We might also think of it as "the bright side of hostile sexism"—although it is not pleasant to experience the hassles of hostile sexism, it can motivate women to work together for a more gender equal society.

When women do engage in collective action, it is good for their well-being. In one recent study, women read about sexism and then were randomly assigned to tweet (or not) about gender discrimination. Compared to controls, tweeters showed a decrease in negative feelings and an increase in psychological well-being (Foster, 2015). Apparently, even a little bit of speaking up about sexism is better than keeping quiet about it.

An end to patriarchal inequality is still a vision for the future, and not yet a reality. The global feminist vision is one of a just and caring society "that will give not only to men but also to women, bread and roses, poetry and power" (Alindogan-Medina, 2006, p. 57). Nobel Peace Prize Laureate and leader of Myanmar's democracy movement, Aung San Suu Kyi, put it this way: "The education and empowerment of women throughout the world cannot fail to result in a more caring, tolerant, just and peaceful life for all."

Exploring Further

∾

Solnit, Rebecca (2015). *Men Explain Things to Me.* Chicago: Haymarket.
> A brilliant collection of feminist essays. The title essay is both funny and scathing (at a party, a man explains the author's own book to her!). The six other essays show that the problems of patriarchal power and entitlement are not so funny, exploring a wide range of issues with intelligence and quick wit.

Fitzpatrick, Ellen. (2016). *The Highest Glass Ceiling: Women's Quest for the American Presidency.* Cambridge: Harvard University Press.
> Did you think Hillary Clinton was the first woman to run for president? Actually, more than 200 have campaigned before her. This book tells the stories of three: Victoria Woodhull (free love, anti-big banks), Margaret Chase Smith (first woman Senator), and Shirley Chisholm (first Black Congresswoman). The history of what happened to them and other politically ambitious women tells us much about the gender system in America.

Society for the Psychological Study of Social Issues, http://www.spssi.org
> APA's Division 9, SPSSI is an international group of psychologists and other social scientists who share a common concern with research on psychological aspects of important social issues facing social groups, communities, our nation, and the world. SPSSI publishes the *Journal of Social Issues* and welcomes student members.

Text Credits

∾

p. 25: Unger, R. K. (1979b). Toward a redefinition of sex and gender. American Psychologist, 34, 1085–1094. **p. 28:** Sources: http://www.malala.org http://www.biography.com/people/malala-yousafzai-21362253 Contributed by Annie B. Fox. **p. 35:** Cameron, D. (1996). The language-gender interface: Challenging co-optation. In V. L. Bergvall, J. M. Bing, & A. F. Freed (Eds.), Rethinking language and gender research: Theory and Practice (pp. 31–53). New York: Addison-Wesley. **p. 41:** Source: Adapted from Klonoff, E. A., & Landrine, H. (1995). The schedule of sexist events: A measure of lifetime and recent sexist discrimination in women's lives. Psychology of Women Quarterly, 19, 439–472. Percentages have been rounded to the nearest whole number. **p. 43:** Tom Cheney/The New Yorker Collection/The Cartoon Bank. **p. 47:** Crosby, F. J., Iyer, A., Clayton, S., & Downing, R. A. (2003). Affirmative action: Psychological data and the policy debates. American Psychologist, 58, 93–115. Crosby, F. J., Iyer, A., Clayton, S., & Downing, R. A. (2003). **p. 50:** Glick, P., & Fiske, S. T. (2001). An ambivalent alliance: Hostile and benevolent sexism as complementary justifications for gender inequality. American Psychologist, 56, 109–118.

CHAPTER 3

Images of Women

Tamika Cross, M.D., was midway through a flight from Detroit to Minneapolis when another passenger suddenly became ill and the flight attendants called for a physician. Dr. Cross moved to help, but a flight attendant told her, "Oh no, sweetie, put your hand down. We are looking for actual physicians or nurses or some type of medical personnel, we don't have time to talk to you." Dr. Cross repeatedly explained that she *was* an actual physician but the flight attendant kept cutting her off and then asked to see her credentials.

What was going on here? Tamika Cross, an African American woman, did not "look like a doctor." When a White man later came forward and said he was a physician, the flight attendants accepted his help without question. The airline later apologized for the incident (Hawkins, 2016).

This example illustrates the power of cultural images and the intersection of race and gender in those images. In this chapter we explore how verbal, visual, and cognitive representations of women affect how we think about and behave toward women, and how women feel about themselves. We'll start with the most basic representation: language about women.

Words Can Never Hurt Me?

When people use language to communicate with others, they make choices that are not only practical but also political. The term *linguistic sexism* refers to inequitable treatment of women and men that is built into the language. Feminists have worked to draw attention to sexist language and to change it (Crawford, 2001).

Language about Women and Men

In the 1970s, research on linguistic sexism identified several varieties. Researchers found that language patterns sometimes trivialized women, with gender-marked terms such as *steward* and *stewardess.* Other terms sexualized and devalued women. There were far more negative sexual terms in English for women than for men, and words referring to women tended to acquire more negative meanings over time (Schultz, 1975). (See Box 3.1.) Linguistic sexism also marked both women and men who deviated from expected occupations and roles with terms such as "career woman" and "male nurse."

Some of these practices have changed, but the transition to nonsexist language is not complete. For example, *stewardess* has been replaced by the gender-neutral *flight attendant,* but women's sports teams are still the "Bronco-ettes" or the "Lady Lions." One college has "Lady Rams," which doesn't even make anatomical sense! Let's look at other varieties of linguistic sexism.

Mrs. Man

Language traditionally marked women as the possessions of men. Until recently, a woman's marital status was designated by the use of *Mrs.* or *Miss; Mr.,* the corresponding title for men, was neutral with respect to marital status. When feminists

Box 3.1 ∼ "He Is . . . She Is . . .": Linguistic Inequality

Consider the following pairs of terms.

Term for Male	Term for Female
Lord	Lady
Sir	Madam
King	Queen
Master	Mistress
Dog	Bitch

Terms used for women often become lower in status over time. *Lord* and *lady* started out as equivalent terms. Today only God and some English nobility are referred to as Lord, but any woman can be addressed as "Hey, lady."

Terms for women also pick up negative sexual connotations over time. *Sir, king,* and *master* are terms of respect, but their formerly parallel terms have taken on new meanings. A mistress is a sexual partner, a madam may be a prostitute or female pimp, and queen is a derogatory term for a gay man.

Even animal terms are not exempt from linguistic sexism. A dog is "man's" best friend—but a bitch is friend to no one!

proposed *Ms.* as a parallel term to *Mr.,* they were accused of being dangerous radicals bent on mutilating the English language (Crawford et al., 1998). Women who used *Ms.* were seen as more masculine and less likable than women who stuck to the traditional titles (Dion, 1987). Although *Ms.* has become much more accepted, women who use it may still be seen as more masculine and less feminine than those who use *Mrs.* or *Miss* (Malcolmson & Sinclair, 2007).

The practice of a woman taking her husband's name upon marriage is a heritage of patriarchy. The majority of women still follow this custom, and choosing to keep one's own name is controversial because of its symbolic meaning. Among a sample of U.S. college students, the majority of women were willing to take their partner's last name if they got married and the great majority of men were unwilling to do so (Robnett & Leaper, 2013). Endorsing benevolent sexism was related to holding more traditional preferences. Women who wanted to keep their name said it was about preserving their own identity.

Because of the practical and symbolic complexities of naming, some married women change their name depending on the situation. For example, a woman may hyphenate her name in some situations but not others, or use her husband's name in family contexts and her birth name in professional contexts. In a study of 600 married women, about 12% engaged in name shifting (Scheuble & Johnson, 2005). This shifting may reflect women's ambiguity about their identity as wives versus individuals, or their concern that others might disapprove of their naming choices.

For same-sex couples, changing names does not carry patriarchal baggage, and there is no social pressure to do so. In a study of 30 lesbian and gay couples in committed relationships, only one woman had changed her name, and most had no plans to do so, although some participants said they would consider hyphenating their names. The main reasons they gave for choosing to keep their own names were maintaining personal and professional identities, avoiding hassles, and resisting heterosexual norms (Clarke et al., 2008).

He/Man Language

In many languages, the word for *man* is used to refer to humans in general—in Spanish, it's *hombre,* in French, *homme,* in Italian, *uomo.* In English, this generic use of *man* was long commonplace in academic as well as everyday language—as in "a history of man," "the rights of man," and "the man in the street." Because English does not have a gender-neutral singular pronoun, speakers must choose either *he* or *she*; traditionally, *he* was chosen to refer to both males and females.

Unfortunately, these "generic" masculine terms are not really generic at all. A great deal of research over the past 40 years has shown that when people read *he, his,* and *man,* they think of men, not people in general (Gygax et al., 2008; Henley, 1989). Moreover, this interpretation affects their behavior. When male and female college students read an essay titled "The Psychologist and His Work," which used *he* throughout, the women later remembered the facts in the essay more poorly than when they had read the same essay in a gender-inclusive (*he or she*) version—despite the fact that they could not remember which form they'd read. The differential language had no effects on memory among the men (Crawford & English, 1984).

Being exposed to language that excludes them is also demotivating for women. In mock job interviews, women faced with gender-exclusive language from the interviewer became less motivated, felt a lower sense of belonging and identified less with the job compared to others who heard more gender-inclusive (he or she) or gender-neutral language (Stout & Dasgupta, 2011). Fortunately, it's fairly easy for people to change their use of sexist pronouns (Koeser & Sczesny, 2015; Koeser et al., 2015).

Only one country in the world has attempted to add a truly gender-neutral pronoun to the language. That country is Sweden. In 2012, a third gender-neutral pronoun *hen* was proposed as an addition to the already existing Swedish pronouns for *she (hon)* and *he (han).* The pronoun *hen* can be used both generically, when gender is unknown or irrelevant, and as a transgender pronoun for people who want to sidestep the gender binary. The majority of Swedes reacted negatively to the linguistic change, but after just two years attitudes had begun to shift and usage of the new pronoun had increased (Sendén et al., 2015). A new pronoun is a much more drastic change then the introduction of *Ms.* or *he and she* was in English, but like these changes in our own language, it seems that people can get used to them in a rather short time. (I'll talk about new English pronouns for transgender and non-binary people in Chapter 5.)

There may be a cognitive bias that goes beyond language. Even when they hear gender-neutral terms, people may still assume a male is the subject. This *people = male bias* has been demonstrated in multiple languages, including English, French, German, and Norwegian (Gygax et al., 2008; Merritt & Kok, 1995; Silveira, 1980). For example, when participants read a set of gender-neutral instructions and were then asked to describe a (sex-unspecified) character, they produced three times as many spontaneous descriptions of males as females (Hamilton, 1991).

There is even an ***animal = male bias.*** When children in three age groups and adults were shown stuffed toys (a dog, a deer, a mouse, and so on) and asked to tell stories about them, both children and adults showed an overwhelming bias toward using masculine pronouns. For example, 100% of 3- to 10-year-old children and 100% of adults used *he* to refer to a teddy bear. Preschool-age children used *he* to refer to a dog (100%), a mouse (95%), a deer (87%), a snail (94%), and a butterfly (88%). Only cats were seen as (sometimes) female, mostly by girls. Even when the experimenters tried to disrupt the bias by using feminine pronouns to introduce the animals ("Here is a panda bear. She's eating bamboo now, but she had fish for breakfast"), 100% of the children still used masculine pronouns in their own stories (Lambdin et al., 2003). As sexist language changes and eventually is eliminated, will these cognitive biases change too? Time will tell.

Babes, Chicks, Ho's, and Bitches

Slang referring to women is much more likely to have sexual meaning than is slang referring to men (Crawford & Popp, 2003). Some sexualized terms refer to women as body parts, from the relatively mild *Big Booty Judy* and *tail* to *piece of ass*, *pussy*, and *cunt*. When students were asked to list slang terms for both sexes, 50% of the terms for women had sexual connotations, compared to 23% of the terms for men (Grossman & Tucker, 1997). The most common terms for women were *chick, bitch, babe,* and *slut;* for men, they were *guy, dude, boy,* and *stud.* As these examples show, the terms for women are not only more sexual, but more negative.

Slang enriches the English language by providing new words to the lexicon, but it can be extremely sexist. As documented on sites like *onlineslangdictionary .com*, women often are referred to as animals (cow, chick, fox) or food (arm candy), and defined in terms of their looks (a butterface is a woman with an attractive body but an ugly face) and sexual availability.

Pop culture gives us ever more models for disparaging women. The spread of the words *bitch, whore,* and *slut* into sexual interaction and everyday talk is partly due to the popularity of rap music and the increased availability of Internet pornography (Wright et al., 2016). But they have long since moved from pornography to become part of the normal way that middle-class college women talk about each other (Armstrong & Hamilton, 2013). All the linguistic biases described so far add up to real, though sometimes subtle, forms of discrimination. Let's look at a specific arena in which language treats men as the norm and women as deviants: media coverage of athletes.

Venus and Mr. Federer: Describing Female and Male Athletes

Media descriptions of female athletes differ from descriptions of male athletes in several ways. Female athletes and their sports are asymmetrically ***gender marked*** when reporters use terms such as "basketball" and "women's basketball" to refer to men's and women's sports, respectively; the underlying message is that men's basketball is the norm while women's is the variation (Messner et al., 1993). The relative social power of women and men is subtly communicated when commentators refer to female athletes as girls, but do not call male athletes boys, or when they use the women's first names (Ana, Serena, Svetlana) but the men's last names and title (Federer or Mr. Federer).

The achievements of women athletes are often described in gender-typical and trivializing ways. Here are just a few examples from the 2016 Summer Olympics (Moran, 2016). As Hungarian swimmer Katinka Hosszu broke a world record to win the 400-meter medley, NBC cameras panned to her husband, who served as her coach, and the commentator said, "And there's the man responsible." Social media users were furious, pointing out that Olympic athletes are pretty much responsible for their own gold medals. When an American athlete won a bronze medal in trap shooting, the *Chicago Tribune* didn't even mention her sport in their headline: "Corey Cogdell, wife of Bears lineman Mitch Unrein, wins bronze in Rio." The story didn't mention that it was her second medal at the games and her third time at the Olympics, either; instead, it digressed into her husband's sports record. Apparently, the most important thing about these talented women athletes is the men in their lives. Another NBC commentator managed to trivialize even the mighty Women's Gymnastics Team USA who were laughing and talking together after a first-round triumph by saying they looked like they "might as well be standing in the middle of a mall."

Often, media commentary focuses on women athletes' physical appearance and sex appeal more than on their performance. Moreover, like other female public figures, female athletes are more likely than male athletes to be identified as parents or spouses in media reports. Thanks to the popularity of beach volleyball and gymnastics, women's sports actually got a slight majority of prime time in the 2016 Summer Olympics. But media researchers report that the coverage is still quite different. "We found things like men being described as fastest, strongest, biggest. For women, it's unmarried, married, references to their age. There is an inequality there." (Rogers, 2016).

Are we affected by language about female athletes? A study at 4-year colleges and universities in the southern United States found a negative correlation between the use of sexist team names, such as those described earlier, and athletic opportunities for women students (Pelak, 2008). The lack of opportunities cannot be attributed to the team names, but both reinforce a cultural bias against women's sports participation. Two studies on the impact of descriptions of female athletes found that when a woman athlete was described in terms of her attractiveness, both male and female readers perceived her as less talented and aggressive (Knight & Giuliano, 2001, 2003).

Worth a Thousand Words: Media Images

Every day, each of us is exposed to hundreds of images of women and men, most of them from the mass media: television, newspapers, magazines, movies, comics, video games, billboards, and the Internet. Most of the time, we pay little attention to these images; however, media images of women and men create a distorted reality that does affect us. Let's look more closely at media images of women compared to those of men.

Representing Women and Men

In general, women are underrepresented in the media. About 51% of the population is female, yet females appear in media less often than males. They are outnumbered 2 to 1 in leading roles in the movies, cable TV shows, network TV, and reality show leads. (See Box 3.2) Every year since 2007, when monitoring began, women have averaged only about 30% of speaking roles in the 100 top earning movies each year (Women's Media Center, 2015). And it's not just the shows; women are underrepresented in commercials for all types of goods except health and beauty products, and this gap has not changed since first measured in the 1980s (Ganahl et al., 2003). Similar patterns of underrepresentation have been shown in other countries, including Great Britain and Saudi Arabia (Nassif & Gunter, 2008), Kenya (Mwangi,

Box 3.2 ∾ Does Your Favorite Movie Pass the Bechdel Test?

The Bechdel test was developed in 1985 by graphic novelist Alison Bechdel in her comic *Dykes to Watch out For*. For a movie to pass the Bechdel test, it must meet the following three criteria:

Does it contain two or more named female characters?
Do they talk to each other?
And, if so, do they discuss something other than a man?

This simple test gives us some insight into the presence of women in film. On face value, the test seems fairly easy—a movie just needs to have two named female characters who speak to one another about *anything* other than men. And yet, the test proves surprisingly difficult for movies to pass! According to the crowdsourcing site bedcheltest.com, about 40% of movies fail the test. Interestingly, a study that used data from movies that were released

between 1990 and 2013 found that movies that pass the Bechdel had a lower median budget, yet made more money at the box office than movies that fail it.

Movies that Fail	Movies that Pass
Avatar	The Hunger Games
Toy Story	Little Miss Sunshine
The Departed	Mystic River
Lord of the Rings Trilogy	The Matrix
Fight Club	Inside Out
Good Will Hunting	Frozen
The Original Star Wars Trilogy	Star Wars: The Force Awakens
Avengers	Titanic
Breakfast at Tiffany's	Jurassic Park
	Harry Potter and the Chamber of Secrets

Source: http://fivethirtyeight.com/features/the-dollar-and-cents-case-against-hollywoods-exclusion-of-women/
[Cartoon source: https://en.wikipedia.org/wiki/Bechdel_test] The Bechdel Test from *Dykes* to *Watch Out For* by Alison Bechdel. Used by permission of Alison Bechdel.
Contributed by Annie B. Fox

1996), Portugal (Neto & Pinto, 1998), and Japan, where the ratio of males to females on TV is 2:1 (Suzuki, 1995). No form of media is immune to the underrepresentation bias, not even psychology textbooks. (See Figure 3.1a and b.) Women and girls are even underrepresented in the comics (LaRossa et al., 2001), in children's picture books (Hamilton et al., 2006), and on cereal boxes (Black et al., 2009).

Sheer numbers may be the least of the problems in media depictions of women. Media images portray women and men quite differently in personality attributes. When researchers analyzed the portrayal of women and men in 1,600 commercials shown on popular TV shows, both the White and African American male characters were more aggressive, active, and gave more orders than female characters did. The White female characters, but not the African American ones, were more passive and emotional than the male characters (Coltrane & Messineo, 2000).

The media also show women and men in different settings and occupations. For example, one study examined nearly 8,000 illustrations of men in magazines

©Time Life Pictures/Mansell/The Life Picture Collection/Getty Images

FIGURE 3.1a   This photo of Ivan Pavlov and his colleagues in his lab appeared in an introductory psychology textbook used by thousands of psychology students.

©Sovfoto/UIG/Getty Images

FIGURE 3.1b   Unfortunately, some of Pavlov's colleagues were erased from the historical record. This is the original, complete photo. How might the selective elimination of women in the history of psychology affect students' attitudes and beliefs about women scientists?

aimed at women, men, and general readers. In male-oriented magazines, men were almost always shown in work and occupational roles, almost never as husbands or fathers. Images of men with their families or taking care of children showed up only in women's magazines (Vigorito & Curry, 1998). Women's work, in contrast, is downplayed. TV ads are less likely to show women than men at their jobs (Coltrane & Adams, 1997) and more likely to show women than men at home (Coltrane & Messineo, 2000). The most recent studies available reconfirm this bias. On prime-time TV, female characters are still mainly involved with romance, family, and friends, while male characters are mainly at work (Lauzen et al., 2008).

These differential gender portrayals occur cross-culturally. In India, for example, TV ads portray women almost exclusively in contexts of choosing products to make them better housekeepers and mothers (Roy, 1998). In Japan, just as in the United States, most women work outside the home, but a study of Japanese TV ads showed that depictions of workers were predominantly male (Arima, 2003). In a comparison of TV ads in Great Britain and Saudi Arabia, women appeared more often in domestic settings, and less often at work or leisure, than men, and were much more likely to promote products for body care and household cleaning (Nassif & Gunter, 2008).

Face-ism

Some differences in how the media represent men and women are less obvious than others. Although most people do not notice, the composition of images of men and women is quite different. This phenomenon has been termed *face-ism* (Archer et al., 1983). Face-ism is measured as the proportion of the overall image devoted to the face.

As Figure 3.2 illustrates, the facial prominence in published images is usually higher for men. In a study of more than 1,700 photos from magazines and newspapers, the average index for men was .65, and for women only .45. In other words, two-thirds of a typical photo image of a man featured his face, while less than half of a typical image of a woman featured hers (Archer et al., 1983).

How prevalent is face-ism? A look at photos published in 11 different countries found similar results—more facial prominence for men. The researchers also examined paintings in art museums, finding that face-ism has occurred from the 17th century onward and increased over time (Archer et al., 1983). In a study of news magazines, the face-ism index favored not only men over women but also European American over African American people; Black women had the lowest face-ism index of all (Zuckerman & Kieffer, 1994).

Research on face-ism has been done since the 1980s. Today, it is still very easy to find examples of face-ism everywhere from advertising to politics, and it may have important implications for women in leadership positions. In the largest study of face-ism to date, researchers used 6,610 politicians' official website photographs from 25 countries to explore the relationship between face-ism and the level of

FIGURE 3.2   Face-ism in images of women and men.

gender equality in each country. Gender equality was measured by macrolevel indicators such as the literacy rate for women and gender differences in life expectancy (Konrath et al., 2012). Surprisingly, there was more face-ism (the male politicians had bigger heads than the female politicians) in the more gender-equal cultures. This study shows that subtle kinds of sexism can persist even in relatively gender-equal cultures.

Why should we care about face-ism? It can have real effects on how individuals are evaluated by others. We tend to associate a person's individuality, personality, and intelligence with their face. When students were asked to rate the same people shown in different photos, they rated an individual higher on dominance, ambition, and intelligence when the photo had a higher face-ism index (Archer et al., 1983; Zuckerman & Kieffer, 1994). In other words, seeing more face and less body in an image leads us to think of the person as more outstanding in character and ability. The widespread tendency to show more of men's faces and women's bodies may function without our awareness to focus attention on men's character and women's physical characteristics. The implications for women leaders are obvious.

Sexual Objectification

Women's bodies are not just pictured more than men's, they are also *sexualized* more than men's. Overall, one of every four White women and one in 10 Black women in U.S. television commercials is dressed or posed in a sexually provocative way, compared with one in 14 men (Coltrane & Messineo, 2000). In ads, women are often shown partially undressed or completely nude, even when revealing the body has nothing to do with using the product. Content analyses of international television and magazine advertising suggest that although levels of female nudity vary across cultures, more female than male nudity is cross-culturally universal (Nelson & Paek, 2005, 2008).

When women's bodies are sexualized in media, the women themselves are often reduced to those bodies—or even just parts of them (see Figure 3.3). This is what is meant by *sexual objectification*. When a woman is objectified, she is being treated as a body or a collection of body parts. Her body is valued mainly for its use by others, and she is not being considered as a person with thoughts and feelings of her own (Fredrickson & Roberts, 1997). Movies and television shows sexually objectify women much more than men, and entire shows focusing on women's bodies are commonplace. Think of all the beauty pageants—Miss America, Miss Universe—modeling competitions, swimsuit specials, fitness competitions, and fashion shows that parade women's bodies to be ranked and judged. Every newsstand features rows of magazines with seductively posed, often scantily clad, young women on the cover, and more inside, and countless Internet sites offer an endless supply of sexually objectified women. Rap, R&B, and hip-hop lyrics focus on women's sexual body parts and hotness (Flynn et al., 2016).

These images of women are not new; what *is* relatively new is the objectification of *virtual* women. Several content analyses of video games have shown that female avatars are far more likely to wear tight, revealing clothing and to be sexualized than are male avatars (Vandenbosch et al., 2016). *Grand Theft Auto V*, which

©Marmorino/Newpress/Ropi/Zuma Press/Newscom

©Maarten Udema/Alamy RF

**FIGURE 3.3   Objectified women. A woman's body is displayed
on an urban street (top). But at least she has a head—unlike
the woman on the bottom.**

earned $1 billion in the first three days after its release, has long been notorious for its depiction of highly sexualized avatars in strip clubs and simulated sex with female prostitutes. Unlike images in other kinds of media, virtual humans are designed to respond to users' actions. Interacting with an avatar is very different from looking at a picture in a magazine, and users often react to a virtual human almost as though it were real. Users can also experience a virtual body almost as though it is their own. Virtual objectification may have powerful and long-lasting effects on off-line behavior (Fox et al., 2015).

Every day we gaze upon myriad objectified images of women. These images not only reduce women to their bodies, they represent women unrealistically—in idealized and distorted ways.

Idealization and Distortion

Media have long been saturated with idealized images of feminine beauty (Banner, 2006). Consider the corseted Gibson Girl of the 1890s, the boyish flapper of the 1920s, the full-figured pin-up of the 1950s, Twiggy in the 1960s, and the ultraslim yet busty models of today. Ideals have changed with the fashions, but what hasn't changed is the fact that all have required substantial modification of women's natural appearance.

Both fashion magazines aimed at women (Elle, Glamour, etc.) and men's magazines (Maxim, Men's Health) feature full-page ads with female models distorted to meet the fantasies of their audiences. In the fashion magazines, the women are both flawless and passive. In the men's magazines, they are symbolically silenced and violence against women is glamorized. In both, women are likely to be shown as sexualized parts (a pair of legs, a close-up of crotch or buttocks), not whole people (Conley & Ramsey, 2011). Of course, the idealized flawlessness of the fashion magazine is unattainable by actual women. For decades, the beauty and fashion industries have employed heavy makeup, deceptive clothing, artful lighting, careful posing, and photo retouching to create ideal images. In recent years, however, digital technology has taken this to a new level, allowing radical alteration and complete fabrication of images of women without viewers realizing how artificial the images are. In real life, even actresses and models don't look like the images we see. In the publicity shots for the film King Arthur, for example, before-and-after photos published online showed that actress Keira Knightley was gifted by the photo retoucher with not only flawless skin but also with bigger breasts, thinner arms, and a smaller waist (Borland, 2008).

The contemporary ideal is characterized by extreme thinness, but this has not always been the case. Published body measurements of Playboy centerfold models and Miss America contestants have shrunk over the past 40 years. Many current models meet the weight criteria for anorexia. At the same time, the actual body size of adult Americans has gotten heavier (Owen & Laurel-Seller, 2000; Spitzer et al., 1999). The latest version of the ideal woman is not only extremely thin but also large-breasted—a size 4 in the hips, 2 in the waist, and 10 in the bust (Harrison, 2003). Of course, this figure rarely occurs in nature—it must be created through surgical intervention. In a sample of college students, both men and women who had more exposure to ideal images on television showed higher levels of approval for women's use of cosmetic surgeries such as liposuction and breast augmentation (Harrison, 2003). It seems that the more TV you watch, the more you believe that real women's bodies are just not good enough.

How does it impact women to be surrounded by idealized, sexualized, and dehumanized versions of themselves? How are women's perceptions of their bodies shaped by being treated as objects? How does the objectification of women's bodies affect their social interactions? We will address these questions by exploring research on women's objectification.

Body Image

The term *body image* refers both to the mental picture one has of one's appearance and the associated feelings about the size, shape, and attractiveness of one's body (Dorian & Garfinkel, 2002). Many researchers have studied the link between body image and overall self-esteem and most have found that women are more strongly invested in their physical appearance and are more dissatisfied with their bodies than men are. These concerns begin in childhood and extend across the lifespan (e.g., Murnen et al., 2003). And they occur in every ethnic group. A meta-analysis of nearly 100 studies of body dissatisfaction showed that White, Asian American, and Hispanic women had similar levels of body dissatisfaction. African American women were only slightly less dissatisfied with their bodies (Grabe & Hyde, 2006).

Many theorists attribute the gender discrepancy in body image, at least in part, to the impact of idealized beauty images on women. Numerous experiments that have exposed women to images of attractive models and then measured their self-esteem, perceptions of their own attractiveness, and mood have found significant negative effects (Grabe et al., 2008; Groesz et al., 2002). Most researchers theorize that these negative effects are the result of the *social comparison* process (Want, 2009). That is, idealized beauty images make women feel bad because their own appearance suffers by comparison. But, there may be more going on than social comparison. In their original context, beauty images are often accompanied by messages that relentlessly remind women that attractiveness is central to femininity, that it matters in every situation, that it is what matters most in women, and that you cannot be beautiful unless you alter the natural body. Perhaps ideal images presented in the laboratory negatively impact women not merely because they set a high standard of comparison, but also because they remind women of these more general messages and of their objectified status.

Some studies on women's responses to idealized images have found no effects or *positive* effects. Why these inconsistencies? One factor that seems to matter is a woman's level of body dissatisfaction at the outset. Women who are more dissatisfied with their bodies respond more negatively to ideal images in experiments and in real life. Another factor is the instructions given to participants. Negative effects are more likely when the participant is *not* thinking about the images in terms of appearance (Want, 2009). This may be counterintuitive, but it seems that the social comparison process is automatic. Actually thinking about that gorgeous model in the image may help women consciously override the tendency to compare themselves with her.

Most of the research on the impact of media images has been done with White college students. But women of color are affected, too. In a qualitative study of personal experiences of objectification, African American women described encountering media images of the always–sexually–available Black woman, along with the "almost-white" model: light-skinned, with straight hair and a slim body. They did not see themselves in these images of the Black woman and found them oppressive and discouraging (Watson et al., 2012). A study of African American college students found that those with a positive racial identity and a multiculturally inclusive outlook were most able to resist the negative effects of such portrayals on their body image (Watson et al., 2013).

As Western media images of women spread across the globe, we may see a worldwide increase in women's body dissatisfaction. A survey of female university students in five Arab countries found a link between exposure to TV and magazines and an increase in dieting and weight concerns (Musaiger & Al-Mannai, 2014). In Iran, where women cover the entire body, facial cosmetic surgery is in demand (*The Economist*, 2015). And African women are using skin bleaching cosmetics that may cause skin cancer. Their goal is to have white, European-looking skin (Cooper, 2016; Lewis et al., 2011). Even in the small Himalayan country of Nepal, women are participating in beauty contests where they are judged by Western norms, and are beginning to report body dissatisfaction and disordered eating (Crawford et al., 2008, 2009).

Self-Objectification

Psychologists Barbara Fredrickson and Tomi-Ann Roberts's (1997) *objectification theory* explains that in a sexually objectifying culture, girls and women learn to "internalize an observer's perspective as a primary view of their physical selves" (p. 1): they engage in s*elf-objectification.* This idea is not original to Fredrickson and Roberts—many writers and researchers before them have described how women perceive themselves as objects that exist to be evaluated by others (e.g., Beauvoir, 1953; Berger, 1972; McKinley & Hyde, 1996)—but objectification theory is important because it delineates the psychological and behavioral consequences of self-objectification.

Self-objectification involves habitual and chronic preoccupation with self-surveillance that disrupts a woman's connection to her subjective experiences and divides her attention. Continual body monitoring not only creates a sort of splitting of self—between the subjective self and the self as object—it also claims cognitive resources and interrupts thinking with feelings about appearance concern. Here are a few examples of U.S. women describing their habitual self-surveillance and body shame:

> If there is a mirror, I will most likely do a quick glance to make sure that my looks are in order (i.e., hair in place, no lipstick on the teeth or smudged makeup) . . . it boosts my confidence to periodically look at myself and reassure myself that I look good. (A 26-year-old.)

> I look and compare myself to other women constantly. (A 24-year-old.)

> I find my weight to be an obsession. I think of it at least 20 times per day. This makes me think that there is something wrong with me psychologically. (A 45-year-old.) (Crawford et al., 2009)

Self-objectification divides attention between self-surveillance and other mental tasks. We know from cognitive psychology that our mental resources are limited. We can only think about so many things at once. As long as women are devoting some of their mental resources to the emotional and cognitive processing associated with self-objectification, fewer resources will be available for other applications. See Box 3.3 for research confirmation of the link between self-objectification and cognitive performance.

Exposure to objectifying media is not the only factor linked to self-objectification, but it is a very important one. More and more studies are showing links between amount of exposure to different kinds of mass media and increases in self-objectification in women, and sometimes in men as well. Exposure to TV, music TV, fashion magazines, and social media all predict self-objectification (Vandenbosch & Eggermont, 2012). Time spent on Facebook is a big predictor of self-objectification, especially if you compare yourself to your Facebook peers (Fardouly et al., 2015). Time spent watching reality TV shows is also linked to self-objectification for both women and men (Ward et al., 2015).

What about those "post-feminist" ads that portray young attractive women who knowingly and deliberately play on their sexual power? These images are objectifying, but in contrast to traditional passive images, they present women's sexual objectification as empowering and women in control. In an experimental test of the effect of these images, researchers randomly assigned undergraduate women to view a group of them, a group of more passively objectified images, or a neutral set of images (Halliwell et al., 2011). Exposure to both kinds of objectifying images led to more self-objectification and weight dissatisfaction than the neutral images, and the "post-feminist" images had a greater effect than the more passively objectifying ones. The pseudo-empowerment of these ads may be even more damaging than the objectification in traditional ads.

Objectification theory has led to a great deal of important research that has confirmed links between self-surveillance, body shame, and negative psychological consequences for girls and women (Moradi & Huang, 2008). Self-objectification is related to eating disorders in adolescent girls and female college students (Tiggemann & Williams, 2012; Tylka & Hill, 2004). It is linked to anxiety, depressed mood, and depressed state in female college students (Muehlenkamp & Saris-Baglama, 2002; Tiggemann & Kuring, 2004; Tiggemann & Williams, 2012), and to a tendency toward dissociation and the likelihood of self-harm (Erchull et al., 2013). Priming thoughts of self-objectification in women increases their intention to undergo cosmetic surgery in the future (Calogero et al., 2014). Just as objectification theory predicts, the cultural images that surround us become internalized, with psychological results that are harmful to women.

Even women who do not suffer from obvious psychological distress related to their appearance are affected by self-objectification in troubling ways. Women in the United States spend tens of billions of dollars annually on makeup, hair care, skin care, and cosmetic surgery, in an attempt to improve or remedy aspects of their bodies that they perceive as flawed. Self-objectification can explain the antagonistic relationship that many women have with their own bodies. Women's language about their bodies is frequently hostile and combative in tone. Women talk about

Box 3.3 ～ Do I Look Fat in That? The Swimsuit/Sweater Study

Nearly twenty years ago, psychologists Barbara Fredrickson and Tomi-Ann Roberts developed what has become one of the most important and influential theories in psychology, Objectification Theory. One of the most famous examinations of Objectification Theory is a creative experiment sometimes referred to as the "Swimsuit-Sweater Study." Fredrickson and her colleagues measured women's and men's performance on math problems after trying on a sweater or a swimsuit. Participants were told they were participating in an experiment related to "emotions and consumer behavior." Men and women were randomly assigned to try on either a swimsuit or sweater in a room with a full-length mirror and told they were to evaluate the item of clothing. While acclimating to the item of clothing (they were asked to wear it for 15 minutes), participants were asked to complete a set of math problems, ostensibly for another experiment being conducted in the education department (there was no other experiment—the math problems were actually part of the experiment they were participating in).

The research team found that men's math performance was unaffected by the experimental manipulation while women's math performance suffered in the swimsuit condition, which temporarily heightened their self-objectification. Wearing the swimsuit produced body shame for women, but not for men. Although men reported feeling more "silly, awkward, and foolish" than women, women reported feeling significantly more "disgust, distaste, and revulsion" than men.

Since the publication of Objectification Theory in 1997, researchers have continued to demonstrate the negative effects of self-objectification for

©Comstock Images/Alamy RF

women, including depression, anxiety, body shame, and disordered eating. This groundbreaking theory continues to provide an important framework for understanding and ultimately reducing the impact that living in a sexually objectifying culture has on women.

Source: Fredrickson, Roberts, Noll, Quinn, & Twenge, 1998
Contributed by Annie B. Fox

"watching" their weight and "fighting" their fat. They "tame" their hair and "control" their tummies. We do not flinch when a woman says she "hates" her butt, thighs, tummy, wrinkles, and so on. When was the last time you heard a man say he "hated" any part of his body?

Invisible Women

Who is left out of media representations of women? A short answer might be, "Any woman who is not White, young, thin, rich, feminine, and sexually available!" Let's look at some of the women who remain underrepresented or invisible.

Women of Color

In 2015, when the Academy of Motion Picture Arts and Sciences announced the nominees for best actor and actress, each and every Oscar nominee was White, prompting a flurry of protests about the lack of diversity. When it happened again in 2016, the protests turned to outrage, the hashtag #Oscarsowhite was born, and host Chris Rock labeled the awards ceremony the "White People's Choice Awards." Most people may notice it only once a year at the Oscars, but women (and men) of color are hard to find in good roles at the movies. Analyses of top 100 films over the years show that about 74% of speaking parts go to white characters, and the proportion is not changing over time despite repeated calls for diversity (Women's Media Center, 2015). For example, in 2013, only 14% of speaking characters were African American; 5% were Hispanic; 5% were Asian; 1% were Middle Eastern; and less than 1% were American Indian. Male characters of color consistently outnumbered female characters of their same racial group.

Latinos are particularly likely to be erased from the media. Between 1950 and 2013, when the Latino population grew by roughly 5 times its size to comprise 17% of the U.S. population, the%age of Latinos with leading roles on English-language TV dropped from 4% to 0% and those with leading roles in the movies dropped from 2% to 0% (Women's Media Center, 2015). The only place Latinas show up in substantial and equal numbers with Latinos on U.S. TV is on Spanish-language *telenovelas* (Rivadeneyra, 2011). When Latinas get roles in the movies, they are either highly sexualized, or they are depicted as maids and housekeepers (Lewis, 2002). For example, in 2013, 69% of all maids in entertainment media were depicted as Latina (Women's Media Center, 2015).

It's not just movies and TV shows. Women of color are rendered invisible in other ways, too. They are less likely to be featured in women's magazines (Covert & Dixon, 2008) and in TV ads (Coltrane & Messineo, 2000). After her brilliant turn as the monstrous mom in *Precious,* the actress Mo'Nique was asked by an interviewer whether she'd gotten a lot of job offers. Her reply? "Ain't a damn soul called me." (Carter, 2010).

Older Women

If Martian observers were to estimate the U.S. population demographics from TV, they might think that some mysterious virus had killed off all the human females over the age of 40. Older women are among the least visible groups in the mass media. TV newscasters can have gray hair and wrinkled brows only if they are male. Studies from the 1970s to the present show that the majority of female characters in commercials are under the age of 35. One study compared the actual proportion of people over the age of 51 in the U.S. population with the representation of characters in a large sample of prime time commercials. Although people over the age of 51 are 27% of the population, they accounted for only 18% of the characters in the commercials. And despite the fact that there are increasingly more women than men the older people get (because women live longer on average), two-thirds of the older characters were men (Ganahl et al., 2003).

The U.S. media are not alone in the bias against older people. A study of prime-time TV characters in Germany showed that only 8% appeared to be over the age of 60 (compared to 22% of the actual population), and two-thirds of those were male. Older women were depicted much more negatively than older men (Kessler et al., 2004). A content analysis of TV ads in the UK and Taiwan showed that only 12% of the ads in Taiwan and 7% in the UK showed people over the age of 50, mostly in background roles (Chen, 2015). About half the ads portrayed the seniors as competent, and 20% as "Golden agers," but particularly in Taiwan, they were also seen as conservative, traditional, in poor health, incompetent, and vulnerable (frightened, suspicious, and sad).

Stereotyped TV portrayals of older people are socially significant for several reasons. Older people watch more TV than younger people do, and these stereotypes can affect their self-image and expectations for aging. There is also evidence that heavy TV viewers of all ages underestimate the proportion of older people in the population—because they hardly ever see them on TV (Chen, 2015).

Bigger Women

One challenge in analyzing images of larger women in the media is that there are so few. One of the first studies examining the prevalence of different body types in prime-time TV was done in 1980, and it found that 88% of individuals shown had thin or average body types. Of the remaining 12%, who were heavier, twice as many were men as women. Since then, other studies have replicated the underrepresentation of larger bodies as well as the more extreme underrepresentation of larger women (Fikkan & Rothblum, 2012). When a token overweight woman is portrayed, she is rarely allowed to be like other women. Her weight defines her, making her unlovable (think Fat Amy in the movie *Pitch Perfect*). In an analysis of sitcoms, male characters directed more positive comments toward thinner female characters, and more negative ones to heavier characters (Fouts & Burggraf, 2000). Most of the negative comments to heavier women were followed by laughter, showing that it is socially acceptable to ridicule overweight women. Food ads often portray thinness as a woman's major goal in life and depict women's appetites and eating behaviors in moralistic terms. Women are told that it is bad or sinful to have an appetite—unless it is for diet foods (Kilbourne, 2002).

A study of images that accompanied online news stories about obesity found that 72% of the images depicting an overweight person were negative and stigmatizing (Heuer et al., 2011). Compared to images of normal-weight people, images of overweight people were significantly more likely to exclude their heads or show only their abdomens, and overweight people were less likely to be shown fully clothed, professionally dressed, or exercising. In another study, participants were assigned to read a news story about obesity that was accompanied by either a typical photo of an obese woman (eating junk food or emphasizing body size) or an atypical photo (nicely dressed or exercising). Participants who viewed the typical photos expressed more negative attitudes toward obese people than those who viewed the atypical photos (McClure et al., 2011). In a content analysis of reports about obesity from major news sources, researchers found that overweight and obese adults and youth were significantly more likely than non-overweight individuals to be portrayed as headless, with close-ups of isolated body parts and unflattering rear views, eating unhealthy foods, being sedentary, and dressed in badly fitting clothing (Puhl et al., 2013). These stigmatizing and objectifying portrayals of overweight people may reinforce societal bias against them.

Studies suggest that overweight women suffer socially and economically as a result of antifat attitudes fostered by the media. For example, being large is a liability for women in education (e.g., discrimination in college admission); in employment (wage discrimination); and in healthcare and mental health treatment (Fikkan & Rothblum, 2012). The prevalence of weight discrimination has increased by 66% in the past decade and is now on a par with rates of racial discrimination (Puhl et al., 2013).

Lower-Income Women

Media critics have noted that the people on TV rarely seem to actually work for a living; instead, they hang out. They wear expensive clothes and live in improbably nice houses and apartments; everybody belongs to a vaguely upper-middle class. The working-class characters and sitcoms of the past (Rosanne, Archie and Edith Bunker) are gone. People who earn the minimum wage or work with their hands show up only on reality TV shows like *Dirty Jobs* (Morris, 2016).

Working-class and poor women in particular are singled out for disdain or, at best, pity in the media. On afternoon talk shows, working-class women are shown as out of control, belligerent, and victims of dysfunctional families. In the print media, newspapers and magazines feature poor women (particularly women of color) in stories about welfare reform or homelessness, but not in stories about other issues. Few women are called upon to comment on issues of poverty, although the majority of poor people in the United States are women and children. Most poor and low-income women, who struggle to work and care for families under difficult conditions, are not considered worthy of air time (Bullock et al., 2001).

One of the few places you will find African American women *over*represented in the media is in discourse about welfare reform. A content analysis of network news coverage of welfare reform from 1992 to 2007 showed that African American women were significantly overrepresented as public assistance recipients and that the language used to describe them was full of racist stereotypes. The "welfare mother" was described as too unintelligent or childlike to ever get off welfare, as hyperfertile, lazy, with a poor work ethic, and as a bad mother who transmits a "culture of poverty" and creates a "cycle of welfare dependency" (Kelly, 2010). Today, the era of welfare reform has passed, but we are hearing similar stereotypical and stigmatizing discourses about other low income people of color: undocumented workers and immigrants, who are said to be criminals and terrorists bent on destroying our country. Politicians seeking election promise to build walls to keep them out and deport their families by the millions.

Voices of Authority

Women are relatively invisible in the media as responsible citizens and experts. The news media focus on the actions, opinions, and expertise of men much more than women. For example, a study of Sunday morning talk shows found that 77% of the 2,150 guests were men (Garofoli, 2007). By 2014, the situation had hardly improved. On the big five Sunday talk shows such as *Face the Nation*, *Fox News Sunday*, and *CNN State of the Union*, all of which have White male hosts, between 73% and 77% of the guests were men (Women's Media Center, 2015). The overrepresentation of White men on TV may be largely due to male control behind the scenes: 93% of TV network and studio heads are White and 73% are male. Even when the voice of authority is merely selling a product, it is usually a man's voice. Studies in many countries—the United States, Australia, Denmark, France, and Portugal—show that 70 to 90% of the authoritative voice-overs in TV commercials are male (Bartsch et al., 2000; Furnham & Mak, 1999; Neto & Pinto, 1998).

No matter the context, women are likely to be presented in a way that focuses on their appearance, family roles, and bodies rather than their words and ideas—a practice that has been documented since the 1970s (Foreit et al., 1980). This kind of bias makes it more difficult for women to be taken seriously. For example, in an article about a presidential campaign appearance by Hillary Clinton (Keller, 2003), women who attended were described in trivializing terms: "a fortysomething from Newton with suspiciously jet-black hair who's risking perspiration stains on her cashmere sweater," "a well-tailored woman in her fifties," "a middle-aged woman wearing expensive glasses," "a fortyish black woman." In contrast, men were described by their names and occupations ("healthcare worker Andy Johnson"). Their age, race, and fashion preferences were not considered relevant. Collectively, Clinton's supporters were referred to as "the chevre and Chardonnay sisterhood," and one was quoted as saying that Clinton has "beautiful skin, and let me tell you, that's important to women." In other words, Clinton's supporters were portrayed as ditzy middle-aged women, not politically informed voters.

Even when women have the authority to be heard, their appearance is paramount. News reporter Katie Couric, the first female solo anchor in network news history, posed for *Harper's Bazaar* (March 2010) in a "tough-and-sexy photoshoot featuring smoky, kohl-rimmed eyes, a one-shouldered Calvin Klein sheath, and a pair of Gucci platform shoes," to accompany an article in which she talked about her current romance and her use of Botox to hide wrinkles (von Pfetten, 2010). We can hardly imagine Anderson Cooper being asked to pose for a fashion spread like this.

It should be clear by now that the language we use about women and the images of women that we see can affect us. A review of experimental studies confirmed that presenting participants with biased media images increases their acceptance of gender-biased beliefs (Herrett-Skjellum & Allen, 1996). Now we will turn to a discussion of those gender-biased beliefs and how they affect our perceptions of, and behavior toward, the real women in our lives.

Stereotypes about Women and Men

Stereotypes can be thought of as theories that people carry around in their heads about how members of a particular group think, look, and behave, and how these attributes are linked. An individual may be unaware that he or she holds stereotypical beliefs or behaves in accordance with them. Still, the network of associations around a group forms a *schema,* or mental framework, that guides people as they experience the world around them (von Hippel et al., 1995). For a particular schema to be considered a stereotype, the content of the schema must be similar to others' schemas for the same group. For example, Charlotte may believe that short people are grumpy, but this belief is idiosyncratic, not stereotypical. On the other hand, if Charlotte believes that women are more likely than men to become emotional in a crisis, her belief, which is shared by many others, is a stereotypical belief. *Gender stereotypes* are networks of related beliefs that reflect the "common wisdom" about women and men.

Stereotyping is not an all-or-none matter; four limitations are especially noteworthy. First, people do not say (unless forced to choose) that women and men are complete opposites; instead, they think that women and men differ *on average,* and they allow for overlap (Deaux & Lewis, 1984). Second, although most people know the stereotypes, not everyone believes them. Third, stereotypes tend to have the biggest influence when you are registering a first impression of a stranger or thinking generally about a category of people (Deaux & Lewis, 1984). Fourth, the activation of stereotypes in our minds tends to be an automatic process that is not under our conscious control, and it happens even if we don't believe the stereotypes. However, we do have some control over whether we use stereotypes or not (Devine & Sharp, 2009).

Think back to the example that opened this chapter. Most people would agree that the stereotypical image of a doctor is a White male, but most would also agree that actual doctors include both genders and a wide array of ethnicities. Stereotypes are most likely to be activated in assessments of a stranger—like the harried flight attendants' situation. Stereotype activation is automatic and unconscious, but it can be overruled by rational thought. If the flight attendants had stopped for just a moment and reflected on their thinking—if they had tried *not* to stereotype—the passenger in medical distress would have been helped more quickly, and Dr. Cross would have been treated with the respect she deserved.

The Content of Gender Stereotypes

In general, people associate gender with a variety of attributes including physical characteristics, personality, behaviors, and roles.

Physical Characteristics

Physical appearance is particularly important because it is the first thing we perceive when we meet someone. In fact, this information is conveyed within one-tenth of a second (Locher et al., 1993). More than any other stereotype component, it activates other components.

The special role of appearance was shown in a classic study in which participants read about a hypothetical woman or man. The target person was described using one component of gender stereotypes: either personality traits, gender-role behavior, occupation, or physical characteristics. Then the participants were asked to judge the probability that the target would have other stereotypical characteristics. When targets were described as having stereotypically feminine physical characteristics, such as being dainty, soft, and graceful, participants were very certain that they would also have feminine personalities, occupations, and gender-typed behaviors. Parallel judgments were made about men: when they were described as tall, strong, and sturdy, participants were very sure they would also have stereotypically masculine personalities, gender-role behaviors, and jobs. If the initial descriptions focused on traits, occupations or behaviors, participants were not nearly as certain that they could tell what the target would be like on the other dimensions (Deaux & Lewis, 1984).

Personality Traits

When people are asked to respond to lists of traits by choosing whether each trait is more characteristic of a woman or a man, or by rating the typicality of each for women and men, they attribute such traits as independent, competitive, decisive, active, self-confident, dominant, competent, unemotional, adventurous, and ambitious more to men. In contrast, they attribute traits such as warm, gentle, understanding, nurturing, helpful, aware of others' feelings, expressive, emotional, submissive, and sensitive more to women. The traits considered characteristic of men are *instrumental* and *agentic:* they describe a person who is an active agent and an effective "doer." The traits considered characteristic of women are *affective* and *communal:* they describe a person who is concerned with feelings and other people. The instrumental/affective (or agentic/communal) dimension of gender stereotypes was first found nearly 50 years ago (Broverman et al., 1972). It has been measured periodically over the years (Spence & Buckner, 2000; Williams & Best, 1990) and is still found in the most recent studies (Andreoletti et al., 2015; Haines et al., 2016).

Several cross-cultural studies have shown that agentic/instrumental traits were associated with men and communal/affective traits were associated with women in virtually every nation studied (Best, 2001; Williams & Best, 1990). This suggests that gender stereotypes of agency and communality are universal. However, there are other explanations. First, cross-cultural studies typically rely on college student samples, which may be exposed to Western cultural influences and which do not represent their countries' population as a whole. Second, most cross-cultural studies have measured only trait stereotypes. Perhaps there is more variability in other components of gender stereotypes—physical attributes, social roles, and so on. Until there is more cross-cultural research, the universality of gender stereotypes is an open question.

Role Stereotypes

Many behaviors and social roles are stereotyped as more typical of women or men. This aspect of stereotyping becomes evident when people are asked to think of particular *types* of women and men. In the first study of gender subtypes (Deaux et al., 1985), participants found it easy to think of subcategories for women and men. For women, the types included the housewife/mother, who was believed to be self-sacrificing, focused on her family, and nurturing. The housewife/mother subtype is closest to the more general stereotype of women, suggesting that a *real* woman is a wife and mother. Another type, the sexy woman, was described less in terms of personality and more in terms of physical characteristics: having a good body, long hair, nail polish, and so on. (The lack of overlap between these two also suggests that moms are never sexy, and sexy women are never moms—a point we'll take up in Chapter 9.) Another type was the athletic woman, described in terms of physical characteristics (muscular, strong) as well as traits (aggressive, masculine). Finally, participants nominated a career woman type, seen as smart, hardworking, organized, and not very feminine.

Corresponding categories for men included blue-collar, athletic, macho, and businessman. Although the characteristics attributed to each type differed, all of the male types were seen as masculine—blue-collar men were described as hardworking, macho men as hairy-chested—and none were seen as having any feminine traits or behaviors. In contrast, some of the female types were seen as more feminine than others (e.g., housewives versus career women). Beliefs about these subtypes of women and men were as strongly held as beliefs about women and men in general.

To a large extent, people still differentiate between the housewife/mother and career woman subtypes, and the housewife subtype remains closest in attributes to the generic female or supposedly typical woman (Irmen, 2006). However, because of changes in the social roles of women, the generic woman stereotype is starting to include attributes previously assigned only to masculine female subtypes such as the career woman (Diekman & Eagly, 2000).

Occupational Stereotypes

Are there specific occupational gender stereotypes? This question, first asked in a 1975 study, was assessed again more than 20 years later (Beggs & Doolittle, 1993). When women and men were asked to classify each of 129 occupations as masculine, neutral, or feminine, 124 of them were classified the same way as they had been in 1975. Most jobs were perceived as gender-typed, not gender-neutral.

Occupational stereotypes are grounded in reality, because most occupations and professions historically have been delegated to one sex or the other, not evenly divided. Children learn these stereotypes by about the age of 6 to 8, and this knowledge shapes their preferences about future careers from an early age (Adachi, 2013). Such stereotypes are just as persistent in other cultures as they are in our own. In a recent study using an Internet sample of Japanese adults, the most masculine-typed occupations included carpenter, pilot, and system engineer, and the most feminine-typed occupations included nurse, kindergarten teacher, and supermarket cashier (Adachi, 2013).

Experiments have shown that using occupational stereotypes may be automatic, rather than under our conscious control (Oakhill et al., 2005). Participants were asked to decide whether pairs of occupation labels and kinship labels could refer to the same person. Some pairs were gender stereotype–congruent (e.g., sister-secretary, father-plumber), some were incongruent but possible (brother-nurse), and some were impossible (uncle-landlady). The accuracy and speed of participants' decision making was worse for stereotype-incongruent possible terms than for stereotype-congruent possible terms, suggesting that gender stereotypes are automatically activated as soon as an occupation name is read and we cannot necessarily suppress them even when it makes sense to do so.

Sexuality Stereotypes

Gender and sexuality are closely linked in most people's cognitive schemas. Gay and lesbian people pose a problem for gender stereotypes because these stereotypes are implicitly heterosexual. Traditionally, people solved this cognitive problem by putting lesbians into the male/masculine schema and gay men into the female/feminine one. This was even true for physical characteristics, which are key to overall stereotyping. For example, early sexuality researchers claimed to find "long clitorises, narrow hips, small breasts, and deep voices" in lesbians (Kitzinger, 2001). Even today, lesbians are stereotyped as "butch" or "mannish" and gay men are stereotyped as effeminate (Blashill & Powlishta, 2009).

Women who are particularly strong, either in personality or physical skills, are likely to be stereotyped as lesbians, a cognitive trick that helps maintain two stereotypes: heterosexual women as the weaker sex and lesbians as mannish. For example, two longstanding and still prevalent myths about women in sports are "Sports make girls masculine" and "Only lesbians play sports" (Hall, 2008). Of course, some athletes are lesbians—and so are some teachers, attorneys, and flight attendants. Most women in all these occupations are heterosexual. "Clearly, any correlation made between athleticism and sexual orientation is misleading" (Hall, 2008, p. 107). One study confronted participants with a challenge to the "woman athlete = lesbian" idea by measuring their perceptions of heterosexual hypermuscular female bodybuilders (Forbes et al., 2004). Participants assumed that these women were less feminine, less popular, less attractive, and worse mothers than average women (and that their male partners were extramasculine).

Both in and outside the realm of athletics, sexuality stereotypes may be a means of keeping women subordinated. As long as the label "lesbian" carries a social stigma, it can be used as a weapon against any woman. On the other hand, the stereotype of lesbians as mannish may protect them from some of the negative evaluation of women's competence discussed in Chapter 2. You may recall that women often face a double bind in leadership and professional situations: if they behave in assertive and dominant ways, they are judged competent but cold, unlikable, and domineering. If they behave in more traditionally feminine ways, they are judged incompetent, though likable. Recent research suggests that lesbians may be judged *more* competent than heterosexual women when they make a traditionally feminine decision. In this case the situation was a hypothetical job interview, and the decision was that they had moved to a new location to accommodate their partner's job (Niedlich et al., 2015). The results in this study suggested that lesbians, because they are believed to be more masculine, may be, like men, relatively immune from the likability versus competence double bind. There may be a similar bonus for gay men, who are judged to have better social skills in the workplace than heterosexual men, perhaps because they are seen as more feminine (Niedlich & Steffens, 2015).

There is a need for more research to explore the intersection of prejudice and positive stereotyping in evaluating lesbian and gay people in the workplace.

The Intersectionality of Gender and Ethnic Stereotypes

Most psychological studies of gender stereotypes have asked participants about "typical" women and men. A big problem with this approach is that participants (who are most often college students) may equate "typical" with White and middle-class. This only becomes apparent when researchers specifically ask about race or class. For example, when researchers asked college students to list traits for "American women" and "Black women," there was no overlap in the top-ranked traits. Typical American women were seen as intelligent, materialistic, and sensitive (similar to stereotypes of White women), whereas typical Black women were seen as loud, talkative, and aggressive (Weitz & Gordon, 1993).

This negative stereotype is related to archetypes of Black women in American culture: Mammy, Jezebel, and Sapphire (Watson et al., 2012; West, 2008). The prototype of the Mammy goes back to *Gone with the Wind,* in which Mammy was a happy slave whose huge breasts and perpetual smile symbolized her role as nurturer, while her dark complexion, bandana-covered hair, broad features, and fat body marked her as asexual. Aunt Jemima, a Mammy symbol for over a century, finally lost her bandana in the 1990s. Originally, Aunt Jemima spoke in a caricature of slave dialect: "Honey, . . . Yo know how de men folks and de young folks all loves my tasty pancakes" (West, 2008, p. 289). Today's Pine-Sol Lady may not wear a slave's bandana but she is still smiling, overweight, motherly, and calling people "Honey" (see Figure 3.4).

The Jezebel is a stereotype of a highly sexed Black woman. During slavery, owners and traders brutalized African women by raping them, forcing them to bear children who would be sold away from them, and forbidding them to marry African men. There was a conscious attempt to destroy Black families. The victims were blamed, and the oppression justified, by portraying Black women as immoral, seductive, and promiscuous. Today, the Jezebel stereotype is represented in music videos, hip-hop music, advertising, and pornography as the hoochie or the "ho."

The Sapphire icon is domineering, aggressive, strong, and unfeminine. This stereotype, too, probably originated in slavery, when Black women were forced to do heavy labor alongside Black men, and it served both to justify their oppression and to separate them from the passive, frail, and domestic role occupied by White Southern women. Sapphire is a hostile, tongue-lashing nag who drives men away and bullies everyone else (West, 2008). She is the Black woman with attitude and anger who gets into seemingly every reality TV show, the gangsta girl of hip-hop legend, and the Madea grandmother who can tell off anyone and follow up with a fistfight. Like the Mammy and the Jezebel, the Sapphire stereotype may be a distortion and exaggeration of coping strategies that enabled Black women to survive centuries of oppression.

There has not been much systematic research on how stereotypes of gender and race or ethnicity are related, for African Americans or any other ethnic group. Intersectionality theory proposes that intersectional gender and ethnic stereotypes

FIGURE 3.4   Diane Amos has a varied career as an actress and comedian, but she is best known as the Pine-Sol lady.

(Asian American men, Middle Eastern women) will contain unique elements—not simply be composed of an addition of separate elements from the overall ethnic and gender stereotypes. This hypothesis was tested by asking more than 600 U.S. undergraduates to generate stereotypical attributes for different ethnic groups overall and by gender: Asian Americans, Blacks, Latinos, Middle Eastern Americans, and Whites (Ghavami & Peplau, 2013). If the intersectionality hypothesis is correct, there should be attributes in each intersectional category that are not present for the more general categories. For example, Middle Eastern women should be stereotyped somewhat differently than Middle Easterners in general. Some of the results of this study are summarized in Table 3.1. You can see that the intersectional ethnic stereotypes comprise both positive and negative characteristics, and a mix of physical characteristics, personality traits, and role behaviors. Which of the stereotypes do you think is most positive? Most negative? Most based on physical characteristics?

With respect to the intersectionality hypothesis, there were unique attributes in every ethnicity-by-gender group. For example, Middle Eastern women, but not Middle Eastern men or Middle Easterners in general, were stereotyped as quiet and oppressed. Latinas, but not Latino men or Latinos in general, were stereotyped as feisty and good cooks. Thus, the hypothesis of intersectional uniqueness was confirmed. Knowing the content and uniqueness of ethnic stereotypes may be useful in educating people about bias and preventing discrimination (Ghavami & Peplau, 2013).

TABLE 3.1   Gender and Ethnic Stereotypes

Participants in this study were asked to list the first 15 adjectives that came to mind when they thought of members of each group. Here are the traits they listed most often. * Indicates a unique attribute.

Asian Men	Asian Women	Asian People
Intelligent	Intelligent	Intelligent
Short	Quiet	Bad drivers
Nerdy	Short	Good at math
Quiet	Bad drivers	Nerdy
Good at math	Shy	Short
Bad drivers	Small build	Shy

Black Men	Black Women	Black People
Athletic	Have an attitude	Ghetto/unrefined
Dark-skinned*	Loud	Criminals
Loud	Big butt*	Athletic
Quick to anger*	Overweight*	Loud
Tall	Confident*	Gangsters
Violent	Dark-skinned*	Poor

Latino Men	Latina Women	Latinx People
Macho	Feisty*	Poor
Poor	Curvy*	Many children
Dark-skinned	Loud	Illegal immigrants
Day laborers	Attractive	Dark-skinned
Promiscuous*	Good cooks*	Uneducated
Short	Dark-skinned	Family-oriented

Middle Eastern Men	Mid. East. Women	Mid. East. People
Bearded	Quiet*	Terrorists
Dark-skinned	Religious	Dark-skinned
Terrorists	Covered*	Oppress women
Sexist	Oppressed*	Muslim
Speak accented English	Conservative	Hairy
Dirty	Dark-skinned	Wear turban

White Men	White Women	White People
Rich	Arrogant	High status
Tall	Blond	Rich
Intelligent	Rich	Intelligent
Assertive*	Attractive	Arrogant
Arrogant	Small build	Privileged
Successful*	Ditsy*	Blond

Source: Ghavami, N., & Peplau, L.A. (2013). An intersectional analysis of gender and ethnic stereotypes testing three hypotheses. *Psychology of Women Quarterly*, 37, 113–127, from Tables 1–5 (p. 118–120).

Are Stereotypes Accurate?

Stereotypes, to some extent, reflect the social world, and some hold a kernel of truth (Jussim et al., 2009). If your stereotypical image of a nurse is female, and a computer scientist, male, you are more accurate than not, because the proportions of women and men in these occupations are in fact different. We saw earlier that occupational stereotypes had changed somewhat as women's actual distribution in the workforce changed. In order for stereotypes to function as effective cognitive shortcuts, they need to be at least somewhat anchored in reality (Ottati & Lee, 1995).

However, it is not always clear what counts as reality. What criteria should be used to defend or refute stereotypical judgments is always open to debate, and often the debater's position depends on their social and political agenda. More important than arguing over whether stereotypes are accurate is to recognize that even when they are somewhat accurate as an overall group judgment, they may be very inaccurate when making judgments about individuals. Relying on stereotypes can cause harm:

> It *matters* when stereotypes are misused. It matters when an employer hires a man rather than a woman for a given job because he believes that men are inherently more suited for it. It matters when girls are told that they should take English rather than mathematics in high school. It matters when a Black family is excluded from the possibility of owning a house in a nice neighborhood because a real estate agent believes that they will have too many children and not take care of the property. In this sense, the critical issues of stereotyping go beyond the question of whether the perceiver, on average, is accurate in his or her perceptions, to the potential negative outcomes . . . (Stangor, 1995).

Even when stereotypes contain a kernel of truth, they are *never* true of every group member. Unfortunately, despite their limitations as cognitive aids and their harmful social potential, stereotypes are not easily dislodged.

Stereotypes Are Hard to Change

Gender stereotypes have been studied for over 60 years. During that time, there have been enormous changes in the status of women. Attitudes toward women's rights have become more liberal, and women have become more visible in politics, the law, medicine, and professional athletics (Haines et al., 2016). However, gender stereotypes have changed remarkably little. Various studies measured gender stereotypes as early as the 1950s, and later studies compared these to stereotypes in the 1970s, 1990s, and 2000s (Lueptow et al., 1995; Spence & Bruckner, 2000; Werner & LaRussa, 1985). In these studies, the traits believed to characterize women and men in the 1950s were still thought to apply many decades later.

As we have learned, there is more to stereotypes than traits. A recent study compared 1980s stereotypes of not only traits but also role behaviors, occupations, and physical characteristics with stereotypes of today by collecting data from an Internet sample of U.S. adults. Just as they did in the early 1980s, people perceive strong differences between typical men and women on instrumental and affective traits, and also on all the other components of stereotypes. In fact, there was a significant *increase* in the stereotyping of female gender roles over time (Haines et al., 2016). The researchers admitted to being surprised at the durability and persistence of gender stereotypes over a 30 year period of social change toward gender equality.

If social reality is changing, why are stereotypes relatively static? People tend to hang on to their stereotypical beliefs even when they are challenged by new or incongruent information, for several reasons (von Hippel et al., 1995). We may cling to stereotypes because they help us feel good about ourselves. Jokes and stories about dumb blondes or effeminate gay men may serve to make others feel superior. And since "everybody" knows that blondes or gay men are "all like that," stereotypes serve to make the ingroup members feel more cohesive and in tune with each other. When someone makes a remark about fags, JAPs, or welfare queens, the ingroup gets to feel superior to the outgroup (Ruscher, 2001).

Stereotypes also persist because they are useful cognitive shortcuts, helping us to allocate cognitive processing time efficiently and get through the day with a minimum of mental effort. Stereotypical thinking helps keep us from getting bogged down as we navigate a complex social world. There is a lot of evidence consistent with this view of stereotyping. For example, people rely on stereotypes more when they are least alert—"morning people" stereotype more at night, and "night people" do it more in the morning. And most people rely on stereotypes more when they are under time pressure or overloaded with incoming information (von Hippel et al., 1995).

Another reason stereotypes survive is that they influence the amount and kind of information that the individual takes in. When you have a well-developed schema, you tend to encode information that is congruent with the schema, then stop encoding. You do not perceive the incongruent information that is all around you. As an example, imagine a group of four women and four men working together on a committee. One of the women is more talkative than average. If other group members hold the stereotypical belief that women talk a lot, they may pick up on her talkativeness and notice it. But perhaps the other three women say very little, and on balance more of the talking is done by the four men (a normative pattern discussed in Chapter 2). Because the silent women are stereotype-incongruent, their behavior is less likely to be encoded into memory and used to form judgments.

Stereotypes about gay, bisexual, and lesbian people may be even more resistant to change than gender stereotypes because people may interact with gays and lesbians quite often without realizing it. Thus, gay or lesbian people who do not match the stereotypes (the lesbian who wears dresses or does flower arranging, the gay man who drives an SUV or plays football) may not be recognized as such (Garnets, 2008).

Another cognitive mechanism that helps stereotypes persist in the face of incongruent information is the formation of subtypes. If Trisha, who believes that women love children, meets a woman who is focused on her career and has little interest in children, she may protect her stereotype by putting the woman into a "career woman" subtype. Career women are unfeminine, Trisha may decide, but real women still love children.

The Impact of Stereotypes

Stereotypes matter! Here we look at three ways in which stereotypes have very real effects: they become part of the self-schema and may cause stereotype threat and create harmful self-fulfilling prophecies; they reinforce differences in status and power; and they prime sexist behavior and lead to discrimination.

Stereotypes, the Self, and Stereotype Threat

Because gender is such an important dimension in perceiving and evaluating others, the gender schema becomes part of the self-schema. In other words, people may come to believe that the attributes of their gender stereotypes are true expressions of their identity.

Research offers both good news and not-so-good news about today's self-schemas. The good news is that, compared to earlier generations, today's college women see themselves as more instrumental. They endorse traits such as "acts like a leader," "self-reliant," and "assertive" just as much as college men do. However, men still rate themselves higher on about 40% of instrumental traits. Thus, the gender gap in instrumentality is narrowing, but not yet closed. The not-so-good news is that women and men still see themselves as very different in expressiveness. Virtually every expressive trait—kind, emotional, understanding, warm, gentle, tender, and so on—still is endorsed significantly more by women than by men (Spence & Buckner, 2000). Thus, gender stereotypes are still being internalized as part of the self. Although the stereotypes are internalized somewhat differently than in the past, the change is not equal for women and men. Women are seeing themselves as more instrumental, but men are not seeing themselves as more expressive.

When people know that there is a negative stereotype about their group's abilities, the pressure caused by their fear of confirming the stereotype can interfere with their performance—a phenomenon called *stereotype threat.* For example, Aisha may perform below par on a math test because she is preoccupied with concern about confirming the stereotype that women are inferior in mathematics. (For research on stereotype threat, see Chapter 4.)

In addition, stereotypes may generate *self-fulfilling prophecies* because they often depict not only a consensus about the way things are but also the way they should be. In other words, they are not just descriptive, but *prescriptive:* they prescribe how the ideal woman or man *should* think, look, and behave. For example, a woman who does not want to have children not only violates the stereotype that women are nurturing but may be judged an inadequate woman; a man who is not ambitious or strong may be seen as not a real man. Prescriptive stereotypes create strong pressure for women to act feminine and men to act masculine—to play by the rules of gender.

Stereotypes, Status, and Power

In general, people with more power engage in stereotyping of people with less power (Keltner et al., 2003). Powerful people pay more attention than less powerful people to stereotype-consistent information, and less attention to information that might contradict their stereotypes. Although both these tendencies contribute to maintaining imbalances, they make sense cognitively and socially. Powerful people may seek to confirm beliefs that work for them. And they do not need to pay much attention to the individual differences among the powerless, because their well-being does not depend on it. For example, a worker must pay more attention to the moods and demands of the boss than the boss must pay to the worker's, because the boss controls important outcomes for the worker.

Group-based power differences also increase the tendency to stereotype. Recall that people who are higher in social power (men compared to women, European American compared to African American) tend to be higher in social dominance orientation, or SDO (see Chapter 2). In turn, SDO predicts the tendency to stereo-type others—with higher SDO scores linked to more stereotyping. Importantly, research on *behavioral confirmation* suggests that when higher-power people (such as men) interact with lower-power people about whom they hold stereotypes (such as women), they may—intentionally or unintentionally—treat those people in ways that actually elicit stereotype-consistent behaviors, even when the stereotype is inaccurate (Chen & Bargh, 1997; Snyder & Klein, 2005). Their stereotypes are then confirmed—the self-fulfilling prophecy described in Chapter 2.

Stereotypes and Sexist Behavior

Another harmful effect of stereotypes is that they can prime sexist behavior. Con-sider the example of an award-winning study grounded in real-world sex discrimination.

In the early 1990s, women workers at the Stroh's brewery in Minnesota sued the company over sexual harassment in the workplace. The attorney representing the women introduced Stroh's infamous "Swedish Bikini Team" beer commercials as evidence that Stroh's tolerated a hostile workplace. Her argument was that any company that produces such sexist and objectifying commercials is sending a clear message to its employees about how to regard women. (These commercials can still be found on YouTube). The case settled out of court, but graduate student Laurie Rudman was inspired to investigate how commercials that portray women as sex objects affect male viewers. Using a computer-timed word-recognition task, Rud-man and her colleague Eugene Borgida found that men who had watched sex-object commercials were quicker to recognize words associated with the sex-object female stereotype (e.g., bimbo) than were men who had viewed commercials that did not portray women as sex objects. Moreover, when they were asked to interview a female job applicant, these men rated her as less competent, and remembered less about her résumé and more about her appearance. In other words, activation of the stereotype distorted men's perceptions of the female applicant and affected their behavior toward her (Rudman & Borgida, 1995).

How Not to Stereotype

Are stereotyping and its negative consequences inevitable? No. Admittedly, it isn't easy to change or eliminate stereotypes. Because they are part of the cognitive pro-cess of categorization, they are relatively automatic, and they are activated without awareness. But people can make conscious decisions to pay attention to their auto-matic stereotyping and to combat their natural tendency to judge others stereotypically.

Although more than 100 studies since the late 1980s have demonstrated auto-matic activation of stereotypes, researchers have identified several types of inter-ventions that disrupt this process and allow people to exercise some control over their stereotyping (Blair, 2002; Lenton et al., 2009). One factor that can make a big difference is the motivation of the perceiver (Blair, 2002).

For example, people rely less on stereotypes when they are trying to be accurate in their judgments of others. In one study, participants were provided with both stereotypical and nonstereotypical information about another individual and instructed to convey their impression to another person. Participants conveyed more balanced (less stereotypical) information when they were in situations that stressed the importance of accuracy (Ruscher & Duval, 1998). Instead of disregarding nonste-reotypical information that was provided to them, they included it in their accounts. This study suggests that a conscious effort to be accurate will reduce stereotyping.

There is also evidence that nonprejudiced people can suppress or override their stereotypes (von Hippel et al., 1995). In other words, virtually everyone is aware of stereotypes such as the mammy, bimbo, hottie, and housewife; the words and images of our culture routinely activate these stereotypes. Prejudiced people—those who score high on the measures of sexism and racism described in Chapter 2—are likely to rely on such stereotypes when they are automatically activated; the stereo-types affect their judgments and behavior. Less prejudiced people stop and think about the stereotypes, and replace them with more accurate information, so they are less likely to respond to others as stereotypes and more likely to respond to them as individuals. *Not* stereotyping requires being open minded, paying atten-tion, and making a conscious choice, but it can be done.

Making a Difference

Sexist representations are everywhere in our culture, and they can be powerful agents in fostering biased attitudes and discriminatory behavior. Feminists view these representations as an important opportunity for education and work toward societal change. Here we look at some of their efforts.

Transforming Language

Feminists from many cultures and societies have taken action to change linguistic sexism through *feminist language reform:* efforts to eliminate gender bias in the structure, content, and usage of language and to provide nonsexist alternatives (Pauwels, 1998). Feminist language reform has modified old language and also cre-ated new language (Crawford, 2001).

One of the biggest successes in feminist language reform has been the adoption of nonsexist language guidelines. By the mid-1970s, major educational publishers and professional organizations (such as APA and National Council of Teachers of

English) had adopted such guidelines. In 1975, the U.S. Department of Labor eliminated gender bias in occupational titles. Government agencies adopted nonsexist language in Germany, Italy, France, Spain, and other countries at around the same time (Pauwels, 1998).

Guidelines for nonsexist language led to noticeable and important changes. Occupational titles and terms are now almost always gender-neutral—letter carrier has replaced mailman, and chairperson is an everyday word. There has been a dramatic drop in the use of pseudo-generic masculine terms in magazines and newspapers in all the countries studied (Pauwels, 1998). Politicians are usually very careful to refer to citizens as "he or she" and troops as "our men and women in uniform." However, nonsexist language guidelines did not address more subtle aspects of linguistic sexism such as the people = male bias. Nor did they address the blatant sexism of referring to women in terms of animals, appearance, and sexuality.

Feminists have provided new words for new times by adding many terms to the English language. Some, such as mansplaining, named aspects of women's experience that had been invisible. The writer Gloria Steinem expressed the importance of naming and the influence of 1970s feminist activism on language when she said, "We have terms like 'sexual harassment' and 'battered women.' A few years ago, they were just called 'life.'" (Steinem, 1983, p. 149).

Lesbian, gay, bisexual, and transgender activists, too, have taken over the power to name. Gay activists coined *heterosexism, homophobia,* and *biphobia.* Rejecting the psychiatric label *homosexual,* they adopted *gay,* and made *LGBTQ* a convenient shorthand term for diverse sexualities. Formerly derogatory epithets such as *queer* and *dyke* have been reclaimed as positive badges of identity (Marecek et al., 2004).

Despite resistance and backlash (such as the term *feminazi*), efforts to change language are ongoing. They are important because "Language is more than just talk. In using language, we create our social reality. By changing language, we can contribute to changing that reality" (Crawford, 2001, p. 244).

Challenging Objectification

Women's objectification is a profitable commercial enterprise. We are unlikely to see significant change in the behaviors of profit-driven organizations until they receive the message that women's objectification is going to cost them.

As consumers, we have tremendous power to influence popular culture. People dismiss women's objectification with the convenient phrase, "sex sells." This is not unlike dismissing sexual harassment or sexual violence against women with "boys will be boys." Just because something happens doesn't mean it has to be accepted. And women's objectification is not sex; it is dehumanization of half the population, a process that strips women of their personhood. Ours is a society that is shaped by economic forces. If anything is going to change with regard to women's objectification in our commercially driven culture, well-informed consumers are going to have to use their voices—*and dollars*—to educate the people producing the images, the products, and the services that rely far too much on objectification of women.

We now know that objectification is harmful to women's health. What if ads that objectify women were required to have warning labels, like cigarette ads are? Body image researcher Marisa Tiggemann and her colleagues tested the effect of

Box 3.4 ❧ Jean Kilbourne: Media Activist

Courtesy of Jean Kilbourne

"Jean Kilbourne's work is pioneering and crucial to the dialogue of one of the most underexplored, yet most powerful, realms of American culture—advertising. We owe her a great debt."

—*Susan Faludi, author*

Jean Kilbourne is an award winning educator, lecturer, film maker, author, and media activist. She is best known for her lectures and advocacy work around how women are portrayed in the media. In her lectures, Kilbourne dissects the many ways in which advertisers use objectifying images of women and create unrealistic beauty standards all in the name of selling products. She also explores how media images are connected to serious issues in society, including teen pregnancy, sexual harassment, violence against women, substance abuse, and eating disorders. The *New York Times* named her one of the most popular speakers on college campuses, and she has lectured at nearly half of the colleges and universities in the United States over the course of her career. She turned her lectures into one of the most popular education films of all time, *Killing Us Softly: Advertising's Images of Women, Still Killing Us Softly, Killing Us Softly 3*, and *Killing Us Softly 4*. Kilbourne is the author of the book, *So Sexy So Soon: The New Sexualized Childhood and What Parents Can Do to Protect Their Kids* (co-written with Diane E. Levin). She also won the Distinguished Publication Award from the Association for Women in Psychology for her book, *Can't Buy My Love: How Advertising Changes the Way We Think and Feel*. In October 2015, she was inducted into the National Women's Hall of Fame. Kilbourne has been a pioneer in recognizing and calling attention to the detrimental impact that advertisers' images of women have had on both women and our larger society. By continuing to speak out about how advertising and the media influence our lives, Kilbourne educates, empowers, and inspires others to take action.

Source: http://www.jeankilbourne.com

Contributed by Annie B. Fox

attaching labels to fashion ads. ("Warning: this image has been digitally altered to smooth skin tone and slim arms and legs".) Unfortunately, the warnings so far have had inconsistent effects (Slater et al., 2012; Tiggemann et al., 2013), showing that more research is needed. Perhaps the warnings need to specify the links between unrealistic images, body dissatisfaction, and depression. It's important, too, to use psychological research to try other ways to inform women about the deception involved in commercialized images and its effects—an example of how experimental psychology potentially can make a difference in women's lives.

Many feminist activists and everyday citizens have worked to raise awareness of the harm done by sexist and stereotyped words, images, and beliefs, and to provide positive alternatives. Those who wish to get involved in education and activism against sexism in the media can find information through groups such as the ones listed at the end of this chapter. One good example of ongoing activism is educator Jean Kilbourne, who has become a familiar presence on college campuses through her videos documenting sexism in advertising (see Box 3.4). Despite a long history of feminist activism on cultural representations of women, the need for change is as great as ever.

Exploring Further

About Face (www.about-face.org). About Face's mission is "to equip women and girls with tools to understand and resist harmful media messages that affect self-esteem and body image." Its lively Web site has a gallery of winners and another of offenders. And catch its "Covert Dressing Room Action" video on YouTube.

Ellen Cole and Jessica Henderson Daniels (Eds.). (2005). *Featuring females: Feminist analyses of media.* Washington, DC: APA.
Psychologists report their original research analyzing the portrayals of women in reality television shows, films, news programming, magazines, video games, and advertising. This book addresses how aging, race/ethnicity, body image, gender roles, sexual orientation and relationships, and violence are treated in the media. The authors maintain that it is important for consumers to become media literate and critical of stereotypical representations of women and gender.

The Feminist Majority Foundation (http://feminist.org) has created a list of alternative feminist magazines on its Web site (http://feminist.org/research/zines.html). Feminist zines such as Bust (www.bust.com) are smart and funny alternatives to the mainstream media, and there are options for younger girls, too, like New Moon Girls (http://www.newmoon.com/magazine/).

Media Watch (www.mediawatch.com) was founded in 1984 to challenge abusive stereotypes and other biased images commonly found in the media through education and activism. Its videos are available on YouTube and it has a Facebook group.

Text Credits

p. 63: Contributed by Annie B. Fox. **p. 63:** The Bechdel Test from *Dykes to Watch Out* For by Alison Bechdel. Used by permission of Alison Bechdel. The Bechdel Test from *Dykes to Watch Out* For by Alison Bechdel. **p. 73:** Contributed by Annie B. Fox. Fredrickson, Roberts, Noll, Quinn, & Twenge, 1998. **p. 81:** Hall, R. L. (2008). Sweating it out: The good news and the bad news about women and sport. In J. C. Chrisler, C. Golden, & P. D. Rozee (Eds.), Lectures on the psychology of women (4th ed., pp. 97–115). New York: McGraw-Hill. **p. 84:** Ghavami, N. & Peplau, L. Al (2013). An intersectional analysis of gender and ethnic stereotypes testing three hypotheses. Psychology of Women Quarterly, 37, 113–127, from Tables 1-5 (p. 118–120). **p. 85:** Stangor, C. (1995). Content and application inaccuracy in social stereotyping. In Y. Lee, L. J. Jussim, & C. R. McCauley (Eds.), Stereotype accuracy: Toward appreciating group differences (pp. 275–293). Washington, DC: American Psychological Association. **p. 90:** Steinem, G. (1983). Outrageous acts and everyday rebellions. New York: New American Library. **p. 90:** Crawford, M. (2001). Gender and language. In R. K. Unger (Ed.), Handbook of the psychology of women and gender (pp. 228–244). New York: Wiley. **p. 91:** Contributed by Annie B. Fox

CHAPTER 4

The Meanings of Difference

❧

*M*ost people believe that women and men differ in many important ways. As one pop-psych best-seller put it, "Men are from Mars, women are from Venus." On the other hand, I once saw a T-shirt that proclaimed, "Men are from Earth. Women are from Earth. Deal with it!"

Certainly, the images and stereotypes discussed in Chapter 3 present women and men in dramatically different ways. But what are the *real* differences between boys and girls or women and men in traits, abilities, and behaviors? Often, students of psychology want "the facts and just the facts," and they expect the science of psychology to be able to provide those facts. Psychology does have powerful research methods. However, the study of group differences is not just a matter of establishing facts, because differences that show up in psychological research are open to debate about their origins, meaning, and importance.

The Politics of Difference and Similarity

Some differences between groups do not matter very much in Western society. Almost no one divides the social world into people with freckles and those without, or people who can wiggle their ears and those who cannot. Other differences, like the ones in Figure 4.1, matter very much. These differences have social and political consequences; they represent dimensions of privilege versus disadvantage (Morgan, 1996). In feminist theory and political movements, there have long been two ways of thinking about gender-related differences (Kimball, 1995, 2001), grounded in liberal and cultural feminism respectively (see Chapter 1). The *similarities tradition* claims that women and men are very much alike in intelligence, personality, abilities, and goals. This tradition stems from liberal feminism and is used to argue for equality of the sexes. After all, if men and women are far more alike than different, shouldn't they be treated equally?

The *differences tradition* claims that there are fundamental differences between women and men that should be recognized and honored. This tradition, stemming from cultural feminism, is used to argue that society should give more recognition to the activities, traits, and values of women. After all, if taking care of other people and relationships (traditionally viewed as feminine characteristics) were rewarded as much as dominance and personal ambition (traditionally viewed as masculine characteristics), wouldn't the world be a better place?

Both these ways of thinking have been used to generate research and to form political strategies. Debates about which approach is better have gone on for a long time in women's studies. Within psychology, the emphasis on quantitative research has provided new ways to think about difference and similarity. The *similarities hypothesis* (Hyde, 2014) proposes that women and men are more similar than different in most, but not all, psychological dimensions and abilities. Those who stress the overall similarity between women and men point out that sex differences have been, in the past, interpreted as female inferiority and used to justify discrimination. Others view the idea of a so-called feminine nature as a kind of benevolent sexism. However, there may be ways in which the characteristics attributed to

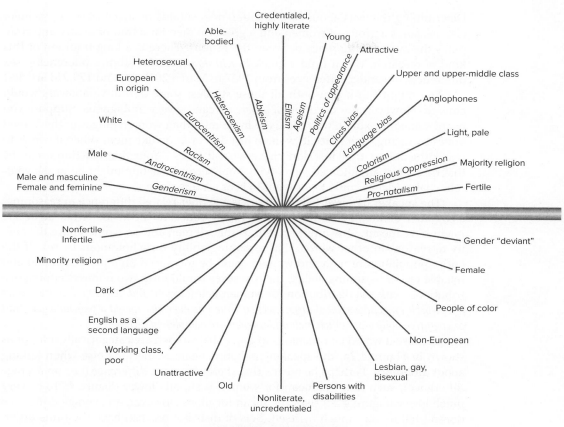

PRIVILEGE

OPPRESSION/RESISTANCE

FIGURE 4.1   Intersecting dimensions of privilege and oppression. An individual may be socially evaluated on any of these dimensions. For each dimension, there is clearly a good and bad end. Some of us are multiply privileged by occupying the favored end of most dimensions; others are multiply oppressed.

Source: Ann Diller, Barbara Houston, Kathryn Pauly Morgan, and Maryann Ayim, *The Gender Question in Education: Theory, Pedagogy, and Politics,* Figure 8.1 (p. 107). Copyright © 1996 by Westview Press, Inc. Reprinted by permission of Westview Press, Inc., a member of the Perseus Books Group.

women *are* undervalued and underappreciated. In this book I explore both traditions, looking at important research from each. The goal is not to decide which tradition is better. Rather, I hope you will decide that there is value in both—that "double visions are theoretically and politically richer and more flexible than visions based on a single tradition" (Kimball, 1995, p. 2).

Because claims about group differences may be politically and socially controversial, there has been a lack of agreement in *defining* difference, problems in *measuring* difference, and issues of *values and interpretation* in understanding results. Let's examine these controversies in more detail.

Defining Difference and Similarity

Determining the facts about gender differences sounds relatively easy: a psychologist measures a group of women and a group of men for a trait or ability and computes the average difference between the groups. There is a long tradition of this kind of research. When I did a quick *PsychInfo* search for studies referencing sex differences or gender differences from 1967 to March 2016, I found 129,218 articles!

You might think that with all these studies, some definitive answers would emerge. However, the meaning of *difference* can be very ambiguous. Suppose you heard someone explain why there are more men than women judges in the United States by saying, "Let's face it, women just don't reason like men. When it comes to reasoning ability, they just don't have what it takes." Your first reaction might be that this is just an outdated stereotype. Your second reaction might be to ask yourself what evidence could be brought to bear on this claim.

The speaker has asserted that there is a gender-related difference in reasoning, a cognitive ability. Before we examine the evidence, let's consider what he or she might have meant. One interpretation is that all men and no women have the ability to reason—in other words, that reasoning ability is dichotomous by sex. If the entire population of men and women could be measured on a perfectly valid and reliable test of reasoning ability, the two sexes would form two nonoverlapping distributions, with the distribution for women being lower. *But despite a hundred years of research on gender-related differences, no one has ever discovered a psychological trait or cognitive ability on which men and women are completely different.*

Because it would be ridiculous to argue that women are categorically inferior as shown in Figure 4.2a, the speaker probably means something else when talking about difference. Perhaps he means that there is a **mean difference** (i.e., an average difference), such that the mean for women is slightly lower (Figure 4.2b) or very much lower (Figure 4.2c) than the mean for men. However, an average difference doesn't tell us very much by itself. Sets of distributions can have the same differences in means but large differences in **variability,** defined as the range or spread of scores. Figure 4.2d shows males more variable than females and 4.2e shows females more variable than males. Looking at the areas in which males' and females' distributions do not overlap in each set shows that the meaning of difference is different for each. That is, the proportion of women who score below the lowest-scoring men and the proportion of men who score above the highest-scoring women differ greatly from one set of hypothetical distributions to the next.

Moreover, these are not the only possible population distributions. Women and men could be equal on average, but one sex could be more variable, as shown in Figure 4.2f; here, the area where females and males overlap is larger than those where they do not.

Most research on gender-related differences reports a mean difference between a sample of women and a sample of men, with statistical tests to determine whether the difference is **statistically significant** (unlikely to have occurred by chance). As noted in Chapter 1, the concept of statistical significance is not the same as the ordinary meaning of "significant." A difference may be statistically significant yet be so small that it is useless in predicting differential behavior in other situations. In other words, statistical significance is not the same as importance.

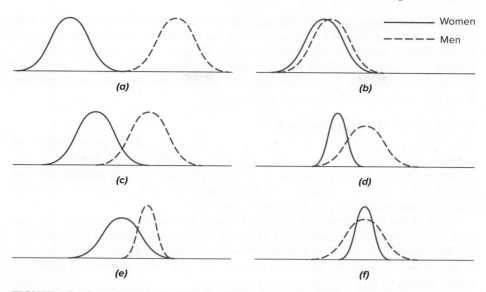

FIGURE 4.2   **Some hypothetical distributions of reasoning ability in females and males.**

How large does a statistically significant difference have to be before we are justified in labeling men and women more different than similar? Should the importance of a sex difference be judged in terms of average scores, in terms of the variability for each group, or in how much the distributions for women and men overlap? And how do we compare the results of several studies of the same trait or ability when the results vary? How many studies are sufficient to settle a question? How consistent must the results be? Is it important to measure the trait or ability in people of different age groups, social classes, ethnic groups, and cultures—or is it safe to assume that what is true for North American college students is true for all people? The answers to these questions involve value judgments about the meaning of difference.

Measuring Differences

Suppose a psychologist wanted to test the claim that there is a gender difference in reasoning ability. She might compare a sample of women and a sample of men on a standard test of reasoning, matching the two groups on any other factors that might affect reasoning ability, such as years of education. She would compare the average scores of her two groups with an appropriate statistical test to determine whether the difference she obtained was likely to have occurred by chance.

The logic of experimental design and hypothesis testing leads psychologists to put more weight on findings of difference than on findings of similarity. Statistical tests allow psychologists to be fairly confident that when a difference is judged to exist, the conclusion is an accurate one. But when a difference is *not* found, psychologists cannot know for certain that there is no difference in the population; the result could be just a failure of this experiment to detect the difference. They may conclude that they should try again, not that the hypothesis about a difference was wrong. Relying on similar logic, as discussed in Chapter 1, professional journals are less likely to publish articles that report similarities between women and men than they are to publish reports of differences. The possibility of overemphasizing differences is a built-in limitation of hypothesis testing.

Sources of Bias in Gender Research

Even when a study is done methodically and ethically (and the great majority of published psychological research is), it may reflect unintended gender bias. As discussed in Chapter 1, bias can occur in deciding what topics are important and how to study them (question formulation and research design), during data analysis, and when interpreting and publishing research results.

One of the most persistent sources of bias in gender-difference research is the difficulty of separating gender from all the other factors it is related to in our society. The interaction of gender with other factors leads to *confounding,* in which the effects of two or more variables are mixed, and it becomes impossible to decide which variable is causing experimental effects.

For example, suppose we were matching participants for our imaginary experiment on reasoning ability. We would certainly not choose to compare a male sample with college degrees to a female sample of high-school graduates, because this would confound gender and educational level. Obviously, the different backgrounds and experience of the two groups could account for differences in reasoning ability. But even when a researcher attempts to measure comparable men and women, it is often hard to decide what characteristics should be matched. Suppose researchers compared female and male college students. Although male and female college students are matched on level of formal education, the women and men may have very different backgrounds in mathematics, science, and the liberal arts and may be concentrated in different majors. These differences may be irrelevant to some research questions but crucial to others.

Meta-Analysis: A Useful Tool

A technique called *meta-analysis* can resolve some of the issues of definition and measurement in research on gender differences. Meta-analysis uses quantitative methods to summarize the results of research done by different people at different times (Hedges & Becker, 1986). It allows researchers to integrate the results of many studies on a topic and to assess the magnitude and consistency of difference effects statistically (Hyde & Linn, 1986).

In doing a meta-analysis, the investigator first identifies all relevant studies on a topic. The next step is to summarize the results of each study in a common unit of measurement. There are different degrees of statistical significance, and the results of some studies may be stronger than others. In meta-analysis, studies can be classified in terms of the magnitude of the gender-related difference. Finally, meta-analysis allows researchers to group studies by subcategory and thereby assess the influence of variables other than gender. For example, if a researcher did a meta-analysis of studies on gender and reasoning ability, she might categorize the studies according to the type of task used or whether there was time pressure in the situation. Perhaps the gender difference only occurs when the task is male-oriented or when there is time pressure. A variable that interacts with another variable to change its effect is called a ***moderator variable.***

Meta-analysis also allows the researcher to estimate the size of a gender-related difference. We noted in Chapter 1 that a difference may be statistically significant but still trivially small. Likewise, in a meta-analysis, the overall difference may be small, medium, or large. When researchers report the size of this difference, called the ***effect size***, it is helpful in interpreting the importance of the gender related difference. For a small effect size, there is about an 85 percent overlap between the distribution for women and men—much more similarity than difference. Even for a very large effect size, there is still about a 45 percent overlap—far from a complete difference between women and men (Hyde, 2014).

You can probably see by now why meta-analysis is so useful. It helps researchers interpret data from large numbers of studies and allows them to estimate the size of a gender-related difference. It simplifies the study of other variables that interact with gender—which is important because there almost always are other factors involved—and helps unravel possible confounding variables. Throughout this book, I report the results of meta-analyses on many gender-difference topics.

But meta-analysis cannot wholly compensate for the biases in the original studies or ensure objective interpretation. Reviewers must still decide which studies are relevant and whether several measures of the same construct (such as different tests of reasoning ability) are measuring the same thing. Moreover, there could be an overlooked source of bias common to all the studies in a meta-analysis, which could lead to an overall conclusion that is biased (Hedges & Becker, 1986). If most of the tests of reasoning ability used in research happened to use problems and examples more familiar to men, for example, a false gender difference might show up in a meta-analysis.

No statistical technique can resolve all problems of interpreting differences. Meta-analysis can show which variables moderate the occurrence of gender differences, but it does not allow conclusions about the *causes* of the differences. Moreover, there is still room for disagreement about how big a difference must be to count as an important one. Recently, researchers used data from over 20,000 individual studies and 12 *million* participants in a meta-synthesis of meta-analyses to evaluate the gender similarities hypothesis (Zell et al., 2015). They found that the average effect size was small to very small, supporting the hypothesis. However, they still maintain that more research is needed and concluded by saying that gender similarities and differences are "an exciting yet challenging task that should occupy researchers for decades to come" (p. 18). The meaning of differences is still at issue, because it is human beings who make meaning out of numbers.

Interpreting Results: Values and Ideology in Research

It is not always easy to see the values and assumptions underlying interpretations of data about gender. Students learn that science is value-free and that scientists are objective, impartial seekers of truth. But values and beliefs related to gender have affected research throughout the history of science (Gould, 1981; Harding, 1986). A brief history of the scientific study of some gender issues will help clarify the connections between values and practice.

Throughout most of Western history, the intellectual and moral inferiority of women was seen as self-evident. The first systematic empirical research on women conducted by scientists of the late nineteenth century took women's inferiority as a given and was aimed at uncovering its biological determinants (Gould, 1980; Hyde & Linn, 1986; Russett, 1989; Shields, 1975). In other words, most scientists at that time were convinced that women were not as intelligent as men and they focused on finding biological differences between women and men to explain what they were sure was true. One way to understand their focus is to think about it in its political context. In an era of agitation over women's rights, members of the dominant social group needed to document the inferiority of other groups in order to defend the status quo. "You are women and hence different," was the message conveyed. "Your differences disqualify you for the worldly roles you seem, most unwisely, to wish to assume" (Russett, 1989, p. 23). Sometimes the scientists' antifeminist bias was expressed directly; one British anthropologist presented an allegedly scientific paper denouncing the "superficial, flat-chested, thin-voiced Amazons, who are pouring forth sickening prate about the tyranny of men and the slavery of women" (cited in Russett, 1989, p. 27).

The Female Brain: Different and Inferior

Historically, sexism, racism, and class bias were often intertwined and the brain often was the battle site (Bleier, 1986; Winston, 2003). First, researchers asserted that the inferiority of women and people of color was due to their smaller brains. One prominent scientist asserted that many women's brains were closer in size to those of gorillas than to the brains of men (cited in Gould, 1981). Similarly, scientists measured cranial size in skulls representing various "races" and concluded that the races could be ranked on a scale of cranial capacity (and hence intelligence) with darker people such as Africans at the bottom, Asians intermediate, and White European men at the top. The brain-size hypothesis foundered when it occurred to scientists that, by this criterion, elephants and hippos should be much more intelligent than people. They then turned to the ratio of brain size to body weight as a measure of intellectual capacity. Little more was heard of this measure when it was discovered that it actually favored women.

Giving up on gross differences such as brain size, scientists turned to examining supposed differences in specific regions of the brain. When it was believed that the frontal lobe was the repository of the highest mental powers, the male frontal lobe was seen as larger and better developed. However, when the parietal lobe came to be seen as more important, a bit of historical revisionism occurred. Women were now seen as having similar frontal lobes but smaller parietal lobes than men (Shields, 1975).

When size differences in brain regions proved impossible to document, the debate shifted to the *variability hypothesis.* It was asserted that men, as a group, are more variable—in other words, although men and women may be similar on average, there are more men at the extremes of human behavior. Variability was viewed as an advantageous characteristic that enabled species to evolve adaptively. The variability hypothesis was used to explain why there were so many more highly intelligent men than women. Only men could achieve the heights of genius.

The Female Mind: Different and Deficient

The history is similar for another type of research, the measurement of human abilities, which began in the nineteenth century with Sir Francis Galton's studies of physical variation and motor skills. Galton measured height, grip strength, and reaction time because he thought they reflected mental ability. When physical abilities failed to correlate with intellectual functioning, the mental testing movement was born. When tests of mental ability failed to demonstrate male intellectual superiority, scientists returned to the variability hypothesis to explain how apparent similarity reflected underlying difference, claiming that men and women might be equal on average, but only men appeared at the upper end of the distribution of mental ability (Hyde & Linn, 1986; Shields, 1982).

Some of the first generation of women who became psychologists worked to dispute these claims. For example, Leta Hollingworth and Helen Montague examined the hospital records of 2,000 newborn infants to test the variability hypothesis. Others examined gender-related differences in emotionality and intelligence (Wooley, 1910). Few differences were found. However, widespread beliefs about innate gender differences in mental abilities persisted. Today, the search for biological differences underlying intellectual functioning continues.

The Lessons of History

The history of attempts to find biologically based sex differences illustrates some important points about the study of gender-related differences. Much of this history shows haphazard testing for a wide variety of differences. Of course, the number of possible differences is infinite, and demonstrating the existence of one or many gives no information about their causes. Perhaps most important, this history illustrates that scientific knowledge is historically and contextually limited. In hindsight, it is easy to see how the racist and sexist prejudices of past eras led researchers to search for justifications of the inferiority of women and people of color. It is less easy to see how personal values affect the work of contemporary scientists, but such influences surely exist. Even today, the traits attributed to women and minorities are less socially desirable than the traits attributed to men. Because White men remain the norm by which others are judged, and because this dominant group is mostly in charge of designing, producing, and interpreting scientific research, science may sometimes be enlisted in support of the social status quo.

How can we begin to make sense of the differences between women and men? One approach is to analyze these differences in terms of the gender system—to consider how they are produced and maintained at the sociocultural, interactional, and individual levels. To make this task easier, I will focus on two areas where differences have been shown to be socially (as well as statistically) significant: mathematics performance and emotionality.

Gendering Cognition: "Girls Can't Do Math"

Women and men are much more similar than different in cognitive ability and skills (Hyde, 2014). However, math ability and achievement is one of a very few areas where past research has shown consistent gender differences. Let's look at these differences in mathematics performance.

There are two widely used ways to measure math ability and achievement: school achievement and performance on standardized tests such as the SAT-M. On standardized tests, boys come out ahead. In school achievement, girls come out ahead. From elementary school through college, girls and young women of all ethnic groups get better grades than boys and young men, even in areas in which the boys score higher in ability tests. Girls are less likely to repeat a grade, get assigned to special education classes, or get in trouble over their behavior or schoolwork, and they are more likely to take honors and AP classes, make the honor roll, and be elected to a class office (Coley, 2001; Hill et al., 2010; Hyde & Kling, 2001). Their higher academic achievement is rarely interpreted to mean that girls are more intelligent. Rather, it is claimed that girls get their higher grades by being quiet and neat, following directions, and trying hard to please their teachers. This may be an example of devaluing the characteristics of a subordinated group. In actuality, girls' higher grades are linked not only to their ability to refrain from disruptive behavior in class but also to their drive for mastery (Kenney-Benson et al., 2006).

Girls' performance on standardized math tests is better than boys' in the elementary school years. In high school they perform as well as boys (Hyde, 2014). A few generations ago, girls lagged behind boys in math performance on these tests, likely because they took fewer math classes in high school. Today, college-bound high school girls are just as likely as college-bound boys to take four years of math (Hill et al., 2010). The historical change in girls' math performance is often cited as an example of what happens when girls are given equal educational opportunity.

There is, however, a well-documented difference favoring males in *advanced* mathematics performance. For the past 40 years, boys have scored consistently higher on the math portion of the SAT than girls. The gender gap has narrowed considerably over time, but it's still a matter for concern. In the 1970s it was about 45 points; in 2015, it was 31 points (College Board, 2015). In national math talent searches using the SAT and similar tests, far more boys than girls are identified as gifted, and the gifted boys score higher than the gifted girls (Hill et al., 2010). The gender gap in math scores occurs within every ethnic group tested (White, Black, Hispanic, Native American, and Asian American), and it also occurs on the GRE test, which is used for admissions to graduate school.

What a puzzle for psychological research to unravel! Girls do better than boys on standardized tests in math and get better grades. Yet, by the time they are in high school, they score lower on advanced math. And they are far less likely than boys *with the same test scores* to major in math or pursue a math-related career (Ben-Zeev et al., 2005; Hill et al., 2010).

What Factors Influence Math Performance?

As you might expect, many factors influence the development of gender differences in math performance. Some researchers emphasize the possibility of biologically based differences in ability. Others emphasize social factors such as gender stereotypes, gender-linked differences in math self-confidence and attitudes, and stereotype threat.

Biological Perspectives

Gender differences, especially in advanced mathematical reasoning, may be in part influenced by gender-linked genetic contributions, hormonal influences, or differences in brain structure (Hill et al., 2010). So far, however, no one has been able to specify exactly what the relevant biological differences are or how they might work to produce performance differences. The existence of a sex-linked gene for math ability was ruled out a long time ago (Sherman & Fennema, 1978). There are some physical differences in female and male brains, but whether these are related to cognitive differences is not yet understood. Some gender-linked differences do not occur cross-culturally (Ben-Zeev et al., 2005), and others have been getting smaller over time (Hill et al., 2010). For example, 30 years ago there were 13 boys for every girl who scored over 700 on the SAT math exam at age 13; today there are just 3 boys for every girl. It's still a big difference, but the fact that it's shrunk so much suggests that environmental influences must be important. In a review of more than 400 articles on why women are underrepresented in math and science, the researchers concluded that the evidence for biological factors was weaker than the evidence for social factors (Ceci et al., 2009). But possible connections between gender-linked biological influences and intellectual performance continue to be explored.

Math as a Male Domain

Close your eyes and visualize a mathematician. Chances are your image is of a cerebral-looking man with glasses and an intense but absent-minded air—an Einstein, perhaps. Early research showed strong stereotypes that math was for men, and nerdy men at that. When elementary and senior high school students were asked about their perceptions of people in math-related careers such as science, engineering, and physics, they described white-coated loners, isolated in laboratories, with no time for family or friends. Not surprisingly, female mathematicians were stereotyped as unattractive, masculine, cold, socially awkward, and overly intellectual (Boswell, 1979; 1985). As we learned in Chapter 3, occupational stereotypes have not changed much since the 1980s (Haines, et al., 2016), and math and science occupations are among those most stereotyped as belonging to men only.

Related to the stereotype of math and science as male domains is the stereotype that boys and men are better at them. At the center of these math stereotypes is the instrumental/affective dimension described in Chapter 3 (Carli et al., 2016). Because gender stereotypes ascribe autonomy and rational thought to men, it is difficult to imagine women enjoying (and being good at) a career that calls for these attributes. Because emotion and connection to others are ascribed to women, a woman who is in a male-stereotyped occupational field such as math or science may be seen as atypical and unfeminine.

In the past, it was thought that the belief that math is for the guys was held largely by girls and women, and that it deterred them from choosing math courses and math-related activities. However, a meta-analysis of math attitudes has shown that males hold this belief much more strongly than females do (Hyde et al., 1990). This finding suggests that gender-related influences on math choices work at the interactional and social structural levels at least as much as at the individual level. In other words, we can no longer conclude that women's underrepresentation in math and science is entirely due to their own choice that math is not for them. Rather, it may be at least partly due to others' beliefs that math is not for women. Such beliefs can create self-fulfilling prophecies (Chapter 2), as others' behavior may put subtle pressure on girls and women to conform to stereotypical expectations.

Learning the Lesson: "I'm Just Not Good at Math."

Even when they take the same courses, boys and girls may experience different worlds in the classroom. Research on classroom interaction confirms that boys and girls are not always treated similarly. At all grade levels, a few males often dominate classroom interaction while other students are silent and ignored (Eccles, 1989). Gender interacts with race: White males get the most attention from teachers, followed by minority males and White females; minority females get the least attention of any group. And this discrimination takes a toll: girls of all ethnic backgrounds, but particularly African American girls, become less active, assertive, and visible in class as they move through the elementary grades (Sadker & Sadker, 1994).

Sexism in the classroom may be benevolent (Hyde & Kling, 2001). Teachers may be trying to protect the feelings of girls by not calling on them for difficult questions or by praising their appearance, not their performance. As we learned in Chapter 2, however, benevolent sexism has its costs. Girls may do their best when they are challenged, not protected, in school. Classroom sexism can also be hostile. For example, girls experience sexual harassment from their peers and teachers more often than boys (American Association of University Women Educational Foundation, 2001).

By the time they are 8 or 9 years old, girls are losing their confidence that they can do math as well as or better than boys, and their change in attitude is independent of their actual performance. When they have trouble with a math problem, they tend to attribute it to their lack of ability, and they are more influenced by what they believe their teacher thinks about them than by their own actual performance (Dickhäuser & Meyer, 2006). Fifth-grade girls report less enjoyment and pride in their math achievement than fifth-grade boys do, and more anxiety, hopelessness, and shame (Frenzel et al., 2007). In middle school, although their grades remain better than boys' grades, girls rate themselves lower in math ability, consider their math courses harder, and are less sure that they will succeed in future math courses. It may start as early as the third grade: In one study of 476 students in second through fifth grade classes in Italy, the second-graders did not differ in their math self-confidence—but by third grade, the boys' self-confidence was higher. By fifth grade, both girls and boys agreed that boys are better at math (Muzzatti & Agnoli, 2007). Meta-analyses have shown that adolescent boys are higher in math self-confidence and girls are higher in math anxiety (Hyde, 2014). The effect sizes in these meta-analyses, while small to moderate, are larger than the effect sizes for actual performance at the same age, and attitudes may be as important as actual performance in predicting future educational and career choices. If Raul thinks that AP math class would be a fun challenge, but Tanya worries that she might not be able to keep up, even though they're both doing fine in tenth grade algebra, their educational paths (and future earning ability) will begin to diverge.

As math self-confidence declines, and the stereotype that boys are better at math is internalized, girls begin to differ from boys in their more general attitudes about math. Compared to boys, they are more likely to say that they don't like math very much and don't consider it very important to their future. They also report that they put in lower levels of effort in math class (Muzzatti & Agnoli, 2007). In other words, they disengage from math, despite performing just as well as boys do, and look elsewhere for sources of self-esteem. Over time, boys' math self-confidence and the value they ascribe to math declines too, but not as much as it does for girls. For adolescent girls, self-esteem is linked more to confidence in their physical attractiveness to boys than it is to confidence in their academic ability (Eccles et al., 2000).

Parents of girls probably play a part in these attitude changes. Parents tend to attribute a daughter's success in math to hard work and effort, and a son's success to talent. They view math as more difficult for daughters and more important for sons. Parents' stereotypical beliefs about gender differences predict children's later beliefs about their math abilities (Tiedemann, 2000). Parents' beliefs may be expressed subtly (just a little more praise for Johnny's math grade than Susan's) or more overtly (only Dad helps with math homework; Mom says it's beyond her) but they may add up to convey the message to boys that they have natural math aptitude. Girls, on the other hand, may learn that hard work cannot entirely make up for their lack of ability.

Stereotype Threat

One important way that beliefs about gender and math ability may affect performance is through stereotype threat. As discussed in Chapter 3, when people know that there is a negative stereotype about their group's abilities, the pressure caused by their fear of confirming the stereotype can interfere with their performance.

Typically, stereotype threat is studied in laboratory experiments. In one such study, college students were given a tough math test after being told that men and women usually do equally well on it. The women and men achieved similar scores. Another group of students took the same test after being told that significant gender differences were expected. In this group, the men outperformed the women. A third group was given the test with no mention of gender similarities or differences (similar to an SAT testing situation). In this group, the men also outperformed the women (Spencer et al., 1999). These results suggest that the gender gap in math performance is at least partly due to stereotype-influenced beliefs and expectations. When women believe that men will do better than they will on a math test (either because they're led to by the experimenter or because they have learned this belief elsewhere), they tend to produce the expected results. However, when the stereotype of female inferiority is explicitly challenged, women perform as well as men.

Hundreds of studies of stereotype threat have been conducted in the past decade, both in the United States and other countries. They have demonstrated effects of stereotype threat on female and ethnic and racial minority students, from elementary school girls through high school, college, and graduate students (Régner et al., 2014). Together, they provide a great deal of information about what activates stereotype threat, the factors that influence it, who may be affected by it, and how it can be prevented or alleviated. A meta-analysis of 151 experiments has shown that the damaging effects of stereotype threat are consistent for both women and minorities (Nguyen & Ryan, 2008). Here, we will focus on stereotype threat related to gender and math performance.

Stereotype threat is likely to be activated whenever the negative stereotype of the group (in this case, that girls aren't good at math) is salient or explicit in the situation. For example, just taking a test in the presence of men may activate stereotype threat for women. In one study, students were tested on difficult math problems in small groups composed of all men, all women, or different male/female combinations. When tested with other women, women got 70 percent of the items correct. When the group was one-third male, their scores dropped to 64 percent. And when women were outnumbered by men, they got only 58 percent correct. Group composition had no effect on the men's performance (Inzlicht & Ben-Zeev, 2000). It seems that being in the minority hinders women's performance by increasing anxiety and stereotype threat. For another example of how stereotype threat directly affects women's math performance, see Box 4.1.

Stereotype threat can be activated just by making gender identity salient. In a classroom study of 7- to 8-year-old French girls and boys, the children were primed to think about gender by being given a picture to color. For boys, the picture was of a boy holding a ball; for girls, it was a girl holding a doll. A control group colored a landscape picture. Following this priming for gender identity, the children worked on math problems from a standardized test. Gender priming disrupted the girls' ability to solve the more difficult problems, but had no effect on the boys' problem solving (Neuville & Croizet, 2007).

Exactly how does stereotype threat disrupt performance? When activated, it arouses stress-related physiological responses; it causes the person to focus too much on how she is doing at the task; and it requires her to try to suppress negative thoughts and emotions (Schmader et al., 2008). All these effects combine to disrupt working memory and interfere with the ability to generate good problem-solving strategies (Quinn & Spencer, 2001).

Stereotype threat may occur quite often for women in male-dominated areas of study. For example, female college students in math, science, and engineering report higher levels of stereotype threat than those in the arts, education, and social science (Steele et al., 2002). Women who pursue math and science careers are in the minority for most of their working lives, and stereotype threat may be an ongoing problem for them. In one intriguing study, female engineers who interacted

Box 4.1 ∾ Research Focus
The Impact of Stereotype Threat on Women's Math Performance

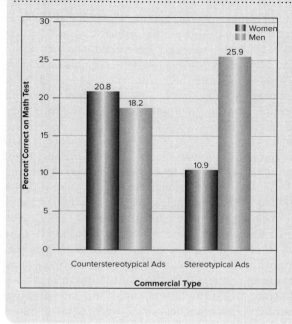

In this study, female and male college students were selected on the basis of having good math attitudes and achievement. The students then saw television commercials. Some of these commercials were gender-stereotypical (a woman bouncing on her bed with joy over a skin product, or drooling with pleasure over a brownie mix); others were counterstereotypical (a woman speaking knowledgeably about health care issues). All students then took a difficult math test. Although none of the ads had anything to do with math, viewing the stereotypical commercials caused the women's subsequent math performance to drop quite noticeably because women became anxious about fulfilling the stereotype. Men's performance was not affected, probably because sexist stereotypes of women were not personally relevant to them.

Source: Adapted from Davies, P. G., Spencer, S. J., Quinn, D. M., & Gerhardstein, R. (2002). Consuming images: How television commercials that elicit stereotype threat can restrain women academically and professionally. *Personality and Social Psychology Bulletin, 28*(12), 1615–1628. doi:10.1177/014616702237644

with men who behaved in sexist ways later performed worse on an engineering test (but not on an English test) than those who interacted with nonsexist men (Logel et al., 2009).

Stereotype threat can affect just about anyone who is a member of a group that is negatively stereotyped. We learned in Chapter 3 that ethnic minorities may be stereotyped as less intelligent than Whites (Ghavami & Peplau, 2013). Low-income people, too, are often stereotyped as less academically capable. What happens when a person belongs to more than one stigmatized group? Research suggests that these individuals experience ***multiple stereotype threat.*** In one study, male and female African American, Latino, and White college students who were low, middle, or high income in background were exposed to stereotype threat conditions. Next, they were given tests of math and working memory (Tine & Gotlieb, 2013). Results showed that stereotype threat based on gender, ethnicity, and income level all affected performance; income level had the strongest effect. These results highlight the intersectionality of multiple identities and how intersectionally identified students are multiply affected by stereotype threat.

Ethnic and gender stereotypes sometimes contradict each other. Asian American women, for example, may be stereotyped as not good at math (because they are female) or good at math (because math ability is stereotypically attributed to Asians). To see how these contradictory stereotypes affected math performance among Asian American women, researchers manipulated the salience of gender or ethnic identity by having one group fill out a questionnaire about gender and another a questionnaire about ethnicity before taking a math test. A control group filled out a general questionnaire that did not reference ethnicity or gender. As predicted, women in the ethnicity-primed group did best on the math test; those in the control group did next best; and those in the gender-primed group did worst (Shih et al., 1999). These studies show another aspect of intersectionality: as shown in the dimensions of privilege and oppression in Figure 4.1, individuals may be simultaneously stigmatized for some aspects of their identity, and privileged for others. Because Asian Americans are stereotyped as good at math, both male and female Asian Americans who are highly identified with their ethnic group may experience a "stereotype boost"—improved performance when the ethnic stereotype is activated (Armenta, 2010).

Stereotype threat can even disrupt the performance of White men. When researchers tested a group of White male students by evoking the stereotype that Asians are better at math than White Americans, their performance on a difficult math test dropped in comparison to a neutral control group—even though these students were all highly competent at math (Aronson et al., 1999).

Research on stereotype threat has shown that several factors influence how likely it is to happen and how severely it impacts performance. For example, women's math performance is more affected by subtle, rather than blatant, priming of stereotypes. A girl or woman is more vulnerable if she identifies with math as a somewhat important domain for her. Task difficulty is important, too—negative effects usually show up only on difficult tasks, not easy ones (Keller, 2007; Nguyen & Ryan, 2008).

Can stereotype threat be prevented? The answer is yes—several strategies have been shown to be effective in preventing its activation. One strategy is simply to teach women about the possibility of stereotype threat—being informed seems to prevent or lessen its effects (Johns et al., 2005). Another strategy is to counter the negative stereotype with a positive stereotype that is relevant to the individual. For example, activating the belief that "college students are good at math" or "students at elite colleges like mine usually don't experience stereotype threat" prevents female college students from being affected by the women-and-math stereotype. Stronger and more direct countermessages work better than subtle ones (McGlone & Aronson, 2007; Nguyen & Ryan, 2008; Rydell et al., 2009). A third strategy is to remind women of other aspects of their identity—in effect, to convey that "you are not only a female, but a writer, a friend, a student," and so on. In one study, students who were asked to draw detailed self-concept maps later performed better on a difficult math test than students asked to draw simple self-concept maps, probably because the task evoked their multiple identities (Gresky et al., 2005). In another study, students who wrote about their most valued personal characteristic were later immune to stereotype threat (Martens et al., 2006).

Providing positive examples is another good strategy for reducing or preventing stereotype threat. When female college students read a newspaper article that highlighted the number of women in science, technology, and math and how much it has increased over recent years before taking a math test, they performed just as well as their male peers on the test (Shaffer, et al., 2013). In another study, sixth-graders read a description of a same-sex role model before a math test. They were told that the role model's math success was due either to working hard or being gifted; in a control condition, no explanation for the success was given (Bagès, et al., 2016). Girls scored as well as boys on the test when they had read about a hard-working role model, but less well than boys in the other two conditions. Exposure to the hard-working role model increased both boys' and girls' self-efficacy in math. Apparently, even a little boost enables girls—and boys, too—to feel and be more effective in math. For girls in particular, anything that makes gender stereotypes less salient in a math testing situation reduces the likelihood that stereotype threat will disrupt their performance.

Social Implications of Gendered Cognition

Girls and boys still grow up in a gendered world (see Chapter 6): dolls and princess attire for girls; microscopes, building sets, and computers for boys. One implication of the gender gap in math performance in the United States is that our society needs to pay more attention to the intellectual development of girls. One way to help young girls develop their cognitive abilities is to provide them with computers and so-called boys' toys. Psychologist Diane Halpern, an expert on cognitive sex differences, has said, "We may be shortchanging the intellectual development of girls by providing them with only traditional sex stereotyped toys" (Halpern, 1992, p. 215). Another strategy is to offer educational environments that optimize chances for girls and young women to do well in math and science. (See Box 4.2.)

A second implication of the math gap is that our society's emphasis on test scores may be misplaced. At least 1.7 million high school students take the SAT each year, and another 1.9 million take the ACT. The purpose of these standardized tests is to predict college grades. But although women score lower on such tests, they get better grades than men in college. In fact, females who score 33 points lower on the math SAT earn the same grades as males in the same college math courses. The tests thus underpredict women's performance (Gender Bias in College Admissions Tests, 2007). This *female underprediction effect* compromises women's right to equal education. Testing activists have charged that a test that underpredicts the performance of more than half the people who take it is so unfair that it should be considered consumer fraud.

The consequences of the underprediction effect are serious. Most four-year colleges and universities use test scores in admissions decisions. Because women's college grades are higher than their test scores predict, some women are rejected in favor of male applicants who will do less well in college. Moreover, women lose out on millions of dollars in financial aid. For example, the majority of National Merit Scholarships go to males (Nankervis, 2013). Girls also lose out on opportunities to participate in special programs for the gifted when SAT and PSAT scores are used to determine eligibility. Finally, an individual's test scores affect her self-confidence and her future academic goals (Hill et al., 2010).

Box 4.2 ⦁ Your Daughter (or Niece or Little Sister) the Rocket Scientist

How to Encourage Girls in Math and Science

Although girls are told from a very young age that they can be whatever they want—a doctor, lawyer, scientist—a recent report from the American Association of University Women found that girls aren't following this advice, particularly when it comes to pursuing careers in fields such as science, technology, engineering, and math. So how do we get (and keep) girls interested in becoming rocket scientists? Here are some of the main suggestions from the AAUW report:

1. Teach her that intelligence grows. Students who have a "growth mindset"—that is, they believe that intelligence can be increased through effort and hard work—are more likely to persevere through academic challenges and succeed in all fields (including math and science) compared to individuals who have a "fixed mindset"—those who believe that their intelligence is innate and unchangeable. Research has shown that there is no gender difference in math and science performance for students with growth mindsets.

2. Talk about stereotype threat. From a young age, children are aware of the stereotype that boys are better at math and science than girls. Unfortunately, research on stereotype threat shows that when people know about a stereotype related to their group, their performance on a task related to the stereotype can be impaired. The negative effects of stereotype threat can be overcome by talking to girls about it.

3. Remind her that Bs and Cs are okay. Girls are often harder on themselves in courses where they think that boys are more innately skilled (namely, math and science). If she doesn't receive an A, she might think she is confirming the stereotype that boys are better than girls in math. Encourage girls to think that tests are fair assessments of their understanding of the material, not their gender. It may also be beneficial to ask your daughter's teachers to set clear standards for assessments.

©Jupiter Images/Brand X/Alamy RF

4. Encourage her spatial skills. One domain where boys consistently outperform girls is in spatial skills, such as the ability to mentally rotate objects. However, it is possible for girls to easily improve their spatial reasoning, and not just through playing with Legos! Activities such as sewing, painting, and video games can all develop and enhance girls' spatial skills, particularly their ability to perform mental rotation.

5. Expose her to women working in science. The low visibility of women in science fields likely contributes to the maintenance of math and science stereotypes for girls. Expose girls to role models and mentors in these fields—even pointing out female television characters who are scientists can be beneficial. Involve her in afterschool programs and camps that emphasize women in science and technology careers—such experiences offer excellent role models.

To read the full AAUW report, go to http://www.aauw.org/learn/research/whysofew.cfm. Then read the full KiwiMagazine blog series from which this list is adapted; go to http://kiwimagonline.com/kiwilog/education/your-daughter-rocket-scientist.

Contributed by Annie B. Fox.

Some colleges and universities, including prestigious ones, have decided to make standardized test scores an optional part of admissions decisions (Simon, 2015). Their decision is based on concerns about excluding talented women and students of color whose scores may underpredict their ability to succeed in college. They recognize, along with some testing specialists, that the tests do not measure areas of human achievement that contribute to success in school and work such as motivation, self-understanding, conscientiousness, and creativity (Teitelbaum, 1989). To date, most of these colleges and universities are finding minimal differences in graduation rates between students admitted with and without test score data (Simon, 2015).

Finally, beliefs about women's alleged inability to do mathematical and scientific thinking foster the continued exclusion of women and ethnic minorities from many careers. Science, math, computer science, and engineering are still among the most male-dominated fields. (See Figure 4.3.) The higher the level, the fewer women there are. The underrepresentation of women in science, math, and technology is a serious problem. These jobs are interesting, prestigious, and will continue to be in high demand over the next decades. Plus, they pay well! Women are losing out on good career opportunities when they forgo these fields. Even more important than individual success is the fact that science, math, and technology are crucial to the future of our country, as we try to solve problems with the environment, resource use, food production, and health care. Ignoring half the population means that we are not getting the full pool of talent needed to meet the challenges of the twenty-first century (Hill et al., 2010).

Researchers in the similarities tradition have tried to demonstrate that, given the same opportunities, women can do math and science as well as men. By questioning the size of cognitive differences and examining how they are socially produced, feminist researchers have made a contribution toward equality. Yet, equality

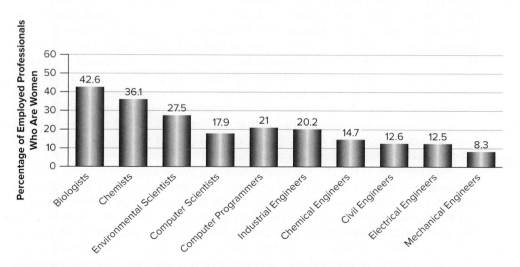

FIGURE 4.3   Women in selected science and technology occupations, 2015.

Source: U.S. Bureau of Labor Statistics, www.bls.gov/cps/cpsaat11.htm.

has not been achieved, although women, particularly White women, have made some very real gains. The belief persists that math and science are male domains; women of color continue to be extremely underrepresented in science; and discrimination against women persists.

Social change requires collective action. One success story started when women scientists at the Massachusetts Institute of Technology (MIT) decided to work together to end gender discrimination at their institution. At MIT's School of Science, there were 197 tenured men and only 15 tenured women. The 15 women, all of whom suspected that discrimination was taking place, demanded an investigation, which showed that they had been given less lab space and lower salaries than their male colleagues and had been excluded from positions of power. In response, MIT raised the women's salaries an average of 20 percent, equalized retirement benefits, and pledged a 40 percent increase in female faculty (Zernike, 1999). The success of the MIT women scientists shows that discrimination can be confronted and successfully challenged through persistence, courage, and collective action.

Gendering Emotion: "Boys Don't Cry"

Who are more emotional—women or men? Chances are the answer that pops into your mind is "Women!" When most of us think of emotion, gendered images come to mind—a woman who cries over the slightest upset, or blushes with embarrassment. Let's look more closely at gender and the experience and expression of emotion.

Emotion Stereotypes

The belief that women are more emotional than men are has been documented for as long as stereotypes have been measured (Broverman et al., 1972; Plant et al., 2000; Shields, 2002). It is widely held not only in the United States, but also in many other countries (Williams & Best, 1990). Not only are women stereotyped as the emotional sex, but particular emotions are attributed to women. Table 4.1 shows the emotion stereotypes of a sample of U.S. college students and working adults. Notice that a far greater number of emotions, both positive and negative, are attributed to women. Only three emotions—anger, contempt, and pride—are thought to be more characteristic of men. Emotion stereotypes are so cognitively ingrained that, in lab experiments, people are actually faster at perceiving angry expressions on men and happy or sad expressions on women than vice versa (Becker et al., 2007; Parmley & Cunningham, 2014).

A closer look at the stereotype of women as the emotional sex reveals that it depends on a peculiar definition of emotion. Emotional displays by men are often not labeled as emotionality. In fact, it is easy to think of examples of men expressing strong emotions: a tennis star throwing a tantrum on the court, a football team hugging each other ecstatically after a touchdown, an angry man yelling at another driver at a stoplight. But when people think of women as the emotional sex, it seems they are thinking of those emotions which women are allowed to express

TABLE 4.1   Emotion Stereotypes for American Males and Females

Male Emotions	Female Emotions	Gender-Neutral Emotions
Anger	Awe	Amusement
Contempt	Disgust	Interest
Pride	Distress	Jealousy
	Embarrassment	
	Fear	
	Guilt	
	Happiness	
	Love	
	Sadness	
	Shame	
	Shyness	
	Surprise	
	Sympathy	

Source: Adapted from Plant, A. E., Hyde, J. S., Keltner, D., & Devine, P. G. (2000). The gender stereotyping of emotions. *Psychology of Women Quarterly, 24,* 81–92.

more than men are, such as sadness, love, surprise, and fear. The stereotype of women as the emotional sex is maintained in part by excluding anger from the everyday definition of emotion (Shields, 2002). A woman who cries when the dog dies may be seen as emotional, but a man who kicks the dog may not be.

Are there gender differences in emotionality that support the stereotype that women are more emotional than men? In studies done in the United States, women and men do show differences in expressing their own emotions and recognizing the emotions expressed by others. In talking and writing, women use more emotion words than men do (Brody & Hall, 2000). When asked about their emotional experiences, women report more intense emotions (both happy and sad) than men do—and the more they believe in emotion stereotypes, the more they report intense emotions for themselves (Grossman & Wood, 1993). They are more aware of their own and others' emotional states than men are (Barrett et al., 2000). Women are also somewhat more skilled at recognizing emotions expressed by others—termed *decoding ability* (Hall et al., 2000), and they tend to score higher on tests of emotional intelligence—a hazy concept that is often used in applied psychology to predict job performance (Joseph & Newman, 2010). But not every study finds these patterns, and some find contrary results. Several meta-analyses of emotional expressiveness have confirmed that overall, the gender difference is trivial, or at most, the effect size in favor of women is small (Hyde, 2014).

Despite the stereotype of the overemotional woman, there is more similarity than difference between the emotionality of women and men. To understand the similarities and differences, and perhaps why the exaggerated beliefs about difference persist, let's look at how emotionality and its meaning are socially constructed at the sociocultural, interpersonal, and individual levels.

Culture, Ethnicity, and Emotionality

Expressing Emotion

Ever since Darwin (1872), scientists have studied how emotions are expressed. Cross-cultural studies can help us understand similarities and differences in emotional expression. Early studies showed that people from different cultures could usually identify the emotions depicted in a set of posed photographs, leading psychologists to theorize that emotional expression is a biological universal with an evolutionary basis. However, a meta-analysis showed that people are somewhat better at recognizing emotions when they are expressed by a member of their own culture than when they are expressed by a member of a different cultural group (Elfenbein & Ambady, 2003).

Although the expression of emotions may be a biological universal, different cultures teach different techniques for channeling emotional expression. Every culture has *display rules* that govern which emotions may be expressed, under what circumstances, and how (Safdar et al., 2009). For example, in some cultures people are expected to shriek, wail, and cry loudly at funerals. If there are not enough family members to provide a suitably loud chorus, professional mourners may be hired to do the job. In other cultures, people are expected to show respect for the dead by quiet, emotionally subdued expressions of grief.

A society's display rules often incorporate gender stereotypes. In the United States, where women are expected to smile more than men are, more women than men undergo medical procedures such as collagen injections in the lips and teeth bleaching to increase the display value of their smiles. In Japan, however, a wide, teeth-baring smile is considered impolite for a woman, and a woman may hide her smile behind her hand (see Figure 4.4). In a cross-cultural study comparing display rules in Japan, Canada, and the United States, Japanese were less emotionally expressive overall than the other groups. However, gender-related display rules were similar in all three cultures: men expressed powerful emotions more than women, whereas women expressed the emotions of powerlessness (fear, sadness) as well as the positive emotion of happiness, more than men did (Safdar et al., 2009).

Do emotion display rules vary for different ethnic groups within our own society? One way to find out is to ask people of different ethnicities about how men and women are expected to experience various emotions. When members of four American ethnic groups (African Americans, Asian Americans, European Americans, and Hispanics) were asked this question, many differences emerged (Durik et al., 2006). Recall that among White European American participants, anger and pride are stereotyped as more suitable for men. Among African Americans, both these emotions were stereotyped as equally suitable for women and men. When asked about the positive emotion of love, European Americans and African Americans were similar to each other: both thought that women express love much more than men do. Asian Americans, however, differentiated less between women and men,

FIGURE 4.4   Cross-cultural differences in smiling.
(left):©Purestock/Superstock RF; (right): ©Glow Images/SuperStock RF

and overall reported less expression of love. Among all ethnic groups, respondents expected women to express more guilt and embarrassment than they expected from men. These patterns of differences and similarities across ethnic groups show that the rules for expressing emotions are learned within specific cultural contexts.

Experiencing Emotion

Cultural differences affect the experience of emotion, not just its display. For example, college students in Japan reported feeling generally happier when they were experiencing emotions tied to interconnections, such as friendly feelings toward another. American college students, on the other hand, were happier when experiencing emotions tied to separateness, such as pride in an achievement (Kitayama et al., 2000).

These findings have been linked to broader differences between two types of cultures: some cultures encourage the development of an ***independent self*** whereas others foster an ***interdependent self*** (Markus & Kitayama, 1991). The United States and Western Europe hold up the independent ideal: each individual is seen as unique, and the task of each individual is to fulfill his or her potential and become an autonomous person. Much of the rest of the world has a very different ideal: individuals are seen as connected in a web of relationships, and their task is to maintain those connections by fitting in, staying in their proper place, and building reciprocal relationships with others. Cultural differences in the sense of self are illustrated in contrasting proverbs from the United States and Japan:

The squeaky wheel gets the grease. (United States)

The nail that sticks up gets hammered down. (Japan)

Most of the research on gender and emotions has been conducted in Western countries that place a premium on independence. Interestingly, gender differences in feeling as well as in expressing emotion are much smaller in collectivist countries than individualistic ones. In collectivist cultures, both women and men are allowed to feel and express emotion. This was made clear to me when I watched a Bollywood movie, *Three Idiots*. The movie's main characters were three male students at an engineering college. At every improbable and melodramatic plot twist, they wept copious tears and hugged each other. They were smart, normal, fun-loving college students—and every bit as emotional as the main female character in the movie, who was a beautiful motorcycle-riding doctor.

Emotionality and Social Interaction

Learning the Emotion Rules

Children learn their culture's rules for displaying emotion at an early age. One important influence is "emotion talk" from parents. Many studies have shown that parents are more likely to talk about people and emotions with their daughters than with their sons (Aznar & Tenenbaum, 2015). Moreover, they talk to daughters and sons about different emotions. In one study of children between the ages of 2 1/2 and 3, 21 percent of mothers discussed anger with a son during a half-hour conversation, whereas not a single mother discussed anger with a daughter. Mothers also used more positive emotion words (e.g., happy) with girls (Fivush, 1989). Other studies show that both mothers and fathers are much more likely to discuss fear and sadness with a daughter than with a son (Fivush et al., 2000; Fivush & Buckner, 2000). And when parents were asked to discuss pictures of gender-neutral children displaying basic emotions (anger, fear, sadness, and happiness) with their toddlers, the parents labeled the angry pictures more often as boys and the sad and happy pictures more often as girls, conveying stereotypical gender messages (van der Pol et al., 2015). This differential attention to girls' and boys' emotions soon has its effects: By the time they are 3- to 4-years-old, girls are more likely than boys to bring emotion talk into a conversation—especially talk about sad experiences (Fivush & Buckner, 2000).

As children begin to think about emotion in gendered ways, the social environment shapes different consequences for girls and boys. In a study of preschoolers, girls who expressed anger (but not those who expressed sadness or distress) were likely to be rejected by their peers, while boys who expressed anger tended to be popular with their peers (Walter & LaFreniere, 2000). And girls learn early to hide their negative feelings, because their emotional expressions are supposed to be "nice." For example, think about how you would act if someone gave you a gift you didn't like. Most adults have learned the social norm that, in this situation, you should pretend to be happy. When researchers presented first- and third-grade children with disappointing gifts, the girls showed more positive and less negative emotion than the boys, indicating that they had already internalized this rule and were better than the boys at masking their true feelings (Davis, 1995).

Children learn not only the display rules but also *feeling rules* (Shields, 2002). That is, they learn what it means to experience an emotion, what others expect them to feel, and how they are supposed to recognize emotions in others. All these lessons are deeply gendered. "Emotion education includes not only 'because you are a boy, feel/show X,'" but also "feel/show X in order to become a boy" (Shields, 2002, p. 91). For example, a study of White suburban teenage boys showed that they valued teasing and bullying because their identity was connected to suppressing emotional reactions. Hostile interactions with others gave them practice in "sucking it up" and "taking it like a man" (Oransky & Marecek, 2002). For both boys and girls, doing emotions appropriately becomes an important part of doing gender, of performing one's identity as a boy or girl.

Through a Gender Lens

Beliefs about the different emotionality of males and females may influence perceptions of others' emotions. Classic studies have shown that observers who are asked to judge the emotions of babies and young children from video clips rely on gender as a cue. When told that the neutrally dressed child they are viewing is a boy, they perceive more anger than when told they are viewing a girl (Shields, 2002).

The influence of gender on perceptions of emotions occurs for adults, too. In one study, participants viewed photos of women's and men's faces displaying specific emotions (Plant et al., 2000). Some photos clearly portrayed anger, others clearly portrayed sadness, and still others showed a more ambiguous blend of anger and sadness. When people looked at the slides, what they saw depended on whether a woman or a man was displaying the emotion. Even though the actors in the photos had identical expressions, participants saw men's blended expressions as angrier than women's, and women's blended expressions as sadder than men's. Moreover, participants used the same gender lens even when the expressions quite clearly represented a single emotion. They rated women's anger as less angry than men's anger, and saw sadness where there was none in women's angry expressions. In another study, participants saw photos from a standardized set that portrayed clear, intense emotions. Again, participants perceived the angry male as showing more anger than the angry female; the angry female, but not the male, was seen as fearful (Algoe et al., 2000).

These studies show that gender stereotypes of emotion are powerful enough to lead people to misperceive others' feelings, even when they are quite clearly expressed. They also imply that, for women, anger is truly the forbidden emotion. An angry woman is so disturbing and unacceptable that people refuse to see anger in a woman's clearly angry expression, and instead choose to see sadness or fear. Furthermore, this research shows that people make gender-biased judgments about the reasons for emotional behavior in order to hold on to their stereotypes.

Gendering Emotion: A Summary

The social construction of females as the emotional sex occurs in many ways. Cultures differ in their rules for displaying and feeling emotion, but most societies have rules that are gender-linked. Emotionality is one of the core characteristics of feminine stereotypes cross-culturally. In our own society, this stereotype is maintained in part by defining emotionality more in terms of the emotions attributed to women than the emotions attributed to men. Stereotypes influence perceptions, so that identical behavior by a woman or a man may be seen as expressing different emotions. Moreover, stereotypes open the way for self-fulfilling prophecies. People expect women to be more emotional; therefore they may treat them in ways that encourage emotion displays.

Social Implications of Gendered Emotionality

Gender differences in emotionality are not socially neutral. Instead, they are linked to power and status, and they affect the roles, occupations, and opportunities considered appropriate for women and men.

Emotion, Status, and Power

Expressing emotion is linked to status and power as well as to gender (Smith et al., 2015). Emotionality may be taken as a sign of weakness if the emotions expressed are sadness, grief, or fear. However, other emotions are reserved for the powerful. People recognize this social fact, and expect different emotions from high- and low-status people in the same situations. For example, when college students read scenarios about employees receiving positive performance evaluations, they believed that a low-status employee should feel more appreciation, whereas a high-status employee should feel more pride. When the scenario described a negative evaluation, participants expected that the low-status employee should feel sad or guilty, whereas the high-status employee should feel angry (Tiedens et al., 2000). Notice that the emotions expected of high-status people—anger and pride—are identical to the ones expected of White men (Plant et al., 2000). The right to get angry and show it is one kind of social power.

Another link between emotionality, status, and power is related to the roles and occupations considered to fit women and men. A person who shows fear and sadness is unlikely to be thought of as a potential leader in government, business, or the military. A person who shows anger, contempt, and pride is unlikely to be thought of as a potential full-time parent, teacher, or nurse.

In all the studies I have described, there is much more overlap than difference in women's and men's emotionality—just as there is in other gender-linked differences. Unfortunately, emotionality remains a core part of feminine stereotypes. As other gender categories (like intelligence and math ability) are challenged and changed, emotion may become more and more important in differentiating men from women. "In an era where neither 'masculine' work nor 'masculine' clothing unambiguously define gender as difference, emotion is one of the few remaining contested areas . . . in which drawing a line between masculine/manly and feminine still works" (Shields, 2002, p. 136).

There is no reason to think that a person cannot be emotionally expressive and also rational, yet the traits seem polarized in the minds of perceivers, with rational man and emotional woman on opposite sides of the divide. Historically, women's presumed emotionality was used to justify their exclusion from education and career opportunities. Earlier in this chapter, I described how nineteenth century scientists considered women's reasoning ability to be lesser than men's. They also considered women's emotions to be more delicate, sensitive, and unstable. Therefore, they reasoned, women had better be confined to the home, where their out-of-control emotions could be contained. If women were allowed to take part in public life, their weaker reasoning capacities might be "swamped by the power of emotion" (Shields, 2002, p. 72). Some of the founders of American psychology shared this view. As late as 1936, Lewis Terman claimed that, compared to men, women were more tender, sympathetic, and loving, but also more timid, fearful, jealous, and suspicious. Luckily, women's submissiveness, docility, and lack of adventurousness tended to keep them out of trouble, according to Terman (cited in Shields, 2002).

Echoes of this age-old prejudice still pop up from time to time. In the 1990s, women attempted to gain admission to two all-male colleges, the Virginia Military Institute and South Carolina's Citadel. These universities serve as openings to the social networks that control political and economic power in the South. Both offer military-type education. Although they were funded by taxpayer money, they continued to deny admission to women long after female cadets had been integrated into the U.S. Military Academies. When their discriminatory admissions policies were challenged, VMI and the Citadel claimed that women were unsuited for the military life because of their feminine natures. In testimony to the U.S. Supreme Court, attorneys for VMI claimed psychological research had proved that

> Women are physically weaker; that they are more emotional and cannot take stress as well as men; that they are less motivated by aggressiveness and suffer from fear of failure; and that more than a hundred physiological differences contribute to a "natural hierarchy" in which women cannot compete with men (United States of America v. Commonwealth of Virginia, 1994, p. 4).

In response, a large group of feminist psychologists (a group I was part of) testified in a friend of the court brief that the VMI witnesses had misrepresented and misused the psychological research on gender differences. In ruling against VMI's discriminatory policy, the Court stated that generalizations about women's natures, even if they may apply to some women, do not justify denying equal opportunity to all.

Emotions and Relationship Conflict

Because women are perceived to be the experts at emotion, they may be expected to be in charge of others' feelings as well as their own (see Figure 4.5). Stereotypes about the emotionally inexpressive male suggest that men need to be coaxed into recognizing and expressing their feelings, and that it is women's job to do so. This also implies that women are responsible for keeping a relationship smooth and free of conflict. Because of these expectations, romantic relationships can become destructive traps for women who put their commitment to the partner and the relationship ahead of their own needs (White et al., 2001). Married women may be expected to take on the role of emotion manager not only for their spouses but also for their children, and to mediate among spouse, children, and other family members. Being responsible for everyone else's feelings can be a full-time job and a major source of stress. (Women's relational work is discussed more fully in Chapter 10.)

FIGURE 4.5   When men are emotionally inexpressive, others are left to guess their feelings.

Source: Tom Cheney/The New Yorker Collection/www.cartoonbank.com

Men in our culture are likely to learn that expressing anger is an acceptable and effective means of controlling others. Societal acceptance of men's anger and aggression puts heterosexual women at risk of violence from their relationship partners. Men who are violent in dating and marital relationships often hold the belief that violence between intimates is acceptable (White et al., 2001). (For more on relationship violence, see Chapter 12.) At the same time, emotional inexpressiveness when it comes to positive feelings may serve to preserve status and power differentials that benefit men. Refusing to recognize the feelings of a partner or a child may be a means of control and a privilege of the more powerful. And as long as women are primarily responsible for maintaining emotional connection, their opportunities in work, achievement, and public life will be curtailed, and they will continue to be at risk for destructive and violent relationships.

Curtailing emotional expressiveness has costs for men, too. Men who score high on measures of stoicism and masculinity tend to show little emotional involvement with others, dislike the expression of feelings, and have little tolerance for emotion. These men report a lower quality of life overall than less emotionally restricted men and women do. A particular concern is that they are unlikely to seek psychological help when they have adjustment problems, which has implications for their long-term mental health (Murray et al., 2008). Such men also minimize their symptoms when they're ill, put off going to the doctor, and have poorer health outcomes than women and less emotionally restricted men (Himmelstein & Sanchez, 2014).

Making a Difference

Claims about sex differences have often been used to justify keeping women in their place. Even today, hypotheses about female inferiority and claims of new gender-linked psychological differences keep turning up. Gender differences are the socially constructed product of a system that creates categories of difference and dominance. Because gender is a system of social classification that operates at the sociocultural, interactional, and individual levels, changing the social consequences of gender difference can take place at all those levels.

The Individual Level: Thinking Critically about Differences and Similarities

In this chapter, I've focused on two areas of gender-linked difference. In the case of mathematics performance, we've seen that there's an overall pattern of similarity except for performance on the standardized tests that are used for admission to college and graduate school. Girls' lower performance on these tests underpredicts their actual performance in college. The size of the gender gap in mathematics performance has decreased over time. In the case of emotional expressiveness, the difference favoring women is small, and cross-cultural differences are large. Other areas of gender difference in personality and behavior will be discussed later in this book. However, it is important to remember that there are many more areas of thinking, reasoning, personality, and behavior that consistently show *no* gender-linked differences. Thus, one important part of thinking critically about gender and difference is to recognize that differences occur against a background of overall similarity, and there are far more areas of similarity than areas of difference (Hyde, 2014).

Moreover, there is much more variability *within* each sex than *between* the sexes on cognitive skills, abilities, and personality traits. Therefore, it is impossible to predict much about a person's behavior by gender alone, even in an area where overall gender-linked differences exist. For example, recall the VMI admissions decision. It may be true that, on average, more men than women are interested in military-style education and prepared to undergo it. However, it is much harder to predict the performance of an individual woman or man. Will Taisha do better than Howard at VMI? That depends not only on their gender, but their fitness, intelligence, and determination. Just knowing Howard or Taisha's gender does not tell us much, because average group differences are not very good predictors of individual behavior.

At the individual level, each of us can try to think about gender-linked differences in all their complexity, resisting the urge to treat women and men as opposites. Even though it is tempting to think that "men are from Mars, women are from Venus," women and men are much more similar than different. Thinking critically and responsibly about alleged gender differences can help foster social change on behalf of equality.

The Interactional Level: Difference and Discrimination

We have seen that gender-linked differences are important to the social definition of masculinity and femininity. Therefore, even when women and men behave in similar ways, they may be seen as different. For example, recall the women scientists at MIT who were treated as though they were not as capable or valuable as their male colleagues, although their scientific work was similar. Emotional displays, too, may be judged differently depending on whether the emotion is coming from a woman or a man. Gender-biased perceptions of behavior create ample opportunities for self-fulfilling prophecies. Being aware of this possibility, and guarding against it, helps ensure gender fairness in evaluations of others.

Even if a gender-linked difference can be reliably demonstrated, it does not justify group discrimination. Suppose you are a parent who is told that your daughter should probably not apply for an AP math class because in the past, girls in this class have had a higher failure rate than boys. You probably would insist that your daughter be evaluated as an individual, not as a gender category. If her grades, motivation, and skills qualify her for AP math, her gender is unimportant. One solution to gender discrimination, then, is to assess people as individuals. However, this is sometimes impossible. If 2,000 people are applying to an elite college that can take only 300, admissions officers feel they must rely on test scores. For this reason, it is very important to ensure that the measures are fair.

Activist organizations are keeping watch on the testing industry. For example, after the group FairTest filed a complaint with the Office of Civil Rights over gender bias in the National Merit Scholarship competition, the test was changed, and the proportion of semifinalists who were female increased significantly.

The Sociocultural Level: Creating Opportunities for Equality

Educators have created many programs to equalize opportunities for girls and young women in science, technology, engineering, and mathematics (STEM). These programs allow girls to explore unfamiliar subjects and discover new areas of interest, or for those already interested, to build their skills and knowledge (Propsner, 2015). Women's colleges have led the way in developing girls-only STEM camps held during the summer. With their tradition of preparing women for leadership roles, and the benefit of already having women in most of or all of their leadership positions, they provide good role models for aspiring young scientists. In the summer camps, girls ranging from seventh grade through high school get to work in the college's science labs and interact with faculty members from the science and math departments. Being in an all-girl setting greatly reduces stereotype threat and enlarges girls' visions of who can be a scientist. Thus, psychologists and educators have created programs to equalize opportunity for girls and women in math and science.

One example is "Calculating the Possibilities," a summer program for high school juniors and seniors funded by the National Science Foundation (Pierce &

Kite, 1999). Girls were selected for this program on the basis of grades, interest in science, and previous course work. For four weeks, the girls lived on a college campus. During this time, they visited corporations where they interacted with female scientists in pharmaceutics, engineering, medicine, and other areas. They met with career counselors who helped them explore their interests and goals. Moreover, each girl worked with a mentor on research projects in chemistry, biology, and other fields. Other activities included guest speakers and e-mail mentoring from women scientists. Asked what they liked about the program, the young women were very positive:

> Everything! This was the best learning experience! I learned about researching science and that it is fun and interesting. I learned women have a place in this world and a right to work for it.
> The visits have shown me that women still have a long way to go to be equal. I liked working with the mentors. Their experiences and stories have been very helpful in ways that are impossible to describe. It shows scientists can be real people. (Pierce & Kite, 1999, p. 190)

Not everyone can go to science camp. But sometimes even very simple efforts can help. In one recent study, middle school girls saw a 20-minute video about the lives of female engineers and the benefits of engineering careers. The video emphasized how engineers can help people and society, and encouraged students to think of themselves as capable of being an engineer. The result? An increase in the girls' interest in engineering careers (Plant et al., 2009). A society that cares about equal opportunity needs to make programs like these more available to girls.

The similarities tradition, grounded in liberal feminism, has provided the impetus for special programs in math and science for girls. It is hard to imagine the federal government sponsoring programs to equalize emotional expressiveness, relational orientation, and empathy. According to the differences tradition, these are so-called feminine characteristics that are less valued by society. Researchers in the differences tradition argue that women and their characteristic activities should be reappraised (Jordan et al., 1991). Women have been assigned the tasks of fostering others' development and taking care of others, tasks that require empathy and communality. Yet neither they nor society as a whole have been encouraged to value these interactions and activities, which may be underpaid on the job (see Chapter 10) and taken for granted at home (see Chapter 9).

Psychology and its theories have failed women by devaluing their strengths, according to researchers in the differences tradition. Many psychological theories of human development focus on *autonomy* as the end point. That is, the ideal adult is seen as one whose sense of self is entirely separate from others, and who is independent and self-reliant. If you are thinking that this sounds like the overall stereotype of men, you are right. But very few people are truly autonomous, and when individuals appear to be so, it is usually because many other people are quietly helping them. The idea that psychological development is a process of separating from others may be an illusion fostered by dominant men. Perhaps instead of the John Wayne/Clint Eastwood ideal of the autonomous man, theories of human development should stress human connection and caring. From this perspective, the criteria for human development should include the ability to engage in relation-ships that empower others and oneself; empathy, not autonomy, becomes the ideal (Jordan et al., 1991).

Can Similarities and Differences Be Reconciled?

Researchers in both the similarities and the differences traditions have recognized that sociocultural aspects of gender govern access to resources; for example, social forces work to keep women out of careers in math and science, and to overvalue the attributes of dominant groups in society. Both traditions also recognize that gender can become internalized—as when women come to think of themselves as bad at math and good at understanding others' feelings. The similarities tradition encour-ages a focus on equity for girls and women in family, work, and educational set-tings. The differences tradition suggests that women's characteristics, such as greater emotional connectedness with others, are strengths, not weaknesses.

Individual feminists may feel an affinity for either the differences or the similari-ties tradition (Hare-Mustin & Marecek, 1990). And a particular kind of research may be useful for a specific political goal. However, both traditions have an important place in feminist theory. Whether we are making comparisons by gender, culture, or some other category, similarities *and* differences can be shown, and they both have strengths and limitations (Kimball, 2001). Becoming familiar with both traditions can help address a very important question: How is the gender system made invisible so that socially produced gender seems inevitable, natural, and freely chosen?

Exploring Further
∾

AAUW (www.aauw.org).
> The American Association of University Women is a nationwide network of more than 100,000 members that advances equity for women and girls through advocacy, educa-tion, and philanthropy. One of its most important contributions is to sponsor and report research on women in math, science, and technology. Its website features many new initiatives in this area.

FairTest (www.fairtest.org)
> An activist organization that works to curtail the misuse of standardized testing and foster testing that is fair to women, ethnic minorities, and economically disadvantaged people.

Fischer, Agneta, and Evers, Catharine (2013). The social basis of emotion in men and women. In M. K. Ryan & N. R. Branscombe (Eds.), *The Sage Handbook of Gender and Psychology* (pp. 183–198). London: Sage.
> It's too simple just to say that women and men differ in emotional expression and regu-lation. The "how" and the "why" offer interesting questions to explore. This chapter looks at cultural stereotypes and norms as well as more individual motives and expecta-tions and the differing roles that women and men are likely to find themselves in. It provides an excellent overview of current research on gender and emotion.

Text Credits

〜

p. 93: Kimball, M. M. (1995). Feminist visions of gender similarities and differences. New York: Harrington Park Press. **p. 95:** Ann Diller, Barbara Houston, Kathryn Pauly Morgan, and Maryann Ayim, The Gender Question in Education: Theory, Pedagogy, and Politics, Figure 8.1 (p. 107). Copyright © 1996 by Westview Press, Inc. Reprinted by permission of Westview Press, Inc., a member of the Perseus Books Group. **p. 100:** Russett, C. E. (1989). Sexual science: The Victorian construction of womanhood. Cambridge, MA: Harvard University Press. **p. 107:** Adapted from Davies, P. G., Spencer, S. J., Quinn, D. M., & Gerhardstein, R. (2002). Consuming images: How television commercials that elicit stereotype threat can restrain women academically and professionally. *Personality and Social Psychology Bulletin*, 28(12), 1615-1628. doi:10.1177/014616702237644 **p. 109:** Halpern, D. F. (1992). Sex differences in cognitive abilities (2nd ed.). Hillsdale, NJ: Erlbaum. **p. 110:** Contributed by Annie B. Fox. p. 111: U.S. Bureau of Labor Statistics, www.bls.gov/cps/cpsaat11.htm. **p. 113:** Adapted from Plant, A. E., Hyde, J. S., Keltner, D., & Devine, P. G. (2000). The gender stereotyping of emotions. *Psychology of Women Quarterly*, 24, 81–92. **pp. 116, 118, 119:** Shields, S. A., (2002). Speaking from the heart: Gender and the social meaning of emotion. Cambridge, MA: Cambridge University Press. **p. 119:** United States of America v. Commonwealth of Virginia, 1994, p. 4. **p. 120:** Tom Cheney/The New Yorker Collection/www.cartoonbank.com **p. 123:** Pierce, R. L., & Kite, M. E. (1999). Creating expectations in adolescent girls. In S. N. Davis, M. Crawford, & J. Sebrechts (Eds.), Coming into her own: Educational success in girls and women (pp. 175–192). San Francisco: Jossey-Bass.

PART 3

❧

Gender and Development

CHAPTER 5

Sex, Gender, and Bodies

❧

"$\mathcal{U}$t's a girl!" or "It's a boy!" At birth, a child's sex is announced to the world. It is the first label attached to this new person, and it will have profound importance throughout the child's life. Why? What does it mean to be male or female?

In the past, three assumptions about sex were so fundamental in our society that most people never thought about them (Kessler & McKenna, 1978). The key assumptions are these:

- There are two, and only two, sexes.
- Sex exists as a biological fact independently of anyone's beliefs about it.
- Sex and gender naturally go together.

According to the first two assumptions, bodies always fall into two clear, natural categories, based on biological facts. The third assumption is that gender follows naturally from sex. In other words, once a child's sex is recognized, either at birth or by imaging during pregnancy, the process of becoming gendered will follow a normal and natural course. A female baby should come to know that she is a girl, accept her female sex as a core part of her identity, act like a girl, and grow into a heterosexual woman. Likewise, a male baby should grow up unambiguously masculine in his identity, interests, roles, and sexuality. These assumptions are the basis of the gender system (Chapter 2), which prescribes different roles for the two sexes and awards more power and status to men.

Are these assumptions valid? Biological sex and its relationship to psychological gender turn out to be surprisingly complex and unpredictable—not at all a neat binary system in which sex and gender are always congruent. This chapter explores sex and its complex relationships with gender and sexual orientation, beginning with the question of how sex develops.

How Does Sex Develop?

Sex is usually defined as two reproductive forms within a species. The female and the male of the species have specialized structures, organs, and hormones that result in different roles in reproduction. Thus, sex involves much more than just being born with a penis and scrotum or a clitoris and vagina. No one characteristic defines sex. Sex involves a cluster of biological attributes—including genetic, hormonal, and anatomical components—that develop gradually before birth. Let's look at how sex is formed during prenatal development—a process called *sexual differentiation.*

Sexual Differentiation during Fetal Development

Each human being has a set of 46 chromosomes in each cell of the body. Each of us inherits these 23 chromosome pairs, one of each pair from the mother and the other from the father. Of these, 22 pairs are *autosomes,* and one pair is composed of the *sex chromosomes,* called the X and Y chromosomes. The X chromosome is similar in size to the autosomes, but the Y chromosome is much smaller; it contains fewer than 50 genes, compared with 1,000 to 2,000 on the X chromosome (Wizemann & Pardue, 2001).

Genetically, a female is defined as a person who has two X chromosomes, and a male is defined as one who has an X and a Y chromosome. The newly conceived embryo inherits one X chromosome from the mother and either an X chromosome or a Y chromosome from the father. Therefore, genetic sex is determined at the moment of conception.

During the first month or so after conception, there is no visible indication of the fetus's sex. The fetus has no internal or external sex organs, only embryonic structures from which these will later develop. For example, the fetus has a structure that will become *either* a clitoris or a penis, depending on whether it follows a male or female developmental pathway (Fausto-Sterling, 2000). However, the fetus does not remain in this unisex state for long. Genes on the sex chromosomes, particularly on the Y chromosome, soon initiate sexual differentiation.

I'll first describe sexual differentiation in males, because it is better understood than in females. Starting at about the sixth week of pregnancy, a gene called the *sex-differentiation region of the Y chromosome* (SRY) causes the embryonic sex glands, or *gonads,* to grow and develop into *testes,* the pair of male sex glands that much later (starting at puberty) will produce sperm (Sinclair et al., 1990). Of course, only genetically male fetuses develop testes, because only they have a Y chromosome.

Once the testes are formed, they produce several steroid hormones collectively known as *androgens*. In turn, these androgens shape the development of a typical male body. The androgen *testosterone* causes the internal structures of male sexual anatomy to develop, such as the tubes that will later transport sperm from the testes. *Dihydrotestosterone* causes the penis to grow and the testicles to form. *Mullerian duct inhibiting hormone* (MIH) prevents the internal embryonic structures from developing into female organs such as a uterus.

When all these hormones are activated at the right times and in the right sequence during prenatal development, the fetus develops male sexual and reproductive anatomy. By the twelfth to fourteenth week of the mother's pregnancy, the process is complete. The fetus is male—genetically, hormonally, and anatomically.

How does sex develop in female fetuses? Much less is known about this process, probably because in the past many reproductive biologists were more concerned with male development and considered females to be the default pathway. In other words, when there is no Y chromosome to stimulate androgen production, the fetus develops as a female. This approach represents females as the product of an absence or lack—as the sex that just happens when there is no Y chromosome. Because of this androcentric view, there has been little research on the processes underlying female development until quite recently (Vilain, 2006).

In the female fetus, the gonads develop into *ovaries,* the pair of female sex glands that contain eggs. At puberty, the ovaries produce steroid hormones called *estrogens*. However, estrogens do not function in the fetal development of females exactly the same way that androgens do in male fetal development. The female structures of vagina, labia, and clitoris develop largely before the ovaries are formed, so their development cannot be due to estrogens. Instead, estrogens may be important later in fetal development—but the processes are not yet fully understood (Fitch & Denenberg, 1998).

Just as in males, the process of sexual differentiation in females is complete by the twelfth to fourteenth week of the mother's pregnancy. The genetically female fetus now has the internal structures (uterus, ovaries, and Fallopian tubes) and external anatomy (vagina, clitoris, labia) of a female. (See Figure 5.1.)

As you can see, sexual differentia-

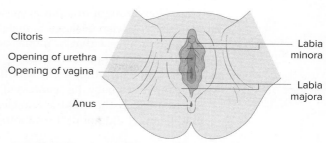

FIGURE 5.1   Female external sexual anatomy at birth.

Source: Adapted from González, J. L., Prentice, L. G., & Ponder, S. W. (2005). *Newborn Screening Case Management. Congenital Adrenal Hyperplasia: A Handbook for Parents.* Texas Department of State Health Services. http://www.dshs.state.tx.us/newborn/hand_cah.shtm, Figure 5.

tion involves coordinated processes influenced by both genetic and hormonal factors. It's a complex process, and there is still much to be learned about how it works. Recent research has shown that both the X and Y chromosomes contain multiple genes, not just *SRY*, that initiate sexual differentiation. There may be environmental effects too, but not much is known about them in humans because most of the research is done on rats and mice (McCarthy & Arnold, 2011).

After the internal structures and external anatomy of sex are established in the developing fetus, the sex hormones are not produced in quantity again until the individual reaches puberty.

Variations in Fetal Development: Intersexuality

In the great majority of cases, all the components of biological sex are congruent with each other. An XY fetus develops testes, produces androgens, and develops a penis and testicles. An XX fetus develops a vagina and clitoris, ovaries and a uterus. Based on the appearance of its genitals at birth, the infant is given the label female or male (its *assigned sex*) and raised as either a girl or a boy.

However, about 1.7 percent of babies vary in some way from the biological norm of two distinct sexes (Fausto-Sterling, 2000). In other words, the components of biological sex are not entirely congruent for these individuals. To put this percentage of the population in perspective, differences in sexual development occur twice as often as albinism, about as often as cystic fibrosis, and about half as often as Down's syndrome (Kessler, 2002). *Intersexuality* is a collective term for a number of specific variations on the theme of biological sex; people with any of these variations are usually referred to as *intersex individuals.*

Intersexuality has been recorded in many cultures and historical eras. People who did not fit either sex category often became sources of social controversy, and their cases have come down to us through historical records:

- In 1843, a Connecticut resident, Levi S., was not allowed to vote because town officials said he was "more female than male," and only men had the right to vote. They brought in a physician who examined S. Seeing a penis and testicles, the physician declared S. male; S. was allowed to vote. However, the physician later found that S. menstruated and had a vagina. It is not recorded whether S.'s vote was cancelled.

- In Italy, in 1601, after a blacksmith and soldier named Daniel Burghammer gave birth to a baby, he "confessed" to being "half male and half female." The Church called the child a miracle, but granted his wife a divorce because Burghammer did not fit the definition of a husband.

Biologist Ann Fausto-Sterling (2000), who provided these historical examples, points out that making a clear distinction between male and female has been central to law, religion, and politics in many cultures. Those who didn't fit in sometimes were forced to choose male or female and stick with the choice; if they could not or would not, they were punished or shunned.

Some intersex variations are visible—the person's genitals or other aspects of appearance are anomalous. Others, such as chromosome irregularities, may not result in any overtly noticeable bodily differences. What variations on the theme of biological sex occur, and do they affect behavior?

XYY Males: Born Criminals?

Some people have a genetic composition of XYY, or even XYYY. Because the Y chromosome and associated hormone production lead to male sexual differentiation, these people look pretty much like other men, except that they are taller than average (usually over six feet in height). Unless they had a genetic test done, most men with this condition would be unaware of it.

Does an extra Y chromosome affect behavior? Early studies showed that XYY men were overrepresented in prison populations. Based on this evidence, many people began to believe that the biology of XYY men determined their criminality. The belief was reinforced when the media (falsely) claimed that one notorious mass murderer was an XYY male and therefore "born to kill."

The evidence about XYY males and violent behavior turned out to be quite different from the media hype. A large, well-controlled study was conducted comparing XYY men to genetically typical men and to men with another chromosomal irregularity—XXY, or *Klinefelter's syndrome.* Klinefelter's syndrome causes men to have a less masculine physique and appearance (small penis and testicles, enlarged breasts, and sparse body hair), along with increased risk of learning disabilities (Diamond & Watson, 2004). The researchers predicted that, compared to the XY men, the undermasculine XXY men would have an exceptionally low rate of criminality, whereas the overmasculine XYY men would have an exceptionally high rate, particularly for violent crimes (Witkin et al., 1976).

The results were a surprise. Contrary to prediction, a man's chromosomal composition was not directly related to his criminal record. What did predict criminality? Lower intelligence and educational level were associated with crime, and both XXY and XYY men were disadvantaged on these factors compared to XY men. As for violence, there was no relationship with chromosomal status. Less-intelligent people, including some of the men with chromosomal irregularities, were most often in prison for nonviolent crimes like burglary. In other words, the notion that an extra Y chromosome causes men to be violent criminals was *not* supported. Rather, some chromosomal irregularities may affect intelligence, which in turn may be linked to lowered educational attainment and greater likelihood of imprisonment. After 50 years of research seeking a link, there is still no evidence that XYY and similar syndromes are associated with violent crime (Re & Birkhoff, 2015).

The furor over "killer chromosomes" illustrates the dangers of simplistic thinking about biological determinism (Dar-Nimrod & Heine, 2011). For example, because of the alleged link between the extra Y chromosome and violence, it was proposed that newborn males be subjected to mass testing for extra chromosomes. One TV crime drama ran a plot line about an angelic-looking but monstrously evil XYY little boy. Mass testing for chromosomal status could have stigmatized all those found to have chromosomal irregularities. In turn, stigma could lead to the kind of differential treatment that creates behavioral confirmation and self-fulfilling prophecies. How might a boy's life be shaped by others' beliefs that he was born to kill?

Androgen Insensitivity

Maria Patiño, Spain's top female hurdler, was on her way to the Olympic Stadium in 1988 to start her first race when she was barred from competition for failing the sex test. Patiño looked like a woman, and believed she was a woman "in the eyes of medicine, God, and most of all in my own eyes." However, the test (mandatory only for female athletes) had shown that Patiño's cells contained Y chromosomes, and examinations revealed that she had no uterus or ovaries, but did have testes. Patiño was publicly humiliated by the press. After devoting her life to her sport, she was stripped of all her titles and medals, deprived of her athletic scholarship, and forbidden to compete in the future. Her boyfriend left her (Fausto-Sterling, 2000, pp. 1–2).

Maria Patiño had discovered, in an exceptionally cruel and public way, that she had a condition termed ***complete androgen insensitivity syndrome*** (CAIS) (Diamond & Watson, 2004). Her genetic composition was XY, but her body was completely unable to process androgens. Therefore, the androgens that had been produced by her testes during fetal differentiation did not prompt the development of male reproductive structures. Externally, she looked like any other woman; her testes were hidden in the folds of her labia. When she reached puberty, her testes and other glands had produced enough estrogens that she developed the breasts and body curves of a typical woman.

Maria Patiño challenged the International Olympic Committee's policy of sex testing. Eventually, she was allowed to rejoin the Spanish Olympic Team (Fausto-Sterling, 2000). However, other Olympic athletes have not had such happy endings to their gender disputes with the IOC, and controversies continue (See Box 5.1).

The Missing X

About once in every 1,900 births an individual is born with an XO chromosomal composition—instead of a second X or a Y, there is a missing sex chromosome, a difference called ***Turner syndrome*** **(TS)** (Baker & Reiss, 2016). The fetus with this condition lacks androgens and estrogens (other than those produced by the mother's body) during development. As a result, the fetus does not develop complete internal reproductive structures. Externally, however, people with Turner syndrome look like normal females, with a vagina, clitoris, and labia (recall that female

Box 5.1 ∾ Controversy: Caster Semenya, Dutee Chand, and Gender Verification of Female Athletes

©Michael Kappeler/dpa/Alamy

In August 2009, Caster Semenya, an 18-year-old South African track and field athlete, dusted her competition in the 800-meter race at the World Championships, winning a gold medal and running the fastest time in the 800 meters that year. However, soon after her win, the International Association of Athletic Federations (IAAF) banned Semenya from competing and ordered her to undergo what they term "gender verification testing." Although never named as official reasons for pursuing gender testing, Semenya's muscular build, deep voice, and masculine facial features likely played a role. Competitors and spectators alike all questioned whether she was female, and at competitions, Semenya often had to go to the bathroom with a member of the competition so they could visually verify her sex.

Gender verification testing is physically and psychologically invasive, requiring a physical examination, as well as the involvement of a gynecologist, an endocrinologist, a psychologist, an internal medicine specialist, and a gender expert. The experts then convene and decide whether the athlete is male or female. But this decision is not as straightforward as some might think. At what point is a female athlete (or anyone else for that

matter) considered a woman? Is it the presence of a vagina? Or ovaries? Even the standards used by the IAAF were unclear.

In 2011, the IAAF stopped gender verification testing and instead instituted a test for hyperandrogenism, arguing that it was the naturally high levels of testosterone associated with hyperandrogenism that gave suspected women a competitive advantage. According to the policy, if a female athlete has a testosterone level that fell in the range for men, she would be banned from competing unless she took steps to lower her testosterone levels (through hormone therapy or surgery). Interestingly, the IAAF does not investigate high levels of testosterone in male athletes, although, presumably, they too would have an advantage.

In 2014, Indian sprinter Dutee Chand challenged the IAAF's hyperandrogenism policy saying it was discriminatory, and brought her case to the Court of Arbitration for Sport (CAS). CAS agreed with Chand and said that there was not enough evidence to suggest that high levels of androgens give female athletes any more of an advantage than other factors that could influence performance, including genetics, coaching, or even nutrition. CAS suspended the IAAF's policy until July 2017, giving the IAAF time to present evidence that high testosterone gives women an unfair advantage.

The controversy surrounding Caster Semenya and Dutee Chand was highlighted once again during the 2016 Olympic games, as both athletes competed. Although Chand did not medal in her event, Semenya won gold in the 800-meter race. Did her elevated levels of testosterone give her an unfair advantage? Some of her competitors might think so. But right now, science and law are on her side.

The need to classify people as either male or female is so embedded in society that individuals

Box 5.1 ～ Controversy: Caster Semenya, Dutee Chand, and Gender Verification of Female Athletes (*Concluded*)

who fail to conform are subjected to questioning, ridicule, and are often dehumanized. Gender verification and hyperandrogenism testing require female athletes to prove they are female. We return to the question we posed earlier—at what point is a woman considered a woman? Cases like those of Semenya and Chand also bring up other important questions. When an individual is intersex or has naturally high levels of testosterone, should they be allowed to compete as male or female? Is there another way of classifying people unrelated to gender that would allow for fair athletic competition? What do you think?

Sources:

Levy, A. (2009, November 30). Either/Or: Sports, sex, and the case of Caster Semenya. *The New Yorker,* pp. 45–59.

Longman, J. (2009, November 19). South African runner's sex verification results won't be public. Retrieved July 25 from http://www.nytimes.com/2009/11/20/sports/20runner.html.

Longman, J. (2016, August 18). Understanding the controversy over Caster Semenya. http://www.nytimes.com/2016/08/20/sports/caster-semenya-800-meters.html.

Padawer, R. (2016, June 28). The humiliating practice of sex-testing female athletes. http://www.nytimes.com/2016/07/03/magazine/the-humiliating-practice-of-sex-testing-female-athletes.html?_r=0.

Contributed by Annie B. Fox

genitals develop in the absence of androgens). Girls with Turner syndrome are short in stature, and they may have cognitive deficits in some math and spatial visualization tasks, such as map reading and mental rotation of objects (Mazzocco, 2009). A meta-analysis of math aptitude studies showed that girls with Turner syndrome had large deficits compared to other girls, especially under time pressure. They did better when they could use verbal strategies than when they had to do calculations (Baker & Reiss, 2016). The exact cause of these specific cognitive deficits is unclear; the overall intelligence of girls with Turner syndrome is normal.

In the strictly genetic definition of sex, people with Turner syndrome are neither male (XY) nor female (XX). However, because their external genitals are female, they are labeled females and raised as girls. When they reach the age of puberty, girls with Turner syndrome are given estrogens to stimulate the development of breasts and an adult woman's body shape.

Ambiguous Bodies

Because people with CAIS and Turner syndrome look like females, they are treated like females and raised accordingly. In contrast, some intersex conditions result in bodies that are visibly ambiguous: the external genitals may be some combination of penis-like and vagina-like structures and the internal glands and organs may be intersex as well. Historically, people with sexually ambiguous bodies were called **hermaphrodites,** after the Greek deities Hermes and Aphrodite, who according to myth produced a child with all the attributes of both its father and mother (Fausto-Sterling, 2000).

Sexually ambiguous bodies may result from a number of genetic, hormonal, and environmental influences. For example, people with *partial androgen insensitivity* **(PAIS)** may have an external sex organ that could be classified as either a large clitoris or a small penis. Internally, they have male testes, but instead of being located in a scrotal sac, the testes may be located in the abdomen or in the labia (Diamond & Watson, 2004).

One of the most common conditions producing a sexually ambiguous body is *congenital adrenal hyperplasia* (CAH), a genetically inherited malfunction of one or more of the enzymes needed to make the steroid hormone cortisol (Berenbaum & Beltz, 2011). This hormone deficiency causes the mother's body to overproduce other hormones, which act as androgens on the developing fetus. When the condition is discovered at birth, the androgen overproduction is stopped (with cortisone). Similar conditions have occurred when pregnant women were prescribed hormones to prevent miscarriage, which had androgenic effects on the fetus.

As we have learned, androgens are responsible for the formation of male reproductive structures and anatomy. Female (XX) fetuses with CAH and related disorders develop female internal structures—the uterus, ovaries, and fallopian tubes. However, at birth their external genitals may look like those of infant males, or may be ambiguous. The clitoris may be enlarged and capable of erection. The labia may fuse (grow together) so that the vagina is hidden and the infant appears to have a male scrotum (see Figure 5.2).

Occasionally, genetic females with CAH are labeled male at birth, and raised as boys. In one study, for example, this had occurred in about 6 percent of cases (Zucker, 2001). Others have been reassigned at their request (Jorge et al, 2008). Today, the condition is usually recognized at birth, at least in developed countries, and CAH infants are assigned as females.

The occurrence of intersex conditions demonstrates that two of the three key assumptions about sex are not universally true. The great majority of human beings do have one of two distinct bodily forms, female or male, along with a corresponding genetic composition and hormonal history. However, some do not. We turn now to the third assumption: that sex and gender naturally go together.

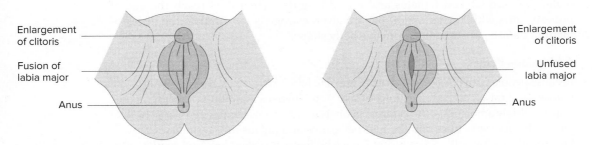

FIGURE 5.2   Ambiguous genitalia of female infants due to CAH.

Source: Adapted from González, J. L., Prentice, L. G., & Ponder, S. W. (2005). *Newborn Screening Case Management. Congenital Adrenal Hyperplasia: A Handbook for Parents.* Texas Department of State Health Services. http://www.dshs.state.tx.us/newborn/hand_cah.shtm, Figure 5.

Sex, Gender Identity, and Gender Typing

For most people, the genetic, hormonal, and anatomical aspects of sex are congruent. At birth, their assigned sex fits these components. As they emerge from infancy, they develop a *core gender identity,* a fundamental sense of belonging to one sex or the other. Almost always, children develop a core gender identity that corresponds to their biological sex. For most children, the core identity is learned by the age of three. Once formed it is usually permanent. Children then become gender-typed, adhering to the rules of the gender system of their culture. For example, girls are expected to engage in whatever behaviors their culture defines as appropriate for girls and to refrain from those defined as out of bounds for girls. Each individual also develops an erotic and affectional attraction to others, most often heterosexual.

The underlying assumption is that all the components of sex and gender should fit together. A genetic female should have a core gender identity as a female. She should also become a girly girl, preferring feminine toys, clothing, and pastimes, and later she should become a heterosexual woman. Echoing the gender stereotypes discussed in Chapter 3, the assumption is that physical attributes, traits, and behaviors are all tightly linked. If they are not, the person is not developing "normally."

Intersexuality and Identity

Is gender identity predicted by an individual's chromosomal makeup, prenatal hormones, external genitals, assigned sex, or some combination of these and other factors? Researchers have addressed this question by studying gender in intersex people. The medical literature often refers to these people as experiments of nature that allow scientists to examine the effects of biological irregularities that they could not ethically induce. (Of course, it would be unethical to do experimental studies of factors influencing human sexual differentiation.) But it is important to recognize that intersex people are *people* first and foremost. Like other people, they have personal identities, friends and families, sexual desire and intimate relationships, achievement goals, and dreams for their future. Although they do not fit the gender categories allowed by society, they have to live in a gender-divided world.

When an individual's biological sex is a variant, what happens to his or her gender? There is a great deal of research attempting to determine which (if any) aspects of biological sex are responsible for one's core gender identity and gender typing.

Growing Up with Turner Syndrome

It is clear that one does not need two X chromosomes to develop a core gender identity as female. Despite their chromosomal differences from the norm, individuals with Turner syndrome are assigned as females, and develop a core gender identity as female. Girls with Turner syndrome are similar to other girls in their interests and activities.

Although Turner syndrome does not cause problems with gender identity and gender typing, it may cause other developmental problems. For example, the short stature of girls with this syndrome, and their lack of the hormones that induce puberty, may lead to problems of social adjustment. They and their families may have to make decisions about taking growth hormones in childhood as well as estrogens to stimulate puberty. There is a need for health care practitioners to be sensitive to the psychosocial development of girls who have Turner syndrome (see Box 5.2).

Box 5.2 ∽ As a Woman with Turner Syndrome

Courtesy of Dr. Jessica Lord Bean

As a woman with Turner Syndrome (TS), I have faced some interesting and unique challenges. TS can result in a variety of physical, neuropsychological, and psychosocial difficulties for the individual, and there is a wide range of functioning within the TS population. Importantly, most women with TS lead happy, healthy, productive lives if they have the right kind of medical, educational, and social-emotional support.

The specific challenges that I have faced as a woman with TS have evolved as I, myself, have evolved as an individual. Having the short stature commonly associated with TS, I remember being in elementary school and wanting so badly to reach five feet. After three years on growth hormone, my interest in height waned and I began asking doctors how I could look more like my friends who were developing breasts, curves, and a "grownup" look. As I entered the professional world, I found myself acutely aware of presenting myself in an age-appropriate manner despite my younger appearance. As an adult woman searching for a partner to share my life with, I wondered when and how it was appropriate to share the details regarding my infertility with a significant other. I was fortunate to find a very special man, and we have been happily married for 12 years. We adopted two beautiful boys, now six and two years old. The gift of motherhood is truly the best gift I have ever been given. My favorite adoption-related quote is: "A child born to another woman calls me mom. The depth of the tragedy and the magnitude of the privilege are not lost on me." (Jody Landers). How true those words are!

The questions and experiences that I have struggled with have made me a better person. As a child psychologist, I believe that my personal experience makes me more insightful and compassionate when working with families. As a mom, I also feel that my experiences are helping guide me as I raise a child with special needs related to his own genetic condition. As I frequently tell others living with TS: although we do not have control over the fact that we have a genetic condition, we do have control over our attitude and the lessons we learn from our experiences. In this way, I view TS as a great opportunity to grow and help others in the process.

Please contact the Turner Syndrome Society of the United States at 1-800-365-9944 or www .turnersyndrome.org for more information.

Contributed by Jessica Lord Bean, PhD

Androgen Insensitivity and Identity

Complete androgen insensitivity is a rare condition, occurring in fewer than 1 in every 100,000 births. Because of their female genital appearance, infants with CAIS are almost always classified as female and raised as girls. In a review of 156 CAIS cases, 100 percent had established and maintained a female gender identity and, as adults, none were dissatisfied with their gender or had attempted to change it (Mazur, 2005). Because the child looks and acts like a normal girl, she is treated like a girl, and her gender identity is congruent with her assigned sex.

Neither the girl with CAIS nor her family may be aware of her condition during her childhood. However, when she reaches the age of puberty, her family may seek medical attention because she does not begin to menstruate. At that point, she may be given vague explanations that do not reveal her XY status. Even her parents may not know the truth (Diamond & Watson, 2004). Like Olympic athlete Maria Patiño, most individuals with CAIS do not know of their intersex condition because they are given selective information by their physicians and family.

The Impact of CAH

A great deal of research has focused on girls with CAH because researchers believed that they could provide evidence about the effect of androgens on core gender identity and gender typing. Certainly, the exposure to androgens during fetal development influenced these girls' bodies. Do the androgens also affect their identity, interests, and abilities?

Girls affected by CAH almost invariably develop a core gender identity as females. In other words, neither the exposure to androgens nor the families' reactions to their ambiguous genitals at birth disrupt gender identity: CAH girls think of themselves as females and are comfortable with their female identity. In the rare cases where CAH girls have been raised as boys, the majority developed a male gender identity because their assigned sex fit their genitals and they were socialized as boys (Berenbaum & Beltz, 2011).

Do girls with CAH act more like boys in their play patterns and other aspects of gender-typing? Dozens of studies have been done in this area. Usually, CAH-affected girls are compared with their non-CAH sisters or other female family members; sometimes they are compared with boys. Typically, CAH-affected girls are somewhat more active and more likely to be tomboys, and they play with so-called "boys' toys" more than other girls do. Some studies report that they are more aggressive than other girls are (Matthews et al., 2009). They are stronger than other girls and perform more like boys on tasks such as throwing balls or darts at a target (Collaer et al., 2009). In summary, it seems that their gender-related behaviors are more masculine than other girls' behaviors (Berenbaum & Beltz, 2011).

The gender-atypical interests of CAH girls persist; as teenagers, they tend to be more interested in electronics, cars and sports than cheerleading, fashion and makeup. As adults they choose more male-typed careers (Berenbaum & Beltz, 2011), preferring occupations related to things (chemist, mechanic) rather than people (social worker, teacher) (Beltz et al., 2011).

The theory that prenatal hormones permanently affect the brain, determining gender-typed behavior, is controversial, and of course it cannot be tested experimentally in humans. One thing missing from the theory is a recognition of the lived experience of gender for people with intersex bodies (Jordan-Young, 2012). CAH affects more than just the appearance of the genitals; it also affects physical characteristics that others can see and use to stigmatize girls. Due to hormonal imbalances, a girl with the condition is likely to be short in stature, overweight, to have excess body hair and severe acne. Because these characteristics do not meet cultural standards for feminine attractiveness, she may be perceived by herself and others as unattractive and more likely to think of herself as unfeminine or masculine. Moreover, girls with CAH undergo intensive lifelong medical scrutiny and psychiatric interventions. As soon as the infant girl's condition is diagnosed, she is under suspicion of being masculine, and this expectation is conveyed to her parents and other family members. Few researchers who endorse the prenatal hormones theory take these expectations seriously and virtually none have systematically investigated their possible effects. However, priming a belief about a child can create a self-fulfilling prophecy (Jordan-Young, 2012).

In summary, gender identity in intersex children seems to be largely (but not entirely) dependent on social factors. Being assigned as a female and brought up as a female usually outweigh biological inconsistencies in the components of sex, particularly when the external appearance is clearly female. However, this does not mean that gender identity and gender typing are unrelated to biological sex. Some girls with CAH develop in less gender-typed ways than unaffected girls; whether this is due to prenatal hormones, physical appearance differences, social factors, or some combination of these and other factors is still unknown. Some intersex people may have problems with gender identity that have not yet been documented by psychological researchers because of the secrecy and stigma surrounding these conditions. What the research does tell us is that there is not a simple, direct relationship between physical sex and psychological gender (see Box 5.3). Instead, the relationships are complex, multidetermined, and still somewhat mysterious.

Box 5.3 ⁓ Research Focus
David Reimer: The Boy Who Was Raised as a Girl

In 1965, Janet and Ron Reimer gave birth to healthy twin boys, who were named Bruce and Brian. Nine months later, during what should have been a routine circumcision, Bruce's penis was destroyed in a surgical accident. Desperate to find a way for their son to live a normal life, the Reimers were referred to Dr. John Money, an expert in gender identity at Johns Hopkins University.

Dr. Money believed that at birth, children were gender neutral. It was nurture—not nature—that determined gender identity. The Reimer case presented a once-in-a-lifetime opportunity for him to demonstrate his nurture theory because Bruce had an identical twin brother who would be raised as a boy—a perfect matched control case. He suggested that Bruce undergo gender

Research Focus

Box 5.3 ∾

David Reimer: The Boy Who Was Raised as a Girl (*Concluded*)

reassignment surgery and be raised as a girl. Bruce's parents, teenagers at the time, believed there was no other option that would allow their child a "normal" sexual life, and agreed to raise Bruce as a girl, renaming him Brenda. Brenda underwent surgery to remove her testicles, as well as procedures to construct a vagina. Later, she was given estrogen therapy to promote female pubertal development (i.e., breasts). Brenda wore dresses and was encouraged to play with dolls, to reinforce her female gender identity.

During Brenda's childhood, the Reimer family made trips to Johns Hopkins to meet with Dr. Money who attempted to reinforce Brenda's female gender identity and heterosexual orientation using questionable techniques such as showing her pornographic images of heterosexual sex. He also involved Brenda's brother in these treatments, having Brenda and Brian simulate sexual positions. Throughout the 1970s, Dr. Money proclaimed the success of the "John/Joan case" (the pseudonym he used to refer to Bruce/Brenda) in medical journals, books, and in speeches all over the country. Although Brenda was not born intersex, Dr. Money used the case to support his theories about the treatment of intersex individuals, arguing that they could adapt to a gender identity consistent with the outward appearance of their genitalia, but inconsistent with their genetic sex.

Despite Dr. Money's claims that Brenda had successfully adopted a female gender identity, Bruce's transition to Brenda was hardly successful. Brenda played with her brother's toys, refused to wear dresses, and was constantly teased and harassed at school for her lack of femininity. Although the Reimers reported Brenda's behavior to Dr. Money, he dismissed it as a phase or a lack of compliance on their part. At the advice of a psychiatrist and against the orders of Dr. Money, the Reimers decided to tell Brenda the truth about her past when she was 14. Unfortunately, the damage had already been done.

Brenda decided to revert back to her biological sex. He began testosterone injections, underwent surgery to remove breasts and reconstruct a penis and testicles, and gave himself the name David. Although he eventually married and adopted his wife's children, he never fully recovered from his traumatic childhood, suffering from severe depression and anger. David's family was also deeply impacted by what had occurred in David's childhood. His mother suffered from depression and attempted suicide, his father became an alcoholic, and his brother, who suffered from depression and drug use, died of a drug overdose in 2002.

When David was 30, he met Dr. Milton Diamond, a longtime critic of Dr. Money who had been interested in the John/Joan case in the 1970s. Dr. Money had stopped publishing reports on the case in the late 1970s and Dr. Diamond wondered what had become of John/Joan. When David found out that Dr. Money had touted his gender reassignment as a success and that the case was used to promote gender reassignment surgery for intersex people and those with genital injury, he decided he wanted to go public about what really happened to him. Dr. Diamond published a report in a medical journal in 1997 and David decided to work with journalist John Colapinto on a book about his life and childhood, *As Nature Made Him: The Boy Who Was Raised a Girl,* published in 2000. David's case was also featured in a BBC documentary, and received a great deal of media attention. As the details of the case became widely known, Dr. Money's research ethics were criticized by many. Although David's story ends tragically—he committed suicide in 2004—going public about his case brought attention to the need for revised guidelines for the ethical and clinical treatment of intersex individuals. David's tortured life also shows that science does not yet fully understand how physical sex and psychological gender are related in the human psyche.

Contributed by Annie B. Fox.

Transgender Identity

James Morris had a full and adventurous life. After serving in the British military as a war correspondent, he became a successful journalist, married happily, and fathered five children.

However, Morris felt that something was wrong. From earliest childhood he believed that he was meant to be a woman, not a man. After much introspection and conflict, Morris began a 10-year process of transitioning to being a woman. Following years of hormone treatments, he underwent what was called at the time *sex change surgery*: his penis and testicles were removed, and a vagina was constructed. Morris and her wife were divorced, but remained emotionally close, bonded by friendship and their mutual love for their children. Jan Morris continued her career as a writer, and now has more than 30 books to her credit.

Morris's book *Conundrum* (1974) articulates one person's struggle with having been "born in the wrong body." After changing sex, this formerly athletic and adventurous man described his pleasure in the ordinary rituals of femininity: wearing makeup and soft clothes, engaging in small talk with neighbor women, being helped with tasks like parallel parking or opening a bottle of wine. Becoming a woman made Morris acutely aware of disadvantages women may face: "addressed every day of my life as an inferior, involuntarily, month by month, I accepted the condition" (p. 149). However, she felt that the benefits—being helped, flattered, and treated more kindly—outweighed the costs.

Jan Morris is certain that she found her true self as a woman. Even the ordeals of hormonal and surgical treatments seemed a small price to pay for having her sex congruent with her gender: "I would have gone through the whole cycle ten times over, if the alternative had been a return to ambiguity or disguise" (p. 145). She describes her journey as "thirty-five years as a male . . . ten in between, and the rest of my life as me" (p. 146).

Jan Morris has a ***transgender*** identity. Transgender is a general term referring to a variety of gender variant identities. Some transgender people, like Jan Morris, eventually live full time in the sex and gender opposite to the ones they were assigned at birth. To make this transition, they may undergo surgeries or hormonal treatments to make their physical sex congruent with their gender identity. Other individuals who identify as transgender or gender variant have fluid gender identities. They may view themselves as not being entirely one gender or the other, or they may construe their gender identity as changeable over time (Levitt & Ippolito, 2014a,b; Williams, 2014).

Gender Dysphoria

Morris's account reflects the view that a person whose biological sex does not fit his or her core gender identity has a psychological disorder. ***Gender dysphoria*** (GD) is an official psychiatric category for those individuals who experience a disjunction between their assigned sex and their core gender identity. The APA defines GD as a strong and persistent desire to be the other sex or belief that one is really the other sex (American Psychiatric Association, 2013, 2000).

In children, GD is diagnosed when the child expresses a strong desire to be the other gender or belief that they are the other gender, experiences significant distress and problems in social functioning, and behaves like the other gender. Parents are asked about toy preferences, dress-up and fantasy play, and peer relationships (APA, 2013). Girls more often meet the criteria for GD in childhood, but boys are far more likely to be referred for treatment (Berenbaum & Beltz, 2011; Ristori & Steensma, 2016). Gender nonconformity is tolerated in young girls, who may be thought of as just "tomboys" who will "grow out of it," but it is more often considered worrisome in boys.

GD diagnoses in adolescents are increasing. Transgender teens face many problems including bullying and social rejection, and often suffer from depression and anxiety. They have a high rate of suicide attempts and self-harm. Some transgender teens and their families choose to suppress puberty with hormone treatments starting at around age 12. This gives the young person time to stabilize gender identity and postpones the decision whether to undergo surgery to change gender. Initial studies suggest that puberty postponement is helpful to long-term psychological adjustment (Fuss et al., 2015; Leibowitz & de Vries, 2016).

What proportion of people have transgender identities? A meta-analysis of studies included data from 12 countries with a total population of 95 million people (Arcelus et al., 2015). Only 4.6 in 100,000 people, or 1 in 21,739, had been treated for an official diagnosis of GD. Of these, there were 2½ times as many men as women. Of course, the number of gender variant and transgender people is likely very much higher, because not all transgender people are diagnosed with the disorder. For example, in a national survey of high school students in New Zealand, 1.2 percent said they were transgender and another 2.5 percent said they were not sure of their gender (Fuss et al., 2015). Studies relying on clinical diagnoses also may underestimate the proportion of women who transition to men. Because it is relatively simple for a woman to don men's clothes and change her body contours with testosterone injections, perhaps more women skip the diagnosis and pass unnoticed as men. Moreover, the norms for masculinity are more restrictive than the norms for femininity in our society. A woman who wears pants, cuts her hair short, or plays rugby is hardly controversial, but a man who wears dresses, uses makeup, or asks for help carrying a bag of groceries would likely be disrespected. Therefore, gender-variant men may be quicker than women to be diagnosed with GD.

Psychological and medical researchers have sought differences in brain structure and function in transgender people. However, the results so far have been preliminary, inconclusive, or negative (Erickson-Schroth, 2013; Kreukels & Guillamon, 2016; Leibowitz & de Vries, 2016). Almost always, the genetic sex, hormonal history, and reproductive anatomy of transgender individuals form an unambiguous biological sex as female or male (Berenbaum & Beltz, 2011; Gooren, 2006). Their childhoods are typically unremarkable except for their growing sense that they are different from other children and their assigned sex is a mistake. This awareness, and their resistance to being gender typed in line with their birth sex, often causes conflicts with parents and leads to the GD diagnosis.

New evidence of a genetic link comes from a twin study in which one or both twins transitioned. Though you might think there wouldn't be a lot of people in this category, the researcher managed to find 112 pairs (Diamond, 2013). Strikingly, among the identical (monozygotic, or MZ) twins, who share all their genes in common, 33 percent of the males and 23 percent of the females shared transgender identities. In other words, if one twin had transitioned, the other had too. Among the fraternal (dizygotic, or DZ) twins, who are only as genetically alike as any other siblings, just 3 percent shared transgender identities. The researcher concluded that transgender identity is much more influenced by genetics than childhood experiences; however, this study tells us nothing about what specific genetic factors might be influential.

Changing Gender

The transition from one gender to the other usually takes place over a long period of time. A woman may change her appearance by binding her breasts and getting a masculine haircut. A man may wear makeup and women's clothes and strap his penis between his legs. Some transgender individuals use hormonal supplements: estrogens to grow feminine breasts and reduce body hair on a male, or androgens to build muscle bulk and deepen the voice of a female (Wassersug et al., 2007). Others undergo surgery. Transmen may have surgeries to remove the breasts, uterus, and ovaries, but not all opt for constructing a penis, because the surgery is complicated and the results often disappointing (Morgan & Stevens, 2008).

The transgender person must adjust to a changing body, learn new ways of behaving, and accommodate to others' reactions to the new body and behavior (Bolin, 1996). As we learned in Chapter 2, innumerable small differences in verbal and nonverbal behavior mark gender in social interaction. A man who transitions to a woman is expected not only to dress like a woman; she should also walk, sit, talk, flirt, sip coffee, and throw a ball like a woman. To pass as a woman, she should have feminine interests and activities. And she must learn how to respond when treated like a woman. One transwoman reported that in addition to hormone treatment, "I spent almost a year going out in public and getting comfortable with myself as a woman, working on my presentation, my voice, my mannerisms, makeup and dress . . . laying the groundwork as best I could for the person I wanted to become" (Wassersug et al., 2007, p. 107).

Surgery to change genital anatomy and secondary sex characteristics to conform to gender identity is now called *gender affirmation surgery* within the trans community. Although the physical characteristics of the body are being changed, which fits the traditional definition of changing sex, not gender, those who identify as transgender conceptualize this change in terms of gender. The surgery or other treatments serve as a means to bring the body into harmony with the individual's core gender identity. Therefore, I will use gender terminology when discussing crossing from female to male (FtM, or transmen) or male to female (MtF, or transwomen).

The outcomes of gender affirmation treatments for trans people are usually positive. A review of 38 studies of the pre- and post-treatment psychological health of transgender individuals showed that before treatment they had a much higher incidence of anxiety and depression than the general population. (Their rates of disorders such as schizophrenia and bipolar disorder did not differ from the population average.) After gender affirmation treatments, either surgical or hormonal or both, they were similar to those in the general population (Dhejne et al., 2016).

Today, transgender celebrities are in the news. Activist Janet Mock's award-winning memoir *Redefining Realness* became a bestseller. Laverne Cox, best known for her role as Sophia on *Orange Is the New Black*, has appeared on the cover of *Time*. Nevertheless, the great majority of transgender individuals still live in a climate of excessive stress. In-depth interviews of 17 gender-variant individuals revealed that they experienced heightened awareness of gender, constantly monitoring their behavior to minimize the risk of rejection, aggression, or violence against themselves. They also experienced rejection and lack of support from friends and family. They reported that they had gained insight into the workings of patriarchy, with those who transitioned to male personas benefiting from male privilege, and those becoming female experiencing job discrimination and other kinds of sexism (Levitt & Ippolito, 2014a).

The good news is that it is becoming easier for transgender and gender variant individuals to form friendships and community. In an online study of 536 individuals who identified as transgender or gender variant, participants described their friendship experiences with other transgender, non-transgender, lesbian, gay, and heterosexual friends. Using an intersectional approach, the researchers asked each participant about the unique benefits and barriers to having friends who were different or similar to them in gender identity and sexual orientation (Galupo et al., 2014). (If you have friends who differ from you on these dimensions, you might think about these questions before reading further about the results.)

Transgender individuals valued their more normative friends because they felt more normal around them, because transgender issues did not dominate the conversation, and because they offered more diverse perspectives and interactions. They valued their transgender friends because of their shared experiences, their mutual understanding, and the fact that they could talk about transgender issues and offer support, mentoring, and resources (Galupo et al., 2014). Being accepted by both LGB and straight friends was important to the transgender people in this study; it provided a validation of their own identity.

Sex and Sexual Orientation

It may seem obvious, but one of the biggest differences between women and men is that the great majority of men are attracted to women, and the great majority of women are attracted to men. *Sexual orientation* is a multidimensional concept involving erotic attraction, affectional relationships, sexual behavior, erotic fantasies, and emotional attachments. The gender of one's sex partners is only one component, and not always the most important one. Often, the various components are inconsistent within the same person (Hoburg et al., 2004; Rothblum, 2000). Moreover, a person's sexual orientation may change over time. Despite the complexity of defining it, researchers have looked for genetic and hormonal influences on sexual orientation.

Is There a Gay Gene?

Several studies have shown that same-sex sexual orientation runs in families. In other words, lesbian, gay, and bisexual (LGB) people tend to have a higher-than-average number of LGB people among their relatives. These studies suggest that either particular family environments or genetic factors could increase the likelihood of LGB orientations, but cannot distinguish between the two kinds of factors. Of course, both could be present in the same families. Twin studies help separate the influences of genes and environment by comparing MZ with DZ twins. (Remember that MZ twins are genetically identical, whereas DZ twins are only as genetically alike as any other siblings are.) If MZ twins share the same sexual orientation more often than DZ twins do, it suggests that there is some genetic contribution to sexual orientation. In general, studies of male twins do suggest a genetic influence. In one study 66 percent of the MZ co-twins of gay men were also gay, compared with 30 percent of the DZ co-twins (Whitam et al., 1993). This study also found one set of MZ triplets who all were gay. For females, however, the story is less clear. Some twin studies show the same pattern as the studies with men. However, others show little or no relationship between genetic similarity and lesbian or bisexual orientation (Hines, 2004).

Recent studies of genetic sequencing have identified specific linkages on the X chromosome related to gay sexual orientation in men (Sanders et al., 2015). Genetic sequencing for sexual orientation is still a new area of research; what it indicates so far is that there are probably multiple genes related to sexual orientation. Scientists do not yet know exactly how these genes influence sexual orientation, but it is clear that they do not solely determine it because there is also strong evidence for nongenetic factors. For example, in the twin studies, overall about half of the MZ co-twins of gay men are not gay (Hines, 2004). For females, there has been less research and the data are even less clear. There are still many unanswered questions about the biological origins of sexual orientation.

Hormones and Sexual Orientation

Recall that XX and XY fetuses experience different exposure to gonadal hormones during fetal development. Male fetuses are exposed to androgens, whereas female fetuses are not. Do fetal androgens play a role in the later development of sexual attraction to women? One way to study the effects of fetal hormonal exposure on later sexual orientation is to assess the sexual orientation of people whose intra-uterine hormonal exposure was atypical.

Individuals with partial androgen insensitivity syndrome (PAIS) are XY males who effectively receive little androgen during fetal development and therefore develop ambiguous genitalia. Depending on the appearance of the genitals at birth, the individual may be assigned as either a male or a female, and the genitals are surgically altered to fit the assigned sex. Regardless of which sex they are brought up as, individuals with PAIS usually develop a heterosexual orientation—those brought up as girls become attracted to men, and those brought up as boys become attracted to women. In these cases, it is clear that a normal dose of fetal androgens was not necessary for the individual to develop a sexual orientation toward the other sex. Despite their similar hormonal histories, the individuals raised as boys and those raised as girls developed different sexual orientations, illustrating that there is a lot of flexibility in human psychosexual development (Hines, 2004).

Other researchers have asked whether an excess of androgens during fetal development could predispose a female to become attracted to women. To answer this question, they have looked at the sexual orientation of women with a history of CAH, which causes exposure to fetal androgens. (Recall that CAH also causes intersex male-appearing genitals that are surgically altered in infancy.)

The majority of CAH women identify as heterosexual. However, when they are compared to their non-CAH sisters or other female family members, CAH-affected women are more likely to report having lesbian orientation, fantasies, or experience—and less likely to have heterosexual orientation, fantasies, or experience (Hines, 2011). However, we shouldn't be too quick to conclude that these differences are entirely due to prenatal hormone exposure. As noted earlier, there are many other differences between women with CAH and other women. Heterosexual intercourse may be painful and unsatisfying for women with the differently formed genitals caused by CAH. Moreover, these women are subjected to intensive lifelong medical scrutiny and psychological intervention, often including multiple genital surgeries and total amputation of the clitoris. Many CAH women have described their treatment as violating and dehumanizing, and their sexual adjustment with men could be negatively affected (Jordan-Young, 2012).

In this area, there is a need for feminist research methods that explore not only biological factors but also the subjective experiences of women (Jordan-Young, 2012). Meanwhile, it is clear that prenatal hormones do not fully determine sexual orientation, because the great majority of women with prenatal exposure to androgens identify as heterosexual, and the great majority of women who identify as lesbian or bisexual have no evidence of abnormal prenatal hormone exposure (Hines, 2011).

Sex as a Social Construction

The presence of intersex bodies challenges the fundamental assumption that everyone is either male or female and that this is an "irreducible fact" (Kessler & McKenna, 1978, p. vii). The presence of naturally occurring variations in biological sex also challenges the assumption that gender follows naturally from sex. If sex is not a distinct binary system, why does gender have to follow a binary pattern of masculinity/femininity?

According to some feminist theorists, sex is a *social construction,* which means that the assumptions underlying our commonsense beliefs about it are the products of a specific culture, not universal or fixed truths about nature (Marecek et al., 2004). In other words, sex is a belief system rather than a fact (Crawford, 2000). However, in every culture, the belief system about sex seems perfectly natural to members of that culture. In our own society, most people firmly believe that sex is a biological dichotomy. It is hard to recognize that what is taken as fact might be the product of social negotiation and cultural consensus.

Even the label "It's a girl!" or "It's a boy!" is a social construction. As we have seen, this classification is usually based on the appearance of the external genitals—but genitalia are only one aspect of biological sex. Relying on genital appearance, and not other determinants of sex, is the product of a social consensus. And sex classification is the crucial first step in creating gender. It is *because* we have already classified someone as male or female that all the other gender attributions we might use—masculine, feminine, lesbian, gay, transgender—make sense. The concepts of core gender identity and sexual orientation, for example, presume that each infant *is* male or female *before* these psychological processes begin.

Questions of how we become gendered are interesting and important, of course. But even more important is the question of how the social reality of two, and only two, sexes is constructed in the first place (Golden, 2008). Here we look at the process of making social decisions that *create* two sexes by exploring the medical treatment of intersex people. These treatments spark heated debate because they involve tailoring bodies that vary from the norm to fit the only two sex categories that are permissible in our society.

Constructing Two Sexes

For many years, the standard treatment for intersex conditions began with assigning a child the label of male or female as soon as possible after birth. This was followed by medical and surgical interventions designed to alter the genitals to look more "normal." These surgeries were done before the child was old enough to consent to them. Often, parents were not given the exact diagnosis. As intersex children grew older, they were rarely told the truth about their condition. Instead, their medical records were sealed. Here, we consider the social implications of each step in this process.

When physicians recognize that an intersex child has been born, they attempt to decide what they term the **optimal gender** for the child. By this they mean, "Which sex will the child fit best?" The criteria for best fit are flexible. Physicians consider whether such children have reproductive potential as a male or female, whether they will be able to function sexually as a male or female, and whether they can be made to look like a typical male or female. If the child is old enough to have formed a core gender identity before the condition is diagnosed, this also must be taken into account.

As you can imagine, deciding a child's optimal gender is a complex matter involving both medical criteria and social norms. Some critics have suggested that the criteria may be applied in sexist ways: for those children who are assigned as males, sexual function is primary, whereas for those assigned as females, reproductive capability is given more weight (Fausto-Sterling, 2000; Kessler, 1998, 2002). In other words, for males, the ability to have an erection and engage in heterosexual sex is the primary criterion, but for females it is the potential for motherhood, not sexual functioning or pleasure.

Although medical professionals use the concept of optimal gender among themselves, they consider the indeterminacy of the child's actual sex too unsettling a concept for parents. Critics claim that in treating intersex children and counseling their families, the medical profession uses a gender doublespeak whereby they deliberately hide the intersex status. Instead of saying that the infant is a mixture of female and male and that they are deciding on an optimal gender, they tell the family that they know the "true" sex and will "correct" the "incomplete development" (Fausto-Sterling, 2000; Kessler, 1998). Even when physicians perform major surgery on intersex children they consider it best not to be too candid. The secrecy, even more than the surgery, may be the most traumatizing aspect of traditional intersex management (see Box 5.4).

Why do physicians conceal the truth about intersex conditions from patients and their families? Traditionally, they have believed that the child's core gender identity might be compromised, and that this would lead to psychological conflict and poor adjustment. This reflects the assumptions that there must be only two sexes and that gender identity and gender typing must follow biological sex. Although physicians know that some infants do not fit the pattern, they have felt obligated to pretend that the sex/gender binary is universal.

Box 5.4 ∾ Research Focus: Life Experiences of Intersex People in Israel

Many intersex individuals grow up unaware of their intersex condition. They may undergo invasive testing, examinations, hormone therapy, and even surgical alterations without ever being told the truth about why they need such treatment. In a qualitative study of the lived experiences of three intersex individuals in Israel, Limor Meoded Danon (2015) examined the ways in which these individuals were impacted by the secrecy surrounding their intersex condition. For example, a woman with Complete Androgen Insensitivity Syndrome (CAIS) didn't know she was born with testicles and that they were removed surgically. Her parents and doctors kept it a secret from her:

In the summer between eighth and ninth grade, I had surgery. My mother told me to say that it was hernia surgery, and that's what I said. . . . I was told that they were removing my residual ovaries, so I wouldn't get cancer or something. I didn't know it was something else. . . .

A man with Classical Congenital Adrenal Hyperplasia (CCAH), who was born with a penis, ovaries, and a uterus, reported feeling objectified during his many trips to the hospital during his childhood:

You're a little kid and all day they strip you and dress you and look at you; that's how it was. I understood that mine was a rare, special case, so they all wanted to see, they all wanted to touch, that's how it was. Just like an exhibit in a museum.

In adulthood, the individuals Danon interviewed spoke of the ways in which they continue to conceal their intersex bodies from their friends and families. One woman with CAH reported that her parents kept her CAH a secret from her siblings, and that has affected her relationships with all of them. She also described the ways in which the secret of her condition has impacted her desire and ability to have intimate relationships. Unable to accept herself, she feels that she is not capable of experiencing love:

How can I tell someone I was born different, that what you see now is the result of a successful plastic surgeon, more or less? I have no idea what I look like compared to someone normal. I would argue that the work they did wasn't one hundred percent perfect, that I'm quite different. I don't know, I mean they forgot to tattoo an orientation map on my genitals [laughs].

The need to assign a binary sex to intersex individuals reflects how uncomfortable our larger society is with ambiguous bodies. Instead of normalizing intersex bodies, the biomedical model calls for treatment and concealment, denying intersex individuals autonomy over their own bodies.

Source: Danon, L. M. (2015). The body/secret dynamic: Life experiences of intersex people in Israel. SAGE Open, April–June 2015, 1–13. DOI: 10.1177/2158244015580370.

Contributed by Annie B. Fox

In constructing unambiguous genitals for intersex infants, the medical profession has enforced a standard that allows no overlap between male and female genitals. For an intersex child to be considered a functional girl, she must have a clitoris that is smaller than the smallest permissible penis for a boy. If her clitoris is "too big," it will be surgically "downsized" (Fausto-Sterling, 2000, p. 60). In the past, surgeons often removed the clitoris of intersex girls entirely. Today, clitoral reduction surgery is performed. Despite considerable natural variability in clitoral size at birth, physicians often rely on their personal impressions or opinions about the appropriate size and appearance of this organ. Psychologist Suzanne Kessler (1998; 2002) compiled a list of the adjectives used in the medical literature to describe clitorises that were perceived as needing surgical reduction. The list includes *defective, deformed, obtrusive, offending, troublesome,* and *disfiguring*. Clearly, these are value judgments. It is the physician, and not necessarily the child, her parents, or her future sex partners, who is troubled by a clitoris that is "too big."

Some intersex individuals have genital surgery several times during the first few years of life, followed by more surgery after puberty (Fausto-Sterling, 2000). Female-assigned children may face repeated surgeries to construct a vagina. Following surgery, instruments must be inserted into the vagina daily by the parents in order to keep the new structure open. A male-assigned child may have genital surgery in order to repair or construct an acceptable penis. The medical literature reports hundreds of techniques for this task, along with techniques to repair the unsatisfactory results of previous surgeries. The costs of genital surgery include visible scarring, loss of sexual sensation, and loss of the ability to reach orgasm. Interviews with adult intersex people, as well as medical data on the results of genital surgery, have shown that poor overall appearance and dissatisfaction with the results are common (Kessler, 2002; Hines, 2004).

The medical interventions aimed at intersex children also have other costs. Because they may not have access to their medical records, the affected individuals may not know about medical conditions that could compromise their health. Moreover, due to repeated experiences of surgery, and the suspicion that they are being deceived, some intersex people distrust the medical profession to the extent that they fail to get help for other conditions, causing overall health to degenerate (Kessler, 2002).

There are encouraging signs that the medical management of intersexuality is changing. In 2006, a group of 50 international experts on intersex published a consensus statement: parents should not be encouraged to pursue cosmetic genital surgery for intersex infants because there is no good medical evidence that it improves quality of life for intersex people (Golden, 2008). For both ethical and scientific reasons, it is better to postpone surgery until the child can consent (Diamond & Garland, 2014). To guide physicians in decision-making with their intersex patients, Europe has established a registry of cases that tracks treatment and long-term outcomes. However, there is not yet a registry in the United States.

The changing norms in medical management of intersex conditions show that sex is not just a biological given. Its meaning is negotiated through social decision making. In social negotiations, members of dominant groups have more power to define reality. In this case, the medical profession has had more power to define the sex of intersex individuals than the intersex people themselves, or their families, have had. The consequences for intersex people have sometimes been tragic, because they have been subjected to life-altering medical treatments without informed consent. Only recently is treatment being revised in a more humane direction.

Rethinking Gender Dysphoria

Transgender people have engaged in a long struggle to have their condition recognized by the medical profession. Their demands for legal recognition and medical care have forced society to recognize and name their problem, and to help them change both physical sex and social gender. However, not everyone believes that labeling cross gender identity as a psychiatric disorder is entirely a positive change. Some argue that the diagnostic category of gender dysphoria contributes to stigmatizing people of diverse gender identities and labels some ordinary behaviors as mental illness based on the gender of the person doing them. Other critics point out that the there is no evidence that cross-gender identity or behaviors in themselves create psychological problems or distress. Rather, it is being stigmatized that creates such problems (Sanchez & Vilain, 2009). A third criticism is that the GD diagnostic category has had the paradoxical consequence of reinforcing the idea that there are and can be two and only two sexes and that gender must conform to one or the other. According to this view, by requesting surgery to make their bodies match their gender, transpeople reinforce the medical profession's philosophy that within an individual's body, sex and gender must conform (Fausto-Sterling, 2000). Their dilemmas of identity may be a result of our binary system of sex and gender. Indeed, the criteria for a diagnosis of GD are entirely based on the binary model. If you do not feel like a man, then you *must* be a woman—there is no other choice available.

In a qualitative study, researchers interviewed medical providers caring for intersex and transgender patients. The providers had robust beliefs in the gender binary, which left no leeway for intersex bodies or transgender identities to be viewed as healthy. They viewed the ideal outcome of their medical interventions as re-creating the binary: producing masculine men or feminine women who led heteronormative lives (Davis et al., 2016). But in an era when gender nonconformity has shifted away from being considered a sin or a mental illness, and the lives of LGBTQ people have become much easier as a result, should heteronormativity still be a universal goal?

The GD diagnostic category remains controversial. Does it pathologize gender nonconformity and increase stigma—or does it open access to psychological counseling and care? Reasonable people disagree on this question (Lev, 2013); stay tuned for further developments.

In summary, the medical and psychiatric treatment of intersex and transgender provides evidence that both sex and gender are processes of social consensus and social enforcement. Constructing two and only two sexes through hormonal and surgical intervention may be done with the best of intentions, but it also may reinforce the belief that these two categories are the only natural and acceptable ones. However, there are other ways to categorize the human body and psyche.

Beyond the Binary

For those of us brought up within a binary system of sex and gender, it may be difficult to think outside the boxes. However, in some cultures, the idea that people come in more than two sexes is commonplace. In other words, these cultures have women, men, and others (Williams, 1987). In our own culture, as well, some people challenge the idea that one must choose between only two sex or gender categories. We turn now to these steps beyond the binary.

More Than Two Sexes

Societies that have a third-sex category are found in many parts of the world. These categories contrast with our own society's binary categories of female/male, masculine/feminine, and gay/straight. They are neither, both, and all of the above. The social roles and social positions of third-sex people vary across cultures. Let's look at a few examples.

Third Sexes across Cultures

In India about a million people identify as *hijras* (Sharma, 2014) or *Aravanis* (Mahalingam, 2003). Hijras and Aravanis, by their own definition, are a third sex or "third nature" people, neither men nor women (Kalra, 2012). Hijras take female names and wear women's clothes, but they set themselves apart from women by being much more sexually overt in their behavior. Unlike proper Indian women, they wear heavy makeup, joke about sex, and wear their hair loose. One's genitals do not determine being a hijra. Some hijras have male genitalia, some were born biologically male but chose to be castrated, and still others were born with intersex genitals. Within their society, hijras are not considered to be women, because they cannot bear children; they are not considered to be men, because they do not function sexually as men. In north India, hijras are considered to incorporate the divine powers of the goddess; they sing and dance at weddings and birth celebrations, and traditionally are asked to bless newborn babies (Kalra, 2012).

In southern India, hijras are known as Aravanis. Like their counterparts in north Indian society, they dress as women, and may use hormones or surgery to change gender (Kalra, 2012). However, they are not merely trying to mimic true women; rather, "gender-bending is central to their identity," and they "pride themselves on being 'superwomen,'" a third gender that both enacts femininity and flouts it (Mahalingam, 2003, p. 491).

Hijras and Aravanis have faced stigma, discrimination, and harassment in an ambiguous social position that leaves them sometimes revered and sometimes persecuted. But they are very visible in Indian society, even in Bollywood films, where they are portrayed in a variety of ways: as figures of fun, as villains, even as sensitive and caring mothers (Kalra & Bhugra, 2015). In 2014, the Supreme Court of India granted them legal status as a third sex, conferring constitutional protection, legal rights, and affirmative action in government jobs (Sharma, 2014).

In the South Pacific, Samoans call the third sex *fa'afafine,* which translates as "in the way of a woman." Typically, fa'afafine are biological males who dress as women and take up women's tasks such as caregiving and teaching. They are highly valued as dancers and entertainers, and usually treated with respect and acceptance (Vasey & Bartlett, 2007). However, although they are treated like women in social interactions, they are clearly differentiated from biological women and men (Vasey & VanderLaan, 2009). A popular nickname for the fa'afafine is "50/50s," because they can be both masculine and feminine. Like men, they are allowed to tell bawdy jokes, engage in dirty dancing, and play baseball; like women, they are allowed to be artistic, concerned with fashion and appearance, and willing to babysit for small children (Fraser, 2002; Vasey & VanderLaan, 2009).

Anthropologists and historians studying North American Indian cultures have found that more than 150 of these societies have (or had in the past) a third-sex category that the anthropologists term the *berdache* and Native Americans themselves term *two-spirit people* (Pullin, 2014). The characteristics of two-spirit people have varied widely across different Native American cultures and across time (Fausto-Sterling, 2000). Most often, they were biological males who wore women's clothes and took up some of the roles and tasks of women. However, they could also adopt men's customs and clothing, switch back and forth, or combine the two (Roscoe, 1996). Thus, their gender was changeable and not always congruent with their sexual anatomy. Two-spirit people were often seen as particularly creative and artistic. Today, Native Americans use the term to encompass their LGBTQ community (Pullin, 2014).

A custom known as *pledged virgin* is unusual because it is a third sex category for women. This custom existed in areas of the Balkans (the former Yugoslavia and Albania) (Gremaux, 1996). A pledged virgin took over a male gender when there was no man available in a family or when she rejected marriage and motherhood. Pledged virgins were no longer thought of as women; they wore men's clothes, did heavy work, and even served as men in the military. Unlike people in other third-sex categories, pledged virgins were not allowed sexual activity. The custom has nearly died out today, but when journalists recently interviewed the last of the pledged virgins, these elderly individuals expressed no regrets at having exchanged the life of a woman in their society for the relative freedom of the pledged virgin (Malfatto & Prtoric, 2014).

Third-Sex Categories and the Gender System

In their respective cultures, third-sex people are not considered to be gay. For example, fa'afafine have sex with supposedly heterosexual men, often initiating young men and giving them practice at having sex before they become sexually active with women. Most straight men in Samoa report having had sex with a fa'afafine at some time in their lives; this is not considered to be gay sex (Vasey & VanderLaan, 2009). In other words, a person's sex is defined in terms of their social role rather than in terms of their anatomy. Third-sex people may be accepted in cultures where homosexuality is strongly tabooed, such as India and Samoa. As one Samoan explained, the preacher might preach that being gay is un-Godly at the same time there is a fa'afafine singing in the church choir every Sunday (Fraser, 2002, p. 74).

Across cultures, there are more opportunities for males than for females to opt for a third category. As we have seen, hijras, Aravanis, and fa'afafine all are biological males (or, more rarely, intersex). Only a few Native American societies permitted females to become two-spirit people by taking up some of the clothing and tasks of men.

Why are third-sex categories more often available to males than to females? Beliefs about sex and gender may hold the answer. One unique study asked 100

Aravanis about their beliefs regarding the possibility of sex change (Mahalingam, 2003). The Aravanis thought that gender nonconformity was equally acceptable for girls and boys. For example, they saw nothing wrong with a boy who wanted to wear flowers in his hair or a girl who wanted to do carpentry. However, when asked whether a girl could *become* a boy, or vice versa, they were virtually unanimous in agreeing that only a boy could change sex, by dressing like the other sex, having surgery, or performing a religious ceremony. In other words, they saw *male* sex as changeable and fluid, but *female* sex as unchangeable and fixed. The only way they thought a girl might become a boy was through reincarnation.

Of course, all the Aravanis were themselves biological males who had changed their sex/gender. They were also Hindus, whose religion emphasizes goddess worship and represents female identity as primordial, strong, and powerful. Thus, the "facts" of sex and gender for the Aravanis were influenced by their culture, religion, and social position, and are quite different from our own "facts."

In summary, the various third-sex categories around the world challenge more than the assumption that sex is a binary category. Societies that include a third sex may view sex and sexual orientation as changeable depending on the social situation (Roscoe, 1996). These views contrast with our own society's belief that sex and sexual orientation are biologically fixed and permanent. They also point out the cultural bias of diagnostic categories such as gender dysphoria. For example, Samoan fa'afafine were unquestionably gender-variant as children, but most report that their difference was a source of joy and fulfillment, not psychological distress (Vasey & Bartlett, 2007).

Genderqueer

In our own society, some people permanently adopt a transgender identity that is neither female nor male. They do not see themselves as in transition from one sex to another. Instead, they see themselves and others like them as a third-sex category. For example, transgender activist Kate Bornstein describes herself as a gender outlaw and has said, "I am not a man—about that much I am very clear, and I've come to the conclusion that I'm probably not a woman either" (Bornstein, 1994). Or they may view sex and gender as continuous, like sliding scales on which a person can place him/herself at any point. Some transgender people take up life as the other sex while keeping their biologically given bodies intact—they are men with vaginas and women with penises.

People whose gender identities are neither exclusively male nor female, but instead are outside the gender binary, often refer to themselves as *genderqueer, gender-expansive, non-binary,* or *agender.* The latter term means having no gender at all. Another term used in this community is *genderfluid,* meaning a person who moves between genders n or whose gender fluctuates and changes across time. As we learned in Chapter 3, changing language can be a way of raising consciousness and drawing attention to a social or political issue. People now even have the option of nonbinary pronouns—which may be a little confusing at first (see Box 5. 5). Transgender activists have certainly succeeded in raising consciousness about gender variability. In 2014, Facebook added 50 custom genders for its users, and agender is now an option on the dating website OKCupid.

Box 5.5 ⮑ Genderqueer pronouns: A new user's guide

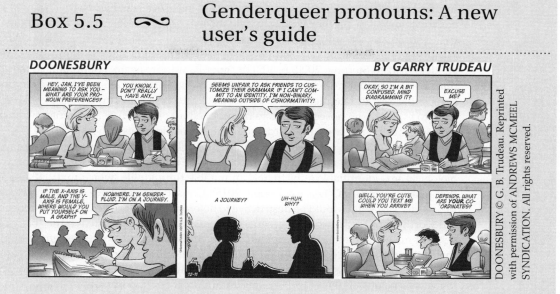

DOONESBURY   **BY GARRY TRUDEAU**

Although many transgender individuals identify as women or men, not everyone identifies within these binary identities. As more people become comfortable expressing their identity outside the binary, pronouns beyond she/her/hers and he/him/his have emerged. But how do you know what pronouns someone uses? How do you get used to using these new terms?

There are many pronoun options for individuals who identify as genderqueer or outside the gender binary, for instance, the gender neutral: they/them/their, ze/zim/zir, sie(zie)/hir/hirs. These are just the more common gender neutral pronouns; there are many others. Such pronouns help create meanings of gender beyond the binary, and give space for more diverse representations of gender. When talking with and referring to someone who is transgender, it is important to use the appropriate pronouns. When transgender individuals experience frequent instances of being misgendered, they may feel increased stigmatization and anxiety.

Asking someone what their pronouns are can feel awkward or uncomfortable. However, when you do not know the pronouns someone uses it is important to gain the courage to ask so you do not contribute to their feelings of being stigmatized. It's okay to simply ask, "What pronouns do you use?" The transition to using a pronoun you may never have used can be difficult. Many people struggle with using they/them/their as singular pronouns ("Have you met my friend Jae? *They* just moved here."). Be forgiving of yourself when you mistakenly use the incorrect pronoun for someone. Simply apologize, try to use the correct pronoun next time, and move on.

Unfortunately, genderqueer people have not had much representation in the media. However, as transgender activism becomes more visible, hopefully genderqueer characters in mainstream media will also increase. This representation will help gender neutral pronouns become more familiar, and possibly reduce the stigmatization of genderqueer identity.

Contributed by Dawn M. Brown.

Sources

FORGE (2016). Publications and resources. Retrieved June 2016 from http://forge-forward.org/wp-content/docs/FAQ-Pronouns.pdf.

McLemore, K. A. (2015). Experiences with Misgendering: Identity Misclassification of Transgender Spectrum Individuals. *Self and Identity*, 14(1), 51–74.

Wentling, T. (2015). Trans* Disruptions Pedagogical Practices and Pronoun Recognition. *TSQ: Transgender Studies Quarterly*, 2(3), 469–476.

Some transgender activists claim that their lives reveal the social construction of sex, and thus their perspectives are crucial to feminist social change. Rather than try to pass or change gender, they wish to "make their crossing visible, to pose it as a counter to the dominant account that there are only two sexes" (Marecek et al., 2004, p. 207). The transgender movement is sometimes heralded as a "radical re-visioning of sex and gender" (Fausto-Sterling, 2000, p. 107) or "guerilla warfare against dominant constructions of sex, gender and sexuality" (Marecek et al., 2004, p. 207). But not everyone agrees that sex and gender should be deconstructed. Other transgender people still want to live as their chosen gender, to fit into the binary system as an ordinary woman or man. They do not want the burden of being revolutionaries (Elliot, 2009).

According to the conservative Family Research Council, the transgender movement is no more than an ideological attack on the "basic reality–that all people have a biological sex, identifiable at birth and immutable through life, which makes them either male or female" (O'Leary & Sprigg, 2015). Conservatives believe that acknowledging gender variability would be destructive to heterosexual marriage and family. Indeed, it is worth asking what would happen to the patriarchal gender system if the "basic reality" of male and female were expanded? Would the acceptance of transgender imply that our current concepts of sex and gender would disappear entirely? Anne Fausto-Sterling (2000) suggests that it would not erase these categories, but would allow us to focus more on variability and less on conformity. If our society were to develop more inclusive definitions of sex and gender, it would become more like the other societies I've discussed that have allowed some people to be neither male nor female, but "other." It would also open up alternatives to the surgical "correction" of intersex people. If the stigma of having an ambiguously sexed body were diminished, some people with unusual bodies might choose to keep them and enjoy them as they are.

But merely recognizing variability or allowing a third-sex category does not guarantee that the gender system will change. As we learned in Chapter 2, the gender system is not just a matter of individual beliefs; it is a system of social classification that governs access to power. If sexual variability were recognized and accepted, laws and customs that regulate marriage and sexual behavior would have to change too.

Making a Difference

Transforming Society: Equality for Gender Minorities

The medical treatment of intersex people is increasingly being questioned. Cheryl Chase is one activist who has broken the silence. Chase's history was not unusual for an intersex person in our society. Born with ambiguous sex glands but the internal organs of a female, she was assigned as a boy at birth because she had a large clitoris, and raised as a boy for the first 1½ years of her life. However, she was then reassigned as a girl. Her clitoris was surgically removed. Her parents took their physician's advice and eliminated all evidence of her past as a boy. Her name was changed, her clothes were replaced, and her baby pictures destroyed (Fausto-Sterling, 2000).

Chase's intersex history was kept secret from her. It was not until much later in life that she entered therapy for severe depression and began to piece together the facts. Cheryl Chase realized that many of the difficulties she had experienced in growing up and her lack of sexual fulfillment were due to her treatment and the stigma attached to her intersex condition by the medical profession and therefore by her family. In 1993, Cheryl Chase founded the Intersex Society of North America, a nonprofit organization "dedicated to ending shame, secrecy and unwanted genital surgeries on people born with an anatomy that someone decided is not standard for male or female" (isna.org). In 2007, ISNA formed a new group, Accord Alliance, which today is a leader in improving health care and outcomes for intersex people and their families. Another activist group is StopIGM (StopIGM.org), which describes itself as an international human rights organization of survivors and allies fighting for the right to physical integrity and self-determination for all children born with variations of sex anatomy.

Sex researcher Milton Diamond has been a leader in uncovering the negative effects of medical treatment of intersex and transgender people and has been influential in calling for the development of better ethical standards in treatment. Moreover, he has repeatedly pointed out the need for a registry of cases, treatments, and long-term outcomes that physicians can refer to when working with intersex and transgender patients (Diamond, 2011). Scientists and researchers have much to contribute to the future of transgender studies, especially when they bring perspectives that integrate medical and biological knowledge with the psychological experience of gender variant people.

Stigma and discrimination are important issues for the intersex and transgender community. *Transphobia* or *genderism*, defined as negative attitudes toward gender-variant people, are prevalent, and a threat to the safety of transgender individuals (Levitt & Ippolito, 2014a). In 2016–17, there was a national furor over transgender people's use of public bathrooms, after North Carolina passed a discriminatory law. In response, the Obama administration issued guidelines to public schools nationally to allow transgender students to use bathrooms matching their gender identity. The Trump administration repealed those guidelines, once again allowing states to discriminate, and the Supreme Court refused to hear a test case brought by a transgender high school student. The great transgender bathroom panic shows the consequences of fear and misunderstanding. But for transgender people, the consequences of transphobia may be even more serious than the stigma of being excluded from a bathroom. In one court case, a jury awarded a mother nearly $3 million in damages after the death of her son following a traffic accident. Paramedics had stopped treating the son, who was cross-dressed, when they discovered his male genitals (Taylor, 2007). Transgender people, particularly trans women, face a high risk of hate crimes, including murder (Levitt & Ippolito 2014a).

The Federal definition of hate crimes now includes crimes committed against people on the basis of their gender, gender identity, and sexual orientation (Levitt & Ippolito, 2014a). The American Psychological Association has stated a non-discrimination policy on the basis of gender identity (APA, 2009). There has been real progress in the transgender movement. But every civil rights movement—from votes for women to racial desegregation to gay rights—has met resistance and backlash. Equality for gender nonconforming people is still a work in progress.

Transforming Ourselves: Accepting Biological and Social Diversity

The contents of this chapter make many students uncomfortable. The most disturbing idea of all may be the idea that not only gender, but *biological sex* is a social construction.

As the conservative Family Research Council claims, the belief in two biological sexes is for most people a "basic fact"—in other words, a belief that is deeply held and stubbornly resistant to change. However, Suzanne Kessler and Wendy McKenna, authors of a pioneering book on the social construction of sex, maintain that as long as "female" and "male" are seen as objective physical facts, sex and gender will be a basis for discrimination and oppression. They pointed out that until we see gender, in all of its manifestations *including the physical* as a social construction, we will be slow to change our thinking about it. Kessler and McKenna urged that "people must be confronted with the reality of other possibilities, as well as the possibility of other realities" (1978, p. 164). In this chapter, I have attempted to explore both realities and possibilities, encouraging you to begin to think of both sex and gender as not just female and male, feminine and masculine, but neither, both, and all of the above.

Exploring Further

∾

Fausto-Sterling, Anne (2000). *Sexing the body: Gender politics and the construction of sexuality.* New York: Basic Books.

  Very few people can claim expertise in reproductive biology, feminist theory, *and* the history of science. Fausto-Sterling is an exception. In this richly detailed book, she shows how cultural assumptions create biological realities.

Reis, E. (2009). *Bodies in doubt: An American history of intersex.* Baltimore: Johns Hopkins University Press.

  An expert historian offers a cultural, social, and medical history of how intersexuality has been regarded in America from early to modern times, showing that the meaning of ambiguous bodies is culturally determined.

Third Wave Foundation (www.thirdwavefoundation.org)

  A feminist activist group that works nationally to support young women and transgender youth ages 15 to 30. The foundation is led by a board of young women, men, and transgender activists and its goal is to work toward gender, racial, economic, and social justice by supporting young feminists and developing their leadership skills.

Text Credits

∾

p. 129, 134: Adapted from González, J. L., Prentice, L. G., & Ponder, S. W. (2005). Newborn Screening Case Management. Congenital Adrenal Hyperplasia: A Handbook for Parents. Texas Department of State Health Services. http://www.dshs.state.tx.us/newborn/hand_cah.shtm, Figure 5. **p. 136:** Contributed by Jessica Lord Bean, PhD. **pp. 132 ,138, 147:** Contributed by Annie B. Fox. **p. 140:** Morris, J. (1974). Conundrum. New York: Harcourt Brace Jovanovich. **p. 142:** Wassersug, R., Gray, R. E., Barbara, A., Trosztmer, C., Raj, R., & Sinding, C. (2007). Experiences of transwomen with hormone therapy. *Sexualities*, 10, 101–122. **p. 153:** Contributed by Dawn M. Brown. **p. 155:** ISNA

CHAPTER 6

Gendered Identities:
Childhood and Adolescence

"As the twig is bent, so the tree will grow." This proverb reflects the belief that what children learn in their early years shapes them for their entire lives. One of the most important tasks of children in all cultures is to learn how to be a woman or a man in their society.

Theories of Gender Development

Some psychological approaches to gender development stress how the environment shapes children's learning and behavior. Others stress cognitive factors within the child. The differences between these theories are relative, not absolute. Most developmental psychologists recognize that becoming gendered is a result of biological, cognitive, and social factors interacting with each other.

Social Learning Theory

Almost everyone can remember childhood events that taught what a good girl or boy should—or shouldn't—do. Perhaps we were expected to do gender-specific household chores—boys may take out the trash, while girls set the table for dinner. We may have been encouraged to follow a same-gender example, "Susan doesn't talk back to *her* mother. . . ." When asked to explain why men and women seem so different from each other, students frequently remember events like these and express the idea that "we've all been conditioned by society." This way of thinking about gender is consistent with *social learning theory,* an approach that emphasizes how children learn gendered behavior from their environment (Mischel, 1966, 1970; Bussey & Bandura, 2004).

Learning through Reinforcement

According to social learning theory, people learn their characteristic behavior patterns mainly through the process of *reinforcement* (Bandura & Walters, 1963). Behavior that is followed by desirable consequences is reinforced, and is more likely to occur in the future. If a behavior is never reinforced, it will eventually stop.

Reinforcement of gender-linked behaviors is not always obvious. Parents do not usually follow their little girl around feeding her candy when she picks up a doll and frowning at her when she picks up a toy bulldozer! But behavior shaping can be effective without being noticeable. If Dad merely glances up from his computer with a warm smile when little Debbie is coloring quietly in her coloring book but stays absorbed in his work when she builds a block tower, she will, according to social learning theory, be more likely to color than to build towers in the future. The newly learned behavior may generalize to other situations—Debbie may begin to prefer coloring books to blocks at preschool as well as at home. The lesson may also be quite broad—Debbie may learn that, in general, quiet play is nicer than active play.

Learning gender-typed behavior is made easier when parents set up the environment in such a way that some activities are more likely to occur (and thus be

FIGURE 6.1   Parental hindsight…

reinforced) than others. And research from the 1970s to the present shows that most kids' physical environments are very gender-stereotyped, so much so that untrained observers can instantly tell whether they are seeing a photo of a boy's room or a girl's room (Sutfin et al., 2008).

According to social learning theory, reinforcement can occur whether or not the adult is deliberately attempting to influence behavior. Even when adults do not *intend* to teach a lesson about gender, their behavior may reinforce gender differentiated behavior in children. Parents, teachers, grandparents, and other adults may sincerely believe that they treat boys and girls the same while they actually are reinforcing very different behaviors. (See Fig. 6.1.)

Learning through Imitation and Observation

Social learning theory proposes that people also learn by observing others and imitating their behavior. *Imitation*—copying someone else's behavior—seems to be spontaneous in young children (see Figure 6.2). Children imitate language, as many a parent has found to their dismay when a swear word used in an unguarded moment is repeated by their toddler. And they imitate all sorts of other behaviors. A young boy shaves with a toy razor while his father does the real thing; a young girl plays with her dolls as her mother feeds the baby. Imitation is often expressed in play, as children play house or play school.

Observational learning occurs through watching others' behavior. Even though it may not always be imitated right away, the lesson is stored for later use. A boy might observe that his father spends a lot of time watching sports on TV and later develop the same interests. A small girl may observe her mother shopping for clothes, planning new outfits, applying makeup, doing her hair, and dieting to lose weight. She learns through these observations that attractiveness is a very important dimension for women, although she might not express that knowledge very much until she is older.

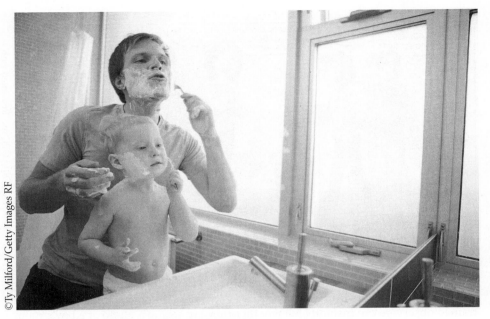

©Ty Milford/Getty Images RF

FIGURE 6.2   Children learn by imitating adults.

A classic study by Albert Bandura (1965) illustrates the operation of both reinforcement and imitation in learning to be aggressive. In Bandura's study, children
were shown one of three films. In all the films, an adult behaved aggressively by
hitting and kicking a large toy clown. In the first film, the adult was rewarded; in
the second, the adult was punished; and in the third, no specific consequences followed the aggression. The children were then given the opportunity to play with
the toy clown. Just as social learning theory would predict, the children imitated the
aggressive behavior most when it had been reinforced; that is, children who had
seen the first film were more aggressive than those who had seen either of the other
films. Overall, boys were more aggressive than girls.

In the next part of the experiment, the children were offered small treats for
performing as many of the adult model's aggressive behaviors as they could remember. Here all the children were more aggressive and overall the girls were nearly as
aggressive as the boys. Bandura's experiment shows that children imitate adult
models even when they are not directly reinforced for doing so. In particular, they
imitate models who are rewarded. Furthermore, children may learn a particular
behavior through observation but show no evidence of learning the behavior until
it is reinforced—like the girls in the second part of the experiment.

Learning Gender

Social learning theory explains gender identity and gender typing as the result of
moment-to-moment, day-to-day interactions between the developing child and the
immediate social environment—mother, father, and other caretakers; the media;

school; and playmates. It assumes that what a child learns about femininity and masculinity will vary according to the child's social class, ethnic group, and family composition—including any and all social and environmental factors.

The easier it is for children see gender-typed behavior, the easier it is for them to learn it. Most preschool children see their mothers in largely gender-typed behavior because mothers typically do more housework and childcare, and children are nearby when they do these activities. When children go to preschool or daycare, their caregivers are usually women, too. When it's mostly women who are seen cleaning house, changing diapers, and looking after young children, both girls and boys learn that these are women's work. Even if these tasks are shared by mom and dad at home, kids usually have plenty of opportunities to see gender-stereotypical behavior in the media. When mom goes to her job outside the home, the child does not observe her work directly and therefore doesn't get a chance to see her in a less gender-stereotyped way.

Although social learning theory emphasizes environmental influences on gender typing, cognitive factors also play a role. Once children know that there are two gender categories and have developed a core gender identity, they pay more attention to same-gender models than to other-gender models. The likelihood that a child will imitate the behavior of same-gender adults depends on what proportion of same-gender adults display the behavior. In other words, a preschool-age girl who sees one TV show about a woman who races sports cars may or may not play with toy cars. However, if she sees dozens of TV shows and commercials featuring women who take care of babies and children, she is very likely to play with dolls and imitate the child care behaviors that she has seen on TV. The more gender typical a behavior is, the more likely a child will imitate it. As the theory has evolved, and cognitive factors have been more emphasized, it is sometimes referred to as *social cognitive theory* (*Bussey & Bandura, 1999; 2004*).

Social learning/social cognitive theory implies that we can reduce gender typing in children. Parents, schools, and the media could choose to reinforce and model more adventurous, instrumental behavior for girls and more nurturing, cooperative behavior for boys. Implicit in the theory is the idea that gender typing can be lessened or even eliminated if we as a society and as individuals choose to do so.

Cognitive Theories

- Neil, age 6, has liked to draw ever since he could pick up a crayon. His drawings have earned him lots of attention and praise from his preschool teachers, and the refrigerator at home is covered with them. His parents are proud of his talent, and even took him to meet a real artist in his studio. They are amazed when Neil suddenly loses interest in drawing, saying that "art is for girls."
- Rosa, age 3½, goes to a female pediatrician for her regular checkups and has an aunt who is a physician. Therefore, her parents are astounded to hear her announce to a playmate, "Girls can't be doctors! Girls are nurses and doctors are boys!"

These behaviors are hard to explain using social learning theory. How did Neil and Rosa learn their gender typed beliefs when *non*stereotypical beliefs and attitudes were being reinforced and modeled for them? One answer to this question is offered by cognitive developmental and gender schema theories of gender development. These two cognitive theories offer the intriguing idea that children willingly socialize themselves to be masculine or feminine (Martin & Ruble, 2004).

Cognitive Developmental Theory

This approach to gender development began by building on the research of Jean Piaget, who observed that young children think in ways that are qualitatively different from older children and adults (Kohlberg, 1966). Piaget believed that children move through a fixed series of stages in their cognitive development and there are concepts they cannot grasp until they have reached the appropriate cognitive stage. Children's predictable errors in thinking indicate that they have different, less mature ways of thinking than adults—less sophisticated modes of cognitive organization. Regardless of what stage they have reached; however, children actively strive to interpret and make sense of the world around them. According to the cognitive developmental approach, gender identity and gender typing are the outcome of children's active cognitive structuring of their physical and social world.

Children understand some things about the concepts of sex and gender long before others. A 2- or 3-year-old child can answer correctly when asked if he or she is a boy or a girl, and is able to classify others too (Zosuls et al., 2009). However, the child may believe that people can change sex by changing their hairstyles or clothing. (At age 2½, one of my children maintained stubbornly that the *real* difference between boys and girls was that only girls wear barrettes.) The child may believe that boys can grow up to be mommies, as the following conversation between two young boys shows:

> Johnny (age 4½): *I'm going to be an airplane builder when I grow up.*
>
> Jimmy (age 4): *When I grow up, I'll be a mommy.*
>
> Johnny: *No, you can't be a mommy. You have to be a daddy.*
>
> Jimmy: *No, I'm going to be a mommy.*
>
> Johnny: *No, you're not a girl, you can't be a mommy.*
>
> Jimmy: *Yes, I can.*
>
> (Kohlberg, 1966, p. 95)

This conversation illustrates that children's understanding of gender is concrete and limited. Johnny, who is slightly older, understands *gender constancy*—he knows that gender is permanent—while Jimmy does not. By the age of 6 or 7, almost all children understand gender constancy. According to cognitive developmental theory, this is a result of cognitive maturation.

Once children know that they are, and always will be, one sex or the other, they turn to the task of matching the societal expectations for people of their sex. Almost immediately after they learn to label themselves and others by sex, children start to engage in gender typed play (Zosuls et al., 2009). They start to value behaviors, objects, and attitudes that are consistent with their gender. In fact, they exaggerate gender. Having adopted the binary construction of gender that is the only one allowed in our society, children make it their own. Boys become obsessed with superheroes, weapons, combat, and symbols of strength such as construction equipment and dinosaurs. Girls adorn themselves as princesses in glittery tiaras and insist on wearing pink frilly dresses even in freezing weather (Halim et al., 2011). None of this behavior needs much encouragement from parents; it is motivated from within. (See Figure 6.3.)

In middle childhood, many girls go through a startling shift from princess to tomboy—they want to play sports, wear pants, and be as active and adventurous as the boys are. About 35 percent to 50 percent of girls in elementary school label themselves as tomboys (Halim et al., 2011). Boys show no corresponding shift; most remain steadily gender-typed from preschool onward. Oddly, theories of gender development largely ignored the tomboy phenomenon for decades—perhaps because it was only about girls (which would be an example of androcentric thinking), or perhaps because their theories couldn't explain it. In a world that largely reinforces gender conformity, and where boys were toeing the line, how could so many girls be gender nonconforming and getting away with it?

Graduate student May Ling Halim and her colleagues (2011) proposed a theory to account for girls' shift to becoming tomboys in middle childhood. First, as girls mature cognitively, they realize their lower status and the possibility of gender discrimination. For some girls, the value they place on masculine attributes may

Courtesy of Mary Crawford

Courtesy of Julia Pallares Apgar

FIGURE 6.3 **According to cognitive developmental theory, young children often seek out gender-conforming activities and roles. This boy and girl have invented their own dress-up outfits.**

increase. Boys' activities and traits are appealing because girls can see that society appreciates and rewards boys and what they do more than girls and what they do. Second, girls' understanding of gender becomes more flexible as they mature cognitively. Being a tomboy is a way to enjoy some of the status privileges of boys while still being an acceptable girl. In support of this theory, an interview study of 5- to 13-year-old girls found that tomboys view themselves as girls with options, who don't necessarily reject "girl stuff," they just like "boy stuff," too. Interestingly, they had more flexible and egalitarian attitudes toward other kids' gender transgressions than more traditional children did (Ahlqvist et al., 2013).

Like social learning theory, cognitive developmental theory has generated a great deal of research. This research supports the idea that children's understanding of gender is related to their cognitive maturity. Research does not support the theory's claim that children become gender typed only after they acquire an understanding of gender constancy. On the contrary, children show a preference for gender-typed objects and activities by the age of 3 (Maccoby, 1998), even though, typically, they do not fully understand gender constancy until several years later. Recent research and theory accounting for gender *non*conformity in the form of tomboyism is an interesting addition to the cognitive developmental approach.

Gender Schema Theory

As discussed in Chapter 3, a schema is a network of mental associations. According to schema theory, it is difficult or impossible to understand information when you cannot connect it to a schema or when you unintentionally connect it to the wrong schema. *Gender schema theory* uses this cognitive approach to explain gender typing. Like other schemas, the gender schema is used by the individual as an aid to thinking and understanding (Bem, 1981). According to gender schema theory, the gender schema is learned very early, and it guides the individual in becoming gender typed. As children learn the contents of their society's gender schema, they learn which attributes are linked to their own sex, and hence to themselves. Gender schema theory conceives of gender typing as a readiness to organize the world in terms of gender and to process information in terms of gender associations. This is more than just learning how boys and girls are ranked on each dimension—that boys are supposed to be stronger than girls, for example— but also that the dimension of strength is more important in evaluating boys (Bem, 1981).

In other words, a difference between people who are highly gender typed and those who are not is that gender typed people have a well-developed gender schema and rely on it spontaneously in making sense of the world—they are *gender-schematic.* Less gender typed people have less developed gender schemas and rely more on other schemas—they are *gender-aschematic.* The difference is a matter of degree because everyone in our society has developed some sort of schema for gender.

Gender schemas lead to selective attention and selective memory. In one experiment, 5- and 6-year old children saw pictures of boys and girls doing stereotype-consistent activities (such as a boy playing with a truck) and stereotype-inconsistent ones (such as a girl using a hammer). A week later, when the children's memory for the pictures was tested, they tended to misremember the stereotype-inconsistent pictures—for example, they thought they had seen a boy using a hammer (Martin & Halverson, 1983). This study suggests that as early as the age of five, children have gender schemas and use them to filter information as they categorize the world around them. By this age, they already believe that certain occupations are for men and others are for women. When asked what they would like to be when they grow up, they are likely to choose an occupation that is stereotyped for their gender (Helwig, 1998).

Gender schema theory suggests that children *can* be brought up in ways that minimize the development of a gender schema, and thus bypass gender-stereotyped thinking and behavior. If others around them paid less attention to gender, children would not automatically categorize by it, any more than they automatically categorize in terms of eye color. If they were taught to use the concept of sex to refer to anatomical differences, they would not assimilate irrelevant dimensions to the gender schema. They would differentiate male and female in sexuality and reproduction, but other aspects of behavior would remain gender-neutral (Bem, 1983). Gender schema theory stimulated a great deal of research in topics such as gender stereotyping in children's books and toys and in psychological comparisons of more or less gender-typed individuals. It has been useful for over three decades as a framework for understanding the social scope of gender (Starr & Zurbriggen, 2016).

In summary, social learning and cognitive theories emphasize different influences on children's gender development. Social learning theory maintains that children are shaped by the people and environments they encounter in everyday life. Cognitive theories emphasize that the child's mind is actively trying to comprehend and categorize gender information. Cognitive developmental theory proposes that this occurs in distinct stages, whereas gender schema theory emphasizes the gradual development of a complex mental network about gender and its assimilation to the self. No single theory has all the answers, but virtually all psychologists agree that social forces interact with biological and cognitive factors in gender development (Powlishta et al., 2001). In what follows, we will look in detail at gender influences in children's lives, showing how these factors interact to produce adults who fit in to the gender system.

Gender in the Child's Daily Life

Starting almost immediately after birth, an infant is viewed differently and treated differently depending on its sex. The effect of this treatment is to mold children into the gender norms of their culture. At first, parents and family are the strongest influence on gender. As the child grows, peers become more important. Meanwhile, toys, books, movies, videogames, and TV provide highly gendered messages. The child's own concept of gender interacts with all these influences, as he or she forms cognitive schemas and progresses to more cognitively mature ways of thinking about gender. These influences—from adults, other children, the media, the physical environment, and the child's own cognitive development—construct gender at the interactional level. They are all important in shaping adults who fit into their society's gender system and we will look at each in more detail.

Parental Influences

As soon as a woman announces that she is pregnant, others ask—boy or girl? Today, parents usually know the sex of their child before its birth via ultrasound imaging. But this is a recent development. Throughout history, there were many superstitious methods of guessing the future baby's sex. If the mother "carries high," it is a boy; if she "carries low," it's a girl. If the fetus is active, moving and kicking a lot, it must be a boy. If the mother is sick during pregnancy, it's a girl. In much of this folk wisdom, the symbolically more negative characteristic of a pair (low/high, sick/healthy) was used to predict a girl. And there are many folk methods for insuring the birth of a son, such as taking herbs, eating particular foods, and even wishful thinking. When I traveled in rural China, I saw an identical large poster tacked up on the wall in several village homes: a pair of adorable fat baby boys, naked from the waist down. I finally asked about it, and found that the reason for its popularity is a folk belief that if a married woman looks at images of boy babies, she is more likely to conceive a son.

The birth of a girl is a disappointment in many traditional cultures, as these proverbs show:

To be born a girl is to have an ill fate. (Nepal)

One daughter is more than enough; three sons are still too few. (South Korea)

Boys: The Preferred Sex

In some societies, the preference to have a son is so extreme that it reduces the survival rate of baby girls. Throughout history, some societies have practiced *female infanticide.* In ancient Greece, infant girls were sometimes left on a mountainside to die of exposure or be eaten by wild animals (Rouselle, 2001). Although no society today officially approves of female infanticide, there are persistent reports that it still takes place in areas where girls are particularly devalued. For example, in rural China, there are far more births of boys than girls recorded. In the southern Indian state of Tamil Nadu, the death rate for female infants—when there is no obvious medical cause—is 5 to 17 times higher than for male infants (Mahalingam et al., 2007). Women describe methods such as poisoning infants over a period of several days by mixing milk with a toxic tree sap (Diamond-Smith et al., 2008). The high rate of female infanticide in this region prompted the government to offer bonuses to parents whose daughters survived childhood (Miller, 2001).

Selecting boys for survival occurs in other ways, too. *Female-selective abortion—*aborting healthy fetuses only because they are female—is widely practiced in East and South Asian countries including South Korea, Vietnam, China, India, Taiwan, and Pakistan. For example, almost immediately after fetal sex-determination techniques became available in Indian cities, social workers reported huge imbalances in the gender ratio of aborted fetuses; one study of 8,000 abortions showed that 7,997 were female fetuses (Hrdy, 1988).

Estimates of the number of women missing from the world's population due to the preference for sons range from 115 million up to 200 million (Grech, 2015). The problem is most acute in societies where there is increasing prosperity (allowing couples to pay for fetal sex tests and medical abortions) along with strong traditional ideas about the greater worth of sons. Methods of sex-selective abortion, female infanticide, and neglect of baby girls are common knowledge in these societies (Diamond-Smith et al., 2008), and have severely affected the sex ratio in many countries. In China, officials predict a future shortage of some 30 to 40 million women, meaning that an equal number of men will never be able to marry (Hesketh et al., 2011; Huang, 2014). Only in South Korea is there now a more normal sex ratio, probably because modernization has weakened traditional attitudes that foster an extreme preference for sons (Chun & Gupta, 2009).

The reasons for son preference are related to patriarchy. The more patriarchal a society is, the more men control economic, political and social power, and the more the ideology of gender supports their continued dominance. In some traditional Asian societies, females tend to be economically dependent on fathers and husbands, have lower social status, and are considered impure or polluting. Tradition holds that only a son can provide for his parents in their old age. All of these factors combine to influence both women and men to prefer having sons and avoid having daughters. Moreover, because of dowry systems that require a bride's family to provide large sums of money and costly possessions to the groom's family, the birth of a daughter is an economic disaster. In southern India, although sex-selective abortion is illegal, mobile ultrasound/abortion clinics cruise rural villages advertising, "Pay 50 rupees now to save 50,000 rupees later" (Diamond-Smith et al., 2008; Miller, 2001).

What about preference for boys in our own society? The Gallup poll, which measures the attitudes of large representative samples of U.S. adults, has asked in ten polls since 1941, "If you could have only one child, which would you prefer to have—a boy, or a girl?" Men's preference, in every poll, was for a boy. In the most recent (2011) poll, men favored a boy over a girl by 49 percent to 22 percent. Women were more evenly divided: 31 percent favored a boy and 33 percent favored a girl. (The remaining men and women expressed no preference.) (Newport, 2011).

There is no way to know how often prospective parents are using sex selection techniques or female-selective abortion in the U.S. In-depth interviews with 65 married Indian women living in the U.S. who had sought prenatal ultrasound services revealed that 40 percent of the women had terminated prior pregnancies with female fetuses and 89 percent of those carrying female fetuses in their current pregnancy obtained an abortion (Puri et al., 2011). The women reported pressure to have a son from female in-laws and husbands; 62 percent described verbal abuse and 33 percent described physical abuse due to failing to produce a male child.

Parents: Not Gender-Neutral

From the first minutes of a baby's life, its parents are forming impressions of this new little person. Do parents perceive their babies in gender-stereotyped ways? In one study, mothers and fathers were asked to rate their newborns on a list of attributes provided by the experimenters. Parents of sons rated their babies as stronger, as well as less delicate, feminine and fine-featured than did parents of daughters. However, when asked to provide their own descriptions of the baby, the parents used language that did not differ according to the baby's sex (Karraker et al., 1995). This study suggests that gender stereotyping of infants can be primed—in this case, by providing a list of gender-stereotyped attributes. Of course, our society provides many ways to prime gender stereotypes about infants (see Box 6.1).

When they were asked the same questions a week later, mothers in this study no longer stereotyped their infants, but fathers still did (Karraker et al., 1995). The mothers may have decreased their tendency to stereotype because they got to know their babies as individuals, whereas the fathers, who had less contact with the infants, did not. Many other studies of infants and young children show that fathers view their children in gender-stereotyped ways more than mothers do. Although fathers may stereotype more, they have less opportunity to convey their gender schemas to their offspring because they spend much less time overall with infants and young children (Tenenbaum & Leaper, 2002).

Differences in parental behavior may provide important models for children to observe and imitate. Everything a father or mother does when the children are present provides an example of expected female and male behavior. Take nurturance, for example. In most societies, young children see that mothers more often take care of their bodily needs, soothe and comfort them, and play gently with them (Bronstein, 2006).

One of the most important ways parents socialize babies and young children is by talking to them. In the toddler and preschool years, girls and boys get different kinds and amounts of talk about emotion, contributing to gender differences in

Box 6.1 ∾ Gender Stereotyping Starts Early
"It's a boy!" "It's a girl!"

A study conducted by Judith Bridges (1993) of the visual images and verbal messages in birth congratulations cards sampled 61 cards announcing the birth of a girl and 61 announcing the birth of a boy from 18 stores and 4 different municipalities in Hartford, Connecticut. Content analysis of the cards revealed stereotypical differences between boy and girl cards. Visual images on boy cards included more physical activity, such as action toys and active babies, than that of girl cards. Girl cards included more verbal messages of expressiveness, including sweetness and sharing. Surprisingly, boy cards presented a message of happiness for the parents and/or the baby more than girl cards.

Even though this study was conducted almost 25 years ago, birth congratulations cards still tend to portray gender stereotyping. When I checked out the greeting card section of a local retailer in 2017, I found that most of the cards portrayed girl and boy babies very differently. In fact, there were only a handful of gender neutral cards in the whole section! In addition to the more obvious pink versus blue distinction, several of the boy cards featured messages that referred to the new baby as the new "little man" or "little guy" of the house. One card had the phrase "Boys will be Boys!" in extra large print on the front. Several cards for boys told parents they were embarking on an "adventure." On the front of one girl card was a poem, "Let's see . . . ten little fingers, ten little toes, 500 pairs of shoes . . ." Another card for girls featured a picture of a baby girl wearing a princess crown and holding a scepter. What activities and traits do these cards imply that parents can expect from their children? How might these expectations create self-fulfilling prophecies?

Contributed by Annie B. Fox and Michelle Kaufman

emotionality (Chapter 4). Overall, mothers talk more to children than fathers do, and their talk is more supportive and emotion-focused, while fathers' talk is more directive and informative (Leaper et al., 1998). These differences in parental behavior are congruent with gender stereotypes of expressiveness for females and instrumentality for males. Mothers also talk more and use more supportive speech to their daughters in particular. This pattern is consistent with socializing girls toward connectedness and communality.

Parents also play with their sons and daughters differently during the preschool years. They do more pretend and fantasy play with girls, and fathers in particular do more rough and tumble, physical, and pretend-aggression play with boys (Lindsey et al., 1997; Lindsey & Mize, 2001). In a meta-analysis of over 150 North American studies, fathers were more likely than mothers to encourage their children toward gender-typed play and activities (Lytton & Romney, 1991).

It is clear that children pick up the messages their parents send. In one study of 4-year-olds, almost half of the boys said that they could not play with girls' toys because their fathers would think they were bad (Raag & Rackliff, 1998). In a meta-analysis, parents' attitudes about their own masculinity/femininity as well as their gender-stereotyped attitudes about others significantly predicted their children's gender-related beliefs and attitudes. The more traditional the parents' gender ideology, the more gender typed their children were. Interestingly, the effect was stronger for mothers (Tenenbaum & Leaper, 2002). Thus, the gender schemas of children, which are applied both to themselves and to others, are formed partly through exposure to their parents' gender schemas.

Before you conclude that parents are entirely responsible for turning out gender typed girls and boys, it is important to remember a few points. First, meta-analyses show that the areas where parents treat their sons and daughters similarly are more numerous than the areas where they treat them differently (Lytton & Romney, 1991). Second, the most recent meta-analysis was done on studies only to the 1980s, which were largely restricted to white middle-class heterosexual families. Perhaps parental attitudes about gender have gotten more flexible since then, and less traditional families may socialize their children differently. For example, a more recent study that compared children adopted by lesbian couples, gay male couples, and heterosexual couples found that the boys and girls in gay and lesbian families were less gender typed in their play than those in heterosexual-parent families (Goldberg et al., 2012). Moreover, parental treatment of children may be influenced by the children's own characteristics. Parents may talk more to girls because girls on average are more responsive to talk. They may play more rough and scary games with boys because boys enjoy them more. The child's characteristics probably interact with the parent's beliefs about gender to influence parents' differential treatment of sons and daughters. Finally, there are plenty of other influences over which parents have little control.

Peer Influences

From an early age, children choose to play with same-gender friends—a pattern called *gender segregation.* This preference emerges around the age of two, when girls start to orient more toward playing with other girls; boys' preference for other boys develops about a year later (Powlishta et al., 2001). Gender segregation increases steadily during the preschool years. By age 4½, about 90 percent of a child's social playtime is with same-gender others (Martin & Fabes, 2001). This spontaneous gender-sorting occurs not only in our own society but also in many others (Fouts et al., 2013).

Adults do not usually initiate or encourage gender segregation. Why then do children self-segregate by gender? One explanation, based on cognitive developmental theory, is that they want to fit into their prescribed gender roles, and it's easier in same-sex play groups. Another theory is that children choose others with compatible play styles. According to this explanation, boys on average have a higher activity level than girls (a difference that may have a biological basis), and may prefer to play with others who are as active as they are. Girls may be more verbally and socially advanced, and prefer to play with others who are as good at sharing and communicating as they are (Moller & Serbin, 1996). Both explanations are supported by research. For example, a study on elementary school kids' attitudes about their same-gender peers showed that they have an ingroup bias and positive expectancies about ingroup interactions (Zosuls et al., 2011). In other words, kids self-segregate by gender both because they prefer the company of other girls (or boys) and because they like to do the same kinds of things that the other girls (or boys) are doing (Leaper, 2015). When kids play in gender-segregated groups their play styles diverge and become increasingly gender typed (Martin & Fabes, 2001). Boys' play in gender-segregated groups involves more competition, confrontation, and risk-taking; girls' play in their groups involves more negotiation, cooperation, talking about oneself, and contact with adults (Maccoby, 1998). The more territorial and physical a game is, the more likely it is that elementary school children will segregate while playing it (Kelle, 2000). In other words, gender differences in play are shaped by the peer context.

Gendered play in turn affects friendship styles. By the time they are in fourth or fifth grade, girls' friendships are organized around confiding in each other and talking about others, whereas boys' friendships are more often organized around sports and other activities. These different friendship styles continue into adulthood. The playgroups of childhood are an important step in creating each new generation of gender-typed adults (Maccoby, 1998).

Gender-segregated play is not just a matter of difference. It is also a matter of status. Boys in particular create in-group solidarity and derogate the out-group (girls). For example, boys taunt other boys who do not conform to group norms by calling them faggot (Thorne & Luria, 1986) or sissy (Edwards et al., 2011). They also reinforce gender segregation by teasing and making jokes about romantic attraction. If Tory is a low-status, unpopular girl, boys may tease another boy by accusing him of liking her and saying that he will get "cooties" from her. Girls rarely tease other girls for being tomboys or accuse boys of having cooties. When a girl picks a fight, she may be called mean, but she is not accused of being like a boy (Shields, 2002). Usually it is boys who patrol the boundaries between groups by encouraging opposition between boys and girls, defining cross-gender contact in terms of sex and pollution, and scapegoating some girls as "untouchables" (Thorne & Luria,

1986). For unpopular girls like Tory, hostile teasing from high-status boys may make playtime into a nightmare (Keltner et al., 2001).

When boys learn competitive, dominance-oriented play styles, and girls learn more cooperative styles, girls are at a disadvantage in mixed groups. The tactics they use to gain power and influence with other girls (persuasion and negotiation) simply do not work with boys. In one early study, children were allowed to play with a movie-viewing toy in groups of four (two boys and two girls). Only one child at a time could see the movie. In this situation, boys ended up with three times as much viewing time as girls (Charlesworth & LaFreniere, 1983). Similar patterns may occur when children have to share computers in a classroom or compete for a teacher's attention. The tactics boys learn in all-boy play groups help them achieve dominance in many different kinds of interactions.

We should not conclude that girls are not competitive or not interested in status. The difference seems to be that girls' play style teaches them interpersonal skills, which they prefer to use over overt physical aggression, whether they are competing or cooperating. When girls want to be aggressive and dominant, they may engage in *relational aggression*—hostile acts that attempt to damage another's close relationships or social standing (Crick & Rose, 2000). In other words, a girl may spread a rumor about another girl, block her from sitting down on the bus or in the lunchroom, or post a photo on Snapchat or Instagram of all her other friends at a party so everyone knows exactly who's being left out (Maybury, 2015). Relational aggression can be just as harmful as physical aggression.

Traditionally, psychologists have claimed that there is a consistent gender difference in aggression, with boys being more aggressive than girls from early childhood (Maccoby & Jacklin, 1974). This supposed gender difference may have been the result of an androcentric definition of aggression, because it included only physical aggression. A meta-analysis showed that there is indeed a moderate effect size for physical aggression in favor of boys (Archer, 2004). However, when relational aggression is added to the mix, the picture is more complicated; the same meta-analysis showed a small effect size in favor of girls. And what about cross-cultural differences and similarities? A study of 7–10 year-old children in China, Colombia, Italy, Jordan, Kenya, the Philippines, Sweden, Thailand, and the United States, which asked the kids themselves to report on their use of both kinds of aggression, found that in all nine countries boys were more physically aggressive, but there were no consistent gender differences in relational aggression (Lansford et al., 2012). In sum, girls and boys may favor different kinds of aggression on average, but there is far more similarity than difference. Boys are somewhat more physically aggressive, and both girls and boys use indirect, relational aggression. Just about every school has its share of both "mean girls" and "mean boys."

Gender segregation and the resulting differences in interaction style are not absolute or inevitable. In a study of a multicultural group of 4-year-olds in a Head Start program, girls and boys who were less gender-segregated and gender-stereotyped in their play were just as well-adjusted and socially competent as their peers (Martin et al., 2012). In a classic observational study of elementary school children on their playgrounds, there was a great deal of variety in play. Unsegregated and nonstereotypical play actually occurred quite often. The strictest segregation was among the most popular and socially visible students; others quietly went their own way, often violating the rules of gender segregation (Thorne, 1993). Cross-gender friendships do occur, though they may be kept out of sight. I remember a middle-school friendship with a boy who, like me, was obsessed with chemistry experiments. We never talked at school, but on Saturdays we happily burned holes in our parents' carpets as we tried to mix potions that could eat through any substance. Our friendship was underground but it was important to both of us.

Gendered Environments

Girls and boys grow up together, but their environments foster different activities, values, and beliefs. Here we look at just one of many aspects of the environment: the toys children play with.

When I was eight I really wanted a chemistry set. I asked for it for my birthday, but got a Cinderella watch instead. I liked the watch but I still wanted a chemistry set. I put it on my Christmas list but Santa failed me. Finally, on my ninth birthday, my wish was granted and my career in chemical catastrophes began. I was not surprised, years later, to come across a study showing that children were more likely to get an item on their Christmas list if it was gender-stereotypical than if it was not (Etaugh & Liss, 1992). My parents weren't being mean; they just relied on their gender schemas when providing me with toys. And they weren't alone. Studies conducted from the 1970s onward, in several countries, show that boys and girls as young as 5-months-old are provided with different toys, such as more vehicles for boys and more dolls for girls (Nelson, 2005; Pomerleau et al., 1990; Rheingold & Cook, 1975). Gender typing in toys is not due only to parents' influence. From an early age, children themselves express strong preferences for gender-typed toys.

Gendered toy preferences increase during the preschool and elementary school years (Powlishta et al., 2001). Both boys and girls continue to play with gender-neutral toys. It is only the supposedly opposite-gender toys that they avoid—and boys do this more than girls do. Children develop activity preferences, too, based on their toys. In general, girls' toys are associated with attractiveness, nurturing, and housework skills, whereas boys' toys are associated with violence, competition, and danger (Blakemore & Centers, 2005).

These gender-typed patterns are blatantly reinforced by stereotypical marketing that is directly aimed at children. Almost all children's toys are color-coded: pink and purple for girls, everything else for boys. Dozens of studies have shown that toddlers develop gender-typed color preferences between the age of 2 and 3 and avoid toys with the "wrong" colors for their gender (Weisgram et al., 2014; Wong & Hines, 2015a, 2015b). Large retailers like Toys "R" Us clearly distinguish boys' aisles, with brightly colored action figures, tanks, trucks, and guns, from girls' aisles, with pastel-colored crafts, dolls, toy appliances, and makeup kits (Bannon, 2000). When researchers analyzed the 410 toys listed for boys and the 208 toys listed for girls on the Disney Store website, they found a similar pattern: brightly colored action figures, building toys, weapons, and vehicles for boys, and pink and purple dolls, beauty gear, jewelry, and domestic tools for girls. The 91 toys listed as suitable for both girls and boys were in colors designed to appeal to boys, who presumably would not go near anything pink or purple (Auster & Mansbach, 2012). Today, every aspect of children's immediate environments is decorated with highly gendered images: their backpacks, T-shirts, pajamas, shoes, even their water bottles. For boys, it's Spiderman or the Transformers, images of aggressive, combative masculinity. For girls, it's Disney princesses or pop stars, images of beauty and hyper-femininity. It seems that no toy or activity is exempt from having gender imposed on it. Even with an undeniably gender-neutral toy, such as a bicycle, manufacturers create two versions—a pink, flower-trimmed bike with a wicker basket for girls, and a black, heavy-duty BMX version for boys. Distinctions like these foster the development of extended gender schemas in young children. It's as though the adults in their lives are telling them, "Gender is the most important category in the world—even your bike has to have one!" Some parents and child development experts are starting to resist gendered toy marketing to kids (see Box 6.2).

BOX 6.2 ∞ The Gendered Toy Marketing Debate

Whether shopping in a physical store or online, you've likely seen the gendered ways that toys are marketed to boys and girls. However, in 2015, two large retailers made efforts to decrease or remove gendered toy marketing. Target announced it was removing gender-based labels for girls' and boys' toys in their stores, and Amazon.com stopped using gender-based categories for toys in its search filters. Gendered toy marketing (GTM) is a hotly debated topic. Recently psychologist Cordelia Fine

and philosopher Emma Rush dissected the debate, analyzing the arguments on both sides of the issue.

Proponents of GTM argue that such marketing reflects fundamental differences between boys and girls, and therefore has either a neutral, or positive effect on children by emphasizing toys that highlight their "natural" characteristics. However, the psychological research on gender, child development, and children's toy preferences fails to support such an argument. Experimental and

Continued on next page

BOX 6.2 ∾ The Gendered Toy Marketing Debate (*Concluded*)

observational studies of children's toy preferences demonstrate substantial overlap between boys' and girls' preferences, and suggests that those preferences are malleable. The research also suggests that GTM reinforces gender stereotypes and can increase stereotyping and prejudice in children. Proponents of GTM also argue that shifting to gender-neutral marketing would be economically untenable. However, marketing toys in gender neutral ways could actually increase profits by opening the potential market of a toy to all children, instead of just half of them.

There are a number of activist organizations and campaigns across the world dedicated to eliminating gender stereotyping in toys, books, clothes, and media. A few of these campaigns are described below.

Resources for Activism

Let Toys be Toys http://lettoysbetoys.org.uk
Let Books be Books http://lettoysbetoys.org.uk /letbooksbebooks/
Parent-led campaign asking the toy and book industries to end GTM and instead focus on organizing and labeling toys and books according to theme or function. Since it launched in 2014, ten book publishers have agreed to remove the "boys" and "girls" labels from their books.

A Mighty Girl http://www.amightygirl.com
World's largest collection of books, toys, movies, and music for those dedicated to raising empowered girls.

Pink Stinks http://www.pinkstinks.co.uk/
Campaign targeting the restrictive and damaging messages directed at girls through the "pinkification" of clothing, toys, and popular media.

Play Unlimited http://www.playunlimited.org.au
Australian campaign that works toward ending GTM and instead promoting non-restrictive play experiences for boys and girls. To counter the heavily gendered toy marketing taking place during the holiday season, they sponsor "No Gender December" where they encourage people to "give gifts not stereotypes."

Source: Fine, C. & Rush, E. "Why does all the girls have to buy pink stuff?" The ethics and science of the gendered toy marketing debate. *Journal of Business Ethics* (2016). doi:10.1007/s10551-016-3080-3

Contributed by Annie B. Fox

Media Influences

The books children read, the TV shows they watch, and the video games they play are all powerful sources of gender socialization. Starting in the 1970s, feminists drew attention to gender stereotyping in children's readers and storybooks. Several studies from the 1970s to the early 1990s showed that boys and men more often were represented as independent, active, competent, and aggressive, whereas girls and women more often were shown as passive, helpless, nurturing, or dependent. Overall, males appeared much more often than females as the main character.

Gender stereotyping declined but did not disappear in the 1990s. A study of 83 children's books published from 1995 to 1999 showed that about half of the main characters were female, a big improvement from the past. But most of the women still were shown as mothers or grandmothers, with the occasional washerwoman or witch thrown in (Gooden & Gooden, 2001). Men were shown in a much greater variety of roles and occupations than women, but they were rarely shown taking care of children, and no man was ever shown doing household chores. A content analysis of school readers during the same time period showed that male characters were more argumentative, aggressive, and competitive, whereas female characters were more affectionate, emotionally expressive, passive, and tender (Evans & Davies, 2000).

Have things changed in the twenty-first century? Not so much. A study of 200 top-selling and award-winning children's books that were published after 2001 showed that there were nearly twice as many male as female main characters—a throwback to the 1970s. Females were far more likely to be shown nurturing others, and both males and females were shown almost exclusively in stereotypical occupations. The good news: Females were no longer more passive or more likely to be rescued (Hamilton et al., 2006).

With help like this, it's not surprising that children learn gender stereotypes at an early age—even when they cuddle up with Mom or Dad for a bedtime story. As psychologist Mykol Hamilton put it, children's books provide "nightly reinforcement of the idea that boys and men are more interesting and important than are girls and women" (Hamilton et al., 2006, p. 764). Fortunately, even very young children can learn to think critically about sexism in their storybooks with a little help (see Box 6.3).

Most children spend a lot more time watching TV and playing video games than they spend with their reader or library book. Kids between the ages of 2 to 11 watch about 24 hours of TV a week (Nielsen, 2015). What they see on children's programming echoes the gender stereotypes in programming for grown-ups: female characters are underrepresented; girls are portrayed as more frail, emotional, fearful, and nurturant; boys are portrayed as more dominant, aggressive, and attention-seeking. What do kids learn about boy-girl relationships? In a content analysis of popular kids' programs (*Drake and Josh, Hannah Montana*, and others), the most common relationship themes were boys valuing girls only for how "hot" they are, and girls objectifying themselves and flattering boys (Kirsch & Murnen, 2015).

Social cognitive theory, cognitive developmental theory, and gender schema theory all predict that children will internalize and imitate what they see on TV, and sure enough, they do. A meta-analysis showed that the more a child watches TV, the more likely the child is to have gender-stereotyped beliefs (Herrett-Skjellum & Allen, 1996). In a study of 134 preschool children, the more time a boy spent watching superhero programs, the more male-stereotyped his play was when measured a year later. For both boys and girls, watching superhero programs predicted more play with weapons a year later (Coyne et al., 2014). And several studies have linked viewing TV violence with real-life violence. For example, a longitudinal study of third-, fourth-, and fifth-grade students found that higher exposure to violence on TV, video games, and movies at the beginning of the school year predicted more verbal aggression, relational aggression, and physical aggression, and less positive social behavior, later in the school year (Gentile et al., 2011).

Fortunately, there are alternatives to simplistic gender stereotypes aimed at kids. Disney characters like Mulan and Elsa in *Frozen* enlarge the possibilities for girls. The cartoon show, *My Little Pony: Friendship Is Magic*, became a cultural phenomenon during its 4-year run (2010–2014). It appealed to young girls with its cute characters, rainbows, and pastel colors, but it also provided a healthy

BOX 6.3 ～ Little Kids Scope Out the Hidden Messages in Their Storybooks— And Come Up with Some Bright Ideas for Gender Equality

©Blend Images/Getty Images RF

Gwendolyn, Milo, and their friends are not even four years old yet, but with the help of their teachers at ChildRoots, a progressive preschool in Portland, Oregon, they are learning to think critically about media influences. One way teachers do it is by encouraging the children to look for "hidden messages" in storybooks; another is by offering them counter-stereotypical stories. Here is a snippet of the children's conversation after their teacher, Morgan, read them a book called *My Mom Is a Firefighter* and asked them what they thought about the story:

MILO: I wish my mom was a firefighter!

MAYA: Yeah, and maybe she would let you use the hose!

API: There is one girl firefighter in this book and four boy firefighters.

GWENDOLYN: What is the real word for firefighter?

TEACHER MORGAN: Do you mean firemen?

GWENDOLYN: Yeah, maybe if you say firemen then girls will think that they can't try. But I'm gonna try.

Some boys noted that they had shirts and socks with fire trucks on them. The children went on to discuss whether firefighting toys and clothes are just for boys.

GWENDOLYN: The people who make clothes are trying to trick girls so they they'll think they can't be firefighters and that is not nice.

MILO: Hey, I have a good idea! We could make some clothes for girls that have fire trucks on them, then show them to girls!

GWENDOLYN: But how can we show them?

MILO: We'll just hold up the shirts so they see! (Milo draws a picture on bright yellow paper.) I'm making a fire truck shirt that's for girls. . . . Here's the hose. I want my mom to see this!

Reprinted by permission of ChildRoots and with thanks to Teacher Morgan and the parents of the remarkable Api, Gwendolyn, Maya, and Milo.

challenge to gender stereotypes, according to a content analysis by media researchers: all the primary characters are female, they are in positions of authority, and they lead the development of the plot in non-stereotypical ways (Valiente & Rasmussen, 2015). Unfortunately, it seems boys are still not allowed to like shows about friendship and empathy; many boys reported being called "gay" for watching the show. In 2014, a North Carolina school district banned nine-year-old Grayson Bruce from bringing his (blue) *My Little Pony* backpack to school because he was being bullied about it. It wasn't until the story went viral that the district relented and decided to educate students about bullying instead of punishing the victim (Heigl, 2014).

Video games surpass all other media both in popularity and in sexism. Gaming is the leading online activity for children over the age of 6—about 84 percent reported that they played a video game in the past month and 20 percent played every day. Gamers also spend time reading gaming magazines, participating in gaming blogs, and talking with friends about games (Dill & Thill, 2007). Boys aged 11 to 14 are the biggest gamers of all.

What are kids learning from video games? One research team summarized the gender messages like this: "a sexist, patriarchal view that men are aggressive and powerful and that women are not healthy, whole persons but sex objects, eye candy, and generally second-class citizens" (Dill & Thill, 2007). Females are consistently underrepresented in video games. However, it may be better when women are absent, since when they do appear it is usually as sex objects, helpless victims, or targets of aggression. Male characters are shown with far more abilities and powers (Miller & Summers, 2007).

Video games are more popular with boys, but Barbie dolls and all the media products connected with them are more popular with girls (see Figure 6.4). Among U.S. girls aged 3 to 10, 99 percent own at least one Barbie doll, and the average number owned is eight. Many girls report going through a phase where they identified intensely with Barbie, thought she was perfect, and wanted to be just like her (Dittmar et al., 2006). But Barbie's proportions give girls an everyday model of extremely unrealistic body shape. If Barbie were a full-size woman, she would have a 42-inch bust, 18-inch waist, and 33-inch hips, and her body weight would be so low that she could not menstruate (Dittmar et al., 2006; Gray & Phillips, 1998). The odds of a real woman having the same proportions as Barbie are 1 in 100,000. Ken is considerably more realistic—the odds of a man having his proportions are about 1 in 50 (Norton et al., 1996).

Should we be concerned about Barbie's effects on young girls? On the one hand, it's just a doll. On the other hand, it's a doll that provides a model of how a girl should look and be. In other words, Barbie is a powerful tool of gender socialization. Let's look at two studies. In the first, 5- to 8-year-old girls saw images of Barbie dolls, Emme dolls (a larger weight woman based on the full-figure model of the same name), or no dolls, and then completed measures of body image. Younger girls exposed to the Barbie images reported a lower satisfaction with their bodies and a greater desire to be thinner than girls in the other conditions (Dittmar et al., 2006). Body dissatisfaction can lead to unhealthy eating, excessive dieting, and ultimately to eating disorders.

FIGURE 6.4 **Barbie is everywhere. These little girls are playing outside their house in Kathmandu, Nepal.**

In the second study, girls aged 4 to 7 years were randomly assigned to play either with a Barbie or Mrs. Potato Head doll for 5 minutes and then asked about 10 occupations for their future: How many could they do, and how many could a boy do? Overall, girls believed that boys could do more occupations than they could, and the difference was larger for girls who had played with Barbie (Sherman & Zurbriggen, 2014). These two studies show that even a few minutes of Barbie play can affect young girls' body image and career beliefs. Maybe Barbie is not just a harmless fashion toy.

It's not just Barbie, either. Another study found that 58 percent of fashion dolls sold at 4 major U.S. stores had moderate to very sexualizing characteristics (Starr & Zurbriggen, 2014), part of a disturbing trend to sexualize girls at younger and younger ages (APA, 2007). *Sexualization* is defined as inappropriately imposing sexuality on a person, sexually objectifying a person, or valuing another for only their sexual appeal (APA, 2007). You don't have to go far to see examples of the sexualization of young girls. Walk down the girls' toy aisle in a local store and you'll find impossibly thin "Monster High" fashion dolls wearing thick make-up and knee high latex boots and "police woman" costumes that display a miniskirt and high heels (but no baton). Venture into the girls' clothing section, and you may find padded bras and thongs aimed at preteens. Sexualization is not rare, even among products and media aimed at young girls. For example, among girls' clothing available in 15 popular U.S. stores, 29 percent were found to have sexualizing characteristics (Goodin et al., 2011).

Given the prevalence of sexualized products and media, it's perhaps not surprising that many girls come to sexualize themselves. When given a choice between looking like a sexualized doll, dressed in a crop top and mini-skirt, and a non-sexualized doll in jeans and a long sleeve shirt, 68 percent of 6-to-9-year-old girls preferred to look like the sexualized doll, and 72 percent believed her to be more popular. Girls who watched more media and had mothers who self-objectified were more likely to want to look like the sexualized doll—in other words, these very young girls wanted to look like the sexually mature women they see in the media and in person (Starr & Ferguson, 2012). Another study among 815 mothers of 4-to-10-year–old girls found that although overt sexualized behavior was rare, many girls engaged in some sexualizing behaviors, such as using beauty products (Tiggemann & Slater, 2014). This is worrisome because internalized sexualization is linked to lower grades and lower test scores among girls, as well as to self-objectification (McKenney & Bigler, 2014, 2016). People may also view girls dressed in sexualizing ways as different from other girls, and treat them differently. Disturbingly, adults in one study viewed young girls dressed in sexualizing clothing as less intelligent, less moral, and more responsible for their own victimization (Holland & Haslam, 2016).

Intersectionality, and Gender Typing

Roxanne Donovan was born in the West Indian nation of Guyana. Like most Guyanese, Roxanne is multiracial, a combination of African, European, South Asian, Hispanic and indigenous heritage. As a child, she had never thought about race until she moved with her family to the US at the age of eight and was constantly asked "What are you?" and "Are you black?" One day, a teacher told the class to raise their hands when their racial group was called. Roxanne did not know what to do. So she raised her hand when the teacher said White… and when she said Black… and Hispanic. Roxanne was ridiculed, even by her best friend, a Black girl. Much later, she realized that her friend might have felt betrayed, might have thought that Roxanne was trying to deny her African heritage (Suyemoto & Donovan, 2015).

As Roxanne's story shows, issues of skin color and physical appearance may prompt children to develop gendered racial identities. In a focus group study of African-American women, one participant remembered realizing she was Black "about the same time I started realizing that I was a girl, about the same time I started realizing that um, my hair wasn't straight and um, I had a wide nose and full lips" (Thomas et al., 2011, p. 536).

Accounts like these remind us that there is no such thing as a generic girl (or boy). Most research on child development has been done with White middle-class samples. It's only recently that researchers have asked about more diverse children. In a study of 229 African-American, Mexican-American, and Dominican American children who were followed each year from age 3 to 5, their gender stereotyped clothing choices, dress-up play, toy play, and gender segregation turned out to be quite similar to the patterns seen in previous studies with White kids of the same age (Halim et al., 2013): the little boys wore "tough guy" clothes and dressed up as superheroes, and the little girls wore pink headbands and dressed up as princesses.

We shouldn't conclude from studies like this, however, that ethnicity doesn't matter. A child's socialization is affected not only by gender but also by ethnicity and social class, and these may be intertwined. Parents' attitudes about gender are often based on their ethnic group's cultural heritage. For example, Asian American families may retain the tradition that women should be nurturing and home-oriented and that men should be strong and stoic, but also family-oriented, and these ideals are still passed on to Asian American children (Bronstein, 2006).

When a sample of Latinas aged 20 to 45 were asked in in-depth interviews what their parents taught them about how girls and boys should behave, the majority recalled traditional role expectations. Their brothers were granted more freedom, while the girls were expected to help with housework, learn to cook, and behave properly. A second, larger sample of Latino/a college students supported these findings and showed that gender socialization messages were usually conveyed by the same-gender parent: fathers taught boys what was expected of them and mothers taught girls (Raffaelli & Ontai, 2004).

In African American families, extended-family relatives and neighbors are often very involved in children's lives, forming an extended community of discipline and guidance. Just over half of all African American children are raised by a single-parent mother who works outside the home. Therefore, African American children see women as both providers and caretakers, which may be particularly important for girls. Several studies show that African American girls and women do less gender-stereotyping and hold less stereotypical attitudes than their European American counterparts, and less than African American boys and men. When African Americans are compared with European Americans from single-mother homes, the differences are smaller. Thus, these ethnic group differences may be due to growing up in different kinds of family structures (Leaper, 2000).

Social class differences in African American households may also create different gender socialization patterns. In an interview study of a class-diverse group of African American parents, there was generally strong support for gender equality. Most parents stressed that they had high educational goals for both boys and girls, and they expected both their sons and daughters to learn independence and equality of roles. As one mother said,

> I will definitely teach my son that men and women are equal; he is not the head of anybody. His wife will always have input and say-so in whatever is going on in their lives. And he needs to know that . . . when we were growing up, boys washed dishes, boys cooked; girls washed dishes, girls cooked. My mother taught us pretty equally to do everything, just in case you were on your own you wouldn't have to depend on somebody. (Hill, 2002, p. 497)

However, some of the families studied were newly arrived in the middle class—they had come from low income families or were less educated than others in the sample. These parents gave more mixed messages to their children. For example, one mother said that she wanted her daughter to be a warrior for racial justice, and also that she wanted her to be respectable, sit properly, avoid being loud, and act like a lady. Fathers in this group were more likely to be worried that their sons would become homosexual if they were not taught traditional masculinity. This study suggests that African American parents' support for gender equality depends on how secure they feel in their middle-class status; more secure families were more able to take the risk of raising gender-flexible children (Hill, 2002).

Children and Poverty

The United States is a wealthy nation and the poverty that exists in the midst of this wealth is often invisible. More than one in five American children lives in poverty (Huston, 2014). Poor children face many obstacles to healthy development, both in their social environments and in their physical environments.

Children from low-income families are exposed to more violence at home, in their neighborhood, and at school than those from middle-income families. They are more likely to experience parents' divorce, family breakup, and foster care (Evans, 2004), and are 2.5 times more likely to develop mental health problems (Reiss, 2013). Poverty makes it difficult or impossible for parents to provide for their children's needs. Poor parents are more likely than middle-class parents to be working two or more jobs and working later hours. For the parents this means having less time to read to children, help with homework, take them to the library, or supervise their play. They often lack basic resources like a reliable car, health insurance, and decent childcare. Moreover, poverty is strongly linked to depression in parents, leading to less consistent and effective parenting (Belle, 2008). From infancy onward, poor children are exposed to more punishment and less positive parental interaction than are middle-income children.

Poverty has a "devastating negative effect on academic achievement" for both girls and boys (Arnold & Doctoroff, 2003, p. 518). Poor children receive less cognitive stimulation and enrichment than wealthier children do (Huston, 2014). They are less likely to have a computer or Internet access at home. Their schools cannot fill the gap because they are likely to have less qualified teachers, outdated facilities, and few educational materials (Evans, 2004).

The physical environment of poverty includes higher exposure to toxins such as lead poisoning and air pollution, along with crowded and inadequate housing. For example, poor children are over four times as likely to have high levels of lead in their blood, 3.6 times more likely to live in houses infested with rodents, and 2.7 times more likely to have not enough heat in the winter, compared with other children. Multiple stressors in the social and physical environment have a cumulative effect on poor children (Evans, 2004).

I have focused on poor children in our own nation but childhood poverty is a worldwide problem. In poor and developing countries, many children lack safe drinking water and basic sanitation. Their housing is particularly inadequate and may be located in flood zones, toxic waste areas, or other undesirable locations (Evans, 2004). They may not be able to go to school or even have a school to go to.

Childhood poverty affects both boys and girls, but it is not gender-equal in its effects. In the United States, because boys are more likely to act out and cause trouble for others, their problems may receive more attention, and more programs are available to help them. The problems that are more likely to afflict girls, such as underachievement, depression, and poor mental health, are less often noticed and treated (Arnold & Doctoroff, 2003). In developing countries, girls are often kept at home to do household work, denying them the education that could help lift them out of poverty. Two-thirds of the world's people who cannot read or write are girls and women (UNESCO, 2016).

Leaving Childhood Behind: Puberty and Adolescence

When does a child become an adult? *Puberty* is a series of physiological events that changes a child into a person capable of reproducing. However, there is much more to being an adult than the capability to reproduce. The period after puberty and before adulthood, termed *adolescence,* is the time that a society allocates for young people to mature and grow into their adult roles. The adolescent must negotiate sexuality, independence, and personal identity, while being not yet an adult.

The biological changes of puberty and the social meanings of adolescence are closely intertwined, because the biological changes take place in a cultural context that defines their meaning. For adolescent boys, the maturing body signifies an increase in status and power. As boys grow taller and more muscular, they are given more freedom. For girls, the maturing body signifies a more mixed status. It is wonderful to become a woman, and some girls eagerly await their first period and first bra. On the other hand, girls may not be granted more freedom—in fact, their independence may be curtailed. In this section, I discuss the physical changes of puberty and their social meaning.

Changing Bodies

Puberty begins with a rise in hormonal production that gradually causes the body to mature. For girls, the first external sign may be a *growth spurt* or the development of *secondary sex characteristics*—breasts and body hair. The growth spurt is not just a gain in height, but also a gain in body fat. This increase is necessary and normal. In order for a girl to begin menstruating, she must reach a critical level of body fat (Frisch, 1983). Healthy adult women have up to twice as much body fat as healthy adult men (Warren, 1983). However, developing womanly curves conflicts with societal norms for extreme thinness at the same time as it makes girls' sexuality visible to all. Many girls are uncomfortable about their changing bodies:

> I was developing very early as a 6th grader and I didn't like my body at all . . . my boobs were just so big that, I mean, I am still busty and I mean, they are huge and I was a small person and they got in my way . . . and I really hated them . . . I just remember feeling that I was going to grow up and the only thing that I would be good for was something like a Playboy bunny. (Lee, 2003, p. 89)

During adolescence, there is a dramatic increase in girls' concern about their weight (Smolak & Striegel-Moore, 2001). In a study of factors that predict body dissatisfaction, the most important factors were not only actually being overweight but also the perceived pressure from others to be thin, a belief in a "thin-is-better" ideal, and lack of social support (Stice & Whitenton, 2002).

White girls in particular tend to tie their self-esteem to their weight, whereas African American girls tend to be more satisfied with their bodies. For example, 40 percent of a large sample of African American girls, and only 9 percent of White girls, said that they felt attractive (Phillips, 1998). Although body dissatisfaction was higher among the White girls, it was present in both ethnic groups. The preoccupation with weight can have serious health consequences. For example, girls may start smoking and using diet pills in attempts to eliminate body fat (Phillips, 1998). Some girls develop eating disorders. (See Chapter 13).

The onset of menstruation—termed *menarche*—is the most visible and dramatic sign of puberty. Menarche occurs at about 12½ years of age on average. European American girls reach menarche several months later than African American and Latina girls, and earlier than Asian American girls; these ethnic differences may be related to average body weight. However, there is a great deal of variability in its timing. Some girls reach menarche as early as age 8 (O'Sullivan et al., 2001).

Virtually every woman remembers the day she got her first period:

> So I was 10 years old and didn't understand any of it. In fact I misunderstood most of it. What I remember about it from the book was that somehow the menstrual blood came out on the outside of your lower abdomen somehow like it seeped through your skin! . . . So I told my mother and it was like "oh," she did seem rather pleased but it wasn't like the kind of pleased where if I got a really good grade or . . . the solo in the school play . . . She pulls out the Kotex kit and that is when I begin to connect, this is what it is, it doesn't come out of your stomach! (Lee, 2003, p. 93)

> When it came, I was a high school exchange student in Europe, staying with the family of a friend. I felt like I was out of control, that something was happening to me that I couldn't stop. I bled terribly all over the sheets and was horribly embarrassed telling my friend's aunt (especially since I didn't know the right words, menstruation is hardly one of the common vocabulary words you have to learn). . . . I felt like it was all happening to someone else, not me, like I was watching myself in a movie and now was this sexual being. (Lee, 2003, p. 87)

> I saw blood on my underwear and it was like I just sat on the toilet . . . and I am like "mom." She comes in and she was like, "What? Well honey, congratulations, you are a little lady now." I am like, "Say what?!!"(Lee, 2003, p. 93)

Girls receive both positive and negative messages about this aspect of becoming a woman. Although some studies have shown that women feel positive about menstruation as a sign of good health and an affirmation of womanhood, menstruation is more often associated with disgust, shame, annoyance, secrecy, and a list of "do's and don'ts" in our society as well as in many others (Johnston-Robledo et al., 2006; Marvan et al., 2006; Reame, 2001). (See Box 6.4.) In-depth interviews with 18- to 21-year-old American women who were asked to recall their menarche revealed that they were concerned with hiding, concealing, and managing menstruation, especially around boys. Even around other girls, they were uncomfortable admitting that they were menstruating except to complain about it. Around each other and around their

BOX 6.4 ∾ Call It Anything But Don't Call It Menstruation

Societies generate euphemisms to disguise or soften the meaning of taboo topics. Menstruation has generated many euphemisms. Which of these have you heard and which are new to you?

Bunny time (Australia)

Monthlies (Australia)

Mary is visiting (Belgium)

I have my moon (Canada)

Blowjob time (England)

Blobbing (England)

Lingonberry days (Finland)

The Reds are Coming (Germany)

Monthly tax (Germany)

Cranberry woman (Germany)

Casual leave (India)

Out of doors (India)

Aunty Mary (Ireland)

Jam Rag (Ireland)

Cookies (Mexico)

Little Miss Strawberry (Japan)

Ketchup (Japan)

The tomato soup overcooked (Netherlands)

Mrs. Noodles (New Zealand)

Doing time (Nigeria)

Aunt Bertha (Scotland)

My aunt parked her red Porsche outside (South Africa)

Granny came in a red Ferrari (South Africa)

Wearing the red beret (Vietnam)

The curse (U.S.)

The plague (U.S.)

Aunt Flow (U.S.)

Riding the cotton pony (U.S.)

On the red (U.S.)

Shark week (U.S.)

Source: Museum of Menstruation & Women's Health (www.mum.org). Contributed by Michelle Kaufman and Annie B. Fox

mothers, they used euphemisms and indirect language to reference "it" (Jackson & Falmagne, 2013). Menstruating women are still stigmatized. In one creative study, college students saw a woman "accidentally" drop either a hair clip or a tampon in front of them. Students were then asked about their attitudes toward the woman, although they did not know that their responses had anything to do with the incident. When the woman had dropped the tampon, participants (both male and female) rated her as less likable and competent, and sat further away from her, than when she had dropped the hair clip (Roberts et al., 2002).

The media contribute to stigmatizing menstruation. For many years menstrual products were banned from TV and radio, and magazine ads were so vague that it was hard to tell what was being advertised. Even today, ads for menstrual products are far from direct. A content analysis of ads in *Seventeen* and *Cosmopolitan* found that they used idealized images—or left women's bodies out of the picture entirely (Erchull, 2013). In 2003, the FDA approved a continuous oral contraceptive, *Seasonale,* designed to suppress menstruation. Medically, menstrual suppression is controversial, and there are *no* long-term studies of its effects. But a study of 22 articles in the popular press just before the debut of Seasonale showed that very few mentioned the lack of long-term research, and most characterized menstrua-tion as messy, annoying, unhealthy, inconvenient, and unnecessary. Advocates of menstrual suppression were quoted twice as often as those who opposed it, and suppression was endorsed not only for women with severe menstrual problems but for just about anyone (Johnston-Robledo et al., 2006). This biased reporting is wor-rying in light of research showing that women's primary source of information about the risks and benefits of menstrual suppression is . . . you guessed it, the media (Rose et al., 2008). Menstrual suppression may be particularly appealing to adolescent girls who are self-conscious about their bodies and wish that puberty would just go away—and big pharmaceutical companies are ready to market to this anxiety and stigma (Barnack-Tevlaris, 2015).

Gender Intensification

In a three-generational study of college students, their mothers, and their grand-mothers, a majority said they had been tomboys during childhood. Most had given up their tomboy ways at around 12½, but it wasn't due to the physical changes of puberty. They still liked active, adventurous play, but they reported that they had quieted down due to social pressure to be more feminine (Morgan, 1998).

The shift from tomboy to young lady illustrates the process of *gender intensifi-cation*—or increased pressure to conform to gender roles beginning in early adoles-cence (Signorella & Frieze, 2008). By the time they are 11 or 12 years of age, girls start to get more messages from parents, other adults, and peers to act feminine, stake their self-esteem on being attractive, and conform to social norms for females. It's not that girls necessarily believe they are really more feminine now, and boys that they are more masculine, but rather that their roles and behaviors change. For example, they become more gender-typed in their household chores, and spend more time with their same-sex parent (Priess et al., 2009).

As you might expect, the timing of puberty affects the timing of these mes-sages. The earlier a girl matures, the earlier she is subject to gender intensification. On the one hand, early maturity may make a girl more popular with boys. Early-maturing girls date more than late-maturing girls and are more likely to get involved with boyfriends in middle school and junior high (Brooks-Gunn, 1988). On the other hand, early-maturing girls experience a more stressful adolescence. For example, they get lower grades and score lower on achievement tests than late-maturing girls. They engage in more risky behaviors such as smoking, drink-ing, and early sexual intercourse, and they have higher rates of depression and eat-ing disorders than late-maturing girls. Altogether, early maturation is associated with a host of developmental problems for girls (Ge & Natsuaki, 2009; Mrug et al., 2014; Vaughan et al., 2015).

These timing effects may occur because early-maturing girls tend to become part of an older, more experienced peer group involved in activities that they imitate. Pressures can come from adults, too, who expect a physically mature girl to behave like an adult woman—as discussed in Chapter 3, physical characteristics are particularly important in triggering gender stereotypes. However, a 12-year-old girl with the body of a woman is still a 12-year-old girl emotionally, cognitively, and in her life experience.

Vulnerabilities of Adolescence

The transition from childhood to adulthood has traditionally been thought of as a time of increasing self-confidence and competence. However, for girls, adolescence may be a time of *decreasing* self-confidence and self-esteem as they learn that speaking out and being themselves leads to trouble, and that others seem to value only their appearance.

Who Is This New Self?

Interviews with adolescent girls during the middle-school and junior-high years showed that many stifled their own feelings and thoughts in an effort to fit in and be seen as a nice girl—a phenomenon termed *self-silencing* (Brown & Gilligan, 1992). The girls in this study were from privileged backgrounds and attended a private school. However, they are not the only ones to experience self-silencing. In another study, girls from diverse racial and ethnic backgrounds were asked to complete the sentence, "What gets me into trouble is _____." More than half the girls answered "my mouth" or "my big mouth" (Taylor et al., 1995). In a Canadian study of 149 teen girls who had eating disorders, self-silencing was strongly correlated with their symptoms; the more anxious they were about social acceptance, the more they were dissatisfied with their bodies, and the more they strove to be thin (Buchholz et al., 2007).

Self-silencing can be contrasted with *relational authenticity*—the congruence between what a girl thinks and feels and what she does in relationship situations—in other words, how much a girl is able to be herself (Impett et al., 2008). Authenticity can promote psychological health and well-being. Self-silencing and a loss of authenticity may occur among adolescent girls because they come up against a "wall of 'shoulds' in which approval is associated with their silence" (Brown, 1998). The pressure to be a perfect girl—not just pretty and smart but always nice and polite, never angry or oppositional—leads a girl to doubt the truth of her own knowledge and feelings.

Self-esteem refers to a person's overall level of positive self-regard and self-respect. It is measured by asking people to agree or disagree with statements such as "I feel good about myself and who I am." Do adolescent girls suffer from low self-esteem? Meta-analyses of hundreds of studies of self-esteem in children and adults of all ages showed that boys and men scored higher than girls and women. This difference is very small in elementary school, increases in middle school, and is largest in high school (Hyde, 2014; Kling et al., 1999; Major et al., 1999). When different ethnic samples were examined separately, the gender self-esteem gap occurred only among European Americans. Self-esteem was also related to social class, with the gender gap largest in economically disadvantaged groups. In other words, a girl's self-esteem is dependent not only on her gender, but also on other factors that influence her place in society. And the notion that all adolescent girls suffer from drastically low self-esteem is a recent media myth (Hyde, 2014). The moderate gender gap in self-esteem scores actually has remained stable since 1991 (Bachman et al., 2011).

Low self-esteem, when it does occur, is a cause for concern because it is linked to problems with psychological adjustment, physical health, and life satisfaction. One reason that an adolescent may develop self-esteem issues is that appearance becomes much more important socially. Of course, this is true for boys as well as girls. In a Canadian study of seventh to eleventh graders, over one-third of both girls and boys said that their overall self-esteem was *determined* by their appearance (Seidah & Bouffard, 2007). But girls, more than boys, find their flesh figuratively and literally squeezed into an unrealistic beauty ideal (Pipher, 1994). The body that was once an ally in exploring the world now becomes an adversary that must be forced into submission to an artificial appearance standard. Girls' self-surveillance, body dissatisfaction, and body shame all increase at puberty (Lindberg et al., 2007).

- "I like my behind. I don't care what nobody says, I love myself!"
- " You're supposed to think of yourself as beautiful and I think I'm beautiful. . . But I can make myself look more beautiful if I lose weight. . . I don't like my stomach or my thighs."
- "Like, there's so much focus on like weight and stuff. . . And people are put into like their categories, like, you're either like, fat, or you're acceptable."
- "But when we have the workshops that come around and they're like 'you're perfect the way you are'. . . And everything like that, most of the girls, we just sit there and, like, 'that's a load of crap'. . . We know that's not true because the first impression is what you look like."

These are the voices of girls. The first two are 13-year-old African-American girls in an interview study about their body image (Pope et al., 2014). The second two are Australian high school students in an all-girls school (Carey et al., 2011). In their voices we can hear the universal struggle of adolescent girls as they realize that their appearance, in the eyes of others, is the most important thing about them. In our media saturated culture, they can hardly escape this realization for a moment, and media exposure is strongly related to their distress. In a study of 11-year-old girls, exposure to magazines, Internet use, and the amount of appearance talk among their friends predicted their self-objectification and body shame, which in turn led to dieting and symptoms of depression (Tiggemann & Slater, 2015). In a study of 11- to 18-year-olds in the Netherlands, use of social media predicted more investment in their appearance and more interest in getting cosmetic surgery—for both boys and girls (de Vries et al., 2011).

The good news is that self-objectification among teens seems to decrease over time. In a longitudinal study that followed 587 White and Latina girls from the ages of 13 to 18, body objectification dropped and self-esteem rose during the high school years (Impett et al., 2011). Girls who decreased the most in self objectification had the highest self-esteem and fewest depressive symptoms.

Peer Culture and Harassment

A school principal in Maine described an incident in which the girls said that the boys were scaring them by saying,

"You're my girlfriend. And I'm gonna marry you and . . . we're gonna have sex." . . . it got pretty aggressive and real loud and pretty soon there were lots of things coming out from all the boys: "Yeah, we're gonna have sex with you," and "Yeah, we're gonna rape you; we're gonna kill you." And "Yeah, 'cause you're our girlfriend." And then one boy said, "I'm gonna put an engagement ring on you 'cause that's what you do when you love someone, but I'm gonna NAIL it on 'til the blood comes out! (Brown, 1998, p. 104)

These children were six and seven years old. Too young to fully understand the meaning of words like sex and rape, they nevertheless acted out a scenario of masculine dominance: "The boys felt powerful using hostile language they knew would strongly affect the girls; the girls . . . felt uncomfortable, frightened, and angry" (Brown, 1998, p. 105).

Research shows that gender-related harassment by peers is prevalent in schools and that it intensifies as children reach adolescence (Petersen & Hyde, 2009). When the American Association of University Women (AAUW) conducted a national survey of students in Grades 8 through 11, they found that 83 percent of girls and 79 percent of boys had experienced harassment. This included behaviors such as spreading sexual rumors, making remarks about one's body or sexuality, forced kissing, and unwanted touching (AAUW, 2001). White girls reported the most sexual harassment, followed by African American, and Latina girls. Although the overall rates were nearly gender-equal, the consequences were not. In this study as well as others, boys tended to view sexualized attention as flattering; they reported that it makes them feel proud of themselves. Girls were much more likely to report that it makes them feel frightened, self-conscious, and embarrassed. Research has shown that peer sexual harassment increases girls' self-surveillance and body shame (Lindberg et al., 2007), which is linked to negative psychological and physical health consequences.

Some studies show that boys get even more harassment than girls do because they are targeted by other boys. In other studies, girls are more often the targets. In a large study of 14- and 15-year-old students in the Netherlands, girls were more than twice as likely as boys to report incidents of unwanted sexual attention at school (Timmerman, 2003). For boys, the most common forms were verbal taunts such as "gay" or "homo." For girls, there was more physical harassment. As one girl reported, "I was pawed and blocked. I was very frightened and helpless. It was a group of boys" (p. 239). In an interview study of Australian high school students and teachers, both boys and girls reported that boys taunted girls with names (like whore, bitch, slut, and skank), as well as comments on body shape (whale), and specific body parts (flat chested, watermelons, nice arse). Some boys reported that "guys just go up to a girl and grab her . . . grab her tits" (Shute et al., 2008, p. 481).

It's not that different in U.S. schools. In a large representative sample of over 18,000 U.S. high school students, 37 percent of girls reported having been sexually harassed within the past year, and boys were 2½ times more likely to report being perpetrators (Clear et al., 2014). When students in a Midwestern middle school, whose average age was 12, were surveyed, the majority had experienced or seen sexual harassment in the hallways, cafeteria, classrooms, and gym classes at their school. More than one-third of both boys and girls said that they'd had someone say hurtful things about their body or how they looked, and 60 percent had witnessed others calling a student sexual names (Lichty & Campbell, 2012). Over many studies, the pattern that emerges is one of homophobic name-calling directed at boys by boys, and a wider range of sexual and sexist harassment directed at girls by both girls and boys. Gender nonconforming students experience more peer harassment than any other group. In an Internet survey of 5,907 LGBT students aged 13 to 18, 72 percent of lesbian/queer girls, 66 percent of bisexual girls and gay/queer boys, and 81 percent of transgender youth reported having been sexually harassed within the past year (Mitchell et al., 2014).

A striking feature of peer gender harassment among children and teens is that it often takes place in full view of adults, who may do little to stop it. Often, teachers stand by and watch without comment as sexual teasing and harassment take place, which provides a powerful message to both boys and girls (Shute et al., 2008). Girls may report harassment only to be told, "Boys will be boys." In a particularly horrifying incident, gang rapes of female students were reported at a major Japanese university. In response, a member of Parliament said in a public forum, "Boys who commit group rape are in good shape. I think they are rather normal. Whoops, I shouldn't have said that" (French, 2003, p. A4).

Girls may be encouraged to interpret their experiences of gender-related harassment and hostility in terms of heterosexual romance. For example, after the "We're gonna rape you" incident described earlier, 7-year-old Melissa struggled to understand how boys who she thought were her friends could be so hostile. She was comforted when she remembered that her grandfather had told her "If boys chase you then that means that they love you" (Brown, 1998, p. 105). Although Melissa's grandfather probably meant well, I doubt whether this is a good lesson for Melissa to learn. For more on the ideology of heterosexual romance and its relationship to violence against girls and women, see Chapters 7 and 12.

Unfortunately, teachers may also be perpetrators of sexual harassment. Students of all ages are legally protected from all sexual contact with teachers (Watts, 1996). However, teacher–student sexual harassment is amply documented. A survey of high school students in the Netherlands found that 27 percent of reported unwanted sexual behavior at school was done by a teacher, principal, or other adult authority. The perpetrators were overwhelmingly male, the victims mostly female. Teacher harassment was more severe and led to more negative psychological consequences than peer harassment (Timmerman, 2003).

The power imbalance between teachers and students leads to under-reporting of this kind of violence because students are afraid of the consequences. When a 13-year-old Japanese girl brought charges against her 51-year-old teacher for fondling her in a school office, more than 40 teachers signed a petition asking that he should be treated leniently. The girl was rejected by her classmates, and her best friend told her that she had ruined the teacher's life. The girl replied that it had been the other way around (French, 2003).

Making a Difference

Feminists have maintained that raising children to be highly gender-typed is harmful to boys and girls because it closes off possibilities for both. As long as kids are raised to believe that there are certain things they cannot or should not do because of their gender, society is losing potentially unique contributions and individuals are losing potential sources of fulfillment.

Transforming Social Interactions: Enlarging the Options for Girls

Many feminist researchers and parents have explored alternative approaches to bringing up children (Katz, 1996). First, what examples can parents offer? Children who grow up in families where parents share child care and house work are less gender typed in the preschool years than those who grow up in more traditional families (Fagot & Leinbach, 1995). Those whose mothers work in gender-neutral or male-dominated occupations have less gender-typed interests and beliefs (Barak et al., 1991). Parents can start by becoming more flexible in their expectations for their children, rather than pushing them into gender-stereotyped activities (Bem, 1998). They can offer gender-neutral toys and counter-stereotypical examples of people and activities in daily life (picture books with a nurturing man, a strong woman). Even when their preschoolers are most gender-stereotyped, they may be storing up these experiences and, later on, they will become more cognitively flexible about gender.

Early sexualization can be thought of as a result of gender typing, since gender-typed girls strive to be like the women they see around them, including in the media. Media literacy, or talking to children about what's happening in the media, is one way to reduce early sexualization. Girls whose mothers talked to them about what was happening on TV were significantly less likely to self-sexualize, and this worked better than simply restricting TV usage (Starr & Ferguson, 2012). The same study also found that dance classes as well as sharing spiritual values with girls were related to reduced sexualization. It's likely that sports (a girls' soccer team) and other values (feminism) would also be protective factors.

In addition, it's important to reduce sexualization in our culture and to become informed consumers of media. Several organizations, such as the SPARK movement (http://www.sparksummit.com/), aim to draw attention to and push back against sexualization in the media. SPARK is unique in that it gives a space for children and teens to write blog posts and create other media to raise awareness. Other organizations like Common Sense Media (www.commonsensemedia.org) strive to inform parents about the media their child is consuming, as well as provide tools to help parents talk to their children and encourage them to become critical consumers of media.

For girls in the vulnerable teen years, the main issues are keeping a healthy identity and self-esteem, becoming comfortable with a woman's body, and expressing sexuality in relationships. We discuss the latter topic in the chapters that follow. For now, let's look at the factors that foster healthy self-esteem and prevent self-objectification in adolescent girls.

In one study of a diverse sample, girls were asked what made them feel good about themselves. Athletics topped the list (Erkut et al., 1997). (See Figure 6.5.) Girls who participate in sports do better academically and are less likely to drop out of school, and they have lower rates of stress and depression and higher self-esteem. Improved self-esteem among girls who participate in sports stems from feelings of physical competence, improved body image, and feeling less constrained by a feminine gender role (Richman & Shaffer, 2000; Schmalz et al., 2007).

There is still a gender gap in high school sports in the U.S., with girls of every ethnic group less likely to participate than boys (Shifrer et al., 2015). This is unfortunate because it's psychologically important for girls to experience being "in the body"—to know their bodies as strong and capable, not just objects to be judged and rated for their looks. There is direct empirical evidence that sports involvement is important in reducing self-objectification: in a longitudinal study of Australian girls, the more time a girl spent in sports activity, the less she objectified herself when measured a year later (Slater & Tiggemann, 2012). Sports are not the only venue in which girls and young women can challenge the limitations of femininity by actively inhabiting their bodies. Outdoor recreation is becoming increasingly popular for women (Henderson & Roberts, 1998) and may offer different benefits than sports. Like sports, outdoor recreation is consistent with traditional masculinity but not with traditional femininity. The idealized feminine form does not have mass or muscles. It does not assume unbecoming postures, such as those required in rock climbing. For girls and young women whose relationship with their bodies is focused on appearance concerns, trading media and mirrors for trees and trails can be a liberating experience. Outdoor educator S. Copeland Arnold (1994) explains,

> My experiences in Outward Bound as a young woman deeply affected my sense of self-acceptance, self-esteem, and body image. I gained an appreciation for my strength and agility. . . Rather than an object to be adorned and perfected, my body became an ally. (pp. 43–44)

Another important influence that girls say helps them feel good about themselves is creative self-expression—music, art, or theater (Erkut et al., 1997). In an ethnically and geographically diverse sample, these activities provided opportunities to meet a challenge (a reason especially important to more affluent girls, European American and Asian American girls, and those in urban areas), and also just because they were enjoyable or involved being with friends (most important to girls from rural areas).

Creative activities like playing a musical instrument, singing in a choir, or learning to dance all demand being "in the body" and reduce the focus on appearance and sexualization. For example, a UK study recruited 55 14-year-old girls to learn contemporary dance. At the end of the classes, their upper body strength and overall fitness had increased significantly and their self-esteem had, too (Connolly et al., 2011).

Service to others is another experience that helps girls feel good about themselves (Erkut et al., 1997). When more privileged girls help those who are disadvantaged, both groups benefit. In one successful program, students from a

©Purestock/Superstock RF

FIGURE 6.5   Involvement in sports and outdoor recreation may help protect girls against self-objectification.

women's college served as mentors to inner-city high school students who were mostly from low income Hispanic and immigrant families (Moayedi, 1999). The high school girls visited the college campus, participating in leadership and career workshops. Both the college students and the high school girls learned from this experience. As one college mentor said, "My friend Elisabeth has nobody to count on. She came here with nothing in her pockets to start a new life from the bottom. That is why I have learned more from her" (pp. 237–238). As for the high school girls, they reported that before the mentoring program they had never been on a college campus, knew few White people, and had never thought about going to college. As a result of the program, their goals were enlarged and their options expanded.

Children from disadvantaged backgrounds particularly need mentoring to help them overcome the deficits induced by poverty. *Big Brothers/Big Sisters* program is a nationwide attempt to foster healthy development in disadvantaged children through mentoring. Involvement in Big Brothers/Big Sisters has been shown to improve children's grades, academic skills, and relationships with parents and peers (Grossman & Tierney, 1998; Herrera et al., 2011).

Transforming Ourselves: Resisting Gender Typing

Girls (and boys) are not just passive victims of gender socialization. On the contrary, many girls actively resist gender pressures and develop identities in opposition to the norms of femininity. And young people who define themselves as gender-nonconforming are becoming more visible in our society. Making a space in society for girls and boys who are less gender-typed (or not gender-typed at all) is an important social justice task that has hardly begun, despite nearly 50 years of second- and third-wave feminism. To date, psychology has contributed a huge amount of research on gender-typing but much less research on how *not* to become gender typed.

Understanding how girls resist becoming gender typed may require close study of their own accounts of their experience. In an ethnographic study of girls in a small town in Maine, psychologist Lyn Mikel Brown (1998) reported that working-class girls, in particular, tend to "fight verbally, and physically when necessary, to speak the unspeakable, to be nurturing and also tough and self-protecting," disrupting the boundaries of femininity. They are not the good girls their teachers want but they may be holding on to their identities in a system that does not understand or value them.

Understanding and supporting girls is a crucial area for feminist research and activism, because girls have the potential to contribute to a post-patriarchal society. Lyn Mikel Brown (1998, p. 224) has suggested that we need to help girls to accept themselves

> as complete and whole beings, with a range of feelings and thoughts connected to their experiences. Teaching girls how to pinpoint what is causing them anger or pain and how to act on their feelings constructively provides a kind of warrior training for social justice.

Exploring Further

❧

Bem, S. L. (1998). *An unconventional family.* New Haven, CT: Yale University Press.
> A personal memoir by a prominent feminist psychologist about how she and her husband tried to bring up ungendered children. The now-grown children, Emily and Jeremy, have their say too. This book is controversial—see the review in the journal *Feminism and Psychology,* 2002, 12, 120–124.

Hardy Girls Healthy Women. (http://hghw.org)
> Founded by feminist psychologist Lyn Mikel Brown, this nonprofit organization is dedicated to providing girls and young women with opportunities, programs, and services that empower them. Hardy Girls programming, resources, and services are grounded in psychological research in girls' development and focus on social structural changes.

New Moon Girls. (www.newmoon.com)
> New Moon Girls is an online community and magazine that is international and multicultural. At New Moon, girls create and share poetry, artwork, videos, and more; chat together; and learn. It provides a safe Internet community for girls 8 to 14 and a print magazine designed to build self-esteem and positive body image.

Plan International: Because I Am a Girl
> Plan's campaign is to fight gender inequality, promote girls' rights and lift girls out of poverty. Across the world, girls face the double discrimination of their gender and age. They are denied access to health care and education, and face violence, abuse, and harassment. You can see Plan's most recent report on the status of girls around the world, and get involved in helping, at their Web site, http://plan-international.org.

PART 4

Gendered Life Paths

CHAPTER 7

Sex, Love, and Romance

$\mathcal{S}$ex, love, and romance seem like natural events—instinctive, unlearned, and universal. For example, think about a kiss. Perfectly natural, right? In Western societies, kissing is seen as an instinctive way to express love and increase arousal. Yet in many cultures, kissing is unknown. When people from these cultures hear about our kissing customs, they agree that these practices are dangerous, unhealthy, or just plain disgusting. When members of one African community first saw Europeans kissing, they laughed and said, "Look at them—they eat each other's saliva and dirt" (Tiefer, 1995, pp. 77–78).

Strange as it may seem, sex, like kissing, is not a natural act. In other words, sexuality is not something that can be understood in purely biological terms. Instead, it is a social construct.

How Is Sexuality Shaped by Culture?

Every culture throughout the world controls human sexuality. Because men have more social and political power, this control usually works to their benefit. For women, cultural constructions of sexuality lead to an ongoing tension between pleasure and danger (Vance, 1984).

What Are Sexual Scripts?

Each of us learns rules and norms around sexual behavior—the "who, what, when, where, and why" of what we are allowed and not allowed to do sexually. These rules and guidelines are termed **sexual scripts** (Gagnon & Simon, 1973; Kimmel, 2007).

Sexual scripts are schemas for sexual concepts and events, used in guiding one's behavior and interpreting others' behavior. For example, when college students back in the 1980s were asked to list what people would typically do on a first date, they agreed on things like go out, get to know each other by joking and talking, try to impress date, kiss goodnight, and go home. In this script, men asked for the date and initiated physical contact (Rose & Frieze, 1989). In more recent studies, much of the old date script is gone, but it is still the guy who makes the first advances (Krahé et al., 2007; Seal et al., 2008).

Contemporary Sexual Scripts

Today's sexual scripts are much more varied than the dating scripts of the 1980s. They include everything from Cinderella-like romance to hooking up and friends with benefits. Let's take a closer look.

Romantic Ideology: A Core Element of Sexual Scripts

Romantic ideology includes the belief that love is all you need; true love lasts forever; true lovers become one; love is pure and good; and anything done in the name of love cannot be wrong (Ben Ze'ev & Goussinsky, 2008). The ideology of love is positive, but it is sometimes used to justify horrible acts such as stalking, sexual assault, and even murder (see Chapter 12).

In our society, the ideology of romantic love is everywhere (see Figure 7.1). From earliest childhood, girls are encouraged to identify with heroines who are rescued by a handsome prince (Cinderella), who are awakened from the coma of virginity by the love of a good man (Sleeping Beauty, Snow White), or who transform an unpromising prospect into a good catch through their unselfish devotion (Beauty and the Beast).

One pervasive source of romantic ideology is romance novels , a $1.08 billion industry each year and still growing (Holson, 2016). Each of their covers features a woman (almost always young, White, beautiful) gazing rapturously up into the eyes of a tall, strong, and handsome man. Romance novels aimed specifically at adolescents are sold through school book clubs, gaining in popularity every year. Although most romance novels are published in the United States, England, and Canada, their readership is global (Puri, 1997).

No one would claim that these novels are great literature. They follow a predictable script: love overcomes all obstacles. The heroine attracts the hero without planning or plotting on her part. In fact, she often fights her attraction, which she experiences as overwhelming, both physically and emotionally—her knees go weak, her head spins, her heart pounds, and her pulse quickens. The hero is often cold, insensitive, and rejecting, but by the end of the novel the reader learns that his coldness has merely been a cover for his love. The heroine is swept away and finally gives in to the power of love and desire.

©Ingram Publishing/SuperStock RF

FIGURE 7.1   Romantic ideology and imagery are all around us.

Why do so many women enjoy these fantasies? Although the hero is initially cold, patronizing, sometimes even brutal, he actually loves the heroine, and the power of her love transforms him into a sensitive and caring partner. In reading the romance, women may learn to interpret a male partner's insensitivity or controlling behavior as evidence that underneath the gruff exterior is a manly heart of gold (Radway, 1984). Not surprisingly, this is an appealing fantasy. It also may be a dangerous one (see Chapter 12).

TV provides another major source of romantic scripts. According to a Harris poll, nearly half of U.S. teens say that it is their major source of information about love and romance (Ben Ze'ev & Goussinsky, 2008). What lessons are they learning? A survey of 625 college students found that those who watched marriage reality TV (*The Bachelor, Millionaire Matchmaker*) had stronger beliefs in love at first sight and finding the perfect partner. Those who watched romantic comedy movies believed that love overcomes all obstacles; and those who preferred sitcoms had the least romantic beliefs of all (Lippman et al., 2014). These results are correlational and cannot determine if the particular kind of media exposure *caused* the beliefs, but it is interesting that the beliefs corresponded to the media messages: in marriage reality TV, people fall in love almost immediately, in romcoms, love always finds a way, and in sitcoms there is often a more cynical view of relationships.

There is another side to the sexual scripts in the media: gender inequality. In a content analysis of the 25 prime-time TV shows most watched by teens, the predominant script was of heterosexual, male-dominant relationships that sustained gender inequity. Males were portrayed as sexually active and aggressive, whereas females were portrayed as willingly objectifying themselves (Kim et al., 2007). In a study of reality TV dating shows, college students who were more involved in watching such shows were more likely to think of relationships as adversarial (males and females are in a contest with different goals). They were more likely to believe that men are driven by sex, that appearance is very important in relationships, and that dating is a game (Zurbriggen & Morgan, 2006).

In summary, romantic ideology encompasses positive aspects of love, such as mutual devotion and intimacy, but also conveys more dubious or even harmful messages: A woman is nothing without a man, and men should be aggressive initiators of love and sex, whereas women should be coy, receptive gatekeepers. A man's controlling behavior is acceptable and even exciting if it is done in the name of love. A woman should objectify herself if that's what it takes to be loved. In contrast, taking care of yourself and your partner by practicing safe sex is rarely part of the script (Alvarez & Garcia-Marques, 2009). And it almost goes without saying that all the scripts are heterosexual.

Hookup Scripts

Hooking up refers to sexual activity between two people who are not in a romantic relationship. When researchers asked college students to describe a typical hookup, the script included going to a party, friends were there, drinking alcohol, flirting, hanging out and talking, dancing, and sexual activity. However, the exact sexual activity in a hookup is ambiguous. It can range from hugging and kissing to oral, anal, or vaginal intercourse (Holman & Sillars, 2012). When sociologist Danielle Currier (2013) interviewed college students about their hookup history she found that 85 percent reported having hooked up at least once. At the same time, they struggled to define it: "anything from kissing to having sex;" "it's so difficult now to actually say what it is;" "it's in the eye of the beholder." Currier's interviews suggested that the ambiguity of the term may be useful, as college men are under pressure to demonstrate their masculinity through sexual conquests, and college women want to avoid the label "slut." By using the generic term "hookup," neither men nor women have to say exactly what sexual activities they are doing.

Other scripts for casual sex include *friends with benefits*, in which two people who are friends, but not romantically involved, sometimes have sex with each other. A *fuck buddy* is a person that an individual only has sex with, not a romantic partner or friend. People can also have a casual sex relationship through the *booty call,* a text or phone call request for a sexual meetup (Wentland & Reissing, 2014). In hookup scripts, sex is acceptable between partners who have no intention of engaging in a committed relationship or even contacting each other again (Boislard et al., 2016).

On the one hand, today's sexual scripts are more egalitarian than in the past—they portray both women and men as interested in sexual pleasure and active in pursuing it (Dworkin & O'Sullivan, 2007). On the other hand, casual sex scripts treat sex as just a game. One group of researchers analyzed all the articles on how to have better sex from 70 issues of various widely read magazines for women (Cosmo, Glamour) and men (Maxim, Men's Health). They found that most of the advice was about technique (try new positions, learn new tricks) and variety (try rough sex, porn, props, etc). Advice that focused on good sex as part of a relationship (intimacy, communication) was far down on the list. Men were depicted as wild, aggressive, and animalistic in their sexuality, whereas women were advised to be coy, indirect, and focused on the man's pleasure (Ménard & Kleinplatz, 2008).

Sexual Scripts Differ across Ethnic Groups and Cultures

Scripts about sex, love, and romance are influenced by race and class as well as by gender (Mahay et al., 2001). Table 7.1, based on a national sample, shows some aspects of scripts that differ among ethnic groups in the United States. In this table, you can see that the intersectionality of gender and ethnicity, along with religiosity, shapes a person's sexual scripts. Scripts about sex, love, and relationships are even more variable from one society to another (Goodwin & Pillay, 2006). For example, people in the United States believe that love is necessary for marriage. But in most of the world, marriages are arranged by family members, not by the bride and groom. Romantic love may be viewed as irrelevant or even destructive. In a study of college students in 11 cultures (India, Pakistan, Thailand, Mexico, Brazil, Japan, Hong Kong, the Philippines, Australia, England, and the United States), participants were asked whether they would marry someone they were not in love with, if the person had all the other qualities they desired. In India and Pakistan, about half said yes. In Thailand, the Philippines, and Mexico, about 10 to 20 percent agreed. However, in the other countries, including the United States, only a tiny minority of people said they would marry without love (Levine et al., 1995).

In a culture like ours, where romantic love is strongly endorsed, not being in a relationship can be pretty lonely. One study compared college students in the United States and Korea, a culture where romantic love is not as important as family obligations (Seepersad et al., 2008). The U.S. students felt lonelier than the Korean students when not in a relationship, and happier when they were in one. Apparently, U.S. culture amplified both the positive and negative feelings around romantic love.

Cultural beliefs about sex and romance affect more than feelings; they lead to ethnic group differences in sexual behavior. For example, compared with American college students, Chinese students start dating at a later age, date less often, and are less likely to have sex with their dates (Tang & Zuo, 2000). A comparison of Asian and non-Asian students in a Canadian university showed that the Asian students were more conservative in their behavior (for example, they were less likely to have had sexual intercourse or to masturbate, and they had fewer partners if sexually active) (Meston et al., 1996).

TABLE 7.1   Societal Scripts about Sexuality Differ in American Ethnic/Racial Groups, Even When Social Class Is Accounted for

| | Ethnic/Racial Group | | | | | |
| | African American | | Mexican American | | White | |
Sexual Script	Male	Female	Male	Female	Male	Female
There's been a lot of discussion about the way morals and attitudes about sex are changing in this country. If a man and a woman have sex relations before marriage, do you think it is always wrong, almost always wrong, wrong only sometimes, or not wrong at all? (% Wrong)	25.5	38.3	27.7	41.8	21.6	30.3
What if they are in their teens, say 14 to 16 years old? In that case, do you think sex relations before marriage are always wrong, almost always wrong, wrong only sometimes, or not wrong at all? (% Wrong)	67.6	83.2	75.9	92.4	73.5	84.6
My religious beliefs have shaped and guided my sexual behavior. (% Agree)	49.5	69.2	51.8	60.9	44.4	56.6
I would not have sex with someone unless I was in love with them. (% Agree)	43.3	77.0	56.6	78.3	53.1	76.4

Source: Mahay et al. (2000). Race, gender, and class in sexual scripts. In E. O. Laumann & R. T. Michael (Eds.), *Sex, love and health: Private choices and public policies* (pp. 197–238). Chicago: University of Chicago Press.

The Western ideal of romantic love is spreading as the rest of the world adopts U.S. and European media. However, it gets interpreted in terms of local norms. In India, for example, dating is usually unacceptable, women are expected to be virgins when they marry, and romantic love has little or nothing to do with choosing a life partner. Yet India may be the world's largest market for romance novels. A study of more than 100 young, single, middle-class Indian women suggested that reading romance novels is a form of cultural resistance. In them, women explored alternative kinds of relationships with men. They admired the spunky, feminine-but-strong heroines. And they gained information about sexuality. As one woman said, she had learned about the biology of sex at school, but it was from romance novels that she learned there is nothing wrong with sex—indeed, that it is pleasurable (Puri, 1997). For better and for worse, romance novels, reality TV, and Hollywood movies are part of the globalization of Western culture.

Adolescent Sexuality

How Does Sexuality Emerge in the Teen Years?

With puberty comes a surge in sexual interest and behavior. During the last 50 years, there have been large changes in patterns of sexual activity in the teen years, both in the United States and around the world:

- More teens are having sexual intercourse outside of marriage.
- The increase has been greater for girls.
- First intercourse is occurring at an earlier age, on average.

In the 1940s, only about 33 percent of U.S. females (and 71 percent of males) had intercourse outside marriage by the age of 25 (Kinsey et al., 1948, 1953). Sexual scripts of the time emphasized virginity before marriage for girls; for boys, not so much. In the most recent national study 70 percent of females and 78 percent of males reported having intercourse prior to marriage (Laumann et al., 1994). The gender gap in sexual experience has almost disappeared. However, boys still have first sex at an earlier age than girls despite reaching puberty at a later age.

Comparisons of countries around the world show that the average age of first intercourse is similar (between 16–18 years in most countries). However, the percentage of unmarried women who have intercourse is lower in Latin American countries than in the United States or Africa, due to the influence of Catholicism. Increasingly, young people experience mass media that expand sexual norms, so that intercourse outside marriage is becoming more globally widespread (Hyde & DeLamater, 2017).

What Factors Influence the Decision to Have Sex?

The initiation of sexual behavior depends very much on social factors. For both boys and girls, one of the strongest predictors of sexual activity is the *perceived* level of sexual activity of their best friends. A meta-analysis of studies on teens' sexual decision-making including nearly 70,000 adolescents in 15 countries found that *beliefs* about others' behavior were more important than the actual sexual attitudes of peers or the direct pressure of peers (Van de Bongardt et al., 2015). In other words, teens start having sex mostly because they think their friends are doing it. In the words of one teen girl, "I just felt like everyone else was doing it and they were all talking about it and I didn't have anything to talk about so I was like, yeah I might as well" (Skinner et al., 2008, p. 596).

This raises troubling questions of free choice. In a study of sexually active girls aged 14 to 19 in urban Australia, the girls participated in in-depth interviews about their first experience of intercourse. Some said that they had been ready for the event—comfortable with the timing and with their first partner, "I waited with my boyfriend for ages just until I felt ready, until I trusted him and that took a long time." Others reported that their first intercourse had been unwanted. Often, they had been intoxicated at the time, "I was 15, I was stupid, young, I shouldn't have done it. It just sort of happened at a party. I was drunk. He was drunk. It was bad."

Some said they had given in to pressure despite being unready. "I just did it to keep him happy" (Skinner et al., 2008, pp. 596–597). In a major national study in the United States, women of all racial and ethnic groups were significantly more likely than men to report that their first sex was unwanted (Laumann & Michael, 2000).

Parents have some influence on their teens' sexual behavior (Miller et al., 1997). In a study of urban African American teens, girls' delaying their first intercourse experience was related to the amount of time spent with their mother and boys' was related to the amount of time with their father (Ramirez-Valles et al., 2002). Both African American and White girls who feel close to their parents and talk to them about sex engage in less sexual behavior than girls who do not (Murry-McBride, 1996). These studies show that it is important for parents to express support, love, and care for their teens while allowing them growing independence. One recent study followed a large sample of teens longitudinally for a year. At the start of the year, none of the teens had yet been sexually active. The biggest factor in these teens delaying sexual initiation over the study's time period was parental caring; parental efforts to control their behavior were less effective (Longmore et al., 2009).

Although adults are quick to attribute teens' behavior to raging hormones, the relationship between hormones and sexual activity is complex. Hormonal levels have a strong effect on the level of a girl's sexual interests but only weak effects on her sexual behaviors (Udry et al., 1986). An earlier age of menarche has been associated with earlier sexual activity among both Black and White adolescents (Smith, 1989; Zelnik et al., 1981), probably due to both hormonal changes and social pressures. As discussed in Chapter 6, early puberty leads to early gender intensification, which has many consequences for girls.

How early is too early for sex? Developmental psychologists agree that having sex before age 15 is harmful because teens at that age are not yet cognitively ready for safe and consensual sex. They tend to be impulsive and easily influenced by social pressure, increasing their risk for unprotected sex, sexually transmitted infections (STIs), and unintended pregnancies (Boislard et al., 2016; Hyde & Delamater, 2017). Long-term studies show less positive outcomes for both boys and girls who have early sex (Vasilenko et al., 2016).

Teens and Safer Sex

We've noted that young people often base their sexual decision making on what they think others are doing. This is true for risky behavior as well as sexual initiation. A large-scale study of U.S. college students showed that the students believed that their peers engaged in more risky behavior than the peers actually reported— and they based their own risk-taking on their perceptions of what others were doing (Lewis et al., 2007). This study and others like it suggest that one way to reduce risky sexual behavior is to provide young people with accurate information about norms for their peer group.

However, peer group norms may be problematic. Romantic sexual scripts suggest that women should be swept away by love; hookups scripts treat sex as just a game. Neither type of script allows much room for women to negotiate condom use and other responsible sexual practices with their partners. The consequence is an increased risk of unwanted pregnancy and sexually transmitted infections (STIs). These include bacterial infections (such as chlamydia and gonorrhea), viral infections (such as herpes and genital warts), and HIV (which causes AIDS). All these STIs are transmitted by genital, anal, or oral sexual contact, and all can have serious long-term health consequences. Although STIs are a risk for sexually active people in any age group, teens are particularly vulnerable because they tend to have more partners and because they are inconsistent in using protection. Half of the STI cases in the U.S. each year occur in young people aged 15 to 24, and one in four sexually active adolescent girls have an STI (Hyde & DeLamater, 2017).

The AIDS epidemic continues. Over 75 million people worldwide are infected, almost half of whom are women. In the United States, women now account for 23 percent of AIDS cases. The great majority (84 percent) of U.S. women living with HIV/AIDS became infected through heterosexual contact; injection drug use accounts for most other cases. HIV/AIDS is now the *leading* cause of death for African American women aged 25 to 34, and the fifth for all women in the same age group (Hyde & DeLamater, 2017).

Condoms are the most effective means of preventing STIs during heterosexual contact. But media depictions of sex and romance almost never include the use of condoms in sexual encounters. This may be one reason why many people do not use condoms consistently even when they know about their effectiveness. In a study of female college students, those who read the most romance novels had the most negative attitudes and intentions about condom use (Diekman et al., 2000). This study also showed that including safe sex scripts in romance stories led to more positive attitudes towards condoms.

Experiencing Sexuality

First Intercourse: Less Than Bliss?

Sociologists and psychologists have studied the factors that influence the decision to have sex for the first time. But what about the *experience* of first sex? There has been much less research. In our society, it's called losing your virginity, and the script is romantic. Here's one example, taken from a Harlequin romance novel:

> For a long timeless moment Roddy gazed down at the sleeping figure, watching the soft play of moonlight on her features. . . . Gently he pulled back the blankets and lay down beside the motionless girl. She turned in her sleep, one hand flung out towards him. Tenderly he stroked a dark strand of hair from her face, then pulled her into his arms. . . . Still half drugged from brandy and sleep, she found herself stroking his hair. "Such a perfect dream," she murmured, her eyes already beginning to close again.
>
> "No dream, my lady," and Roddy's mouth found hers, silencing her words. Tenderly he slipped the ribbon straps of her nightdress over her shoulders, and her body arched up towards him as his fingers traced a burning path across her breast. A groan vibrated deep in her throat as he threw her nightdress to the floor. Then his body was pressed along hers and she gasped at the feeling of skin on naked skin. . . .

Driven now only by pure instinct, she moved against him, raining kisses down on his hair-roughened skin, tracing her fingers down the hard strength of his muscled chest. His breathing became ever more ragged, his hands slipping under her to pull her closer still, and she gave a tiny cry of surrender as he finally claimed her body, her fingers digging his shoulders as they moved together in frenzied rhythm. A vast well seemed to surge up within her, and as the room exploded into fragmented light she heard a voice crying "I love you" . . . (Elliot, 1989, pp. 116–118).

There may be a gap between the romantic ideal and reality. In a study of 1,600 American college students, women reported more guilt and less pleasure than men did when remembering their first sexual intercourse. When asked to rate the pleasure of their first intercourse on a 1 to 7 scale, the women gave it an average score of 2.95 (Sprecher et al., 1995). This account is from a sexual autobiography written by a college sophomore, reproduced here exactly as she wrote it:

I don't think I will ever forget the night that I did lose my virginity. It was this past September (September 7th to be exact). My boyfriend and I had been going out for six months. I met him at a party late that night, but, by the time I had gotten there, he was extremely drunk. We came back to my room because my roommate was not going to be there. . . . Well, my boyfriend was very drunk and very amorous to say the least. Once we got into bed, I knew exactly what he had in mind, he was all hands and lips. I figured that we might as well have sex. . . . So, I made the decision to let him do whatever he wanted. For the actual act of sex itself, I hated it the first time. Not only was it painful but, it made a mess on my comforter. I hated my boyfriend at that time. I actually kicked him out of my room and sent him home. I was upset for a lot of reasons: My boyfriend was too drunk to remember the night so, I had made the wrong decision in letting him do whatever he wanted; there had been no feelings involved; I hadn't enjoyed it in the slightest; I had lost my virginity and betrayed my parents. I was upset for just a couple of days.

After that first night, the sex between my boyfriend and myself has been great (Moffat, 1989, pp. 191–192).

The experience of first intercourse tends to be different for young women and young men. In a sample of White, African American, Asian-American, and Latino college students who were asked to describe their first experience of sexual intercourse, the top descriptors were both positive ("special and perfect and memorable") and negative ("We didn't really know what we were doing"), ("Not pleasant. Didn't feel good"). As in past research, men were more likely than women to describe first intercourse as generally positive and physically pleasurable and women to describe it as painful and negative. However, women more often than men described it as a positive *emotional* experience (Walsh et al., 2011).

Losing one's virginity has many meanings. Researcher Laura Carpenter (2005) explored those meanings by interviewing a diverse sample of 61 young people— straight, gay, lesbian, of varying religions, socioeconomic backgrounds, and ethnicities. Three ways of thinking about sexual initiation stood out in the interviews. The first, mentioned by about half the respondents, was that virginity is a gift given by one partner to the other. Not surprisingly, the gift metaphor, which may be influenced by abstinence-only sex ed programs in schools, was used more by heterosexual women. The second view, endorsed by more than one-third of respondents, was that virginity is a stigma to be gotten rid of. The stigma metaphor was used more by heterosexual men, but some women used it, too, in rejecting traditional notions of femininity. The third view was that virginity loss is a step in a process—for heterosexuals, a process of becoming an adult—for LGBTs, a process of coming out. The qualitative research method used in this study does not permit us to make conclusions about the general population, but it does provide a rich picture of how the people in the sample made meaning of their own experiences. It seems that virginity means different things to different people.

Women's Experiences of Orgasm

Women who have not had a lot of sexual experience are sometimes unsure about whether they have had an orgasm because they do not know how it is supposed to feel. One way to get an idea of the subjective experience of orgasm is to ask women to describe their own behaviors and sensations. Shere Hite (1976) did just that in a survey of more than 3,000 women. Although her research methods were not very systematic, Hite appealed woman-to-woman to her prospective sample and used open-ended questions. Many of her respondents wrote lengthy, detailed answers. *The Hite Report* was a feminist sensation in its day because it described orgasm and other sexual experiences in women's own voices.

Is the experience of orgasm different for women and men? Research suggests that the experiences are similar. In a study in which college students were asked to write descriptions of their orgasms, judges (psychologists and physicians) could not reliably distinguish women's and men's descriptions (Vance & Wagner, 1976). In a recent qualitative survey of British young adults, both the men and women described orgasm as the main goal of sexual activity and the ultimate pleasure. Both men and women experienced better orgasms when they were comfortable with their partner and aware of each other's sexual preferences (Opperman et al., 2014).

Evils of Masturbation or Joys of Self-Pleasure?

Stimulating one's own genitals is a very common sexual practice. Traditionally, this practice was given the clinical term *masturbation,* which made it seem like a disorder. Indeed, masturbation was thought to cause everything from dark circles under the eyes to insanity. However, the majority of people today believe that it is neither harmful nor wrong (Petersen & Hyde, 2010). More positive terms for masturbation include *self-pleasuring* and *self-gratification.*

Women usually masturbate by stimulating the clitoris, either by hand or with a vibrator. Other methods include pressing the clitoral area against a pillow or using a stream of water while in the bath or shower. Most women who masturbate engage in sexual fantasies while doing so. Hite's survey respondents described both their techniques and their fantasies.

There is a persistent gender difference in masturbation experience. Curiously, women do not report more negative attitudes toward masturbation than men do, but they are definitely less likely to say they do it (Das, 2007; Petersen & Hyde, 2010). Only about 42 percent of women in a national study reported that they had ever masturbated, compared to virtually all the men (Laumann et al., 1994), and African American and Asian American women have lower rates than white women (Das, 2007). For young women in our society, developing a positive attitude about masturbation may take time, due to the cultural silence and shame around it. When college women were asked to write narratives about their feelings and experiences with masturbation, stories like these were common:

- When it comes to sexuality, my mom was open to discussing anything I had questions about. . . However f or some reason I missed ever learning about masturbation, or being in any discussions about masturbation.
- I grew up in a very Christian household, and I thought sex and sexual play was shameful before marriage. I thought all forms of sexual experience was dirty. . . (Kaestle & Allen, 2011, pp. 986–7).

Self-pleasuring can be an important way for a woman to learn about her pattern of sexual arousal and satisfaction. Through practice, she can learn what fantasies are most arousing, what kinds and amounts of stimulation are most enjoyable, and what to expect from her body. For these reasons, sex therapists frequently use education in self-pleasuring for women who are unable to experience orgasm with a partner (LoPiccolo & Stock, 1986). Feminist writers have encouraged women to use self-gratification as a route to erotic skill and sexual independence (Dodson, 1987) (See Box 7.1).

Box 7.1 ∽ Research Focus: Women's Masturbation and Sexual Empowerment

In an anonymous survey study of 765 American women, Christin Bowman asked women about their attitudes toward masturbation, why they masturbated, and how they felt about masturbation. About 96 percent of the sample reported ever masturbating, and about 62 percent had done so in the past week. Women were presented with 17 different reasons for why they might masturbate and were asked how frequently they did so for each reason. The responses clustered into five main categories (listed in order from most frequent reason to least frequent reason): sexual pleasure, substitute for partner sex, release, learning about body/pleasure, and sexual dissatisfaction. Responses to the question "How does the fact that you masturbate make you feel?" clustered into three categories: Sexual Empowerment, Shame, and Fears of Selfishness.

In general, the women in Bowman's sample had positive attitudes toward masturbation. In fact, 85.5 percent reported that they felt little or no shame about masturbating, and nearly 92 percent felt that they were not being selfish. Bowman also looked at predictors of sexual empowerment. She found that women were more likely to feel sexually empowered if they masturbated for sexual pleasure or to learn more about their bodies, if they felt sexually efficacious (i.e., feeling comfortable asking for what one wants sexually), and if they had a positive genital self-image (i.e., having a positive attitude toward one's vagina).

Source: Bowman, C. P. (2014). Women's masturbation experiences of sexual empowerment in a primarily sex-positive sample. *Psychology of Women Quarterly, 38*(3), 363–378.

Contributed by Annie B. Fox

Lesbian and Bisexual Women

So far, the discussion in this chapter has been about heterosexuality, because it is the dominant, socially approved form of sexual expression and the one that has clear, pervasive scripts. Let's turn now to other sexual identities and experiences, those of lesbian and bisexual (LB) women.

Defining Sexual Orientation

A lesbian is a woman who is emotionally and sexually attracted to other women; a bisexual woman is capable of emotional and sexual attraction to both women and men. Although these definitions are straightforward, sexual orientation is a complex matter involving not just attraction but also love, intimacy, fantasies, behavior, and—most important—the individual's subjective sense of her sexual identity.

Non-heteronormative identities are hard for the dominant culture to assimilate. Individuals identifying as "bi" do not fit the gay/straight binary; traditionally, some researchers and clinicians maintained that there is no such thing as a true bisexual, implying that they are just confused or indecisive and will eventually decide to be either gay or straight (Rust, 2000). Some bisexuals may feel marginalized by both gay and straight culture. They may be accused by the gay community of wanting to avoid the stigma of the homosexual label and of using cross-sex relationships to hide from their homosexuality (Rust, 2000; Hayfield et al., 2014). On the other hand, some feminists maintain that bisexuality is a revolutionary concept because it challenges the "little boxes" of sexual orientation and pushes society beyond dualistic thinking about sexuality (Firestein, 1998). Indeed, some bi people say that their bisexual identities reflect their gender politics—they are attracted to *people*, not gender categories (Rust, 2000).

As transgender individuals are becoming more socially visible, so is the question of who counts as a woman. If a lesbian identified woman transitions to a transman, is she still part of the lesbian community? What about people who identify as genderqueer (both male and female, or neither) but self-identify as lesbians? Social psychologist Charlotte Chucky Tate has proposed new models of sexual orientation that define "woman" as any female identified person even if the person was not labeled female at birth, thus including transgender and genderqueer self-identified lesbians in the category (Tate, 2012; Tate & Pearson, 2016). Tate maintains that if we truly believe that gender is socially constructed, then female gender identity, the lived experience of being female, and being a lesbian are open not just to those who were assigned female at birth but those who identify as female later in life.

Even among cisgender women (those whose gender identity matches their birth sex), people do not always mean the same thing when they say, "I am a lesbian." A pioneering study done in England by psychologist Celia Kitzinger (1987) compared the explanations or stories about the experience of lesbian identity of 41 self-identified cisgender lesbians ranging in age from 17 to 58. Five viewpoints emerged from a close comparison of the accounts.

The first viewpoint was the idea of lesbianism as personal fulfillment. Women who viewed themselves primarily in this way were sure of being lesbians, were unashamed of their orientation, and thought of themselves as happy, healthy individuals:

> I have never stopped feeling relief and happiness about discovering myself and, you know, accepting about myself and finding all these other women, and it means that I'm happy almost every day of my life. . . . I've never regretted being a lesbian. . . (Kitzinger, 1987, p. 99)

A second viewpoint defined sexual preferences in terms of love: being a lesbian was seen as the result of falling in love with a particular person, who just happened to be a woman. Though defining themselves as lesbian, these women felt that they could or would have a heterosexual relationship if they fell in love with a man. A third viewpoint had to do with the feeling of being "born that way," yet resisting sexual labeling:

> I'm me. I'm . . . a social worker; I'm a mother. I've been married. I like Tchaikovsky; I like Bach; I like Beethoven; I like ballet. I enjoy doing a thousand and one things, and oh yes, in amongst all that, I happen to be a lesbian; I love a woman very deeply. But that's just a part of me (Kitzinger, 1987, p. 110)

The fourth view included women who came to identify as lesbians through radical feminism:

> It was only through feminism, through learning about the oppression of women by men and the part that the enforcement of heterosexuality, the conditioning of girls into heterosexuality plays in that oppression, it was through that I decided that whatever happens I will never go back to being fucked by men . . . that decision was made because I'm a feminist, not because I'm a lesbian. I take the label "lesbian" as part of the strategy of the feminist struggle. (Kitzinger, 1987, p. 113)

A final view identified a few women who saw their sexual orientation as a sin or weakness—a "cross to bear." These women were sometimes ashamed of being lesbians, said they would not have chosen it, and would be happier if they were heterosexual.

This classic study explored the multiple meanings women give to their sexuality and its relationship to the rest of their lives. Each of the ways these women subjectively experienced their sexuality had both costs and benefits for the individual. The social meaning of sexual orientation has changed over time, and individuals' self-definitions have likely changed with it. Definitions now have moved beyond the little boxes of gay or straight and are becoming more inclusive of transgender and genderqueer people. Stay tuned for further developments.

Developing a Lesbian or Bisexual Identity

Coming out is the process of acknowledging to oneself, and then to other people, that one is LGB or genderqueer. Usually, LGB people experience coming out as a series of milestones: their first sexual attraction, first self-identification as LGB, first LG sexual activity, and first disclosure to another person. In a randomized sample of over 1,200 LGB adults ranging in age from 18 to 84 years, most had self-identified at an early age. Women had had their first sexual experience later than men, but disclosed earlier, possibly because being a lesbian is somewhat less stigmatized than being a gay man. Bisexual individuals had experienced the milestones about a year later than LG individuals on average. However, there is a lot of individual variability in the timing of these milestones (Calzo et al., 2011).

Gay, bisexual, and lesbian adolescents do not have an easy time. They are at higher risk for low self-esteem, emotional isolation, poor school performance, dropping out, and a variety of other problems. Being rejected by their families is strongly related to mental health problems in LGB youth. In one study of White and Latino/a young people, those who reported higher levels of family rejection during adolescence were 8 times more likely to report having attempted suicide, 6 times more likely to report high levels of depression, and 3 times more likely to use illegal drugs or engage in unprotected sexual intercourse compared with peers from families that did not reject them (Ryan et al., 2009). Bisexual girls have particularly high rates of early sex, risky sex, depression, and drug use in high school (White Hughto et al., 2016). These studies show that it is important to provide for the psychosexual needs of LGB teens in school counseling programs.

Coming out as bisexual or lesbian can be hindered by stereotypes. In a qualitative study of bisexual-identified college women, participants reported others' stereotypes that a bisexual orientation is just a phase ("bisexual until graduation") or a display that women do for the enjoyment of heterosexual men ("kissing girls" when drunk or having threesomes) (Wandrey et al., 2015). These stereotypes discredited the participants' identities by equating bisexuality with sexual promiscuity. Linda Garnets, a lesbian feminist psychologist and professor of LGBT studies, described her own moment of truth:

> I remember the first time I met a lesbian couple. I was beginning to think that I might really be a lesbian, so I wanted to meet some other people who were gay. I knew very few gay people, and I had numerous fantasies about how they were going to look and act. I vividly remember standing by my front door waiting for them to arrive and having every possible stereotype about them. I thought they were going to ride up on motorcycles and have greasy hair and tattoos. I was shaking. But when I opened the front door, there stood two of the most ordinary-looking women. I thought they must be at the wrong apartment. (Garnets, 2008, p. 233).

Although coming out may be difficult, it has many benefits. In a national sample of more than 7,800 LGBT high school students, being out was related to higher self-esteem and lower depression. But being out isn't all positive; in the same study, it was also linked to verbal and physical harassment (Kosciw et al., 2015). For LGBT high school students, coming out is a form of resilience in the face of risk, one that promotes psychological well-being despite its hazards. Being out is related to greater social support, better relationships, and lower psychological distress for LB women of all ages (Jordan & Deluty, 2000; Legate, et al., 2012; Morris et al., 2001). (See Figure 7.2.)

So far, I've been describing sexual identity as though it is fixed and unchangeable: Once a woman recognizes the essential truth that she is gay, straight, or bi, she's set for life. However, women's sexual identity seems to be potentially more changeable than that (Bohan, 1996; Golden, 1987; Rust, 2000).

Sexual fluidity refers to changes that occur over time in one or more components of sexual orientation. This could include sexual attraction (a person could

©McGraw-Hill Education/Christopher Kerrigan, photographer

FIGURE 7.2 **For women who love women, coming out is associated with better psychological adjustment.**

change from being attracted only to men to being attracted to both women and men), identity (a change from identifying as a lesbian to identifying as bisexual), or behavior (having same-sex activity for the first time). Using interview and survey methods, and following participants over time in longitudinal studies, psychologists have found that sexual orientation is not a "done deal" for everyone. Sexual fluidity is not at all uncommon, particularly in women.

In a study of lesbians and bisexual women aged 14 to 21 years, self-identification had changed over time for many of the young women; more than half who identified as lesbian had identified as bisexual at some time in the past, and the majority had had sexual activity with both other women and with men (Rosario et al., 1996). In a survey of 155 lesbian and gay young adults aged 18 to 26, the young women were significantly more likely than the young men to report sexual fluidity in attraction and identity. The women also were more likely to believe that sexuality is changeable and influenced by the environment (Katz-Wise & Hyde, 2015). Recent studies also show considerable sexual fluidity in gender-nonconforming, transgender, and polyamorous people (Katz-Wise et al., 2015; Manley et al., 2015). (Polyamorous individuals are those who engage in more than one intimate relationship at a time.)

In the first longitudinal studies of lesbian and bisexual women, participants were first interviewed when they were 16-23 years old and followed up two years later. Half had changed their sexual orientation more than once, and one-third had changed between the two interviews. Psychologist Lisa Diamond (2000, 2008), after tracking the sexual orientation and behavior of her sample over a ten-year period, concluded that sexual fluidity is characteristic of female sexuality.

Intersections of Ethnic and Sexual Identity

Lesbians and bisexual women are underrepresented in psychological research (Lee & Crawford, 2007; 2012). Lesbians and bisexual women of color are even more invisible, a minority within a minority (Sung et al., 2015). Does identity development differ for women of different ethnic and racial backgrounds? Intersectional identities may create more stress. For example, LGB people may remain closeted in African American families. On the other hand, intersectional identities may bring strength and resilience. For example, the strong family loyalty in Asian American families may override the stigma of a LGB family member, or the coping skills that an African American or Latino family learns to deal with racism might help in dealing with homophobia (Kuper et al., 2014).

In some ways, the development of diverse groups of lesbian and bisexual women may be more similar than different. In a study that directly compared White, African American, Asian-American, and Latina LB women, an Internet sample of 967 women whose average age was 21 was surveyed on their identity development and well-being. The four ethnic groups had reached developmental milestones such as the first same-sex sexual experience at about the same age. They had about the same levels of internalized homophobia and the same amount of involvement in the LGBT community. The only major difference was that all the women of color were less out to their families than the White women were. Despite having more objective stressors such as unemployment, the women of color in this study had managed to connect with an LGBT community and maintain a positive LB identity, indicating resilience and resourcefulness (Balsam et al., 2015).

There are differences in the experiences of African American, Latina, and Asian American LG women due to their cultural backgrounds, and differences within these cultural groups, too. Oliva Espin, a pioneering lesbian psychologist who conducted the first research on Latina lesbians in the early 1980s, noted:

> Because as a Latino she is an ethnic minority person, she must be bicultural in American society. Because she is a lesbian, she has to be polycultural among her own people. The dilemma for Latina lesbians is how to integrate who they are culturally, racially, and religiously with their identity as lesbians and women (Espin, 1987, p. 35).

Latina lesbians are perhaps more likely to remain in the closet, keeping their orientation secret from family and friends, than White lesbians because most members of their ethnic group strongly disapprove of lesbians. However, families who become aware of a daughter's lesbianism are unlikely to openly reject or disown her. They will remain silent, accepting the situation tacitly but not openly (Castañeda, 2008).

In a questionnaire study of 16 Latina lesbians, the respondents, like White participants in previous research, showed a wide range of subjective understandings of their lesbianism. They also wrote eloquently about the difficulty of integrating their ethnic and sexual identities. This woman had earlier said that being a Cuban and being a lesbian were equally important to her:

> I guess that if the choice were absolute, I would choose living among lesbians . . . but I want to point out that I would be extremely unhappy if all my Latin culture were taken

out of my lesbian life. . . . I feel that I am both, and I don't want to have to choose (Espin, 1987, p. 47).

The Roman Catholic religion, which teaches that homosexuality is a mortal sin, is the predominant religion in the Latino community, creating dilemmas of loyalty for Latina lesbians. To date, there has been little research on how Latina women reconcile the demands of religion with their sexual identities as lesbians or bisexual women. Oliva Espin (2012) eloquently described how she has resolved her own spiritual identity:

> Nothing matters to me more than my relationship with God. Yet, I refuse to let religious institutions and authorities determine how I should or will live. Religion and spirituality are not about rules and holy books. They are about our innermost being, our expectations, hopes, and desires for transcendence. . . . It is not God, or the sense of the sacred and divine, who is punishing or persecuting (us) for being lesbians. But, rather some of the self-declared agents of God who transmit their own sexism and heterosexism *as if* it were God's word. (Espin, 2012, p. 53).

African American lesbians also have described issues of integrating multiple identities and group memberships: as lesbians, as members of the Black community, and as part of the larger culture with its racism, sexism, and heterosexism, as this case study shows:

> Diane (hesitated) to discuss her lesbian feelings while in college. The college she attended was predominantly White, and Diane relied a great deal on the Black community there for support. She considered that coming out to these individuals might jeopardize her acceptance in this group. Although Diane continued to explore her lesbian feelings internally, she also continued to date men. Several years later, as she did begin to come out to others, she feared that identification as a lesbian might pull her away from what she considered her primary reference group—Black Americans (Loiacano, 1993, pp. 369–370).

In African American communities, the African American Church often plays a central role, and religion has helped African Americans cope with oppression throughout American history. However, many pastors teach their congregation that homosexuality is a sin, and justify this belief by quoting the Bible (Trahan & Goodrich, 2015; Walker & Longmire-Avital, 2012). Therefore, LGB African Americans may delay or avoid coming out. As one young woman told a researcher:

> We're all Christian, and we're all Baptist . . . I don't know if you know, in a black family, being gay is like, wow, really, really taboo . . . We've all been going to church all of our lives and raised in church. That's the reason I didn't come out right away, because of that (Trahan & Goodrich, 2015, p. 152).

In a study of African American LGB young adults, being religious was associated with a high level of resilience, but also with a high level of internalized homophobia (Walker & Longmire-Avital, 2012). In other words, more religious people had more strength to handle challenges in their lives, but also were more ashamed of their sexuality. For these young people, religion was truly a mixed blessing.

Although Asian American LB women share some experiences with other ethnic minority LB women, their intersectional experiences are unique in other ways. Traditional Asian cultures are strongly patriarchal and have very negative attitudes toward homosexuality. Therefore, Asian LB women may be devalued both as women and as sexual minorities (Sung et al., 2015). Because traditional Asian values place great emphasis on the extended family, women are expected to continue the family line through marrying and bearing children; being lesbian or bisexual brings shame to the whole family. On the other hand, traditional East Asian religions such as Buddhism do not specifically condemn homosexuality, and sexual behavior is considered a private matter within families (Chan, 2008).

How do Asian American women cope with the challenges of their intersectional identities? Mi Ra Sung and her colleagues (2015) addressed this question with an Internet sample of 50 Asian American women whose average age was 24 and whose ethnic background was diverse: Chinese, Korean, Vietnamese, and others. They were asked open-ended questions about the challenges they face as LB women, how they cope, and the positive things about being an LB Asian American woman. Among their biggest challenges were conflicts with Asian American family members and being afraid to come out to family members. Many women said that they coped by just not talking about their personal life at home, instead emphasizing their academic achievement. Because of the Asian cultural taboo on open discussion of sex and sexuality, they were able to steer conversations away from sensitive topics and keep their sexuality and lesbian relationships hidden from their families. Despite the challenges of being an Asian American LB woman, participants also believed there were benefits. For example, they felt part of an LGBT community. Some reported that they had developed a positive sense of self and a "unique and intersectional perspective on the world" that allowed them to view society "more critically and intelligently" and "find commonalities with a lot of different communities" (Sung et al., 2015, p. 60).

Hookups, Dating, and Romantic Love

Returning to the heteronormative scripts for female sexuality, let's look at heterosexual women's experiences of sexual and emotional satisfaction in casual sex, dating, and romantic relationships.

Hookup Culture?

The media have proclaimed that we now live in a "hookup culture." Indeed, research indicates that between 60 and 80 percent of college students have experienced a hookup at some point (Garcia et al., 2012). But before you conclude that romance is dead and college is all about "girls gone wild," remember that the definition of a hookup is vague (Currier, 2013). There has not been a huge and sudden change in sexual attitudes or behavior. Results from the U.S. General Social Survey in the 1990s and 2012 show that people have not changed their attitudes about teenage sex or extramarital sex. They aren't having more different sexual partners or more frequent sex, either. However, they are more likely to report sex with a casual date or a friend, and they are more accepting of LGB sexuality (Monto & Carey, 2014). Social change, yes, but hardly a whole new culture. Instead, older scripts of romance and commitment coexist with newer scripts of sexual freedom and independence.

Those who endorse hooking up express the belief that it's a harmless and fun way to have sexual satisfaction without emotional commitment. It allows individuals to assert control over their sexuality and it reflects their sexual freedom and autonomy (Boislard et al., 2016). In one study, for example, college students described the benefits of hookups: sexual satisfaction and positive emotional experiences. However, the hookups were better when they were with a previous partner, and they were emotionally better for the men than the women (Snapp et al., 2015). Other studies show that the majority of college students (both female and male) say that they prefer committed romantic relationships to hookups, and engage in hookups hoping that they might turn into a dating relationship (Garcia et al., 2012). Positive feelings are the norm after hookups; however, regrets are also very common, and are probably related to the high level of alcohol use typical of hookup situations. In one study, about one-third of women and nearly as many men who had hooked up in the past year said they likely would not have done it or would not have gone as far physically as they did if they had not been drinking (LaBrie et al., 2014).

There are some gender differences in the hookup experience. Women are far less likely to have an orgasm in a hookup than in relationship sex, and men report more orgasms and sexual satisfaction in hookups than women do (Boislard et al., 2016; Garcia et al., 2012). There are several reasons for this orgasm gap. For women, experience with a particular partner, commitment, and affection all are linked to having an orgasm. Typically, these are lacking in hookup sex. Perhaps most important, when in-depth interviews have assessed attitudes about hookup partners, they have often shown that neither women nor men believe that women are entitled to pleasure in a hookup—it's more about his pleasure. The focus on male pleasure was expressed by a female student who said "I will do everything in my power to, like whoever I'm with, to get them off. Just because it makes me feel like I'm good at sex . . . because in a hookup, that's really all you have." Another woman described a "degrading" experience at a fraternity party when she gave oral sex to a partner and waited for a mutual response only to have him fall asleep. A male student said, "I'm all about just making her orgasm," but when asked if he meant any specific "her" replied, "Girlfriend her. In a hookup her, I don't give a shit" (Armstrong et al., 2012, p. 456).

Despite the rhetoric of sexual freedom, hookups take place in a context of gender inequality. In the hookup script, men are still more likely to be the initiators of sexual activity. They sometimes gain more sexual and emotional satisfaction from the interactions. Women may be pressured to exceed their sexual boundaries. When college students were asked to write about sexual encounters, nearly half the women said that the men should make the first move or the male should always chase the female. Men agreed: they expected to take the lead "because I'm the guy."

The majority of students also felt that oral sex was for women to give and men to receive. As one man said, "She can give me a blow job, but she's not getting any." A substantial minority of men said they would use aggressive tactics to get women to have sex with them (Jozkowski & Peterson, 2013).

And hooking up is not totally okay in the eyes of others. In a national survey, about half of college students said they would lose respect for both men and women who hook up "a lot." Others, more men than women, said they would lose respect only for women who hook up a lot (Allison & Risman, 2013). These results suggest that there is a line one must walk when engaging in casual sex, and that line is different for women. Although women aren't judged as negatively for casual sex today as they were in the past, those who participate in "too many" hookups are still called sluts (Boislard et al., 2016). Of course, nobody knows exactly how many is too many; an invisible line is the hardest one to walk.

Internet Dating

My neighbor Lauren had been married and divorced twice, but she wasn't ready to give up on love. Living in rural New England, on a small farm with ducks, chickens, dogs, cats, and two horses, she didn't get out a lot and didn't meet many eligible men. Then she signed up on an Internet dating site for horse owners. Lauren figured that anyone who had the empathy and nurturance to take care of a horse had to be a nice guy. She soon met the man of her dreams; within six months, after many intense online chats and two brief meetings, Lauren sold her farm, shipped her horses across the country and married Ethan. To date, Lauren, Ethan, and their seven horses are living happily ever after on his farm. (This is a true story. I've changed Lauren and Ethan's names, but not the number of horses!)

Ever since Internet dating was invented, it has revolutionized the way people find romantic partners. Instead of being limited to the people in your hometown, your church, or the local bar scene, you now have access to millions of potential partners. Not only that, you can communicate with them for as long as you like before you actually meet them, by email and chatting on the computer. And many dating websites promise that they can find your "perfect mate" by using scientific methods or mathematical algorithms to match you with compatible partners. In other words, they claim to know better than you do who is 100 percent right for you (Finkel et al., 2012).

Online dating is different from old-fashioned conventional dating, but is it better? In some ways, it is. As Lauren and Ethan's story shows, it can bring people together who otherwise never would have found each other. This can be a huge benefit, especially for minority groups, people in rural areas, and so on. Where women and men are kept segregated from each other, such as the Middle East, Internet dating sites allow young women and men to talk to each other and begin to understand each other as human beings (Hatfield, 2016). Even if they cannot meet in person, the ability to talk freely with someone of the other gender is an important step in loosening traditional gender restrictions.

On the other hand, the thousands of people that one can "meet" on dating websites are not really people, they are profiles—two-dimensional representations of people. Because there are so many individuals, and they are represented by photos and carefully crafted profiles, it's easy to objectify them and shop around as if buying a pair of shoes. Sadly, the attributes that are searchable—things like education, income—don't predict relationship satisfaction very well. Other attributes that aren't searchable, because they take time to develop in interaction with another person—things like rapport—are better at predicting long-term relationship satisfaction (Finkel et al., 2012). And, curiously, the attributes that people say they prefer when looking for a partner often turn out not to be the same ones they actually prefer when they meet people in person. It seems we don't always know what we want in a partner.

Men are more active in initiating encounters on dating websites; women are more likely to wait to be contacted (Hitsch et al., 2010). Both women and men tend to contact extremely attractive and high-income people, the superstars of the websites, regardless of their own attractiveness or income. In other words, dating websites place a premium on attractiveness and income even more than conventional dating does (Finkel et al., 2012). Another drawback is that it's easier to lie and misrepresent oneself online than in person, and harder for the partner to detect deception. Almost everybody engages in some deception, taking a few years off their age or a few pounds off their waistline (Ellison et al., 2011). Fortunately, the deception is usually minor—but how to know when it's serious, like omitting a prior marriage or three?

Dating websites that make extravagant promises about finding your soulmate contribute to a romantic myth that there exists one perfect partner in the universe for each of us. By the way, there is no published scientific research to support the claims made by these companies that their "scientific methods" or "mathematical algorithms" produce more compatible matches. Instead, over 40 years of social science research has shown that the individual personality traits and attitudes they use for compatibility matching do not predict relationship outcomes very well at all (Finkel et al., 2012). The long-term outcomes of relationships are affected more by social stressors (poverty, illness) and the interaction patterns of the couple—but you can't factor these in before the partners have even met.

The Subtle Scripts of Sexual Initiative and Pleasure

The hookup script is one of sexual freedom and the enjoyment of casual sex without shame. However, underneath the freedom lurk some old-fashioned beliefs: that it is still more often the man's right to initiate sex; that his pleasure is more important than hers; and that how much hookup sex is "too much" may be different for him and her. In online dating, too, men still initiate more interactions, and it is easy for people to be treated like commodities. It seems that some age-old beliefs about gender and sexuality still pervade contemporary sexual scripts.

People are emotionally vulnerable in sexual encounters; the woman who wants to initiate sex and the man who wants to say no may fear being rejected and labeled as deviants. It feels more comfortable and secure to follow familiar patterns, as expressed by this British 16-year-old girl being interviewed by a researcher:

INTERVIEWER: Do you think boys always take the lead?
RESPONDENT: Yeh.
I: Yeh? And do you want them to or—
R: Yeh! Definitely! It's tradition (laughs).
I: Yeh? Why? Does it feel better or does it—
R: I don't know? I just think they should.
I: Yeh.
R: 'Cause I wouldn't, so I would expect them to, really.
I: So why wouldn't you?
R: I don't know? 'Cause I am the girl? (both laugh) (Sieg, 2000, p. 501)

Boys seem to agree and research shows that this aspect of sexual scripts is slow to change. In a study of male college students in ongoing relationships, more than half said that they initiated sex either all or most of the time. The reasons they gave included "I'm the man," "She's a girl," "It's not in her nature," and "I'm more aggressive/more of a top/more dominant." Interestingly, most of the men who were in charge of sexual initiation in their relationship said they would like it to be more equal, although they were not actively trying to make this change happen (Dworkin & O'Sullivan, 2007).

Satisfying sex depends on communication, learning, and initiative on the part of both partners. In a study of a community sample of 104 couples in long-term relationships, the (unsurprising) results showed that sexual self-disclosure helps the partners understand each others' needs and contributes to overall relationship satisfaction as well as sexual satisfaction. These results held for both women and men. Being able to talk about sexual likes and dislikes helps couples establish and maintain mutually pleasurable sexual scripts (MacNeil & Byers, 2009).

Sexual Scripts and Sexual Dysfunction

Because our society does not give women the same permission to be fully sexual that it gives men, women may experience less sexual joy. A meta-analysis showed that women express somewhat more anxiety, fear, and guilt about sex than men (Petersen & Hyde, 2010), as well as less sexual satisfaction. Other research suggests that women in heterosexual relationships experience less pleasure in sexual activity than their partners. In national samples, women were much more likely than men to report lack of interest or pleasure in sex (Laumann et al., 1999), and men reported more emotional and physical satisfaction in their relationships (Waite & Joyner, 2001).

Acceptance of traditional sexual scripts is implicated in women's sexual dysfunction and suppression of desire. Sexual pleasure and orgasm require an awareness of one's own needs plus a feeling that one is entitled to express those needs and have them met. Women's recognition of themselves as sexual beings is blocked in many ways by cultural influences. For example, women may feel guilty or selfish about having needs and fear their partners' disapproval if they express their needs. In a study of over 600 dating couples, the women on average reported that they felt less confident about their ability to talk about sexual health, pleasure, and sexual limits than their male partners reported. Those with less traditional attitudes about sexuality were better at communicating about sexual issues and more comfortable with initiating or refusing sex (Greene & Faulkner, 2005).

Objectification also affects women's sexual pleasure. Objectification theory predicts that when women are sexually objectified they will come to objectify themselves, causing alienation from their own bodies, including sexual dysfunction (Fredrickson & Roberts, 1997). Several studies have found relationships between self-objectification and women's sexual functioning (Tiggemann & Williams, 2012). Women who self-objectify worry about their appearance during sexual activity, which interferes with joyous sex (Vencill et al., 2015). When a woman is treated like an object for the gaze of others, she may lose the ability to distinguish between her sexual desire and her desire to please. Her sex life may feel like a part she is acting or a service she performs on demand.

Social Contexts of Sexual Expression

Sexuality, including beliefs, values, and behavior is always expressed in cultural context. It is social, emergent, and dynamic (White et al., 2000).

Cultural Variations in the United States

African American women are burdened by sexuality stereotypes that they are promiscuous, sexually available, and seductive. The Jezebel archetype discussed in Chapter 3 lives on. In one recent study, college students judged paired photos of an African American and a White woman; they judged the African American woman is having had sex with more people, less likely to use birth control, and more likely to have been pregnant in the past, reflecting the stereotype of Black women's sexuality as less disciplined and controllable (Rosenthal & Lobel, 2016). Ironically, research shows few differences in the sexual behavior of African American and White women of similar social class, but when there are differences they tend to be in the direction of more conservative behavior for African American women (Hyde & DeLamater, 2017).

Like Black women, Latinas in the United States are a diverse group with respect to social class. In addition, their families come from many different countries, including Cuba, Puerto Rico, Guatemala, and Mexico. Despite this diversity, there are some commonalities affecting romantic and sexual attitudes and behaviors. Because of historical influences and the Catholic religion, virginity is an important concept. In Hispanic cultures, the honor of a family depends on the sexual purity of its women. The Virgin Mary is presented as an important model for young women, and abstaining from sex before marriage is stressed (Castañeda, 2008). The religious influence on Latino/as affects behavior: in research using national data sets of teens and young adults, those who identify as more religious consistently engage in less risky sexual behavior (Edwards et al., 2011).

The traditional Hispanic ideal for men is one of *machismo*—men are expected to show their manhood by being strong, demonstrating sexual prowess, and asserting their authority and control over women. Women's complementary role of *marianismo* (named after the Virgin Mary) is to be sexually pure and controlled, submissive, and subservient. Their main sources of power and influence are in their roles as mothers. These traditional roles vary widely with social class, urban versus rural locations, and generational differences (Castañeda, 2008). Nevertheless, the cultural imperatives of virginity, martyrdom, and subordination continue to exert influence over the experience of love for Hispanic women. Marianismo can be seen as moral superiority and strength: women are put on a pedestal because they are purer and better than men. It may be an age-old form of benevolent sexism, a coping strategy for countering machismo (Hussain et al., 2015). However, the marianismo ideology continues to influence young people. In a recent study, female and male Mexican-American teens agreed that women should be pure and virginal; boys believed even more than girls did that Latinas should self-silence to maintain harmony in relationships and should be subordinate to men (Piña-Watson et al., 2014).

In Asian cultures the public expression of sexuality is suppressed and sexual matters are rarely discussed. Yet sexuality is viewed as a healthy and normal part of life. The Confucian and Buddhist roots of Asian cultures stress women's roles as wives, mothers, and daughters and place strong importance on maintaining family harmony. Influenced by these traditions, Asian Americans tend to be more sexually conservative than people of other ethnic groups; for example, Asian American college students are less likely to be sexually active than their White peers (Chan, 2008).

Because Asian American families tend not to talk openly about sex, messages from parents are implicit. For example, a mother might criticize a scene in a TV show and make a moral lesson out of it for her daughter. When researchers surveyed Asian American college students about the messages they had picked up from parents and peers about sexuality, the women reported that they had been taught abstinence, traditional gender roles, and the importance of sex within relationships (e.g., sexual intercourse is a special experience only for people in love) (Trinh et al., 2014).

Cross-cultural and ethnic group differences in attitudes toward sexuality and sexual practices remind us that there is no "right" way to think about sexuality. They also show once again the importance of intersectionality: a woman's identity as a sexual being is formed at the intersection of her Latina (or Asian or African American, or other ethnic) identity and her gender.

Attractiveness and Sexual Desirability

Physical attractiveness is an important factor in romantic relationships (Sprecher & Regan, 2000). Good looks are especially important to men choosing a prospective sexual partner or mate, as shown by research in many cultures (Ha et al., 2012). Typically when asked to list the qualities they want in a romantic partner, men emphasize physical attractiveness and women emphasize earning ability and/or personal qualities (Eastwick & Finkel, 2008). This attractiveness bias may seem a bit depressing for ordinary-looking women with great personalities, but there are other aspects to consider. First, it may apply only to hookups, not steady relationships. When college students in the United States (Nevid, 1984) and in India (Basu & Ray, 2001) were asked to rate physical, personal, and background characteristics they consider important in a sexual relationship, the predictable results were that males favored physical characteristics; whereas, females favored personal qualities. However, when rating characteristics they considered important in a long-term, meaningful relationship, both men and women emphasized personal qualities more than looks. And in both studies there was considerable overlap between the traits desired by women and men.

Another limit to the importance of attractiveness is that what people *say* they want may not be the same as what they actually choose. To illustrate this, I'll describe a study that used speed dating followed by questionnaires to assess partner preferences (Eastwick & Finkel, 2008). College students were recruited to participate in rounds of 4-minute speed dating, in which they kept notes about the interaction and recorded their interest in seeing the speed-date partners again. After the event, they were repeatedly asked whether they'd be interested in seeing each of their partners again, by means of questionnaires over a one-month period. Unexpectedly, both women and men valued looks, earning power, and personality equally. The most curious result was that there was no relationship between what they said and the choices they made, either on the questionnaires or in real life. For example, participants who said that physical attractiveness was very important in a dating partner were no more likely than others to like, be attracted to, or feel "chemistry" with partners they found physically attractive. It seems that when it comes to romance, people may not know what they really want.

Preferences for romantic partners' qualities are related to sexist attitudes about gender. Women's benevolent sexism beliefs predict their preference for a partner with high earning power and resources, and are also linked to their right-wing authoritarian attitudes. Men's hostile sexism beliefs predict their preference for an attractive partner and are related to their social dominance orientation (Sibley & Overall, 2011). These studies suggest that the dual motives of women and men who have sexist beliefs perpetuate gender inequality when they seek romantic partners. Women who believe that they should be put on a pedestal seek men with the resources and attitudes to keep them there, and men who dislike women except when they are "in their place" seek attractive women that they can dominate.

Disability and Sexuality

Disabled girls and women, like nondisabled women, are judged by their attractiveness. Additionally, they are judged against an ideal of the physically perfect person who is free from weakness, pain, and physical limitations. Interviews with women who have cerebral palsy and spinal cord injuries showed that one of the psychological tasks they faced was reconciling their bodies and experiences with society's norms for women (Parker & Yau, 2012; Tighe, 2001).

Parental attitudes and expectations for their daughter with a disability can have an important effect on the daughter's sexual development. In a study of 43 women with physical and sensory disabilities (including cerebral palsy and spinal cord injury), many of the parents had low expectations of heterosexual involvement for their daughters because they saw them as unable to fulfill the typical role of wife and mother. Some of these daughters became sexually active partly out of rebellion and a desire to prove their parents wrong, while others remained sexually and socially isolated. In contrast, other parents saw their daughters as normal young women, with the disability being only one of their many unique characteristics. These young women became socially and sexually active as a matter of normal growing up. One interviewee reported:

> In childhood, I was led to believe that the same social performance was expected of me as of my cousins who had no disabilities. I was a social success in part because my mother expected me to succeed (Rousso, 1988, p. 156).

Women with disabilities confront stereotypes that sexual activity is inappropriate for them; that people with disabilities need caretakers, not lovers; that they cannot cope with sexual relationships; that they are all heterosexual; that they should feel grateful if they find any man who wants them; and that they are too fragile to have a sex life. When people express these stereotypical beliefs, it is difficult for a woman with disabilities to see herself as a potential sexual and romantic partner. These beliefs can interfere with a disabled woman's sexual expression and her chances for having relationships. In a national survey that compared women aged 18 to 83 with and without disabilities, the disabled women were less satisfied with the frequency of dating and perceived personal and societal barriers to dating relationships (Rintala et al., 1997). Indeed, disabled women are less likely to be married than disabled men, and more likely to be abandoned by their partners when a disability like multiple sclerosis is diagnosed (Chrisler, 2001; Fine & Asch, 1988).

Critics have charged that psychology has contributed to the marginalization of people with disabilities because there has been little psychological research on healthy functioning, sexual identity, and sexual relationships within this group, and almost none that includes people of color (Greenwell & Hough, 2008). Despite stereotyping and marginalization, many women with disabilities manage to maintain healthy identities and relationships. (See Figure 7.3.) Internet dating is an asset for people with disabilities because it allows people to get to know each other without the disability taking center stage. And women with disabilities emphasize that the need for intimacy and eroticism can be fulfilled in many ways. As one woman said to an interviewer, "There is more to sex than intercourse" (Parker & Yau, 2012, p. 20).

Is Sex Talk Sexist?

A negative evaluation of female sexuality is deeply embedded in language, as Chapter 3 discussed. Linguists agree that languages develop an abundance of terms for concepts that are of particular interest or importance to a society. English has many terms describing women and their genitals in specifically sexual ways, and most of these are negative—*whore* (*ho*), *bitch, cunt,* and *gash* are a few examples. Absences in language are also revealing. For men, *virile* and *potent* connote positive masculine sexuality, as do other, more colloquial terms such as *stud, macho man,* and *hunk.* However, there is no English word for a sexually active woman that is not negative in connotation.

Slang words for sexual intercourse (*ramming, banging,* and *nailing*) suggest that it is something violent and mechanical done to women rather than a mutual pleasure. The same verb can even be used to describe harm and sex—as in "she got screwed." One anthropologist who studied college students in their natural habitat (the dorm), reported that about one-third of the young men talked of women, among themselves, as "chicks, broads, and sluts." Their "locker-room style" was character-

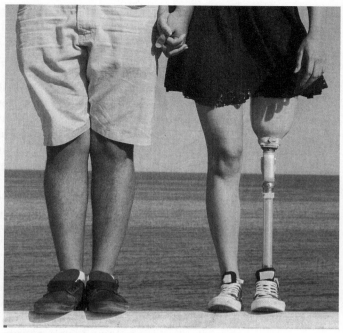

FIGURE 7.3   Together.

ized by "its focus on the starkest physicalities of sex itself, stripped of any stereotypically feminine sensibilities such as romance, and by its objectifying, often predatory attitudes toward women" (Moffat, 1989, p. 183).

In another study, New Zealand psychology students were the researchers. They observed how their friends talked about sex in their daily life settings for a week and then analyzed the metaphors used. The four most common kinds of metaphor were food and eating (*munching rug, tasty, fresh muffin,* and *meat market*), sport and games (*muff diving, getting to first base, chasing,* and *scoring*), animals (*pussy, spanking the monkey,* and *hung like a horse*), and war and violence (*whacking it in, sticking, pussy whipped,* and *launching his missile*). Males were two and a half times more likely to be the active agent, reflecting the tendency to objectify women (Weatherall & Walton, 1999).

U.S. college students, too, have been studied, by asking them to report the sexual language they used. Male students, especially those who were members of fraternities, were more likely than female students to use degrading terms to refer to female genitals and aggressive terms to refer to sex acts. These same students next listened to a conversation in which one speaker told another about having sex with someone they had recently met. When the sex partner was talked about using the more degrading terms, they were viewed as less intelligent and less moral (Murnen, 2000).

It is easy to see how women might become ambivalent about sexual pleasure when the very language of sex suggests that the female role is degraded, and random sexual insults are hurled at women. An anti-harassment campaign found that in a single three-week period, Twitter users sent 200,000 aggressive tweets using the words "slut" and "whore." (That's about one every 10 seconds.) (Dewey, 2016).

Studs and Sluts: Is There Still a Double Standard?

The *sexual double standard* is the belief that women and men should be judged differently for the same sexual behaviors. Traditionally, women were expected to remain virgins until marriage and monogamous after marriage, whereas sexual activity before marriage and infidelity afterward were tolerated in men. The double standard remains in place in much of Asia and Latin America, but by the 1970s it had decreased in the U.S. except among conservative religious groups. Evidence that the double standard is gone comes mainly from laboratory experiments in which college students are asked to judge the sexual behavior of a hypothetical woman/man. In recent studies, the results usually (but not always) show women and men being judged equally for sexual behavior (Bordini & Sperb, 2013; Crawford & Popp, 2003).

However, we should not be too quick to believe that women and men are now equally free to be sexual. First, several recent studies of hypothetical situations have shown that there is still a double standard for behavior that is unusual or out of bounds. Women who get a sexually transmitted infection or engage in threesomes are still judged more negatively than men who do (Bordini & Sperb, 2013). Second, although people may deny the double standard when asked about it hypothetically on a questionnaire, they do not always behave that way in their daily lives. Researchers who have done their studies by interviewing their participants, meeting with them in small groups, or just hanging out with them find that the double standard is still used to control girls and women's sexual autonomy (Bordini & Sperb, 2013; Crawford & Popp, 2003). For example, a study of African American mothers and their teens showed that the mothers used a double standard in educating their offspring about sexuality. Only girls were talked about as clean or dirty, slutty or not. Boys were just told to be careful and take precautions (Fasula et al., 2007).

Two major research reviews a decade apart both found that researchers' choice of methods strongly affected their results about sexual double standards (Bordini & Sperb, 2013; Crawford & Popp, 2003). Qualitative methods such as interviews, focus groups, and ethnographic analysis were more sensitive; quantitative methods such as questionnaires and hypothetical scenarios tended to find no evidence of double standards. Perhaps when people are asked about hypothetical scenarios they try to be liberal and fair-minded, but when they are engaged in thinking about themselves and their peers, more nuanced attitudes are expressed. Also, most of the quantitative studies had been done with college students, while the qualitative studies had been done with more varied populations. Whatever the reason, this methodological effect brings back points made in Chapter 1: it is important for psychological researchers to use and compare a variety of quantitative and qualitative methods and to study diverse people (Kimmel & Crawford, 2000).

Studying people in their social contexts reveals new evidence for sexual double standards. For example, longitudinal studies of adolescents show that boys who have a lot of sexual partners or more sexual experience are more accepted by their peers than boys with fewer partners or less experience, but for girls the correlation is in the other direction: more sexual experience leads to less peer acceptance (Kreager & Staff, 2009; Kreager et al., 2016). In interview studies, young people frankly give their opinions:

- (For guys, it's) "Oh, you scored last night! That's great!" But when it goes back to the girl, she's a "whore!" She put out too early. . . . (Kayla, age 17, in Lyons et al., 2011, p. 444).
- I think if a girl has sex with 25 guys she's labeled a slut .. But if a guy has sex with 25 girls, that's sweet dude—nice job. (Jed, a college junior, in Stinson et al., 2014, p. 66).

Silencing Girls' Sexuality

Body shame can start in early childhood, with the simple task of learning to name the sexual parts of the body. Surely, 21st-century U.S. children are taught anatomically correct names for their own genitals? Not so much. A web based survey of mothers of children aged 3 to 6 showed that only about 46 percent of boys and 40 percent of girls were taught to use "penis" and "vagina." Boys were taught other correct terms such as *scrotum* and *testicles*, along with childish terms such as *pee-pee* and *willie*. Girls were more likely to be taught vague terms such as *privates, coochie, thingy, down there, booty,* and *butt*. Not a single one of the 631 mothers in this study had used the word *clitoris* with a daughter (Martin et al., 2011). Because of inaccurate and incomplete labeling, girls may approach adolescence not knowing the difference between their vaginal and urethral openings, and not knowing that they have a clitoris or understanding its role in sexual pleasure. And many parents are uncomfortable providing sexuality education to their teenagers (See Figure 7.4).

Can schools fill the education gap? In many U.S. schools sex education has been shaped by pressures from conservative parents and religious groups who believe that knowledge about sexuality encourages sexual activity. There is a war being waged between conservative and liberal politicians adolescents are in the line of fire. Many schools have adopted federally funded programs like *Sex Respect*, which teach that abstinence is the only safe and moral approach to sexuality.

Sex ed 101?

Middle-school children are taught to chant slogans such as "Don't be a louse, wait for your spouse," and take chastity pledges in class (Hyde & DeLamater, 2017).

These programs present heterosexual marriage as the sole place for sexual expression. They encode gender stereotypes of boys as sexually insatiable aggressors and girls as defenders of virginity. At best, girls are taught that they should avoid being victims of teen pregnancy and STIs. They also learn that "good girls just say no" to sex. But nowhere do they hear the suggestion that girls and women might like, want, need, seek out, or enjoy sexual activity (outside of heterosexual marriage). Even in the more enlightened programs, girls see educational videos only about menstruation while boys are seeing films about wet dreams, erections, and penis size. And LGBT students' need for information may be ignored altogether.

This kind of sex education does not allow young women to come to terms with their own feelings of sexuality. It "allows girls one primary decision—to say yes or no—to a question not necessarily their own" (Fine, 1988, p. 34). By emphasizing to girls how easily they can be victimized, it may also convey the idea that women are weak and vulnerable, and all men are predatory. Black feminist theorist bell hooks (1989) poignantly described how as a teenager, she began to think of men as enemies of her virginity. "They had the power to transform women's reality—to turn her from a good woman into a bad woman, to make her a whore, a slut" (p. 149).

Because society constructs sexuality in terms of the presumably dangerous and uncontrollable urges of boys and men, girls and women are assigned the role of keeping everything under control (Tolman & Brown, 2001). Young women get little opportunity to learn how to say no at whatever stage of sexual activity suits them, and no chance to learn when they would rather say yes—or be the one who asks. By assuming that girls and women are not active agents in their own sexuality, sex education contributes to muting women's desires:

> The naming of desire, pleasure, or sexual entitlement, particularly for females, barely exists in the formal agenda of public schooling on sexuality. When spoken, it is tagged with reminders of "consequences"—emotional, physical, moral, reproductive, and/or financial. . . . A genuine discourse of desire would invite adolescents to explore what feels good and bad, desirable and undesirable, grounded in experiences, needs, and limits (Fine, 1988, p. 33).

Abstinence-based sex education programs place teenage girls in the position of gatekeepers. Their task is to say no to sex and to keep on saying no. But these programs fail to recognize the power imbalances that may exist in their relationships, and give them no skills in negotiating with their partners if they no longer want to say no. For example, in a national sample of U.S. teens in relationships, condom use was predicted by the boy's attitude about condoms; the girl's attitude had little influence (Vasilenko et al., 2016).

Sexuality education based on abstinence until heterosexual marriage is opposed by the American Psychological Association, the American Civil Liberties Union, the American Academy of Pediatrics, and dozens of scientific and public health organizations, yet Congress continues to fund these programs (Hyde & DeLamater, 2017). The information such programs present is scientifically limited and inaccurate. They reinforce harmful gender stereotypes for both boys and girls, and contribute to alienating girls from their sexuality. They fail to teach adolescents how to negotiate sexual relationships with mutual respect. Moreover, research has shown that abstinence-based programs are completely ineffective; in fact, teen pregnancy rates *increase* in states where they are used in schools (Hyde & DeLamater, 2017). (For another dubious approach to controlling girls' sexuality, see Box 7.2.)

Box 7.2   ∽   Purity Balls and Virginity Pledges

Two phenomena to come out of the "abstinence only" movement are purity balls and virginity pledges. At a purity ball, girls and their fathers dress up in formal attire, have a nice dinner, and dance the night away. But the key event of the ball is a ceremony where fathers vow to live a moral life and protect their daughter's chastity, and daughters sign a virginity pledge, vowing to remain sexually pure until marriage. In some ceremonies, fathers present purity rings to their daughters, or daughters present a key (symbolizing their virginity) to their fathers that they must protect and present to her husband on her wedding day. They also may lay a white rose on a cross symbolizing the giving of their virginity to God. The first purity ball was held in Colorado Springs in 1998, and since then, balls have taken place in 48 states and 17 countries.

©Rick Wilking/Reuters/Alamy

Advocates argue that these balls are more than just about virginity pledges, but about encouraging fathers to be more involved in the lives of their daughters. And in fact, research demonstrates that girls who have strong relationships with their fathers have higher self-esteem and do better academically. They are also more likely to go to college, and are less likely to get pregnant as a teenager, go to jail, or experience mental health issues. But purity balls are less about strengthening father-daughter relationships, and more about controlling girls' sexuality. Further, research suggests that virginity pledges don't work and may actually lead to *increased* risky sexual behavior. According to data from the National Longitudinal Study of Adolescent Health, 88 percent of girls who pledge their virginity go on to have sex before marriage. Girls who take virginity pledges are also less likely to use condoms and birth control and may be more likely to get a sexually transmitted infection or have an unwanted pregnancy compared to girls who do not take virginity pledges. There can be psychological and emotional consequences, too. When girls or young women break their pledge, they may feel guilty and worthless because they have been taught to equate their sexuality with their worth as a person.

Sources: Baumgartner, J. (December 31, 2006). Would you pledge your virginity to your father? Glamour Magazine. http://www.glamour.com/story/purity-balls
Paik, A., Sanchagrin, K. & Heimer. K. (201X). Broken Promises: Virginity Pledge Breach and Health. *Journal of Marriage and Family.* https://www.umass.edu/sociology/sites/default/files/Paik-Broken_Promises-Prepublication.pdf
Khazan, O. (May 4, 2016). Consequences of purity pledges. The Atlantic Online. http://www.theatlantic.com/health/archive/2016/05/the-unintended-consequences-of-purity-pledges/481059/#article-comments

Contributed by Annie B. Fox

Controlling Women's Sexuality

Radical feminist perspectives suggest that male dominance is fundamentally sexual. In other words, the power that men have over women is expressed and acted out in male control of female sexuality. Male dominance can define and shape the very meaning of a woman's sexuality (MacKinnon, 1994). One place where cultural control is particularly overt and harmful to women is the practice of genital cutting in order to insure that women are properly subordinated.

Female genital mutilation (also termed *female circumcision,* although it involves much more drastic procedures than male circumcision) is a common practice in 28 African countries as well as parts of Asia and the Middle East. It is usually done to girls between the ages of 4 and 12. It may involve removal of part or all of the clitoris (*clitoridectomy*), cutting away the clitoris plus part or all of the inner lips of the vulva (*excision*), or in addition to excision, sewing the outer lips of the vulva together to cover the urinary and vaginal entrances, leaving only a small opening for the passage of urine and menstrual blood (*infibulation*). A woman who has undergone infibulation must be cut open for childbirth (Abusharaf, 1998).

Genital surgery is usually performed by a midwife who has no medical training. The surgery often takes place under unsanitary conditions; therefore, complications such as infection and hemorrhaging are common. The presence of open wounds makes women extremely vulnerable to HIV infection. Other long-term health consequences, especially for infibulated women, include chronic pelvic and urinary tract infections, difficult and painful urination, and complications in childbirth. Psychological consequences can be severe as well. A review of studies found that up to 44 percent of affected women suffered from posttraumatic stress disorder; anxiety disorders and depression were also common (Mulongo et al., 2014). Because the clitoris is amputated or scarred, and the vagina may be partially obstructed, circumcised women may experience painful intercourse, no sexual desire, and no orgasms (Berg & Denison, 2012a). "Circumcision is intended to dull women's sexual enjoyment, and to that end it is chillingly effective" (Abusharaf, 1998, p. 25).

According to Amnesty International, which has investigated genital mutilation as a human rights issue, 135 million women living today have been subjected to the process. The World Health Organization estimates that each year another 3 million girls are cut (Odeku et al., 2009). Genital mutilation is spreading to countries where there are large numbers of refugees from Africa, Asia, and the Middle East. These include Canada, France, Sweden, and the U.S., among others. For example, it is estimated that in the small country of Belgium there are now more than 6,000 adult women who have been genitally cut, and 2,000 young girls at risk each year (Dubourg et al., 2011). Most European countries have outlawed genital cutting; Great Britain outlawed it in 1985 when three girls bled to death after the procedure but no one has ever been prosecuted under the law (Laurance, 2001).

Why does this custom persist? It is believed to purify women and control their sexual desire, making them more docile and obedient. Women who remain uncut are disrespected and become social outcasts. Those who have been cut are marriageable (Berg & Denison, 2013). The practice of genital surgery has been very resistant to change. However, studies show that the more educated women are, the less willing they are to allow their daughters to be cut. As women in developing countries make gains toward social equality, becoming less dependent on marriage for survival, their attitudes may change. Meanwhile, the genital cutting of girls reflects the social and economic powerlessness of girls and women (Berg & Denison, 2012b; Odeku et al., 2009).

The custom of genital mutilation is the result of a cultural construction of sexuality that may seem barbaric to outsiders. However, it was actually a common practice in England and the United States only a century ago, when clitoridectomies were done by physicians to cure upper-class women of having too much interest in sex. One health expert advised parents of girls who masturbated to apply pure carbolic acid to the clitoris (Michael et al., 1994). And some current Western practices seem barbaric to outsiders, too. What counts as normal depends on one's cultural standpoint:

> Today, some girls and women in the West starve themselves obsessively. Others undergo painful and potentially dangerous medical procedures—face lifts, liposuction, breast implants, and the like—to conform to cultural standards of beauty and femininity . . . people in the industrialized world must recognize that they too are influenced, often destructively, by traditional gender roles and demands (Abusharaf, 1998, p. 24).

Making a Difference

Sexual norms are changing rapidly in Western societies and these changes have global impact (see Box 7.3). The increasing acceptance of same-sex and extramarital

---

BOX 7.3   ∾   A New View of Women's Sexuality

Beginning in the 1980s and 1990s, academic and popular thinking increasingly emphasized the medical, biological, and genetic bases of behavior and behavioral problems. It suddenly seemed like hormones and the brain featured in every news story and research study about learning, memory, gender, sexuality, children's behavior problems, mental health, moods, emotions, drinking problems, criminal offenses, and on and on. The trend was valiantly resisted by feminists and social scientists who called it "medicalization" and insisted it was a bias that underestimated the importance of culture, learning, personality and other psychosocial and political influences. Medicalization wasn't entirely a recent trend, but it escalated due to publicity about new genetics and neuroscience research.

In 1998, medicalization in sex research and sex therapy made a huge leap forward with the

Leonore Tiefer, Ph.D.

Courtesy of Leonore Tiefer

appearance of Viagra, the first "sexuopharmaceutical," and shortly after that I became active in challenging this new direction for sexology.

Continued on next page

BOX 7.3 ∞ A New View of Women's Sexuality (Concluded)

During the 1980s and 90s I was employed in men's sexual health clinics in NYC hospitals. These clinics, based in urology departments, gradually replaced the sex therapy clinics in departments of psychiatry. It seemed to me that turning sex therapy over to urologists, who are trained as surgeons concerned with medical conditions of the urogenital organs, was resulting in fewer patients learning about sexual psychology and technique, fewer couples receiving counseling, and most patients receiving medical treatments and prescriptions.

I started by writing critically about the "medicalization of sex" that I was observing—about how sex was becoming more like digestion than dancing! I was concerned that this would produce some negative effects: more pressure to be sexually 'normal,' standardized sexual performance goals, sexual self-consciousness and insecurity. I believed that people would have less understanding of how culture, emotions and individuality get expressed in sexuality.

In 1998 the publicity surrounding Viagra was immense, and journalists began to ask, "Where is the Viagra for women?" I thought the growth of a medicalized women's sexuality could be a harmful trend and eclipse twenty years of research on the social context of women's sexualities (e.g., gendered double standards, prevalence of violence against women, pervasive media objectification).

As a result of this, in 1999 I used the feminist organizing skills I had learned in the early second wave women's liberation 1970s to start "The New View Campaign (NVC)," a grassroots initiative to challenge the over-medicalization of sex and emphasize the aspects of sexuality that celebrate sexual culture, diversity and variety rather than medical norms and treatments. Our activities have included:

- a website (newviewcampaign.org) with coverage of our activities and many resources about women's sexuality; it's a great website if you are interested in women and sexuality
- a manifesto that criticized "female sexual dysfunction" and offered an alternative view of women's sexual problems (translated into many languages)
- producing a book, A New View of Women's Sexual Problems
- five conferences (San Francisco in 2002, Montreal in 2005, Las Vegas in 2010, Vancouver in 2011, and Bloomington, IN 2016)
- a manual for classroom and workshop use
- an online listserv
- online courses for health professionals
- testifying at the US Food and Drug Administration's advisory hearings in 2004, 2010, and 2015 when drugs for "female sexual dysfunction" came up for approval
- a street demonstration to protest female genital cosmetic surgery
- an art gallery event to celebrate genital diversity
- expanding into Facebook and Twitter social networking
- YouTube videos (especially emphasizing the importance of satire as a tool of activism)
- interviews, op-eds, and blogs in the media

Our membership has been intergenerational and interdisciplinary, and we have focused equally on academic scholarship and political activism. We hope our lasting legacy will be to contribute to several movements: feminism, critical health studies, anti-corporate public health, and humanistic sexology.

Source: Contributed by L. Tiefer, PhD.

sexual behavior have been liberating in some ways, but a sexual double standard remains, and women's sexuality is still suppressed, both overtly (genital mutilation) and covertly (the double standard). Here I will focus on efforts to empower women to protect themselves and to make sexual choices without coercion or shame—to be in charge of both the dangers and the pleasures of their sexuality.

Safer and Better Sex

What can be done to reduce risky sexual behavior? Psychologists have developed strategies that work for a wide variety of groups including urban minority teenagers and college students (Fisher & Fisher, 2000; Fisher et al., 1996; 1999). Successful strategies depend on giving people *information* about how STIs are transmitted, increasing their *motivation* to reduce their own risk, and teaching them *specific skills and behaviors.* These skills and behaviors might include practice in talking about condoms with a partner, avoiding drinking or drug use before sex, or learning how to buy and use condoms.

Community-based efforts are important, partly because school-based programs are often inadequate, and partly because many students are not invested in school learning. One example is *Esperanza,* a peer-education program serving urban teens of diverse race, class, and sexual orientation (Ashcraft, 2008). Esperanza's peer educators offer programs to schools and youth organizations about STIs, pregnancy prevention, sexual decision making, and healthy relationships. The information is beneficial to recipients and to the peer educators, who themselves are low-income urban teens, both gay and straight. One peer educator said, "You can't always believe what you hear . . . and that's why they (friends) come to me now for all this sex stuff, because it's like, '*She* has the information . . . *She's* got the lowdown on it' " (Ashcraft, 2008, p. 645).

Another example is the program developed by psychologist Michelle Kaufman for the Big Sisters/Little Sisters organization (Kaufman, 2010). This program provides accurate information on sexuality and how to talk about it to big sisters whose little sisters are approaching adolescence. The girls in this program come from difficult family situations and are at high risk for early sexual initiation, unintended pregnancy, and STIs. Helping them to understand and claim their sexuality, through talking with the big sister they trust, is an important initiative.

In educating about sexuality, what works depends on the norms of the group. For example, messages that stress risk to the individual may work better in more individualistic cultures, whereas messages that stress harm to one's family may work better in more collectivist cultures (Murray-Johnson et al., 2001). Generic appeals like "just say no" or "practice safer sex" are unlikely to change behavior. Most important, researchers need to develop feminist approaches that recognize the diverse realities of women's lives: male control of sexual decision making, coercion by male partners, economic dependence on men, and substance abuse are all factors in women's risky sexual behavior. Even those who are not disadvantaged by these factors are shaped by sexual scripts that tell them that love is all you need and a woman should do anything to please her man. Empowering women to control their own bodies is key to their sexual health (Amaro et al., 2001).

There are alternatives to androcentric thinking about sexuality. Feminists are actively creating and supporting theories of sexuality that celebrate diversity and integrate the social context of sexual expression.

Feminist theorists have developed the concept of **sexual subjectivity** to encompass aspects of sexuality from a feminist perspective. Sexual subjectivity includes three key components:

- Awareness of one's own sexual desires and responses

- A belief that one is entitled to sexual pleasure
- The ability to stand up for one's sexual safety and sexual pleasure (Schick et al., 2008)

In other words, it "consists of knowing what one wants and how to get it as well as knowing what one does not want and how to stop it" (Schick et al., 2008, p. 226). Of course, for women, achieving healthy sexual subjectivity is easier said than done because it conflicts with norms about gender-appropriate behavior.

Sexual attraction and erotic arousal are not merely programmed into us by the culture. Often, they may even contradict cultural dictates, as shown when some women develop healthy lesbian and bisexual identities or use feminist thinking to claim their sexuality. Research has demonstrated links between being a feminist and developing a healthy sexual subjectivity. In a study of 342 college women, three groups were compared: those who endorsed feminist values and self-identified as feminists; those who endorsed feminist values such as equal pay but did not label themselves feminists (termed egalitarians); and nonfeminists, who rejected everything about feminism. Feminists had the most positive attitudes about sexuality. Egalitarians had ambivalent attitudes. On the one hand, they were confident that they could be sexually assertive; on the other hand, like nonfeminists, they endorsed the sexual double standard. Egalitarians seem to think that sexual freedom is fine for themselves, but not for other women, whereas feminists were more aware of cultural constraints on all women and still positive about sexuality (Bay-Cheng & Zucker, 2007).

Other studies also have found that feminist beliefs and rejection of traditional gender roles are linked to sexual subjectivity and sexual satisfaction (Emmerink et al, 2016; Schick et al., 2008). People with feminist beliefs and attitudes are more aware of their sexual desire and engage in sex for positive reasons. They are comfortably assertive about condom use, taking care of their own health and safety. In one study, even when they were challenged by being in a hostile sexist environment, women with strong feminist beliefs maintained that they would initiate using a condom in their next sexual encounter (Fitz & Zucker, 2014). Blatant sexism did not deter their sense of sexual self-efficacy.

In spite of the social control placed on women's sexuality, most women desire and enjoy sexual pleasure with men and/or with other women. It is well to remember that in spite of social pressures from all sides, some women, some of the time, do manage to love their bodies, define sexual pleasure in their own terms, and have good sex!

Exploring Further

～

Boston Women's Health Book Collective and Judy Norsigian (2011). *Our bodies, ourselves: Informing & Inspiring Women Across Generations.* New York: Touchstone.
 This is the latest edition of the book that started a feminist revolution in women's health by establishing women as the experts on women's bodies. The diversity of women's

sexual identities and expression is respected in this indispensible reference book for women of every age and life stage.

Hyde, Janet S., & DeLamater, John (2017). *Understanding human sexuality* (13th ed.). New York: McGraw-Hill.
A matter-of-fact, nonsexist college text on human sexuality. This book, written with wisdom and humor, provides a great deal of factual information.

Braun, Virginia (2012). Female genital cutting around the globe: A matter of reproductive justice? In J.C. Chrisler (Ed.) *Reproductive Justice: A Global Concern* (pp. 29–56). Oxford: Praeger.
A comprehensive look at all kinds of female genital cutting, including surgery perpetrated on intersex individuals and that done by choice on Western women for cosmetic reasons. Braun discusses the ethics of each in its social and cultural context.

The Vagina Monologues. (DVD). (2002). An HBO Production.
Created and performed by Eve Ensler, this dramatic performance captures Ensler's unique performance of her controversial work. She performs interviews she conducted with other women about their vaginas, sex, orgasms, and menstruation.

CHAPTER 8

Commitments:
Women and Close Relationships

- **Marriage**
  Who Marries and When?
  Who Marries Whom?
  Varieties of Marriage
  Power in Marriage
  Happily Ever After? Marital Satisfaction and Psychological Adjustment
- **Lesbian Couples**
  Lesbian and Heterosexual Couples Compared
  Characteristics of Lesbian Marriages and Relationships
  Power and Satisfaction in Lesbian Relationships
- **Cohabiting Couples**
  Who Cohabits and Why?
  Does Living Together Affect Later Marriage?
- **Ending the Commitment: Divorce and Separation**
  What Are the Causes and Consequences of Divorce?
- **Remarriage**
- **Making a Difference**
  Marriage Equality for Lesbian and Gay Couples
  True Partnership: Equality in Heterosexual Marriage
- **Exploring Further**

*R*osalynn Carter and her husband, former President Jimmy Carter, have been married for 70 years. According to the Carters, their marriage has been long and happy because of their shared ideals and because they enjoy activities together: skiing, birdwatching, biking. They both are working for world peace through the Carter Center (Alter, 2016).

When people marry they hope it will last a lifetime. These hopes are encouraged by couples like Rosalynn and Jimmy who have made lives of mutual love and respect together. It's not just a Democratic thing either—former President George Bush and his wife Barbara have beat the Carters' record by being married for 71 years!

However, despite these examples, not all marriages work out well. And there are enduring commitments to a partner other than marriage. Until recently, gay and lesbian couples did not have the right to marry, and more and more heterosexual couples live together without getting married. In this chapter we explore the kinds of commitments couples make to each other and the consequences of these commitments for women.

Marriage

As a very old joke puts it, "Marriage is an institution—but who wants to live in an institution?" This joke recognizes that marriage is a way that societies regulate private relationships between couples. Laws and statutes stipulate who may marry whom—for example, in the past, interracial marriages were forbidden. Laws also regulate the minimum age for marriage, the division of property when marriages dissolve (indeed, whether they are permitted to dissolve), and the responsibilities of each partner within the marriage (what behaviors constitute grounds for divorce). Religious codes and social norms also regulate marriage and divorce.

Although people in Western societies are aware that marriage is a legal contract subject to regulation by the state, they rarely think of it that way in relation to themselves. Rather, they are influenced by the ideology of love and romance, choosing their partners as individuals and expecting to live out their married lives according to their own needs and wishes. (See Figure 8.1.) Nevertheless, the rights and responsibilities imposed by the state may have consequences for both partners, especially when a marriage ends.

As an institution, marriage has a strong patriarchal heritage (Grana, 2002). Historically, wealth and titles were passed on only through male heirs. In many countries married women are still regarded as the property of their husbands. In the United States most women still give up their own name and take their husband's name upon marriage.

Patriarchal traditions are slow to change. Even in the 21st century, people expect a man to propose by getting down on one knee and presenting a woman with a diamond ring. In a survey, two-thirds of U.S. college students said they would definitely want the man to be the one to propose, and not a single student,

©LWA/Jay Newman/Blend Images LLC RF

FIGURE 8.1   Most people look forward to marrying.

male or female, said they would definitely want the woman to propose. The reasons they gave for leaving it to the guy were mostly gender based traditions. One man said simply, "Because I'm the man." A woman said, "It would be more romantic. I'd be able to tell the story to my girlfriends . . ." (Robnett & Leaper, 2013, p.106).

> When people marry, they are not just establishing a personal relationship, they are fitting into a scripted social institution. "The idea of marriage is larger than any individual marriage. The role of husband or wife is greater than any individual who takes on that role" (Blumstein & Schwartz, 1983, p. 318).

Who Marries and When?

More than 90 percent of people in the U.S. marry at some time in their lives, according to U.S. Census data (Lewis & Kreider, 2015). Marital patterns are divergent across ethnic groups. For example, African American women are the least likely of any group to be married. However, there has been very little research on marriage using African American, Hispanic, Asian American, or other ethnic group samples, and little on working-class people (Orbuch & Brown, 2006). Most research on American marriage has been done with White, middle-class samples, and it's helpful to keep this bias in mind while exploring this topic.

In general, women marry at younger ages than men do. Women in developing areas of the world marry very young. In many parts of Africa and Asia, the average young woman is married before she reaches the age of 20, and child marriage is a persistent form of oppression (Callaghan et al., 2015; United Nations, 2000). In the U.S., women are marrying later than they used to. According to the most recent (2010) census, the median first-time bride is 26.5 and the median groom is 28.7 years old. Just a generation or so ago, she was 20 and he was 22.8. A similar trend toward later marriage is occurring in other developed countries.

Why are American women marrying later? They are more likely than women of previous generations to invest in higher education. Also, advances in contraception have made premarital sex and living-together arrangements less risky. For Black women, there is a shortage of marriageable men, due to a number of socioeconomic forces (Orbuch & Brown, 2006). (See Chapter 9 for more on African American family patterns.) Economic factors may play a part, too, when young people find it difficult to become financially independent (Teachman et al., 2006).

Whatever the causes, the tendency to marry later has important implications for women. A woman can do a lot of living between 20 and 26.5. She can finish job training, college, or internships. She can get started on a job or career, support herself independently, learn how to manage her money, and live on her own. She can have relationships, exploring her sexuality and what she wants in a partner. All in all, she is likely to enter marriage at a later age with a well-developed identity and broad horizons for her life.

Who Marries Whom?

In a cross-cultural study, more than 9,000 people from 37 nations representing every part of the world were asked to assess the importance of 31 characteristics in a potential mate (Buss et al., 1990). The characteristics included good health, chastity, dependability, intelligence, social status, religious background, neatness, ambition, and sociability.

The biggest difference across cultures was in a cluster of characteristics reflecting traditional values such as premarital virginity, being a good cook and housekeeper, and desire for a home and children. For example, samples from China, Indonesia, India, and Iran placed great importance on virginity; those from Scandinavia considered it irrelevant.

Overall, cultural differences were much more important than gender differences. Men and women from the same culture were more similar in their mate preferences than were men from different cultures or women from different cultures. In fact, men's and women's rankings were virtually identical overall, with a correlation of +.95. This gender similarity suggests that each culture—whether Bulgarian, Irish, Japanese, Zambian, Venezuelan, or whatever—socializes men and women to accept its particular script for marriage. When all 37 cultures were considered, an overall picture of an ideal mate emerged. Both women and men rated mutual attraction and love, dependable character, emotional stability, and pleasing disposition as the four most important characteristics in a potential marriage partner.

There were some gender differences, however. Across cultures, women were more likely to emphasize a partner's earning capacity, while men were more likely to emphasize physical attractiveness. Women's desire for a man with material resources became a matter of theoretical controversy, because some evolutionary psychologists claimed it is a cross-cultural universal built into the human species, related to the female's need for a male to invest in offspring (Buss, 2011). Other psychologists, those with a sociocultural orientation, believed that this preference might be largely due to women's historical lack of opportunities to provide for themselves. Psychologist Alice Eagly was the first to test this theory by showing that women's preferences for men with material resources was greatest in countries where the women had the least ability to gain resources on their own—where they were denied equal access to education and jobs (Eagly & Wood, 1999). Since then, using more sophisticated measures of gender equality in more nations around the world, and re-analyzing the data from the original 37-nation study, researchers have shown that gender differences in mate preferences shrink as women gain more equality in each country. As women make progress toward gender equality, what they look for in a mate changes. They focus less on a prospective mate's financial prospects and ambition, and more on his sociability, education, intelligence, and their mutual attraction (Zentner & Mitura, 2012; Zentner & Eagly, 2015). This flexibility in women's mating preferences suggests that choosing a high-status, wealthy man is not so much a result of evolutionary pressures as a way of coping with patriarchy.

Varieties of Marriage

In the United States, many marriage patterns coexist. I will classify marriages into three types (traditional, modern, and egalitarian) based on three important characteristics: the division of authority, how spousal roles are defined, and the amount of companionship and shared activities they provide (Peplau & Gordon, 1985; Schwartz, 1994).

Traditional Marriage

In a *traditional marriage,* both the husband and wife agree that the husband should have greater authority; he is the head of the family, or the boss. Even in areas in which the wife has some decision-making responsibility (such as household shopping), he retains veto power over her decisions. The wife is a full-time homemaker who does not work for pay. Clear distinctions are made between the husband's and wife's responsibilities. She is responsible for home and child care, and he is the breadwinner. Couples in these marriages may not expect to be best friends; rather, the wife finds companionship with other women—neighbors, sisters and other kin, or members of her church. The husband's friendship networks are with male kin and coworkers, and his leisure activities take place apart from his wife.

Attitudes toward traditional marriage have changed a great deal in the past few decades. These changes do not mean that marriages based on traditional beliefs and values are entirely a thing of the past. Certain religious groups still strongly endorse traditional marriage. For example, Orthodox Jews, Latter-Day Saints (Mormons), some evangelical Christian sects, the Promise Keepers, and Nation of Islam insist that distinct gender roles and submission by the wife to her husband are necessary for marital and societal stability (Hewlett & West, 1998). About 29 percent of women with children under 18 are stay-at-home moms, a proportion that has increased in recent years (Pew Research Center, 2014). A couple may plan for the wife to keep on working after they have children, but change their minds once the first baby arrives, and their marriage soon becomes more traditional than they expected. Here, two traditional husbands describe to an interviewer how they decided their wives would stay home with their children:

> My daughter wasn't 18 hours old and . . . I was holding her in the room, that night with my wife there and I just looked at my daughter and I told my wife I said, "There's no way I can put this child in day care."

> I was afraid to touch this boy all the time because he was so small. That was not even an option for me to stay home. I'd have to call her all day asking, "Honey, how do you do this? How does this thing go on him?" Ah, no, that was never even a question (Kaufman & White, 2016, p. 1593, 1594).

Modern Marriage

In *modern marriage,* the spouses have a "senior partner–junior partner" or "near-peer" relationship. Modern wives work outside the home, but, by mutual agreement, the wife's job is less important than the husband's. He is the breadwinner and she is just working to help out. Moreover, it is expected that her paid employment will not interfere with her responsibilities for housework and child care. Within modern marriage, the husband and wife may spend an equal amount of time on paid work, but that work has different meanings because of the belief that the man is the real provider (Steil, 2001). Modern couples emphasize companionship and expect to share leisure activities. They value togetherness and may discuss husband/wife roles rather than taking them for granted as more traditional couples do.

Modern marriage may seem to be a relationship of equality when compared with traditional marriage, but the equality is relative, because wives have more responsibility for the home and the children. Modern wives do a *second shift* every day—they put in a day's work for pay and another day's work when they get home (Amato et al., 2007; Hochschild, 1989). The kids expect Mom to do the second shift of childcare and think it would be unfair if Dad had to do it (Sinno & Killen, 2011).

The unequal division of labor in modern marriages is normative and hard to change. So too is the greater priority given to the husband's job or career. In a national dataset of couples surveyed during the recession of 2007–2009, wives were more likely to say they would move 500 miles if their husbands were offered a good job than husbands were to say they would do the same for their wife (Davis et al., 2012). Even in the tough economic climate of a recession, couples were not willing to prioritize a wife's career.

Egalitarian Marriage

Egalitarian marriage, once relatively rare, is becoming more common (Knudson-Martin & Mahoney, 2005; Schwartz, 1994). In *egalitarian marriages,* the partners have equal power and authority. They also share responsibilities equally without respect to gender roles. For example, one partner's paid job is not allowed to take precedence over the other's. In practical terms, this means that either partner might relocate to accommodate the other's promotion, or either would agree to miss work to care for a sick child. Egalitarian fathers do not believe that their wives are uniquely qualified to do all the childcare. They are comfortable with using daycare and preschool helpers. As one father of two said, children with stay-at-home moms are not necessarily better off:

> . . . when they're 5 years old and they have been at home their whole life, they don't do very good in getting into school. I mean, they are suddenly not used to sharing things, they're not used to having all these other people, they're not used to being away from mom (Kaufman & White, 2016, p. 1598).

The ever-present tasks of running a household—cleaning, cooking, bill paying, errands—are allocated by interest and ability, not because certain jobs are supposed to be women's work and others men's work. One wife in an egalitarian relationship described her commitment to nonsexist task allocation like this:

> I believe that people should be flexible. A woman, if she can fix (the) light, she should fix the light . . . I don't believe in taking care of husbands . . . when I'm still showering, he irons my clothes for me . . . even cooking is not fixed, although I love to cook (Quek & Knudson-Martin, 2006, p. 64).

Such marriages are *post gender relationships;* the partners have moved beyond using gender to define their marital roles. More than any other type of marriage, an egalitarian relationship provides the couple with intimacy, companionship, and mutual respect. This husband, whose wife's educational and job status are equal to his own (both have master's degrees and their job rank is similar), says that he has no need to feel superior to her:

> I need (the relationship) to be equal. If I am in a more dominant kind of position, this will not make me feel right. I would only feel as if I'm not able to engage with the most important person in my life at the level I would like to engage in (Quek & Knudson-Martin, 2006, p. 61).

©BananaStock/Alamy RF

FIGURE 8.2   Egalitarian couples enjoy doing activities together.

Because egalitarian couples share a great deal, they are likely to understand each other, communicate well, and choose to spend a lot of time together (see Figure 8.2). Often, each partner says that the other is their best friend, precious and irreplaceable, and that their relationship is unique (Risman & Johnson-Sumerford, 1998; Schwartz, 1994).

Power in Marriage

Different marriage types reflect different beliefs about what the duties of husband and wife should be and how they should relate to each other. Completely egalitarian marriages are still relatively rare. Although Americans like to think of marriage as an equal partnership, men may still end up having more power. Why is it that the result of a stroll down the aisle and the words "I do" is often a long-term state of inequality?

One definition of power is the ability to get one's way or influence decisions. In classic studies of marital power in the 1960s and 1970s, sociologists found severe imbalances. For example, 60 percent of men decided whether their wives were allowed to hold a paying job (Blood & Wolfe, 1960). In a study of Canadian households, 76 percent of wives said that the husband was the boss and only 13 percent said both had equal power (Turk & Bell, 1972). Although the imbalance is no longer so extreme, more recent research confirms that marital equality is still not the norm (Bulanda, 2011). Fewer than one-third of heterosexual dual-career couples share marital roles in egalitarian ways (Amato et al., 2007; Gilbert & Kearney, 2006). For the majority, although roles and responsibilities are more balanced than in traditional marriages, there may still be a consistent pattern of inequality that is accepted by both partners. For example, even though women and men agree that women do far more housework and child care in most marriages, most don't see it as a problem. In a major survey first conducted in 1980 and replicated in 2000, the majority of respondents in both time periods said that this imbalance was fair (Amato et al., 2007). Couples may construct a *myth of equality,* refusing to acknowledge how gender socialization and social forces have steered them toward traditional roles (Knudson-Martin & Mahoney, 1996; 2005).

How Do Couples Justify Marital Inequality?

Power in marriage is both structural and ideological—it is related to societal structures that give men greater status and earning power and also to beliefs about who is better at nurturing or more suited to doing housework (Dallos & Dallos, 1997). How is marital power exerted and justified? How do couples create myths of equality and explain away inequalities in their own marriages?

When a sample of highly educated dual-career couples was asked about other couples' relationships, they defined equality in terms of task sharing. However, when asked about their own relationships, they talked less about who did the cooking and cleaning than about abstract concepts like mutual respect (Rosenbluth et al., 1998). In fact, most of the couples had not achieved their ideal of equality: the women did more household work and their careers were secondary to that of their husbands' careers. They did not focus on adding up who did what around the house, perhaps because it would make the inequality painfully apparent. Redefining the situation is a common way to avoid perceiving injustice of all kinds (Steil, 2001).

In an in-depth study of 17 British couples, the wives and husbands were first interviewed together and then, 18 months later, they were interviewed separately (Dryden, 1999). The researcher was aware that, in general, married couples might not openly acknowledge inequality. Ideologically, most couples believe that marriage is supposed to be about love, sharing, and mutual respect. Wives might be particularly unable to challenge inequalities in their marriages because of being dependent on a husband's income or having young children to take care of. Openly admitting their dissatisfactions might be emotionally almost "too hard to bear" (p. 58). For husbands, admitting inequality might lead to a loss of power and privilege. Therefore, the researcher analyzed the interview data for subtle ways that the women and men justified the status quo.

The women used distancing, talking about behavior and roles in vague, hypothetical terms rather than challenging their husbands openly ("*Some* men sit around watching the telly all day . . ."). They minimized conflict or blamed themselves when it happened ("It's only silly little things we fight about and maybe I take them too seriously"). They also made positive comparisons between their husband and other people's husbands ("Some women have it really bad, their husbands don't do a thing to help, so I'm in a fairly equal situation"). These strategies helped the women create a vision of relative marital fairness for themselves and the interviewer.

Although the women's challenges were indirect and hedged with self-blame, the men often tried to deflect them, without actually mentioning inequality. Their strategies included describing their wives as inadequate ("If she were better organized, she could get all her work done with time left over") and themselves as "hard done by" (having to work long hours and needing more time out with the boys). The researcher noted that the husbands reflected back to their wives a negative identity that the wives had already created through self-blame—a "subtle undermining process that had the power to exacerbate in women a sense of lack of confidence, low self-esteem, and in some cases, depression" (p. 86). Clearly, these couples were doing gender in ways that preserved and perpetuated inequality in their marriages.

What Are the Sources of Men's Greater Power?

Many factors are associated with husband dominance in marriage (Steil, 1997). Social class and ethnicity make a difference: Black and working-class couples have less of a power differential than White middle- and upper-class couples. Wives who are employed have more power than those who work only at home. White middle-class women in traditional marriages may have less marital power than any other group of women (Bulanda, 2011).

One reason the power balance in marriage is weighted in favor of men is the influence of traditional gender ideology. If either or both spouses believe that the man *should* be in charge, he is likely to have more decision-making power. Traditional gender ideology is strongest in collectivist cultures, which stress responsibility to one's family and society above individual needs. Women in collectivist cultures are not allowed to prioritize their careers, to say no to serving men and children, or to place their own needs first. In a study of newly married couples in Singapore (a highly developed and economically successful Asian republic), some were working toward egalitarian relationships while others were still voicing traditional values about gender. One wife stated, "The man must always be the man of the house. He will make the major decisions." Another couple, asked about power and authority in their marriage, agreed with each other:

> She: *I have to be supportive. I still believe that behind every successful man is a wife, a loving wife.*
> He: *I would have more authority because our mindset is of the older generation* (Quek & Knudson-Martin, 2006, p. 60).

This traditional gender ideology is not limited to collectivist cultures. In the United States, it is often related to faith-based attitudes (God intended women and men to play different roles) or beliefs about human nature (gender differences are natural and built in to the species). For example, James (a school counselor) and Kwan (an accountant) have one child and another on the way. It is Kwan who insists that James is rightfully in charge, "I want the father to be the head of the house and I want him to lead or make important decisions." She describes her husband as "a big thinker" and "stronger" than she is, and describes herself as emotional. He says it's "not natural" for him to notice housework that needs doing, and that is why Kwan usually does it (Knudson-Martin & Mahoney, 2005).

Another explanation for greater male power in marriage comes from *social exchange theory* (Thibault & Kelley, 1959). This theory proposes that the partner who brings greater outside resources to the relationship will have the greater influence in it. The partner who has less to offer, be it status, money, or knowledge, will likely take a back seat. Gender confers status on men in itself, and husbands usually earn more than wives, even when both are employed full time. (This is true for a variety of reasons that I will discuss in Chapter 10.) As already noted, wives who have no income or employment of their own have the least power of any group of married women. Moreover, the husband in most marriages traditionally has had a higher level of education than the wife. In American society, educational attainment brings status and prestige in itself and is also associated with higher income. When the husband earns more, many couples agree that he automatically has the right to make financial decisions for the family. But the money he brings in also may give the husband the right to make other decisions that have nothing to do with money. In a British study, one wife described how things changed when she began to earn money on her own:

> Before, I had five children and was very vulnerable, I avoided raising some issues because I was worried that he would stop giving me any money . . . he threatened it a couple of times and that was enough . . . now I'm earning things have changed, I'm not so quiet about things I don't like now (Dallos & Dallos, 1997, p. 58).

Because of its practical and symbolic importance, it's not surprising that fights about money plague many marriages. In a study where 200 husbands and wives kept diaries about the conflicts they had with each other, money was not the topic they fought about about most often—children and chores topped the list. However, the fights about money were more severe, more problematic, and more likely to recur, even though couples (particularly the wives) kept trying to resolve them (Papp et al., 2009).

Social exchange theory is limited; it has focused on economic exchange while ignoring the symbolic value of gender roles. The breadwinner or provider role, still more important for men than women, means that men's capacity to earn money is more highly valued than their capacity to nurture children. For women, on the other hand, providing nurturance to husband and children is more valued than the ability to earn money. Even if a wife brings in as much money as her husband, she may not have equal power because her success is seen as undermining his provider role and interfering with her nurturing role. In other words, the same resource (in this case, earned income) may function differently for husband and wife.

Just how central is earning power to marital equality? Does its influence work the same way for husbands and wives? To answer these questions it is necessary to study couples in which the wives earn as much or more than their husbands. Couples like these used to be rare but today about 30 percent of wives earn more than their husbands (Commuri & Gentry, 2005).

In one study, 30 couples in which the wife earned at least one-third more than the husband were compared with an equal number of couples in which the husbands earned at least one-third more than the wives (Steil & Weltman, 1991). Respondents were asked questions about the relative importance of careers ("Whose career is more important in the relationship?") and decision-making power ("Who has more say about household/financial issues?"). Consistent with social exchange theory, spouses who earned more saw their careers as more important and also had more say at home than spouses who earned less. Nevertheless, wives overall had less say in financial decisions, had more responsibility for children and housework, and felt that their husbands' careers were more important than their own.

In a more recent study, couples were interviewed repeatedly over a 2-year period. In each couple, the wife earned at least $10,000 more than her husband, and in some couples the gap was as much as $120,000. These couples struggled with how to honor the man's provider role even though he was not bringing home most of the bacon. One strategy they used was to pool their money into a shared account, making the gendered earning difference less obvious (Commuri & Gentry, 2005). A comparison group of couples in which the men earned more did not use this money management strategy nearly as much. Instead, each spouse paid expenses in proportion to his/her income.

The meaning of earning more money differs between White and racial/ ethnic groups. For African American women, who traditionally have had vital roles as wage earners for their families, earning more than their husbands affected their marital happiness negatively only if they also were highly religious and traditional in gender beliefs (Furdyna et al., 2008).

To sum it up, equal access to money can be an equalizer of power in marriage— but even when wives earn more money than their husbands, beliefs about the appropriate roles of women and men may still influence the balance of power in favor of men. This implies that in order to change power imbalances in marriage, both women's economic power and couples' gender ideology will have to change. Because women's earning power seems to be changing faster than gender ideology, couples where the woman out-earns the man use strategies like pooling their incomes to cope with the embarrassment of being gender-deviant. The good news is that marriage equality is increasing in many parts of the world. Women are becoming more educated and economically equal relative to men and are marrying at a later age, so they bring more resources of their own to relationships. The traditional ideology of patriarchy is losing its hold (Xu & Lai, 2002). Egalitarian marriage is not yet the norm, but it is becoming more and more common, and may be the wave of the future (Esteve et al., 2012; Kulik, 2011).

Happily Ever After? Marital Satisfaction and Psychological Adjustment

"Happily ever after" is our society's romantic ideal of marriage. Does marriage bring happiness and fulfillment? At first glance, the answer is a resounding "Yes!" Over 20 years of research has consistently shown that married people report being happier than single, divorced, widowed or cohabiting people—happier with themselves, their relationships and with life in general (Vanassche et al., 2013). (See Figure 8.3.) Social scientists attributed this to two main causes: the intrinsic benefits of marriage (social support, economic security, a sexual partner, basis for family) and selection bias (more stable and happy people are more likely to marry and stay married in the first place).

For a long time, no one thought to look at the larger social context of this research: the fact that marriage is normative, something that is expected of everyone. Would unmarried people be just as happy as married people if they weren't under pressure to get married? If they weren't considered rejects or deviants? A recent 24-nation study tested this idea by measuring the extent to which each nation did not stigmatize other ways of living (staying single, living together without being married, LGB relationships). In these countries, there was no relationship between marriage and happiness for women! (Vanassche et al., 2013). This and other new research (Lee & Ono, 2012; Stavrova et al., 2012; Wadsworth, 2016) suggests that heterosexual marriage is linked to happiness only when it's the norm. If other ways of being in relationship were equally acceptable, perhaps marital status and happiness would be totally unrelated. What do you think?

Does Marital Happiness Change Over Time?

The happiness and satisfaction of married couples varies greatly across the course of a marriage. Almost all studies of marital satisfaction over time show an initial "honeymoon period" followed by a substantial decline in happiness with the birth of the first child. Wives are more likely than husbands to become dissatisfied with the marriage over time. Satisfaction often hits its lowest point when the children are school-aged or adolescents. Some studies have shown that the happiness of the early years is regained or even surpassed in later life, when the children have grown

FIGURE 8.3   Affection and companionship are among the benefits of marriage.

and left home. In other studies, the happiness trend has been all downhill (Amato et al., 2007; Bulanda, 2011; Wendorf et al., 2011).

What accounts for the changes in marital happiness after the birth of children? When more than 700 women were studied during pregnancy and three months after the birth of their first child, they reported doing much more of the housework and child care than they had expected. Their negative feelings about their marriages were related to the violation of their expectancies of equal sharing. In other words, it was not the added domestic chores that made these new mothers less happy than they had been, but their feeling that the new division of labor was unfair. The more they had expected equality, the more dissatisfied they were (Ruble et al., 1988). Other studies have documented higher levels of depression in women whose hopes for shared child care were not achieved. Following up on this early research, 119 expectant couples in an ethnically diverse sample (White, African American, Asian American, and Hispanic) completed questionnaires about actual and expected household responsibilities before and after the birth of their baby, and were also observed interacting with the baby (Khazan et al., 2008). The study found that the more the women's wishes were unfulfilled, the more their marital satisfaction declined. In addition, when women's expectancies for (equal) help regarding infant care had been violated, parents' interactions regarding their infant showed subtle signs of conflict and poor coordination between the parents. To put it bluntly, when new dads refused to change diapers or get up at night, parenting interactions became a lot less friendly and cooperative, and parenting was less effective.

You might expect that happiness would decline less among women who feel respected and appreciated by their husbands, and this is just what was found in a study that followed couples for 6 years. Women whose marital satisfaction stayed the same or increased after giving birth were those who said that their husbands expressed love and were "tuned in" to their wives and their relationships. Those women whose marital satisfaction declined were those who perceived their husbands as negative or their lives as out of control and chaotic (Shapiro et al., 2000).

When children leave home, couples have fewer demands on their money and time. Many couples experience this stage of their marriage as a time of greater freedom and flexibility, and therefore their marital happiness increases. In a study of 300 middle-aged and older married couples, partners were observed as they discussed a current conflict and also as they collaborated on a task (planning errands). The older couples had higher marital satisfaction overall. When collaborating, they were both warm and assertive. Even when they disagreed they were less upset about it than the younger couples (Smith et al., 2009).

Is Marriage Linked to Psychological Well-Being?

Marriage is associated with better psychological adjustment in both women and men. However, the benefits are unequally distributed: Men are more satisfied than women with their marriages and receive greater mental health benefits from being married. Compared to single men, married men have fewer alcohol abuse problems, are less likely to commit crimes, and are less likely to have psychological disorders such as depression. They have greater career success, earn more money, are healthier, and live longer than never-married, widowed, or divorced men (Steil & Hoffman, 2006).

The psychological benefits of marriage are related to the balance of power. Both husbands and wives are most satisfied with their marriages when decision-making is relatively equal (Amato et al., 2007). The relationship between balance of power, marital satisfaction, and women's psychological well-being has been most studied in White middle-class dual career couples (Steil & Turetsky, 1987), but the relationship between relative equality and satisfaction seems to hold in other groups too, such as a community sample of African-American couples (Stanik & Bryant, 2012). In a sample of first-generation immigrant Latino/a couples, the more traditional the man's attitudes about gender roles were, and the more different from the woman's, the lower the satisfaction in their marriage (Falconier, 2013). Compared to relationships in which either partner dominates, more egalitarian relationships have more constructive communication, more affection and intimacy, greater sexual satisfaction, and more overall happiness with the marriage (Steil & Hoffman, 2006). Women in traditional marriages have the poorest psychological adjustment (Steil, 1997; Steil & Turetsky, 1987).

One cause of men's better outcomes in marriage is that wives may provide more emotional support for husbands than they receive in return (Steil & Hoffman, 2006). We will look at women's emotion work more closely in Chapters 9 and 10. Briefly, it includes things like confiding thoughts and feelings, asking about their partner's thoughts and opinions, offering encouragement, listening, and respecting the partner's point of view. Studies from the 1980s onward suggest that husbands usually depend on wives for emotional support; but too often, they do not offer equal support in return. Lacking the return of emotional support, women are less happy than their partners. In one study of more than 4,000 married persons—aged 55 and over—husbands said they were most likely to confide in their wives, while wives were less likely to confide in their husbands and more likely to turn to a friend, sister, or daughter. Both men and women who confided in their spouses had markedly higher marital satisfaction and overall psychological well-being than those who did not (Lee, 1988). The work of caring and emotional support that married women do may partly account for their husbands' better psychological adjustment.

Lesbian Couples

In small-sample surveys conducted over the past several decades, the majority of lesbians were in a steady relationship (Peplau & Spalding, 2000). But for a long time it was difficult to estimate how many lesbian couples there are. It was only in 2000 that the U.S. census added a category for unmarried partners. The 2010 census recorded 646,464 same-sex couple households, with 332,887 of these being lesbian couples. (The Census Bureau does not distinguish married same-sex couples from those in civil unions or registered domestic partnerships or those who are not in a legally recognized relationship. All these groups are designated as same-sex couple households.) More than one in five same-sex couples is interracial or interethnic, compared to less than one in 10 heterosexual married couples (Gates, 2012). The number of gay and lesbian households grew rapidly in the past decade.

Lesbian and Heterosexual Couples Compared

When two women make a commitment to live together as lovers and friends, their relationship has some similarities to conventional marriage—but without the institutional aspects or the label. To date, there has been very little research on legally married lesbian or gay couples, because they are few and newly married.

Like heterosexual people, most LGBTQ people believe in marriage. (See Box 8.1.) In an Internet survey of more than 1,500 LGBTQ people in 27 countries, 95 percent agreed that same-sex couples should be allowed to marry just like different-sex couples are (Harding & Peel, 2006).

BOX 8.1 ∾ A Marriage to Remember: Del Martin And Phyllis Lyon

Del and Phyllis moved in together on Valentine's Day. It was 1953, and they'd already been partners for two years, sharing a passion for feminist and gay rights activism. The couple went on to found the first political organization for lesbians in the U.S., Daughters of Bilitis, and were editors of its pioneering journal, *The Ladder*. They were the first lesbian couple to join the National Organization for Women and were active in its leadership, incorporating lesbian issues into its agenda. They also wrote two books together, *Lesbian/Woman* (1972) and *Lesbian Love and Liberation* (1973). As they grew older together, they engaged in elder activism; both served on the White House Conference on Aging in 1995.

Del and Phyllis were the first same-sex couple to marry when it became legal in San Francisco in 2004. However, their marriage was voided by the California Supreme Court six months later, along with those of thousands of other same-sex couples. Phyllis said, "Del is 83 years old and I am 79. After being together more than 50 years, it is a terrible blow to have the rights and protections of marriage taken away from us. At our age, we do not have the luxury of time."

On June 16, 2008, the day when same-sex marriage was once again legalized in California, Phyllis and Del were once again the first couple married. Sadly, their time as a married couple was short.

©Marcio Jose Sanchez/AP Images

Del Martin died in August of that year at the age of 87. After more than 55 years with her beloved Phyllis, she did not live to see the Supreme Court ruling that legalized same-sex marriage nationwide. When Phyllis, then age 90, heard the news of the Supreme Court decision, she laughed with joy. "Well how about that?" she said. "For goodness' sakes."

Sources: http://www.nytimes.com/2008/08/28/us/28martin.html
http://lgbthistorymonth.com/del-martin-phyllis-lyon?tab
=biography
http://www.cbsnews.com/news/calif-same-sex
-marriages-voided/
http://www.latimes.com/local/la-me-california-gay-marriage
-20150627-story.html

Contributed by MC and Annie B. Fox

For many years, researchers and the public alike assumed that lesbian couples mimic traditional heterosexual roles, with one partner being the "husband" ("butch") and the other the "wife" ("femme"). This belief applies a heterosexual script to lesbian relationships. Most research shows there is no clear preference for masculine/feminine roles among lesbians (Peplau & Spalding, 2000). Instead, they tend to be more like friendships between peers. When lesbian partners describe their relationships, they use terms such as mutual respect, compatibility, shared decision-making, equal rights, and equal value for both partners (Garnets, 2008).

Among lesbian and queer women, the terms butch and femme are usually used simply to distinguish between those who reject feminine ways of dressing and acting, and those who choose more stereotypically feminine ways of dressing and acting (Goldberg, 2013). Therefore, when lesbians do endorse butch/femme roles, it may be with different meanings than heterosexuals might assume. When a researcher asked a sample of 235 self-identified lesbians to define and apply these concepts to themselves, 40 percent of the sample said they were neither. The higher a woman's education and income, the more likely she was to have an independent (not butch/femme) identity (Weber, 1996). Only about 26 percent identified themselves as butch and 34 percent as femme. However, these women did not use butch/femme to represent husband/wife roles. To them, butch signified that they did not enjoy girly things such as makeup, dresses, and hair styling. Femme signified the freedom to enjoy a feminine personal style, while still being committed to loving women. They stressed that butch did not mean they were dominant, acted like men, or disliked being a woman, and femme had nothing to do with being submissive. In summary, the butch/femme dimension has been important to some lesbians, and it is linked to social class, but it is not about relationship dominance.

Characteristics of Lesbian Marriages and Relationships

Lesbian marriages and relationships can be described on the same dimensions as heterosexual marriages: companionship, communication, roles and the division of labor, power, and satisfaction.

Most lesbians reject gender roles (Peplau & Spalding, 2000). When looking for a long-term partner, they prefer characteristics such as intelligence and interpersonal sensitivity (Regan et al., 2001). They are more likely than gay men to live with their partner, to desire sexual fidelity and a steady monogamous relationship. They value emotional closeness and intimacy (Garnets, 2008).

Same-sex couples cannot assign the breadwinner role on the basis of gender, and they tend to value independence. Therefore, the importance of the work interests of each partner is more likely to be fairly equal than in heterosexual marriages. The great majority of lesbian and gay couples are in dual-earner or dual-career relationships. Just as they balance work roles, lesbians are highly likely to share household duties. They assign housekeeping chores on the basis of preference, skills, and ability(Goldberg, 2013). As one woman explained to an interviewer:

> There are certain things that one of us is just better at than the other, so it's divided that way. I'm much more mechanically inclined, so if something needs to be put to-

gether, fixed or something like that, I'm just better at it. My partner is very good at remembering to water the plants. . . . I didn't even know we had plants (Kelly & Hauck, 2015, p. 455).

However they divide the chores, the basic principle is fairness. For example, one couple (I'll call them Sue and Tonya) described to researchers how Sue managed the money and retirement funds for both, and in return, Tonya put in extra time caring for Sue's elderly mother (Bailey & Jackson, 2005). Each partner got to do what she did best, and each was grateful to the other for the mutually agreed-on division of labor.

Same-sex couples tend to share more leisure activities than heterosexual couples. They are more likely to socialize with friends together, belong to the same clubs, and share hobbies and sports interests. Perhaps, due to socialization, two women are more likely to have interests in common than a woman and a man; or perhaps most people need same-gender best friends, and lesbians can find a same-gender friend and a spouse in the same person. These ties may be one reason that when a relationship ends many former lesbian partners remain good friends (Clarke et al., 2010).

Power and Satisfaction in Lesbian Relationships

Most lesbians desire egalitarian relationships. Power differences in a lesbian relationship are usually due to the same factors that influence power in heterosexual relationships, such as one partner having greater resources (more money, status, or education), or one partner being more committed than the other. However, the egalitarian ideal may be more important than status and money in determining power relations among lesbians. Unlike heterosexual couples, many of whom believe that the man should be the head of the family, lesbian couples are more likely to start out with a belief in total equality. Therefore, money and other resources do not automatically equate to power. Pam (an office manager) and Linda (a writer) have been a couple for 15 years. Pam describes the "give and take" in their relationship:

A couple of times I have been out of work and Linda has been really supportive. Also, she's been out of work, and I've had to support us. So, it's flip-flopped. And it's never any of that "I'm sick of supporting you" . . . Never. That would never happen in our relationship (Bailey & Jackson, 2005, p. 61).

The equality in lesbian relationships compared to heterosexual relationships has led some researchers to suggest that heterosexual couples may be able to learn from lesbians about how to negotiate egalitarian relationships (Clarke et al., 2010). Comparing the two kinds of relationships can also help researchers learn more about factors in the partners and in the social structure around them that foster more egalitarian patterns of living. For example, in contrast to heterosexual couples, where the partner who earns more money often has more power, lesbian couples' balance of power tends toward equality even when one works for pay and the other does housework, cooking, and childcare. This may be because both are socialized as women to appreciate and value women's domestic work, to see it as important, creative, and meaningful (Goldberg, 2013).

Studies that have compared the self-reported satisfaction and happiness of lesbian and heterosexual couples show few differences between the two. Like heterosexual women, lesbians are likely to enjoy sex in committed relationships more than casual ones (Garnets, 2008; Mark et al., 2015). Satisfaction in lesbian relationships is higher when the two partners are equally committed to the relationship, when they have similar attitudes and values, and when they perceive their relationship as fair and equitable. Lesbian relationships tend to decline in satisfaction over time at about the same rate as those of heterosexual married people (Clarke et al., 2010; Kurdek, 2007). In one study of 75 lesbian couples in the United States and Canada, both partners in each couple took part in an Internet survey that measured personality factors, perceptions of equality, and relationship satisfaction (Horne & Biss, 2009). When partners perceived their relationship to be unequal, their anxiety about it, particularly among those whose attachment was insecure, led to lower relationship satisfaction. These results reinforce a conclusion drawn from earlier research: Equality is very important to lesbian partners.

External pressures affect relationships, too. Women who love women have to cope with prejudice and discrimination. Parents and other family members may reject or disown a lesbian daughter, remove her from a will, refuse to acknowledge the partner or the relationship, exclude the couple from family gatherings, or encourage them to break up. One important factor in relationship satisfaction for lesbians is having a good social support network. Receiving social support from friends and family is related to individual psychological adjustment as well as happiness in the relationship for both lesbian and gay couples (Berger, 1990; Kurdek, 1988).

Are gay activists right in encouraging lesbians to come out to friends and family despite the risk of rejection? The evidence is mixed. Although some studies show that women who are out to significant others in their lives (family, friends, and employers) report more satisfaction with their partners, others find that relationship satisfaction is unrelated to disclosure about being a lesbian (Jordan & Deluty, 2000; Beals & Peplau, 2001). Interviews with lesbian couples suggest that being out does influence satisfaction with the relationship because it helps them support each other in coping with homophobic prejudice and discrimination, and to feel connected to their communities. One woman expressed her feelings this way:

> I want the same community connection that heterosexuals have. I want people to be glad for us when we're happy, I want them to be there for us when we're having difficult times, I want to be able to talk about our lives . . . And if we're not out, we don't have that (Knoble & Linville, 2012, p. 335).

Now that lesbians and gay men are finally able to participate in civil unions and legal marriage in the U.S., will they gain the same psychological and health benefits that people in heterosexual marriage have had? The research is preliminary, but the answers so far are positive. Lesbians in civil union relationships, compared to those in non-legalized relationships, report that their lesbian identity is more central, they receive more support from their partner, they conceal their lesbian identity less, and experience less isolation and more self-acceptance as a lesbian (Riggle et al., 2016). A study using population data from a state health survey showed that legally married LGB people had significantly better psychological adjustment than cohabiting LGBs—the same pattern of results typically found for heterosexual people. This is the first large-scale study showing that same-sex marriage provides the same psychological benefits that straight people have from heterosexual marriage (Wight et al., 2013). Of course, we can make the same objection about selection bias: maybe better-adjusted LGBs are more likely to marry in the first place. But it is also worth thinking about the psychological effect of removing an age-old stigma and allowing people to legally acknowledge their love for their partner.

Cohabiting Couples

Today many heterosexual couples choose to live together without being legally married. Sociologists give this arrangement the unromantic name *cohabitation.* Couples who do it usually call it living together.

The rise in cohabitation is one of the most striking social changes of the past fifty years. Today, more than half of all first marriages in the United States are preceded by living together. Increasingly, cohabitors are having children together as well. Cohabitation is becoming not just a prelude to marriage but a substitute for it. (Barr et al., 2015). In a nationally representative sample of U.S. women, most cohabiters intended to marry, and most did, but the proportion of cohabitating relationships that lead to marriage has been getting steadily smaller over time. Increasingly, women are likely to be in one cohabiting relationship after another. Many of these consecutive cohabiters are uninterested in marriage; they don't believe in it as an institution (Vespa, 2014).

Who Cohabits and Why?

People choose to cohabit for a variety of reasons (Noller, 2006). For some, it is a trial period or a prelude to marriage, "Let's see if we're compatible." Others cohabit more as a matter of convenience than commitment; it's easier for two to pay the rent and cover the bills. And some, as I've noted, live together because they don't believe in marriage or feel that they are not ready for marriage. In interviews, working-class couples more often talked about practical reasons like housing needs and finances; middle-class couples talked about spending time together and compatibility (Sassler & Miller, 2011).

A longitudinal study of nearly 200 married couples assessed the commitment and quality of their relationships first when they were dating, then yearly until they'd been married for an average of 7 years. The results showed that, overall, the women were more committed to the marriage than the men were. And there were interesting differences among the men: When the couple had cohabitated before becoming engaged, the man was less committed and dedicated to his wife than those who had cohabited only after getting engaged or not at all (Rhoades et al., 2006). In this study, commitment was measured in terms of working as a team, desire for a long-term future together, giving the partner high priority, and willingness to make sacrifices for the partner and the relationship. This study suggests that when a couple lives together before being engaged, a discrepancy between his and her commitment exists, and this discrepancy may persist even after years of marriage.

People who choose cohabitation tend to be liberal in attitudes about religion, sexuality, and gender roles (Willoughby & Carroll, 2012). They are more sexually experienced and sexually active than non-cohabiters, and their relationships are less likely than married relationships to be monogamous. In a national sample of more than 1,200 women aged 20 to 37, the cohabiters were 5 times more likely than the married women to have sex with someone other than their partner—about 1 in 5 had sex with someone else while cohabiting. This was true for all ethnic groups studied (Forste & Tanfer, 1996).

As with married couples, issues of money, power, and the division of labor inside and outside the home can be sources of conflict. Cohabiting couples usually have a division of labor similar to modern marriage. They almost always expect that both partners will work outside the home. However, as with most married couples, women do more housework than men. Time use surveys of cohabiting and married couples in five European countries (Spain, Italy, Germany, France, and the United Kingdom) showed that women who weren't officially married to their partners fared only slightly better on housework than married women did: they did 70 percent of routine housework, while wives did 76 percent (Dominguez-Folgueraz, 2013). In the U.S., interviews of working-class and middle-class people in cohabiting relationships showed that only about half of the women expected equality in sharing housework. Middle-class women expected it more, and were more likely to get it, both because they had more power in the relationship and because middle-class men were more willing to cooperate. Still, the majority of the women did most of the housework, and only one third of the sample reported relative equality in this domain (Miller & Carlson, 2016).

In general, cohabiting relationships are lower in quality than marital ones, with more disagreements, fights and violence, and less perceived fairness and happiness. In a cross-cultural study of eight European countries, cohabiting couples were more likely to have plans to break up and were less satisfied in their relationships than married couples. The gap between the two kinds of couples was biggest in countries where cohabitation is more marginalized (Wiik et al., 2012). Cohabiting relationships in the U.S. have had a high breakup rate, too, with more than half ending within two years, and 9 out of 10 ending within five years (Noller, 2006). Over the past 15 years, U.S. cohabitation unions have become more likely to break up and less likely to transition to marriage, even if the couple were engaged when they moved in together (Guzzo, 2014).

Does Living Together Affect Later Marriage?

Cohabiting couples may experience an unplanned pregnancy, which brings up the question of whether to get married (Sassler et al., 2009). Cohabitation is associated with premarital pregnancy among all ethnic groups and the likelihood of pregnancy during cohabitation is greater for Latina than White or African American women.

Does pregnancy push cohabiters toward marriage? This, too, depends on the couple's ethnic group and on the quality of their relationship. One study showed that White women who got pregnant while cohabiting were likely to marry; there was no effect for African American women; and for Puerto Rican women, pregnancy lowered the odds of marrying before the birth of the child (Manning & Landale, 1996). A study that relied on in-depth interviews with 30 couples reported that those who believed they had a future together said they would be upset and dismayed over a pregnancy but would bear the child. A smaller group of couples said they would terminate the pregnancy. Other couples could not agree on what they would do (Sassler et al., 2009). In an interview study, cohabitors with children often said that they stayed together because it is a practical way to co-parent and share expenses, but becoming parents did not increase their commitment to each other or the relationship (Reed, 2006).

Is cohabitation related to later marital satisfaction? It would seem that if people use living together as a trial marriage, those who do go on to marry should be better adjusted and less likely to divorce. However, many studies have shown that former cohabitants are *more* likely to divorce (Noller, 2006; Teachman et al., 2006). There are ethnic and racial differences, too. Living together before marriage predicted later divorce in a U.S. national survey sample, but only for White women, not for African American or Mexican American women. (Phillips & Sweeney, 2005). Of course, a higher divorce rate for people who had previously cohabited is not necessarily an indication that cohabitation is a mistake. Because women who cohabit (and their partners) are more unconventional, independent, and autonomous than those who do not, they may be less likely to make a commitment and more likely to leave a marriage that does not meet their expectations (Rhoades et al., 2006; Teachman et al., 2006). Recent research suggests that couples who cohabit before marriage may no longer be divorcing at higher rates than those who don't (Manning & Cohen, 2012). Perhaps living together is becoming such a normal pattern in our society that it will become disconnected from both marriage and divorce. Time— and further research—will tell.

Ending the Commitment: Separation and Divorce

The United States has the highest divorce rate of any industrialized nation, a rate that has only recently leveled off after rising more or less steadily for over a century. About 40 percent of American marriages end within 15 years (see Figure 8.4). The U.S. Census Bureau predicts that the U.S. divorce rate will continue to be among the world's highest. Using past trends to predict the future, statisticians estimate that today's new marriages will have a 44 percent chance of ending in divorce. Other countries have experienced similar increases in divorce rate, though none as extreme as the United States (Copen et al., 2012; Orbuch & Brown, 2006; Teachman et al., 2006).

There is a large amount of research on divorce. In contrast, few studies have examined the process or consequences when a relationship ends without a formal divorce (Teachman et al., 2006). This can happen in several ways. Some spouses simply desert or abandon their families, leaving them without a division of assets or child support. Little is known about how these families fare. In others, marital partners separate permanently but do not get a divorce (McKelvey & McKenry, 2000). When relationships between cohabiting couples end, breakups occur without legal divorce. In one of the few studies that compared gay, lesbian, and heterosexual individuals who had broken up with a partner, the respondents from each group gave similar reasons and reported similar levels of distress (Kurdek, 1997). There is a need for more research on how non-marital relationships end. But for now, I will mainly focus on heterosexual married couples who divorce.

What Are the Causes and Consequences of Divorce?

At the societal level, several factors have been correlated with the rising divorce rates. Divorce rates rise along with women's participation in

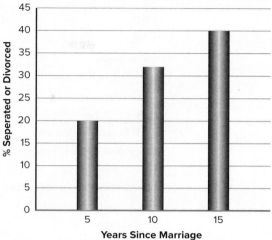

Probability that a First Marriage will End

FIGURE 8.4   In the United States a large proportion of first marriages end in divorce within 15 years.

Source: National Center for Health Statistics (2012). *National Health Statistics Report: First marriages in the United States.* Hyattsville, MD: National Center for Health Statistics.

the paid workforce, both in the United States and in many other countries. Wives' paid employment is not usually a direct cause of divorce. Rather, it seems that when women don't need a husband's income to survive, they are less likely to stay in unsatisfactory marriages (Teachman et al., 2006). Age at first marriage is also highly correlated with divorce: The younger the man and woman are when they marry, the more likely they are to divorce (Bramlet & Mosher, 2001). Other factors related to the rising divorce rate are changes in laws and attitudes; divorce is no longer the disgrace it once was and no-fault laws make it easier.

At the personal level, women and men tend to give somewhat different reasons for the break up of their marriages. In a study based on a national random sample of divorced people, women were more likely than men to mention their partner's infidelity, substance abuse, and mental or physical abuse as reasons for their divorce. Men were more likely to mention poor communication or say that they did not know the cause of the divorce. Other causes, such as incompatibility, were cited equally often by women and men (Amato & Previti, 2003). (See Table 8.1.)

Events and feelings early in a marriage may predict later divorce. Large population surveys in Germany, the United Kingdom, and Australia found that when women were less happy than their husbands in the first year of marriage, this "happiness gap" predicted later divorce (Guven et al., 2012). In another study, those who were disillusioned within the first 2 years (as reflected in decreased love and affection and increased ambivalence) were more likely to end up divorced several years later (Huston et al., 2001). Substance abuse by either partner is an important

TABLE 8.1   Perceived Causes of Divorce: Women's and Men's Accounts

Cause	Women (%)	Men (%)
Infidelity	25	16
Incompatible	19	20
Drinking or drug use	14	5
Grew apart	10	9
Personality problems	8	10
Lack of communication	6	13
Physical or mental abuse	9	0
Loss of love	3	7
Not meeting family obligations	5	1
Employment problems	4	3
Don't know	0	9
Unhappy in marriage	3	3

Source: Amato, P. R., & Previti, D. (2003). People's reasons for divorcing: Gender, social class, the life course, and adjustment. *Journal of Family Issues, 24,* 602–626, from Table 3 (p. 615). Percentages have been rounded to nearest whole number.

predictor of divorce in people who marry young (Collins et al., 2006), as shown in a longitudinal study of more than 450 people who were married by the age of 23. Those who used alcohol or marijuana to excess were more likely to be divorced by the age of 29.

Whatever the reasons for divorce, it has serious and long-lasting consequences for women. I will consider three types of consequences, each intertwined with the others in its effects: psychological adjustment, economic effects, and responsibility for children.

How Do People Psychologically Adjust to Divorce?

A considerable number of divorcing women (from 17 percent to 33 percent in different samples) describe their divorces as causing little or no psychological disturbance or pain. These women view their divorces as the end of a stressful or unbearable situation and the beginning of increased freedom. In a study of remarried couples who were asked to describe the effects of their earlier divorce, one woman reported that it was "a total weight lifted off my shoulders. . . . no tears were shed" and another said, "I breathed a sigh of relief because it had been so bad for so long" (Brimhall et al., 2008). For most women, however, adjustment to divorce includes feelings of anger, helplessness, and ambivalence, especially if the woman did not initiate the divorce; in an interview study, these women felt abandoned and vulnerable (Sakraida, 2005). Cohabiting couples who separate follow the same trajectories: loneliness, distress, and disappointment that decline over time as they adjust to the end of the relationship (Halford & Sweeper, 2013). Stress during divorce is related to a variety of physical health problems. (As with all correlational research, it is not possible to determine cause and effect in these studies.) Compared with married people, divorced people of both sexes have higher rates of illness, death, alcoholism, and serious accidents.

In general, the adjustment to divorce seems to be more difficult for men than women. Although both divorced men and women are more likely to commit suicide than their married counterparts, divorced men are 50 percent more likely to do so than divorced women. They are also more likely to show serious psychological disturbances (Price & McKenry, 1988). Women appear to be better at building and maintaining networks of close friends and family during and following divorce (Gerstel, 1988), and men may miss their partner's caretaking more (see Figure 8.5). However, women and men are similar in their responses to divorce in many other ways (Gove & Shin, 1989).

"This is goodbye—there are one thousand, eight hundred, and twenty-five meals for you in the freezer."

FIGURE 8.5

Source: © Barbara Smaller/The New Yorker Collection/www.cartoonbank.com

Adjustment to divorce depends on social support. A meta-analysis of 21 studies confirmed that having good friends and being part of a supportive network, such as a church or community group, help both women and men adjust to divorce (Krumrei et al., 2007). Post-divorce coping varies for different groups of women. In a study using a national sample of divorced or separated women with at least one child, Black women felt more positive about their personal ability to master their lives and their economic situation (McKelvey & McKenry, 2000). Three factors have been shown to help African American women adjust to divorce better than White women: they are more likely to live in multigenerational households, to have strong ties to their parents, and to have support from their church and their friends (Orbuch & Brown, 2006).

Divorce is usually discussed as a personal and social tragedy. But divorce may be an important way that women counter marital inequality, a way out of an oppressive situation and a turning point for women in developing healthy sexual subjectivity (Montemurro, 2014). Women who were in marriages with unsupportive, critical spouses report being more satisfied with their lives after a divorce (Bourassa et al., 2015). Research on remarried people shows that they interact with their partners in more egalitarian ways; for example, wives have more control over finances and share decision-making more with their husbands than in their first marriages (Ganong et al., 2006). Most research on divorce has assessed negative consequences. Few researchers have asked about positive ones, but when they do, many people report that their self-esteem increased, their enjoyment of life grew, their careers benefited, and they enjoyed the freedom and independence that followed the end of a troubled relationship (Tashiro et al., 2006). Divorce is a painful family transformation but also a potential opportunity for growth and change (Stewart et al., 1997).

What Are the Economic Effects of Divorce?

Divorce in the United States is an economic disaster for women. Research from the 1960s to the present has conclusively shown that the economic status of men improves upon divorce, while the economic status of women deteriorates (Sayer, 2006). The decline is greater for Black women than for White women. And no-fault divorce laws, designed to ensure equitable division of assets, have actually made the situation worse. As one divorce expert noted, the popular discourse is that relationships are based on romantic love and commitment, not "base financial motives." But marriage and divorce are also "economic arrangements with economic consequences" (Sayer, 2006, p. 385).

Why do women lose out financially with divorce? There are several reasons but structural factors are probably more important than individual ones (Sayer, 2006). The majority of state property laws assume that property belongs to the spouse who earned it. Since husbands usually have had greater earning power during the marriage, these laws result in men being awarded more of the couple's assets. The economic value of the wife's unpaid labor may not be considered. In other states, attempts to make divorce fairer for women have led to laws that order equal division of property. However, most divorcing couples (especially younger ones) have very little in the way of valuable property—perhaps a car (complete with loan payments), household furnishings, and a modest bank account, offset by credit card debt. Fewer than half have equity in a house. The biggest asset for the large majority of couples is the husband's earning power, at the time of the divorce and in the future.

As discussed earlier, the husband's career usually takes priority in both single-earner and dual-earner marriages. Couples invest more in his advancement; frequently the wife will do the unpaid work at home that allows him to concentrate on his paid job. Courts have been slow to recognize that the benefits husbands gain from traditional and modern marriage patterns translate into economic advantages upon divorce. Only about 15 percent of all divorced women in the United States are awarded spousal support. Most awards are for a period of about 2 years; and in the past, less than half of the men ordered to provide such support have actually complied (Faludi, 1991; Price & McKenry, 1988).

Who Is Responsible for the Children?

Two-thirds of divorces involve children. More than half of all children in the United States will experience their parents' divorce before the age of 18, and they will then spend an average of about 5 years in a single-parent home, the great majority with their mothers (Arendell, 1997). The presence of children is an important factor in women's adjustment to divorce. The benefit of awarding custody to women is that most divorced women stay connected with their children and receive the emotional rewards of parenting more than most divorced men do. However, current custody arrangements also have costs for women. Being a single parent is not easy. The single mother may feel overwhelmed with responsibility, guilty at having separated the children from their father, and under pressure to be a supermom.

The lack of a husband's income is a big handicap for divorced women and their children. About 60 percent of divorced mothers with custody of their children are awarded child support. However, the average amount is only about $5,600 a year. Child support payments clearly do not cover the actual costs of bringing up a child. And few fathers provide extra help voluntarily. In recent studies, the majority of fathers no longer living with their families provided *no* monetary help with children's clothes, vacations, or uninsured medical expenses, and only one-third included their children on their health care coverage (Sayer, 2006).

Moreover, the majority of women entitled to child support do not receive it. Several national studies from the 1970s to the 1990s showed that only 25 percent to 50 percent of men ordered to pay child support did so, whether voluntarily or through having their wages garnished by the courts. Many who complied paid less than the designated amount; and one-fourth to one-third of fathers never made a single payment despite court orders. The most recently published studies show that the situation has gotten worse. The proportion of divorcing mothers who are awarded child support has decreased to 43 percent in the past decade, possibly because more fathers are sharing custody, but also because there are more low-income or out-of-work dads (Meyer et al., 2015). If the parents have cohabited instead of marrying, the mother's chances of getting a child support award and actually getting any of the funds are even lower (Allen et al., 2011; Sayer, 2006).

When a relationship ends, the divorced or formerly cohabiting woman and her children must adjust to a lower standard of living. The economic impact of break-ups was systematically studied in a national longitudinal survey of divorced and cohabiting couples (Avellar and Smock, 2005). Overall, the end of a relationship caused more economic harm to women than to men; to ethnic minority women than to white women; and to cohabiting women than to married women. Without the earnings of their male partners, women and their children often drop to a lower socioeconomic class. In this study, the former cohabiters were particularly vulnerable: almost one in four of the White women and one in two of the African American and Hispanic women lived at or below the poverty level when their relationship ended. For many women with children, the financial hardship that comes with the end of a marriage or live-in relationship becomes the central focus of their lives, dictating where they can live, determining whether they and their children can afford health care, healthy food, or a college education, and affecting their psychological well-being (Sayer, 2006).

Remarriage

Most people who get divorced marry again—in the United States, about 85 percent do. The median time between a first divorce and remarriage is about 3 years (Ganong et al., 2006). Men are more likely to remarry than women, and White women more likely than Black or Hispanic women. Middle-class women have better odds of remarrying than poor and low-income women (Shafer & Jensen, 2013). In the United States, about one in four marriages involves two people who are marrying for at least the second time (Lewis & Kreider, 2015). A cynic might say that remarriages represent a triumph of belief over experience; most people do not question the institution of marriage after they have been divorced. Rather, they believe that they chose the wrong partner last time and now know how to choose the right one. The rate of third (and fourth, and fifth . . .) marriages continues to increase. Apparently, people are determined to keep trying until they get it right (Ganong et al., 2006).

Are second marriages more successful? In general, the level of satisfaction in second marriages is about the same as in first marriages; as in first marriages, husbands are more satisfied than their wives (Ihinger-Tallman & Pasley, 1987). Decision making may be more equal than in first marriages, but remarried women still do more housework than their partners, and more child care, too, regardless of whether they are the mother or the stepmother of the children in the family (Ganong & Coleman, 2000; Ganong et al., 2006). Second marriages are even more likely to end in divorce than first marriages (Lewis & Kreider, 2015). Well over half of women who enter a second marriage later experience a second divorce.

The complex family structures and dynamics of second marriages ("his," "her," and "their" children, stepparents, ex-spouses, in-laws, and ex-in-laws) may be a source of stress. (See Figure 8.6.) Financial problems may be increased by lack of support payments from former husbands and many families have conflicts over how to allocate money to various household members (Ganong et al., 2006).

FIGURE 8.6　Blended families may lead complicated lives.

(Who should pay Tiffany's college tuition—mother, father, or stepparent?) Second marriages may also be less stable because, once having violated the ideal of lifelong marriage, people are even less inclined to stay in unsatisfying relationships.

Many blended families develop strength and resilience, but there is little research on how they do it. In a small-scale study conducted among White South Africans, a parent and teenage child from each of 38 blended families were surveyed and asked an open-ended question about what had helped the family through stressful times (Greeff & Du Toit, 2009). Among the factors that correlated with good family adjustment were positive family relationships, communication, mutual support among family members, a reliance on spirituality and religion, and activities that helped the family spend time together. Other blended families report problems with role confusion among parents and stepparents and interference with parenting decisions by ex-spouses (Martin-Uzzi & Duval-Tsioles, 2013). These studies cannot separate cause and effect; there is much more to learn about what makes blended families healthy for parents and children.

Making a Difference

To close this chapter, I consider two important sites of struggle for equality for relationship partners. First, although social justice for LGBTQ partners has made tremendous progress, same-sex relationships are not yet universally accorded the same respect and rights as heterosexual relationships. Second, women in relationships with men often have less power than their partners, even when both partners believe in equality. Equality in heterosexual marriages is an individual-level and interactional-level problem as well as a sociostructural one.

Marriage Equality for Lesbian and Gay Couples

The long, hard battle for same-sex marriage in the U.S. was ended by a 5-4 vote in the Supreme Court in 2015 (See Box 8.2). In other words, *one* vote in the other direction could have denied marriage equality for the forseeable future. The Supreme Court decision was a milestone in social justice movements and one about which many progressives are proud and grateful. However, LGBT individuals are not unanimously agreed that same-sex marriage is the best goal for LGBT activism. Some have argued that marriage is a deeply flawed patriarchal institution, and that LGBT people can create better alternatives within their own communities. Others reject the right of the government to legalize any relationships. These are minority

---

Box 8.2 ∾ Key Dates in the History of Marriage Equality

The fight for marriage equality in the United States has been a long one, punctuated by a back-and-forth of triumphs and defeats, culminating with the 2015 Supreme Court ruling legalizing same-sex marriage in all 50 states. Below are some of the key dates in the battle for marriage equality over the past 20 years.

September 21, 1996: President Clinton signs the Defense of Marriage Act (DOMA). DOMA defined marriage as a union between one man and one woman for federal purposes.

September 22, 1999: California becomes the first state to pass a domestic partnership statute

July 1, 2000: Civil unions legalized in Vermont

November 18, 2003: Massachusetts becomes the first state to legalize same-sex marriage

November 2, 2004: 11 states pass constitutional amendments denying same sex-marriage (Arkansas, Georgia, Kentucky, Michigan, Mississippi, Montana, North Dakota, Ohio, Oklahoma, Oregon, and Utah)

November 7, 2006: 7 states pass constitutional amendments denying same sex-marriage (Colorado, Idaho, South Carolina, South Dakota, Tennessee, Virginia, and Wisconsin)

October 10, 2008: Connecticut Supreme Court legalizes same-sex marriage

November 4, 2008: California voters approve Proposition 8 which banned same-sex marriage; Proposition 8 is later ruled unconstitutional in federal court

November 6, 2012: Maine, Maryland, and Washington State pass constitutional amendments permitting same-sex marriage

May 2013: Governors of Rhode Island, Delaware, and Minnesota sign laws permitting same-sex marriage

June 26, 2013: Supreme Court upholds federal court ruling that California's Proposition 8 was unconstitutional, legalizing same-sex marriage in California

November 2013: Hawaii, Illinois and New Mexico legalize same-sex marriage

November 6, 2014: U.S. Court of Appeals upholds same-sex marriages bans in Kentucky, Ohio, Tennessee, and Michigan

June 26, 2015: Supreme Court legalizes same-sex marriage across the United States in a 5-4 decision

Source: http://www.usatoday.com/story/news/politics/2015/06/24/same-sex-marriage-timeline/29173703/

Contributed by Annie B. Fox

views within the LGBT community, but they reflect the diversity of opinion on the issue. To learn more about the diversity of feminist views on both gay and straight marriage, see the resources at the end of this chapter.

Globally, the outlook for same-sex marriage is mixed. Many countries have legalized same-sex marriage and the majority of the population, when surveyed, say they approve of its legality. These include Canada, the United Kingdom, New Zealand, France, and Spain, among others (Valenza, 2015). Many more countries allow civil unions and other forms of officially recognized domestic partnerships (Clarke et al., 2010). However, in still other countries, encompassing billions of the world's people—countries such as China, Israel, Japan, Russia, Saudi Arabia, and India—gay marriage still is prohibited or criminalized.

True Partnership: Equality in Heterosexual Marriage

Egalitarian marriage may be emerging as a life pattern of the future. But equality in marriage or long-term cohabitation is unlikely to happen just by wanting it. How many times have you heard people express the belief that "If two people love each other enough, their marriage will work"? This belief is part of a romantic ideology and a variation of "love conquers all." A related belief is that if the husband does not *intend* to oppress or dominate the wife, oppression and domination will not occur. Happy marriage, then, should be mainly (or entirely) a matter of picking the right person. One major conclusion that can be drawn from the research reviewed in this chapter is that power differentials between husbands and wives are *not* solely the result of individual differences. Rather, the *institution* of marriage has been organized around gender inequality. Even couples who try very hard to change their own behavior have problems achieving gender balance in marriage.

To have an egalitarian marriage, both wife and husband must be willing to integrate their work and family responsibilities despite social pressures to conform to more traditional roles. Women who value their work outside the home and set limits on the sacrifices they make for husbands and children may be perceived as cold, unfeminine, and selfish; men who do housework and child care and set limits on their career involvement may be perceived as weak and unmasculine. (One of my children once *begged* my husband not to wear an apron in front of the child's friends!) Fortunately attitudes toward the work and family roles of women and men have changed a great deal in the past 30 years and continue to become more flexible (Amato et al., 2007).

Women may have to lead the way to more egalitarian relationships because men are unlikely to fight a status quo that gives them many benefits. However, only when women perceive gender roles in relationships as unequal and unjust can they begin to change them. To recognize their position as unjust, women must be aware that other possibilities exist, must want such possibilities for themselves, must believe they are entitled to them, and must not feel personally to blame for not having them.

Women who are assertive in asking for equal sharing of housework and child care are more likely to get what they want. In a study of 81 married women with children, participants provided information about their and their husbands' work hours, incomes, and division of labor in the home. Also, they were interviewed twice over a 2-month period and asked to tell the story of the last time they'd discussed whether the husband should help more with housework or child care (Mannino & Deutsch, 2007). As predicted, power in marriage was related to the usual factors: the couple's gender ideology, their relative earnings, and so forth. But the woman's attempts to instigate change were important, too. At the second interview, the women who had tried to negotiate a fairer marriage had achieved change by assertively discussing their feelings and wishes with their husbands. The researchers concluded that change is most likely to happen when women are aware of inequality and willing to persist in discussing it with their husbands. In other studies with male participants, husbands often report that they had to first become aware of their gender entitlement before they could see the inequality and try to change: "When we first got married I thought I could make the decisions on money. But, I quickly learned we need to talk things over," one said, and another reported that he now reminds himself to do a fair share because "This is my house, these are my dishes, this is my baby just as much as hers" (Knudson-Martin & Mahoney, 2005, p. 243).

What social factors give women more negotiating power in relationships with men? If society allows more flexible commitments to paid work by both women and men, there will be less likelihood that the man's job or career will take precedence. (The interaction of work and family life will be discussed further in Chapter 10.) Economic power is a key factor. The single biggest obstacle to egalitarian marriage and cohabiting relationships is men's greater earning power, which steers couples into investing in his career and leaving the work at home to her. If our society invested resources in guaranteeing gender-equal pay, marriage and other committed relationships would quickly change in the direction of equality.

As the number of couples who are consciously trying to build egalitarian relationships increases, it should be easier for them to find each other and build supportive networks. Nontraditional arrangements are coming to be seen as legitimate, normal, and even routine (Knudson-Martin & Mahoney, 2005). Similar needs can be met for lesbian and gay couples by being part of a LGBTQ community, and by seeing their unions legitimized and accepted.

The movement toward egalitarian relationships will bring benefits for both women and men. Relieved of some of the economic burdens of traditional marriage, men will be freer to become involved with their children's growth and development. Women will experience better psychological adjustment. For both men and women, equality is linked to more satisfying relationships and greater intimacy. Equality in committed long-term relationships offers both women and men a chance to become more fully human.

Exploring Further

∾

Change (www.change.org) is designed to provide information about a broad range of social movements, including women's rights, gay rights, and the environment. Online petitions at the Web site are a quick and easy way to get involved in activism for equal rights.

Feminism & Psychology: Special Issues on Marriage.
>This noted journal asked feminist women and men to write about their views on LGBTQ and heterosexual marriage. The result is a superb collection of research articles, personal observations, and critical commentaries that spans three issues of the journal:
>Volume 13, 4, November 2003.
>Volume 14, 1, February, 2004.
>Volume 14, 2, May, 2004.

Traister, Rebecca (2016). *All the single ladies: Unmarried women and the rise of an independent nation.* Simon & Schuster. Not only are U.S. women marrying later, but more and more are choosing not to marry at all, instead cohabiting sequentially and staying single. This well-researched book explores how independent women are becoming a new political and social force with a voice of their own.

Text Credits

༄

p. 240: Quek, K., & Knudson-Martin, C. (2006). A push toward equality: Processes among dual-career newlywed couples in collectivist culture. Journal of Marriage and Family, 68 (1), 56–69. **p. 243:** Dallos, S., & Dallos, R. (1997). Couples, sex, and power: The politics of desire. Philadelphia: Open University Press. **p. 245:** ROSE IS ROSE © 2011 Pat Brady and Don Wimmer. Reprinted by permission of ANDREWS MCMEEL SYNDICATION for UFS. All rights reserved. **p. 248:** Contributed by MC and Annie B. Fox **p. 250:** Bailey, D., & Jackson, J. (2005). The occupation of household financial management among lesbian couples. Journal of Occupational Science, 12, 57–68. **p. 255:** Source: National Center for Health Statistics (2012). National Health Statistics Report: First marriages in the United States. Hyattsville, MD: National Center for Health Statistics. **p. 256:** Source: Amato, P. R., & Previti, D. (2003). People's reasons for divorcing: Gender, social class, the life course, and adjustment. Journal of Family Issues, 24, 602–626, from Table 3 (p. 615). Copyright © 2003 by SAGE Publications, Inc. Percentages have been rounded to nearest whole number. **p. 257:** Source: Barbara Smaller/The New Yorker Collection/www .cartoonbank.com **p. 262:** Contributed by Annie B. Fox

CHAPTER 9

Mothering

❧

- **Images of Mothers and Motherhood**
- **The Decision to Have a Child**
  Why Do Women Choose to Have Children?
  Childless by Choice or Circumstance?
  Restricting Women's Choices
  Technology and Choice
- **The Transition to Motherhood**
  How Does Motherhood Change Work and Marital Roles?
  Psychological Effects of Bodily Changes during Pregnancy
  How Do Others React to Pregnant Women?
  Motherhood and Women's Identity
- **The Event of Childbirth**
  Is Childbirth a Medical Crisis?
  Family-Centered Childbirth
  Depression Following Childbirth: Why?
- **Experiences of Mothering**
  Teen Mothers
  Single Mothers
  Black Mothers and the Matriarchal Myth
  LGBT Mothers
- **Making a Difference**
  Transforming Social Policy: Redefining Family Values
  Transforming Social Meanings: Redefining Parenthood
- **Exploring Further**

The day my husband and I took our newborn son home from the hospital I sat on my bed with him in my arms. All of a sudden, I realized I was in love. It is an indescribable love, comparable to nothing else in life. I never would have believed it before becoming a parent. (Deutsch, 1999, p. 228)

*M*otherhood is one of the most transforming events of a woman's life. It may seem the most natural thing in the world, a biological privilege accorded only to women. However, those aspects of society that seem most natural often are the ones most in need of critical examination. Like marriage, motherhood is an institution. Its meaning goes beyond the biological process of reproduction, encompassing many customs, beliefs, attitudes, norms, and laws. Like other institutions, it also has a powerful symbolic component. Yet women who become mothers are individuals. "Mother is a role; women are human beings" (Bernard, 1974, p. 7).

Motherhood raises troubling questions for feminist analysis. Liberal feminists have stressed that the institution of motherhood has been used to exclude women from public life, and they have shown how the myths and mystique of motherhood keep women in their place. Some radical and cultural feminists, on the other hand, have pointed out that motherhood is a woman-centered model of how people can be connected and caring (McMahon, 1995). Although the institution of motherhood can be oppressive, the lifelong process of being a mother can be powerful and rewarding (Bem, 1998; Rich, 1976).

In this chapter, I use a variety of feminist perspectives to address questions about mothering. What are the images and scripts that define mothers and motherhood? How do women go about choosing whether to have children, and to what extent are they allowed to choose? How does the transition to motherhood change women? What are women's experiences of birth and mothering? Finally, should motherhood be redefined?

Images of Mothers and Motherhood

Western society has strong beliefs about motherhood. Mothers are wonderful. We love them and celebrate them with flowers and breakfast in bed on Mother's Day. However, underlying the positive images of mothers is an ideology of motherhood that has been termed the *motherhood mystique.* It includes the following myths:

1. Motherhood is the ultimate fulfillment of a woman. It is a natural and necessary experience for all women. Those who do not want to mother are psychologically disturbed and those who want to but cannot are fundamentally deprived.
2. Women are instinctively good at caregiving and should be responsible for infants, children, elderly parents, home, and their husband. Good mothers enjoy this kind of work; a woman who doesn't is maladjusted or poorly organized.
3. A mother has infinite patience and the willingness to sacrifice herself to her children. If she does not put her own needs last, she is an inadequate mother.
4. A woman's intense, full-time devotion to mothering is best for her children. Women who work are inferior mothers (Johnston-Robledo, 2000).

Although these beliefs may seem outdated, the motherhood mystique lives on. Surveys in 21 European countries showed that people disapprove of women who choose not to have children more than they disapprove of men who make the same choice (Eicher et al., 2015). In the U.S., college students judged a hypothetical married person who chose not to have children as less psychologically fulfilled than one who did, and they expressed moral outrage (disapproval and anger) toward that person (Ashburn-Nardo, 2017). In this study, the negative attitudes were directed at both women and men. There is a persistent belief that voluntarily childless people are psychologically disturbed. In response, some have adopted stigma management strategies such as using the term "child free" (Morison et al., 2016).

And what about the notions that women are instinctively good caregivers and children always need to be with their mothers? Intensive mothering, in which young children spend virtually all their time with their mother, is believed to be best for children by many parents, and is also promoted by conservative media and evangelical religious groups. National organizations such as MOPS (Mothers of Preschoolers) run support groups for full time mothers who accept the ideology of intensive mothering—although, if it is instinctive and women are naturally inclined to do it, it is unclear why a support group would be needed (Newman & Henderson, 2014). U.S. college women overestimate the negative effects of working mothers on child development, probably because they are more familiar with the stereotypes than the data (Goldberg & Lucas-Thompson, 2014). In national samples and meta-analyses, the amount of time mothers (vs. other responsible adults) spend with children actually shows very little correlation with their behaviors or academic achievement; socioeconomic variables are much better predictors (Goldberg & Lucas-Thompson, 2014; Milkie et al., 2015).

Mothers of young children who work outside the home still face social disapproval. The same European surveys that found disapproval of voluntary childlessness also found disapproval of mothers (but not fathers) who work full-time when children are young (Eicher et al., 2015). In U.S. studies using hypothetical scenarios, working mothers are judged to be less good mothers than non-working mothers, especially when they work in a male-typed occupation, when they are successful at it, and when they're working because they want to (Okimoto & Heilman, 2012). Occupational success doesn't make a man look like a bad father, but it undermines a woman because it makes her seem less communal, and communality is a central component of the feminine gender stereotype. "Working mom = bad mom" is still, in the 21st century, a part of the motherhood mystique that can be used to guilt-trip women.

The motherhood mystique persists because it has important functions for the patriarchal status quo. Women are encouraged to sacrifice other parts of their lives for motherhood, which creates economic dependence on men and is used to justify women's lower status and pay at work. The mystique may persist also because it is the one area in which Western society values connectedness and caring over individual achievement. Groups that have the most power economically and politically benefit by glorifying motherhood and defining it in ways that constrict and burden women.

The Decision to Have a Child

Having a child profoundly changes a woman's life. The emotional and economic costs of bringing up children are high. Yet the great majority of women have children.

Why Do Women Choose to Have Children?

There are practical reasons for having children, particularly in traditional societies. Children are necessary as workers (both at home and at jobs), as a path for passing on property and a customary way of life, and as a form of personal immortality. In post-colonial and underdeveloped societies, many children are lost to disease and malnutrition. Five or more children may have to be conceived for two to live to adulthood; these children may provide the only economic support for their parents' old age.

In industrialized societies, children have little economic value—in fact, they are a big economic liability—and psychological reasons for having children are given more weight. There is considerable social pressure on women to have children, pressure that has been called the **motherhood mandate** (Russo, 1979) (see Figure 9.1). And one child is not enough. Stereotypes have portrayed the only child as socially inadequate, self-centered, unhappy, and unlikable. (There is no evidence that only children actually are maladjusted.)

Has the motherhood mandate decreased because of feminism? When I ask my students, "Why have children?," they provide a long list of reasons: the desire to experience pregnancy and birth, to participate in the growth of another human being, to please a husband, to strengthen a relationship, to become an adult, to be needed and loved, and to pass on a family name or one's genes or one's values. Few people mention that the decision to have a child may still be influenced by the motherhood mandate. However, in American society , and in most nations around the world, parenthood is still expected of women and, to a lesser extent, for men, and childlessness still is

"So, have you two been doing anything reproductive?"

FIGURE 9.1

Source: © Marisa Acocella Marchetto/The New Yorker Collection/The Cartoon Bank

deviant (Eicher et al., 2015). Procreation within marriage is endorsed by all major religions and has been characterized as a developmental stage of adulthood by psychologists, showing that it is still the normative choice.

The expectation that everyone should become a parent is related to the ideology of **pronatalism.** Pronatalism assumes that having children is a natural human instinct and a normal part of heterosexual adulthood. Without children, a person cannot lead a happy or meaningful life. Political and religious institutions enlist pronatalist discourse for their own ends, for example by encouraging citizens to procreate as a patriotic duty or promoting large families as a way of disseminating a religion (Morison et al., 2016).

Childless by Choice or Circumstance?

Fewer than 7 percent of American women remain childless voluntarily (Pew Research Center, 2010). Compared to women with children, these women are more likely to be highly educated, employed in high-status occupations, less conventional, and less conservative in gender ideology (Park, 2005). Throughout history, the childless woman has been regarded as a failed woman (Phoenix et al., 1991; Rich, 1976). Given this negative image, why do some women choose not to have children? Reasons include financial considerations, a desire to pursue their education or career, the dangers of childbirth, the possibility of bearing a child with disabilities, and a belief that they are not personally suited to nurturing and caring for children (Landa, 1990). Increasingly, young Americans worry about overpopulation and the fact that Americans use an outsize proportion of the world's natural resources, contributing to climate change; remaining child free is an ecologically responsible decision (Hymas, 2013; Ludden, 2016).

In a qualitative study, some women reported that their decision had been based on the models of parenting they'd seen. For example, Rose, an Italian American woman in her early 30s, said:

> My mother worked in the home all of her life . . . Not only did she take care of my sisters and I, but she took care of her mother and a sister with Down's syndrome. So her whole life was this caretaking. I guess I looked at that and saw her life and said I don't think I want that for myself . . . She doesn't have a life. Her children are her life . . . It's just . . . I don't know . . . I guess I want something *different* for my life. (Park, 2005, pp. 387–388)

Other people talked about need for work and leisure time. Some women said they lacked a "maternal instinct" or just were not interested in children. As one put it, she did not dislike children but did not have the personality for taking care of them. "They're fine if they belong to somebody else and I can leave" (Park, 2005).

In this study, women sometimes agonized over their decision, even questioning whether they were normal:

> I do wonder what is not quite right with me that I have *no desire whatsoever* to have a child. Somehow that doesn't seem quite right. Because, you know, the persistence of the species *demands* that we procreate, to want children. And I have *nothing* there. (p. 394)

Other studies show reasons such as a strong need for autonomy. This childfree woman explained that she doesn't even live with her long-time partner:

> I'm in control over my own time to 100 percent. I have a real strong need to be alone. That's why we are still living apart together. I need to be in control of my alone time. (Peterson, 2015, p. 188)

One problem for people who choose not to have children is how to deal with the stigma of being different in a pronatalist world. Their task is to maintain a positive identity when others think of them as maladjusted and selfish. In a study of individuals who posted on childfree Internet websites, respondents used two kinds of discourse to justify their childfree status. The first was a discourse of choice, in which they described themselves as rational, responsible, and making wiser choices than childbearers, who they felt followed the crowd unthinkingly. The second was a discourse of nonchoice—"It's just the way I am" (Morison et al., 2016).

Of course, childlessness is not always a matter of choice. In the U.S., about one woman in six experiences fertility problems, and only about half who seek medical treatment are able to conceive. Women who want to but cannot bear children may be stigmatized, leading to feelings of guilt and failure:

> His parents wouldn't leave me alone. They felt I wasn't trying. I was just feeling a failure—failure as a woman because you know this is what you are here for and I actually felt as though I had failed my husband because I wasn't giving him an heir to the throne. (Ulrich & Weatherall, 2000, p. 332)

In the past, infertility was often a hidden shame leading to depression, decreased life satisfaction, and social isolation. Today, individuals and couples have access to social media forums for networking and social support (Jansen & Onge, 2015). However, women of color with infertility are still largely omitted from infertility research and social visibility, although they are at least as likely to experience infertility as White women.

Taking an intersectional perspective, Rosario Ceballo and her colleagues (2015) interviewed 50 African American women from diverse backgrounds who were coping with infertility. Virtually all the women experienced silence and isolation about their infertility. They hid it even from their sisters and their closest friends. They explained this choice in terms of a sense of shame, cultural expectations about privacy in African American communities, and their internalization of stereotypes that African American women are always fertile and can "pop out" babies easily. A third of the women reported strongly stereotyped beliefs about the motherhood mandate: they would be failures as women if they could not produce a baby. Some specifically connected this belief with teachings from the Bible or the strong communal and family orientation of the African American community. This intersectional study—the first to focus on African American women's experiences of infertility—showed that their identities with respect to gender, race/ethnicity, and socioeconomic class were all relevant in how they viewed themselves and how they were perceived by others.

Accepting childlessness is a gradual process. The primarily White middle-class participants in a study of women who had given up trying to conceive after years of treatment reported coming to a point where they realized that further efforts were futile. Exhausted and worn out, they felt profound grief and emptiness. At the same time, however, they felt relief at being out of the "medical machinery" and recognized an opportunity to take back their lives, moving on to other goals (Daniluk, 1996).

Does not having children (by choice or by chance) lead to unhappiness? In a classic study of American women at midlife, there was no relationship between whether a woman had children and her psychological well-being (Baruch et al., 1983). The women in this study grew up in an era when the motherhood mandate was in full force, yet their well-being at midlife did not suffer because of childlessness. In a more recent interview study, most childfree married women at midlife (menopause) showed no regrets about their path in life (DeLyser, 2012).

Studies of elderly people in several countries show that those who never had children had fewer social ties in old age than those who were parents, and were more likely to live alone or in an institution, but they were no less satisfied with their lives (Koropeckyj-Cox & Call, 2007; Park, 2005). However, in surveys done in 36 nations, childless adults in more pronatalist nations were unhappier and less satisfied with their lives than those in less pronatalist nations—indicating that the larger social context matters for childfree people's well-being (Tanaka & Johnson, 2016). Overall, research contradicts the ideology that having children is necessary for a woman's happiness—but motherhood and remaining childfree are not yet equally respected choices in many societies, and until that happens women are not yet fully liberated (Morell, 2000).

Restricting Women's Choices

Women's choices about child rearing do not take place in a social vacuum. Most societies regulate women's rights to have—or not have—children. Moreover, practical and economic factors restrict options, especially for low-income and minority women.

Feminists advocate *reproductive freedom* for all women, an ideal that has not yet been achieved. This concept includes a range of issues, such as the right to comprehensive and unbiased sex education, access to safe and reliable contraception, an end to forced sterilization and forced birth control for poor and minority women, and access to safe and legal abortion (Baber & Allen, 1992; Bishop, 1989).

At the heart of the concept of reproductive freedom is the idea that all choices about reproduction should be made by the woman herself: It is her body and her right to choose. For this reason, feminist perspectives on reproductive freedom are often termed *pro-choice*. Because reproductive freedom affects every aspect of a woman's life, it has been a goal of every feminist movement throughout history. "Without the ability to determine their reproductive destinies, women will never achieve an equal role in social, economic, and political life and will continue to be politically subordinate to and economically dependent on men" (Roberts, 1998).

Abortion

Each year, about 56 million abortions occur worldwide, terminating 25 percent of all pregnancies. Women in developing countries are more likely to have an abortion than those in wealthier and more developed nations. Globally, nearly 75 percent of abortions are provided to married women (Guttmacher Institute, 2016b).

North America has one of the world's lowest abortion rates. In the U.S., about 1.6 million abortions take place each year, representing about 21 percent of pregnancies. Women who choose abortion tend to be young; more than half are in their 20s. However, less than 4 percent are 17 or younger. Nearly half have incomes below the federal poverty level. Compared to their proportion in the population, Black and Hispanic women are more likely to experience an unintended pregnancy than White women are. Of all abortions, 39 percent are for White women, 28 percent for Black women, 25 percent for Hispanics, and 9 percent for women of other ethnic groups (Guttmacher Institute, 2016d). The majority of women who obtain abortions already have at least one child.

Abortion has been legal in the U.S. since 1973, when the Supreme Court, ruling in *Roe v. Wade,* affirmed that women have a right to decide whether to terminate their pregnancies on the basis of the constitutional right to privacy. Abortion, the Court ruled, is a matter to be decided between a woman and her physician. Although the principle of choice was affirmed by this ruling, in practice there are many limitations and legal restrictions on women's choices.

How is abortion restricted? The *Hyde Amendment,* in effect since 1976, prohibits the use of federal Medicaid money for abortions except in cases of incest, rape, and when the mother's life is (medically) endangered. Because Medicaid provides health care for low-income families, poor women are the ones affected by this restriction, which forces them to choose between paying for an abortion out of their own inadequate incomes or carrying an unwanted fetus to term. Today, 99 percent of the public money spent on abortions for poor women must come from state (rather than federal) funds. But states may do little to provide for poor women, even those who are victims of incest or rape. As I noted earlier, low-income women and ethnic minority women particularly make use of safe and legal abortion. Women of color are disproportionately affected by the Hyde Amendment.

Those who oppose abortion, having been unable to persuade the Supreme Court to revoke *Roe v. Wade,* have turned to enacting restrictive laws on a state-by-state basis, and those efforts are intensifying. In 2000, 13 states had major abortion restrictions and were classified as hostile to abortion rights by pro-choice organizations; by 2015, the number had more than doubled, to 27 states. Between 2011 and 2016, states enacted 334 new restrictions on abortion, such as parental notification and parental consent laws, mandatory waiting periods, consent of a husband or partner, and "educational" sessions that are designed to discourage women from the abortion option (Guttmacher Institute, 2016c; Mollen, 2014). Some states require counseling that includes misinformation about the alleged negative psychological and medical effects of abortion—such as South Dakota's "suicide advisory law" (Kelly, 2014).

In 2016, Indiana Gov. Mike Pence (elected vice president of the U.S. later in 2016), signed legislation forbidding women to choose abortion of genetically defective fetuses and requiring burial or cremation of the remains of all miscarriages and abortions. The latter requirement inspired a group of Indiana women to start a Facebook page, *Periods for Pence.* Noting that a fertilized egg can be expelled during a woman's period, without her even knowing that she might have been pregnant, Indiana women realized they could be at risk of breaking the law by disposing of a tampon or menstrual pad. Better keep the governor informed by calling his office to let him know the status of their periods, since he was so concerned about their welfare! (The Indiana law was later suspended by a federal court.)

Unfortunately for women's right to choose, state-imposed restrictions have been quite effective. However, in 2016 the U.S. Supreme Court ruled that abortion restrictions in Texas were unconstitutional, calling into question similar restrictions in 19 other states. The Court recognized that these laws were not intended to benefit women's health, but to restrict abortion access, and specified that a restriction must not impose an undue burden on women.

A nonsurgical abortion procedure, developed in Europe in the 1980s, is *mifepristone* (Mifeprex), formerly known as RU-486. This drug, taken as a pill, safely induces abortion early in pregnancy by causing the uterine lining to slough off. Antiabortion groups prevented legalization of RU-486 in the U.S. for over a decade because they believed that it would make abortions more private and easy to obtain (the patient can go to her doctor's office for the pill, instead of an abortion clinic) and therefore less vulnerable to political pressure (Hyde & DeLamater, 2017). After a long campaign by women's health advocates, Mifeprex was finally, in 2000, made available to American women. Nonsurgical methods now account for 23 percent of all abortions in the U.S. (Jones & Jerman, 2014).

A different kind of restriction comes from harassment and violence at abortion clinics. For example, 84 percent of clinics report frequent picketing and harassing phone calls (Jerman & Jones, 2014). The number of doctors who perform abortions has been dropping significantly for the past 4 decades, partly because of stalking, death threats, Internet hit lists, and murders of physicians and clinic staff (Cozzarelli & Major, 1998; Jerman & Jones, 2014; Solinger, 2005; Vobejda, 1994). The most recent counts show that 89 percent of all counties in the U.S. do not have a medical practitioner who provides abortion (Jones & Jerman, 2014). Picketing, bomb threats, and demonstrations affect clients, too. Studies of women who faced antiabortion protesters as they went to a clinic show that the encounters made women feel angry, intruded on, and guilty. However, they had no effect on the women's decision to have an abortion (Cozzarelli & Major, 1998). Medical abortions, which do not require clinic visits, are becoming more common, and fewer women are being subjected to the trauma of clinic harassment. However, students and low-income women, who are more likely to rely on clinics such as Planned Parenthood for healthcare, testing, and wellness visits, remain particularly vulnerable to this kind of interference with their reproductive health care.

In many developing countries in Africa and Asia, safe abortion is unavailable because medical facilities are scarce and laws are restrictive. Under these conditions, wealthy women can still obtain abortions, but poor women may resort to attempting self-induced abortion by taking caustic drugs or inserting objects into the vagina. In these countries, abortion mortality rates are hundreds of times higher than in the U.S. (Cohen, 2007; Guttmacher Institute, 2002).

Feminists and conservatives agree that preventing unwanted pregnancies is a better option than terminating them through abortion. However, they disagree on how to reach this goal, with conservatives emphasizing abstinence and legal restrictions, and feminists emphasizing sex education and contraceptive options. The good news about abortion rates is that they are dropping steadily, both in the U.S. and worldwide. The decrease is bigger in developed countries, and particularly in those countries where abortion is legal and readily available. These are the same countries where use of contraception has been increasing. It may seem paradoxical, but restricting women's right to abortion does not reduce it as much as more liberal approaches do. The research suggests that the best way to reduce abortion is to provide women with other options that are in addition to it: comprehensive sexuality education, family planning programs, a variety of safe and effective contraceptive methods, and culturally sensitive approaches to empowering women toward reproductive control (Foster, 2016).

Science, Censorship, and the Information Wars

One argument used in efforts to restrict abortion is that it has harmful physical and/or psychological consequences. In their zeal to abolish abortion, opponents have misrepresented the scientific evidence showing that it is generally safe for women. One example of misinformation is the claim that abortion causes breast cancer, a claim that has no scientific basis. Another example is the claim that women who have an abortion typically suffer guilt, shame, and lasting psychological damage—a *post abortion syndrome* (Major et al., 2009; Russo, 2008). This pseudo-fact has been widely disseminated on the web by abortion opponents and influenced state legislatures. At least 20 states now require that women seeking abortions be told that there are potential psychological effects; 8 states mention only negative effects, and some distribute medically inaccurate or exaggerated information (Kelly, 2014). Although psychology cannot resolve moral differences of opinion about abortion, empirical research can answer questions of the relationship between abortion and psychological well-being. Let's look at the evidence for and against "post abortion syndrome."

To determine the effects of abortion on women's mental health, the American Psychological Association sponsored and published several studies of the scientific research. These research reviews established that the legal termination of an unwanted pregnancy does *not* have negative effects on most women, and is no riskier to mental health than carrying an unwanted pregnancy to term (Major et al., 2009). Measurements of psychological distress usually drop immediately following the abortion and remain low in follow-up assessments. When a woman freely chooses a legal abortion, the typical emotion that follows is relief. In fact, abortion may be a milestone for a woman in taking control over her own life (Travis & Compton, 2001). The majority of women remain satisfied with the decision they made even years later (Major et al., 2009).

This does not mean that women are always perfectly well-adjusted after an abortion. In different studies, between 0.5 percent and 15 percent of abortion clients have experienced psychological problems that lasted from 1 week to 10 years following the abortion. The most important factor in a woman's adjustment after abortion is her adjustment prior to the abortion (Major et al., 2009; Russo, 2008). A history of mental health problems prior to the unwanted pregnancy greatly increases the chances that a woman will have mental health problems after an abortion (or, for that matter, after giving birth). Women obtaining abortions have a much higher average rate of past physical, sexual, and emotional abuse than other women, a factor that strongly affects their pre-abortion well-being and makes them more vulnerable to the effects of any life stress (Russo, 2008). Therefore, post abortion psychological problems may not be *caused* by the abortion, but co-occur with it.

Most women contemplating an abortion have mixed feelings about it. Even a woman who has no prior history of psychological problems may experience distress following an abortion if she was committed to the pregnancy, is aware of stigma surrounding abortion, feels the need to keep it a secret, has received little support from her family or friends, or believed in advance that she would have problems in coping (Major et al., 2009).

Women who experience severe distress following abortion may want to obtain psychological counseling. However, women should not have to deny their conflicts for fear of being labeled emotionally disturbed:

> Abortion, like other moral dilemmas, does cause suffering in the individuals whose lives are impacted. That suffering does not make the choice wrong or harmful to the individual who must make the choice, nor should the individual be pathologized for having feelings of distress. In fact, the shouldering of such suffering and of responsibility for moral choices contributes to psychological growth. (Elkind, 1991, p. 3)

Technology and Choice

The development of new reproductive technology does not always increase choices for women. The reality is that reproductive technology has introduced troublesome questions of ethics, morality, power, and choice. Indeed, the body may be the major battleground of women's rights for decades to come.

In Vitro Fertilization

Some couples who are unable to conceive a child use technologies such as *in vitro fertilization,* or *IVF,* commonly known as the test-tube baby procedure. A woman's ovaries are stimulated with strong fertility drugs so that they produce multiple eggs, which are then surgically removed. Her partner's sperm, obtained by masturbation, is combined with the eggs in a glass dish. If fertilization occurs, the embryos are inserted into the woman's uterus to develop (Williams, 1992).

The media are upbeat about the new reproductive technologies. They frequently feature heart-rending stories of a woman's quest for a child but rarely do these stories analyze how the need to have children is socially constructed. In an analysis of 133 news articles on IVF, 64 explicitly endorsed the pronatalist belief that bearing children is the single most important accomplishment of adult life, and only two articles countered that belief (Condit, 1996). This suggests that our society creates a market for IVF by making fertility seem so central to a woman's identity that infertility becomes an intolerable problem to be fought at any cost (Williams, 1992).

IVF carries many risks. The fertility drugs and surgeries can lead to side effects and complications. The emotional costs are high and the success rate is low. A pregnancy through IVF leads to higher levels of psychological distress than a natural pregnancy, and the majority of couples have to cope with repeated failure as IVF does not work for them. On the other hand, those who succeed in having a child through IVF or other medically assisted methods generally report more positive relationships between mother, father, and child than comparison mothers who conceived naturally, and IVF children are as well-adjusted as others (Hahn, 2001).

Surrogacy: Women Helping Women or Exploitive Rent-A-Womb?

Today, many couples pay a surrogate mother to bear a child for them. A fertilized egg is implanted into the surrogate's uterus and she carries the pregnancy to term. Surrogate parenthood is a site of ethical and moral debate; many feminists believe that it exploits women (Baber & Allen, 1992; Raymond, 1993). Others believe that it can have substantial benefits to all parties if it is carefully regulated. In early cases, it seemed that the technology had moved faster than our ethical sense of how to manage it. For example, Robert and Cynthia contracted for a baby with Elvira, a working-class Latina, but Robert failed to tell Elvira that he was planning to divorce Cynthia. When Robert filed for divorce, biological father, biological mother, and surrogate mother got into a three-way custody battle. In a more recent case, a 60-year-old British woman has won the latest round in a legal battle to obtain the frozen eggs of her daughter, who died of cancer in 2011, with the intention of bearing her own grandchild, although the daughter left no specific permission for her mother to do so (BBC News, 2016).

A particularly difficult ethical issue is the practice of transnational surrogacy—heterosexual and gay male couples in wealthier countries paying surrogates in less developed countries. For example, India had a thriving international surrogacy industry until recently, with clients from the U.S. and Europe. Ironically, India has one of the highest maternal mortality rates in the world for natural pregnancies. The impoverished Indian women who take on this task are medically better off as surrogates than when they are pregnant with their own children. Indeed, they may have to leave their own children behind to become surrogate mothers. The contracts they sign require them to live in dormitories for a year, where their diets and activities are monitored and they are provided with prenatal healthcare. The money they earn helps them provide for their families, but not to escape poverty on a long-term basis (Fixmer-Oraiz, 2013). The affluent Western couples who pay for their services believe that transnational surrogacy is a beautiful and altruistic deed, women helping women around the world; another perspective is that the need for women in less developed countries to rent their wombs for a few thousand dollars is a symptom of profound global injustice. In 2016, the Indian government outlawed international surrogacy.

Many feminists argue that women are at risk for exploitation by technologies that separate the genetic and physiological aspects of pregnancy. It is women's bodies that are manipulated and experimented on with these techniques. It is poor women, more often than wealthier ones, who are recruited as wombs for hire. More than ever, women may be viewed solely as egg providers and incubators, and motherhood defined to suit those with the most social power (Fixmer-Oraiz, 2013; Raymond, 1993; Ulrich & Weatherall, 2000).

The Transition to Motherhood

Becoming a mother changes a woman's life perhaps more than any other single life transition. Pregnancy, birth, and the transition to motherhood include both biological and social events. These events interact to produce changes in life circumstances, lifestyle, and work, as well as changes in relationships with partners, parents, and others. Once a woman becomes a mother, the role is hers for life, and she will be defined largely through that role, much more than men are defined through their roles as fathers. It is not surprising that motherhood profoundly affects a woman's sense of self. Let's look more closely at some of the changes that occur with pregnancy and motherhood and their effects on women's identities.

How Does Motherhood Change Work and Marital Roles?

More than 20 longitudinal studies have shown that the birth of a child can negatively affect family relationships, reducing psychological well-being and marital satisfaction (Walzer, 1998). Studies using large national samples show that parenthood results in bigger changes in women's lives than in men's, as they take on more child care and housework (Sanchez & Thomson, 1997). This gender-linked change was expressed in an interview by one new mother in a British study of adjustment to parenthood:

> I felt that once he'd gone out through that door then he didn't have to think about it until he came back through the door . . . When he went off in the morning his life hadn't changed.

. . . It was the same as the day before we had her. But everything for me had just gone completely, you know, up in the air. Everything was different. (Choi et al., 2005, p. 174)

Many women experience the change from paid worker to unpaid full-time mom as stressful. The changes from a 9-to-5 schedule to being on call 24 hours a day, from adult company to isolation with an infant, from feeling competent to feeling overwhelmed with new tasks, all require adjustments. Women who return to paid work have their own stresses, juggling many old and new demands. Mothers are encouraged to evaluate themselves against images of ideal mothers such as the radiant, serene earthmother and the superwoman who juggles the demands of house, children, husband, and job while providing her children with unfailing love and plenty of quality time. One new mom, asked by a researcher what she'd expected before becoming a mother, said that she'd thought the baby would eat and sleep and she could "get on and do lots of things . . . be sort of Supermum, Superwife and Supereverything." Unfortunately she'd discovered that "it's not like that at all" (Choi et al., 2005, p. 173). Women often are not prepared for negative and ambivalent feelings and may feel like failures when they occur. One woman remembered how she felt a few weeks after the birth of her first child:

> I couldn't seem to do anything right; I felt so tired, the baby kept crying, and I kept thinking that this was supposed to be the most fulfilling experience of my whole life. It felt like the most lonely, miserable experience. (Ussher, 1989, p. 82)

The difficulties of being a first-time mother may be offset by the rewards of getting to know one's growing baby, the belief that caring for one's children is worthwhile and important, and the sense of mastery that comes from learning how to do it well. In one study of Australian women who were assessed while pregnant and 4 months after the birth of their baby, the majority of women said that their experience was largely positive and exceeded their expectations (Harwood et al., 2007).

When conflict occurs, it often is linked to a discrepancy between the woman's expectations of her partner's involvement and the partner's actual behavior once the child is born (Choi et al., 2005). In one study, new mothers kept time-use diaries and were also interviewed twice. Their workdays ranged from 11 to 17 1/2 hours a day, and they spent an average of 6 hours a day alone with their babies. Although they said the babies' fathers were their main source of support, fathers actually contributed only 0 to 2 hours a day of primary care (Croghan, 1991). The perceived unfairness contributes to marital disharmony during the first year of parenthood. ("How can he have time to play computer games when I don't even have time to take a shower?") (Sevón, 2012).

These studies suggest that new mothers are stressed when there is inequality in marital roles. When fathers become more involved with their babies, it benefits the family. In an intensive study of the first year of parenthood in a small sample of mothers in Finland, couples who shared responsibility for child care had the smoothest transition and the best marital relationships. The moms were proud of the dads for how trustworthy and reliable they were with the babies (Sevón, 2012).

Psychological Effects of Bodily Changes during Pregnancy

The hormonal changes of pregnancy are much greater than those of the menstrual cycle. The levels of progesterone and estrogen in pregnant women are many times higher than in nonpregnant women, and many of the physical experiences of early pregnancy may be related to rapid hormonal changes. These include breast tenderness, fatigue, and "morning sickness" (which can actually occur at any time of the day): nausea, revulsion at the sight or odor of food, and sometimes vomiting.

In addition, other physiological changes may alter the functioning of the central nervous system. The level of the neurotransmitter norepinephrine drops during pregnancy while the levels of stress-associated hormones rise (Treadway et al., 1969). Norepinephrine and progesterone have both been related to depression. In a study of mood changes during pregnancy, women were interviewed both before and during their pregnancies and compared with a control group of women who did not become pregnant. For the pregnant group, changes in mood increased compared with both their prepregnancy baseline and compared to the control group, mainly during the first three months of the pregnancy (Striegel-Moore et al., 1996).

Pregnancy also has implications for women's sexuality. When women become pregnant, they are confronted with many of the contradictions about sexuality that characterize Western society. (See Figure 9.2.) Becoming pregnant and giving birth highlight a woman's sexuality. At the same time, society may downplay the sexuality of the pregnant woman or the mother, fostering a split between the woman's body and sense of self (Ussher, 1989). The predominant image of motherhood in centuries of Western art is the Virgin Mary, the mother of Jesus. The idea of a mother who has sexual desires and acts on them conflicts with the ideal of maternal selflessness and purity.

Pregnancy is a time of dramatic weight gain and changes in body shape. Many women feel extremely ambivalent about these changes (Ussher, 1989). Reactions include feeling temporarily free from cultural demands to be slim, feeling awe and wonder, feeling afraid and disgusted

©Frank Micelotta/PictureGroup/Newscom

FIGURE 9.2   Singer Beyonce, pregnant with twins, was a sexual and sensual goddess at the 2017 Grammy awards.

by their size, and feeling alienated and out of control (see Box 9.1). In a study of more than 200 women, changes in body image were among the most frequently reported stressors of pregnancy and early motherhood, second only to physical symptoms (Affonso & Mayberry, 1989). As young women's body image concerns increase due to the pervasive objectification of women in American culture, these stressors may increase as well. "The idealized feminine body is expected to be

BOX 9.1 ∾ A Brand New Body: One Woman's Account of Pregnancy

©LWA/Dann Tardif/Blend Images LLC RF

One woman's reactions to her changing body are captured in these entries from a journal she kept during her first pregnancy. Her pregnancy was planned and wanted, and she was in a stable relationship with a supportive male partner. How might the reactions of women to their changing bodies differ in differing social circumstances?

- I have the feeling that I brought a brand new body home from the doctor's office. I'm a new me. Nobody else would look at me and call me pregnant, but it's wonderful to know that I really am, and I look for every tiny sign to prove it's true. My developing breasts are encouraging, and my nipples have become much larger. My nipples stand erect at times, and they're at least three shades darker.

- I really do feel beautiful. In fact, I feel like I'm a pretty good place for a baby to stay and grow in. Nice, round, firm, with just enough fat all over to make it really soft and safe for the baby.

- I rub cocoa butter on my tummy and breasts every morning after showering. The skin has become pink and smooth and I can't help feeling it all the time. The other day we were in the bookstore, and I was absent-mindedly rubbing myself and staring into space. A young woman with a child called to me from across the store, "That's a lovely belly you have there!"

- I've begun to feel huge. I remember hearing other pregnant women hassle themselves about getting fat. I never could figure it out. To me they looked beautiful, round, and blooming. I assured myself that I would never feel that way, and I would love my tummy and all the extra pounds. Well, that's great in theory—but suddenly the day comes when I look in the mirror and my face is round and I really do look like an orange! even holding my stomach in. So yesterday I spent the whole day feeling fat, ugly, and unlovable. Despite every nice thing John has said, I knew he would soon see how unappealing I am.

- I never thought it would come to this. I can't reach over my stomach to get to my feet. John has to lace up my hiking boots!

- Sometimes it seems as though I've been pregnant all my life. I can't remember being unpregnant.

Source: ©Suzanne Arms, www.BirthingTheFuture.org. Used by permission.

blemish free, young, smooth, sexual, tight, and always available for heterosexual viewing and pleasure" (Malacrida & Boulton, 2012, p. 751). The weight gain, stretching, and messiness of pregnancy and birth violate the heteronormative feminine ideal.

Stressors may interact during pregnancy. In a study of 413 young Black and Latina pregnant women, those who experienced discrimination were far more likely to also gain excessive weight, putting them at risk for later obesity and its associated health risks (Reid et al., 2016). This study demonstrates the complex relationship between psychological and physical health during pregnancy, and is a reminder that, as we saw in Chapter 2, systems of dominance have far-reaching consequences. For all pregnant women, their status as gendered beings is highlighted.

Indeed, the pregnant woman does lose some control over her body. Changes will occur no matter what she does. She is helpless (short of terminating the pregnancy) to govern her own body. And yet society defines her mainly in terms of her body. Thus it should not be surprising if pregnant women feel unfeminine, moody, or insecure, even apart from hormonal causes.

How Do Others React to Pregnant Women?

Pregnant women are powerful stimuli for the behavior of others. A woman who is visibly pregnant has already begun to be defined as a mother in the eyes of society. Her body symbolizes the eternal power of women:

> The atmosphere of approval in which I was bathed—even by strangers on the street, it seemed—was like an aura I carried with me, in which doubts, fears, misgivings, met with absolute denial. This is what women have always done. (Rich, 1976, p. 26)

Pregnant women may be genuinely cherished. One woman, who married into a Puerto Rican family, was delighted by her special status when she became pregnant:

> I'm treated like a precious, fragile person by my in-laws. I . . . get the best seat on the couch and am served dinner first. When my mother-in-law found out I was pregnant with my first child, she created a special ritual for me that involved a warm, scented candle-lit bath. She placed my husband's baby picture on the mirror and told me all about her experiences with pregnancy and birth. (Johnston-Robledo, 2000, p. 132–133)

On the other hand, pregnancy may elicit sexist behavior. Benevolent sexism is primed because pregnant women are seen as fragile and in need of protection. Hostile sexism may occur if the pregnant woman seems not to accept her traditional role. Benevolent sexists believe that it's okay to restrict pregnant women—for example to tell them not to eat fat or exercise too much (Sutton et al., 2011). Hostile sexists have negative attitudes toward pregnant women who don't follow all the rules (i.e., they drink tap water instead of filtered water or have an occasional beer (Murphy et al., 2011). Ambivalent sexists disapprove of a woman's right to an abortion even when her life is in danger (Huang et al., 2014).

A field study demonstrated ambivalent sexism directed at pregnant women in a real-world setting (Hebl et al., 2007). Female experimenters (with the help of a little padding) posed as pregnant women who were job applicants or customers at retail stores in a large mall, and the researchers observed and recorded the behavior of store employees toward them. The good news from the results was that employees did not overtly discriminate against pregnant women—they weren't ignored or refused job applications. However, observations of subtle sexism yielded some not-so-good news. The employees showed more patronizing and benevolent behavior (being over-friendly and overhelpful, touching) toward the supposedly pregnant women posing as customers (a traditional and nonthreatening female role), but more hostile behavior (rudeness, staring) to the pregnant women applying for jobs. The hostility was greater when the women were applying for gender-incongruent (masculine) jobs. The researchers pointed out that this combination—rewards for conventionally feminine women, and punishments for those who violate gender roles—is exactly the kind of subtle sexism that sustains social inequality. Pregnant women may get an extra dose of sexism because their visible condition primes sexist attitudes.

Unfortunately, sexist attitudes may be primed in actual workplace situations, too. Most U.S. women are working when they become pregnant for the first time, but there has been very little research on how pregnant women are treated at work. In a groundbreaking longitudinal study of 142 pregnant women during and after their pregnancies, participants both expected and encountered stigma and discrimination related to their pregnant status: they were viewed as more emotional, likely to quit their jobs, and less committed to their work. When they encountered this kind of discrimination, their job satisfaction and psychological well-being decreased, and they became more likely to intend to quit their jobs after the birth of their children (Fox & Quinn, 2015). These dramatic changes in their lives were not caused by the pregnancy, but by the stigma and discrimination that their pregnancy elicited at work.

Motherhood and Women's Identity

Pregnancy and mothering affect women's sense of self. In a Canadian study, for example, the women experienced themselves as profoundly changed. Middle-class women described the changes in terms of personal growth and self-actualization; working-class women described a process of "settling down." For both groups, motherhood involved a moral transformation in which they became deeply connected to their babies. However, the flip side of such connectedness—feeling totally responsible for the child—was described as one of the hardest things about motherhood (McMahon, 1995).

In another study, women who were interviewed during pregnancy described several ways their identities were changing. They talked about creating themselves as mothers and beginning to develop a relationship with their unborn child. They also described changes in social identity—learning how to situate themselves with family and societal expectations about motherhood. They said they had to "add motherhood to the mix"—to integrate their new identities with the other parts of their lives (Messias & DeJoseph, 2007).

An intensive case study of one woman's pregnancy illustrates the experience of personal identity change (Smith, 1991). Clare's change during early pregnancy involved imagining the child-to-be. As she explained, "In one respect, it's—it's a person, a whole person that just happens to be in there, and in another way, it's something different" (p. 231). In the middle phase, Clare experienced a growing sense of psychological relatedness with others—partner, mother, and sister. Near the end of the pregnancy, Clare believed that she had changed in important ways, saying "I'm one of two and I'm one of three." Her identities as a partner to the baby's father and as a mother were now an integrated part of her self.

The prototypical mother in research studies is White, middle-class, heterosexual, and married. However, when we think about mothering more inclusively it becomes clear that attitudes toward pregnant women and mothers vary by social class, ethnic group, and sexual orientation. Middle-class women in heterosexual marriages may be treated as delicate and special when they're pregnant, but low-income single women are labeled "welfare moms," undeserving of respect. Middle-class moms are urged to stay home with their children, but low-income women are forced to look for employment. Heterosexual women's connectedness with their children is seen as positive, but lesbians' connectedness with theirs may be pathologized. Women's identities as mothers are shaped not only by their individual experiences but by the social context in which they are judged as mothers.

The Event of Childbirth

If a woman were training to run a marathon, climb a cliff, or go on an Outward Bound trek, she would probably think of the upcoming event as a challenge. She would acknowledge that her body would be worked hard and stressed, her courage tested, and her life put at some risk. Yet she could feel in control and prepare for the challenge. She might undertake the experience as a way of knowing her own self or of developing her strengths and resources. Childbirth is a normal physical process with some of the same potential for empowerment, yet women are rarely encouraged to think of it in this way (Reiger & Dempsey, 2006). Instead, they are taught to think of it as an event in which they will be dependent, passive, subject to authority, and in need of expert medical intervention.

In virtually all cultures, birth is associated with fear, pain, awe, and wonder; it is viewed as both the worst pain anyone could suffer and as a peak experience. Yet there are surprisingly few literary accounts of childbirth *by women,* and women's experiences of childbirth are invisible in Western art. Images of war and death are innumerable but images of birth are virtually nonexistent (Chicago, 1990). (See Figure 9.3.)

Is Childbirth a Medical Crisis?

In some countries, birth is considered a natural phenomenon that needs no medical intervention in the majority of cases. For example, the Netherlands is well known for its high percentage of home births and low rate of medical procedures

©Reg Innell/Toronto Star/Getty Images

FIGURE 9.3   Artist Judy Chicago with her image "The Crowning," which represents the moment the baby's head first becomes visible at the vaginal opening.

(Christiaens et al., 2008). The Dutch philosophy is that a healthy woman can best accomplish her task of birthing her baby if she is self-confident, in familiar surroundings—preferably her own home—and attended by a birth specialist such as a midwife.

In contrast, the U.S. has adopted a ***medical model of birth.*** Over 99 percent of U.S. births take place in hospitals (Hyde & DeLamater, 2017). Nurse-midwives attend only about 8 percent of U.S. births, with the rest attended by physicians. Even the language of childbirth reflects the centrality of the physician: People routinely speak of babies being *delivered* by doctors instead of birthed by women.

Is the medical model of birth best for women? On the one hand, basic health care and education for pregnant women can save lives and improve maternal and infant health. On the other hand, the medical monopoly may lead to women being regarded as incompetent and passive patients, depriving them of control during one of life's most awesome experiences. Many of the customary procedures surrounding birth in the U.S. are virtually unknown in other societies and are not necessarily in the best interest of mother or baby. For example, in hospital births the woman lies on her back during delivery, whereas in most cultures women give birth in a squatting or semi-seated position. The supine position puts pressure on the spine, may slow labor, works against gravity, increases the risk of vaginal tearing, and makes it more difficult for the woman to push actively during the process. Why, then, do hospitals insist on this position? It is easier for the physician, who can view the birth more conveniently.

American women experience childbirth with feet in the air, drugged, shaved, purged with an enema, denied food and water, hooked up to machines and sensors, and psychologically isolated to a degree that is virtually unknown in other parts of the world (Nelson, 1996). Research shows that giving birth in an unfamiliar environment, being surrounded by strangers, and being moved from one room to another during labor affect the birth process adversely even in nonhuman animals, yet these practices are routine in medicalized childbirth (MacFarlane, 1977; Newton, 1970).

In the U.S., women have also been routinely taught that they will need pain relief during normal birth. The use of tranquilizers, barbiturates, and anesthetics during childbirth has become routine, but it is also controversial. On the one hand, drugs can spare women unnecessary pain. On the other hand, there are well-documented negative effects on both mother and baby (Hyde & DeLamater, 2017). Anesthetics in the mother's bloodstream are passed to the infant, depressing its nervous system. Anesthetics may prolong labor by inhibiting contractions and making the mother unable to help push the baby through the birth canal. Psychologically, they reduce the woman's awareness and her ability to control one of the most meaningful events of her life.

The medical model of birth encourages physicians and pregnant women to focus on possible complications and emergencies and may cause them to react to even remote possibilities with drastic medical interventions. In the past 25 years, there has been a dramatic increase in the number of caesarean (surgical) births in the U.S., from about 4 percent to nearly 33 percent of all births (Martin et al., 2014). This rate is much higher than in other developed countries such as Great Britain (where it is about 10 percent) and is *not* associated with lower infant mortality. Other medical procedures such as artificial induction of labor are also rising dramatically in the U.S. (NCHS, 2009).

Why the epidemic of medical intervention? Some critics have rather cynically suggested that scheduled surgical births are more convenient and profitable for physicians. Others have attributed the increase to physicians' fear of malpractice suits. It has also been suggested that the high rate of surgical deliveries is an attempt by the medical profession to keep its dominant role in childbirth, despite women's increasing insistence on viewing birth as a normal process.

Many feminist activists and health specialists are concerned about the over-medicalization of birth. When birth is defined as a medical event, helping and supporting the laboring woman seems inadequate, and heroic medical measures seem appropriate. Because medical and surgical interventions are now so common, normal vaginal delivery is starting to be seen as difficult, even unattainable by the average woman. Young women, it seems, increasingly express fear of giving birth and lack of confidence in their bodies' ability to cope with pregnancy and childbirth (Reiger & Dempsey, 2006).

Family-Centered Childbirth

After undergoing medically managed childbirth, many second-wave feminists began to write about their experiences and work toward more woman- and family-centered birthing practices. Women organizers founded the International Childbirth Education Association in 1960. Widely read books such as *Our Bodies, Ourselves; Immaculate Deception; Of Woman Born;* and *The Great American Birth Rite* helped change public attitudes in the 1970s.

At about the same time, methods of ***prepared*** or ***natural childbirth*** were introduced to the American public. The most popular type of prepared childbirth is the ***Lamaze method,*** named after a French obstetrician. Women who use this approach learn techniques of relaxation and controlled breathing. Relaxation helps to reduce tension, decrease the perception of pain, and conserve energy during labor. Controlled breathing helps the woman work with, not against, the strength of each uterine contraction. The Lamaze method does not rule out the use of pain-relieving drugs, but it emphasizes that with proper preparation they may not be needed, and it leaves the choice to the laboring woman.

Another part of the Lamaze technique is the help of a "coach," or trusted partner—usually the baby's father—during labor and birth. The coach helps the mother with relaxation and controlled breathing and provides emotional support and encouragement. Men had been banished from the delivery room at the heyday of the medical model, regarded as unhygienic and likely to get in the way (MacFarlane, 1977). Today, many men feel that participating in the birth of their child is an important part of becoming a father.

Studies comparing women who used Lamaze and other methods of prepared childbirth with women who had no special preparation have shown benefits associated with prepared childbirth. These include shorter labor, fewer complications, less use of anesthetics, less reported pain, and increased feelings of self-esteem and control (Hyde & DeLamater, 2017). These studies must be interpreted carefully. Perhaps women who sign up for Lamaze training are largely those who are motivated to experience childbirth positively under any circumstances. In other words, the studies do not rule out the sampling bias of self-selection.

One study of support during childbirth does rule out self-selection effects (Kennell et al., 1991). More than 600 pregnant women, mostly Hispanic, poor, and unmarried, were randomly assigned to one of three groups in an experimental design. One group received emotional support during labor from a specially trained female helper. The helpers, who were recruited from the local community, stayed with the laboring women to provide encouragement, explain the birth process, and offer soothing touch and handholding. A second group had a noninteractive female observer present, and the third group had standard hospital care.

Women in the emotional support group had a caesarean rate of 8 percent, compared with 13 percent in the observed group and 18 percent in the standard procedure group. They experienced less pain during labor: The standard group was almost seven times as likely to need anesthesia as the emotional support group. Moreover, for women in the supported group their labor time was shorter, and they and their babies spent less time in the hospital. Clearly, emotional support made a large difference. The study's director estimated that investing small amounts of money in providing this kind of support would save $2 billion a year in hospital costs.

Women's efforts to regain control of the event of birth have resulted in many changes from the extreme medical model of thirty years ago. Today, fathers are more likely to be with the birthing woman. More births are taking place in home-like birth centers, attended by nurse-midwives. Women and their partners are far more likely to be educated about the normal processes and events of pregnancy and birth. This knowledge reduces fear and helplessness, and thus reduces discomfort. Learning techniques to use during labor can replace passive suffering with active involvement and coping. However, new technology is continually being introduced, and each new intervention can readily be overused.

One area where there is still room for improvement is helping fathers feel welcome during their partners' pregnancies and childbirth. Although many couples today attend childbirth education classes, these classes may not be enough to meet the support needs of men whose partners are pregnant for the first time. A review of 25 studies found that partners of pregnant women often feel a sense of unreality and exclusion at the beginning of the pregnancy. (The first ultrasound or the first time they can feel the baby moving when they touch the "baby bump" is often significant for prospective dads.) During childbirth education classes, prospective dads want information that tells them how they can help and be useful to their partners. They worry about her pain during childbirth and they want to be involved and respected (Poh et al., 2014). It seems that not enough attention has been paid by healthcare professionals to integrating *both* parents into childbirth education, an integration that could foster more egalitarian marriages and parenting.

Depression Following Childbirth: Why?

The first weeks following childbirth (the **postnatal period**) are often characterized as a time of mood swings and depression. For the first few days after giving birth, most women feel elated: the waiting is over, the labor complete, and the baby has arrived. Soon, however, they experience depression and crying spells. Between 50 percent and 80 percent of women experience mood swings for a day or two. Longer-lasting depression (6 to 8 weeks) occurs in about 13 percent of women; it includes feelings of inadequacy and inability to cope, fatigue, tearfulness, and insomnia. The most severe form, a major clinical disorder, affects one-tenth of 1 percent of new mothers (Hyde & DeLamater, 2017).

Are postnatal mood disorders due to hormonal changes? Birth is followed by dramatic decreases in the high levels of estrogen and progesterone that characterize pregnancy. However, hormone changes have not been shown to *cause* depression; in fact, there is no direct link between postnatal hormone levels and mood (Johnston-Robledo, 2000; Treadway et al., 1969). The hormonal changes of pregnancy and the postnatal period are real. They give rise to bodily changes and sensations that must be interpreted by the woman who is experiencing them. But the social context of interpretation is crucial; postnatal depression may be more of a social construction than a medical condition. It is virtually unknown in many countries, including India, China, Mexico, and Kenya, suggesting that the causes are at least partly cultural (Mauthner, 1998).

Many physical, social, and interpersonal factors may contribute to depression and mood swings among new mothers. A large-scale study of over 1,200 women showed that caesarean births did not lead to more postnatal depression, but women who experienced severe pain following childbirth (regardless of type of delivery) had a three times greater risk of depression in the following weeks compared to those whose pain was mild (Eisenach et al., 2008). In a study of 42 Australian women with major clinical depression after childbirth, the psychosocial risk factors were being 16-years-old or younger, having a past history of psychiatric illness, experiencing stressful life events during the pregnancy, being in an unhappy marriage, having little social support, having a vulnerable personality, and having a baby of the nondesired sex (Boyce & Hickey, 2005). In a sample of middle-class French women, risk factors for postpartum depression included depression during the pregnancy, migrant status, physical abuse by the partner, and physical complications after the baby's birth (Gaillard et al., 2014). In a Canadian sample, a previous history of depression, migrant status, depression during the pregnancy, and not breast-feeding were risk factors (Davey et al., 2011). There is a higher risk of depression following an unintended pregnancy than a pregnancy that was wanted and planned (Abbasi et al., 2013).

In an intensive study of a small sample of English women experiencing postnatal depression, a key factor was conflicts between their expectations of motherhood and their actual experiences. Different mothers resolved these conflicts in different ways, but in all cases a woman's recovery was a process of accepting herself and rejecting the impossible ideals of motherhood (Mauthner, 1998). This result was echoed in a larger study of 71 first-time mothers who completed questionnaires during pregnancy and at 4 months postpartum. Most of the women's expectations were fulfilled and their experiences as new parents were positive. However, when experiences were negative compared to expectations, there was greater depression following the birth (Harwood et al., 2007).

Ethnic minority, low-income, and socially disadvantaged women are at higher risk for postpartum depression than other women are, because the combination of stressors that they face is likely to be greater. In developing interventions, it is important to keep in mind that postpartum depression is more than just a medical problem that can be cured by hormones or antidepressant medication. A meta-analysis showed that the most effective interventions, particularly for disadvantaged groups of women, are those that are culturally sensitive and based on interpersonal therapy and support (Rojas-Garcia et al., 2014). The context of the new mother's life is crucial to understanding why some mothers and not others experience depression after childbirth.

As a mother, I believe that sleep deprivation has been overlooked as a factor in postnatal mood disorders. During the last weeks of pregnancy, a woman may not sleep well due to the discomfort caused by the heavy, restless fetus. Next, the hard physical work and stress of birthing a child are followed by many consecutive nights of disturbed sleep. Babies rarely sleep for a 6- or 7-hour stretch before they are 6-weeks-old, and some take much longer to settle down. I know of no studies of postnatal depression that have examined sleep deprivation as a factor or compared moodiness in new mothers with moodiness in a sleep-deprived comparison group, though new moms readily talk about it in interview studies (Choi et al., 2005). Going without sleep for a few days can make anyone cranky and depressed. The lack of attention to this possibility is a striking example of how sociocultural influences are often overlooked in studying women's lives.

Countries in which postnatal depression is rare offer a period of rest and special care for the new mother, practical and emotional support from other women, and positive attention to the mother, not just the baby (Johnston-Robledo, 2000; Mauthner, 1998). For example, in Guatemala, a new mother gets an herbal bath and a massage. In Nigeria, she and her baby are secluded in a "fattening room" where her meals are prepared by others. Customs like these may help the new mother interpret her bodily changes and sensations more positively and ease her adjustment to motherhood. One U.S. psychologist who studied new mothers suggests, "Next time a friend or relative has a baby, in addition to a gift for the baby, bring her a meal and offer to help around the house" (Johnston-Robledo, 2000, p. 139). And maybe somebody else could get up with the baby so she can get a good night's sleep.

Experiences of Mothering

The realities of mothering are as different as the social circumstances of women who mother. In this section, let's look at what motherhood involves for diverse groups of women.

Teen Mothers

Each year in the U.S. more than half a million young women under the age of 20 become pregnant—about 5 percent of all women in this age group. Most of these teens are unmarried. Over half of teen pregnancies result in the birth of a child; about 31 percent are terminated by abortion and the rest end in miscarriage. The rate of births to teen mothers is much higher for young women of color than for Whites (Guttmacher Institute, 2016a).

The rate of teen pregnancy in the U.S. has been dropping since the 1990s and has declined dramatically in the past decade in all racial and ethnic groups, due to more contraceptive use by teens (Lindberg et al., 2016). However, the U.S. still has the highest teen pregnancy rate in the developed world—more than 7 times as high as Switzerland, for example (Sedgh et al., 2015). (See Figure 9.4.) U.S. teens are not more sexually active than their European counterparts, but countries like Switzerland provide comprehensive sex education in schools, positive attitudes toward contraceptive use by teens, and free family planning as part of healthcare services.

What factors put girls at risk for early pregnancy? First and foremost, teen pregnancy and childbearing are related to social class disadvantages. Living in a poor or dangerous neighborhood, growing up in a poor family with a single parent, and

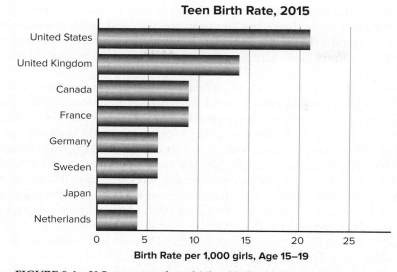

Teen Birth Rate, 2015

Birth Rate per 1,000 girls, Age 15–19

FIGURE 9.4   U.S. teenagers have higher birthrates than adolescents in other developed countries.

Source: United Nations Department of Economic and Social Affairs, Population Division (2015). *World Population Prospects: The 2015 Revision.* New York: United Nations.

being sexually abused are all linked to teen pregnancy. Parents who supervise and regulate their teens' activities and teach them to avoid unprotected sex may lower the risk to some extent (Miller et al., 2001).

Adolescent motherhood has serious consequences for the young women involved, their children, and society as a whole. These include interrupted education and lowered job opportunities for the mothers, health problems for the babies, and the costs of public assistance and interventions (Barto et al., 2015; Gibb et al., 2015; Venkatesh et al., 2014). In one longitudinal study, 281 teen mothers in Indiana were followed through pregnancy and when their children reached ages 3, 5, and 8. The average age of the mothers at the time of childbirth was 17; almost two-thirds were African American, one-third White, and 4 percent Hispanic. Although most of the children were of normal weight and health at birth, they suffered increasing physical, emotional, and behavioral problems. By the age of 8, more than 70 percent were having problems in school. The mothers were suffering disadvantages, too. They did not know very much about taking care of children and did not have the cognitive maturity to be effective parents. Five years after their child's birth, most remained undereducated, underemployed, and weighed down by depression, anxiety, and stress.

However, there was a great deal of variability in the group. About 18 percent of the mother–child pairs were thriving: The mothers were working, had continued their education, and showed high self-esteem and little depression or anxiety. Their children were developmentally normal. The women who had managed to overcome the disadvantages of early motherhood were those who started off with more advantages in the first place (for example, they had more education before they got pregnant), those who received emotional support from a partner, and those whose coping skills and cognitive readiness for parenthood were high (Whitman et al., 2001).

Another study focused on a group of disadvantaged inner-city teens from New York. Ranging in age from 14 to 19, most were African American or Puerto Rican; two-thirds came from families on welfare. The young mothers who were doing best at a 5-year follow-up had active lives that typically involved working, going to school, spending time with their partner and families, and taking care of their children. What contributed to their strengths? In-depth interviews revealed themes of having been raised in a strict home environment, receiving support from their family with the expectation that they would make something of themselves, having role models and support for education, and having confidence, a strong will, and a passion to succeed (Leadbeater & Way, 2001).

These research findings show that statistics alone do not convey the meaning of teen pregnancy. Teen pregnancy is often used as a symbol of moral and social decay, and teen mothers are accused of undermining family values. Research shows that adolescent mothers are a diverse group who are often struggling to overcome disadvantages that go far beyond just having a baby. Many teen mothers show resilience and courage in overcoming the obstacles they face. Surprisingly, early motherhood does not always result in permanent disadvantage. The majority of teen mothers eventually finish high school, get stable jobs, move into their own apartments or houses, and raise children who do not go on to become teen parents themselves (Leadbeater & Way, 2001).

I am not arguing that early childbearing is desirable. But its meaning and consequences depend on its cultural context. Though teen pregnancy is seen as a huge social problem today, rates were actually higher in the 1950s than now (Nettles & Scott-Jones, 1987). It was less of an issue then, because most teen mothers were married, or hastily got married on becoming pregnant.

Today, there are ethnic and cultural differences in the acceptance of teen pregnancy. Most African American teen mothers live with and receive support from their own mothers. Among Hispanic families, teen pregnancy may not be seen as problematic as long as it results in marriage. Some young women see any child as a gift from God, no matter how unfortunate the circumstances of its birth (Leadbeater & Way, 2001; Whitman et al., 2001). And some teen mothers become inspired to better their lives for the sake of their child (Leadbeater & Way, 2001).

Young mothers need access to programs to help them learn parenting skills, complete their education, and take control of their contraceptive use. Moreover, they need support from their families, their communities, and the educational system (Barto et al., 2015). There is also a great need for more research on teen fathers—it takes two to make a baby. A particular need is programs that help fathers take responsibility for birth control, family planning, and their children's economic and social support. With help, the negative effects of early childbearing can be overcome.

Single Mothers

The number of families headed by single women has increased dramatically over the past 30 years. Minority children are more likely to grow up in single-parent families; according to the most recent U.S. census, 21 percent of White, 31 percent of Hispanic, and 55 percent of African American children are in single-parent households (Vespa et al., 2013). The great majority of these families are headed by women. For Whites, the primary reason for single parenthood is the high separation and divorce rate (see Chapter 8). For Hispanic and Black women, the primary reason is a rise in births to single women.

Single mothers, whether they are unmarried, separated, or divorced, are more likely to be holding down jobs than mothers with husbands present in the home. Over half of single mothers work full time, and another 28 percent work part time. Yet families headed by women are far more likely to be poor than other families; their poverty rate is twice that of the general population (Grall, 2009). Poverty among women-headed families is one of the most serious social problems in the U.S. today.

Why are women-headed households so likely to be poor? Some of the reasons for women's poverty are the same as men's: they may lack education or job skills, or live in a region with few jobs. But women are poor for gender-related reasons as well: women in general are underpaid and underemployed (see Chapter 10). In addition, the lack of publicly subsidized child care makes it nearly impossible for a single working mother to get ahead. If she works full time at minimum wage, child care will consume a large part of her income—if she can even find decent child care. Of all the Western industrialized nations, only the U.S. fails to provide family support benefits as a matter of public policy (Lorber, 1993). These are sociocultural-level problems, not ones that a single mom can easily solve by herself.

Another gender-related reason for single mothers' poverty is men's failure to provide financial support for their children. In Chapter 8, we looked at the problem of defaults in child support from absentee fathers after divorce. When all single mothers are considered as a group—those who never married as well as those who divorced—the data show that only 54 percent are awarded child support through a court or legal agreement. Of those, 47 percent get the full amount; another 30 percent get some but not all. The average amount received by a mother-headed family is just $3,350 per year (Grall, 2009).

The primary response to the feminization of poverty in the U.S. seems to be to blame the victims. Women who accept public assistance are accused of causing the very problems they are trying to cope with. In 1996 welfare reform legislation mandated that mothers of young children who receive benefits find paid employment. Consider that many middle-class mothers, with safe homes, good child care, decent jobs, and employed husbands find it difficult or impossible to manage full-time employment when they have babies or toddlers—then think about doing it alone, poor, at a minimum-wage job, and in a dangerous neighborhood.

Many conservative policymakers assume that marriage is the answer to poverty among women and children. However, the majority of women who have children outside of marriage are poor before they become pregnant. Even if these women married the fathers of their babies, they would still be poor, because the fathers are likely to be unemployed and living in economically depressed areas (Dickerson, 1995). Many of the fathers are simply not available or have so many problems of their own that they cannot help support a family. For example, in a study of inner-city young mothers, by the time their first child was 6, 10 percent of the fathers were dead, 25 percent were in jail, and 24 percent were selling or using drugs. Only a few couples had managed to stay together (Leadbeater & Way, 2001). Even among middle-class divorced women, remarriage is not always an option for mothers of small children, and second marriages are more likely than first marriages to end in divorce (see Chapter 8).

But there is more to single-mother families than poverty and despair. Studies show that single mothers are proud that they are handling a difficult job well. They are just as satisfied with motherhood as married mothers are. Among White families, single-parent homes seem to be less gender-typed than two-parent homes. They encourage more gender-neutral play in children and create more flexible attitudes about gender roles (Smith, 1997). This result makes sense when we consider that fathers are more prone than mothers to treating children in gender-stereotypical ways (see Chapter 6), and that children of single mothers see their moms as both the provider and nurturer. Among African American single-parent families, strengths include role flexibility (many adults may "mother" a child), spirituality (relying on inner strength rather than material possessions for happiness), and a sense of community ("It takes a village to raise a child") (Randolph, 1995).

Black Mothers and the Matriarchal Myth

African Americans, under slavery, experienced the systematic, widespread destruction of their families. In addition to this legacy of slavery, there has since been a scarcity of Black men to be providers and husbands. The causes for this scarcity include poor health care and other effects of poverty and discrimination, leading to drug use, imprisonment, and violent death. Thus, Black women have been (and still are) more likely than White women to be raising families without a resident father/husband. For African American women, motherhood is not equated with being dependent on a man (Collins, 1991; Dickerson, 1995).

Black women have coped with oppression in many ways. They often form extended households, with two or three generations living together and sharing resources. Grandmothers, sisters, cousins, and aunts care for the children of young mothers. Black families are less likely than White ones to give children up for adoption by strangers, and more likely to take in the children of friends and relatives. In the Black community, these informal adoptions are seen as better than stranger adoption, because children can stay in contact with their mothers and live with people they know and trust. This collective, cooperative child rearing may reflect a West African heritage (Collins, 1991; George & Dickerson, 1995; Greene, 1990).

Unfortunately, Black women have long been judged against a White middle-class norm of female submission and traditional marriage arrangements (Collins, 1991). Sociologists and psychiatrists have accused them of castrating their husbands and sons by being unfeminine and domineering (Giddings, 1984). Blaming Black women for social problems avoids confronting the real problems of racism, classism, and sexism. Moreover, it obscures the unique contributions of African American family patterns. Black women's involvement in social activism often stems from their definition of motherhood: A good mother does not just take care of her own offspring, she works to meet the needs of her entire community (Collins, 1991; Naples, 1992). In interviews with three generations of middle-class African-American women who had been married and raised families, the women voiced themes of helping to support their families by working, bringing up children to be respectful and obedient, and mothering in the church and community (Fouquier, 2011).

LGBT Mothers

About 6 million Americans have an LGBT parent. Today, about one in five same-sex households includes children under the age of 18 (Gates, 2013). Some women who marry or cohabit with men and have children within these relationships later identify as lesbian and bring up their children in lesbian households. Other lesbians have a child through adoption. A growing trend is medical methods such as donor insemination and IVF. Given the biological and social obstacles to lesbian and gay parenthood, it is safe to say that most children born to LGBT parents are the result of pregnancies that were wanted and planned (Renaud, 2007).

What are the special issues and stresses that confront lesbian mothers? One of the biggest potential problems is negotiating the marginalized identity of lesbian with the mainstream identity of mother (Ben-Ari & Livni, 2006). Lesbian mothers may feel little in common with heterosexual families, whose kids do not have to deal with being taunted at school for having two moms (Breshears, 2011). Turning to the lesbian community for support, they may find that the lives of their child-free lesbian friends are very different from their own. As more lesbians decide to have children, support groups and networks of lesbian families are growing, and family counselors are more aware of their needs (Erwin, 2007).

Lesbian couples, in keeping with their egalitarian ideals, usually try to share parenting duties equally, but it isn't always easy. Even in Sweden, a country that provides generous family leave for both parents in heterosexual and same-sex couples, a discourse analytic study of interviews with lesbian parents found that many couples had to work hard to achieve equal parenting, and not everyone did. (Malmquist, 2015)

Do lesbians raise children differently than heterosexual mothers, and do their children turn out differently? Research suggests that the children of lesbian families are similar to those of heterosexual families.

One study of African American women compared the attitudes of 26 heterosexual and 26 lesbian mothers. The two groups were similar in the value they placed on independence and self-sufficiency for their children. The lesbian mothers, however, were more tolerant about rules, less restrictive of sex play, less concerned with modesty, and more open in providing sex education. They also viewed boys and girls as more similar to each other than the heterosexual mothers did and expected more traditionally masculine activities from their daughters (Hill, 1987). Another study of 33 heterosexual and 33 lesbian couples measured the gender development of their preschool children (Fulcher et al., 2006). The children's gender role attitudes were related to the parents' behavior, not their sexual orientation. In other words, parents who divided the chores and jobs equally, thereby setting an example of mutual respect, had kids with less traditional attitudes, regardless of whether the parents were gay or straight.

In the United Kingdom, children in a representative sample of lesbian families were compared with those in two-parent and single-mother heterosexual families. Parents, teachers, and a child psychiatrist assessed the children's adjustment. There were few differences in lesbian and heterosexual mothers' parenting styles except that the lesbian mothers hit their children less often and engaged in more imaginative play with them. Overall, the children of lesbian mothers were well-adjusted and had positive relationships with their parents and peers (Golombok et al., 2003). Another British study tracked 78 children, half raised by lesbian mothers and half by heterosexual single mothers, from middle childhood to young adulthood (Tasker & Golombok, 1997). As young adults, these participants were asked to look back on their family life. Children of lesbians were more positive about their family life than children of heterosexuals, especially if their mother was open about her sexual orientation and active in lesbian politics. Children of lesbians were no more likely to identify as gay or lesbian, but those who did were more likely to be involved in a relationship than were gay children of heterosexuals. Children raised by lesbians reported that their mothers had been more open and comfortable communicating with them about sexual development and sexuality as they were growing up. There was no difference in psychological adjustment in the two groups.

On the whole, it seems that lesbian family life produces children who are very much like children from heterosexual families. Research reviews (Fulcher et al., 2006; Tasker, 2005) have found no detrimental effects of lesbian or gay parenting on children's cognitive abilities, self-esteem, gender identity, peer relations, or overall psychological adjustment. This research has decreased discrimination against LG families and fostered changes in laws and public policy in some U.S. states and other countries (Short, 2007).

Even people who accept lesbian and gay parenting may still be uncomfortable with the idea of a gender nonconforming, non-binary, or transgender parent. However, many transgender people are already parents when they transition and they do not want to leave their children behind (Haines et al., 2014). Other transgender and gender nonconforming people consider creating a family an important part of life and want to have options such as foster care, adoption, donor insemination, and assisted reproductive technology to make that possible (Dickey et al., 2016).

Taking an intersectional perspective, parenting is a privileged status, given our society's pronatalist bias. However, transgender is still a marginalized status. In short, moms and dads are considered great people, but transgender moms and dads—not so much. The intersection of these two conflicting social positions creates unique challenges for transgender parents. In an online national survey, 50 transgender parents were asked about the challenges they faced (Haines et al.,

2014). They described concerns with their children's well-being due to their parent's transgender status. For example, their children faced bullying at school, and the transgender parents worried about when and where they could be out without stigmatizing their children. Second, transgender parents dealt with ongoing conflict with their co-parents. Usually, the transition had led to a breakup of their relationship, which affected the children. Third, transgender parents worked at balancing their own transition with parenting and changes in family structure. For example, one MtF parent told how her eight-year-old daughter grieved losing a dad. To date, there is very little research on trans parenting, and it is due for more attention from psychologists.

Making a Difference

Bringing up children is a great joy and an awesome responsibility. Traditionally, in Western societies it has been divided into a nurturing role, assigned to women, and a provider role, assigned to men. This arrangement has many limitations. It does not allow for individual differences in personality and ability—some men might make better nurturers than providers, and some women better providers than nurturers. It keeps women and children economically dependent on men; when men default, families live in poverty. It overlooks the diversity of families. Single-parent families, LGBT families, and families from different cultural traditions do not conform to the patriarchal ideal. Social change over the past several decades has been uneven. Although the majority of women now participate in the provider role, the majority of men have not correspondingly increased their participation in nurturing. How might our society support mothers and children and help fathers develop their parenting potential?

Transforming Social Policy: Redefining Family Values

Public policy on families in the U.S. lags behind policies in every other industrialized country in the world, and even behind some that are much poorer and less developed (Crittenden, 2001). For example, new mothers and fathers are guaranteed not a single day of paid leave from work in the U.S. To those of us who live in the U.S., this situation seems normal. But the U.S. is the *only* advanced economy in the world that does not offer federally supported paid maternity leave. In many countries, new mothers get 52 weeks or more. New fathers are guaranteed paid leave in at least 74 countries, which can help them become involved in caring for their babies from the start (Etehad & Lin, 2016). The U.S. is one of just 9 countries that refuse to provide for the needs of families. Here, moms and dads are expected to depend on the goodwill of their employers for paid parental leave and other family-friendly policies. But only 12 percent of companies provide paid maternity leave and only 7 percent offer paid paternity leave (Heymann, 2010). Fortunately, some employers are getting the message that to keep the best and brightest employees, and keep them happy, they need to accommodate their family lives (see Box 9.2).

BOX 9.2 ∽ Redefining Fatherhood

©zhang bo/E+/Getty Images RF

In the U.S., it is common, or even expected, that women will be the primary caretakers of the children, while men serve as breadwinners. Maternity and parental leave policies in the U.S. reflect these stereotypical expectations. Women often receive between six and twelve weeks of (typically unpaid) maternity leave, while men often get a week or less! Unfortunately, the U.S. lags significantly behind other countries when it comes to providing equal opportunity for both men and women to take care of their children.

In Sweden, laws are far more progressive. Although women still take more time off to take care of children, their husbands are expected to take time off, too. Laws in Sweden provide a 13-month parental leave to be shared by mothers and fathers, and at least two months of that leave is required to be taken by fathers. Consequently, 85 percent of men in Sweden take parental leave, and those who do not face criticism from their families and workplaces.

While many companies in the U.S. balk at the thought of a man asking for an extended parental leave, top technology companies appear to be *competing* with one another to have the best parental leave policies. In 2015, Netflix announced unlimited parental leave for the first year following the birth of a child. Microsoft followed up with an announcement that they were increasing their paid leave to 20 weeks for new mothers and 12 weeks for new

fathers. Most recently, the e-commerce company Etsy announced it would be providing employees up to 6 months of paid parental leave. Google, Facebook, and Twitter have also established generous parental leave policies, ranging from 16 to 30 weeks of paid leave (see below). Why have tech companies made the move to improve parental leave policies? It may reflect both a generational shift in employees' expectations regarding work-life balance, as well as an acknowledgement among technology executives of how such leave policies foster company loyalty and help retain top talent.

Of course, there are both economic and social benefits when fathers take time off to help raise their children, too. In Sweden, divorce rates have gone down. Children get to spend time with both of their parents. Women are earning more money, and men are not penalized for taking leave when they come up for promotion. And most interestingly, conceptions of masculinity have begun to shift. Birgitta Ohlsson, the European affairs minister and an advocate for parental leave stated, "Machos with dinosaur values don't make the top-10 lists of attractive men in women's magazines anymore . . . Now men can have it all—a successful career and being a responsible daddy," she added. "It's a new kind of manly. It's more wholesome." Hopefully, more companies in the U.S. will follow the lead of the technology industry and we will begin to see similar benefits in the U.S.!

U.S. Technology Companies with Strong Parental Leave Policies

Netflix: up to 1 year paid parental leave (limited to salaried employees in the streaming division of the company)

Etsy: up to 6 months

Google: 18 weeks paid maternity leave; up to 12 weeks parental "bonding" time during first year

Facebook: 16 weeks paid parental leave

Continued on next page

BOX 9.2 ∾ Redefining Fatherhood (Concluded)

Microsoft: 20 weeks (8 weeks maternity disability, 12 weeks parental leave)

Intel: 13 weeks paid maternity leave, 8 weeks of parental bonding leave (mothers or fathers)

Twitter: 20 weeks for birth mothers, 10 weeks for all other parents

Sources: Bennhold, S. (2010, June 15). Paternity leave law helps to redefine masculinity in Sweden. *The New York Times Online.*

Retrieved August 3, 2010 from http://query.nytimes.com/gst /fullpage.html?res=9F0CE5DD1338F936A25755C0A9669D 8B63&sec=&spon=&pagewanted=all CBS News (2015, August 5). Parental leave by the numbers. Retrieved June 6, 2016 from http: //www.cbsnews.com/news/parental-leave-by-the-numbers/ Reed, E., & Borison, R. (2016, March 16). 8 best companies for paid parental leave. Retrieved June 6, 2016 from http://www.thestreet .com/story/13249442/1/7-best-companies-for-paid-parental-leave .html

Contributed by Annie B. Fox

Parents in the U.S. need parental leave, subsidized child care, flexible working hours, and other policies that contribute to family well-being. These socially progressive changes will not come about by wishing for them. They will take organized activism: electing local, state, and federal representatives who recognize the realities of modern family life, and keeping these issues at the forefront of policy debates. Fortunately, women are over half the population, and their concern for their children's well-being is a perennial source of energy for activism (see Box 9.3).

BOX 9.3 ∾ MomsRising: Women and Organizations Joining Forces for Grassroots Advocacy

MomsRising is an online and on-the-ground grass-roots advocacy organization that started in 2006. Today, they have more than a million members, 1,000 bloggers, and an estimated online readership of 3 million people.

MomsRising works to improve the lives of women, children, and families by advocating for important policies such as paid family leave, earned sick days, affordable childcare, improving childhood nutrition and health, as well as ending wage and hiring discrimination.

In 2013, Forbes.com named Momsrising.org one of the Top 100 Websites for Women for the 4th year in a row.

For more information about how MomsRising is trying to improve the lives of women, children, and families, check out their website at http://www.momsrising.org

Source: http://www.momsrising.org

Contributed by Annie B. Fox

Transforming Social Meanings: Redefining Parenthood

Our society has assigned mothers sole responsibility for their children's well-being to an extent that few other cultures around the world or throughout history have done. It has asked them to fulfill their responsibilities in relative isolation, often without the support they need. Moreover, it has created myths that disguise the realities of parenting. Despite their enormous responsibilities and lack of resources, mothers get blamed for everything that goes wrong with children.

"Mother-blaming is like air pollution"—so pervasive that it often goes unnoticed (Caplan, 1989, p. 39). Psychology and psychiatry have a long tradition of viewing Mom as the source of all problems. A review of 125 articles published in major mental health journals between 1970 and 1982 found that mothers were blamed for 72 different kinds of problems in their offspring. The list included aggressiveness, agoraphobia, anorexia, anxiety, arson, bad dreams, bedwetting, chronic vomiting, delinquency, delusions, depression, frigidity, hyperactivity, incest, loneliness, marijuana use, minimal brain damage, moodiness, schizophrenia, sexual dysfunction, sibling jealousy, sleepwalking, tantrums, truancy, an inability to deal with color blindness, and self-induced television epilepsy (Caplan & Hall-McCorquodale, 1985)!

Excessive mother blaming is not just a thing of the past. In one more recent study, participants imagined they were jury members in a case where a distracted parent left their baby in a car on a hot day, resulting in the baby's accidental death (Walzer & Czopp, 2011). When the offending parent was the mother, participants blamed her more and rated her as a less competent parent, and male participants recommended a longer prison sentence, than when the offending parent was the father. The downside of all those benevolent stereotypes of mothers is that we expect more of mothers than fathers and are quicker to condemn them for mistakes and failures. Today, women are criticized for being "tiger moms" and "helicopter parents," and accused of participating in "mommy wars" between those who work for pay and those who stay home with the kids (Crowley, 2015). It seems there is still no way to escape criticism as a mother.

It is important to value fathers' contributions to their families and support their efforts to be good fathers. This would give men an equal opportunity for intimacy and emotional connection with their families. Fathering is being recognized as a feminist issue. Many feminists have called for redefining fatherhood and helping men become better fathers. There is more to being a father than providing a paycheck; good fathers are responsive and emotionally available to their children (Silverstein, 2002) (see Figure 9.5). At present, much of the poverty and dysfunction among women and children in the U.S. can be linked to men who father children and then fail to take care of them. Rather than condemn these men as "deadbeat dads," our society could consider them "dads in training" and provide social programs to help them be better fathers (Leadbeater & Way, 2001).

What are the payoffs for redefining parenthood? Research reviews have shown that a father's love is good for children, whose cognitive and emotional development is better when their fathers are involved in their lives (Rohner & Veneziano, 2001; Silverstein, 1996). Father involvement is good for couples, who report greater

FIGURE 9.5   A father who is emotionally involved with caring for his children fosters their healthy development.

marital satisfaction, and for mothers, who report decreased stress. And it is good for fathers themselves, who report higher self-esteem and satisfaction with their role as parent (Deutsch, 1999). In a study of 20 first-time fathers in Sweden (a country with generous paternity leave), the men described the experience as fun, amazing, exciting, and much more wonderful than they ever could have imagined (Fägerskiöld, 2008).

Redefining motherhood *and* fatherhood is a revolution that is past due. What is needed is a post-gender definition that allows for flexibility and diversity of family patterns (Silverstein & Auerbach, 1999).

Exploring Further

Joan. C. Chrisler (Ed.) (2012). *Reproductive justice: A global concern*. Oxford: Praeger. Thirteen chapters by leading scholars on topics ranging from contraception and abortion, pregnancy and prenatal care, breastfeeding, infertility, assisted reproductive technologies and STI prevention to female infanticide, sex trafficking, and an international view of public policy on reproductive justice.

Goldberg, Susan, & Chloe Brushwood Rose (2009). *And baby makes more: Known donors, queer parents, and our unexpected families*. Ontario, Canada: Insomniac Press.

An entertaining and thoughtful collection of memoirs by lesbian and gay couples about their experiences with various means of conception and diverse ways of parenting.

Planned Parenthood (www.plannedparenthood.org) 1-800-230-PLAN.

With more than 650 healthcare centers across the country, Planned Parenthood offers sexual and reproductive health care for both women and men, including LGBT services, HIV and STI testing, pregnancy services, birth control, emergency contraception, abortion, and wellness checkups. Planned Parenthood also promotes and sponsors responsible sex education for teens.

Waldman, Ayelet (2010). *Bad mother: A chronicle of maternal crimes, minor calamities, and occasional moments of grace.* New York: Anchor Books.

She's not every mother, but Waldman, a middle-class mother of four, writes honestly about her conflicts over the motherhood mystique, her abortion, and her marriage.

Text Credits

∽

p. 267: Deutsch, F. (1999). Halving it all: How equally shared parenting works. Cambridge, MA: Harvard University Press. p. 267: Bernard, J. (1974). The future of motherhood. New York: Penguin. p. 269: Marisa Acocella Marchetto/The New Yorker Collection/The Cartoon Bank. p. 270: pp. 387–388 Park, 2005. p. 270: Park, K. (2005). Choosing childlessness: Weber's typology of action and motives of the voluntary childless. Sociological Inquiry, 75 (3), 372–402. p. 272: Roberts, D. E. (1998). The future of reproductive choice for poor women and women of color. In R. Weitz (Ed.), The politics of women's bodies: Sexuality, appearance, and behavior (pp. 270–277). New York: Oxford University Press. p. 279: Choi, P., Henshaw, C., Baker, S., & Tree, J. (2005). Supermom, superwife, supereverything: Performing femininity in the transition to motherhood. Journal of Reproductive and Infant Psychology, 23 (2), 167–180 p. 279: Ussher, J. M. (1989). The psychology of the female body. London: Routledge. p. 281: Copyright © Suzanne Arms, www.BirthingTheFuture.org. Reprinted by permission. p. 282: Rich, A. (1976). Of woman born: Motherhood as experience and institution. New York: Norton. p. 282: Johnston-Robledo, I. (2000). From postpartum depression to the empty nest syndrome: The motherhood mystique revisited. In J. C. Chrisler, C. Golden, & P. D. Rozee (Eds.), Lectures on the psychology of women (pp. 129–148). Boston: McGraw-Hill. p. 291: Source: United Nations Department of Economic and Social Affairs, Population Division (2015). World Population Prospects: The 2015 Revision. New York: United Nations. p. 298: Contributed by Annie B. Fox. p. 299: Contributed by Annie B. Fox.

CHAPTER 10

Work and Achievement

*W*ork is a part of almost every woman's life, but the world of work is a gendered world. Often, women and men do different kinds of work, face different obstacles to satisfaction and achievement, and receive unequal rewards. This chapter examines the unpaid and paid work of women, the differing work patterns of women and men, and factors affecting women's achievement. We listen to the voices of women as they talk about their work: its problems, its satisfactions, and its place in their lives.

If She Isn't Paid, Is It Still Work?

Much of the work women do is unpaid and not formally defined as work. When women's work caring for their homes, children, and husbands is taken into account, virtually everywhere in the world women work longer hours than men and have less leisure time (United Nations, 2010). (See Figure 10.1.) However, this pattern is gradually becoming less extreme as women gain more social and political power (Geist & Cohen, 2011).

©Halfpoint/Shutterstock RF

FIGURE 10.1   Women's unpaid work of housework and child care often involves multitasking.

Housework As Real Work

Women's disproportionate contributions in housework and child care were documented in Chapters 8 and 9. Let's think about this unpaid work in comparison to paid work. First, it demands more hours each day than many paid jobs. In developing countries, housework may include gathering firewood, carrying water, and grinding grain for cooking. In industrialized countries, new tasks have taken the place of old ones. For example, taking care of large houses and driving children to sports and music lessons keeps many suburban moms busy. Second, the unpaid domestic work of women is often taken for granted. As one stay-at-home mom said:

> The garbage could overflow and no one would dump it, or the dog may need to be fed . . . and everybody relies on mother to do it . . . some days I feel that they're taking me for granted. They know I'm not going out into the work force, and every once in a while I hear one of my sons say, "Well, you don't do anything all day long." . . . If they didn't have clean clothes or their beds weren't changed or something like that they might realize that their mother does do something. But most of the time they don't. I don't think men feel that a woman does a day's work. (Whitbourne, 1986, p. 165)

Obviously, many families rely on the unpaid work of a woman. But exactly how much is her work worth? Its dollar value is difficult to compute. One way is to estimate the cost of replacing her services with paid workers—cook, chauffeur, babysitter, janitor, and so forth. Another method is to calculate the wages the homemaker loses by working at home instead of at a paid job. If she could earn $500 a week as a bank clerk, for example, that is the value of 40 hours of housework. By this method, however, housework done by a woman who could earn $300 an hour as an attorney is worth 30 times as much as the identical chores done by a woman who could only earn $10 an hour as a food server. Neither method of calculating the value of women's unpaid work really captures its unique characteristics, because it does not fit androcentric definitions of work.

Relational Work: Keeping Everybody Happy

Women are largely responsible for caring for others' emotional needs. Keeping harmony in the family has long been defined as women's work (Parsons & Bales, 1955). In a study of marital interaction in which more than 100 couples kept diaries about their communication patterns, wives did more relational work than husbands. They focused on their husbands, friends, and family; spent time talking and listening with them; talked about relationships more; and worked to keep harmony in the family (Ragsdale, 1996). In another study of dual-earner couples, both partners were asked about how much time they and their spouse spent confiding thoughts and feelings, trying to help the partner get out of a bad mood, trying to talk things over when there was a problem, and so on. Women reported doing more of this emotion work than men did and were less satisfied with the division of emotion work between the partners (Stevens et al., 2001).

Relational work goes beyond a woman's immediate family to a wider network of relatives (Kahn et al., 2011). Women are more likely than men to be in charge of visits, e-mails, texting, and phone calls to distant family members. They buy the presents and remember to send the card for Aunt Anna's birthday. They organize weddings, family reunions, and holiday celebrations, negotiate conflicts, and allocate tasks. Although the specifics of the family rituals vary according to social class and ethnic group, families' dependence on women's labor is similar, whether they are upper-class Mexican, working-class African American, middle-class Italian American, migrant Chicano farm workers, or immigrants to America from rural Japan (research reviewed in Di Leonardo, 1987).

Like housework, the relational work of women is largely ignored in traditional definitions of work. The time it takes may be considerable, as everyone relies on Mom to smooth emotional crises. After all, aren't women the relationship specialists? Relational work also has economic and social value. Exchanging outgrown children's clothes with a sister-in-law or sending potential customers to a cousin's business are ways of strengthening relationships that also help families maximize financial resources (Di Leonardo, 1987).

Perhaps most important, relational work fosters marital satisfaction and happiness. Couples who balance emotion work, with each partner doing about the same amount, are more satisfied with their marriages than couples in which one person is responsible for doing it all (Holm et al., 2001; Stevens et al., 2001). When partners are equally adept at relational work, they become attuned to each other, and negotiations about their life together become easier. In an interview study of married couples, the attunement to each other produced by mutual relational work allowed each partner to feel listened to, loved, and cherished. For example, Bob and Paula did not need to have a lot of discussion about sharing care for their baby:

> They formed a system of care in which Paula feeds the child, then Bob burps him. They say they feel "very lucky" to share responsibility when the baby needs to have his diaper changed or cries in the night (p. 102).

In contrast, this couple were "out of tune" because the relational work was delegated only to Lily:

> Ed and Lily discuss the stressors of being newly married, having demanding jobs, and raising a newborn. Ed suggests that he "tries" and "attempts to understand" his wife. He says, however, that he is "blissfully ignorant of emotions". . . with all going on in his life and what he calls "Mars and Venus stuff" he misses her cues (p. 103).

Because Ed cannot do relational work, he and Lily are experiencing stress and misunderstanding in their marriage (Jonathan & Knudson-Martin, 2012).

In their 60s, some men catch up to women in doing relational work. They get involved in caring for grandchildren and helping other family members with yardwork and home repair. It's not exactly the direct emotion work that women do, but it is a way of expressing caring (Kahn et al., 2011). Other men learn relational work through life challenges. In an interview study of older couples, Gwen and Hal described how at different points each had been faced with cancer. Hal said that he had learned through this experience that emotion work was necessary and important for both partners to do (Thomeer et al., 2015).

Status Work: The Two-Person Career

Women's unpaid work benefits their husbands' careers. The terms *status-enhancing work* and *two-person career* describe situations in which wives serve as unofficial (and often unacknowledged) contributors to their husbands' work (Papanek, 1973; Stevens et al., 2001). The most studied example is the corporate wife (e.g., Kanter, 1977); the wives of military personnel and college presidents are other examples. So is the politician's wife, who must be able to "give the speech when he can't make it but to shut her mouth and listen adoringly when he is there" (Kanter, 1977, p. 122). The role of helper to a prominent man may be rewarding, but it restricts a woman's freedom of action and ties her fate to her spouse's. If the man does not succeed, or if the marriage ends, the woman may be left with little to show for her unpaid work.

What kinds of work do women do in the service of their husbands' careers? The specific tasks vary, depending on the husband's job and career stage (Kanter, 1977). She may entertain clients in her home and make friends with people who can be useful in advancing her husband's career. She is expected to be available at any time for complete care of their children so that he can travel or work evenings and weekends. She participates in volunteer work or community service related to his position. She may also contribute direct services in place of a paid employee—taking sales calls, keeping his books or tax records, or scheduling his travel. Finally, she provides emotional support. She is expected to listen to his problems, cheerfully accept his absences and work pressures, avoid burdening him with domestic trivia, and motivate him to achieve to his fullest potential. She is, indeed, "the woman behind the man."

The clergyman's wife is a classic example of the two-person career. If you grew up belonging to a Protestant denomination in the U.S., you likely had a male pastor (about 85 percent are), that pastor likely was married (about 94 percent are), and the pastor's wife was expected to be involved in her husband's work in a two-for-one deal. She often teaches Sunday school, leads Bible studies, heads a women's group, visits the sick, attends services, sings in the choir, hosts the bake sales, and generally serves as a full-time unpaid assistant (Murphy-Geiss, 2011). Even today, congregations expect the pastor's wife to be playing the piano and baking cookies.

Now that several mainstream Protestant denominations are ordaining women, what will happen to the role of the pastor's spouse? A survey of more than 3000 United Methodist clergy spouses, 22 percent of whom were male, found that the female pastors' husbands were more than twice as likely to be employed full-time, and were much less traditional in their church-related activities, than the male pastors' wives (Murphy-Geiss, 2011).

What Are the Costs and Benefits of Invisible Work?

Obviously, housework, relational work, and the church bake sale do not provide a paycheck. Traditionally, women were supposed to be rewarded by a sense of *vicarious achievement* (Lipman-Blumen & Leavitt, 1976). In other words, a woman is supposed to identify with her husband and feel gratified by his successes. Many women do report this kind of gratification; others feel exploited. One corporate wife complained to an interviewer, "I am paid neither in job satisfaction nor in cash for my work. I did not choose the job of executive wife, and I am heartily sick of it" (Kanter, 1977, p. 111).

Women who achieve through their husbands are vulnerable. If the marriage ends through the husband's death or divorce or if he does not achieve fame and glory, she may have little to put on a résumé and few skills that prospective employers would regard as valuable. The availability of some women as unofficial employees for their husbands' companies also has implications for women who are employed and competing with men. There is no corporate husband position to match that of the corporate wife. Instead, the world of work assumes that workers are men and that these men have wives to take care of them (Wajcman, 1998).

A female employee may appear less talented and motivated than her male colleague because she lacks his invisible support staff. High-level female executives are much less likely to be married than high-level male executives. If she is married, her husband is unlikely to invest his future in vicarious achievement. A study of more than 1,600 U.S. corporate employees showed that men at the highest executive levels were significantly more likely to have spouses who were full-time homemakers than men at lower levels and women at all levels (Burke, 1997). Similar results were found in a U.K. study of high-level managers: 88 percent of the married women, and only 27 percent of the married men, had partners who were employed full-time. In other words, the career success of men is given an invisible boost by their at-home support staff. Corporations know this very well; men are seen as bringing two people to their jobs, and women, because of their family duties, as bringing less than one (Wajcman, 1998).

Working Hard for a Living: Women in the Paid Workforce

More women are working outside the home than ever before, a worldwide social change. About 57 percent of American women (and 69 percent of American men) are in the workforce. Among these workers are nearly 70 percent of all women with children under the age of 18 (U.S. Bureau of Labor Statistics, 2015). Legally, U.S. women have equal opportunity for employment in virtually all jobs. In reality, the workplace in the United States and elsewhere is still very much shaped by gender.

Occupational Segregation

The different distribution of women and men in employment is termed *occupational segregation*. When groups of workers, such as people of color or women, are concentrated in particular jobs, it fosters inequality, because disadvantaged groups are clustered in jobs that are less respected, less secure, and lower paid (Gauchet et al., 2012). In the U.S., gender-based occupational segregation is so extreme that 40 percent of women or men would have to switch jobs to end it (Cha, 2013; Sierminska, 2016). We will look at two varieties: *horizontal segregation* (the tendency for women and men to hold different jobs) and *vertical segregation* (the tendency for women to be clustered at the bottom of the hierarchy within occupations).

Horizontal Occupational Segregation

There are not many occupations in which the proportion of women and men is about equal. Instead, there are women's jobs and men's jobs. For example, 99 percent of all dental hygienists and speech pathologists, 91 percent of receptionists, 90 percent of billing clerks, and 89 percent of registered nurses are women. In contrast, 98 percent of auto mechanics, 85 percent of TV and video cam operators and editors, and 84 percent of computer systems administrators are men (U.S. Bureau of Labor Statistics, 2015). Some occupations have an overall equal ratio of women and men but remain segregated at the level of the individual workplace or task (Gutek, 2001). For example, in retail sales, men more often sell appliances, computers, and cars (the big-ticket items), while women more often sell clothing and cosmetics. Women are more likely to wait tables in diners; men are more likely to be waiters and chefs in upscale restaurants.

The fact that workplaces tend to be "his" or "hers" is a product of the gender system. The jobs where women are clustered tend to be relatively low in pay and status, with little job security and few opportunities for career advancement. Most are service-oriented and associated with stereotypical feminine characteristics such as caring. (See Box 10.1.) Globally, women are more likely to be trapped in work that is underpaid and unprotected by labor laws (U.N. Women, 2016).

The good news is that horizontal sex segregation has declined considerably since the 1970s, in the U.S. and Europe. Professional and management careers are much less gender-typed than they used to be. Still, gender ratios in lower-level jobs, such as those held by high-school graduates, have changed less. Overall, women made fewer gains in the 1990s relative to the 1970s and 1980s, and horizontal occupational segregation is still substantial (Sierminska, 2016).

Vertical Occupational Segregation

Vertical segregation is present when men tend to hold positions that have higher status and better pay than the jobs women hold within an organization or occupation (Sierminska, 2016). For example, in the health care industry the nurses' aides, social workers, laboratory technicians, dental hygienists, medical receptionists, and nurses are more likely to be women; physicians, surgeons, dentists, and hospital administrators are more likely to be men. Women more often get stuck in dead-end jobs—even in Sweden, a country committed to gender equality. When researchers analyzed wage mobility for more than one million Swedish workers over a 4-year time period, they found that women were more likely to hold dead-end jobs with little chance of a raise or promotion (Bihagen & Ohls, 2007).

The closer to the top of the hierarchy, the fewer women there are. Although women are 51 percent of those employed in managerial and professional occupations, they are seldom near the top of the pay scale (U.S. Bureau of Labor Statistics, 2015). Women hold 26 percent of CEO positions overall but only 4 percent of those at Fortune 500 companies (Catalyst, 2016). In Canada, women hold only about one-third of managerial positions, and there is "clear evidence that females face an economy-wide glass ceiling" because higher paying firms discriminate against them (Javdani, 2015, p. 530). In Australia, women are only 15 percent of CEOs. In fact, there is not a single field open to both women and men in which there are more women than men at the top, in any country in the world.

The pervasive phenomenon of women being blocked from advancement has been called the *glass ceiling:* The woman can see her goal, but she bumps into a barrier that is both invisible and impenetrable (Casini, 2016). Women are not totally excluded from business and the professions, but they find it difficult to move past mid-level positions. Women on their way up perceive the glass ceiling as very real, but men in power do not agree. In one survey of women who were corporate vice presidents, 71 percent said there was a glass ceiling for women in their organization. However, 73 percent of the male CEOs in the same organizations said there was not (Federal Glass Ceiling Commission, 1998).

Women's Work as "Only Natural"

Looking at the top occupations for women in Box 10.1, you may notice that many of them involve service to others, similar to the unpaid work wives and mothers do. For example, administrative assistants take care of others' to-do lists

BOX 10.1 ∾ Where the Women Are . . . And Where the Money Is

Top Ten Occupations for Women

In 2014, for women who were full-time, wage and salary workers, the ten most prevalent occupations were:

1. Secretaries and administrative assistants
2. Elementary and middle school teachers
3. Registered nurses
4. Nursing, psychiatric, and home health aides
5. First-line supervisors of retail sales workers
6. Customer service representatives
7. Managers, all other
8. Cashiers
9. Accountants and auditors
10. Receptionists and information clerks

But if you want to earn a high income, these jobs are not the place to go. Women who earn the most are in pharmacy, upper management, and computer science. Note that none of the top paying occupations appear in the list of the most prevalent occupations for women.

Top Ten Highest Paying Occupations for Women

Among women who were full-time wage and salary workers, the ten occupations with highest median weekly earnings in 2015 were:

1. Pharmacists, $1,902
2. Nurse practitioners, $1,682
3. Lawyers, $1,590
4. Chief Executives, $1,572
5. Computer and information systems managers, $1,529
6. Software developers, applications and systems software, $1,457
7. Physical therapists, $1,307
8. Human resource managers, $1,300
9. Purchasing managers, $1,276
10. Civil engineers, $1,275

Source: 2014 Data from Current Population Survey
https://www.dol.gov/wb/stats/most_common_occupations_for_women.htm

and health care aides look after their physical needs. Even when women and men are in equivalent jobs, such as corporate management, women are expected to be more caring and supportive than men. In a study of corporate senior managers and CEOs, both male and female respondents believed that women were more effective than men at caretaking leader behaviors like supporting others and giving praise, whereas men were more effective than women at take-charge leader behaviors like delegating and problem solving (Prime et al., 2009). These expectations reflect the prescriptive nature of gender stereotypes discussed in Chapter 3—women *are* nurturing, and they *should* be. The expectation that women are supposed to be more nurturing, supportive, and helpful than men can affect their job evaluations. In online university courses, female (but not male) instructors got lower evaluations from students when they didn't post a lot in discussion forums (Parks-Stamm & Grey, 2016). Students expected more helpful interactions from female teachers and downgraded them when their expectations were not met.

Because caring fits into a feminine stereotype, it is often seen as a natural by-product of being female rather than an aspect of job competence. When *The New York Times* described new customer-service software that can detect an irate caller, the article suggested that the software could be used to route "an angry man on the line" to "a soothing female operator" ("New York Times," 2002). Reading this, I wondered if the female operators will get bonuses, promotions, or raises for their "soothing" skills. Somehow, I doubt it. After all, women just naturally know how to calm down angry men.

Is it only natural, too, to be sexually objectified at work? Some women's jobs take place in sexually objectified environments, such as Hooters-style restaurants where food servers are required to wear revealing clothing. Not surprisingly, women in these jobs experience objectification from others as part of their everyday work environment, and this is linked to self-objectification, body shame, depression, and lower job satisfaction (Szymanski & Feltman, 2015). When stereotypes of women—whether the nurturing mother or the sex object—are allowed to shape ideas about what they are "naturally" suited for in the world of work, the result is to limit and distort human potential.

The Wage Gap

Women earn less money than men. Indeed, as you can see in Figure 10.2, no group of women has a median income equal to the men in her group. Journalist Barbara Ehrenreich has documented just how hard it is to get by on the jobs available to ordinary working women (see Box 10.2). And the difference between men's and women's wages holds for every level of education. Although young people are urged to get a college education to increase lifetime earnings, the financial payoff of education is much greater for men. Economists have calculated that a female college graduate will earn, over a lifetime of work, $1.2 *million* less than a male college graduate.

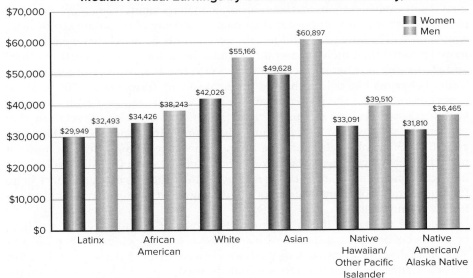

FIGURE 10.2   Median annual full-time earnings by gender and race/ethnicity, 2015.

Source: U.S. Census Bureau, 2015 American Community Survey 1-Year Estimates.

BOX 10.2 ∽ Undercover at Wal-Mart: Life as a Low-Wage Worker

Can America's low-wage workers survive on their weekly paychecks? This is the question journalist Barbara Ehrenreich set out to answer when she went undercover as a minimally skilled laborer. Shedding the privileges of her education and social class, Ehrenreich took on the identity of a home-maker of modest education and job skills attempting to reenter the job market. Ehrenreich traveled to several states, spending approximately 1 month in each location and working at jobs such as house-cleaner, waitress, and sales clerk. Using only the money she earned from her jobs, Ehrenreich attempted to pay for housing, food, transportation, and other living expenses.

Ehrenreich soon learned that minimum wage does not equate to a living wage. Although she was

Continued on next page

BOX 10.2 ∾ Undercover at Wal-Mart: Life as a Low-Wage Worker (*Concluded*)

physically fit, a native English speaker, and had no dependents, she had difficulty financially sustaining her simple needs on her earnings. Even working two jobs, seven days a week did little to help. Additionally, being short of money created many unforeseen problems for Ehrenreich, who found it difficult to obtain safe inexpensive housing, pay for reliable transportation, and maintain a healthy diet. For example, because she could not afford security deposits for an apartment, Ehrenreich had to live in a motel, which was more expensive and less safe. Living in a motel room created additional hardships. Lacking a refrigerator or stove, Ehrenreich had to make do with fast food, an expense she had not anticipated.

Ehrenreich's experience makes it clear that those who fill the low-wage rung on America's economic ladder are greatly disadvantaged. This includes especially the millions of women forced into the workforce because of welfare reform. The American dream of attaining wealth through hard work does not take into account the reality of the working poor, whose hard labor is not even enough to pay the bills.

Sources: Barbara Ehrenreich, *Nickel and dimed: On (not) getting by in America.* (Holt, 2001). Contributed by Roxanne Donovan.

The gender gap in wages has decreased somewhat over the past 55 years. As shown in Figure 10.3, this is partly because women are earning more, and partly because men are earning less. Women now earn about 80 cents for every dollar of men's annual earnings. Earning 20 cents less out of every dollar has huge costs to women workers. The National Committee on Pay Equity has (not so jokingly)

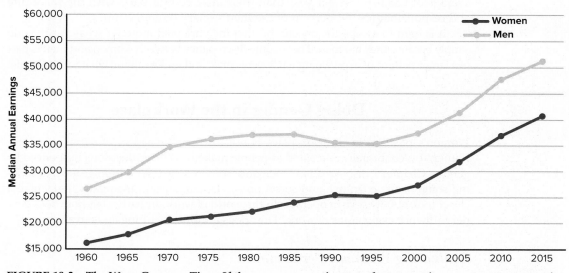

FIGURE 10.3   The Wage Gap over Time. If the wage gap continues to decrease at its current rate, pay equity will be achieved in the year 2059.

Source: U.S. Census Bureau reports and data, Current Population Reports, Median Earning of Workers 15 Years Old and Over by Work Experience and Sex.

proposed that all working women should get a Pay Equity Coupon offering 20 percent off on housing, food, clothing, transportation, and all the other expenses of life! Around the world, the wage gap is even greater, with women in most countries earning about 60 to 75 percent of the wages earned by men (U.N. Women, 2016).

Why this large and persistent inequity in earnings? One traditional explanation is that women invest less in their work roles than men—they are less committed to their work, less likely to obtain extra training and education, more likely to be absent or to quit a job. However, little evidence exists to support these claims. On the contrary, women are more likely than men to invest in higher education—they are 57 percent of all college students (Anderson, 2014). The gender gap in earnings remains substantial when variables such as education, absences, number of hours worked, and years on the job are controlled (Gutek, 2001; Tsui, 1998; Valian, 1998; Wajcman, 1998). The individual investment hypothesis also does not explain why women's jobs that require high levels of education and skill (like preschool teacher) pay less than men's jobs with lower requirements (like drywall installer).

Another explanation focuses on the jobs rather than the gender of the worker—secretaries and clerks are paid less than electricians and truck drivers, and since more women choose to be secretaries and clerks, they earn less on average. It is certainly true that women are clustered in a few low-paying job sectors, but is this entirely a matter of choice? For generations, women who tried to get into male-dominated trades and professions were faced with overt discrimination and harassment, so that even now they are still underrepresented in senior positions in those fields. Moreover, there may be discrepancies even when women and men do exactly the same job. For example, in an international study of high-level buyers (Chief Procurement Officers) in various industries, women were earning an average of €38,076 less per year than their male counterparts with the same title and responsibilities—84 percent of the men's salary (Webb, 2016).

It is hard to escape the conclusion that men are paid more for whatever they do simply because they are men. The income discrepancy between women and men is part of a larger pattern of overvaluing whatever is male and undervaluing whatever is female.

Doing Gender in the Workplace

Women's position in the workplace is not just a static aspect of social structure. Rather, it is continually re-created as people make workplace decisions influenced by gender. Chapter 2 discussed how men and women do gender within groups, describing some of the cognitive and social processes that sustain inequality. Let's take a closer look at how sexism operates in the world of work. In particular, how does gender influence evaluations of work? How does it influence hiring and advancement?

Evaluating Women's Performance

"Are women prejudiced against women?" is a question asked in a study that set off a wave of research on how people judge the performance of women versus men (Goldberg, 1968). Female college students were asked to rate the quality and importance of several professional articles. Some of the articles were from stereo-typically female professions, such as dietetics; others from stereotypically male professions, such as city planning; and others from relatively gender-neutral areas. Each article was prepared in two versions, as though written either by "John MacKay" or "Joan MacKay." Except for the authors' names, the two versions of each article were identical. The students rated the articles more highly when they thought the articles had been written by a man (including the articles from stereotypically feminine fields). Other researchers found that male raters showed similar prejudice (Paludi & Bauer, 1983; Paludi & Strayer, 1985).

Another early study used psychologists as the participants. Fictitious sets of credentials for psychologists were sent to psychology department chairpersons; the credentials were identical except for the gender of the applicant. The chairpersons were asked how likely they would be to hire the individual described and what level of job they might offer. When the chairpersons thought they were evaluating a female psychologist, "she" was rated less favorably and considered qualified for a lower-level position than when "he" was evaluated (Fidell, 1970).

Are these experimental studies of the past relevant today? Unfortunately, yes. They have been replicated not only with psychology credentials but other fields, too (Moss-Racusin et al., 2015). The bias against women is particularly strong in science-related fields. When science faculty members rated lab manager applications, which were identical except for the applicant's gender, both male and female faculty members rated the male applicant as more competent. They said they would be more likely to hire and mentor him than her, and they proposed a starting salary almost $4,000 higher for him than for her (Moss-Racusin et al., 2012).

This study got a lot of publicity, and when the *New York Times* published an article about it, the authors of the original study analyzed the online comments. They found that many agreed that gender bias exists and offered constructive suggestions. However, 24 percent of commentators asserted that gender bias does not exist, claimed that bias against men is a problem, or criticized the study's methods or authors (Moss-Racusin et al., 2015). People still find it hard to believe in pervasive bias against women.

Most of the research on evaluation bias has asked about generic (read White) women and men. There has been almost no intersectional research, so we know little about how racial/ethnic bias interacts with gender bias in evaluating women's performance. In one study, White college students evaluated hypothetical task performance and rated the competence of mixed-race and mixed-gender pairs in a masculine task (software development at an engineering company). They rated the pair with the White male as more competent and deserving higher pay, but they did not devalue the Black female. The researchers suggested that the Black female was protected from bias because she did not fit White female gender stereotypes (Biernat & Sesko, 2013).

Evaluation bias often happens unintentionally, as the result of implicit attitudes and beliefs. Let's look at an example that is close to home: the teacher evaluations that many college students fill out at the end of every semester. Evaluations are important for faculty members' pay raises, promotions, and tenure. They also give your professors feedback about the job they are doing and how to improve their teaching. Unfortunately, there may be gender bias in those evaluations. In one recent study, researchers examined student evaluations from a French and a U.S. university (Boring et al., 2016). The French students were randomly assigned to either male or female section leaders in required courses. Male French students rated male instructors more highly even though the students did slightly worse on the (uniform and anonymously graded) final exam than male students who'd had female instructors. The American study used a different method. Students took an online class with either a male or female instructor—but half the instructors switched names. Students—especially female students—rated teachers they believed to be male more highly on dimensions like caring, responsive and so on, and even on supposedly objective measures like returning assignments on time.

Evaluation bias seems to occur because women's agency, competence, and leadership are incongruent with gender stereotypes, and people rely on stereotypes when evaluating others. This gives us some clues about how to reduce evaluation bias. Asking raters to focus on specific positive and negative behaviors of the person being rated helps them to get beyond stereotypes, as does asking them to remember specific incidents about the person instead of making general statements. Instead of rating a teacher on a "caring" scale, students could be asked if they had attempted to talk to the teacher outside of class and if the teacher was available.

Some corporations and universities have instituted workshops to educate employees about bias and help them overcome the implicit and unrecognized ways they judge women differently. Often, women and men alike are surprised to learn that they have been unwittingly participating in bias. This male faculty member described how hard it is to confront one's own prejudices:

> I don't spend much of my time thinking about gender issues. I probably devote less than 1 percent of my brain power to this issue . . . And so, when you're sort of being faced with questions, which you've never really thought about in any depth before, it hurts your brain, you know what I mean? (Carnes et al., 2012, p. 70).

In these workshops, participants make a commitment to improve gender equality in their organization.

Discrimination in Hiring and Promotion

Sex discrimination in employment has been illegal since 1964, when the Civil Rights Act was passed. Before that time, many employers discriminated as a matter of policy. For example, AT&T allowed women to only work up to certain pay levels and in a limited range of tasks (Gutek & Larwood, 1987). Many states had laws that "protected" women by excluding them from certain jobs. For example, women were banned from jobs that required working at night, working around chemicals, serving drinks, or lifting more than 30 pounds (McCormick, 2002). (And just how much does the average 3-year-old weigh?)

Although employers today cannot directly refuse to hire or promote applicants because of race or gender, a great deal of discrimination still occurs. One source of evidence comes from experimental studies of evaluation bias that used simulated job résumés or applications. A meta-analysis of 49 such studies showed a strong preference for men when the job was seen as masculine and a somewhat weaker preference for women when the job was seen as feminine (Davison & Burke, 2000). Unfortunately, leadership roles are still usually perceived as masculine (Eagly & Karau, 2002). In a real-world study of managers at a major corporation, the managers were less likely to promote women because they believed that the women weren't a good fit to their jobs and were likely to have work-family conflicts (Hoobler et al., 2009). In a Wall Street law firm, male junior attorneys were far more likely to get the top ratings that would guarantee promotion to partner, although there was no difference between them and the female junior attorneys in technical competence (Biernat et al., 2012).

More direct evidence of discrimination comes from sex discrimination lawsuits. Companies that have been sued (and the costs of the settlements) include State Farm ($200 million), Home Depot ($104 million), Novartis ($250 million), Lucky Stores ($95 million), AT&T ($66 million), Mitsubishi Motors ($34 million), Citigroup ($33 million), and smartphone chipmaker Qualcomm ($19 million). Trendy clothing retailer Abercrombie & Fitch paid $40 million in a race and sex discrimination suit that awarded compensation to thousands of African Americans, Asian Americans, and Latinos who applied for a job and were turned down or handed a broom instead of being put on the sales floor. The settlement required A & F to increase diversity in hiring and promotion and also in its ads and catalogs, which had featured almost exclusively White models (Greenhouse, 2004). However, A & F found itself in trouble again in 2015, when the Supreme Court ruled against it for refusing to hire a qualified applicant who wore a hijab (Jamieson, 2015).

Discrimination in promotion may occur because overt displays of competence in a woman are a threat to the gender hierarchy. A study of evaluations in the U.S. military found that women were most likely to be negatively evaluated when they were objectively very good and close to the evaluator in pay grade and status. Follow-up experimental studies with nonmilitary adults also found that evaluators discriminated against highly competent women—but only those evaluators who were male and high in social dominance orientation (Inesi & Cable, 2015). This is a disheartening finding, because when applying for a job or promotion most of us, male or female, try to put our best foot forward, listing our accomplishments with pride. It is hard to accept that high achievement could actually count against you—if you are a woman.

Unfortunately, patterns of discrimination are often very hard to see. For example, if you are a woman with a bachelor's degree who has been with a company for 5 years and you are not promoted, you might compare yourself with a male coworker who was promoted. Suppose this man has been with the company for only 3 years but he has a master's degree: It's hard to decide whether or not you have been discriminated against. But suppose you look further in the company and find a man who was promoted with only a high school diploma and 10 years of service and a woman who was not promoted with 2 years of college and 8 years of service. A pattern begins to form. That pattern is apparent only when many cases are averaged and discrimination is usually examined one case at a time (Crosby et al., 1986). One important function of affirmative action programs is to keep records so that patterns of discrimination become evident over time. You can't fix a problem if nobody knows the problem exists (Crosby, 2004).

Social Reactions to Token Women

From the local fire department or welding shop to the U.S. Senate, the corporate boardroom, and everywhere in between, women in nontraditional careers are likely to work mostly with men. They are a minority in workplaces where the environment is highly masculine. Just by being there, a woman in a male-dominated field sticks out. This is true for other disadvantaged groups, too. The "odd person," whether Black, Hispanic, disabled, or female, becomes a *token.* Generally, researchers define a token as a member of a group that is less than 15 percent of the larger group. Female firefighters and male nurses, for example, are usually tokens in their workplaces.

Because of their visibility, tokens feel a lot of performance pressure. As one woman commented, "If it seems good to be noticed, wait until you make your first major mistake" (Kanter, 1977, p. 213). When a White male employee makes a mistake, it is interpreted as an individual error and no more; if the token woman or minority makes a similar mistake, it may be taken as evidence that "those people" should not have been hired and are bound to fail. Paradoxically, the token must also worry about being too successful. Because all eyes are on the token employee, a token who performs well enough to show up members of the dominant group may be criticized for being a workaholic or too aggressive.

Tokens are also socially isolated and stereotyped. They get pigeonholed into familiar roles such as mother, wife, or sex object. One female commercial pilot reported that her copilot questioned whether she was following the directions from air traffic control, saying "Oh well my wife gets lost when she goes to the supermarket" (Davey & Davidson, 2000, p. 213). When the token does not play along with stereotyped roles, she may be cast as the archetypal unfeminine iron maiden or bitch.

The experiences of faculty women of color in colleges and universities illustrate the intersectionality of race and gender in tokenism. Ethnic minority women are underrepresented in academia. Of all faculty positions held by women, American Indian women hold fewer than 1 percent, Latinas 4 percent, and Asian American and African American women about 7 percent each. In a focus group study of ethnic minority female professors at predominantly White universities, the women reported being highly visible and closely scrutinized. Typical of tokenism, their ability and competence were also questioned, which they attributed to racism. Their hiring was attributed to affirmative action, or students were disrespectful and confrontational (Turner et al., 2011).

Women and ethnic minorities are much more likely than men to experience token status. When men are the tokens, it seems they suffer no disadvantages. Men in female-dominated occupations (nurse, librarian, elementary teacher, and social worker) fare better than women in the same occupations in several ways—they are more satisfied with their jobs, get better evaluations, and advance faster. This has been dubbed the *glass escalator* to contrast with the glass ceiling experienced by women (Sierminska, 2016; Williams, 1992). However, an intersectional analysis shows that it is only straight White men who catch a ride on the glass escalator. African American men who become nurses, for example, do not advance faster than women. They are often mistaken for janitors or orderlies and suffer discrimination on the job. Gay men who become elementary teachers likewise do not benefit from their token status (Williams, 2013). In a large workforce study in the U.K., ethnic minority men and men with disabilities were more likely to be in the lowest category of jobs (along with women) and less likely than other men or women to ride the glass escalator out of that category (Woodhams et al., 2015).

Such comparisons show that the negative effects of being a token are not due just to numbers. Rather, they reflect differences in status and power. When women or ethnic minorities enter a group that was formerly all White and male, they are perceived as interlopers and deviants (see Figure 10.4). The negative effects of tokenism for women and ethnic minorities decrease once they are about 35 percent of the larger group (Yoder, 2002). But increasing their numbers alone is not the answer, because tokens are still seen as lower in status.

How can people in the token slot become more respected and effective? Just getting the job and having the expertise to do it are not enough. In one experimental study, when women were appointed leaders of all-male task groups and supplied with task-relevant expertise to help them lead the groups, they still were not very

FIGURE 10.4

Source: DILBERT: © Scott Adams / Dist. by United Feature Syndicate, Inc.

successful or appreciated as leaders. However, when a male experimenter specifically told group members that the woman leader had special training and useful information for their task, she was able to be effective despite being in a token position (Yoder et al., 1998). While it is worrisome that women's leadership still needs to be given legitimacy by high-status men, this study suggests that fair-minded men can use their organizational power to support token women.

The Importance of Mentoring

Knowing the formal rules in a workplace is rarely enough. Whether you are working in a corporation, factory, hospital, or office, there is inside knowledge that is not written down in the employee manual. Instead, workers rely on informal social networks to work the system to their advantage (Lorber, 1993). A *mentor* is someone who takes a personal interest in a newcomer to guide them toward success (Yoder et al., 1985). Successful older men frequently serve as mentors to young men on their way up, providing them with introductions to important people, special training, and hints about office politics. They may also stand up for the young man if he makes a controversial decision and they raise his status simply by associating with him.

Having a mentor increases future earnings, career satisfaction and advancement for both women and men. Positive benefits of mentoring have been shown for female business school grads (Dougherty et al., 2013), attorneys (Wallace, 2001), and psychologists (Dohm & Cummings, 2002). However, women have more difficulty finding a mentor than men do. In fact, it seems that just about everybody is disadvantaged compared to White men. A study of more than 6,500 faculty members in a variety of academic fields at 259 top universities showed that they were less likely to reply to an e-mail asking for a mentoring meeting from a prospective graduate student if it came from a woman, a Hispanic, an African American, an Indian, or a Chinese student than if it came from a White American male (Milkman et al., 2015).

Women may lack access to the *old-boy network*, who look out for each other's interests (Lorber, 1993). In a national survey, 56 percent of men, and only 28 percent of women, had received help from a White male contact in a job search. People in White male job networks got twice as many job leads as others did, and the connections were to higher status people (McDonald, 2011). As one female corporate executive put it: "It's always been men at the top of this company and the top of the company I was in before. They all know each other. They've all come up the same route together, all boys together" (Wajcman, 1998, p. 97).

Often, high-status men are reluctant to mentor women. Quite simply, they feel more comfortable with people that they perceive as more similar to themselves. Also, young women may not always realize the importance of finding mentors. Or they may be reluctant to ask senior men for mentoring because they fear the relationship would be misinterpreted as sexual (Gutek, 2001). Having a senior male mentor may be particularly beneficial for women in male-dominated and masculine-typed occupations (Dougherty et al., 2013). This was shown in a study of more than 3,000 U.S. college graduates that assessed their career status 15 years after graduation. In industries where there were few women—and/or an aggressive, engineering-intensive, competitive culture—women who had male mentors were earning more money and were happier with their career progress than women with female mentors or no mentors at all. In a tough corporate climate, senior male mentors gave them legitimacy and sponsorship (Ramaswami et al., 2010). (See Box 10.3.)

BOX 10.3 ∽ Where are the women in start-up companies and venture capital?

Each month, women throw away pads and tampons filled with blood that could contain important indicators of health. Instead of using needles or other invasive and painful testing methods, what if you could collect and test menstrual blood for health-related conditions? Uniquely positioned as both an engineer and a woman, Harvard inventor Ridhi Tariyal saw the untapped potential of using menstrual blood for diagnostic medical testing. Together with her business partner, Stephen Gire, Tariyal developed and patented a method to collect menstrual blood for medical testing—the "tampon of the future."

Originally, Tariyal and Gire thought the technology could be used for at-home testing of sexually transmitted diseases. However, when they were pitching their invention to investors, they encountered a lot of resistance. Investors—mostly men—were turned off by the thought of using menstrual blood in such a way. Or, they thought it wasn't a worthwhile investment because it only helped half the population. In response to the negative reception they received, Tariyal and Gire re-envisioned their product as one that could help diagnose endometriosis (a painful disorder of the uterine lining) and cancer, and then were able to attract investors. One of their first big investors was billionaire philanthropist Len Blavatnik. After Blavatnik had his adviser, Patricia Benet, follow their start-up to get a female perspective, he invested even more. Another

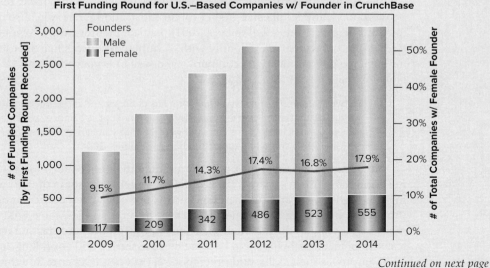

U.S. Venture Funded Companies by Founder Gender
First Funding Round for U.S.–Based Companies w/ Founder in CrunchBase

Continued on next page

BOX 10.3 ∽ Where are the women in start-up companies and venture capital?
(*Concluded*)

investor in Tariyal's start-up is a leading researcher from Harvard, Pardis Sabeti (who also happens to be a woman). Tariyal's start-up experience speaks to the important role female networks can play in getting investor support, especially for products or inventions that focus on women's health.

Unfortunately, there is a dearth of women in both start-up companies and venture capital. Crunchbase, which collects and analyzes business data from thousands of companies across the globe, recently conducted studies examining women in venture capital. They found that overall, women make up 7 percent of investing partners in the top 1,000 venture or micro-venture firms. They also looked at the percentage of women who had founded or co-founded a start-up company between 2009–2014. Of the 14,341 start-up companies funded during that time, about 16 percent had at least one female founder. When looking at the trend over time, the percentage of female founders nearly doubled between 2009 and 2014, suggesting an upward trend for female founded companies (see figure above). Hopefully, the upward trend continues, although there is a long way to go before we might see equal numbers of women and men in start-ups and venture capital.

Sources: http://www.nytimes.com/2016/04/03/opinion/sunday/the-tampon-of-the-future.html?_r=0 https://techcrunch.com/2015/05/26/female-founders-on-an-upward-trend-according-to-crunchbase/ Contributed by Annie B. Fox

What about women mentoring other women? Women may be better mentors for women in creating a professional self-image, empowerment, and supportive personal counseling (Burke & McKeen, 1997; Gilbert & Rossman, 1992). Among a sample of female attorneys, those mentored by women reported less conflict between work and family and greater career satisfaction. They were also more likely to continue practicing law (Wallace, 2001). Female mentors also provide models of leadership that women can identify with. A human resources manager for an international telecommunications company, who was interviewed as part of a study of global managers, put it this way:

> Of the two women mentors that I had, one has children and it has been really refreshing for me to see that she is very senior, that she has kept a balance in her life, and she hasn't become macho. . . . it is refreshing to see that you can get there and not sacrifice yourself in getting more like men (Linehan & Scullion, 2008).

Because women are most underrepresented in science-, technology-, engineering-, and mathematics-related (STEM) fields, which offer some of the most satisfying and high-paying jobs for the 21st century, there has been particular attention to providing mentoring for women in STEM. Several studies show that providing mentors for women during medical school and when they are starting out on medical school faculties helps them become more assertive and confident, feel less isolated, improves their skills, and predicts career success (Geber & Roughneen, 2011; Mayer et al., 2014; Stamm & Buddeberg-Fischer, 2011).

I hope I've convinced you how important it is to find mentors along your career path. It's especially important if you are a woman or an ethnic minority person, although you may have to work harder to do it. As an undergraduate, getting involved with a professor's research lab is a great start. As a grad student or young professional, there are formal mentorship programs. For example, APA's Division 35, The Society for the Psychology of Women, matches beginning researchers with accomplished ones for mentoring. APAGS, its graduate student organization, sponsors a mentoring program for LGBT students.

As I've noted, a particular need is mentoring for students and young professionals in STEM professions, where women are seriously underrepresented and have a high dropout rate. MentorNet, a national e-mail network, offers opportunities for women in engineering, math, and science majors to connect with supportive experts in their fields (www.mentornet.net). MentorNet reports that 95 percent of its mentored students complete their degrees. An online mentoring program, CareerWISE, (https://careerwise.asu.edu) features more than 50 educational modules for communication skills, overcoming stereotype threat, recognizing sexism and other strengths for persisting in STEM fields, along with video clips from interviews with more than 200 successful women in those fields. The modules are based on psychological research, and the program has been empirically tested and shown to improve coping skills (Dawson et al., 2015). Sponsored by the National Science Foundation, this is a free and internationally available alternative to one-on-one mentoring. As the world of work becomes more diverse and integrated, more mentors will become available for all. (See Figure 10.5.)

©digitalskillet/Getty Images RF

FIGURE 10.5   As the world of work becomes more diverse, problems of tokenism and lack of mentors for women and ethnic minorities will probably ease.

Leadership: Do Women Do It Differently?

More and more women are moving into positions of leadership. Once they are in leadership positions, do women lead differently from men? This question was not considered important throughout most of psychology's history. Most leadership research was done with men; women, and particularly women of color, were simply left out of the studies. With the second wave of the women's movement in the 1970s, research on women's leadership began, including studies of how prejudice, discrimination, stereotyping, and group context affect the perception of leaders (Eagly & Heilman, 2016).

Since that time, stereotypes of leaders have been repeatedly measured using several different methods. No matter how they are measured, stereotypes of leaders are much more similar to stereotypes of men than they are to stereotypes of women: more agentic than communal, more masculine than feminine. The most recent meta-analysis shows that this still holds true, but that the leader stereotype is changing over time to include qualities such as sensitivity and warmth. However, men still hold the old-fashioned masculine leader stereotype more than women do (Koenig et al., 2011). Therefore, being accepted as leaders may still be a problem for women due to the lingering stereotype that they don't have "the right stuff" to be a leader.

Contrary to stereotype, there are no dramatic gender differences in leadership style. In a meta-analysis of 370 studies, women were somewhat more democratic and participative leaders than men. However, the difference depended on the situation; for example, it was larger in laboratory studies than real-life settings (Eagly & Johnson, 1990). In laboratory studies, people are usually strangers to each other and the manager role is simulated; gender roles may be salient. In actual workplaces, where people have clear job responsibilities and long-term relationships, the demands of the manager role may be more important than gender roles (Eagly & Johannesen-Schmidt, 2001).

Are women more effective as leaders? Effectiveness is usually defined as how well the leader helps the group reach its stated goals. A meta-analysis of 95 studies of leadership effectiveness showed no overall gender differences. However, women were rated as more effective than men in business, and men were rated as more effective in government and military organizations (Paustian-Underdahl et al., 2014). Again, the effect of situation is apparent—military leadership takes place in an extremely masculine realm where women are a small minority in each work group.

In contrast to these findings of overall similarity, a study of managers from the United States and eight other countries found some significant gender differences. Women were rated higher on several positive attributes such as motivating others, showing optimism about goals, mentoring others, being considerate, and rewarding others for good performance. Men were more likely to be critical about others' mistakes, to be absent or uninvolved during a crisis, and to wait until problems were severe before trying to solve them. Overall, in this study the women were perceived as more effective managers (Eagly & Johannesen-Schmidt, 2001). In the most recent meta-analysis, too, when leaders' own self-ratings were excluded and only ratings by others were analyzed, women were rated as more effective than men (Paustian-Underdahl et al., 2014).

In summary, the evidence suggests that once women are seen as legitimate leaders, they behave similarly to men in the same kinds of positions and they are equally likely to succeed. However, where there are differences in leadership style, the styles that women are more likely to use may enhance the effectiveness of their organizations. But any advantage that women may have in leadership style may be offset by the resistance of men in power to accept women's leadership. Meta-analysis of self-ratings shows that men still rate themselves as more effective leaders than women rate themselves (Paustian-Underdahl et al., 2014). It seems that women are reluctant to accept "bragging rights" about their abilities, but men are not (Smith & Huntoon, 2014). As more women enter formerly masculine domains, gender will become less noticeable in leadership contexts, and we can hope that leaders will be evaluated as individuals.

Sexual Harassment from Nine to Five

In 2016, sexual harassment exploded onto the national consciousness. First, Roger Ailes, the powerful chairman of Fox News Network, was forced to resign, and Fox News paid $20 million to settle a sexual harassment lawsuit that opened up a long-standing culture of harassment and abuse of power at Fox (Grynbaum & Koblin, 2016).

Then, as anyone who did not spend the year on Mars knows, Republican presidential candidate Donald Trump was caught on tape bragging about groping and sexually assaulting women. As Mr. Trump claimed that his talk was just "locker room banter," several women came forward with accounts of harassment by him. Mr. Trump insisted that all the women were lying and retaliated with claims about the sexual misbehavior of former President Bill Clinton. Soon the national media were flooded with arguments and counterarguments about predatory men, lying women, and what constitutes normal masculinity versus sexual harassment. The ugliness of harassment, how it affects women, how difficult it can be to verify, how women are treated when they allege harassment, the excuses that are made for the perpetrators – all these were in full public view in the crudest possible terms. First Lady Michelle Obama spoke out about the Trump tape:

> This is disgraceful. It is intolerable. And it doesn't matter what party you belong to — Democrat, Republican, independent — no woman deserves to be treated this way. (National Public Radio, 2016).

Although it became a media spotlight in 2016, sexual harassment has been around for a long time, and it has been formally defined and studied for at least the past 35 years (Gutek & Done, 2001; Pina et al., 2009).

Defining Sexual Harassment

The legal definition of sexual harassment distinguishes two kinds. ***Quid pro quo*** harassment is unwanted sexual advances or behavior that is a condition of employment. In other words, the harasser makes it clear that the employee will be fired, given unpleasant tasks, receive a negative evaluation, or otherwise suffer bad consequences unless she complies with sexual demands. For example, one woman reported, "This man went after every girl in the office and he went after me . . . We got fired if we did not go out with him" (Gutek, 1985, p. 82).

The second kind of harassment is the creation of a *hostile work environment.* This could include obscene remarks, demeaning jokes about women, or suggestive comments about the worker's sexuality or personal life, as well as threatening or aggressive sexually-toned materials in the workplace. In one case, a female shipyard worker was subjected to pornographic pictures and graffiti at work. Her male coworkers also put up a dartboard drawn like a woman's breast with the nipple as the bulls-eye (Fitzgerald, 1993).

There is room for confusion and disagreement even in legal definitions of sexual harassment. What seems like an unwanted advance or a hostile environment to one person may seem like a friendly invitation or innocent fun to another (Pina et al., 2009). Sometimes the victim herself is not sure whether she is being harassed. In a qualitative study of the sexual harassment experiences of women of color, this participant described the sexual remarks at work and her ambivalence about them:

> I think, just someone saying, "You have big beautiful breasts" or whatever. Or, "she's got that Black girl ass or that's that Jennifer Lopez booty." You know, but that's what you run up against and sometimes it's hard to deal seriously with people when people are telling a joke you don't know if they are meaning it or what all their words are meaning (Richardson & Taylor, 2009, p. 259).

The Supreme Court has changed and enlarged its definition of sexual harassment several times over the past decades to encompass changing social definitions, and will most likely continue to do so. Some researchers have created psychological definitions that differ from the legal ones, classifying a behavior as sexual harassment if the recipient perceives it as offensive and detrimental to her well-being (Fitzgerald et al., 1997). In the courts, both the victim's perspective and the outsider's perspective are taken into account. The victim must show that the behavior is severe or pervasive and detrimental to her well-being, and the behavior must be such that a reasonable person would call it harassment (Gutek & Done, 2001).

Legal and psychological definitions are important in distinguishing sexual attention from sexual harassment; the latter must be severe, pervasive, and unwanted. For example, if a supervisor asks an employee to go out on a date, it is not sexual harassment (although it may be unwise, divisive in the office, or contrary to company policy). However, if the supervisor repeatedly asks for a date despite the worker's evident dismay or disinterest, or suggests directly or indirectly that she might get that raise or that vacation time if they get together, the supervisor is violating the law and committing sexual harassment. In the case of hostile environment harassment, an occasional sexist joke or sexual remark does not qualify as a hostile climate, but a pattern of sexist behavior that interferes with work or creates an offensive tone in the office does.

The Prevalence of Harassment

Like other forms of violence against women (see Chapter 12), harassment is likely to go unrecognized and under-reported, and only the most extreme cases go to court. A meta-analysis showed that when women are asked directly if they have been sexually harassed, the reported rate is much lower than when they are presented with a list of sexually harassing behaviors and asked to check any that have happened to them (Ilies et al., 2003). This indicates that victims may not label what happens to them as harassment, which means that they are unlikely to report it even though it fits into the legal definition.

Random-sample surveys indicate that 35 to 50 percent of women have experienced workplace sexual harassment (Gutek & Done, 2001). Other U.S. estimates suggest that between 14 percent and 75 percent of women have been sexually harassed at work; in European countries the highest estimate is 81 percent (McDonald, 2012). Some of the most consistent data come from periodic random sample surveys of federal employees (U.S. Merit Systems Protection Board, 1981, 1987, 1995). In these surveys, 42 to 44 percent of women workers reported that they had experienced harassment within the past 24 months, a proportion that remained steady over the 14 years covered by these studies.

Anyone may be vulnerable to harassment, but there are some factors that may elevate a person's risk. For example, women in male-dominated occupations are particularly likely to experience harassment. When women are in a numerical minority or token position, the risk increases (Gutek & Done, 2001; Pina & Gannon, 2012). Among military veterans of the Iraq and Afghanistan war era, 41 percent of women and 4 percent of men experienced sexual harassment or assault during their service (Barth et al., 2016). Younger women and those who are unattached to men (unmarried, divorced, or lesbian women) are more likely to be harassed than older, married women. Women of color may be more likely to be harassed than White women, although too few studies have been done to reach a definite conclusion. Ethnic minority women may be particularly vulnerable because stereotypes portray them as sexually available (African Americans and Latinas) or docile and submissive (Asian Americans). Women of color, as a group, also hold less power and status in the workplace than White women, which may increase their risk. Men can be sexually harassed, too, although this happens much less often than male-to-female harassment. In these cases, the harasser may be either another man or a woman (Gutek & Done, 2001; Pina et al., 2009). Sexual harassment often, but not always, goes downward in the power hierarchy. In about half the cases, the harasser is a supervisor, but may also be a coworker, a customer, or even a subordinate of the victim (Gutek & Done, 2001; Pina et al., 2009). In a study of graduate students, women who experienced sexual harassment were actually more likely to be harassed by other students (58 percent) than by faculty or staff (38 percent) (Rosenthal et al., 2016). In this situation, peer harassment was more common than hierarchy-based harassment.

What Are the Causes of Harassment?

There are several theories about the causes of sexual harassment (Tangri & Hayes, 1997). The *sex-role spillover theory* suggests that harassment occurs when a woman's gender is more salient than her role as a worker, so that men see her first and foremost as a sex object. Gender is most salient when the woman is in a token position; thus this theory predicts that the more male-dominated the occupation, the more harassment will occur. Gender can also be salient when the job has objectification built in to it—as when waitresses are required to wear short skirts or tight T-shirts (Szymanski & Feltman, 2015).

Another theory stresses that sexual harassment is an abuse of power. Men have more formal power in organizations and often have more informal influence as well. They can misuse their power to treat women as sex objects, then claim that the incidents never occurred or that the woman was trying to sleep her way to the top. This theory is consistent with evidence that sexual harassment is more prevalent in hierarchical organizations such as the military than in less hierarchical ones such as universities (Ilies et al., 2003).

A third theory points to the broader sociocultural context of male dominance. Men are still being socialized toward taking the sexual initiative, being sexually persistent, and feeling entitled to have what they want. Women are still being socialized toward being compliant, considerate, taking the role of sexual gate-keeper, and putting others' needs first. Thus, according to the sociocultural theory, sexual harassment at work is just part of a larger pattern of societal dominance by men (Tangri & Hayes, 1997). Each of these theories has been supported by some research, suggesting that sexual harassment may stem from all these causes, and differ from one setting (and perpetrator) to another.

To date, there has been little research on the characteristics of men who harass (Pina et al., 2009). Men who score high on a scale indicating the likelihood of sexually harassing tend to hold adversarial beliefs about sexual relationships. They are more accepting of interpersonal violence, higher in authoritarianism and hostile sexism, and they believe more in rape myths than men who score lower on the harassment scale (Pina & Gannon, 2012). These attitudes are similar to the attitudes of men who engage in other kinds of violence toward women — see Chapter 12.

The Consequences of Harassment

Workplace sexual harassment has enormous costs for organizations. Many studies have shown that targets of sexual harassment detach and withdraw from their coworkers, their organization, and their work as they struggle to cope with a hostile environment or unwanted sexual advances (Pina & Gannon, 2012). Employers lose money when employees are less productive, take sick leave, or quit their jobs to cope with the effects of harassment. Organizations have to recruit and train new people, pay the costs of investigating and settling complaints, and deal with lowered morale and damage to the firm's reputation (McDonald, 2012). Quitting may seem better than protesting, as one woman explained:

> I was the only woman and the only Black woman . . . but I didn't want to react to it like the way they thought I would. Like "she's Black and she's going to get all angry." I didn't even want to give them that satisfaction. That's another reason why I just quit (Richardson & Taylor, 2009, p. 263).

The psychological consequences of harassment can be devastating. Harassment interferes with women's commitment to their jobs and the satisfaction they get from doing them, as well as with their physical and psychological health (McDonald,

2012; Pina & Gannon, 2012). An award-winning meta-analysis of 88 studies with nearly 74,000 working women found that it isn't just the most overt and intense kinds of harassment that affect women's occupational well-being. The smaller, day-to-day experiences of minor gender harassment are equally damaging. Over time, working in an organization that tolerates low-intensity sexism affects women's work attitudes and health just as much as major harassment does (Sojo et al., 2016).

A woman's initial reactions to harassment may include self-doubt, confusion, and guilt, as she asks herself if she did anything to cause or encourage it (Richardson & Taylor, 2009). She may worry about losing her job or fear that the harassment will escalate into rape, and her anxiety may become chronic. Her self-confidence and self-esteem drop. The experience of sexual harassment can lead to depression, irritability, physical symptoms (extreme fatigue and headaches), and psychological distress (Gutek & Done, 2001; Pina & Gannon, 2012). A national study of over 3,000 women found that prior harassment was linked with major depression and post-traumatic stress disorder (PTSD). The effects were large: only 9 percent of non-harassed women, and nearly 30 percent of those who had been harassed, suffered from PTSD (Dansky & Kilpatrick, 1997). And in a survey of 13,000 U.S. military women, those who had experienced recent sexual harassment had poorer mental and physical health than their peers and experienced difficulties in performing their military duties and activities (Millegan et al., 2015).

Sexual harassment is not inevitable. Organizations can reduce it by educating people about the problem, and many have developed policies and programs designed to do so. However, these programs may be designed primarily to protect the company from potential lawsuits. This kind of education is not enough. Organizations must also have a strong policy in place, send clear messages to employees that harassment will not be tolerated, and punish those who violate standards (Gutek, 1985). Meta-analyses have shown that organizational climate is a good predictor of whether sexual harassment will occur (Pina & Gannon, 2012). Moreover, they should provide support systems for women who have been harassed and protect them from retaliation when they report it. There is also a need for more research on why some men harass women, whereas the majority of men do not (Pina et al., 2009). Preventing sexual harassment is more than just a matter of preventing lawsuits; it is a matter of creating an organizational climate that is healthy for all its workers.

Women's Career Development

So far our discussion of obstacles to women's job and career satisfaction has focused on forces in the social environment. We now turn to psychological factors—individual differences in beliefs, values, motives, and choices.

Expectancies, Values, and Career Paths

For more than 60 years, psychologists have explored the question of why some people strive for success. *Achievement motivation* is the desire to accomplish something valuable and important and to meet high standards of excellence. Starting in the 1950s, researchers devised tests for measuring achievement motivation and predicting achievement oriented behavior (McClelland et al., 1953). Achievement behaviors of any sort—from running a marathon to winning a beauty contest—could theoretically be predicted by one's score on an achievement-motivation measure. For research purposes, however, scores were used to predict performance in academic settings and competitive games in the laboratory.

Early research showed that achievement-motivation scores predicted the achievement behavior of men but not women. Reflecting the strong gender bias of research at that time, the intriguing question of why women behaved less predictably than men was not explored. Instead, researchers just excluded women from their future studies, concluding that they must lack achievement motivation (Veroff et al., 1953).

Today, it is recognized that women and men have similar motivation to achieve, but that motivation may be channeled in different directions. As they are growing up, girls and boys continually make choices, both consciously and unconsciously, about how they will spend their time and efforts. This decision making is complex and multidimensional (Hyde & Kling, 2001). The most important current theory for understanding these choices and their relationship to achievement motivation is the *expectancy X value model*, developed by feminist psychologist Jacqueline Eccles (Eccles, 1994; 2011).

The expectancy part of the theory involves the individual's *expectations of success*. Research shows that junior high and high school students have gender-linked expectations for success: boys are more confident in math, and girls in English. But even if a girl believes she can succeed at a task, she is unlikely to attempt it unless it is important to her—this is where the value part of the theory comes in. The *subjective value* of various options (Do I enjoy English more than math? Will I really need math for my chosen career?) strongly affects decision making; for example, girls typically view math as less useful and important to them than boys do.

Expectancies and values are shaped by parental attributions ("My daughter got an A in math because she works hard, my son because he's bright"), gender-role beliefs ("Scientists are nerdy guys"), and self-perceptions ("I can't do physics"). Because gender socialization affects values, definitions of success, and the kinds of activities seen as crucial to one's identity, it affects virtually every aspect of achievement-related decision making.

One example of differently socialized values is the importance placed on being a parent. Gender differences in the subjective value of having children, and its effects on career planning, were demonstrated in a study of college students (Stone & McKee, 2000). When they responded to surveys, both women and men were strongly career oriented. However, interviews with the same students gave a different picture. Men consistently planned to put their career first, whereas most of the women planned to cut back or stop their careers once they had children. As one said, "Once I'm a parent, my career is on hold." Perhaps because of these differences in the value attached to parenthood, women had much less knowledge than men did about the fields they planned to enter (the graduate training needed and how much they could earn) and were not gaining as much relevant work experience. Although they expected to work and to be successful, the women's values about family life were leading them to do less planning and preparation for their future career. This study was conducted more than 15 years ago. Do you think it would get the same results if replicated today?

A more recent study asked college students directly about their values in four areas: future income, power, time with family, and helping others. There was no gender difference in power motivation, but male students scored higher on motivation for money, and female students scored higher on wanting time with family and helping others. These values predicted their planned future occupations for example, women chose more traditionally feminine careers such as teaching (Weisgram et al., 2011).

Economists point out that value differences are crucial to the gender wage gap because they point students toward specializing in different fields. College majors in the U.S. and Europe remain largely gender segregated, with men concentrated in science and technology, and women concentrated in the humanities and caring fields (Barone, 2011). These majors lead to very different job opportunities and career paths with a pay differential favoring men.

Expectancy-value theory has fostered a great deal of research, especially on the reasons why girls tend not to pursue STEM careers even though they get higher grades than boys in math and science throughout high school (Eccles, 2011). This theory has succeeded in showing that subjective expectancies and values predict career decisions at least as well as objective measures of ability. For example, a longitudinal study of more than 10,000 Australian high school students showed that their self-concepts about math and the value it held for them predicted whether they took advanced math courses, whether they went on to college, and whether they chose STEM fields (Guo et al., 2015). A longitudinal study of U.S. high school students showed that their occupational and lifestyle values and self-concepts about math ability more strongly predicted both individual and gender differences in the likelihood of entering STEM careers than math scores on the Differential Aptitude Test (Eccles & Wang, 2016). Expectancy-value theory applies equally well to diverse ethnic groups. Among White, African American, Latino, and Asian American high school students, the male students in all the groups had higher math self-concepts and higher expectations of success in math (Else-Quest et al., 2013). With a group of Latina, White, African American, and Asian American high school and middle school girls, several social factors were linked to expectancies for success in math and science. Support from mothers and peers, previous learning about feminism, and belief in gender equality all were positively correlated with the girls' motivation to excel in math and science. These beliefs and knowledge helped girls overcome the stereotype of math and science as boys' territory (Leaper et al., 2012). Overall, expectancy-value theory suggests that a long-term way to encourage young women to enter rewarding nontraditional careers (and ultimately reduce occupational segregation) is to present these fields in ways that fit their values.

High-Achieving Women

It is still the case that relatively few women achieve professional success. Yet despite the many obstacles, some women do. How are these women different? What factors in their personalities and backgrounds make the difference?

What Factors Affect Women's Career Development?

In general, high-achieving women come from backgrounds that provide them with a relatively unconstricted sense of self and an enriched view of women's capabilities (Lemkau, 1983). Their families and their upbringing are unusual in positive ways (see Table 10.1). As social learning theory would predict, girls who are exposed to less gender-stereotyped expectations are more likely to become high achievers. Attending all-girls' schools and women's colleges can provide role models and opportunities for leadership. Not surprisingly, parents play an important role. Employed mothers—especially when they enjoy their work and are successful at it—provide an important model for achievement. Because fathers usually encourage gender typing in their children more than mothers do, a father who supports and encourages his daughter's achievements may be especially influential (Weitzman, 1979). One Black woman who became a distinguished physician provided an eloquent description of her parents' belief in her:

> As a woman, I was told, I would be able to do whatever I wanted. I was taught that my skin had a beautiful color. This constant, implicit reinforcement of positive self-image was my parents' most valuable gift to me. I grew up loving my color and enjoying the fact that I was a woman. . . . In school, I performed well because my mother and father expected it of me. When I entered high school, I elected the college preparatory program as a matter of course (Hunter, 1974, pp. 58–59).

TABLE 10.1   Characteristics Linked to Achievement in Women

Research has shown that certain characteristics tend to predict later achievement in women:	
Characteristics of the Individual	**Characteristics of Family and Background**
high self-efficacy	nontraditional mother
nontraditional values and attitudes	supportive father
both instrumental and expressive traits	highly educated parents
(androgynous personality) high self-esteem	family emphasis on hard work and achievement
Characteristics of Education and Work	
work experience as an adolescent	
attending all-girls' schools and women's colleges	
continuing to take math courses	
higher education	

Sources: Betz, N. & Fitzgerald, L.F. (1987). *The Career Psychology of Women.* Boston: Academic Press. Betz, N. (2008). Women's career development. In F.L. Denmark & M. A. Paludi (Eds.), *Psychology of Women: A Handbook of Issues and Theories* (2nd ed., pp. 717–752). Westport, CT: Praeger. Whiston, S. C., & Keller, B. K. (2004). The influences of the family of origin on career development: a review and analysis. *The Counseling Psychologist, 32,* 493–568.

Setting high goals and being persistent despite setbacks are important factors in women's career development. In a survey of more than 200 African American women attorneys, 80 percent said that their families and teachers had encouraged them to work hard and set high goals. They also said they had benefited from having access to Black women role models and to equal opportunity programs (Simpson, 1996). In a longitudinal study, an ethnically diverse group of high school girls who expressed interest in math and science careers in 1980 were followed up to 13 years later. Those who had achieved their goals had taken more elective math and science in high school, set high standards for themselves, and stressed how important it is to "hang in there" when difficulties arise. Those who had experienced their parents' divorce were especially motivated to be financially independent because they had seen what happens to women who have to support their children on their own. Among the group that had not achieved their goals, some were stopped by family socialization (they were taught that the most important goal for a woman is marriage) or critical life events such as an unplanned pregnancy (Farmer et al., 1997).

Variations among Successful Women

The research summarized in Table 10.1 has been useful in helping psychologists understand the dynamics of achievement in women, but it does have limitations. Obviously, all these characteristics are not true of all high-achieving women. Some women who do not have any of the characteristics manage to succeed anyway, and some even report having been spurred on by a disapproving parent or an attempt to hold them back (Weitzman, 1979). In one study, Black and White women who came from poor families in which neither parent had finished high school were extensively interviewed. Despite their disadvantaged backgrounds, these women had achieved extraordinary success in business, academia, or government service. The odds-defying achievers had an unusually strong belief in their ability to control their lives. They believed that "You can do anything if you put your mind to it" (Boardman et al., 1987).

Research on high-achieving women has been done mostly with White women. More intersectional research is needed on diverse groups of women achievers to give a complete profile of successful women. Family background and socialization probably affect Hispanic, Asian American, and African American women differently. For example, Black women generally grow up expecting to support themselves; some Asian American groups stress academic achievement but also expect subservience to family. It is likely that racism and sexism interact in the career development of women of color (Sanchez-Hucles & Davis, 2010).

Models of career development based on heterosexuals may have limited applicability to lesbian and bisexual women. The process of coming out and accepting a lesbian identity is personally demanding (see Chapter 7) and, in some cases, may delay career development. However, coming out is a normal phase for lesbian and bisexual women, one that should be taken into account in career counseling (Boatwright et al., 1996).

Cause—Or Effect?

Studying the factors leading to success by looking at successful women is an example of *retrospective research* in which participants look back at factors influencing them at an earlier time. It can show us what characteristics successful women tend to share. However, it can also lead us to assume that we know the *causes* of success when we may be observing its *results*.

In other words, women who—for whatever reason—have the opportunity to test themselves in a demanding career may develop high self-esteem, assertiveness, independence, and achievement motivation as a consequence of their success. From this perspective, opportunity creates a "successful" personality, rather than vice versa (Kanter, 1977). Retrospective memory is not always accurate, either. Successful women may remember more achievement emphasis in their backgrounds and childhoods than less successful women simply because this dimension is relevant to them as adults (Nieva & Gutek, 1981).

Women who have achieved top-level career and leadership success often forge independent paths rather than copying a masculine model of success. Their career success is *not* due to spending all their time at work. The research on these high-performing women, particularly those who achieve while also having a spouse and family, shows that they set clear goals and priorities with both family and work in mind. They are good at time scheduling and multitasking. They do not feel guilty about not baking cookies or sewing little Blake's Halloween costume. Instead, they delegate and outsource at home just like they do at work. Far from being superwomen who try to do it all, these women define their roles as mothers, spouses, and workers in ways that suit their own abilities and let all the rest go (Cheung & Halpern, 2010; Ford et al., 2007; Friedman & Greenhaus, 2000).

Putting It All Together: Work and Family

Combining the multiple obligations of spouse, parent, and worker has often been described as a balancing act. Let's look at some costs and benefits of the balancing act for working women and their families.

What Are the Costs of the Balancing Act?

There is no doubt that combining work and family is hard for both women and men. The double day of paid and unpaid work done by many women is particularly demanding. *Role conflict* refers to the psychological effects of being faced with sets of incompatible expectations or demands; *role overload* describes the difficulties of meeting these expectations. Think of a secretary who is asked to work overtime on short notice and must scramble to find child care. She may experience both conflict (feeling torn between her two obligations) and overload (as she calls baby-sitters while formatting the overdue report). Here her mother and worker roles are incompatible with each other and there is no really satisfactory resolution of the conflict. Research has consistently shown that women workers experience role conflict (Crosby, 1991; Gilbert, 1993; Wajcman, 1998). Chronic role conflict and overload are linked to guilt, anxiety, and depression, and contribute to fatigue, short temper, and lowered resistance to illness.

Both women and men may struggle to keep a balance between work and family obligations. In a survey of more than 24,000 workers in 27 European countries, participants were asked about how well they managed the balance and about their health. For both men and women, poor work-life balance was linked to more health problems. The best balance was found in the Scandinavian countries, where government policies are most family-friendly (Lunau et al., 2014). In U.S. studies, women are much more likely than men to adjust their jobs around their family responsibilities (Mennino & Brayfield, 2002). For example, women are more likely to arrange flextime schedules, work part-time, turn down opportunities for promotion or overtime, and use their own sick days to care for others.

Separating private life from work is harder than ever in the age of' smartphones, e-mail, and instant messaging, when the boss can find you anywhere, anytime. A Dilbert cartoon strip showed a boss saying, "We're no longer using the term 'work-life balance' because it implies that life is important" (Brett, 2011).

What Are the Benefits of the Balancing Act?

Side by side with research showing widespread problems with role conflict and overload is a great deal of research showing *benefits* associated with multiple roles. Indeed, study after study shows that involvement as a spouse, parent, and worker is beneficial for both women and men. The value of the balancing act is reflected in better mental health, physical health, and relationship quality as well as more satisfaction at work (Barnett & Hyde, 2001; King et al., 2009).

Why does involvement in many roles benefit well-being? One reason may be that a job or career is generally a source of self-esteem and social involvement (Steil, 1997). Another reason is that success in one domain may help people keep a sense of perspective about the other domains (Crosby, 1982, 1991). Being passed over for promotion might seem less of a disaster if one is happily involved in leading a Girl Scout troop; dealing with a difficult teenager at home may be made easier by being respected at the office.

Employment also increases women's power in the family (see Chapter 8). And it provides families with higher incomes, which benefits everyone and reduces the pressure on spouses (Barnett & Hyde, 2001). Men who get involved with the care of their children are often surprised to find how deeply rewarding this can be and say that they would never give it up (Deutsch, 1999).

There are some limitations to the research in this area. Research samples are self-selected—people have sorted themselves into employed and non-employed groups before being studied. It is possible that multiple roles and happiness go together simply because better-adjusted people are more likely to attempt multiple roles in the first place. Furthermore, most of the research on the benefits of multiple roles has been done on White heterosexual married people with high incomes and status. It is less clear whether those benefits extend to low-income or LGBT families.

Making A Difference: Women, Work, and Social Policy

Clearly, the world of work presents women with many problems. Equity for women workers is not an impossible dream, but it involves more than striving by individual women.

A structural-level approach focuses on the impact of organizations on the people in them. It proposes that the situation a person is placed in shapes his or her behavior. From this perspective, women will advance if real opportunities for advancement become available to them. The system, not the individual, must change for equity to be achieved (see Box 10.4). Rather than viewing women as

BOX 10.4 ∾ The Lilly Ledbetter Equal Pay Act

©Mark Wilson/Getty Images

. . . Equal pay is by no means just a women's issue—it's a family issue. . . . And in this economy, when so many folks are already working harder for less and struggling to get by, the last thing they can afford is losing part of each month's paycheck to simple and plain discrimination. . . . Ultimately, equal pay isn't just an economic issue for millions of Americans and their families, it's a question of who we are—and whether we're truly living up to our fundamental ideals; whether we'll do our part, as generations before us, to ensure those words put on paper some 200 years ago really mean something.

—*President Barack Obama, on signing the Lilly Ledbetter Fair Pay Act into law, January 29, 2009*

In 1998, Lilly Ledbetter, who had worked at Goodyear Tire and Rubber Company for almost 20 years and was one of very few female supervisors,

decided to sue her employer for pay discrimination after she found out that male supervisors were making significantly more money than she was for the same work. A jury awarded her more than $3 million in back pay and punitive damages. However, the case was eventually overturned and made its way to the Supreme Court.

In 2007, the Supreme Court ruled that employees could not sue their employers for wage discrimination if the discriminatory event had taken place more than 180 days earlier. That meant that employees who'd been underpaid due to discrimination over a long time period could not sue if the pay decision had occurred in the past. Of course, employees may not know about pay discrimination until some time has gone by, because they don't have access to pay data for others. Previous interpretations of the law treated each new paycheck as

Continued on next page

BOX 10.4 ∼ The Lilly Ledbetter Equal Pay Act
(*Concluded*)

a new discriminatory act, allowing individuals to sue for pay discrimination even if the original event took place more than 180 days ago. The Supreme Court ruling essentially tied the hands of employees, making it extremely difficult to sue an employer for pay discrimination.

On January 29, 2009, President Barack Obama signed into law the Lilly Ledbetter Fair Pay Act, a law that overturned the Supreme Court's decision. Once again, in claims of pay discrimination, a "paycheck accrual rule" will be used, meaning that discriminatory paychecks an employee receives accrue over time, resetting the clock for when someone can file a discrimination claim. Since the bill was signed by President Obama, the courts have reinstated many of the pay discrimination claims that were overturned as a result of the Supreme Court's ruling in 2007. And Lilly Ledbetter got the money she rightfully earned.

Sources: http://www.nwlc.org/fairpay/ledbetterfactsheets.html
http://www.pay-equity.org/index.html
Contributed by Annie B. Fox.

unique, it sees their problems as similar to the problems faced by other disadvantaged groups such as racial and ethnic minorities. Legislation for equal opportunity is one route to change. Affirmative action helped women, African Americans, and Native Americans gain a few percentage points in professional jobs over the past 30 years. Most of these gains had peaked by the early 1990s (Kurtulus, 2012; 2016), showing that affirmative action, while valuable, is not the only answer. Family leave policies and affordable, high-quality child care are important structural changes, too.

Another approach is based on intergroup power, which has been stressed throughout this book and is the focus of Chapter 2. From this perspective, when men have more social power, women are treated as an out-group. This model explains why women's work is devalued, why male career patterns and definitions of work and achievement are taken as the norm, and why occupations so frequently end up segregated by gender. Stereotypes about differences between women and men reinforce the in-group–out-group distinction.

The intergroup perspective views change in the workplace as dependent on societal change. Educating people about stereotyping might help in the short run, but fundamental change depends on altering the power structure. Power-oriented strategies include passing and enforcing equal-opportunity legislation, increasing women's political power, and forming women's organizations and networks to exert pressure for social change. Many women and men today are engaged in these strategies.

By showing how discrimination works, psychological research can help point the way to change. How can gender bias in hiring and promotion be eliminated? Both individuals and organizations must change (Valian, 1998):

- Develop clear, specific criteria for performance evaluation, and make people responsible for meeting the criteria.

- Allow enough time and attention for performance evaluations. The quicker and more automatic the decision making, the more people rely on cognitive biases that disadvantage women.
- Increase the number of women in the pool, which reduces the salience of gender.
- Appoint leaders who are committed to gender equality.
- Develop clear institutional policies about gender equality and sexual harassment. Make sure they are communicated and implemented consistently.

Parallel changes are also needed to eliminate bias due to race, ethnic group, sexual orientation, age, disability, and other dimensions of disadvantage.

The information and analysis in Chapters 8 through 10 show that women's and men's experiences in relationships, families, and workplaces are interdependent. Women who cannot achieve economic parity at work are disadvantaged by having less power in their marriages. Much of the work women do is unpaid and undervalued. Sex discrimination at work affects productivity and quality of life. If women are to have the same career opportunities as men, they must be able to decide if and when they will bear children. Families suffer when social policy is based on myths of motherhood instead of the realities of contemporary life. These are just a few examples of the complex relationships among family roles and workplace issues. Today, the accomplishments and achievements of working women take place in spite of social policy that does not meet their needs and power imbalances that lead to subtle (and unsubtle) discrimination. Much progress has been made in remedying these inequities — and more must be made, toward a world where every woman can achieve her fullest potential.

Exploring Further

❧

Alice H. Eagly, & Linda L. Carli (2007). *Through the labyrinth: The truth about how women become leaders.* Boston: Harvard Business School Press.

A readable analysis of the psychological and other social science research on how and why women have been excluded from leadership, how the situation is changing, and how to reach the feminist ideal of diversity in leadership.

Crosby, Faye, Sabattini, Laura, & Aizawa, Michiko (2013). Affirmative action and gender equality. In M. K. Ryan & N. R. Branscombe (Eds.), *The Sage Handbook of Gender and Psychology* (pp. 485–499). London: Sage.

Affirmative action policies have helped to create gender equality in the US as well as in other countries. This chapter explains how affirmative action works to promote equal opportunity by describing exactly what affirmative action policies are. Next, the authors document the effectiveness of affirmative action programs. Finally, they explore attitudes toward affirmative action and why people resist it even though they claim to believe in gender equality and fairness.

Institute for Women's Policy Research. www.iwpr.org

The Institute works with policymakers, scholars, and public interest groups around the country to design, execute, and disseminate research that clarifies social policy issues affecting women and families, and to build a network of individuals and organizations that conduct and use women-oriented policy research.

National Committee on Pay Equity. www.pay-equity.org

NCPE is a coalition of women's and civil rights organizations, labor unions, religious, professional, legal, and educational associations, commissions on women, state and local pay equity coalitions and individuals, all working to eliminate sex- and race-based wage discrimination.

Text Credits

~

p. 307: Kanter, R. M. (1977). Men and women of the corporation. New York: Basic Books. p. 310: Source: U.S. Department of Labor. (2010). Employment status of women and men in 2008. Retrieved May 27, 2010, from http://www.dol.gov/wb/factsheets/Qf-ESWM08.htm. p. 312–313: Source: U.S. Census Bureau, 2015 American Community Survey 1-Year Estimates. p. 312: Sources: Barbara Ehrenreich, *Nickel and Dimed: On (Not) getting by in America*. Contributed by Roxanne Donovan. p. 313: Source: U.S. Census Bureau reports and data, Current Population Reports, Median Earning of Workers 15 Years Old and Over by Work Experience and Sex. p. 319: DILBERT: © Scott Adams / Dist. by United Feature Syndicate, Inc. p. 322: Lineham, M., & Scullion, H. (2008). The development of female global managers: The role of mentoring and networking. *Journal of Business Ethics, 83,* 29–40. p. 321: Contributed by Annie B. Fox. p. 326: Richardson, B. K., & Taylor, J. (2009). Sexual harassment at the intersection of race and gender: A theoretical model of the sexual harassment experiences of women of color. *Western Journal of Communication, 73,* 248–272. p. 321: Sources: http://www.nytimes.com/2016/04/03/opinion/sunday/the-tampon-of-the-future.html?_r=0 https://techcrunch.com/2015/05/26/female-founders-on-an-upward-trend-according-to-crunchbase/ p. 328: Richardson, B. K., & Taylor, J. (2009). Sexual harassment at the intersection of race and gender: A theoretical model of the sexual harassment experiences of women of color. *Western Journal of Communication, 73,* 248–272. p. 332: Sources: Betz, N. & Fitzgerald, L.F. (1987). The Career Psychology of Women. Boston: Academic Press. Betz, N. (2008). Women's career development. In F.L. Denmark & M. A. Paludi (Eds.), *Psychology of Women: A Handbook of Issues and Theories* (2nd ed, pp. 717–752). Westport, CT: Praeger. Whiston, S.C., & Keller, B.K.(2004). The influences of the family of origin on career development: a review and analysis. *The Counseling Psychologist, 32,* 493–568. p. 332: Hunter, G. T. (1974). Pediatrician. In R. B. Kundsin (Ed.), *Women and Success: The Anatomy of Achievement* (pp. 58–61). New York: Morrow. p. 336 Contributed by Annie B. p. 336

CHAPTER 11

The Second Half:
Midlife and Aging

- **Not Just a Number: The Social Meanings of Age**
  Is There a Double Standard of Aging?
  Ageism
  Cross-Cultural Differences
  Self-Identity and Social Identity

- **Images of Older Women**
  Invisibility
  Grannies and Witches: Images and Stereotypes of Older Women
  The Effects of Age Stereotypes

- **In an Aging Woman's Body**
  Physical Health in Middle and Later Life
  Menopause and Hormone Replacement Therapy
  The Medicalization of Menopause
  Constructing the Object of Desire
  Exercise and Fitness
  Sexuality in Middle and Later Life

- **Relationships: Continuity and Change**
  Friends and Family
  Becoming a Grandmother
  Caregiving: Its Costs and Rewards
  Loss of a Life Partner

- **Work and Achievement**
  Women in Their Prime
  Retirement
  Poverty in Later Life

- **Making A Difference**
  Transforming Society: Elder Activism
  Transforming Social Interaction: Taking Charge of the Second Half
  Transforming Ourselves: Resisting Ageism

- **Exploring Further**

- Cynthia, who is White, was born in 1930. As a teenager, she felt attraction to other women but had no words for it and no idea anyone else might feel the same way. She was 41 when the gay rights movement began, 45 when homosexuality was removed from the *DSM*, and 70 when the TV character Ellen came out on TV. After years of secrecy and stress, Cynthia feels that she has a positive lesbian identity in her old age (Kimmel & Martin, 2001).
- Rebecca is White, upper-middle-class, 58-years-old, and has been married for 40 years. Her husband, age 67, is a retired executive. When their five children were still at home, she took care of her husband's elderly father, who lived with them for several years until his death. Now she takes care of her 84-year-old mother. She always hoped that she would travel and take up new interests when her children left home, but that is not possible. Rebecca suffers from depression (Brody, 2004).
- Dorothy, who is African American, was born in a small southern town and grew up under racial segregation. She earned a high school diploma and wanted to be a secretary, but at that time, only White women could get clerical jobs. She worked all her life cleaning the houses of White families. A widow, she survives on $6,000 a year and has to ask her family to help out with necessities like food and medicine (Ralston, 1997).
- Mercedes is a Mexican American woman now in her late 60s. When she was growing up, her father did not see the point of sending a daughter to school. She married very young and remembers wanting to play jump rope with her friends but having to cook for her husband instead. She had six children, all of whom now live nearby. People call her *la abuela,* the grandmother, as a sign of respect. Mercedes is sought out by many people in her community as a *curandera*—a person who can heal mind and body (Facio, 1997).
- Annette is a Baby Boomer, one of the large group of Americans born between 1946 and 1964. Hers was the first generation to have the Pill and she was in no hurry to get married. She has worked outside the home ever since her only child started school. After some early struggles against sex discrimination at work, she had a satisfying career. Divorced, living alone, and with little money saved, she is looking forward to retirement with mixed feelings (Scott, 1997).

It is often said that age is the great leveler—it happens to everyone. As these real-life examples show, individuals experience aging differently depending on social class and ethnic background. Another important factor is an individual's **age cohort**—the group of people born in about the same decade. For example, women who graduated from college in the 1950s are more likely to say they regret prioritizing family over career than women who graduated in the 1970s are (Newton et al., 2012). Unlike those in the 1950s, those in the 1970s cohort grew up with second wave feminism.

In this chapter we explore the lives of women at midlife and beyond. Midlife is usually defined as the period that begins at 45 and ends at 65 years of age, and old age as the period beyond age 65. Psychology traditionally has paid less attention to the second half of life than the first. This is unfortunate because the second half of life can be as full of surprises, challenges, and rewards as the first. Let's start by looking at how age is socially defined.

Not Just a Number: The Social Meanings of Age

To a teenager, a 45-year-old may seem ancient; but my 85-year-old aunt says that *old* is anyone five years older than she is. How would you define *old*? Are you old once you reach a certain age? Does it happen when you become a grandparent? When you retire? Or are you only as old as you feel? Age is subjective. Its meaning is defined by social consensus. Age in years is only loosely correlated with abilities or roles; at best, it is a convenient number that lumps together quite different people. One 70-year-old woman might be in a nursing home, whereas another is volunteering on an archaeological dig, teaching math at a university, or delivering meals to the elderly.

Is There a Double Standard of Aging?

Many people hold a ***double standard of aging.*** They think women are old at an earlier age than men, and they see being old as more negative for women. Historically, women's value and status often depended on their sexual attractiveness and reproductive ability. Men's status, in contrast, was derived from their achievements. Therefore, a woman was considered old when she could no longer attract men or reproduce, whereas a man was not old until he became mentally or physically incapacitated. Many experimental studies show that the physical characteristics of age (such as wrinkles and gray hair) are rated more negatively for women than for men (Canetto, 2001).

The double standard of aging can often be seen in the portrayal of older women and men in the media. I'll discuss media images in more detail shortly, but for now here is one example. In a content analysis of a British magazine aimed at older people, all the women shown in ads were well under the age of 50, except for one gray-haired woman shown using a vacuum cleaner. In contrast, a gray-haired man was featured in an ad for a senior rail pass, which showed him in a wetsuit, carrying a large surfboard into the waves. The ad claimed, "60 isn't what it used to be. There are sights to see, friends to visit, waves to catch" (Blytheway, 2003, p. 46).

Although the double standard of aging is prevalent, it's not only women who lose status as they age. Men may be seen as less competent (Kite et al., 2005) and older women are sometimes rated *higher* than older men on positive characteristics such as friendly, cooperative, patient, and generous (Narayan, 2008). It seems that the "women are nicer" stereotype can trump the double standard of aging.

Do people apply the double standard to themselves? A survey of a random national sample of people aged 20 to 85 years in Sweden examined perceptions of age (Öberg, 2003). Figure 11.1 shows the proportion of people over 30 who said they were disturbed by age related changes in their appearance. You can see that there is a gender gap; women expressed more body dissatisfaction than men did. However, the gap does not increase with age. In an interview study done in England, older women were more distressed about changes in *appearance,* and older men by changes in their bodies' *function* (loss of stamina, running speed, etc.). Men spoke of their aging bodies as a holistic entity, whereas women spoke of parts (legs, thighs, and neck) (Halliwell & Dittmar, 2003). Both these studies' results reflect the pervasive objectification of the female body.

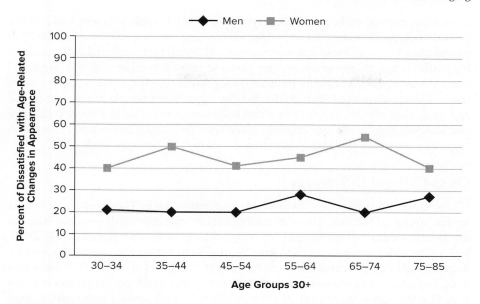

FIGURE 11.1   Gender- and age-related changes in appearance.
In a study of Swedish adults, women in every age group were more likely than men of the same age to be dissatisfied with the effects of age on their appearance. Do you think the results would be similar or different in the United States?

Source: Adapted from Öberg, P. (2003). Images versus experience of the aging body. In Christopher A. Faircloth, (Ed.), *Aging Bodies: Images and Everyday Experience* (New York: Alta Mira Press), Figure 4.4 (p. 118).

Ageism

Prejudice and discrimination based on age is termed ***ageism.*** Psychological research shows that ageism is very real. A meta-analysis of 232 studies comparing attitudes and beliefs about younger/older people found an overall preference for the young. Younger adults were rated less stereotypically, seen as more attractive and competent, and evaluated more favorably than older adults (Kite et al., 2005).

Middle-aged people, not young people, hold the most ageist attitudes (Kite et al., 2005). Among college students, however, certain factors predict ageism. In a sample of ethnically diverse college women (Asian American, African American, Latina, and White) the more they believed that a thin, youthful appearance is central to a woman's value, the more negative were their attitudes toward the elderly (Haboush et al., 2012). In both male and female college students, self-objectification and anxiety about looking or being old are linked to ageism (Gendron & Lydecker, 2016). These studies suggest that, as the media exert increasing influence on body image and self-objectification, ageism may increase.

Why should we care about ageism? First, it is widespread. In a survey, nearly 80 percent of seniors reported experiencing it (Palmore, 2001). Second, anyone is vulnerable to ageism because aging happens to everyone who lives long enough. Third, ageism leads to discrimination in medical care and employment (Palmore, 2015).

In an experimental study, participants saw profiles of job applicants who had positive traits stereotypically associated with older workers (e.g., dealing with people politely) or younger workers (e.g., rapid decision-making). Although they were told nothing about the worker's age, they overwhelmingly chose to hire the worker with the "younger" traits (Abrams et al., 2016). The traits were all positive, but there was a strong bias in favor of those associated with youth. Finally, when older people are discriminated against due to their age, they may turn that discrimination inward and develop negative and self-defeating beliefs and attitudes about their own aging minds and bodies, attitudes that contribute to depression in later life (Han & Richardson, 2015).

Cross-Cultural Differences

White American culture is individualistic and materialistic. These values work best for the young and strong. Those at midlife usually can cope fairly well but "the old are bound to fail" when judged on "rugged individualism" (Cruikshank, 2003, p. 10). The older one gets, the less possible it is to maintain total autonomy and independence. Aging brings the need for help from others and in U.S. culture this need is often seen as shameful. In cultures that value interdependence and connection, the willingness to rely on others may not be so different for older people than for younger ones. Thus, the meaning of old age depends on culture.

Some cultures, past and present, have respected and venerated the old as keepers of knowledge. For example, Buddhist tradition honors old teachers, and Native American tribes relied on the old to pass on knowledge. The wise elder, most often personified as male, is an ancient archetype still with us (think Obi Wan Kenobi and Gandalf).

When old people have meaningful roles in a society, there is less emphasis on their bodies and more on their contributions. The old may have special status as peacekeepers, mediators, healers, or keepers of tradition. In some Asian societies, spiritual power is thought to increase as the body becomes frailer. Old women are honored with the right to name children in some African and Native American groups. In North American society, meaningful roles for the old are most evident in minority communities. For example, older African American women are an important source of influence in Black churches and civic groups.

Nevertheless, the idea that old people are always venerated elsewhere compared to our own society is oversimplified. In pre-industrial societies, just as in our own, how an old person is treated depends on gender, status, and power, aside from age. In developing countries, old people may have to do hard physical labor as long as they can, and retirement is an unknown concept. Women may be valued primarily as caregivers for others, a role that is increasingly difficult to fill as one gets older. Religious beliefs may stress respect for the old but this does not always happen in practice. Physical infirmities, illness, and disabilities seem to lower one's status almost everywhere.

What about the differences between collectivist and individualistic cultures? These are comments by two male college students in separate focus group discussions about attitudes toward older people. Which student do you think is Chinese and which is American?

Older people nowadays are tossed to the edge of the society. . . . this is a new era. It is about technology and new ideas. It is about the young people.

I feel like they always have something interesting to say and I always try to extract a little bit of wisdom from older people . . . (Luo et al., 2013, p. 57).

You may be surprised to learn that it is the first student who is Chinese. China is a collectivist culture, with a tradition of filial piety, which teaches respect for parents and an obligation to provide physical and financial care for their old age. However, China has undergone rapid modernization and economic growth in the past half-century. Everywhere in the world, older people's status declines with modernization (Luo et al., 2013; Vauclair et al., 2016). When Chinese and U.S. college students were compared on their attitudes toward the elderly, the Chinese students had more negative attitudes than the U.S. students. As one Chinese female grad student explained:

Respecting elders is a slogan. Most young people I know think they are burdens. (Luo et al., 2013, p. 58).

When attitudes of young people toward the elderly in the United Kingdom and Taiwan were compared, Taiwanese people showed more prejudice about things like spending time with an older person, or having one for a neighbor or a boss (Vauclair et al., 2016). It seems that the idea that there is little or no ageism in Asian societies is more a stereotype than a reality.

Self-Identity and Social Identity

Like other forms of bias, ageism can be internalized, affecting the individual's identity and self-esteem. "This is the heart of ageism: We deny that we are aging, and when we are forced to confront it, we treat it as ugly and tragic" (Calasanti & Slevin, 2001, p. 186). For example, a 65-year-old may refuse to go to a senior citizen center or retirement community because she does not want to be around "all those old people."

In one study, older adults in Finland were asked to look in a mirror and describe their reflection. One 79-year-old woman said, "It isn't a reflection of me. I know myself pretty well . . . Spiritually I don't feel old, like 'oh dear how old I am.' But I can see it in the appearance" (cited in Öberg, 2003, p. 107). This woman is making a distinction between her *self-identity* (her own subjective feeling of age) and her *social identity* (the way she looks to others).

The discrepancy between self- and social identities was explored in a Swedish study (Öberg, 2003), where participants aged 20 to 85 answered these questions:

In my inner self I feel as if I am _____ years old.

I would most like to be _____ years old.

I think that other people see me as _____ years old.

Figure 11.2 shows that every age group except the 20-year-olds reported a difference between their chronological age and their subjective age. The great majority of

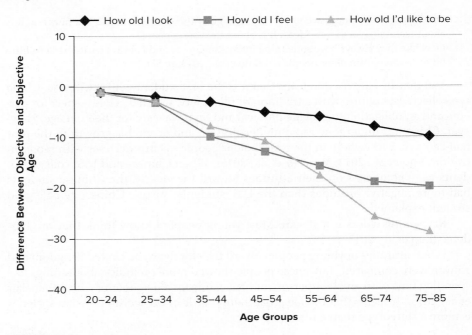

FIGURE 11.2
The discrepancy for respondents in different age groups between how old they think they look, how old they feel, and how old they would like to be.

Source: Öberg and Tomstam, 2001, as summarized in Öberg, 2003.

people said they felt younger, wanted to be younger, and thought that others saw them as younger than they actually were. The gaps between self, ideal, and social identities increased with age. Respondents in their 80s wanted to be 50, felt like 60, and thought that they looked like 70 to others.

Distancing yourself from your age may be a form of resistance against the stigma of being old. When a 91-year-old woman laughingly says that the term "older woman" "describes someone else, not me," she may be refusing to allow the negative stereotypes of old women to define her identity (Quéniart & Charpentier, 2012, p. 992). However, dissociating from one's age is dissociating from an important part of the self. And when each old person thinks of himself or herself as the exception, it is unlikely that older people will bond with each other or act collectively to change the sociocultural forces that construct old age so negatively. Instead, each of us believes that getting old is something that only happens to other people.

Images of Older Women

Think about the last few TV dramas or sitcoms you watched. Were there any women over 40 in leading roles? As I noted in Chapter 9, older women in the media are few and far between, and those who do appear are often depicted negatively.

Invisibility

As women grow older, they become less visible in all forms of media, as though they are so repulsive that no one would want to look at them. Older men, too, are underrepresented, but to a much lesser degree. In an analysis of top movies, major male characters outnumbered major female characters almost 3 to 1; the majority of male characters were in their 30s and 40s, and the majority of female characters were a decade or two younger. Both women and men in their 60s and older were underrepresented compared to their proportion of the population—for example, 60ish women got only 8 percent of the roles although they are 22 percent of the population. It wasn't just the numbers that differed. Men in their 40s, 50s, and 60s had more roles involving leadership, power, and achievement than women in the same age groups (Lauzen & Dozier, 2005). It seems that, to some extent, men are allowed to mature in popular culture, but women are expected to remain 20-something babes, frozen in time.

Women disappear from TV faster than men do as they get older. Women in their 40s show up in significantly fewer roles than men in their 40s. By the time they are in their 60s, both women and men have been all but banished from your TV screen (Women's Media Center, 2015). They still show up occasionally in commercials, but it seems that advertisers think older women buy only laxatives and floor mops. Negative and simplistic depictions of older women in TV commercials are found cross culturally. In Japan and the UK, they are shown half as often as older men are, and they are more often shown at home, while men are shown at work or outdoors, being autonomous and independent (Kay & Furnham, 2013; Prieler et al., 2011).

The most invisible aspect of older women is their sexuality. Although young women's bodies are sexually objectified and exploited by the media, old women are almost never portrayed as sexual, unless their sexual desire is targeted for ridicule. The bodies of young women are used to sell everything from fishing tackle to vodka, but the bodies of old women are evaded. This invisibility "deprives women of all ages from knowing what old bodies look like . . . the ways beauty can be expressed through old female forms is yet to be known" (Cruikshank, 2003, p. 149). Older men's virility is displayed by showing them with much younger women, not women their own age. In movie romances, Jack Nicholson at age 60 was paired with Helen Hunt, 34; Michael Douglas, 53, with Gwyneth Paltrow, 25; and Jeff Bridges, 60, with 32-year-old Maggie Gyllenhaal.

Older LGBTQ people have been invisible not only in mainstream media but even in media aimed at the gay community. In an analysis of LGBTQ magazines such as *Out* and *The Advocate,* there were only 2 articles on older people in the 542 pages of text, and no pictures at all of anyone who looked to be age 60 or older (Apuzzo, 2001). Fortunately, increasing social acceptance has brought more lesbians of all ages into public life: Rachel Maddow, 43; Ellen DeGeneres, 58; and in the over-60 group, actress and comedian Lily Tomlin and financial expert Suze Orman (Rose & Hospital, 2015).

Grannies and Witches: Images and Stereotypes of Older Women

Stereotypes about the elderly are both positive (gentle, kind) and negative (slow, senile) (Chrisler et al., 2015). Positive age stereotypes are related to warmth, while negative ones are related to competence (Cuddy & Fiske, 2002; Nelson, 2009). The overall result is a "doddering but dear" stereotype: old people are thought of as cute and cuddly but not too bright or capable (Andreoletti et al., 2015; Cuddy et al., 2005).

One of the most pervasive images of old women is the kindly grandmother, a portrayal that is consistent with trait stereotypes of warmth and nurturance (Canetto, 2001). Granny images are reinforced by the clothes and props assigned to older women in media representations. The granny figure wears a shawl or an apron. She sits in a rocking chair, knitting, or stirs a pot over the stove. Her gray hair, worn in a bun, and her outdated, unfashionable clothes signify that she has not kept up with the times. This grandmother figure abounds in films made over the past 6 decades (Markson, 2003) and in children's picture books. Although grandparents in children's books are generally portrayed positively, even in books published in the 21st century, one in four grandmothers wears an apron or has gray hair in a bun (Crawford & Bhattacharya, 2014; Danowski & Robinson, 2012).

Other prototypes of older women in the media are the mother-in-law from hell, the manipulative, selfish elderly mother, and the comical but powerless "little old lady" (Cruickshank, 2003) – not to mention various evil queens (Cersei in *Game of Thrones*) and wicked Disney stepmothers. An analysis of Disney movies concluded that old women were depicted as ugly, evil, greedy, power-hungry, and crazy (Perry, 1999). It wasn't until Gramma Tala in Moana that Disney offered a wise and protective older woman character – and even Tala called herself the "village crazy lady."

The Effects of Age Stereotypes

Age stereotyping can have insidious effects on judgments about older people. In one study, college students listened to a taped lecture read by a gender-neutral and age-neutral voice and rated the "professor" on teaching skills. Some were told that the professor was under age 35, and others that he/she was over age 55. Although the lecture was identical for all participants, students rated the professor as more enthusiastic, vocally expressive, and showing more interest when they thought he was young and male than in any other condition (Arbuckle & Williams, 2003). This study shows an interaction of age and gender stereotypes: students' evaluations were filtered though their negative stereotypes about older professors as well as female professors.

Age stereotypes can even affect medical care for older people. Physicians are not immune to age stereotypes, and may base treatment decisions in part on their beliefs about older patients' reduced cognitive abilities and motivations (Chrisler et al., 2016). But the worst effects of age stereotypes may be the damage they do when they are internalized by older people themselves. When an old person comes to believe in the negative stereotypes of aging, she may experience very real effects on her skills and abilities. Let's look at a few examples.

When people talk to the elderly, they sometimes switch to *elderspeak* (Nelson, 2009). Elderspeak is like baby talk (speech by adults to young children) or the way people talk to their pets: it is grammatically simplified, repetitious, slowed down, and exaggerated in pitch. Only listeners who suffer from hearing loss or dementia are likely to find elderspeak helpful. For the majority of older people, it is patronizing, conveying the expectation that they are not competent to understand normal speech. Because elderspeak is simplified, it conveys less information, thereby leading the old person to respond in a more simplistic way and reinforcing the belief in his or her incompetence (Ruscher, 2001). The end result is that older people may be *infantilized,* or treated like children: They are given overly simple information about complex issues, they are protected from information that others think may upset them, and their opinions are disregarded (Nelson, 2009).

Stereotypes can also make their mark in other ways. A meta-analysis of 82 measures of stereotype threat showed that when older people are at risk of confirming the negative stereotype that they have bad memories or cannot do cognitive tasks, their performance on these tasks is negatively affected (Lamont et al., 2015). Evoking positive stereotypes has the opposite effect. Indeed, age stereotypes can become self-fulfilling prophecies.

In an Aging Woman's Body

As bodies grow older, they change. Acknowledging and accepting this is an important part of aging. But the meaning of an aging body is not just a matter of its physical state; it depends on the social context. Track and field athletes are relegated to Masters status at age 35 (women) and 40 (men). In contrast, symphony conductors often lead major orchestras into their 80s, and some U.S. Senators have served into their 90s (Calasanti & Slevin, 2001). When Hillary Clinton, 68, ran for President, she was openly called a witch, and Rush Limbaugh asked his listeners, "Will this country want to actually watch a woman get older before their eyes on a daily basis?" (Talbot, 2016b). Her stamina and health were repeatedly questioned, and she was said to be too old for the job, although her opponent was 70. Because women, more than men, are evaluated throughout their lifetimes by their bodies, living in an aging body is a particular challenge for women.

Physical Health in Middle and Later Life

Measures of women's health in later life are somewhat contradictory. On the one hand, women as a group have a long life expectancy, outliving men on average. On the other hand, women are more likely than men to have chronic illnesses and disabilities as they age (Canetto, 2001; Chrisler et al., 2015). Here we look at some of the most common health problems of older women.

Heart Disease

What is your best guess about the three leading causes of death for U.S. women? Many people's list would include breast cancer. Although one woman in nine will be diagnosed with breast cancer during her lifetime, the top three causes of death for U.S. women are heart disease, all types of cancer, and chronic respiratory disease, with stroke a close fourth (CDC, 2013). Lung cancer kills more women than breast cancer does (Lobo, 2016). Over the past 35 years, death from heart disease has actually decreased for men while increasing for women, and the death rate is higher for ethnic minority women than for other women. In fact, African American and Native American women have the highest mortality rates from heart disease of any group (Mather, 2008).

Because most research on heart disease was conducted with men, there has been a shortage of information about women's symptoms, which may differ from men's. There is also a serious gender gap in treatment. Analyzing a national U.S. database of over 10 million cases, psychologist Cheryl Travis (2005) found that men were twice as likely to have lifesaving bypass surgery as women with similar medical symptoms. No one knows for sure why physicians and others in the medical system are slow to recognize and treat heart disease in women, but one likely explanation is that their cognitive biases interfere. When thinking of a person with heart disease, most people's image is of an overweight, sedentary White male. Because women with heart disease don't fit the prototype, their lives are put at risk.

The effects of gender bias in the diagnosis and treatment of heart disease were evident in a survey of over 200 female cardiac patients (Marcuccio et al., 2003). Some said that their condition was initially misdiagnosed as panic disorder, menopausal symptoms, or hypochondria. Only 60 percent of the sample was referred to a cardiac care program. Other studies also have shown that women receive very little counseling about exercise, diet, and weight control, and much less than men do, after heart disease is diagnosed. Fortunately, healthcare providers, policymakers, and scientists have campaigned during the past decade to raise awareness about women's risk for heart disease and reduce gender bias in research and care (Mosca et al., 2011).

Chronic Illnesses

Midlife and older women are likely to live with chronic illnesses such as arthritis and diabetes. Conditions that limit activity (such as spinal degeneration, varicose veins, and joint problems) are two to three times more prevalent in women over the age of 75 than in men of the same age group. The probability of all these conditions increases with age. It is not uncommon for a woman in her 70s to have several chronic health concerns simultaneously, such as arthritis, heart disease, high blood pressure, back pain, and diabetes (Canetto, 2001).

Chronic illness has psychological effects on identity. It forces a continued focus on the body: on good days, life goes on, but on bad days, the damaged body defines and limits the person (Gubrium & Holstein, 2003). The patient must face the fact that her disorder cannot be cured. Instead, she must cope with whatever physical pain and limitations it brings. Illness and loss of the ability to do everyday activities decrease the quality of life for older people (Bourque et al., 2005). It is not surprising that many people with chronic illnesses experience depression (Chrisler, 2001). On the other hand, learning to manage a chronic condition can be empowering for a woman, as she takes time to care for herself after a lifetime of caring for others (Chrisler, et al. 2015).

Ethnicity and Health

Women of Hispanic and African American heritage have poorer health than European American women, and they are more likely to die from diseases that could be treated and managed if they had access to good health care (Cox, 2005). For example, Black women are more likely to have high blood pressure, which can lead to strokes if untreated (Cruikshank, 2003). African American, Native American, and Hispanic women also have higher death rates from diabetes than European Americans (Canetto, 2001). People of color, both men and women, have shorter lives than White people, with more chronic illnesses and disabilities as they age (Carreon & Noymer, 2011; Warner & Brown, 2011).

Socioeconomic status is the single most important predictor of health in old age and probably is the root cause of many ethnic differences in health status as well as the shorter lifespans of people of color. Poverty is linked to ill health and early death because it is connected to many physical and psychological stressors such as unemployment, crowding, poor diet, unsanitary living conditions, pollution, and violence (Chrisler, 2001). Poor people are unlikely to get consistent high-quality care for the chronic illnesses associated with poverty. The link between poverty and ill health is dramatically obvious in the health status of Native Americans, whose rates of serious chronic diseases are 600 percent higher than for the rest of the population, and whose disabilities at age 45 are similar to the disabilities of 65-year-olds in the rest of the population (Cox, 2005). The effects of low socioeconomic status accumulate over a lifetime, reducing quality of life and shortening the lifespan.

Menopause and Hormone Replacement Therapy

The U.S. medical and pharmaceutical system does seem eager to cure one huge problem affecting millions of women. Unfortunately, the "problem" is not a disease or disorder but a natural aspect of aging, and the "cures" may be unnecessary and even harmful.

Menopause refers to the end of the menstrual cycle and monthly periods. It is caused by a decrease in the production of estrogen and progesterone by the ovaries. It can occur any time between 40 and 60, but the average age is around 50.

Physical Signs of Menopause

The menopausal transition takes place over several years, as periods become less regular. A woman can be sure that she has reached menopause when she has not had a period for a full year.

Other bodily changes may accompany menopause. In Western societies, about 50 to 85 percent of all women experience *hot flashes:* brief episodes of suddenly increasing heart rate, warmth, and sweating. Hot flashes may occur as infrequently as once a month or as often as several times an hour. They are caused by the decline in estrogen that triggers menopause. Over time, the body accommodates to the lower estrogen levels and the hot flashes disappear.

Many women also experience vaginal changes with menopause: the skin and membranes in this area become thinner and drier, which may make sexual penetration by a partner uncomfortable. However, this can be remedied with lubricating gels. In a community-based study, 20 percent of postmenopausal women reported this condition, and only 15 percent of those reported it as bothersome (Boston Women's Health Book Collective, 1998).

The physical signs of menopause are not universal. Women in Japan and China and Mayan women in Mexico very rarely experience hot flashes with menopause (Richard-Davis & Wellons, 2013). Ethnic and cultural differences in menopausal symptoms are affected by socioeconomic status, personal and societal attitudes toward older women, marital status, diet, smoking, exercise, and physical fitness (Richard-Davis & Wellons, 2013). Even where menopausal symptoms are common, they may not be experienced as stressful. In several studies, women have reported that they accept them as a normal and temporary part of midlife, and are not particularly bothered by them (Hyde & DeLamater, 2017).

Psychological Experiences of Menopause

There is a long history of attributing women's psychological distress to their reproductive systems. Starting in the 1860s, psychiatry developed diagnostic categories for the supposed craziness of postmenopausal women, including "old maid's insanity" and "involutional melancholia," a form of depression (Markson, 2003). Psychiatric diagnoses like involutional melancholia were part of the myth that women are mentally unstable because of their reproductive hormones: Raging "PMS" hormones make us crazy in our reproductive years and waning hormones do so later in life. The belief that women become depressed, moody, irritable, and hypersensitive at menopause is still prevalent among health care providers and women themselves (Avis, 2003).

Contrary to these beliefs, research shows no evidence that the onset of normal menopause leads to depression or that women suffer more depression after menopause than before. Instead, the evidence suggests that depression during the menopausal transition is predicted by a prior history of depression, health problems, and social factors. Depression is not a normal part of menopause (Avis, 2003; Georgakis et al., 2016).

Menopause may be linked with short-term moodiness and irritability in some women (Prairie et al., 2015). In the U.S., White women report psychological changes more than Black women do (Richard-Davis & Wellons, 2013). Moodiness may be partly due to hormonal changes and partly due to their associated physical changes; when sleep is disturbed by hot flashes, irritability can result. It may also be due to expectations created by stereotypes. If everyone expects a menopausal woman to be moody, mood changes caused by stressful life events may be misattributed to her hormones.

An old expression for menopause is "change of life." Indeed, like menarche, it marks a major life change that is unique to females. In one study of 2,500 women, the majority experienced this change with neutral or positive feelings (Avis & McKinlay, 1991). In studies comparing African and European American women, the Black women had more positive attitudes than the White women, viewing menopause as a normal and unremarkable part of life (Sampselle et al., 2002; Sommer et al., 1999). A woman may be relieved that she no longer can become pregnant and can stop using birth control; she may be happy to say goodbye to pads, tampons, and cramps. Very few 50-year-olds want to have a baby. Contrary to the stereotype of crazy, moody menopausal women, most women cope with the signs of menopause with little fuss and the transition is not the biggest thing in their lives.

Exercise and fitness are important factors in keeping the menopausal transition smooth. A correlational study of 133 women whose average age was 51 showed that being physically active was linked to higher feelings of self-worth, fewer physical symptoms, and better quality of life (Elavsky & McAuley, 2005). Following up on these results, the same researchers conducted a 4-month randomized controlled exercise trial in which participants (164 relatively inactive women whose average age was 50) were assigned to a walking, yoga, or no-exercise control group. Both walking and yoga led to very positive outcomes, including better mood, better self-rated quality of life around menopausal issues, and, as physical fitness increased, fewer menopausal symptoms (Elavsky & McAuley, 2007). There were also fewer mental health problems in the exercise groups compared to the no-exercise control group. The researchers concluded that increasing cardio fitness is one good way to reduce the physical and psychological impact of menopausal symptoms on women.

The Medicalization of Menopause

Because menopause happens to over 50 percent of the adult population, there is a great deal of money to be made in treating it as a disease. Increasingly, U.S. society defines age as a sickness that can be treated and cured (Calasanti & Slevin, 2001). This trend was apparent in the use of reproductive hormones to relieve signs of menopause and prevent signs of aging, termed *estrogen replacement therapy* (ERT) or *hormone replacement therapy* (HRT) depending on whether estrogen alone or a combination of hormones is used. Proponents argued that ERT/HRT could prevent osteoporosis (bone density loss), heart disease, and some types of cancer. Some claimed that it also could prevent age-related changes in cognition (memory loss and dementia) and appearance (wrinkles and weight gain). Pharmaceutical companies, some scientists, and many physicians urged women to stay forever young by taking hormones to offset menopause.

However, these claims were made before there was sufficient research. Later, a national study of 25,000 women aged 50 to 79 examined the effect of diet, exercise, and ERT/HRT on heart disease, cancer, and osteoporosis. The HRT part of the study was ended early when results showed that HRT was associated with a slightly *increased* risk of breast cancer, heart attack, and stroke (Mather, 2008). Soon after, the ERT results were analyzed and also showed that the risks outweighed the benefits. ERT was linked to an increased risk of stroke and had no effect on preventing heart disease (Women's Health Initiative Steering Committee, 2004). Moreover, both HRT and ERT were linked to increased cognitive impairment such as memory loss and dementia (Espeland et al., 2004; Shumaker, 2004). Women's health activists were outraged that this "therapy" was prescribed to so many women in the absence of scientific evidence for its benefits. In the process, many women probably were harmed.

Research on HRT has continued; new studies and meta-analyses suggest that it may have more benefits than risks when used to relieve *severe* menopausal symptoms and prevent osteoporosis in high risk women. It should be used in the lowest possible doses for the shortest possible time. However, medical experts still disagree about the most effective dose of HRT, and few physicians have received training in its use during the past decade (Lobo, 2016). Clearly, more research is needed on its risks and benefits. Overall, women can have more control over their lives by resisting the medicalization of menopause and aging.

Constructing the Object of Desire

Increasingly, both women and men are expected to spare no effort to disguise or eliminate the bodily changes that come with age. For men, Viagra is aggressively marketed as a way to restore the sexual vigor of youth. For women, much more than a pill is required. As they grow older, many women view their bodies as the site of an ever-more laborious project in which the goal is to masquerade as a younger woman (Calasanti & Slevin, 2001).

Of course, attempts to avoid old age are ultimately futile. Nevertheless, attempts to avoid the *appearance* of old age are rapidly increasing in Western societies, aided by aggressive marketing of anti-aging products. Women are exhorted by advertisers to go to war with their own bodies, to "fight," "resist," "overcome," and "outwit" aging. These messages are directed most strongly to White middle-class and affluent women. Research suggests that the most privileged women are most concerned about their appearance and most invested in treating their body as an improvement project, while working class women regard their body more in terms of how well it functions (Calasanti & Slevin, 2001).

Almost 16 million cosmetic procedures were done in the U.S. in 2015, 92 percent of them on women (American Society of Plastic Surgeons, 2015), many designed to reduce the appearance of aging: breast lifts, abdominoplasties (tummy tuck), and facelifts. Nonsurgical medical techniques such as Botox (injections of a neurotoxin that paralyzes facial muscles), dermabrasion, and chemical skin peels are becoming more popular, too, and women are encouraged to have them every few months to avoid the dreaded appearance of facial lines. TV programs like *Extreme Makeover* (which ran for five seasons) raised the bar, justifying even the most radical, gruesome, and painful surgical procedures in the quest for perfect (youthful) features. What the hype doesn't say is that cosmetic surgery and other medical procedures are expensive, not covered by health insurance, carry risks of disfigurement and death, and must be repeated periodically to maintain the effect. Nevertheless, 38 percent of a sample of middle-aged women reported having had at least one cosmetic procedure, and 81 percent said they would if cost were not an issue. Whether they identified as feminist made no difference to their desires (Chrisler et al., 2012).

Feminist theorists are divided about the meaning of the "beauty work" that so many middle-aged and older women do. Some have argued that it represents a kind of false consciousness, as women accept the sexist attitude that their youthful attractiveness is the only important thing about them, and give in to self-objectification. Others have argued that a focus on appearance is a rational choice for aging women, because there is ample evidence of ageism, and women face prejudice and discrimination based on looks more than men do. Therefore, working on her face and body is one way for a woman to hold on to social power as she ages (Clarke, 2007; Clarke & Griffin, 2008).

Women seem to be conflicted about beauty work. In an interview study of 44 women aged 50 to 70, many participants wished that they could look young without trying to; their ideal was to age "naturally" or "gracefully." However, their behavior was anything but natural, as they reported using a variety of methods to avoid the appearance of aging, ranging from makeup (84 percent) and hair dye (61 percent) to Botox injections, chemical peels, injections of fillers under the skin, microdermabrasion, liposuction, and cosmetic breast surgery (Clarke & Griffin, 2008). One reason they gave was age discrimination at work:

> I'm 52-years-of-age. . . . It happened today to me—she's tall and blonde and long-legged and flirts with the bosses and has no computer skills and only has reception experience. I have 15 years' experience and a computer background. I get along awesomely with the staff. They kept her and they're letting me go. (p. 663)

Another reason for undertaking beauty work was the belief that it was necessary to catch or hold on to a man, as this 59-year-old single woman said:

> My face is sagging and I'm at a stage in my life when I'm looking for a new partner, hopefully to spend the rest of my life with. . . . So, my appearance is very important to me right now. It's difficult to find men in my age range who are not going out with younger women . . . I am seriously thinking about . . . major surgery on my face. (p. 665)

A third reason was painful awareness of the social invisibility of older women. One 55-year-old said,

> Men of all ages find youthful women attractive. What the fuck is that all about? . . . What a shame that the ideal is young as opposed to being old and wise. What a shame. What a reflection on our society that we don't see the beauty in ageing. (p. 667)

Only two of the 44 women interviewed did not use any beauty work interventions, but even they were conflicted about their choice. One woman, 65, put it this way:

> As I grow older, it's very difficult to see the wrinkles appearing and the skin losing its elasticity. My radical feminism, on the one hand, is saying, "Don't be so absurd." The other side of me struggles. When I look through magazines and see all of these advertisements for wrinkle creams and . . . cosmetic surgeons . . . I am just absolutely appalled at what's going on . . . but I've considered getting rid of these wrinkles, and the facelifts and all that. Whether I'll ever do it or not, I don't know, but certainly I've considered it. (p. 668)

Some women respond to the pressure to maintain a youthful appearance by opting out at midlife. If society is saying that they must do what they manifestly cannot do (be slim, toned, smooth-skinned, and young), they choose not to participate in the game of objectification. Instead, they wear relaxed clothes and comfortable shoes, defining a feminine appearance in terms of ease and freedom of movement (see Figure 11.3).

FIGURE 11.3

Source: © Roz Chast/The New Yorker Collection/www.cartoonbank.com

Exercise and Fitness

One of the most important factors in maintaining good health in the second half of life is regular exercise. The benefits of exercise are both psychological (improved mood stability, energy levels, and body self-esteem) and physical (lowering the risk of life-threatening conditions such as diabetes, high blood pressure, obesity, and heart disease) (Gutiérrez et al., 2012; Klusmann et al., 2012). Exercise relieves arthritis pain, maintains strength and posture, strengthens the immune system, benefits thinking and memory, and improves skin tone. In the elderly, exercise helps prevent the loss of muscle tone that causes falls, broken bones, and permanent disability Chrisler et al., 2015. Scientific research has unequivocally shown the benefits of exercise for older people, not only those who are already fit but those who have been sedentary for years and even those in their 90s (Cruikshank, 2003).

In every age group, women exercise less than men, and the amount of exercise women get decreases as they age (Milne et al., 2014). Two-thirds of older U.S. women don't exercise regularly at all (Chrisler & Palatino, 2016). While younger women may feel guilty if they don't work out, women in the 65–75 age group are less likely to be concerned; a focus group study showed that they wrongly think they get enough exercise by walking to the bus stop or doing housework (Milne et al., 2014).

Fortunately, it is never too late to start exercising (see Figure 11.4.). Strength training can actually reverse muscle loss at any age. Pioneering studies at Tufts University showed that frail elderly men in nursing homes greatly increased their muscle strength, walking ability, and balance after strength training. The studies were extended to postmenopausal women, also with dramatic results: compared to a control group, the exercise group gained bone density, muscle tone, balance, and flexibility, and became more energetic and active (Nelson, 2000).

Exercise programs for older women may be most successful if they are realistic about the barriers that exist and if they offer opportunities for social interaction

©Ariel Skelley/Getty Images RF

FIGURE 11.4   **Exercise provides physical and psychological benefits at every stage of life.**

with age peers (Chrisler & Palatino, 2016; Kelly et al., 2016). Tai chi, yoga, water aerobics, mall walking, group birdwatching hikes, and line dancing classes are all ways to increase fitness and have fun, too.

Sexuality in Middle and Later Life

Visualize an old woman wearing a miniskirt. What is your first reaction to this image? What reaction do you think your friends would have?

A mini-skirted old woman is deviant because she dares to appear sexual past her reproductive years (Calasanti & Slevin, 2001). Sexuality and sexual activity in older people are widely considered disgusting or ridiculous. In one study, college students judged that people over 65 were less interested in cuddling, intercourse, and looking at erotic material than people their own age were—and older women least interested of all (Lai & Hynie, 2011). Whether the (hypothetical) sex was for intimacy or pleasure, older women were seen as pretty much sexless. Even jokes about old people and sex are gender biased—there are plenty of approving jokes about Viagra, but an immense cultural negativity about the sexuality of older women. Yet, many older people express continued interest, pleasure, and satisfaction with sexual activity, and in qualitative research studies, describe positive, sustained, and varied sex lives in middle and later life (Bradway & Beard, 2015; McHugh & Interligi, 2015; Ussher et al., 2015).

One factor limiting sexual expression for older heterosexual women is that there aren't enough men to go around. Because women live longer than men, there are more women than men in the population starting at around age 60. The gender differential is greater for women of color, especially African American women, than for European American or Asian American women, and it increases with age. There are about twice as many women as men aged 85 and older (U.S. Census Bureau, 2014). This means that heterosexual women are likely to spend the last decades of their lives without a marital or sexual partner.

Opportunities for relationships are limited not just because of a man shortage, but because men usually choose younger partners. Research has consistently shown that one of the biggest factors influencing the sexual activity of middle-aged and older women is the lack of a partner (DeLamater & Sill, 2005; McHugh & Interligi, 2015).

Is a new sexual script emerging for the over-40 woman? No longer the middle-aged reject, cast off for a younger woman, she is the "cougar," in "strappy heels, cleavage, a little too much make up," with "a glint in her eye," the older single woman aggressively pursuing younger men for casual sex (Montemurro & Siefken, 2014, p. 35). This stereotype of older women, which emerged in the 1990s, has met with mixed reactions. In interviews with 84 women, the majority had negative or mixed feelings about the cougar label. Their main objection was the cougar's link with predatory behavior. They did not like to think of women as aggressively focused on mere conquests. They felt that when older women and younger men dated it was often out of mutual interest and affection, not an older woman being "on the prowl." Others said that it perpetuated the double standard, because there is no nickname for older men who date younger women. Still others thought the older woman chasing a younger man was ridiculous, an object of pity or scorn.

Those who liked the term felt that it referred to women who took charge of their sexuality and acted assertively to get what they wanted. However, they believed that only women who were rich, celebrities, or exceptionally attractive could be cougars.

The image of the cougar transcends notions of the older women as asexual and unattractive. Is the cougar a hot older woman, who knows what she wants sexually and pursues it? Is she out of place, too aggressive, or just pathetic? Or should we avoid labeling women's sexual and relationship choices altogether? What do you think?

Sexual Desire and Satisfaction in Old Age

Older adults have been almost entirely neglected in sex research. However, medical and behavioral studies show that many people desire and are capable of enjoying sexual intimacy into old age (see Box 11.1). Both women and men often remain sexually active into their 70s and 80s if they are in good physical and psychological

BOX 11.1 ∽ Research Focus: Online Dating among Older Adults

©Ingram Publishing RF

Online dating has become one of the most popular ways for adults of all ages to find romantic partners. Although commercials for Internet dating sites would have you believe that it is only young, twentysomethings who are online looking for love, older adults also use the web to find romance. In addition to popular sites like Match .com and eHarmony.com, there are also a number of online dating platforms specifically targeting older adults, including SeniorMatch.com and OurTime.com.

What are older adults looking for in a match? A study examining online dating profiles found that older adults were less likely than younger adults to use self-referential language in their profiles, which may reflect an increased focus on relationships, rather than the self, in later life. Older adults were also more likely to mention money and health in their profiles compared to younger adults, suggesting that financial stability and good health are important considerations for entering into relationships in later life.

In addition to these generational differences, research suggests there are also gender differences when it comes to what older men and women are looking for in potential partners. A study of online personal ads found that women of all ages seek men of higher status, whereas men seek women who are attractive. In general, men preferred a younger partner and women preferred an older one. Interestingly, as men aged, there was a larger discrepancy between

Continued on next page

BOX 11.1 ❧ Research Focus: Online Dating among Older Adults
(*Concluded*)

the man's age and the age of his desired partner. In other words, while a 25-year-old man might prefer a woman who was no older than 24, a 60-year-old man preferred a woman who was no older than 52, and a 75-year-old man desired a woman no older than 65. For women, the difference between their age and their desired partner's age gradually decreased over time. By age 75, women sought younger men. A qualitative study of older online daters found differences in the types of relationships older men and women are seeking. Older men sought committed relationships, whereas older women were less likely to be interested in remarrying. Instead, women sought intimate companionship without having to

take on the role of caretaker. These differences highlight the ways in which gendered relationship norms and experiences shape online dating expectations later in life.

Sources: Alterovitz, S., & Mendelsohn, G. A. (2009). Partner preferences across the life span: Online dating by older adults. *Psychology and Aging, 24*, 513–517.
McWilliams, S., & Barrett, A. E. (2014). Online dating in middle and later life: Gendered expectations and experiences. *Journal of Family Issues, 35*(3), 411–436.
Davis, E. M., & Fingerman, K. L. (2016). Digital Dating: Online Profile Content of Older and Younger Adults. *The Journals of Gerontology Series B: Psychological Sciences and Social Sciences,* 71, 959–967.
Contributed by Annie B. Fox

health, have a positive attitude about sex, and have a healthy partner (DeLamater, 2012). In a study of over 400 married people recruited from centers for the elderly in Greece, more than 50 percent of participants aged 60 to 90 reported still being sexually active, enjoying intercourse once a week on average. Socioeconomic and interpersonal factors were more important than biomedical ones. For example, couples who had married for love and said they were still in love were more sexually active (Papaharitou et al., 2008).

There has been very little research on sexuality among older lesbians. It seems that the idea that not all old people are heterosexual has not yet occurred to most researchers. And it is not easy to do research with older cohorts of LGBTQ people. Among women who are now in old age, those who have had relationships with other women often were not out and did not use the word lesbian to describe themselves; therefore they may be overlooked in research.

A British study of more than 300 LGB people aged 50 to 70 found that 60 percent of the women were currently in a relationship, and almost half of these were living with their partners (Heaphy et al., 2004). Participants said that being in a relationship was very important and became even more so as they got older. An online survey of more than 450 U.S. lesbians whose median age was 62 showed that 60 percent were in a relationship, most in a lifetime partnership. They said that, over time, their relationships had changed in the direction of "less physical passion and greater emotional maturity"; they had less "drama" than when they were young, but the bonds between them were strong (Averett et al., 2012).

Relationships: Continuity and Change

There is much more to the second half of life than changes in the physical self. Midlife is often a time of major changes in relationships with partners, friends, and family. Children grow up and leave home. Grandchildren are born. A husband may become dependent on his wife for daily help and care, or die unexpectedly. Here we look at some important relationships for women in middle and later life.

Friends and Family

Older women tend to be involved with rich networks of friends and family. Compared to men in the same age group they have more friends and feel closer to their friends (Canetto, 2001). Being connected to other people contributes to healthy aging. In a nationally representative sample of U.S. citizens over the age of 65, those with more diverse social networks of friends, family, religious and community groups were happier, and less lonely, anxious, and depressed, than those with more restricted networks, even when background variables such as health and wealth were controlled (Litwin, 2011; Litwin & Shiovitz-Ezra, 2011).

Close friends may be particularly important for older lesbians; in studies of lesbian and bisexual women in their 60s and older, friends are named as a very important source of support by virtually all the participants (Grossman et al., 2001; Heaphy et al., 2004). Lesbians now in their 70s likely grew up with a history of hiding their sexual orientation and being estranged from their families. They are more likely than heterosexual women of the same age to live alone, and less likely to see family members on a regular basis (Wilkens, 2015), making them more vulnerable to social isolation in old age. Older lesbians tend to solve this problem by relying on "families of choice," and organized social groups that meet on a regular basis (Traies, 2015; Wilkens, 2015).

Consistent with their extended family patterns, African American women are more involved with family than European American women. Older Black women are closer to their adult children and have more frequent contact with them than do older White women. They are also more involved with their grandchildren and may develop a particularly close guiding relationship with a granddaughter (Ralston, 1997).

Fortunately, technology makes it easier to stay in touch with friends and family. Contrary to stereotype, most older adults have positive attitudes toward modern technology. In a nationally representative sample, three quarters of adults in their late 60s reported that they enjoyed using e-mail, social media, instant messaging, smartphones, and video chats, and found them easy to learn (Chopik, 2016). People who used more of these technologies were less lonely and depressed and reported a better sense of overall well-being. Even very old people are going high-tech. In a nationally representative sample of 80- to 93-year-olds, using technology to connect to loved ones was related to higher life satisfaction, lower loneliness, and greater goal attainment (Sims et al., 2016). Communication technologies help keep older adults connected to others—and that's good for their well-being.

Involvement with friends and family has costs as well as rewards. Like the younger women discussed in Chapters 8 and 9, older women provide more care and more different kinds of care for other people than older men do, regardless of whether they also work outside the home (Canetto, 2001). We will return shortly to a discussion of the costs and benefits of care work in later life.

Becoming a Grandmother

The grandmother is one of the few positive images of older women. She is easy to visualize: white haired, kind, and warm, she dishes out homemade cookies, babysits for free, and indulges her grandchildren. A Google search for grandma turns up dozens of sentimental quotes like this one: "Grandmas are moms with lots of frosting."

Adapting to a New Role

Grandparenting gives midlife and older women a meaningful and important place in their families. Grandmothers are often relied on for advice, babysitting, help in a crisis, emotional support, financial assistance, and maintaining family customs and rituals. All these provide an important cushion for young families. For the grandparents, it can be very satisfying to see the family line continue and to once again experience the love of a small child (Scott, 1997) (see Figure 11.5.). However, becoming a grandmother is an involuntary role change. Its meaning, and its effects on women's lives, is more complex than its image suggests.

©Leah Warkentin/Design Pics RF

FIGURE 11.5   The rewards of being a grandmother.

A woman may become a grandmother at any time from her 30s to her 70s. The timing of grandparenthood is an important factor in how women adapt and whether they suddenly feel "old" (Bordone & Arpino, 2016). Younger grandmothers may not be ready:

> When my daughter called me from Florida to tell me I was now a grandmother, I was not in the least elated. I had recently remarried and was seeing myself as a young, passionate lover. I didn't want to think of myself as a grandmother. (Doress-Worters & Siegal, 1994, pp. 139–140)

Because the role expectations for grandmothers are so strong, some grandmothers feel the need to set limits. For example, in a study of middle-age Chicanas, one woman said about being a grandmother, "I love it, but I'm not the kind of grandma where I'm going to sit down and only knit little things." Another said that she would help out when needed, but not "stay home and take care of children so (the daughter) could have a good time . . . grandparents have the right to be free and enjoy themselves when they're old" (Facio, 1997, p. 343). These women recognized that a grandmother's caregiving may be taken for granted, and they chose to define grandparenthood for themselves.

Ethnicity, Social Class, and Grandmothers' Roles

A woman's ethnicity is a key determinant of how she will experience her grandmother role. Among Native American families, the grandmother is the center of the family and the one who holds it all together. Native American women often become grandmothers at a young age, and this transition is seen as even more important than becoming a mother because of the symbolic responsibilities it carries. Relationships between grandmother and grandchildren are characterized as warm and loving, and the grandmother is not just a caregiver but a storyteller and teacher who passes on tribal knowledge to the next generation. In Native American communities, it is not unusual for a child to ask to live with his or her grandparents, and the request is usually granted (John et al., 1997).

In African American communities, too, extended multi-generational families offer scope for grandparental involvement in grandchildren's daily lives. The greater contact and involvement of Black grandparents holds even when socioeconomic status is controlled, implying that it is a cultural difference rather than an economic one (Ralston, 1997). When the Obamas moved to the White House, Michelle Obama's mother, Mrs. Marian Robinson, went with them to help care for the girls (Gibson, 2014).

Due to high rates of divorce and births to single mothers, as well as HIV/AIDS and drug epidemics in working class and minority communities, increasing number of grandparents are taking primary responsibility for grandchildren. Some grandmothers provide full-time day care for working single moms; others take in their grandchildren and raise them, with or without legal custody. Women in ethnic minority groups are much more likely than European American women to have primary responsibility for one or more grandchildren. The most recent U.S. census estimated that 4.9 million children are living in grandparent-headed households, and 2.5 million grandparents have full custody of grandchildren (U.S. Census

Bureau, 2010). Many grandmothers who became full-time caregivers report that it seemed like a nondecision: faced with grandchildren whose parents were incapacitated by drug addiction, physical illness, or mental disability, the grandmother's attitude was "you do what you have to do" (Scott, 1997).

Over 57 percent of grandmother-alone households are poor (Calasanti & Slevin, 2001). Women in this situation have multiple stressors that detract from physical health, emotional well-being, and financial security (Crowther et al., 2015). They report more depression and poorer physical health than other grandparents (Calasanti & Slevin, 2001). Grandmothers bringing up children often mourn their dreams of financial security and freedom in later life. These women are unsung heroes who give to the next generation, often at their own expense. As one 69-year-old African American grandmother stated:

> I love the child and pray God gives me life to see him grow up. . . . he doesn't know the sacrifices I made for him. . . . I don't want him to know; I only want him to know Grandma is here. (Conway et al., 2011, p. 122)

Caregiving: Its Costs and Rewards

Women's care work is not limited to their children and grandchildren. They also provide care to their aging parents and spouses.

Caring for Elderly Parents

There is more and more need for care work for the elderly because their numbers are increasing. According to national surveys, about 17 percent of people over the age of 65 have some form of disability that requires long-term help from others (Brody, 2004). Older people with physical or cognitive disabilities may need assistance with basic personal care, such as getting in and out of bed, bathing, dressing, eating, and toileting, as well as help with life tasks such as cooking, housework, shopping, transportation, and money management.

The great majority of caregivers to the old are women. Women who take responsibility for elderly parents, in-laws, and other relatives are often called "women in the middle" because they are most often in their middle years, they are the middle generation in their families, and they are caught in the middle between the requirements of being a wife, parent, worker, and caregiver (Brody, 2004). They are also in the middle of conflicting values, because they may have jobs, careers, or activities they want to do, yet traditional values still prescribe care work as their responsibility. Their numbers and their problems have been virtually ignored by society until quite recently.

Caring for a Spouse

Because women marry men older than themselves, and men have shorter life expectancies, it is highly likely that the husband in a heterosexual couple, rather than the wife, will receive spousal care during his old age and final illness (Calasanti & Slevin, 2001; Cox, 2005). Our society assumes that old women will be responsible for their even older husbands. The older a married woman is, the more likely she will take on the physical and emotional work of elder care despite health problems of her own.

Lucy's case history is typical of a White, working-class caregiver:

> Her husband is bedridden and his entire care is left up to her. She feels tremendous pressure from this responsibility, and she attributes her heart problems to it. Inadequate finances, approximately $500 a month for the two of them, also contribute to her un-happiness. . . . At 74, Lucy wishes she were still working not just because she needs the money but also because she needs to get out of the house. She told an interviewer that her only trips outside the home were to the doctor, the pharmacy, and the grocery store. "Honey, I haven't been in a store downtown for years." (Calasanti & Slevin, 2001, p. 136)

Caring for an elderly spouse can be heartbreaking when it involves prolonged deterioration of physical or mental abilities. One woman, Sara, spoke of her concerns in a support group for Alzheimer's caregivers:

> Can I ever finally close him out of my life and say, "Well, it's done. It's over. He's gone"? How do I really know that the poor man isn't hidden somewhere, behind all that confusion, trying to reach out and say, "I love you Sara"? (Faircloth, 2003, pp. 217–218)

Lesbian couples have similar experiences of care work as heterosexual couples do, but they may also have to cope with heterosexist treatment that adds to their stress. Getting help for a partner may mean coming out about the relationship, and the partner's relatives may withhold help if they do not approve of the relationship (Hash, 2001).

The Costs of Care Work

Care work takes a toll on a woman's economic security, largely because it's impossible to combine it with full-time paid work. In a national study of elder care, 33 percent of women caregivers had cut back their hours at work, 29 percent had passed up an opportunity for job advancement, 22 percent had taken a leave, and 13 percent took early retirement (Cox, 2005). These decisions lead not only to an immediate loss of income for caregivers, but to lower Social Security and retirement benefits when they themselves get old. A national longitudinal study of women age 59 to 61 assessed how many hours a week they spent caring for elderly parents and, 9 years later, how well they were doing economically (Wakabayashi & Donato, 2006). Women who put in the most hours of caretaking (over 20 hours per week) were more likely to end up living below the poverty level and receiving public assistance such as food stamps. Their caretaking responsibilities had forced them into poverty.

The economic cost of caregiving falls most heavily on women who are poorer to begin with. Other negative effects fall on middle-class and poor alike, affecting the caregiver's psychological well-being, physical health, family relationships, and lifestyle. Symptoms of emotional strain are the most prevalent consequence of being a caregiver. In study after study, caregivers report depression, anger, anxiety, guilt, feelings of helplessness, and emotional exhaustion (Friedemann & Buckwalter, 2014; Unson et al., 2016).

Women often try to enlist others in helping with care work, but with limited success. One husband rigged up buzzers so that his wife could respond immediately whenever his 95-year-old mother called from her upstairs room—but did not offer to respond himself. Another woman, desperately needing a respite, sent her mother to her sister's house for a visit, but reported that "after a couple of weeks, my brother-in-law put her in a taxi back to us" (Brody, 2004, p. 105). Although some family members do share care, it is most often left to a daughter who is perceived as suitable by others—or is the only one who offers. The huge sacrifice on the part of women who take care of the elderly and infirm is largely taken for granted by society.

Why Do Women Do More Care Work?

Given its psychological and economic costs, why do women continue to do care work, even into their old age? Some women who care for spouses or parents say they do the job willingly and that they derive many benefits from it: satisfaction from fulfilling a big responsibility, following religious teachings, expressing their love, and returning care received in the past. As these two daughters express:

> I never regret caring for her. She's the only mother I have. (Brody, 2004, p. 118)

> He (her father) gave me so much and so caringly, and so completely. There's no way there's too much I could be doing. It's not an exchange. He just deserves it. (Brody, 2004, p. 137)

Some psychologists and sociologists have argued that nurturing is central to a woman's identity. Others have said that women have less attachment to their paid work and therefore are freer to do unpaid work. However, research shows that personality makes little difference in who gets assigned care work, and over half of female caregivers keep on working despite their caregiving responsibilities (Martire & Stephens, 2003).

Care work is not just a free choice. Rather, responsibility for caring for others is structured by the gender-based division of labor in families, the devaluing of unpaid work, and the reluctance of society to provide social services for those in need. Paid care is too expensive for most families, and federal funding has been cut back over several decades. As one researcher said, women's lifelong devotion to taking care of others "may seem 'natural' and a 'choice,' but what are the alternatives?" In the words of female caregivers themselves, "Who else is going to do it?" (Calasanti & Slevin, 2001, p. 149).

Loss of a Life Partner

Nearly half of all U.S. women over the age of 65 are widows (Koren, 2016). On average, women live for more than 15 years after their partner's death (Canetto, 2001), but African American women are widowed at a younger age, and live longer portions of their lives as widows than White women do (Williams et al., 2012).

Losing a spouse to death is one of life's most difficult experiences. A Danish study of widowed women and men whose average age was 75 showed that, shortly after the spouse's death, 27 percent of the bereaved partners met the official criteria for post-traumatic stress syndrome (Elklit & O'Connor, 2005). Sadness, loneliness, anguish, and hopelessness are common and a normal part of grieving (Dutton & Zisook, 2005). Although the symptoms of psychological distress decline over time, they may never disappear entirely. One woman in her late 70s said, "Once you have had your husband to fall asleep with for 53 years, it never gets any easier to be alone at night" (Covan, 2005, p. 11).

Women seem to cope with the loss of a spouse better than men do (Koren, 2016). Although they report high levels of emotional pain and distress, they have less severe depression and fewer serious physical health problems than men in similar circumstances. They are less likely to abuse alcohol, suffer a heart attack, or commit suicide following the death of a spouse (Canetto, 2001; Stroebe et al., 2001).

The gender difference in coping with spousal loss may be due to several factors. First, men who lose a wife lose a caregiver, whereas women who lose a husband usually have been providing work on his behalf. Second, women may cope better because widowhood occurs at a younger age than for men and "women expect to spend part of their lives as widows" (Canetto, 2001, p. 187). It is sad but true that almost every woman over 60 knows others her age who have been widowed and to some degree she may mentally prepare for becoming a widow.

Many psychologists believe that women cope better with spousal loss because of their support networks. However, a study that tested this hypothesis using a prospective longitudinal method found surprising results. Measures of the size and quality of participants' social networks were obtained and their well-being was measured before they were widowed and at several time points afterward. If social support helps people adjust to widowhood, those with better networks would be expected to adapt better by returning to their previous levels of well-being over time. Using nationally representative samples from three countries (Germany, Great Britain, and Australia), researchers found no evidence that better social support made losing a life partner any easier for either men or women (Anusic & Lucas, 2014). It may be that a wife or husband is so central to one's social network that all the other people in one's life cannot make up for the absent spouse.

Little is known about partner loss in lesbian couples. Coping with the loss of a lesbian life partner is made more difficult by heterosexism (Cruikshank, 2003). In an online survey of diverse lesbians over the age of 55, most of those who had lost a life partner had experienced legal, financial, or social obstacles because of having been in lesbian relationships (Averett et al., 2011). If the couple has not been out to friends and family, the grief may have to be borne alone. Others do not recognize that the "friend who died" was more than just a friend.

With time, most people who have lost a life partner report that they experience life positively again. In a study of resilience following bereavement (Dutton & Zisook, 2005, p. 884) many participants, like this 54-year-old woman, spoke of how they had coped and what they had learned:

> My experience in losing my precious husband has made me more aware of the beauty in everyday life, the need to share the hurts and joys of others. . . . It sustains me and I look forward to the challenge of each day with an appreciation much keener than before.

Work and Achievement

For women who are socioeconomically privileged, midlife can be a very positive and fulfilling time. Moreover, women in recent age cohorts are likely to be invested in multiple roles as partner, mother, and paid worker, which is associated with better psychological adjustment. Is midlife the prime of life for (some) women?

Women in Their Prime

Several studies have shown that for college educated women midlife typically is a time of self-confidence, achievement, and happiness. A sample of Canadian women between the ages of 45 and 65 described themselves as satisfied with themselves and their accomplishments and optimistic about growing older (Quirouette & Pushkar, 1999). Samples of U.S. women show similar results. For example, in a longitudinal study, women's positive identity and self-confidence in their personal power increased from their 20s to their 60s. A woman's belief that she was contributing to the world and caring for the next generation increased up to midlife and then leveled off (Zucker et al., 2002). This belief is linked to successful aging (Versey et al., 2013).

In another study of college graduates between the ages of 26 and 80, women in their early 50s had the highest life satisfaction. Compared with other age groups, both older and younger, these midlife women had fewer childcare responsibilities, better health, and higher income. They were self-confident and involved in the world (Mitchell & Helson, 1990). The researchers suggested that women's prime time of life is their 50s.

For some women, midlife is a chance to explore new career directions or return to school. Psychological theories of personality development have overlooked this developmental pathway because they have largely been based on a White middle-class male norm (finish school, get a job, work until you retire or die, whichever comes first). For women, the stimulus for making a change varies. For some, the death or serious illness of a friend or family member who is near their own age prompts the realization that time is limited and it is important to make the most of it. For other women, divorce is the catalyst for forging a new path. Still others, relieved of childcare responsibilities for the first time, decide to follow a long-postponed dream:

> All my life I had wanted to be a nurse but instead was a secretary. Finally, at age 57, when the youngest of our children graduated from college, I took a year from the workaday world to attend school and become a licensed practical nurse. I made the highest grade in our class on the state board exam. (Boston Women's Health Book Collective, 1998, p. 552)

Midlife patterns of change vary by socioeconomic class. Women from poor or working-class backgrounds often experience health problems sooner than more advantaged women do, because they do more physically demanding and hazardous work and have poorer health care. For these women, slowing down, not speeding up, may be a major midlife goal (Boston Women's Health Book Collective, 1998). However, for others, education becomes an important means of redefining the self. Some of the most hard-working and dedicated college students are older working class women who are making up for the education they could not afford at 18 (Cruickshank, 2003). Education can be a lifelong process (see Figure 11.6).

Retirement

Psychological theories of men's retirement conceptualize it as a major life change. The retiree's social status, power, and income drop. His daily activities and interpersonal interactions change drastically as he gains large amounts of free time but loses daily contact with coworkers.

FIGURE 11.6   **For some women, midlife is a time to achieve long-postponed goals.**

This model of retirement is a poor fit for women (Canetto, 2001; Duberley et al., 2014). Until quite recently, very few women had the kinds of jobs that provide high status, power, and income. Retirement for women more often meant leaving low-status work and subordinate positions. Furthermore, women, more often than men, make the decision to retire because of events unrelated to work itself: a husband retires and pressures his wife to do so, or someone in the family needs care (Duberley et al., 2014; Duberley & Carmichael, 2016). Many low-income workers must keep working as long as possible to make ends meet. Often, low-income women work "off the books" into their old age, without accumulating pensions or benefits (Cruikshank, 2003).

When women, especially working class women, retire from paid work, their total workload may not change a great deal because of all the unpaid work they do. For a woman who is caring for her elderly parent, cooking and cleaning for her husband, and babysitting for active grandchildren, retiring from her job may make little difference. In fact, her unpaid work may expand. As one woman said in an interview, she liked being retired because "Now I got time to do my work" (Calasanti & Slevin, 2001, p. 130).

Divorced or never-married women tend to work longer than married women, because they cannot afford to retire as early. There has been very little research on retirement among gay and lesbian individuals or couples. In one study, lesbian couples had a lower average income before retirement than gay male, heterosexual married, or heterosexual cohabiting couples (Mock, 2001). Lesbians are more likely to have been continuously employed through their adult years than heterosexual women, but their long years of work may not lead to a financially secure retirement (Kitzinger, 2001).

In media images, retirees are eager consumers of travel and leisure products— healthy, smiling seniors cycling country roads, going on cruises, and sipping wine in outdoor cafes. And it's probably a good idea to keep a positive attitude about it. When researchers measured older adults' stereotypes about retirement, then followed up on them 23 years later, they found that, with objective factors controlled, those with the most positive attitudes had lived several years longer (Ng et al., 2016).

Poverty in Later Life

Women's poverty in old age reflects the accumulation of a lifetime of gender-linked inequities. Women now in old age have earned less than men for their work, and are far less likely to have pensions. They have probably taken time out from paid work to take care of their children (Sugar, 2007). For every year a woman works taking care of her children, her spouse, or her elderly family members, a zero is entered into her Social Security account, unless she has done over 35 years of paid work. "Defining an older woman's caregiving years as 'zero years' is blatant gender discrimination. Women are penalized for doing the work society expects of them" (Cruikshank, 2003, p. 128).

About two-thirds of all poor older adults in the U.S. are women, and the majority of these are ethnic minority women (Schein & Haruni, 2015). Poverty among old women is a problem in less-developed nations due to sex discrimination in education, employment, and access to wealth such as land. However, the United States is alone among industrialized nations in having large numbers of old women living in poverty. In Sweden, France, and the Netherlands, the poverty rate of old women living alone is less than 2 percent; in the United States, it is 17 percent (Cruikshank, 2003; Schein & Haruni, 2015).

Older married women are better off than single or widowed women of the same age because of their partner's economic resources. However, a middle-class woman who is relying on her husband's retirement plan may slip into poverty as she ages. Often, savings are depleted during his final illness. His pension may end with his death, and her Social Security benefits drop.

A woman's social class during her earning years makes a huge difference in the odds that she will be poor in her old age:

> A middle-class professional woman in her twenties can afford to buy an IRA (retirement saving fund) each year, but the woman who cleans her office cannot. Forty-five years later, the former may have accumulated several hundred thousand dollars, the latter nothing. To acquire this wealth, all the first woman has to do is keep breathing. . . . The working-class woman's parents will probably need her caregiving help sooner. . . . In late life, home ownership is often the key to financial security, but when working-class people of color own a home, it may have declining value in an inner-city neighborhood. (Cruikshank, 2003, pp. 116–117)

The plight of old women who are poor is not what anyone would look forward to in the last years of life:

> I try to buy the cheapest things. I always make my own milk from powder. . . . If I need clothes I go across the street to the thrift shop. I watch for yard sales. . . . If I have 80 cents I can go to the Council on Aging for a hot lunch. But the last two weeks of the month are always hard. . . . I'm down to my last $10, and I've got more than two weeks to go. (a woman in her 70s, quoted in Doress-Worters & Siegal, 1994, p. 192)

Will future cohorts of women escape poverty in old age? Economists calculate that even today's working women face a steep climb to save enough money to cover basic living expenses in retirement. According to their computations, women now at the lowest income levels could not save enough no matter how soon they started or how hard they tried. More than one-third of Baby Boomer women will be single when they retire. In 2011, the median net worth of households headed by single women was $22,184, compared to $139,024 for households of married couples (U.S. Census Bureau, 2011). The gap in resources reflects the fact that women's lifetime earnings are still much lower than men's.

Making a Difference

Age is a dimension of life that is both biological and cultural. Physical, psychological, and social factors all interact to define a person's age and its meaning. Although aging and death are inevitable, poor quality of life in later years is not.

Transforming Society: Elder Activism

Because older people are an increasingly large proportion of the population, their political clout is growing. The U.S. Census Bureau predicts that by 2050, there will be nearly 84 million Americans aged 65 and over, almost double the current number. The large Baby Boomer cohort began turning 65 in 2011; by 2050, the surviving Boomers will all be over the age of 85. The aging of the population will have wide-ranging effects on programs such as Social Security and Medicare (Ortman & Velkoff, 2014). It may also affect families, businesses, and pop culture in unforeseen ways.

There are many organizations dedicated to political activism on behalf of people over 60. However, these organizations have sometimes treated the old as a gender-neutral group, ignoring issues of particular concern to women. Women's organizations have often focused on issues crucial to younger women, such as reproductive rights. Moreover, organizations dedicated to women's issues and those dedicated to older people's issues have sometimes failed to connect with each other. Thus, the problems of aging *women* in our society are only beginning to be recognized and addressed.

Activism on behalf of older women and men is likely to increase now that the Baby Boomer cohort has reached retirement age. This cohort grew up with the civil rights movement, the women's movement, and the peace and environmental movements. They are better educated than previous cohorts, they expect a higher standard of living, and they know that "the squeaky wheel gets the grease" when it comes to changing social policy. Moreover, they have a network of organizations already in place to educate and advocate for older people (see Box 11.2).

Transforming Social Interaction: Taking Charge of the Second Half

Among the current cohort of midlife women are some who are envisioning new paths for their later years. Women are more likely to be single, widowed, or divorced at midlife now than in previous cohorts, and such women are realizing that they cannot look forward to a spouse's companionship—or retirement pension—in old age. Some women are choosing to live collectively with other women for companionship, mutual support, and economic benefits. This option builds on one of women's strengths, their lifelong bonds with women friends (Adams, 1997).

BOX 11.2 ❧ Resources for Activism

There are many ways for you to become an activist on behalf of older women. Below are some national organizations committed to the social advancement of women, particularly issues of women's health and well-being later in life.

www.blackwomenshealth.org
Black Women's Health Imperative: An African American health education, research, advocacy, and leadership development institution. This organization is the leading force for health for African American women, promoting optimum health for black women across the lifespan—physically, mentally, and spiritually.

www.graypanthersnyc.org
Gray Panthers: A national organization of intergenerational activists dedicated to changing social policy on issues such as peace, employment, housing, antidiscrimination (ageism, sexism, racism), and family security. Over the years, the Gray Panthers have stopped forced retirement at age 65, exposed nursing-home abuse, and worked toward universal health care.

www.latinainstitute.org
National Latina Institute for Reproductive Health: Works toward the goal of reproductive justice and advancing the health and dignity of Latinas through health advocacy, community organizing and outreach, leadership development, and public policy.

www.justiceinaging.org
Justice in Aging: Provides legal services support for poor senior citizens. Advocates to promote the independence and well-being of low-income elderly and those with disabilities.

www.womenshealth.gov
National Women's Health Information Center: A service of the Office on Women's Health in the Department of Health and Human Services, this website provides an array of women's health information and resources, including minority women's health.

www.nwhn.org
National Women's Health Network: Develops and promotes a critical analysis of health issues to affect policy and support consumer decision making.

www.sageusa.org
Services and Advocacy for Gay, Lesbian, Bisexual and Transgender Elders (SAGE): World's oldest and largest organization devoted to meeting the needs of aging gay, lesbian, bisexual, and transgender elders.

www.owl-national.org
Older Women's League (OWL): A grassroots organization focused exclusively on issues related to women in midlife and later. OWL has more than 60 chapters nationwide and its members conduct research and advocate for economic, social, and health equality for women 40 and older.

Contributed by Michelle R. Kaufman and Annie B. Fox

A *New York Times* article (Gross, 2004) profiled some women who are teaming up for old age. Christine P., a contractor in her 60s, built a house for herself and three friends to share, complete with exercise room and hot tub. Two other women in their mid-60s bought adjoining apartments in a city high-rise, planning to help each other enjoy life as long as they are able. There are no official statistics on how many older women are creating family-of-choice living arrangements, but interest in this option is growing rapidly. Baby Boomer women often have previous experience of communal living and are used to controlling their own lives. Laura Young, executive director of the Older Women's League, commented, "We lived together in dorms and sororities. We shared apartments after graduation. We traveled together. We helped each other through divorce and the death of our parents. Why not take it to the next level?" (Gross, 2004).

At present, the new collective living seems to be largely a middle-class trend. However, activists for the elderly have long pointed out that publicly subsidized housing usually is designed on the assumption that tenant will be either a married couple or a woman living alone. Why not have units for two women, designed with both private and shared space? (Cruikshank, 2003). Because friendship is so important to women, the quality of older women's lives may depend on being able to choose how and with whom they would like to live. The stakes are high, as women seek to avoid isolation and poverty in old age.

Transforming Ourselves: Resisting Ageism

You've probably seen hundreds of ads for creams and cosmetics that claim to halt or reverse aging, but it's hard to find an ad for a workshop or seminar on eliminating ageism (Palmore, 2015). It is one of the least recognized forms of prejudice and discrimination in our society. A review of 58 studies of how to change knowledge and attitudes toward older people among college students found that knowledge can easily be provided through course materials, but the best way to change attitudes is through direct contact with older adults in the community (Chonody, 2015). Often, our social networks are so age-segregated that the only older people students know are their grandparents.

As members of an ageist society, none of us can claim to be completely free of ageism. However, we can try to analyze and resist it. How often do we stereotype old women? When we compliment someone by saying "you don't look your age" the implicit message is that if she did look her age it would be a misfortune. When we praise an older woman for being active or busy all the time, we are forgetting that young people do not have to stay frantically busy in order to be seen as worthwhile people. When you meet a person who says she is retired, do you think she has nothing much to talk about? Do you stay silent when someone uses the word *old* as a putdown?

Even stereotypes that seem positive can be harmful, because they treat all members of the category as if they are alike and set standards for behavior. The media tend to pay attention only to seniors who run marathons or go bungee jumping, implying that older people who are not superbly healthy or incredibly active are somehow not aging successfully. Another positive but perhaps insidious image is the wise elder stereotype. Not everyone who is old is wise! The old, like the young, are individuals. What they want is to define themselves and to have the social support they need in order to thrive. As a society, we owe no less to our elders.

Exploring Further

∾

Cruikshank, Margaret (2003). *Learning to be old: Gender, culture, and aging.* Westport, CT: Greenwood Press.

As its title says, this book puts gender first in its analysis of aging. Its feminist perspective leads to many new insights about women's aging and many concrete suggestions for social change.

Muhlbauer, Varda, Chrisler, Joan C., & Denmark, Florence L. (Eds.) (2015). *Women and aging: An international, intersectional power perspective.* New York: Springer.

Differences in power shape how women age in every culture. This volume brings together a diverse group of researchers on topics such as older women, power, and the body; multiple roles; leadership; sexuality, including older lesbians; and interventions to empower older women.

Positive Aging. www.positiveaging.net

This e-newsletter is coordinated by psychologists Mary Gergen and Kenneth Gergen. It offers summaries of new research on aging and a variety of resources for making the most of the second half of life.

Text Credits

∾

p. 343: Adapted from Öberg, P. (2003). Images versus experience of the aging body. In Christopher A. Faircloth, (Ed.), *Aging bodies: Images and everyday experience* (New York: Alta Mira Press), Figure 4.4 (p. 118). **p. 346:** Öberg and Tomstam, 2001, as summarized in Öberg, 2003. **p. 347:** Cruikshank, M. (2003). *Learning to be old: Gender, culture, and aging.* Lanham, MD: Rowman & Littlefield. **p. 355:** Clarke, L. H., & Griffin, M. (2008). Visible and invisible aging: beauty work as a response to ageism. *Aging & Society*, 28, 653–674. **p. 356**: Roz Chast/The New Yorker Collection/The Cartoon Bank. **p. 360:** Contributed by Annie B. Fox. **p. 363:** Doress-Worters, P. B., & Siegal, D. L. (1994). *The new ourselves growing older.* New York: Simon & Schuster. **p. 365:** Calasanti, T. M., & Slevin, K. F. (2001). *Gender, social inequalities, and aging.* New York: AltaMira Press. **p. 365:** Faircloth, C. A. (Ed.). (2003). *Aging bodies: Images and everyday experiences.* New York: AltaMira Press. **p. 366:** Brody, E. M. (2004). *Women in the middle: Their parent care years* (2nd ed.). New York: Springer. **p. 367:** Canetto, S. S. (2001). Older adult women: Issues, resources, and challenges. In R. K. Unger (Ed.), *Handbook of the psychology of women and gender* (pp. 183–197). New York: Wiley. **p. 367:** Dutton, Y. C., & Zisook, S. (2005). Adaptation to bereavement. *Death Studies*, 29, 877–903. **p. 368:** Boston Women's Health Book Collective. (1998). *Our bodies, ourselves for the new century.* New York: Simon & Schuster. **p. 372:** Contributed by Michelle R. Kaufman and Annie B. Fox. **p. 373:** Gross, J. (2004, February 27). Older women team up to face future together. *The New York Times*, p. A1.

PART 5

∾

Gender and Well−Being

CHAPTER 12

Violence against Women

Annie B. Fox and Mary Crawford

❧

*P*erhaps the clearest demonstration of the worldwide harm done by patriarchal social systems is violence against girls and women. Gender-based violence shares some common features. First, even though it is pervasive, it is very often hidden. Second, it tends to be underreported; statistics on crimes against girls and women are often unreliable and they typically err in the direction of underestimating the problem. In previous chapters we have described female infanticide, gender-linked harassment of girls by peers and teachers (Chapter 6), forced genital surgery or mutilation (Chapter 7), and sexual harassment in the workplace (Chapter 10). In this chapter, we examine other forms of gender-linked violence and describe how violence against women involves all levels of the gender system: cultural, interpersonal, and individual. Let's look at an example of patriarchal violence against women in our own society to see how these levels are linked.

In 2012, a female student at Baylor University was raped twice by a Baylor football player. She reported the rape to the Waco Police, and the football player was arrested for sexual assault. He was eventually kicked off the football team, expelled from the university, and convicted of two counts of sexual assault. Although on the surface it seems as if justice was served, there is much more to the story. When the student, who felt her safety was in jeopardy because the assailant had been a student and he remained in the area, reported the rape to campus police, they told her there was nothing they could do. The student health center and academic services department also told her there was nothing they could do for her. Denied access to resources that would have helped her recover—services that colleges and universities are required by law to provide to victims of sexual assault—the student eventually left the university and enrolled in a community college (Lavigne, 2016).

This was not an isolated incident. Five other women reported that they had been raped or assaulted by the same football player between 2009 and 2012, yet he remained on campus and playing football during that time (Lavigne, 2016). And he wasn't the only Baylor Football player to be accused of sexual assault. In fact, sexual assault complaints against members of the Baylor University football team were quite prevalent—but disturbingly ignored. An independent investigation revealed that between 2011 and 2015, 17 women reported sexual assault or domestic violence perpetrated by 19 different football players, including four gang rapes (Reagan, 2016).

At the broadest level of the gender system, the men who held social and political power at the university—the football coaches and players, as well as top administrators—tolerated a climate that was hostile and dangerous for women. The independent investigation of Baylor's handling of sexual assault cases revealed that football coaches met with victims and their parents, actively tried to discredit them, avoiding reporting incidents, and fostered an environment where football players were treated as if they operated outside the rules, with little to no accountability (Baylor Report). At the interpersonal level, the football players who assaulted their classmates abused the status and power they held as football players, and *as men*. At the individual level, the assaults were traumatizing to the women; being disbelieved, having coaches trying to discredit them, and being denied services to aid in recovery when they did speak up added to the trauma.

Unfortunately, the scandal at Baylor is not an isolated incident. Instead, it is just one of several high profile sexual assault scandals to erupt in the past few years, including cases at the University of Montana (Krakauer, 2015), Stanford University (Chappell, 2016), Vanderbilt (Ellis, 2016), and the University of Tennessee (Andrusewicz, 2016). In fact, sexual violence on college campuses has become so prevalent it has garnered a national-level response (e.g., The Cleary Act; Campus SaVE Act; White House Task Force to Protect Students from Sexual Assault).

How can this kind of violence be stopped? Interventions must encompass all the levels of the gender system. At the end of this chapter, we will return to the case of Baylor University and the larger question of how to end violence against girls and women by intervening at all three levels of the gender system. If you were in charge of solving this problem, which level would be your starting point?

Violence against Girls and Women: A Global Perspective

According to the United Nations (García-Moreno, 2005; UNIFEM, 2007) violence against women is one of most widespread human rights violations across the globe. An estimated 35 percent of women worldwide have experienced physical and/or sexual violence in their lifetimes. In some countries, that number is as high as 70 percent (WHO, 2013; United Nations, 2015). Often, when thinking about violence against women, people focus on the perpetrators or the victims as individuals. However, the pervasiveness of violence against women suggests that its origins and mechanisms lie at the sociocultural level of the gender system.

The Gender System and Violence

Gender-linked violence is often justified, condoned, or overlooked. In virtually every culture, some kinds of violence against girls and women are taken for granted. Some forms of violence, such as stoning women (but not men) for adultery, may be officially permitted by the state; others represent a kind of semiofficial or unofficial terrorism.

Research has documented many examples of the prevalence of gendered violence:

- Globally, 38 percent of female homicide victims were killed by their male partners (WHO, 2013).
- Rape and other violent acts against women are widespread in war zones and refugee camps throughout the world (Kristoff & WuDunn, 2009).
- More than 125 million girls and women alive today have been subjected to female genital mutilation (United Nations, 2015).

Not every woman will experience violence directly but the threat of it is an important part of the fabric of life for all women. Such violence can be seen as a culturally useful way of controlling girls and women. The danger attached to simply being a woman can be seen in the profound negative effects of gender-based violence on women's physical health and psychological well-being. For those who experience it directly, it can lead to not only physical injury, but also chronic pain, disability, unwanted pregnancy, sexually transmitted diseases, depression, anxiety, elevated suicide risk, substance abuse, and post-traumatic stress syndrome (United Nations Development Program , 2014). The inequalities and oppression suffered by women led one expert in public health to state, "Being born female is dangerous for your health" (Murphy, 2003, p. 205).

According to the World Health Organization (WHO), gender-linked forms of violence share an underlying cause: "The lower social status of women and the belief that women are the property of men" (as cited in Murphy, 2003, p. 208). Violence against women is inextricably bound to the social context of male domination and control. The patriarchal view of society gives men a higher value than women. It is taken for granted that men should dominate in politics, economics, and the social world, including family life and interpersonal relationships. This is seen as normal and natural. Violence against women is an assertion of the power and control men have over women (White et al., 2000).

Rape-Prone Societies

The status of women is strongly correlated with rates of violence against women across cultures (Archer, 2006; Vandello & Cohen, 2006). In societies in which women have access to power and resources, there are fewer incidences of violence against women like wife abuse (Rudman & Glick, 2008). In rape-prone societies, the occurrence of rape is high, is connected to expressions of masculinity, and is viewed as an acceptable tool for punishing and controlling women. In contrast, in rape-free societies, rape and sexual aggression are rare because these societies value and respect women and there is relative balance in power between men and women (Sanday, 1981; 1983). As one might predict, there are many more rape-prone societies than there are rape-free societies. Let's look at one rape-prone society as an example.

In South Africa, where women have limited access to power and resources, rape and sexual violence are commonplace. One study found that 40 percent of women reported being sexually assaulted (Kalichman et al., 2005). Additionally, survey studies suggest that nearly one-third of adolescent girls' first sexual experiences involve coerced sex (Jewkes & Abrahams, 2002). Cultural views and social norms connect masculinity to the sexual domination and control of women. Both South African men and women endorse the view that women are expected to be passive and submissive and a significant percentage endorse rape myths that place the blame for sexual violence on women (Kalichman et al., 2005). Because women are expected to be subordinate and men are expected to control relationships, women are unable to refuse sex, ask their partners to use condoms, or to prevent their partners from engaging in multiple sexual relationships, placing them at greater risk for sexual violence and acquiring a sexually transmitted infection like HIV/AIDS. A 2002 study estimates that 13 percent of women in South Africa are HIV positive and the women who have HIV are more likely to experience sexual violence (Shisana & Simbayi, 2002).

'Honor'-based Violence

'Honor'-based violence is another example of violence against women stemming from sociocultural factors. Honor-based violence encompasses any form of violence directed at women as a result of patriarchal family and social values that often tie 'honor' to the regulation and control of women's sexuality (Gill & Brah, 2014). Honor killings occur when a woman's actions are thought to bring shame to her male relatives; dishonor can occur for any number of reasons. The woman may have refused an arranged marriage, may have married outside her religion or caste, or may have been accused of an extra-marital affair. Or, she may have been sexually assaulted or raped. In these instances, honor can be restored only by killing the woman. The U.N. estimates that 5,000 women are murdered each year in honor killings (UNFPA, 2000), a number that likely underestimates the prevalence of honor killings since many go unreported (Solberg, 2009). Honor killings occur in countries all over the world, including Afghanistan, Pakistan, Iran, Egypt, Israel, Lebanon, the United Kingdom, and the U.S. In Pakistan, there were nearly 2,000 honor killings from 2004 to 2007, accounting for nearly one-fifth of all homicides during that time period (Nasrullah et al., 2009).

In many countries where honor killings occur, laws reduce or eliminate punishment for men who kill their wives; other countries have laws that are designed to protect women from violence, but they are ignored (Parrot & Cummings, 2006). In Brazil, men who kill their wives, daughters, or sisters can argue for the "legitimate defence of honour" to avoid punishment. Although such a defense cannot be found in any Brazilian penal code, it is nevertheless used and sometimes successful (Pimental et al., 2006). That honor killings are condoned, ignored, or legally sanctioned by the law enforcement and governments of countries in which they occur demonstrates how embedded the devaluation of women is in many societies.

In countries engaged in armed conflict and war, such as Sierra Leone, Liberia, Sudan, Uganda, and the Congo, mass rape has become a tool of war. *Honor rapes* are designed not only to shame the victim, but to shame her tribe, clan, or ethnic group. Often, the women who are raped have no recourse. If they seek treatment at a hospital or tell the police, they can be thrown in jail for having sex outside of marriage (Kristoff & WuDunn, 2009). A U.N. report estimated that during the Liberian civil war, 90 percent of girls and women over the age of 3 were sexually assaulted (cited in Kristoff & WuDunn, 2009). A former U.N. commander commented that, "It has probably become more dangerous to be a woman than a soldier in an armed conflict" (cited in Kristoff & WuDunn, 2009). Only recently has rape been acknowledged as a war crime. In March 2016, the International Criminal Court at the Hague convicted the former vice president of the Democratic Republic of Congo of crimes against humanity, including rapes committed by his forces while he was in command (UN News, 2016).

Sex Trafficking

The trafficking of girls and women takes place in virtually every country in the world, including the U.S. (Banks & Kyckelhahn, 2011; McCabe & Manian, 2010;

U.S. Department of State, 2016). In Southeast Asia alone, UNICEF estimates that 1 million children are trafficked into commercial sex work each year (Meier, 2000). (See Box 12.1.) This sex trafficking takes many forms. In Thailand, children in urban slums near resort areas may be prostituted to Western tourists who are pedophiles (Montgomery, 2001). In Nepal, rural girls may be lured or sold to traffickers who take them to India to work in brothels where they are held as prisoners (Crawford, 2010). The United Nations has recognized human trafficking, including trafficking for sexual exploitation, as a global problem (United Nations, 2000). It is the third largest criminal activity worldwide, behind drug and weapons trafficking (Crawford, 2016). Yet, accurately estimating the size and scope of the sex trafficking industry remains elusive. Nevertheless, we know that sex trafficking is still a huge and profitable industry. Millions of women and children have been trafficked into the sex trade. Global estimates of the profits associated with the sex trade range from 30 to 50 billion US dollars (Belser, 2005; Kara, 2009). In the U.S., the illegal sex industry in the city of Atlanta, Georgia alone brings in an estimated $290 million a year (Dank et al., 2014).

Patterns of trafficking are shaped by gender-related inequities in material resources (Farr, 2005). In general, countries that are less developed, less wealthy, and less politically stable serve as source countries, from which girls and women are trafficked. Underdeveloped countries such as Nepal and Cambodia as well as industrialized ones with high unemployment, such as the independent states of the former Soviet Union, are where trafficking most often originates. More affluent countries

BOX 12.1 ～ Lek: The Story of a Child Prostitute

Lek grew up in a slum near a tourist resort area in Thailand. Her story, documented in an ethnographic study by anthropologist Heather Montgomery, is one of exploitation from a very early age:

> Lek was introduced to commercial sex at the age of three by Ta, her eight-year-old neighbour . . . She was taken by Ta to meet James, a British businessman . . . Lek . . . remembers watching as Ta was paid to masturbate him. A few weeks later Lek did the same and continued to do so until she began, at the age of six, to have intercourse with him. In return for this, James gave money to Lek's family . . . She has been a prostitute ever since, averaging around twenty men a year, although her most regular source of income is still James. She refuses to call him a client or a customer, referring to him instead as a boyfriend. She also refuses to see him as an exploiter; she says "he is so good to me, how can you say he's bad?"

When I met her, Lek was twelve and pregnant by another of her foreign customers. She gave birth prematurely . . . to a daughter . . . Lek debated putting the child into an orphanage, but eventually decided against it, returning to prostitution as a means of supporting the child. There was no money in the family for the medical expenses of the birth, and so she turned to her cousin Nuk's client, a sixty-year-old Australian called Paul, for help. Paul paid all her medical expenses, and in return she traded sex after she gave birth. Six weeks after the birth, she was back at work as a prostitute . . .

Source: From Heather Montgomery, *Modern Babylon? Prostituting Children in Thailand* (New York: Berghahn Books, 2001), p. 80. Reprinted by permission of the publisher. All rights reserved.

serve as destination sites, where trafficked girls and women are enslaved in brothels or otherwise constrained to participate in prostitution. Some countries are hubs, with venues where women can be bought and sold by multinational traffickers. Hub countries typically have highly developed sex industries (Thailand, the Philippines) and/or powerful organized crime sectors (Albania, Turkey, and Nigeria).

Although extreme poverty often plays a significant role, women and children are vulnerable to trafficking for a variety of reasons, including globalization, social and political instability, war, gender inequality and oppression, and limited choices that make families vulnerable (APA, 2014). In Thailand, for example, some parents allow their children to be sexually abused because the only survival alternative is for the child to work 12-hour days picking through garbage and trash in dumps (Montgomery, 2001). In Nepal, rural poverty, civil war, and lack of educational opportunities make many girls want to head to India despite the risk of ending up in a brothel (Crawford, 2010). Moreover, the HIV/AIDS epidemic has increased the market value of very young girls in many parts of the world, as men seek virginal sex partners to avoid acquiring HIV.

Trafficking is a grave violation of the fundamental human rights of women and girls. There are many testimonies from survivors and their advocates about the misery, pain, and degradation of forced prostitution (Crawford, 2010; Kristoff & WuDunn, 2009; McCabe & Manian, 2010). Although research on the physical and psychological consequences of trafficking is limited, the studies that do exist suggest that survivors are at increased risk of anxiety, depression, post-traumatic stress disorder, sexually transmitted diseases, HIV/AIDS, as well as a wide range of physical problems, including chronic headaches, dizziness, fatigue, and memory problems (APA, 2014; Crawford, 2017). Survivors of sex trafficking may also face difficulties returning home because they have been severely traumatized, and because they are stigmatized for having been in the sex trade.

Efforts to eliminate trafficking include anti-trafficking legislation, educational programs for those at risk and their communities, rescue, shelter, and medical/psychological care for survivors, and prosecution of traffickers. International organizations dedicated to ending the sex trade in children, and the poverty that fuels it, include Oxfam (www.oxfam.org.uk) and the Asia Foundation (www.asiafoundation.org). But it is not just poverty that causes sex trafficking; it is also the devaluation of women and the belief that they are property, not people.

Violence and the Media

We have noted that violence against girls and women is often normalized or even condoned. Often, media coverage of violence participates in this process by de-emphasizing the perpetrator, the violence, or its consequences.

Gender Violence as Entertainment

Both children and adults see gender violence every day on television and at the movies. Unfortunately, the violence portrayed on television often presents an inaccurate picture of the real perpetrators and victims of violent crime. A recent content analysis of crime-based dramas on network television found that White women were more likely to be raped, murdered, or attacked by a stranger on television compared to White men, Black men, and Black women (Parrott & Parrott, 2015). However, national crime statistics show that men are more often the victims of violent crimes such as homicide (FBI, 2015). The prevalence of violence against women on television is designed to scare women and give them the false impression that they are in danger of murder or rape by a stranger. However, the real threat for women may come from someone they know or love.

Children's exposure to violence in the media is a particular cause for concern. The majority of TV programs and video games contain violence, and the violent acts are usually portrayed as trivial, justified, or funny. By the time a U.S. child finishes elementary school, he or she has seen more than 100,000 acts of violence on TV, including 8,000 murders. Thirty years of research have definitively shown that exposure to media violence is related to an increase in aggressive emotions, thoughts, and behavior in children and adolescents (Anderson et al., 2003; Anderson & Carnagey, 2009). Media violence desensitizes people to real violence, and at the same time builds schemas of the world as a dangerous, scary place where a person must be aggressive in order to survive (Fanti et al., 2009; Larson, 2003).

Video games are the newest technology for teaching children to be aggressive. (See Figure 12.1.) Over 85 percent of popular video games in the U.S. and Japan contain some violent content. Many psychologists are concerned that video games have an even greater potential for fostering violence than other forms of media because the child actively participates in the game's violence. Meta-analyses demonstrate that exposure to violent video games is related to increases in aggressive thoughts, beliefs, attitudes, emotions, and behavior, and decreases in socially positive behavior such as helping others (Anderson et al., 2003; Greitemeyer & Mügge, 2014). Longitudinal studies of children and adolescents have found that habitual or sustained playing of violent video games is associated with increases in aggression months and even years later (Anderson et al., 2008; Willoughby et al., 2012). Another recent longitudinal study of teens found that extensive use of aggressive media (such as violent video games) lead to more accepting attitudes toward violence. More accepting attitudes toward violence were then associated with increased incidence of dating violence (Friedlander et al., 2013).

Female characters in video games are rare, but when they do appear, they are often portrayed as promiscuous sex objects or targets of aggression (Burgess et al., 2007; Dill & Thill, 2007). In the top-selling video game series *Grand Theft Auto,* a player can hire a prostitute, engage in explicit and demeaning sex talk, have sex, and then kill the prostitute to get his money back. What effect does engaging in such behavior in video gaming have on attitudes and behaviors toward women? Karen Dill and her colleagues (2008) asked college students to view either sex-stereotypical images of men and women from video games (including *Grand Theft Auto*) or neutral images. They were then asked to read a real-life story involving a complex and ambiguous sexual harassment incident and were asked whether the incident constituted sexual harassment. They found that men who viewed the stereotypical images of women from video games were more tolerant of the sexual

©Andrey_Popov/Shutterstock RF

FIGURE 12.1   Research suggests that when children play violent video games extensively, they may become more aggressive later on.

harassment incident compared to those who viewed neutral images, and that in the long-term, violent video game use was positively associated with rape supportive attitudes (Dill et al., 2008).

When violence against women is treated as a form of entertainment, people may view it as more acceptable and less harmful. It also reinforces the view that women are weak and that it is acceptable to use force to control them. The technological advances in television graphics viewing equipment (e.g., high definition and 3D television) means that the violence against women shown on television is increasingly graphic and vivid. Virtual reality technology is also increasing in popularity, allowing people to immerse themselves in a virtual world. High-tech graphics and virtual reality are meant to enhance the viewing experience, but what effect do they have on people's attitudes toward violence against women, and how do they affect the already established relationship between media violence and aggressive behaviors? These are questions that still need to be addressed.

Pornography

Probably the most controversial of all the depictions of women are those found in pornography. What to do about pornography is a subject of debate among feminist researchers and activists. Some maintain that pornography is a form of violence against women and should be prohibited. Others believe that whether an image is pornographic depends upon the perspective of the beholder: what some consider pornographic, others consider artistic; what some consider morally objectionable or sexist, others defend as free speech. Here, we consider pornography from multiple perspectives.

What Is "Pornography"?

It may seem difficult to pin down exactly what is pornography and what isn't, but sexual images can be distinguished in terms of their potential psychological impacts and social consequences. Social psychological experiments demonstrate that the sexual explicitness of the material does not matter nearly so much as whether the sex is presented in a violent or degrading context. Several scholars therefore suggest that the term *pornography* should be reserved for material that combines sexual themes with violence, dehumanization, degradation, or abuse, whereas material that is merely sexually arousing without these other themes might best be called *erotica* (e.g., Longino, 1980; Russell, 1993; Scott, 2008; Steinem, 1980). In most pornography, *women* are the ones subject to the degradation and abuse. When researchers content analyzed a random sample of 122 scenes from 44 of the most-rented adult videos for 2004 and 2005, they found a total of nearly 1,500 acts of physical or verbal aggression, 87 percent of which were directed toward women (Sun et al., 2008).

Pornography Is Pervasive

In the past 3 decades, pornographic images of women have become *much* more available to all citizens in the U.S. male and female, adults and children. The porn industry grew dramatically starting in the 1990s, due primarily to the popularity of adult videos, the availability of subscription cable TV, and the growth of the Internet. Internet porn is prolific. Out of the one million most popular websites in 2010, 4.2 percent were classified as pornography, and from 2009–2010, about 13 percent of internet searches were for pornography (Ogas & Gaddam, 2011). Pornography websites receive more unique monthly hits than popular sites such as Amazon, Netflix, and Twitter (*Huffington Post*, 2013). Researchers estimates that, 250 million people will soon be using their mobile phones and tablets to access adult content on the web (Juniper Research, 2013).

As the pornography industry has flourished, it has had a tangible influence on U.S. popular culture. Pornography has been mainstreamed in unprecedented ways. Advertisers use themes from porn to sell mundane objects such as wristwatches and jeans, and porn stars are recruited to hawk products such as athletic shoes. References to porn and appearances by porn stars are increasingly common on prime time TV and in Hollywood films (Farrell, 2003). Perhaps the most striking evidence of the mainstreaming of pornography is the abundance of Internet "tube" channels featuring an enormous variety of sexually explicit videos uploaded by amateurs as well as pros (Hyde & DeLamater, 2017).

Is Pornography a Form of Violence against Women?

Those feminists who believe that porn should be restricted argue that pornographic images are of particular concern not just because they portray sexual violence but also because of the ways that the creation and use of pornography are intimately linked to actual violence against women. Many of the blatantly violent pornographic images of women from recent years are not merely "images" but are *documentation* of actual sexual violence or humiliation. Women in these pictures may have volunteered for such treatment in exchange for money or other rewards, but according to first-hand accounts, some may have been coerced. For example, it is difficult to believe that images of women being burned by cigarettes, slashed with knives, forcibly penetrated by objects such as vacuum cleaner hoses, covered in excrement, etc., were produced with women's eager consent (Russell, 1993).

Women involved in the making of porn are not the only ones hurt by it. We know from experimental research that pornography, more so than erotica, has at least temporary negative effects on men's attitudes and behaviors toward women. Sexually violent or degrading images, explicit or not, increase men's dominant behaviors toward and objectification of women, their belief in rape myths, and their acceptance of violence against women, and lowers their support for sexual equality (e.g., Linz et al., 1987; Mulac et al., 2002; Wright & Tokunaga, 2016). For practical and ethical reasons, experimental research cannot be used to test the relationship between pornography and violence against women in the real world; however, correlational studies support the link. Meta-analyses of non-experimental studies have found positive associations between men's use of pornography and their attitudes supporting violence against women (Hald et al., 2010) as well as their likelihood of committing acts of sexual aggression (Wright et al., 2015). In interviews with battered women, researchers have found that 40 to 60 percent of the abusers used pornography and tried to force their victims to act out violent scenes from it (Cole, 1987; Cramer & McFarlane, 1994; Sommers & Check, 1987).

We cannot conclude from this research that pornography *causes* male violence against women, but it is clear that pornography is associated with sexual violence and that it can provide sexually arousing behavioral scripts for men with aggressive impulses. When men masturbate to pornography, they may be conditioning their bodies to respond pleasurably to violence against women (e.g., Reed, 1994; Seto et al., 2001).

Among all the popular media images of women in our culture, some feminists believe that pornographic ones are potentially the most damaging. Jensen (2007) argues that pornography reflects and perpetuates how our society views women: as objects for men to sexually dominate. On the other hand, there are feminists who want to keep a clear distinction between words or images and actions. Some feminists argue that censoring pornography could lead to the censorship of women in general. Historically, women were denied information related to their own sexuality in the name of "protecting" them. Treating pornography as obscenity and therefore censoring it is a slippery slope that could lead to the censorship of any material that anyone finds offensive, such as lesbian erotica or woman-focused sex education.

Not all pornography is consumed by heterosexual men. Heterosexual women, lesbians, and gay men also purchase and use pornography. Some fear that because of disagreements about where to draw the line, attempts to censor porn could lead to denying people access to material that they find interesting, enjoyable, and related to their normal, healthy sexual expression. According to this view, pornography can help women interested in sexual experimentation. Moreover, some couples use pornography to stimulate consensual sexual activity.

The feminist debate over the porn problem is unlikely to be resolved any time soon. There are convincing arguments on both sides. However, the debate is productive if it keeps people on both sides engaged in thinking critically about the depiction of women in erotic and pornographic media.

Violence and Social Media

According to one recent study, approximately 75 percent of teens have or have access to a cell phone, and 92 percent of teens report going online daily, mostly from their mobile devices (Lenhart, 2015). The ubiquity of cell phones and our instantaneous access to the Internet has changed the landscape of how children, teens, and adults communicate with one another. Although there are a number of benefits to the connectivity provided by these technological advances, there is also a downside. Social media has become a tool for harassment and bullying, and the ease with which photos and videos can be shared means that material that was once private can be quickly distributed to millions of people at the push of a button.

"Sexting," or sending sexually explicit photos or videos of oneself via text message or email, has become increasingly common among teens and adults. Research on sexting is limited. However, a descriptive study of college students' use of sexting found that more than three quarters of participants had sent sexually explicit text messages to a relationship partner, and between one-third and one-half of the sample had sent sexual pictures or videos (Drouin et al., 2013). Another study of college-aged students found that while 30 percent of those who had sexted did so voluntarily, more than 50 percent reported they felt pressured or coerced at least some of the time, and 12 percent said they always felt pressured or coerced to send sexts (Englander, 2015). Pressured sexters were more likely to be female, and to be sexting a potential boyfriend (Englander, 2015).

One of the dangers of sext messages is that they can easily be forwarded to a much larger audience than originally intended. Two studies of teenagers found that 25 to 30 percent of those surveyed had forwarded nude photos they received to others (Englander, 2014, Strassberg et al., 2013). In some cases, the photos or videos are posted online as a form of ***non-consensual pornography***. Non-consensual pornography is the distribution of sexually explicit material without the permission of the person featured in the photos or videos. When such images are distributed online as payback for ending a relationship, it is referred to as revenge porn. Names, addresses, and other personal information may be published alongside the sexual material, subjecting the victim to further harassment. For example, in one case, a woman found out that her ex-boyfriend had posted nude photos of her, along with her full name, phone number, street, and town on an X-rated website. Her photos and identifying information were posted alongside an invitation to contact her for oral sex (Talbot, 2016a). In another case, a woman's ex-boyfriend created fake social media, escort, and porn site profiles for her, publishing her face next to pictures of vaginas. If that wasn't enough, he included that she "enjoyed gang bangs" and had sexually transmitted diseases (Talbot, 2016a). Although both men and women can be victims of non-consensual pornography and revenge porn, women and girls are disproportionately affected (Cyber Civil Rights Initiative, 2014).

Because material on the Internet spreads quickly, it can be extremely difficult to have non-consensual pornography fully removed. Even after a victim spends hundreds of hours scouring the Internet and sending legal take-down notices, the images and information can still pop-up on other websites. Victims of non-consensual pornography may find their lives upended. They may fear their friends, family, or employer may find the images. They may experience psychological distress, including depression, anxiety, or social withdrawal. They may also fear for their personal safety when their names and addresses have been published online.

In 2013, only three states had laws against non-consensual pornography. However, that number has risen substantially in just three years. In 2016, 34 states and the District of Columbia now have revenge porn laws. Additionally, the Intimate Privacy Protection Act was recently introduced to Congress. This act would make it a federal offense to distribute revenge porn, punishable by up to 5 years in federal prison (Franks, 2016).

Violence against Children

Violence against girls and women can occur at any phase of life and in virtually any setting. Here we examine violence against children that takes place largely within family relationships.

Child Sexual Abuse

Childhood is not always a time of toys and books, safety and security, and a loving Mom and Dad. Because they are small and dependent on others, children are vulnerable to victimization and exploitation by adults. It is unfortunately true that some children learn far too young "the major lesson of patriarchy: The more powerful control the less powerful" (White et al., 2001).

A significant minority of children experience *childhood sexual abuse,* defined as coercive sexual interaction between a child and an adult. According to 2014 data from the National Child Abuse and Neglect Data System, 8.3 percent of suspected abuse reports involved the sexual abuse of a child. Additionally, national and international studies have shown that girls are more likely to be abused than boys (Barth et al., 2013; White et al., 2001). In one such sample of adults, 27 percent of women and 16 percent of men reported that they had experienced sexual abuse as children; in another sample of young people aged 10 to 16, 15 percent of girls and 6 percent of boys reported a history of abuse. It is likely that over one-quarter of U.S. women have experienced sexual abuse during childhood (Gazmarian et al., 2000). Tragically, children, and particularly girls, are most often abused by someone they know and trust. Family members and acquaintances are responsible for almost 90 percent of child rapes. Older relatives, brothers, and the child's own father or stepfather are the leading abusers of girls within the family (Laumann et al., 1994).

Who is most at risk for child sexual abuse? Any child can be abused, and there seem to be few differences in rates of abuse among various ethnic and racial groups. Rather, there are particular kinds of families that provide a context in which abuse is likely. Abusive families are most often emotionally distant and unaffectionate. They tend to be strongly patriarchal: Father is the head of the household, Mother is subservient, and children are taught to obey without question. Finally, they are families with a lot of conflict among family members (White et al., 2001).

Before the abuse starts, the perpetrator may gradually earn the child's love and trust by treating her as special. The perpetrator may buy her toys, tuck her in at night, or take her out for treats. He may increase his inappropriate contact gradually, for example proceeding from tucking in, to touching and patting the child's back, to sexual touching. By the time the child realizes that the behavior is sexual and wrong, it is already part of an established pattern. After each abusive episode, he may apologize and promise it will never happen again. However, the loving, apologetic behavior gives way to another period of building the child's trust, and then to more sexual transgressions, in a cycle of abuse. Because the abuser has power and authority over the child, and may even live in the same home, the child may feel overwhelmed, with nowhere to turn to for help. Living in a patriarchal, authoritarian family, the victim of childhood sexual abuse may be emotionally neglected and afraid to question the power and authority of adults. Under these conditions, the perpetrator may succeed in convincing the child that their relationship is a special, loving secret, rather than the crime and betrayal of trust it is (White et al., 2001).

Sexual abuse may negatively affect many aspects of a child's emotional, cognitive, and social development. For example, the child may show seemingly irrational emotions like fear of the dark, of going to bed at night, or of being alone. Later, the child may experience depression and withdrawal. Behavioral responses include problems in school, bedwetting, nightmares, and, later, running away from home or becoming sexually active at an early age. In adulthood, abuse survivors may have impaired relationships with intimate partners, be at increased risk for intimate partner violence, and experience lower relationship satisfaction (Daigneault et al., 2009; Walker et al., 2009). A research review found that survivors of childhood sexual abuse are more at risk for depression, anxiety, eating disorders, sexual dysfunction, personality disorders, and substance abuse (Mangiolio, 2009). They are also at increased risk for suicidal ideation, suicide attempts, and completed suicide (Devries et al., 2014; Miller et al., 2013).

In a study of adult survivors' recovery narratives, some survivors noted that while they felt recovery was possible, actual healing was not. Take the following quotation from one survivor:

> I don't think you can ever be healed. If you were in an accident and your right arm was cut off, you're never going to get that arm back, but you will learn to go on and manage. It doesn't mean that you can't have a good life. It's just that it's always going to be there. (Anderson & Hiersteiner, 2008, p. 418)

Healing was associated with being cured or made whole again—something these survivors did not think was possible. Instead, their recovery was advanced through disclosure, supportive relationships, and trying to make meaning of their experiences (Anderson & Hiersteiner, 2008). A study of survivors who managed to function well as adults showed that these women had developed coping strategies that kept them from giving in psychologically to the abuse. They dreamed about the future and immersed themselves in school achievements or creative activities such as writing in order to cope with their pain (DiPalma, 1994). Despite attempts to develop coping strategies, the majority of adult women who have survived childhood abuse say that it has significantly affected their entire lives (Laumann et al., 1994).

How Can Abuse of Children Be Ended?

In the U.S. many schools now sponsor programs to teach children that they have the right not to be touched inappropriately and encourage them to tell an adult if someone acts in a sexual way toward them (Wurtele, 2002). However, these programs have limitations because they place the responsibility for prevention largely on the child. Other programs designed to end child abuse focus on educating parents and families, as well as the community at large. The Child Abuse Prevention Association (www.capacares.org) operates a national child abuse/neglect hotline and promotes a variety of family support and counseling services. They offer a program for families that teaches effective communication skills, and they also provide an in-home assessment and intervention for families that are at high risk for violence. As children progress through the school system, teachers and school officials need to be attuned to signs and symptoms of potential abuse. Identifying and ending abuse early in childhood may improve outcomes for victims as they get older. As we have seen, abusers play on the cognitive limitations and emotional vulnerability of their child victims, whose minds may become even more traumatized than their bodies. Childhood sexual abuse is a form of exploitation that no child should have to endure.

Violence in Intimate Relationships

Overall, men are more likely to be victims of violence from the hands of strangers, and women are much more likely to be victims of violence at the hands of friends, lovers, acquaintances, and family members.

Here we look at verbal, physical, and sexual aggression in relationships. When physical aggression and violence occur in a relationship, it is often referred to as *intimate partner violence* (IPV). IPV occurs in all types of intimate relationships, including those in which the partners are dating or married.

Dating Violence

Dating and romantic relationships can provide a host of valuable experiences such as intimacy, companionship, sexual experimentation, and learning how to negotiate conflicts and differences (White et al., 2001). However, there is another, less positive side to many dating relationships. Relationship problems can lead to anger, frustration, and confusion. Unfortunately, violence is an all-too-common means of exerting control in sexual encounters and romantic relationships.

Dating violence is a pervasive problem. It is so common that virtually everyone has witnessed a couple screaming, arguing, or yelling ugly names at each other, or one partner sulking resentfully or stomping off in a huff. In national U.S. surveys, over 80 percent of college students say they have been on the sending or receiving end of this kind of verbal aggression within the past year. Moreover, over one-third reported having engaged in physical aggression during the same time period: grabbing, shoving, throwing something, or hitting. The rates are similar for women and men, across different ethnic groups, regions of the country, and types of colleges and universities.

Some studies have shown that women are more likely to initiate aggression against their partners than vice versa (Archer, 2000; Capaldi et al., 2012). However, qualitative research on women's initiation of partner violence found that although women said they initiated violence more than their partners, there was a lot of variability in how women defined "initiation." For some, it was getting angry or upset, bringing up a conflict, or trying to get their partner to talk about something repeatedly (Olson & Lloyd, 2005). Gender stereotypes define women as the caretakers of relationships. Therefore, women may feel responsible when violence or aggression occurs in their relationships and thus respond affirmatively when asked if they initiated the violence. However, when delving deeper into how women conceptualize initiation, it is clear that women's so-called initiation of violence may be anything but violent.

Although women and men report similar rates of aggression, their motives tend to be different. For men, staying in control is often an important relationship goal (Lloyd, 1991). Men are more likely to say that they aggress in order to intimidate and frighten the partner and control the relationship, while women say that they do so in self-defense or because they lost control of themselves (Campbell, 1992). Another motive for women's aggression is sensitization to the possibility of harm. Women who have experienced aggression in the past—for example, those who witnessed parental violence or were in a prior abusive relationship—may be primed to respond to aggression with more aggression, and even to initiate violence (White et al., 2001).

Is it possible to predict whether a partner is likely to be violent? Studies show a consistent pattern of characteristics in violence-prone men and women. For both men and women, financial and parental stress are associated with perpetration of IPV (Capaldi et al., 2012). For men, the characteristics are related to a need for dominance and control. Violent men are quick to anger and have used violence to get their way in the past. They believe that violence helps win arguments and that violence against a partner is justifiable. They do not hold benevolent and protective beliefs about women. They are likelier than other men to use drugs, have divorced parents, and to be undergoing life stress. For women, the predictors are somewhat different: a history of child abuse, as well as anxiety, depression, low self-esteem, and drug and alcohol use, all increase the likelihood of being aggressive (Capaldi et al., 2012; Sullivan et al., 2005;

White et al., 2001). However, there are some gender similarities: for both women and men, the single biggest predictor of aggressive behavior is having an aggressive partner. Truly, violence begets more violence.

The consequences of dating violence are more severe for women than for men. Women report more fear in violent situations, and they are three to four times as likely to sustain major emotional trauma and serious physical injuries due to dating violence than are men (Makepeace, 1986; Sugarman & Hotaling, 1989). Women who have experienced IPV are more likely to report having diabetes, gastrointestinal symptoms, as well as pain, respiratory, and cardiovascular disorders (Dillon et al., 2013). The psychological effects can spread to virtually every area of life, affecting emotional states (hyperarousal, anxiety, depression), cognitive functioning (lack of ability to concentrate and poor performance in school or at work, memory loss), and identity (low self-esteem) (Dillon et al., 2013). Dating violence also is associated with risk of unwanted pregnancy, substance abuse, suicide, eating disorders, and high-risk sexual behaviors (Hanson, 2002; Silverman et al., 2001). In sum, being on the receiving end of dating violence can disrupt a woman's healthy development in many serious ways.

Stalking

Another way in which psychological or physical violence can manifest in interpersonal relationships is through stalking. Generally, *stalking* refers to repeated, unwanted harassing behaviors where the victim feels threatened or fearful (Sptizberg & Cupach, 2014). Contrary to media portrayals involving a crazed stranger pursuing a celebrity, approximately 80 percent of stalking cases involve perpetrators and victims with past romantic relationships (Spitzberg & Cupach, 2007). Stalking often involves the desire for an intimate relationship, although this is not always the case. When relationship motives are present, stalking behaviors are sometimes referred to as *unwanted pursuit behaviors (UPBs)*. Unlike stalking, UPBs do not necessarily involve the victim feeling fearful or threatened (De Smet et al., 2015). Stalking and UPBs range from less severe behaviors such as phone calls, text messages, or sending unsolicited gifts, to more serious and threatening behaviors, including threatening physical harm, damaging property, or even kidnapping.

Estimates of the frequency of stalking victimization vary based on the sample (e.g., college students versus general public) and how stalking is defined (i.e., whether fear or threat is included in the definition). Regardless of the definition or sample, women are more likely to be victims of stalking compared to men (Lyndon et al., 2012). A comprehensive meta-analysis found that 28.6 percent of women and 13.9 percent of men had been the victim of stalking (Spitzberg et al., 2010). While stalking victims are more likely to be women, stalking perpetrators are more likely to be men. The most recent meta-analysis of stalking perpetration found that nearly 24 percent of men had engaged in stalking behavior, compared to only 12 percent of women (Spitzberg et al., 2010).

As technology has advanced, so too have the ways and methods in which stalking occurs. *Cyberstalking* involves repeated, unwanted and unwelcome pursuit behaviors that take place virtually with the use of computers and other electronic devices like cell phones (Reyns, Henson, & Fisher, 2012). Text messaging, social media, and even GPS tracking apps can all be used for stalking. Research on cyber-stalking is limited, but growing. The only national-level study of cyberstalking found that 26 percent of those surveyed had experienced cyberstalking, and nearly 8 percent reported they had been monitored electronically (Baum et al., 2009).

Because stalking victims often live under constant stress, they may experience a range of negative physical and psychological effects. Women who have been stalked may experience anxiety, depression, suicidal ideation, post-traumatic stress, headaches, or difficulties with sleeping and eating. They may become hypervigi-lant, isolating themselves from family and friends. They may need to move to a new city or state or find a new job. Family members and friends may also be affected or even targeted, especially when the stalker views them as a threat. Clearly, stalking can have detrimental effects on all aspects of women's lives.

Sexual Coercion and Acquaintance Rape

Rape is defined as sexual penetration without the person's consent, obtained through force or threat of harm, or when the person is incapable of giving consent (Bachar & Koss, 2001). The more general terms *sexual assault* and *sexual coercion* include other kinds of unwanted sexual contact (such as groping and fondling) (White et al., 2004). Here, we examine sexual coercion within relationships.

According to data from the National Intimate Partner and Sexual Violence Sur-vey, nearly 20 percent of women are estimated to have been raped during their lifetimes, and almost 44 percent have experienced other forms of sexual violence, such as sexual coercion or unwanted sexual contact (Breiding et al., 2014). The Association of American Universities (AAU) recently conducted one of the largest survey studies of campus sexual assault to date (Cantor et al., 2015). They found that about one third of college senior females had experienced at least one incident of non-consensual sexual contact during their college years, and about half of those incidents were forced penetration. Unfortunately, one-third of victims who experi-enced forced penetration—rape—did not report because they felt nothing would be done about it, and 35.9 percent did not report because they felt "embarrassed, ashamed or that it would be too emotionally difficult" (Cantor et al., 2015).

Most unacknowledged rapes are committed by someone known to the victim.

> Lenore stopped by her boyfriend's apartment to hang out, but her boyfriend wasn't there. His roommate, a foreign exchange student, invited her in to wait for her boy-friend and then suggested that they watch a sex video. Lenore felt uncomfortable but thought that maybe he did not know how to act around American girls and did not want to embarrass him. She said no to the sex video by changing the subject. Then he pro-ceeded to kiss and fondle her, although she said that her boyfriend might come back and that she wasn't interested in him in that way. He forced her to have sex on the couch and then held the door open for her to get up and leave. Lenore did not think she had been raped but she knew that she felt terrible because she had not wanted to have sex. (From an account told to me by an anonymous student, with her permission.)

Sexual assault by a dating partner or someone known to the victim is termed *acquaintance rape.* Most of the public thinks of rape in terms of a stranger jumping out of a dark alley but acquaintance rape occurs far more often than stranger rape. Like other forms of violence against women, it has largely been a hidden crime (Parrot & Bechhofer, 1991). Acquaintance rape is fostered by sexual scripts that encourage women to be passive and offer token resistance. This encourages men to take the initiative physically and ignore a woman's refusals.

In one study, about 20 percent of college students reported experiences of sexual coercion, such as this one where the woman was too impaired to give consent:

> We were drunk. I didn't have control over myself & I didn't have the cognitive ability to say NO. I can't remember everything, but I know we had sex and if I were sober it would not have happened. I just could not control myself at all. (Kahn et al., 2003, p. 241)

Women also commonly reported giving in to unwanted sex because a partner would not stop begging, whining, and pleading: "If he was really in the mood and I wasn't, he couldn't take no for an answer. We would just argue and argue about it until I gave in . . ." (Kahn et al., 2003, p. 240). Even though some of the women's experiences qualified as rape, a woman was likely to use that term only if the man had used force and intimidation or if she woke up to find him sexually penetrating her. If the woman was too drunk to consent, she was less likely to call the incident rape. Some feminists argue that using the label rape is important; without it, the incident is not recognized as a crime, and goes unreported and unpunished. Moreover, the woman is unlikely to get the help and support she needs. Others point out that a woman's choice of label may be part of how she copes with sexual assault, and she has the right to define her own experience (Kahn et al., 2003). The difficulty of defining and labeling rape may partly be due to the way our society defines normal heterosex to include some degree of male aggression and subtle coercion (Gavey, 2005).

Many studies have shown that victims of sexual coercion, like victims of other kinds of violence, suffer psychological consequences in such areas as emotional functioning (anxiety, phobias, and depression), social relations (loss of trust and sexual dysfunction), and identity (lowered self-esteem). The physical aftereffects include injuries sustained during the rape, unwanted pregnancy, and infection with an STI. The victim may also suffer from physical effects of trauma and anxiety, such as nightmares and inability to sleep. The psychological effects of rape are more severe when the assailant is an acquaintance or boyfriend than when he is a stranger, because the acquaintance rape violates not only the woman's body but also her trust. When the woman knows her rapist, she is also more likely to blame herself for what happened (Katz, 1991). The physical, emotional, and psychological aftereffects of rape interact with each other to impair the woman's ability to function, sometimes very severely (Koss & Kilpatrick, 2001).

In March of 2016, former Stanford University student Brock Turner was convicted of sexually assaulting an unconscious 23-year old woman behind a dumpster. The judge who sentenced Turner to only 6 months in jail (of which he had only to serve 3), justified the light sentence by saying that prison would have a "severe impact on him." However, the impact statement given by the victim at the time of sentencing describes in detail the dramatic ways in which her life has been forever altered (by what Turner's father dismissively called "20 minutes of action"). She stated,

"My damage was internal, unseen, I carry it with me. You took away my worth, my privacy, my energy, my time, my safety, my intimacy, my confidence, my own voice, until today . . . My independence, natural joy, gentleness, and steady lifestyle I had been enjoying became distorted beyond recognition. I became closed off, angry, self-deprecating, tired, irritable, empty (Baker, 2016)."

In her statement, she also describes the ways in which she felt re-victimized during the trial, as every detail of her personal life and actions that night were questioned and dissected. One of the reasons so many women decide not to pursue legal action when they have been raped or assaulted is just this—they fear being made to relive the experience or having the assault recast as their fault.

Who is likely to inflict coercive sex? Unfortunately, there is no easy way to spot a potential rapist in advance, because most men who commit acquaintance rape look and act much like other men. However, certain factors in a man's background, personality, and social setting have been associated with sexual aggression toward women. Background factors include coming from a violent or abusive family, getting into trouble with the authorities as a teen, and being exceptionally sexually active at a young age. Personality factors include impulsivity, a need to dominate women, and low self-esteem. Factors in the social environment include involvement in a sports team or fraternity, alcohol use, exposure to pornography, and having friends who encourage sexual conquests and objectification of women (Frintner & Rubinson, 1993; Koss & Gaines, 1993; Seto et al., 2001; White & Koss, 1993).

Rape myths also play an important role in coercive sex. *Rape myths* are widely held, stereotypical, false beliefs about rape, rape victims, and rapists that perpetuate and normalize male sexual violence against women (Brownmiller, 1975; Burt, 1980; Lonsway & Fitzgerald, 1994). They provide powerful cultural messages about victims and perpetrators of sexual assault. The idea that all women secretly desire to be raped, that women "ask for it," and that women are responsible for rape if they were drunk or dressed provocatively, are all examples of rape myths (see Box 12.2). Rape myths justify male sexual aggression as natural, minimize sexual assault, and encourage victim blaming (Lonsway & Fitzgerald, 1995).

Men tend to endorse rape myths more than women (Aosved & Long, 2006; Hayes, Lorenz, & Bell, 2013; Hayes, Abbott, & Cook, 2016) and men who endorse rape myths are more likely to endorse a proclivity to rape (Ben-David & Schneider, 2005). Additionally, rape myth endorsement is associated with higher levels of oppressive and intolerant attitudes, including hostile sexism, racism, homophobia, ageism, classism, conservatism, and right-wing authoritarianism (Aosved & Long, 2006; Chapleau et al., 2007; Hockett et al., 2009). Rape myths also serve a purpose for women. They may provide a sense of control because they suggest that there are actions that women can take to avoid being raped. For example, one common rape myth is that women who dress provocatively are asking to be raped. Because what a woman wears is up to her, she presumably has the power to choose more conservative clothing, and hypothetically reduce her risk of being raped. Unfortunately, although women's endorsement of rape myths might provide a sense of control, there is no evidence that it would reduce their risk, and rape myth acceptance makes it easier to blame women who are raped.

BOX 12.2 ∽ Research Focus
Measuring Attitudes about Rape

Researchers have designed a number of scales to measure the extent to which people endorse rape myths. One of the more popular scales is the *Illinois Rape Myth Acceptance Scale,* which contains either 45 items (long form) or 20 items (short form). Items in the scale represent seven broader rape myths. Below are a few items from the scale and the broader rape myth they represent (in italics).

1. If a woman is raped while she is drunk, she is at least somewhat responsible for letting things get out of control. *She asked for it.*

2. Although most women wouldn't admit it, they generally find being physically forced into sex a real "turn-on." *She wanted it.*

3. If a woman is willing to "make out" with a guy, then it's no big deal if he goes a little further and has sex. *Rape is a trivial event.*

4. If a woman doesn't physically fight back, you can't really say that it was rape. *It wasn't really rape.*

5. Men from nice middle-class homes almost never rape. *Rape is a deviant event.*

6. Rape accusations are often used as a way of getting back at men. *She lied.*

7. Men don't usually intend to force sex on a woman, but sometimes they get too sexually carried away. *He didn't mean to.*

Source: Payne, D. L., Lonsway, K. A., & Fitzgerald, L. F. (1999). Rape myth acceptance: Exploration of its structure and its measurement using the *Illinois Rape Myth Acceptance Scale. Journal of Research in Personality, 33,* 27–68.

Contributed by Annie B. Fox.

Rape myths also have implications for how victims feel about themselves and what happened to them. An analysis of victim narratives from a national crime survey found that 20 percent of the narratives contained at least one rape myth (Weiss, 2009). For example, women blamed themselves for the incident or justified it by saying that male sexual aggression is natural. Rape myths are so much a part of our cultural understanding of sex that even victims themselves use them to understand their experiences. Unfortunately, as long as women blame themselves instead of the perpetrator and hesitate to report the crime, sexual coercion remains acceptable.

Violence in Long-Term Relationships

Millions of women around the world have been subjected to violence from their male partners—husbands, boyfriends, cohabiting partners, and ex-partners. According to a report published by the UN, the number of women who had ever been physically or sexually assaulted by a partner ranged from 6 percent (Comoros) to 64 percent (Democratic Republic of the Congo) United Nations, 2015. A generic term for this abuse, used by sociologists as well as law enforcement personnel, is "domestic violence." However, this seemingly gender-neutral term obscures the fact that by far the most serious "domestic" violence is perpetrated by men against women.

Abuse by a partner is one of the most frequent causes of physical injury for women across cultures (United Nations Children's Fund, 2000). In the U.S. researchers estimate the lifetime prevalence of physical violence by an intimate partner is 31.5 percent, with 22.3 percent of women experiencing at least one act of severe physical violence in their lifetimes (Breiding et al., 2014). Rates in Europe are similar to the U.S. (European Union Agency for Fundamental Rights, 2014), and rates in Africa, Asia, and Latin America are even higher with estimates in the range of 13–62 percent (WHO, 2012). Statistics probably underestimate the actual incidence of partner abuse, which tends to be underreported due to shame, fear, and the belief that nothing will be done about it (Ellsberg et al., 2001). Additionally, women with physical or mental disabilities may be more susceptible to violence in relationships (Brownridge, 2009). One study found that 68 percent of the disabled women who were sampled reported at least one instance of abuse (physical, emotional, or sexual) in the past year (Curry et al., 2009). Using self-reported data, a World Health Organization study found that worldwide, women who reported experiences of partner violence also reported overall poorer health (Ellsberg et al., 2008). In the U.S. between one-third and one-half of all women seen in hospital emergency rooms have been injured by their husband or boyfriend (Warshaw, 2001). Clearly, the impact of violence against women by intimate partners is a worldwide public health problem.

Physical violence against a partner is almost always accompanied by psychological abuse—the woman may be threatened, publicly humiliated, criticized, and belittled. The abuser may be extremely jealous, using accusations of infidelity to keep her from seeing friends or going out. Psychological abuse may be equally as traumatic as physical abuse (Walker, 2000), and the combination of the two can be devastating, as a woman's life becomes governed by the threat of harm:

> But each day I lived in fear. I was afraid he was gonna come in while I was taking . . . I would wait to take a shower. I would hurry up and wash up. I mean, I know I wasn't getting clean enough, under my arms, between my legs but that was it, because I had to make it a minute and a half . . . because I was afraid he was gonna come in and just, you know, go off. (Smith et al., 1999, p. 184)

Recognizing a Hidden Problem

For many years, domestic violence was a hidden problem, because it takes place within the privacy of the home. Moreover, traditional attitudes condone a man's right to dominate and control his wife or partner. Wife beating was considered a normal, if regrettable, part of life. Even today, in countries where patriarchal ideology is strong, wife-beating may be viewed as a morally acceptable means of control (Crawford, 2010; Nordberg, 2014). For example, in Afghanistan patriarchal values make it acceptable for men to beat their wives. Divorce is unacceptable and there are few options available to women trying to leave abusive relationships (Nordberg, 2014). In the U.S. the scope and impact of partner violence has been made visible through two important kinds of research: random-sample surveys and studies of women in hospitals, courts, and battered women's shelters. Surveys of the general population and studies of abuse survivors reveal different kinds and amounts of violence (Johnson, 1995).

In surveys, women and men both report inflicting violence on their partners about equally often (Straus, 1999). This kind of relatively gender-neutral violence has been called *common couples violence* (Johnson, 1995). It does not occur often in a relationship, it rarely escalates over time, and it is sparked when the couple's coping skills are not sufficient for dealing with a particular conflict. In other words, common couples violence results from a breakdown in the couple's ability to handle a conflict constructively. It probably is as likely to occur in gay and lesbian as in heterosexual relationships. However, common couples violence in heterosexual couples is not entirely gender-neutral. When mutual violence occurs in relationships, men are more likely to be the primary perpetrators. Surveys reveal that women's violence against their partners was not as frequent or severe as the violence they experienced (Weston et al., 2005). Women are also much more likely to sustain physical injury than to inflict it and their aggressive acts are often done in self-defense.

Studies of battered women show a pattern of severe, escalating male violence in which women rarely fight back and almost never initiate aggression. This kind of violence, termed *patriarchal terrorism* or *intimate terrorism,* has been the main focus of feminist research and activism (Johnson, 1995; Johnson & Ferraro, 2000). (See Figure 12.2.) It is much more frequent in a relationship than common couples violence, pervading the whole context of the couple's interaction. Its motives are rooted in patriarchal tradition: the male perpetrator feels that he owns his woman and is entitled to control her by any means necessary. Both women who have been victims (Eisikovits & Buchbinder, 1999) and men who have been perpetrators (Anderson & Umberson, 2001; Reitz, 1999) report that without this control the batterer does not feel like a real man. To exercise and display his control, the abuser uses a variety of psychological techniques. Such techniques may include using coercion and threats, intimidation, or emotional abuse. For example, he may insult her, call her names, or humiliate her in front of her friends. He may prevent her from getting a job or keep her on an allowance, exerting his control economically. He may use isolation tactics, controlling where she goes and with whom she interacts, and may try to create a division between her and her friends and family. He might treat her like a servant or use her children against her. He may even blame her for the abuse, or threaten self-harm or suicide if she tries to leave. The ongoing psychological abuse is punctuated by episodes of physical violence, which escalate in intensity and frequency as time goes on. Thus, patriarchal terrorism is a continuous process for its victims, one that exposes them to prolonged and severe stress and fear (Frieze, 2005). The following items, from a scale designed to measure women's experiences of battering (Smith et al., 1999, p. 189), were developed from battered women's own accounts:

> He makes me feel unsafe even in my own home.
>
> I feel ashamed of the things he does to me.
>
> I try not to rock the boat because I am afraid of what he might do.
>
> I feel like he keeps me prisoner.
>
> He can scare me without laying a hand on me.
>
> He has a look that goes straight through me and terrifies me.

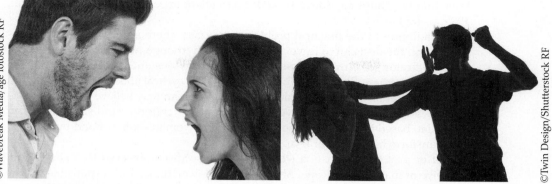

©Wavebreak Media/age fotostock RF

©Twin Design/Shutterstock RF

FIGURE 12.2   Some researchers make a distinction between common couples violence (left), which occurs when couples fail to deal constructively with conflicts, and patriarchal terrorism (right), a severe and escalating pattern of abuse aimed at controlling a woman.

"Why Doesn't She Leave?"

Attitudes about the abuse of women in marital and cohabiting relationships are changing. In U.S. studies, the majority of respondents believe that partner abuse is wrong (Drout, 1997; Locke & Richman, 1999). As a result of feminist activism, it is no longer a hidden problem; more people now acknowledge that abuse happens all too often and that any woman—rich, poor, middle-class, married, cohabiting, of any ethnic or racial group—is vulnerable. However, some myths about abuse remain. The most prevalent is the idea that there is a quick and easy solution for abuse: "Why doesn't she just leave?" Let's look at the evidence about ending an abusive relationship.

Women face many obstacles to leaving an abusive partner. Some of these are practical: She may have no money, no job, and no safe place to go. She may not have a car to leave in. If she takes the children out of school, she will upset them and draw the attention of authorities; if she leaves them behind, the abuser may harm them or she may lose custody.

One very important practical consideration is that attempting to leave may increase the violence. Research shows that a woman is more likely to be seriously injured or killed by her partner *after* she leaves him than when they are living together (Jacobson & Gottman, 1998). It is chillingly common to open the newspaper and see a headline like, "Man, Woman Die after Apparent Murder-Suicide in West Haven" (Becker, 2010). The article explained that the 25-year-old murdered woman had received a protective order against her husband two days prior, and that her husband had been arrested for assault a few months earlier. Their case was pending in a family violence program. The day of the murder, police went to the home twice after receiving 911 calls. On their second visit, they found the woman shot to death and her husband dead of a self-inflicted gunshot wound. According to data from the Bureau of Justice Statistics (Catalano, 2013), in 2010, 39 percent of all female murder victims—and only 3 percent of male murder victims—were killed by current or former partners. Violent men often make it clear that there is no escape. One survivor reported, "He'd always threaten me saying that if I decided to ever leave that he'd hunt me down like a dog and shoot me and the girls" (Smith et al., 1999, p. 185).

In addition to the practical problems and risks, there are psychological issues involved in the decision to leave an abuser. Much (though not all) abuse is **cyclical:** the perpetrator goes through a period of increasing tension, a violent episode, and then a loving phase (Frieze, 2005; Walker, 2000). A cyclical abuser is apologetic and repentant after an episode of violence, and the woman may believe his promises to change. She may feel tied by love for him and their children, and she may accept the belief, based in romantic ideology, that it is a woman's job to stand by her man and transform him with her love.

After prolonged abuse, a woman may be so disempowered that she cannot conceive of making an escape. She feels stupid, worthless, and responsible for the violence. More than half of abused women become clinically depressed (Warshaw, 2001). As one said, "He programmed me over a long, long period of time" (Smith et al., 1999, p. 186). She may develop **battered women's syndrome,** a type of post-traumatic stress disorder (Stein & Kennedy, 2001; Walker, 2000). She may become incapable of taking action on her own behalf.

Nevertheless, women in abusive relationships do try to cope with the violence and get help. Women may withdraw emotionally, or minimize the abuse in an attempt to deal with the stress they are experiencing (Frieze, 2005). Another coping strategy is "managing," in which a women tries to keep the peace by anticipating and avoiding anything that might make her partner angry. However, ultimately, the effort fails because it is the man who gets to decide whether he has a good reason to be angry. One battered woman concluded, "There was no way to tell what was going to happen because most of our arguments were not about anything serious . . . it was like, 'you got the wrong kind of bread' or 'I don't like that kinda candy bar'" (Smith et al., 1999, pp. 184–185).

When coping strategies fail, women often seek help from clergy, family members, police, counselors, and helping agencies. When women turn to their families for help, they may be told that marriage is sacred, that they should go home, apologize, and try harder, or simply, "You made your bed, now lie in it." Often, they are disbelieved or blamed for the abuse, even by those trained to help (Dutton, 1996). Feminist therapy (see Chapter 13) is a useful approach to helping women in abusive relationships because feminist therapists are likely to understand the patriarchal basis of wife abuse. However, not everyone can afford therapy or has access to a feminist therapist. And some groups of women, for example, immigrant and African American women, tend to be distrustful of social services and do not want to take their troubles to a stranger (Joseph, 1997).

The limited research on long-term outcomes suggests that the great majority of women in abusive relationships do manage to end them. However, leaving is a long process, and some women go back to the abuser more than once before they are able to make a final break (Bell et al., 2009). Perhaps this is partly due to the mixed messages they receive from the abusive spouse as well as from others.

In a longitudinal study, Margret Bell and colleagues (2009) examined the relationship between staying and leaving and the amount of violence women experienced over the course of a year. They found that women who consistently stayed away or who consistently remained with their partners experienced less violence (although they still experienced some violence) than those women who exited and re-entered the relationship multiple times over the course of the year. Bell and colleagues (2009) suggest that when women are thinking of leaving a relationship, they may be better off waiting until they have the emotional and financial resources to do so, so that they are in a better position to stay away.

How Can Relationship Violence Be Ended?

Patriarchal ideology is a root cause of violence against women. To the extent that a society accepts men's right to dominate women and women's second-class status, violence in heterosexual relationships is inevitable (Bograd, 1988). The ideology of patriarchy contributes to material inequalities that make women vulnerable to violence. Husbands usually earn more money, have higher status jobs, and have more decision-making power than their wives (see Chapter 8). When women reach out for help, they may encounter patriarchal attitudes from social services, law enforcement, and the court system. In order to truly end relationship violence, it is necessary to change not just individuals, but social structures as well.

The *battered women's movement* is an international movement to educate the public about domestic violence, reform the legal system, and provide direct help to women whose partners are violent. In three decades of activism, this movement has made huge changes in society's view of partner abuse. For example, all 50 U.S. states have passed laws designed to protect battered women and criminalize marital rape (Roberts, 1996). Police in many areas are now better trained to recognize domestic abuse and intervene to protect the woman. Physicians increasingly are being taught to screen for domestic abuse when interviewing female patients (Eisenstat & Bancroft, 1999). These changes make it easier for women to report abuse and get help, despite the powerlessness, shame, and fear they may feel.

Unfortunately, change is uneven and progress may even be reversed. Recently, Russian President Vladimir Putin signed a law that decriminalizes some forms of domestic violence. With the new law, the first incident per year of family or domestic violence that does not cause "substantial bodily harm" is no longer a criminal offense. Such a law puts women and children in an even more vulnerable position. According to data from a Russian state-run news agency, 36,000 women are beaten by their husbands *each day*, 26,000 children are beaten by their parents each year, and 12,000 women die each year from domestic violence (Sebastian & Mortenson, 2017; Staglin, 2017).

Battered women's shelters are refuges where a woman can find temporary safety, emotional support, information about their legal rights, and sometimes counseling. The first shelter for battered women opened in London in 1964, followed by the first U.S. shelter in 1974. Currently, there are shelters in at least 44 countries (Global Network of Women's Shelters (GNWS), 2012), and about 1,500 shelters in the U.S. Unfortunately, this is not nearly enough; thousands of women each year are turned away from shelters that have no space for them (Global Network of Women's Shelters (GNWS), 2012). Shelters are often underfunded, which means that they must rely on volunteers, and staff have to spend time fund-raising rather than offering services to women.

In fostering the development of shelters, the battered women's movement created safe havens for women and saved many thousands of women and children from further harm. When asked what helped them the most in dealing with abuse, women most often said that it was access to a shelter (Gordon, 1996). However, the shelter initiative may be more useful in individualistic societies like the U.S. than in collectivist societies, where women are part of a much larger family structure. In India or Pakistan, for example, a woman who left her family home would lose a web of vital social connections and her identity as a member of her society. In collectivist societies, and in working with more collectivist groups within our own society, such as African American and Native American women, other approaches need to be developed (Haaken & Yragui, 2003).

In the case of dating violence and acquaintance rape, prevention programs on college campuses are often aimed at women, offering advice on how to reduce the risk of assault (don't drink too much, don't be too trusting, say no clearly). Often, these programs are designed to help women avoid stranger rape, do little to help them avoid being attacked by someone they know, and may lead to women blaming themselves if they are raped (Frieze, 2005). Furthermore, would adopting these restrictions actually protect women from sexual assault? The evidence is limited. In one of the first randomized controlled trials of a rape prevention program, researchers in Canada found that participation in a sexual assault resistance program lowered the risk of rape and attempted rape for first-year college women, compared to a control group (Senn et al., 2015). The multi-faceted program contained information about assessing and acknowledging risk of assault by acquaintances, self-defense strategies, and content related to exploring sexual attitudes and sexual communication strategies. While this study demonstrates that rape prevention programs directed at women can reduce their risk of being assaulted, they need to be part of a multi-pronged approach that addresses the root causes of violence against women.

One important feminist initiative for preventing dating violence and rape is to focus on the perpetrators. Studies suggest that programs run *by* men *for* men are most effective in changing men's behavior. Some of these programs are organized through men's fraternities or athletic teams. For example, high schools, colleges, universities across the country, the NCAA, and even the military take part in the MVP program (Mentors in Violence Prevention) for athletes, educating them to become involved in preventing violence against women (www.mvp-national.org). Men can make an important contribution to feminism and to women's lives by working to end violence against women. This goal has spurred international movement by and for men, including the White Ribbon Campaign (www.whiteribbon.ca) and HeForShe (heforshe.org).

In the case of domestic abuse, a focus on the perpetrators includes doing research to understand the attitudes, personality characteristics, and family histories of violent men. This research is difficult because most abusive men deny and minimize their violence and blame their wives or girlfriends for it. In one innovative study, men who were domestic violence offenders in court-ordered programs participated in interviews where they described their own perceptions of violent incidents they had perpetrated. One man had broken his wife's neck; another had held a knife in his wife's face and threatened her with death. These men framed relationships with other people as win/lose situations in which they either felt good, up, and strong, or bad, down, and weak. From their perspective, the world was a threatening place where they could easily be rendered powerless, and their response was to try to subjugate their partners (Reitz, 1999). Such research has implications for counseling violent men. For example, cognitive therapy that helps men restructure their oppositional view of relationships may be useful, along with behavioral therapy that helps them manage anger.

To date, there have been few studies on the effectiveness of treatment programs for men. Few violent men volunteer to participate in programs aimed at changing them, and of those who do, many drop out. When court-ordered to attend, men who manage to complete a treatment program are less likely to be charged with abuse in the future, suggesting that such programs do help change attitudes and behavior (Shepard et al., 2002). However, meta-analyses of batterer intervention programs suggest they are not as effective as they could be (Feder et al., 2008). This may be because most of the programs take a "one size fits all" perspective and focus on issues of power and control, and not other factors that may be contributing to the violence. For example, alcohol and substance abuse are associated with IPV. Without first addressing the alcohol or substance problem, violence prevention programs may not be successful (Cantos & O'Leary, 2014). It is also important that the criminal justice system take a firm stand against violence by arresting and prosecuting offenders. Research suggests that arrest and conviction effectively deter a man from perpetrating future abuse (Garner & Maxwell, 2000; Wooldredge & Thistlewaite, 2002). Clearly, the psychological and physical abuse of women in relationships is a complex problem demanding intervention on many fronts: Changing patriarchal social structures, helping the victims, and stopping the perpetrators.

Violence in Later Life

Even in old age, women are not free from the threat of violence. Unfortunately, the abuse that older women experience is often a hidden problem with devastating consequences. Across the globe, older women experience physical, emotional, and sexual abuse, often from those who are their caretakers. Here we examine some of the types of violence that women may experience in later life.

Elder Abuse

Violence against the elderly, termed *elder abuse,* may involve physical abuse, emotional or psychological abuse, sexual violence, neglect, and misappropriating the victim's possessions or money (Carp, 1997; Lachs & Pillemer, 2015). Most of the harm caused by elder abuse is borne by women, and most elder abuse occurs when the older person lives with family members. Old people are reluctant to complain about abuse when complaining could mean losing their homes, and family members are reluctant to report each other (Carp, 1997).

Elder abuse has much in common with other forms of intimate violence. It reflects patriarchal power imbalances, it takes place in private settings, and it is fostered by secrecy and the isolation of its victims (White et al., 2001). Like other forms of domestic violence, elder abuse can be chronic yet still remain a family secret. Unfortunately, research on elder abuse lags far behind research on other areas of violence research (U.S. Department of Justice, 2014). Too few studies have been done to fully assess the prevalence of elder abuse, but one recent random-sample study found past year prevalence rates of 1.9 percent for emotional abuse, 1.8 percent for physical abuse, and 1.8 percent for neglect, with an aggregate prevalence rate of 4.6 percent (Burnes et al., 2015). The incidence of elder abuse is likely to continue to increase as the percentage of people over age 65 in the population increases; by the year 2030, more than 2 million elder adults may be victims of abuse (Baker, 2007).

Older women are not immune from violence at the hands of husbands and boyfriends. Unfortunately, they are not likely to report the abuse. In a qualitative study of older women who had experienced domestic violence, women identified a number of barriers to seeking help. They felt powerless and blamed themselves. They wanted to protect their family members or spouses from going to jail. In cases where the abuser was also elderly, the oldest women in the sample reported wanting to take care of their spouses rather than report the abuse. Some women reported that they felt there was nothing to be done to end abuse in a long-term marriage. Generational values prohibited divorce as an option and encouraged secrecy with respect to family matters. Many women also reported they felt that domestic violence services were targeted at younger adults and that they would not be comfortable with the help they would get from those services (Beaulaurier et al., 2008).

Sexual abuse of old people is still largely a taboo topic, although it is beginning to receive attention. One study in the United Kingdom reported that the victims were female by a 6:1 ratio, and the perpetrators were usually family members, more often sons than husbands. Elderly women in nursing homes may be raped and sexually abused. Memory impairment and physical frailty in nursing home residents make their victimization easy and prosecution unlikely (White et al., 2001). Rape myths contribute to the under-acknowledgment of elder sexual abuse. Older women are not usually seen as physically or sexually attractive and do not fit the stereotypical image of someone who could be raped. Because today's elder generation grew up when sexist beliefs dominated, they may blame themselves and feel guilty if they are assaulted (Vierthaler, 2008).

Like other types of violence against women, elder abuse is associated with a number of negative physical and psychological outcomes. Victims of elder abuse may experience depression, PTSD, chronic stress, or other psychological distress. The stress associated with experiencing abuse may exacerbate existing physical or mental conditions, contributing to early mortality (Baker, 2007).

Widow Abuse

As discussed in Chapter 11, the loss of a spouse or partner is a difficult time, as a woman adjusts emotionally and financially to living without her husband. Unfortunately, in many countries across the world, the loss of a husband is compounded by experiences of ostracism, homelessness, poverty, neglect, and physical or sexual abuse. Widow abuse is largely an unacknowledged problem. Widows are often left out of reports of development, health, and poverty in the developing world. According to the United Nations Division for the Advancement of Women (2001), "there is no one group more affected by the sin of omission" (p. 2). This omitted group is not just a small number of women. UN Women (2013) estimates there are more than 115 million widows currently living in poverty, and 81 million who have been physically abused. Widows are numerous in developing countries because of the practice of marrying younger women to much older men. For example, India has one of the highest rates of widowhood, with 54 percent of women over age 60 being widowed.

In Africa and Asia, widows are thought to be evil, and may be referred to as whores or beggars. In countries such as Nepal and India, some widows are subjected to shunning, torture, and even murder because they are thought to be witches (Crawford, 2010). In higher castes, women are not permitted to remarry. Often, they are seen as a burden for their families and may be cast out of their homes. Inheritance laws and practices in many countries prohibit a widow from inheriting money or property, leaving her destitute and homeless. Widows may be physically abused or even murdered so that their husband's family may keep the widow's dowry.

How Can Elder Abuse Be Ended?

Elder abuse is a hidden problem with devastating consequences. As the proportion of older adults increases over the next few decades, more than a million women may experience abuse in later adulthood, making the issue a timely one. More systematic research is needed in order to understand the nature and extent of elder abuse. In order to reduce and eliminate elder abuse, health care professionals who attend to older adults on either a regular or emergency basis must be educated on the risk factors associated with abuse (Baker, 2007; Lachs & Pillemer, 2015). Because a great deal of elder abuse goes unreported, accurate assessments are needed to determine if someone is being victimized. Many elderly women who are abused are unable to advocate for themselves.

Collaboration between community providers appears to be one way of increasing the quantity and quality of services for those experiencing sexual abuse, at least in developed countries such as the U.S. For example, a 3-year project, The Pennsylvania Elder Sexual Abuse Project, was conducted to encourage the collaboration of rape crisis centers and adult protective services to better address the issue of elder sexual abuse (Vierthaler, 2008). Initial interviews with workers from both sectors found that these service providers had very little contact with victims and did not know the signs and symptoms of elder sexual abuse. Workers from both sectors were cross-trained on elder sexual abuse, and the project funded an elder sexual abuse awareness campaign. Rape crisis advocates were invited to serve on elder sexual abuse task forces, and in some cases, adult protective services workers were invited to serve on sexual assault response teams. The overall reaction to the project was positive—awareness of the issue was increased and community service providers were successfully collaborating (Vierthaler, 2008).

Making a Difference

At the beginning of this chapter, we highlighted how the sexual assault scandal at Baylor University reflected the links between the three levels of the gender system. Thinking in terms of the gender system can also be useful in designing interventions to prevent, reduce, and eliminate violence against women. Let's return to the Baylor case to see how the gender system is involved in ending violence against women.

Since the scandal erupted, Baylor University has begun to take action to prevent sexual harassment and assault and provide appropriate resources for women who have been victimized. At the sociocultural level, task forces have been created to ensure structural and administrative changes are made to how sexual assaults are handled, as well as to foster a culture of care and respect on campus. Under the direction of the Title IX coordinator, researchers at Baylor are conducting quantitative and qualitative studies of the campus climate that might create barriers to reporting sexual assault. At the interpersonal level, faculty, staff, and students all receive mandatory sexual assault training at the beginning of the school year. Incoming freshmen also take part in the *It's On Us* Challenge (see Box 12.3), a sexual assault awareness program spearheaded by the White House and former Vice President Joe Biden. At the individual level, students who have been assaulted now have access to a variety of support services from the university, including counseling services from trauma-informed providers, a victim advocate, and an after-hours crisis phone line.

It remains to be seen what kind of impact the changes Baylor University has made will have on the incidence of and response to sexual assault. As we noted earlier, sexual assault is a problem on college campuses across the country. Findings from the AAU campus sexual assault survey indicate that one-quarter of college students have experienced at least one incident of unwanted sexual contact during their college years, and about 12 percent experienced nonconsensual sexual contact by physical force, threats of physical force, or incapacitation (Cantor et al., 2015). As of January 2016, 159 colleges and universities were being investigated for Title IX violations. Although there has been progress, there is still quite a lot of work that needs to be done to address sexual violence on college campuses.

A Multifaceted Approach to Interventions

Many interventions designed to prevent, reduce, or eliminate violence against women occur at the individual level of the gender system. In schools and colleges

BOX 12.3 ∾ It's On Us

©Mark Ralston/AFP/Getty Images

Eliminating campus sexual violence was a priority of the Obama Administration. In March 2013, President Obama reauthorized the Violence Against Women Act (VAWA), which included the addition of the Campus Sexual Violence Elimination Act (Campus SaVE). Campus SaVE expands upon the Clery Act, providing additional rights to victims of sexual, dating, and domestic violence. In 2014, President Obama created the White House Task Force to Protect Students from Sexual Assault, and launched the *It's On Us* Campaign to End Sexual Assault on Campus. The driving force of the *It's On Us* campaign is to "reframe the conversation surrounding sexual assault in a way that empowers, educates, and engages college students to do something, big or small, to prevent it." Anyone can go to the website and take the It's On Us pledge (below). *It's On Us* also runs a National Week of Action, where each day of the week centers around an important theme (for example, consent, supporting survivors, or being more than a bystander). The comprehensive website provides ideas, resources, and tools students can use to organize *It's On Us* events on their college campuses.

At the 88th Academy Awards, Vice President Joe Biden spoke about preventing sexual assault on college campuses and encouraged people to visit the *It's On Us* website to take the pledge. He then introduced Lady Gaga, who performed, "Til It Happens to You," the song she co-wrote for the sexual assault documentary *The Hunting Ground*. A sexual assault survivor herself, Lady Gaga's moving performance was made even more memorable when she was joined on stage by 50 sexual assault survivors with words like "survivor" and "not your fault" written on their arms. In an act of inspiring solidarity and courage, all of the survivors—both men and women—joined hands and raised them at the end of the performance. The moment was probably one of the most powerful and emotional ones in Oscar history.

The It's On Us Pledge

To RECOGNIZE that non-consensual sex is a sexual assault.

To IDENTIFY situations in which sexual assault may occur.

To INTERVENE in situations where consent has not or cannot be given.

To CREATE an environment in which sexual assault is unacceptable and survivors are supported.

Take the pledge at: http://itsonus.org/#pledge

Sources: The "It's On Us" website (http://itsonus.org); http://clerycenter.org/article/vawa-reauthorization

Contributed by Annie B. Fox

throughout the U.S., girls and women are educated on ways in which they can avoid being assaulted. For example, women are often told never to walk alone at night and to avoid drinking excessively. Children are also taught to tell an adult if anyone ever touches them inappropriately. Although such self-protective strategies can be useful, they can be problematic. First, they place the responsibility for prevention on the individual. However, some women and children may be unable to speak for themselves due to their age, physical or mental disability, or because speaking out may jeopardize their safety. Second, by addressing potential victims rather than potential perpetrators, the likelihood of victim blaming may be increased. If a woman wears suggestive clothing and walks alone at night, people might be more inclined to blame her if she is assaulted because she failed to act in ways that would protect her. Consequently, while it is good to teach women and children ways in which they may be able to protect themselves, interventions that address both the perpetrators and cultural norms that perpetuate violence against women must be developed.

As mentioned previously, interventions run *by* men and *for* men are effective in changing men's behaviors and reducing sexual assault. More of these types of interventions are needed in order to begin to change attitudes towards the acceptability of violence against women on a larger scale. Colleges and universities across the U.S. are beginning to implement rape prevention programs that are primarily directed at men and women separately. For example, "The Men's Program," is run by and for men and is designed to teach participants how to help women who have been raped with the hope that it will also decrease men's likelihood of raping. Other types of rape prevention programs can also be effective in ending violence against women. Some advocate for focusing on the role of social norms in rape prevention (e.g., Fabiano et al., 2003), while others focus on empowering bystanders (e.g., McMahon & Farmer, 2009).

At the sociocultural level, movements such as the battered women's movement help address the structural barriers to ending violence against women. Women who experience violence often encounter resistance when they seek help or report abuse. Although strict laws protecting women from violence are in place throughout the U.S., these laws need to be enforced by the police and court system. Police officers, as well as legal and medical professionals, need to be educated on the signs and consequences of abuse, and be vigilant in enforcing the law and protecting women. Other local and national campaigns that bring attention to the prevalence of violence against women are also beneficial. For example Sexual Assault Awareness Month, and the *It's On Us* campaign (see Box 12.3) are all ways of educating people on preventing violence against women.

Women's Rights Are Human Rights

Violence against women occurs in every country and is one of the most widespread human rights violations across the world (see Box 12.4). Women of all ages are vulnerable to abuse because of the patriarchal power imbalance that exists in most societies. In many countries, women are denied basic rights. They are treated as

BOX 12.4 ～ Nicole Kidman and UNIFEM

©George Pimentel/WireImage/Getty Images

Nicole Kidman, UNIFEM, and the Global Fight to End Violence Against Women

Nicole Kidman is not only an Academy Award–winning actress; she also serves as a UN Women (formerly UNIFEM) Goodwill Ambassador. Kidman's primary focus is to bring international attention to ending violence against women across the globe. As an advocate for ending violence against women, Kidman has received a Cinema of Peace Award and testified before Congress in support of the International Violence Against Women Act (I-VAWA). In her testimony, Kidman discussed her work with UNIFEM and the women she has encountered who have survived extreme violence. She stated,

> These champions need and deserve our support. Not with a box of band-aids, but with a comprehensive, well-funded approach that acknowledges that women's rights are human rights. It is time for policies that intentionally involve society's key communities—from

health and education departments to the police and judiciary—to deliver on that commitment. To succeed, it requires political will at the highest levels.

In addition to her duties as a UN Women ambassador, Kidman is also the international spokesperson for UN Women's *Say NO—UNiTE to End Violence Against Women Initiative.* The *Say NO* campaign (www.saynotoviolence.org) began in November 2009 and their goal is to encourage individuals, organizations, and governments to take action to stop violence against women.

One way in which the UNiTE campaign is trying to increase attention to the issue of violence against women is through "Orange Day," which occurs on the 25th of each month. Each month has an "action theme" designed to increase attention to global development goals that will help end violence against women. For example, the theme for August 2016 was to "promote sustained, inclusive and sustainable economic growth, full employment, and decent work for all." More information about Orange Day can be found at http://endviolence.un.org/orangeday.shtml

Most recently, Kidman is a spokesperson for the UN's "Face It Together" campaign. "Face It Together" launched in March 2016 and encourages people all over the world to take a picture of themselves and share it as a pledge of support in ending violence against women.

Sources: UNIFEM (2009). UNIFEM Goodwill Ambassador Nicole Kidman and UN Trust Fund Grantee testify at U.S. House Committee on Foreign Affairs—Press release. Available at http://www.unifem.org/news_events/story_detail.php?-StoryID=959

Say NO—UniTE to End Violence Against women website. Available at: http://www.saynotoviolence.org

http://www.dailymail.co.uk/tvshowbiz/article-3475497/Nicole-Kidman-lends-famous-features-s-Face-campaign-end-violence-against-women.html

Contributed by Annie B. Fox

property, to be bought, sold, used, and abused. Women are denied access to education, employment, and the right to own property. The widespread gender inequality that exists across the globe makes women more susceptible to violence.

One of the most important ways in which gender-based violence can be ended is by encouraging women's economic empowerment. For example, some banks in developing countries are offering poor women microcredit, or small loans, to start a small business to employ themselves. Microcredit allows for women to work and begin to independently increase their wealth. Such programs have been successful in decreasing the number of women living in poverty. Some microcredit programs, such as the *Hand in Hand* program in India, go beyond just providing a small amount of money. Hand in Hand also provides extensive business and financial training that is designed to increase the likelihood of the business succeeding. Hand in Hand was so successful it has expanded to Afghanistan, South Africa, and China (Colvin, 2009).

In Pakistan, women can get microfinance from the Kashf Foundation. Kashf lends money to groups of women who meet every other week to make their payments and discuss important social issues. Once women pay off their initial loans, they can return for larger loans. Although Pakistani women are not permitted to leave their homes without their husbands' permission, their husbands allow them to participate because they benefit from the success of their wives' businesses. According to one woman, "Now women earn money and so their husbands respect them more. . . . If my husband starts to hit me, I tell him to lay off or next year I won't get a new loan. And then he sits down and is quiet" (Kristoff & WuDunn, 2009).

Empowering women economically is one way in which women may achieve greater equality with men and decrease their vulnerability to violence. According to Kristoff and WuDunn, "Microfinance has done more to bolster the status of women, and to protect them from abuse, than any laws could accomplish. Capitalism, it turns out, can achieve what charity and good intentions sometimes cannot" (p. 187). But we also need to challenge existing views of gender, power, and inequality. Advocates, lobbyists, and international organizations such as UN Women (see Box 12.4) and Amnesty International continue to try to bring attention to this important human rights issue, but until governments take action and work together, violence against women throughout the world will continue.

Exploring Further

~

Crawford, M. (2010). *Sex trafficking in South Asia: Telling Maya's story.* New York: Routledge. The author lived in Nepal and worked with a women's organization that offered shelter, counseling, and rehabilitation to girls and women who had been rescued from Indian brothels. Her book is a personal memoir of this work as well as a feminist analysis of how to end sex trafficking.

Krakauer, J. (2015). *Missoula: Rape and the justice system in a college town.* New York, NY: Doubleday. A noted journalist investigates how student athletes are not held accountable for a widespread pattern of sexual assault at a Montana university. A compelling look at the complexities of campus sexual assault.

Gavey, N. (2005). *Just sex? The cultural scaffolding of rape.* New York: Routledge.

This important book uses a social constructionist perspective to analyze how normative scripts for heterosexual relationships endorse a degree of coercion that fosters cultural acceptance of rape.

Mendes, K. (2015). *SlutWalk: Feminism, activism, and media.* Palgrave Macmillan.

This book is a study of the global anti-rape movement that started after a Toronto police officer suggested that women could avoid sexual assault by "not dressing like sluts." It documents the scope of the movement, with organized marches in eight countries, and its support both in mainstream news and the feminist blogosphere. Interviews with 22 organizers of the movements and critique of the movement provide a rich analysis of this 21st century activism using social media to challenge rape culture.

Text Credits

∾

p. 381: From Heather Montgomery, *Modern Babylon?: Prostituting children in Thailand* (New York: Berghahn Books, 2001), p. 80. **p. 389:** Anderson, K. A., & Hiersteiner, C. (2008). Recovering from childhood sexual abuse: Is a "storybook ending" possible? *The American Journal of Family Therapy*, 36, 413–424. **p. 393:** From an account told to me by an anonymous student, with her permission. **p. 394:** "Kahn, A. S., Jackson, J., Kully, C., Badger, K., & Halvorsen, J. (2003). Calling it rape: Differences in experiences of women who do or do not label their sexual assault as rape. *Psychology of Women Quarterly*, 27, 233–242. **p. 396:** Contributed by Annie B. Fox. **p. 397:** "Smith, P. H., Smith, J. B., & Earp, J. A. (1999). Beyond the measurement trap: A reconstructed conceptualization and measurement of woman battering. *Psychology of Women Quarterly*, 23, 177–193. **p. 407:** The "It's On Us" website (http://itsonus.org). http://clerycenter.org/article/vawa-reauthorization **p. 407:** Contributed by Annie B. Fox.

CHAPTER 13

Psychological Disorders, Therapy, and Women's Well—Being

$\mathcal{R}$ead the title of this chapter. What do you think it means? Does it imply that women's disorders are cured by therapy, thereby enhancing their well-being? Not exactly. Does it suggest a simple list of topics that will be addressed in turn: first women's psychological problems, then how to treat them, and then something about women's psychological health? Not quite. Replace "and" with "versus" and you'll get a better sense of the gist of much of this chapter. Before discussing how feminist therapy contributes to women's well-being, and how you can make differences in society and in yourself do the same, we'll first address the ways that traditional psychiatry and psychological practice have sometimes done the opposite. Topics include sexist bias in the diagnosis of disorders, the ways in which gender roles and stereotypes interact with our understanding of disordered behaviors, and some history of how psychiatrists have responded to women's nonconformist behavior by incarcerating or sedating them. After describing ways that traditional approaches to mental health have been less than woman-friendly, we'll look at feminist alternatives.

Sexist Bias in Defining Disorders

In her autobiographical memoir, *Girl, Interrupted,* Susanna Kaysen (1993) contemplates the etiology or causes of mental illness. She invites the reader to select from a list of explanations for atypical behavior, including that the person in question is "possessed," "a witch," "bad," "ill," "a victim of society's low tolerance for deviant behavior," and "sane in an insane world." Most of us living in the U.S. today would be unlikely to invoke demon possession or witchcraft as explanations for unusual behavior. We are much more comfortable with the idea of mental illness, which we now attribute to biological and social causes, rather than spiritual ones. We consider mental distress and disorders treatable and individuals suffering from them deserving of treatment. But how do we decide who is mentally ill and who is normal? Sometimes the decision depends not on the behavior itself, but on society's perception of that behavior.

The Social Construction of Abnormality

"Normal" is a relative term. We can define something as normal based on statistical probability. We could say, for example, that if it falls within a certain range around the population mean, then it is normal. This may seem like an objective way to define normality, but in everyday life we rarely know the statistical probability of a characteristic or behavior before we label it. And even when we do have a sense of the numbers, we are not necessarily guided by them. Take the example of height. The average height of women in the U.S. is five feet, 3.8 inches (National Center for Health Statistics, 2012), yet "petite" sizes begin at five-foot-four. Why are sizes for average women labeled with a special designation? Social factors (in this case, fashion industry standards) affect whether something that is statistically probable is considered "normal."

Social factors also influence whether a behavior is statistically probable in the first place. Behaviors vary with culture and historical period. For example, piercing body parts other than ears, which has been common in many indigenous cultures for thousands of years, has become commonplace in the industrialized West only recently. Just 25 years ago, a college student with a nose ring was considered abnormal by conventional standards, whereas today she is seen as a bit alternative, but not far outside the norm.

The norm itself is also determined by social factors such as the status and relative power of the persons making the judgment and the persons being judged. Those of dominant status in the population are in a position to designate what is normal, and will likely define the norm in relation to themselves. In patriarchal societies such as the U.S., there is a pervasive tendency to consider men the norm, and women a special category (Tavris, 1992). This can have negative consequences for women.

Women's Behavior as Abnormal

In general, women have been labeled the unreasonable and crazy ones in androcentric cultures. Feminine "madness" has been contrasted with masculine "rationality" in science, religion, literature, art, and humor (Showalter, 1986; Ehrenreich & English, 1973). Women were called mad for challenging the limitations of a traditional feminine gender role, and they have experienced genuine psychological distress as a result of how this devalued role has limited their access to education, economic independence, sexual self-expression, and political power.

In psychology, the male as norm perspective has influenced researchers' and clinicians' views of women's behavior. Until feminist scholarship gained a solid foothold in psychology in the late 1970s, psychiatrists and psychologists routinely labeled women's behavior as disordered or deficient when compared to a male standard. They attributed the disorder to reproductive pathology and natural feminine frailty (e.g., Chesler, 2005; Ussher, 1992).

A male-as-norm bias has permeated not only academic psychology, but pop psychology as well. Most advice columns and self-help books are aimed at women. Women are told they have low self-esteem, are too emotional, and too dependent. But compared to whom? If *women* were the standard of comparison, would there be more self-help books for men guiding them to temper their inflated self-esteem, develop sensitivity skills, and become less overly independent? Instead of women reading books about *Men Who Can't Love* and *Women Who Love Too Much,* might men read books about how to love as much as women do? Perhaps men would be the target audience for self-help books in general, instead of women constantly getting the message that they are the ones who need to change.

Blaming Women for Distress and Disorders

In 1909, Sigmund Freud was invited by former APA President G. Stanley Hall to make his first and only trip to the U.S. Freud delivered a series of lectures on psychoanalysis at Clark University, stirring up enthusiasm among progressive listeners who were excited about his candid acknowledgment of human sexuality. Feminists thought his early ideas about female sexuality held promise and encouraged him to write more about women; however, when he did, many women were dismayed. Freud defined female sexuality and the feminine personality in terms of their difference from a male norm. According to Freud, in the process of resigning themselves to their inferior genitalia, females develop specific feminine personality characteristics, including masochism (Freud, 1933). Masochism is defined as deriving pleasure from one's own pain.

The idea that women are masochistic caught on, perhaps because it provided a rationalization for women's subordinate status and the pain they experienced at the hands of abusive men; if women *like* to suffer, then there is no need to critically examine the circumstances that promote their suffering. Many psychoanalysts embraced Freud's proposition, and so did many other psychiatrists and psychotherapists. The assumption that women are naturally masochistic leads logically to the conclusion that they bring their problems on themselves by seeking out unhealthy relationships and damaging situations. Paula Caplan (1985) relates a vivid example in her book *The Myth of Women's Masochism,*

> [A graduate student] had been doing an internship at a local hospital, seeing patients for psychotherapy. One of her patients was Sylvia, a woman whose first husband, after they married, had refused to have any sexual relationship with her at all and had also begun to beat her. They were soon divorced and, some time later, Sylvia married another man. While married to her second husband, she became bulimic, going on massive eating binges and then forcing herself to vomit until her throat began to bleed. [The supervising psychiatrist explained] that Sylvia was a masochist. "You see how beautifully her masochism works," he said. "When her first husband isn't there to beat her anymore, she *becomes* her first husband and forces herself to vomit until she bleeds. He's not there to hurt her, so she hurts herself." (p. 192)

What other explanations might there be for Sylvia's bulimia besides "she is a masochist"?

Women have been blamed for their own distress and disorders, and they have also been blamed for the distress and disorders of others around them. In particular, mothers have been blamed for the psychological problems of their children. The mother-blaming described in Chapter 9 has a long history. An early example appears in the book *The Borderland of Insanity,* published in 1875 in London. The author claimed that insanity is inherited from the mother twice as often as it is from the father; however, he had no scientific evidence to support this assertion (Russell, 1995).

In the U.S., mother-blaming became fashionable during and after World War II. Mothers were considered responsible not only for the well-being of their own children, but for the health of society in general. One popular author who pointed the finger at mothers for social problems was Phillip Wylie, who, in his 1942 book, *A Generation of Vipers,* put it this way,

> Mom got herself out of the nursery and the kitchen . . . she also got herself the vote and, although politics never interested her (unless she was exceptionally naïve, a hairy foghorn, or a size forty scorpion), the damage she forthwith did to society was so enormous and so rapid that even the best men lost track of things. Mom's gracious presence at the ballot box was roughly concomitant with the start toward a new all-time low in political scurviness, hoodlumism, gangsterism, labor strife, thuggery, moral degeneration, civic corruption, smuggling, bribery, theft, murder, . . . financial depression, chaos, and war. (pp. 188–189)

Of course, it wasn't mothers who were mugging people and starting wars, but Wylie (and others) held them responsible. Wylie's hostile tirade continues with a description of the typical middle-aged, middle-class mother as a useless, repulsive, smothering, and manipulative drain on society whose demand for devotion from her son saps him of his masculine autonomy. According to Wylie and his contemporaries, the American man was a coddled, simpering, emasculated mother-worshiper.

This epidemic flight from manhood that mothers were supposedly causing was deemed especially severe among African Americans because of the so-called Black matriarchy (Buhle, 1998). African American men were criticized for being childlike, impulsive, manipulative, and irrational—and these characteristics were attributed to the fact that most African American families were headed by relatively economically independent working mothers. As noted in Chapter 9, the role of systemic racism in shaping the African American family structure—and in distorting perceptions of African American men—was overlooked by the mother-blamers.

During the post-World War II baby boom, an intensely pronatalist era, mothering was elevated to the status of patriotic public service. Women had been called to the paid workforce while men were away fighting during both World Wars. Women were the primary breadwinners while men were unemployed during the Great Depression between the wars. After World War II, women were encouraged (even pressured) to resume their place at home. The country as a whole was counting on population growth and scientific technology to restore the prosperity and progress that had been disrupted by the wars and the Depression. In the home, science was applied not only through innovations in gadgetry, but also through expertise-based approaches to childrearing. Mothers faced unprecedented scrutiny of their efforts. Women's magazines regularly featured authoritative warnings about the dangers of improper parenting, from sources such as the now legendary Dr. Benjamin Spock (Ehrenreich & English, 2005; Walker, 1998). More than ever before, physicians and psychologists emphasized the primary influence of mothers to raise psychologically healthy—or unhealthy—children.

Dr. Edward Strecker, author of the mother-blaming book *Their Mothers' Sons: The Psychiatrist Examines an American Problem*, gave a lecture to 700 medical students at Bellevue Hospital in 1946 in which he identified various types of (unfit) mothers who were responsible for the nearly two million men found psychologically unfit to serve in World War II and for the 600,000 psychiatric discharges (Hartwell, 1996). Apparently, the Depression and the horrors of a World War II were not as compelling an explanation for these men's psychopathology.

The Diagnostic and Statistical Manual (DSM)

The *Diagnostic and Statistical Manual of Mental Disorders* (DSM) is produced by the American Psychiatric Association for use by clinicians. It catalogs recognized disorders, listing them with background information and diagnostic criteria. Including the first *DSM*, published in 1952, there have been seven versions (I, II, III, III-Revised, IV, IV-Text Revision, and 5). The most recent version, *DSM-5*, was published in May 2013. Revisions have been necessary in some cases because of research findings that have clarified known disorders or suggested new ones. Revisions have also occurred because of more subjective factors. For example, until

1973, homosexuality was included in the *DSM* as a mental illness. Due to both advances in research on sexual orientation, and political pressure, the American Psychiatric Association opted to exclude it from *DSM-III*.

According to *DSM-5*, a "mental disorder" is characterized by "clinically significant" impairment in an individual's thoughts, emotions, or behaviors. These impairments may be the result of "dysfunction in the psychological, biological, or developmental processes" that impact mental functioning. Mental disorders may negatively impact one's relationships, occupational functioning, or other daily activities. An "expectable or culturally approved response" to an event such as the death of a loved one is not considered a mental disorder. Several of the terms in this definition are subjective. Who decides whether something is "clinically significant," "an expectable or culturally sanctioned response," or a "dysfunction"? Just as sex and gender are socially constructed (as described in Chapter 5), so too are mental disorders.

The ways in which we define both the broader construct of mental illness and specific mental illnesses themselves reflect the dominant societal view of what constitutes "normal" human behavior. Further, the bio-medical model that dominates our understanding of sex and gender also shapes our understanding of psychological disorders. Instead of acknowledging the unique lived experiences of those who are experiencing psychological difficulties, the emphasis has been on listing symptoms and categorizing disorders.

In her essay calling for a phenomenological perspective with respect to psychological diagnosis and treatment, psychologist Gail Hornstein (2013) asks two important questions:

> "What happens if we listen at a far deeper level to what people actually say about their experiences (even of severe distress) instead of seeing their mental lives primarily as a vehicle for advancing our own categories and theories? What if we took people's own accounts not as gibberish, or as some kind of code for us to decipher, but instead as meaningful and accurate (even if fragmentary and contradictory) ways of making sense of their own minds and life histories? (p. 32)

The DSM is more than just a catalog of mental disorders. Its reach and influence are wide-ranging. The DSM is used to set research agendas and funding. It is used to determine eligibility for insurance coverage, disability payments, and special education services. And it is frequently used in the legal system to determine criminal responsibility (Marecek & Gavey, 2013). But it is not without controversy. One of the most significant criticisms of *DSM-5* relates to the influential role of the pharmaceutical industry. Of the individuals who were on the *DSM-5* taskforce and oversaw the revision, 69 percent had ties to the pharmaceutical industry (Cosgrove & Krimsky, 2012; Cosgrove & Wheeler, 2013). Financial conflicts of interest were also the highest within specialized *DSM-5* panels for disorders whose first-line treatment is often pharmaceuticals (e.g., mood disorders, schizophrenia, and psychotic disorder) (Cosgrove & Krimsky, 2012; Cosgrove & Wheeler, 2013).

DSM-5 has 15 new diagnoses, including binge eating disorder (BED, described below), which could now be targeted by pharmaceutical companies looking to

Source: *Diagnostic and Statistical Manual of Mental Disorders*, Fifth Edition

profit from these "new" disorders. In February 2015, the FDA approved the use of the drug Vyvanse to treat BED. Vyvanse was originally used to treat ADHD, but can now be marketed to the nearly 3 million people thought to suffer from BED. *DSM-5* also relaxed some of the diagnostic criteria for disorders. Within the mood disorders category, *DSM-5* removed the bereavement exclusion for depression. Previously, someone grieving the death of a loved one could not be diagnosed with depression within the first two months following the death. Removing this exclusion opens the door for pharmaceutical companies to market anti-depressants to those who are grieving, although the two are distinctly different psychological experiences (Wieczner, 2013).

Some feminist critics of the *DSM* have suggested that gender, race/ethnicity, and class all affect whether a behavior is tolerated from particular individuals within a given cultural context. They object to the sharp lines delineating normal from abnormal, and distinguishing one disorder from another, claiming that such pigeonholing obscures the complex variability of behavior and its causes in a given social environment (e.g., Caplan, 1995). For example, at what point should a clinician conclude that a woman's unhealthy pattern of desperate dieting and depriving herself of adequate nutrition is an eating disorder? If a college student lives in a dorm where binging and purging are accepted and even encouraged as a reasonable way to respond to social pressure to be thin, is she suffering from bulimia nervosa if she joins in?

Another concern raised by critics of the *DSM* approach is that the manual has the potential to legitimize labels that have far-reaching implications, even when sound scientific support for the labels is lacking. One of the appendices in the *DSM* lists provisional categories needing further study. Even though diagnostic labels in this appendix are pending, they may be applied by clinicians. For example, Pre-menstrual Dysphoric Disorder (PMDD) was included in the Appendix in DSM-IV, and clinicians were using it as a diagnosis without solid research evidence of its existence (Chrisler & Caplan, 2002). Further, even without "official" status as a disorder, the FDA approved the use of the antidepressant Prozac (rebranded as Sarafem) to treat PMDD.

Another concern feminist critics have raised is the presence of gender bias in diagnostic criteria. For example, in a study examining the criteria currently used to diagnose personality disorders (according to DSM-IV), researchers interviewed nearly 600 participants and found that women and men with similar levels of pathology responded differently on six specific criteria; men were more likely to endorse some items, and women were more likely to endorse others. It seems these items are not gender-neutral (Jane et al., 2007). The question remains whether gender bias should be remedied by the inclusion of gender-specific criteria, or by the creation of more gender-neutral criteria (Riecher-Rössler, 2010). What do you think?

Gender-Linked Psychological Disorders

Among the diagnostic labels used today, several are applied at different rates to women and men. Women are more likely than men to be diagnosed with eating disorders, mood and anxiety disorders, and some personality disorders. On the other hand, women are less likely than men to be diagnosed with substance abuse disorders, some antisocial conduct disorders, and all of the sexual disorders. First we will consider some general reasons why these gender-related differences in diagnostic rates may exist, and then we will take a closer look at explanations for why specific disorders appear more often in women. We will refer to these differences in diagnostic rates between women and men as gender-related rather than sex differences because it is not possible to decide whether they are more closely related to biological sex, cultural gender, or whether the causal factors differ from one disorder to the next.

Why Are There Gender-Related Differences in the Rates of Some Disorders?

Before answering the question about why gender-related differences in rates exist, we must first consider the possibility that the reported gender ratios are inaccurate. Clinical samples are not random and may not represent the gender ratios in the general population (Hartung & Widiger, 1998). The samples employed in research studies on disorders also are typically non-random and non-representative. This bias in sampling can lead to bias in the understanding of the disorder, which can then lead to bias in diagnostic criteria, which may lead to differences in application of the criteria . . . it is a vicious cycle. For example, the DSM-IV diagnosis of *somatization disorder,* characterized by the presence of physical symptoms with no known physical cause, was originally diagnosed as *hysteria,* which literally translated, means "wandering womb" (Hartung & Widiger, 1998). The name of the disorder was changed, but the diagnostic criteria continued to include symptoms that applied only to women (e.g., irregular menstruation). In an effort to prevent diagnostic gender bias, the authors of the *DSM-IV* added what they considered a parallel set of symptoms for men (e.g., erectile dysfunction), but this was not based on any research with men. The diagnostic criteria were based entirely on research with samples of all women and, therefore, may have led to more frequent diagnosis in women, whether or not the disorder actually occurred more often in women.

Assuming that at least some of the reported gender ratios in disorders are fairly accurate, it may be tempting to name biology as the source of the differences. It would be convenient to conclude that women get depressed because of their hormones and men develop sexual fetishes because of theirs. Certainly, biological factors predispose some individuals to particular psychological disorders, but for the most part these factors are found in both women and men; for example, both women and men can have a genetic predisposition for depression. There is some evidence that the genetic and hormonal differences between men and women may contribute to a few specific gender-related differences in disorders, such as the tendency for women with bipolar disorder to cycle more rapidly between bouts of depression and mania than men do (Leibenluft, 1996). Still, most gender-related differences in psychological disorders have thus far not been accounted for by biological factors.

Some disorders may be diagnosed more frequently in women because women may be more likely to report their distress and seek help; help-seeking is more consistent with a feminine gender role than with a masculine one (e.g., Addis &

Mahalik, 2003). Some studies comparing women's and men's likelihood to seek psychological help have found that women report greater willingness (e.g., Oliver et al., 2005); however, the fact that some disorders are diagnosed more frequently in men suggests that even if women are more willing than men to seek psychological or psychiatric care, this is an inadequate explanation for all the observed gender-related differences in diagnosis frequency.

A close look at the disorders that are diagnosed at different rates for men and women reveals a pattern consistent with traditional gender roles and gender stereotypes. Gender socialization may influence women's higher rates of *internalizing disorders*, where negative affect is turned inward, and men's higher rates of *externalizing disorders*, where negative behavior is expressed outwardly (Rosenfield, 2000). Moodiness and fear are more characteristic of stereotypical femininity, whereas heavy drinking, aggression, and sexual expression are seen as more masculine behaviors.

Gender stereotypes may also influence how the same behaviors are perceived and labeled differently when exhibited by a woman versus by a man. Therapists' own preconceptions about gender may color their interpretations of female and male clients differently, causing them to overdiagnose certain conditions in women and underdiagnose others. For example, given the same set of symptoms, clinicians may be more inclined to diagnose depression in women than in men (Potts et al., 1991), or to diagnose women with "borderline" or "histrionic" personality disorders and men with "antisocial" personality disorder (Becker & Lamb, 1994; Samuel & Widiger, 2009). Stereotypes about women may lead to paradoxical diagnostic biases: sometimes they contribute to overdiagnosis of psychopathology in women—because women are the crazy ones—and sometimes they cause clinicians to overlook women's actual problems—because, after all, emotional distress is common in women, right? (Lopez, 1989; Robinson & Worell, 2002).

Finally, some disorders may be diagnosed more frequently in women because they actually occur more frequently in women—not just because of biology, but because of gender roles and gender prejudice. For example, women may be more likely to develop eating disorders because of the strong link between femininity and appearance pressure (Mussap, 2007). They may be more prone to other disorders including depression and anxiety because of gender-specific stressors such as sex discrimination. Elizabeth Klonoff and colleagues (2000) found support for this idea when they compared women and men on psychiatric symptoms after assessing how frequently the women had experienced sexist events, such as being called a sexist name (bitch and chick) or hearing sexist jokes. Only the women who had frequently experienced sexist stressors reported more symptoms than the men. As described in earlier chapters in this book, daily sexist hassles, micro-aggressions, sexual harassment, and the worldwide prevalence of violence against girls and women take a huge toll on women's psychological well-being.

Which Disorders Are Diagnosed More Frequently in Women?

The disorders discussed below all are diagnosed at higher rates in women than in men. Although they are discussed separately, keep in mind that they commonly occur together; women who suffer from depression often exhibit anxiety disorders, eating disorders, and borderline and dependent personality disorders (Sprock & Yoder, 1997; Widiger & Anderson, 2003).

Depressive Disorders

Women are twice as likely as men to suffer from *major depressive disorder (MDD)* and two to three times as likely to experience the more long-lasting variant, *Persistent Depressive Disorder* (*DSM-5*; formerly known as Dysthymic Disorder). Both of these disorders are characterized by chronically low mood and disabling symptoms such as marked loss of interest in activities, appetite changes, sleep disruption, fatigue, inability to concentrate, and excessive negative thinking. The higher incidence of depression in women emerges in adolescence (Hilt & Nolen-Hoeksema, 2009) and has been found cross-culturally (Grant & Weissman, 2007). Explanations for higher rates of depression in girls and women have focused on internal factors, such as genetics, hormones, and cognitive style, and on external influences such as sexism, poverty, and violence. The most recent theoretical models propose that these factors interact in complex ways to cause the observed gender difference in depression (e.g., Hyde et al., 2008).

Depression and other mood-related disorders have a genetic component. For example, individuals who inherit the tendency to have low levels of the neurotransmitter serotonin are more likely to suffer from depression than individuals with average levels of serotonin. Depression runs in families, but it is equally inherited by men and women (Agrawal et al., 2004), so genes alone don't explain the gender difference. We still know very little about specific genetic markers of depression. Genome-wide association studies (GWAS) look across the genomes of a large group of people to see if there are relationships between genetic variants (called single nucleotide polymorphisms, or SNPs) and specific diseases or conditions (NIH Fact Sheet, 2015). Meta-analyses of MDD GWAS have failed to find evidence of a single SNP associated with depression, suggesting that the gene-environment interaction may be key to understanding the genetic etiology of depression (Ripke et al., 2013; Hek et al., 2013). Some research suggests that sex hormones may interact with stress hormones to make women more vulnerable to depression and anxiety (Solomon & Herman, 2009), but, in general, hormonal explanations are insufficient to fully account for the gender-related difference in depression (Kessler, 2003).

Cognitive explanations for the gender-related difference in depression suggest that girls and women may respond to negative life events with thinking patterns that contribute to low mood. For example, women engage more than men in *rumination,* passively dwelling on distress, its causes and consequences, instead of actively distracting themselves or seeking social support (see Figure 13.1). Rumination predicts the onset of depression and makes it worse (Nolen-Hoeksema et al., 2009). Relatedly, gender differences in rumination can partially account for gender differences in both depression and anxiety (Nolen-Hoeksema, 2012). Women's subordinate social status may cause them to feel less control than men do over their life circumstances and emotions and yet more responsible for maintaining positive relationships with others; therefore, they tend to worry rather than act (Nolen-Hoeksema et al., 1999; Nolen-Hoeksema & Jackson, 2001). The attributions people make to explain negative life events may also make them vulnerable to

©Yuri Arcurs/Cutcaster RF

FIGURE 13.1 **Women's lower social status relative to men may predispose them to rumination, which is predictive of depression.**

depression. Women, more so than men, tend to exhibit a "hopeless" style, attributing negative events to stable, global, internal causes instead of thinking, "Well, it's a one-time event, it's just one aspect of my life, and it wasn't my fault!" (Abramson & Alloy, 2006; Hankin & Abrahmson, 2001).

Biological and cognitive vulnerability alone won't necessarily lead to depression. Most times depression is triggered by negative or stressful life circumstances or events. An example of a stressful life circumstance is poverty, which disproportionately affects women. Poverty and its associated hardships are correlated with depression, especially among mothers with small children (Belle & Doucet, 2003; Heflin & Iceland, 2009). Another external factor that predicts women's depression is interpersonal violence (Golding, 1999). Childhood sexual abuse, rape, and battering are all associated with elevated levels of depression in women (Koss et al., 2003). Most research on depression has been done with White women in the U.S., but research suggests violence also predicts depression in women from varied cultural backgrounds including African American women (Banyard et al., 2002), Latina women (Hazen et al., 2008), Native American women (Bohn, 2003), Chinese American women (Hicks & Li, 2003), and women in Norway (Nerøien & Schei, 2008), Northern Ireland (Dorahy et al., 2007), Brazil (Ludermir et al., 2008), and sub-Saharan Africa (Gelaye et al., 2009).

As mentioned previously, ***Premenstrual Dysphoric Disorder (PMDD)*** was a provisional diagnosis in DSM-IV and became an official diagnosis with the publication of *DSM-5*. PMDD is categorized as a depressive disorder. Symptoms of PMDD occur during the luteal phase (the phase before the onset of menses) and must subside a few days into the menstrual phase. Symptoms may include marked mood swings, irritability, anger, depressed mood, or anxiety, decreased interest in activities, difficulty concentrating, lethargy, sleep disturbances, and physical symptoms such as bloating, headaches, and weight gain. To receive a diagnosis, women must experience at least five of the symptoms (at least one of which much be related to mood) during the majority of menstrual cycles over the past year and they must cause clinically significant distress (*DSM-5*). According to *DSM-5*, risk factors for PMDD include stress, trauma, and sociocultural aspects of women's gender roles. As critics of PMDD have pointed out (Caplan, 2004, 2008; Chrisler & Gorman, 2015), it seems as if most women of child-bearing age are at risk!

Controversy continues to rage regarding the inclusion of PMDD in the *DSM*. Supporters claim it is an identifiable clinical syndrome and its inclusion in the *DSM* is important to legitimize some women's cyclical suffering (e.g., Pearlstein, 2010). Some critics agree that the validation of women's experience is important, but assert that women should not require a mental illness diagnosis to receive attention for physical and emotional symptoms commonly associated with menstruation (Browne, 2015; Caplan, 2004).

The pharmaceutical industry may also have had a hand in creation of PMDD. Eli Lilly marketed the anti-depressant Sarafem (see Box 13.1) as a treatment for

Box 13.1 ∽ Prozac, Sarafem, and the Rebranding of Psycho-Pharmaceutical Drugs

Fluoxetine, the active ingredient in the antidepressant Prozac, was discovered by pharmaceutical giant Eli Lilly in 1972. It was originally tested as both a medication for high blood pressure and obesity before scientists discovered the positive effect it had on a small sample of people suffering from depression. The drug eventually received FDA approval to treat depression. In 1988, Eli Lilly began marketing the newly named Prozac and within a year, nearly 2.5 million prescriptions had been written. At its height, Eli Lilly was making $2.6 billion dollars a year off of Prozac.

In the late 1990s, the patents Eli Lilly held for fluoxetine were approaching expiration, and were being challenged in court by a generic drug competitor. Looking for ways to extend the profitability of Prozac, Eli Lilly investigated several "extension strategies." If Lilly was able to show that fluoxetine could successfully treat another mental illness, they could renew the patent. With a push from Eli Lilly to establish that PMDD was real and treated successfully with Prozac, the FDA ultimately approved its use for the so-called disorder. Eli Lilly was then able to extend one of its patents for fluoxetine—rebranded as Sarafem—to treat PMDD. Although Lilly eventually lost most of their patents (and profits) for fluoxetine, they were still able to make $285 million in sales in 2001. Sarafem was heavily marketed, targeting women with premenstrual symptoms. They were even forced to pull one of their early advertisements for failing to define PMDD. Ads also failed to mention that Sarafem was Prozac, making it possible that women prescribed the drug had no idea they were taking an antidepressant.

The rebranding of Prozac into Sarafem to maintain patents and profits is not an isolated case. It is not uncommon for drug makers to start tweaking their profitable antidepressants before their patents expire. If they are able to slightly alter the chemical structure of their existing antidepressant, they can get a new patent and extend profitability. Effexor, manufactured by Wyeth, has been reformulated as Pristiq. Both contain the same metabolite, although they are processed slightly differently in the body. Not surprisingly, Wyeth encouraged psychiatrists to switch their patients from Effexor to Pristiq. Celexa and Lexapro also share a similar history, and were both manufactured by pharmaceutical company Lundbeck. In 2013, the FDA approved the use of a rebranded antidepressant Paxil (renamed Brisdelle) to treat hot flashes. However, an FDA advisory committee had advised that the drug be rejected because the results of its effectiveness were only marginal compared to a placebo. Nevertheless, Brisdelle was approved and is now marketed as a "non-hormonal" treatment for hot flashes.

Sources: Psychiatry Report, T. (2013). Pristiq vs. Effexor. *Psych Central.* Retrieved on February 17, 2017, from https://pro .psychcentral.com/pristiq-vs-effexor/003676.html

Mukherjee, S. (2012, April 19). Post-Prozac Nation. *The New York Times Magazine.* Retrieved from http://www.nytimes.com/2012/04 /22/magazine/the-science-and-history-of-treating-depression.html

Shorter, E. (2014). The 25th anniversary of the launch of Prozac gives pause for thought: Where did we go wrong? *The British Journal of Psychiatry, 204,* 331–332.

McLean, B. (2001, August 13). A Bitter Pill Prozac made Eli Lilly. Then along came a feisty generic maker called Barr Labs. Their battle gives new meaning to the term 'drug war.' *Fortune Magazine.* Retrieved from http://archive.fortune.com/magazines /fortune/fortune_archive/2001/08/13/308077/index.htm

Contributed by Annie B. Fox

PMDD. FDA approval of the use of this drug to treat menstrual distress was contingent on expert opinion that PMDD was a distinct mental disorder. Of course, a so-called mental disorder that can affect half the population under 50 every month is a lucrative one for drug companies. Five of the six psychiatrists who made the decision to include PMDD in the *DSM-IV* had financial ties to Eli Lilly (Cosgrove et al., 2006).

Some scholars argue that PMDD is a *culture-bound syndrome.* A culture-bound syndrome is a set of symptoms that together define a disease or illness in one culture but not in others (Browne, 2015; Chrisler, 2012). In a study looking at the prevalence of PMDD among ethnic minorities in the U.S., Pilver et al. (2011) found that the likelihood of having PMDD increased the longer a woman had lived in the U.S. In other words, the more ethnic minority women were exposed to American culture, the more likely they were to have PMDD.

Critics also argue that the medicalization of women's distress ultimately harms women because it ignores or mischaracterizes the causes of such distress (Browne, 2015; Chrisler, 2012; Chrisler & Gorman, 2015). For example, studies of women with premenstrual syndrome (PMS) or PMDD find that they have higher rates of life stress, trait anxiety, depression, and trauma such as sexual abuse or assault than women not experiencing PMS or PMDD (Chrisler & Gorman, 2015). Further, pathologizing women's moods suggests that when women experience intense negative emotions, there is something wrong with them and they need treatment.

Many women do experience normal, cyclical changes in their bodies and moods related to their menstrual cycle. For a very small percentage of women, those monthly changes impair daily functioning. Does that mean PMDD should be considered a mental disorder and the first line treatment anti-depressants? What do you think?

Anxiety Disorders

Generalized anxiety disorder is somewhat more common in females than in males, but a more pronounced gender-related difference is found for panic disorder. *Panic disorder* is diagnosed when an individual has experienced repeated, unexpected periods of sudden intense fear or discomfort (accompanied by physical symptoms such as heart palpitations, dizziness, trembling, and a feeling of choking) followed by at least a month of worry about having another panic attack. Because these attacks can occur in public, it is not surprising that panic disorder is associated with *agoraphobia,* which is intense fear of being in places from which it might be difficult or embarrassing to escape (e.g., outside the home alone, in a crowd, or traveling on an airplane). Panic disorder and agoraphobia are diagnosed twice as often in women as in men (Kessler et al., 2012).

Feminine socialization may contribute to women's greater fear of being in public spaces. Traditionally, girls and women have been encouraged to reside in the domestic, private sphere and discouraged from asserting themselves in the public sphere. Also, public places can be aversive for women because they may experience sex discrimination, sexual objectification, sexual harassment, and sexual violence. Other explanations for the gender-related diagnostic difference suggest that the difference may be an artifact: Perhaps men also fear public spaces, but, because of masculine gender role expectations that they boldly enter the arena of the public sphere, men may be unwilling to admit their fear and instead choose to mask it with coping behaviors such as drinking alcohol (e.g., Bekker, 1996).

Most other phobias are about twice as common in women as in men, but the gender ratios vary across phobia type. For example, 75 to 90 percent of individuals with natural environment and animal phobias are women (*DSM-5*). This is particularly interesting given the long tradition in many cultures and religions of associating women more closely than men with nature as nurturers and creators of life (Merchant, 1995). Earth-based spiritual traditions honor earth goddesses and Mother Nature, yet women in the U.S. today are much more likely than men to exhibit an intense fear of nature. Perhaps the roots of women's phobias about the natural environment and animals lie in gender socialization that discourages girls from exploring wild places and accepting their natural physical selves.

Eating Disorders

Ninety percent or more of individuals diagnosed with ***anorexia nervosa*** and ***bulimia nervosa*** are female (*DSM-5*). The word anorexia refers to a loss of appetite, but individuals with anorexia nervosa do not usually lose their appetites; instead, they exert rigorous control over their food intake and physical activity level so as to achieve a lower than normal body weight. Distorted perception of body shape and size is typical. Although widespread concern about the prevalence of anorexia nervosa among girls and women is relatively recent among medical professionals and the general public, self-starvation behaviors among women have been documented as far back as the Middle Ages (Bemporad, 1996; Brumberg, 2000; Liles & Woods, 1999). Like anorexia, bulimia is related to extreme concern about weight gain, but individuals exhibiting bulimia are very often of normal weight or above normal weight. They do not tend to restrict their food intake, instead engaging in food binges followed by purging through vomiting or use of laxatives. Many girls and women engage in unhealthy eating habits and suffer from distressing body preoccupation but do not meet the specific diagnostic criteria for these disorders.

Binge-eating disorder (BED) became an official diagnosis in *DSM-5* and is characterized by recurrent episodes of eating large amounts of food (i.e., binging) and feeling out of control during the binge. During a binge-eating episode, the person may eat faster than normal, may not feel hungry, and may experience embarrassment, disgust, depression, or guilt later on (*DSM-5*). Although there are gender differences in the prevalence of BED, they are not as pronounced as they are with anorexia and bulimia. Women are diagnosed with BED about twice as often as men (*DSM-5*; Kessler et al., 2013). Binge eating is associated with stress, and women who binge may experience more stress than women who do not (Wolff et al., 2000).

Both depression and anxiety in women often co-occur with eating disorders (e.g., Godart et al., 2007; Swinbourne & Touyz, 2007), though the precise nature of the relationship is unclear. It is possible that depression and anxiety predispose women to eating disorders (Keel et al., 2001; Strober et al., 2007). Or it may be that other factors, such as negative social comparison, interpersonal problems, low self-esteem, and body dissatisfaction affect both mood and eating disorders (Ansell et al., 2012; Green et al., 2009). Objectification theory suggests two possible pathways for the development of disordered eating. Eating disorders may be a direct consequence of self-objectification, or they may develop from the body shame and appearance anxiety also associated with chronic self-objectification (Roberts, 2016). Most of the research on the associations between these factors is correlational, so it is difficult to determine causal links between them. However, the few experimental studies of objectification theory do suggest that state self-objectification leads to eating-related outcomes (Fredrickson et al., 1998; Moradi et al., 2005; Moradi & Huang, 2008).

What we do know is that the associations between depression, anxiety, body dissatisfaction, and eating disorders vary in different populations of women. For example, a study of Mexican American women found that endorsement of U.S. societal values (which include the emphasis on thinness for women) was significantly correlated with bulimic symptoms, while a study of African American women conducted by the same researchers found no association between these factors, nor between depressive symptoms and bulimic symptoms (Lester & Petrie, 1995; 1998). One study with postpartum women found that weight gained during pregnancy is associated with depression for White women, but not for African American women (Cameron et al., 1996), perhaps because African American women are less likely than Caucasian women to perceive body changes related to pregnancy negatively (Walker et al., 2002).

The prevalence of eating disorders in general also varies among different populations of women, although the discrepancies may be shrinking. Some populations of women may be less prone to eating disorders because of their greater social distance from the mainstream beauty ideal, which is not only thin, but also young, White, heterosexual, and middle-class. It may be easier for women who do not fit into these categories to reject the dominant standard (e.g., Gilbert, 2003). As ethnic minority girls and women identify more with mainstream society (known as *acculturation*), they are more vulnerable to eating disorders (Gowen, et al., 1999; Cachelin, et al., 2000). This may be due not only to acculturation itself, but also to the stress associated with trying to fit into a culture that is different from one's culture of origin (Gordon et al., 2010; Kroon Van Diest et al., 2014).

Another explanation for racial and ethnic differences in the rate of eating disorders may be cultural differences in the experience and reporting of eating disorder symptoms. For example, a study comparing Asian Americans and non-Latino Whites found that although Asian American women were just as likely to report binge eating, they were less likely to endorse other symptoms of BED, including loss of control and feelings of distress, compared to White women (Lee-Winn et al., 2014). It may be that the diagnostic criteria used for eating disorders do not capture the ways in which women from other cultural backgrounds experience disordered eating (Cummins et al., 2005).

Borderline and Dependent Personality Disorders

Several personality disorders show gender-related discrepancies in prevalence rates, including antisocial and narcissistic disorders (diagnosed more in men) and dependent and borderline disorders (diagnosed more in women). There is a large amount of literature debating whether these differences are real, artifacts of imprecise sampling, the result of bias in diagnostic criteria, or due to assessment bias by clinicians or self-report instruments.

Borderline personality disorder (BPD), the diagnosis applied to the author of *Girl, Interrupted,* is characterized by a pattern of instability in relationships, self-concept, and emotions accompanied by impulsivity and a severe fear of abandonment (*DSM-5*). Seventy-five percent of the individuals diagnosed with BPD in clinical settings are female; however, some studies of BPD prevalence in the general population find no gender difference, so there may be a sampling bias (Skodol & Bender, 2003). Taking the clinical rates as representative, several researchers have explored the possibility that the diagnostic criteria for BPD are sexist. In one study, undergraduate students sorted the diagnostic criteria for the personality disorders on the basis of how characteristic they were of women versus men (Sprock et al., 1990). All of the BPD criteria were rated as more characteristic of women, with the exception of intense, inappropriate anger.

Dependent personality disorder (DPD) is characterized by an excessive need to be cared for that leads to submissive and clingy behavior (*DSM-IV-TR*). Individuals with dependent personality traits experience intense longings to be loved, nurtured, and protected. They have extreme trouble making independent decisions, even minor daily ones, and they require a lot of reassurance and advice. They have difficulty expressing disagreement with others because they fear it will lead to a loss of support or approval. They have trouble initiating projects because of low self-confidence in their abilities. Importantly, these dependent behaviors are to be considered signs of the personality disorder only when they exceed age-appropriate or culturally-appropriate norms. What about gender-appropriate norms? How about differences in gender socialization and gender roles? And what about factors confounded with gender, such as economic dependence and being the victim of domestic abuse?

Sexist Bias in the Treatment of Psychological Disorders

Broadly speaking, treatment for psychological disorders can be defined in terms of two general approaches: a psychiatric model that relies on medical therapies including drugs and hospitalization, and a non-medical psychotherapeutic approach. Psychoanalysis, the therapy originally developed by Freud, falls into both categories in that it is a nonmedical "talk" therapy but is practiced by a (relatively small) subset of psychiatrists. Both the psychiatric and psychotherapeutic approaches have suffered from gender bias. This section will first address the sexism that has pervaded psychiatric institutionalization and drug therapies, and then will describe criticisms of traditional psychotherapy.

Institutionalizing Women

Residential facilities for severely mentally ill or developmentally disabled people serve important caretaking and rehabilitative functions in our society today. Sometimes, however, people are wrongfully incarcerated in these institutions (e.g., Szasz, 1973). A look at the history of women's institutionalization in the U.S. and Europe reveals a pattern of unwarranted involuntary commitment: women have been punished for unwillingness or inability to conform to the limits of a socially-prescribed feminine gender role (Appignanesi, 2008; Showalter, 1986; Ripa, 1990; Chesler, 2005; Ussher, 1992).

Charcot, Freud, and the Salpêtrière

From the seventeenth to the nineteenth centuries, the Salpêtrière in Paris was an infamous institution housing primarily women. Initially built as a gunpowder factory, it was remodeled and expanded under the reign of Louis XIV into an alms house to shelter some of the 40,000 homeless Parisians, 10 percent of the city's population (Vallois, 1998). Many of the women forcibly housed in the Salpêtrière were prostitutes who were later shipped to Louisiana and Canada to help populate France's new territories. Women considered (in the parlance of the time) "feeble-minded" or "deranged" were routinely chained to the walls.

Women who were homeless, suspected or known prostitutes, or merely deviant in their behavior (e.g., were loud or aggressive) were likely candidates for involuntary commitment in the Salpêtrière during the nineteenth century. Jean-Martin Charcot, the founder of modern neurology, opened a clinic in the Salpêtrière to study individuals who displayed *hysterical symptoms,* physical problems with no apparent organic cause. Charcot disagreed with predecessors who thought hysteria was caused by a wandering womb (he saw hysteria in men as well), but he did attribute hysteria to sexual dysfunction. The majority of Charcot's patients were women. The most famous and favored of these was Blanche Wittmann, nicknamed the "Queen of Hysterics," whose dramatic displays of hysteria on demand served Charcot well in his theatrical lectures to colleagues, as depicted in André Brouillet's painting, *Une leçon clinique à la Salpêtrière* (see Figure 13.2).

Charcot's work on hysteria was highly influential to a young Sigmund Freud. Freud was impressed with Charcot's ability to use hypnosis to produce and relieve hysterical symptoms. Here was the first hint that the unconscious mind might be connected to some forms of physical distress. Freud was also impacted when he overheard Charcot assert quietly to a colleague that the cause of hysteria *"c'est toujours la chose genitale . . . toujours . . . toujours . . . toujours"* (translation: "it is always something genital . . . always . . . always . . . always") (Freud, 1914, p. 14).

It was while in residence at the Salpêtrière that Freud first developed his own ideas about hysteria and its origins in childhood sexual trauma. Later, Freud retracted his claim that the hysteria he observed in his women patients at his clinic in Vienna was due to actual childhood sexual trauma and developed the alternative explanation that the symptoms stemmed from unconscious conflict regarding wishful sexual fantasies. This about-face in Freud's thinking may have been due to the negative reaction his theory elicited from his peers in the medical community; after all, he was essentially claiming that childhood sexual abuse was commonplace in

FIGURE 13.2   *Une leçon clinique à la Salpêtrière* by Andrè Brouillet.

their high-status households (Masson, 1984). Undoubtedly, this shift had a significant impact on the treatment received by women who actually had been abused.

True Women and Madwomen in the Victorian Era

In the mid-to-late-nineteenth century U.S. involuntary commitment of "madwomen" by their husbands or other family members who found their attitudes or behaviors inconvenient, unacceptable, or uncontrollable was not unheard of among the middle and upper classes. At the time, economically privileged women were expected to aspire to "True Womanhood," to be passive, pious, domestic, and morally pure (Welter, 1966). According to medical wisdom of the time, intellectual activity—such as that required when pursuing higher education or engaging in social reform activism—was contraindicated for women. The only recommended activity was childbearing; however, this was somewhat of a double bind due to the fact that pregnancy and lactation were also seen as causes of women's mental illness (Geller & Harris, 1994).

Because women's reproductive organs were believed to be the primary source of their mental distress, physicians used woman-specific therapies including the surgical removal of ovaries, electrical shocks to the uterus, hot water injections into the vagina, and clitoral cauterization (Geller & Harris, 1994; Russell, 1995).

An influential doctor, Silas Weir Mitchell, popularized the "rest cure," months of confinement in bed with no activity, not even a book to read. Weir Mitchell's idea was that women enjoyed being ill, and that making the conditions of illness extremely aversive would hasten their recovery. His approach treated women as unruly children in need of paternal discipline. In her short story, *The Yellow Wallpaper*, suffragist and feminist foremother Charlotte Perkins Gilman (1892) relates a first-person account of a woman's descent into madness *caused* by her physician husband's implementation of the rest cure,

> If a physician of high standing, and one's own husband, assures friends and relatives that there is really nothing the matter with one but temporary nervous depression—a slight hysterical tendency—what is one to do? . . . I am absolutely forbidden to "work" until I am well again . . . Personally, I believe that congenial work, with excitement and change, would do me good. (p. 1)

The woman in the story proceeds to develop delusions about a female prisoner lurking behind the garish designs on the peeling wallpaper in her room. Perkins Gillman, herself, was institutionalized and put on the rest cure by Weir Mitchell for a month in 1887. She suffered from "nervous prostration" following the birth of her daughter (today she would probably be diagnosed with postpartum depression). When she was sent home she was instructed to "live as domestic a life as possible," to limit her intellectual activity to 2 hours per day, and to never write another word. After complying with this protocol for several months, Gilman "came perilously near to losing [her] mind." She recovered after her divorce. (See Figure 13.3.) Stories from other women confined to asylums during the latter nineteenth century are in Box 13.2.

FIGURE 13.3   Charlotte Perkins Gilman

Women and Deinstitutionalization

In the 1960s and '70s, a number of writers in the U.S. and Europe penned anti-psychiatry critiques that focused on the social construction of madness and the authoritarian abuses perpetrated by psychiatric institutions (e.g., Goffman, 1961; Laing, 1970; Szasz, 1970). The claim that the so-called mentally ill were yet another marginalized group, labeled and punished for their nonconformist behavior, had a particular appeal against the backdrop of the civil rights movement and counter-culture activism. There followed a trend promoting the deinstitutionalization of mental patients and reliance on community-based care facilities. Unfortunately, these facilities were underfunded and limited in number. The result was that many psychologically distressed individuals ended up homeless (Isaac & Armat, 1990).

Deinstitutionalization has had particular implications for women. When family and community care take the place of institutional care, who are the primary

---

Box 13.2 ∾ Women's Voices from the Nineteenth—Century Asylum

My youngest brother I loved with all the tender love of a sister, and I wanted him to have an education, and I worked in the factory to get money to help educate him; and is it possible that a brother, or a human being, could be so hardened or cruel, on account of difference of religion, to put a sister in prison and hire men to try experiments, and to commit rape on a sister, and to delight in her sufferings! . . . Is this the state of our country, that the rights of a female are trampled upon . . .

—*Elizabeth T. Stone (1840–1842)*

It is now twenty-one years since people found out that I was crazy, and all because I could not fall in with every vulgar belief that was fashionable . . . I find that active nervous temperaments that are full of thought and intellect want full scope to dispose of their energy, for if not they will become extremely excitable. Such a mind cannot bear a tight place, and that is one great reason why women are much more excitable than men, for their minds are more active; but they must be kept in a nut-shell because they are women.

—*Phebe B. Davis (1850–1853)*

It was in a Bible-class . . . that I defended some religious opinions . . . which brought upon me the charge of insanity. . . . Early on the morning of the 18th of June, 1860, as I arose from my bed, preparing to take my morning bath, I saw my husband approaching my door with two physicians, both members of his church and of our Bible class . . . Fearing exposure I hastily locked my door . . . [but] my husband forced an entrance into my room through the window with an axe! . . . And I, for shelter and protection against exposure in a state of almost entire nudity, sprang into bed . . . The trio approached my bed, and each doctor felt my pulse, and without asking a single question both pronounced me insane.

—*Elizabeth Parsons Ware Packard (1860–1863)*

Here, women of intelligence, of spirit, of refinement, with homes, with families, and possessing the power to comfort, cherish, and adorn these, are left to stagnate . . . they are prisoners. It is very generally believed . . . that an asylum confines only the violent, dangerous, or utterly imbecile . . . This is a remarkably wide-spread error.

—*Adeline T. P. Lunt (Date unknown)*

Source: All excerpts from Geller, J. L., & Harris, M. (1994). *Women of the asylum: Voices from behind the walls, 1840–1945.* New York: Anchor Books.

---

caregivers? Most of the time, it is women (Ascher-Svanum & Sobel, 1989; Bachrach, 1984; Thurer, 1983). Deinstitutionalization is related to women's role as the primary caregivers in their families in other ways as well: women with serious mental disorders are more likely to be at home raising their children than they were when community-based outpatient services were unavailable (Oyserman et al., 2000). And, deinstitutionalized women may be more likely to become mothers than women living within a facility that provides family planning services (Bachrach, 1984).

Medicating Women

Like institutional care, when properly applied, psychotropic drugs can serve as an effective component in treatment programs for many forms of psychological distress. As in the case of institutionalization, however, an historical look at the use of psychiatric medications suggests that women have been disproportionately targeted as candidates for this form of therapy, especially when they experienced distress related to their traditional feminine roles as mothers and homemakers.

"Mother's Little Helper"

Since tranquilizers and sedatives were first introduced for widespread use in the 1950s, they have been prescribed more often for women than for men (Herzberg, 2009; Metzl, 2003). This difference may be due, in part, to women's higher rates of disorders appropriately treated with these types of drugs. It can also be attributed to a sexist bias stemming from the perception of certain behaviors in women as disruptive to the social order. Concurrent with the mid-century mother-blaming described earlier in this chapter, tranquilizers were promoted in magazines such as the *Ladies Home Journal* and *Cosmopolitan* as the cure for women's frigidity, infidelity, single status, career-mindedness, and rejection of motherhood (Herzberg, 2009; Metzl, 2003).

Miltown, a muscle relaxant, was introduced to the American public in 1955. Demand for it soon exceeded that for any previous prescription drug. By the end of 1956, 1 in 20 Americans, the majority women, were taking tranquilizers (Metzl, 2003). In 1969, Valium became the most widely prescribed medication in the U.S. with 1 in 10 Americans taking it, three-quarters of whom were women (Chambers, 1972). Tranquilizers were so commonly prescribed to married, middle-class women in North America and Europe that they earned the nickname "mother's little helper," popularized in a 1966 Rolling Stones song by the same name and satirized by artist Judy Olausen (see Figure 13.4). In the 1950s, '60s, and '70s, tranquilizers were recommended for women not only to relieve their own distress, but also to relieve the distress men experienced living with troublesome women (Metzl, 2003).

FIGURE 13.4 "Mother's Little Helpers" by Judy Olausen.

Mother's Little Helpers, ©Judy Olausen

Advertising Drugs to Psychiatrists

Pharmaceutical companies spend an enormous amount of money marketing drugs to both the medical community and consumers. The investigative journalist group ProPublica maintains a database of payments from drug companies to doctors and hospitals across the U.S. According to their data, drug companies pay about $2 billion a year to physicians and another $600 million to teaching hospitals (Jones et al., 2016). And long before it was legal to advertise prescription drugs directly to consumers, pharmaceutical companies targeted physicians through ads in medical journals. Still today, more than 80 percent of promotional funds are spent on advertising to physicians (U.S. General Accountability Office, 2002). Researchers have found gendered patterns in the content of these ads that contradict reality.

A study of more than 200 ads for a variety of prescription drugs from American medical journals found that when both women and men were pictured, women were twice as likely to be portrayed as consumers of the drugs. However, national health statistics at the time suggested that women made fewer office visits and spent fewer days in hospitals than men did (Hawkins & Aber, 1993). Consistent with the face-ism in advertising described in Chapter 3, just parts of women's bodies were pictured significantly more often than just parts of men's, and women appeared naked four times as often as men. An analysis of portrayals of women in U.S. and Canadian medical journals found that drug advertisements reinforced negative stereotypes of women (Ford, 1986). For example, one ad pictured a male bus driver on one page, with the copy, "He is suffering from estrogen deficiency"; on the next page was a picture of an older woman passenger who appeared to be talking loudly, and the rest of the copy, "She is the reason why." Other ads portrayed women as childlike, complaining, and unable to cope.

An analysis of all the psychotropic drug advertisements appearing in a family physician journal for a period of four years revealed that 77 percent of them depicted women patients (Hansen & Osborne, 1995). In this family practice journal, and a psychiatry journal the researchers also analyzed, nearly all of the ads for antidepressant medications portrayed women consumers—100 percent and 80 percent, respectively. These percentages are distinctly inconsistent with the typical 2:1 gender ratio of depression diagnosis.

Ads for antidepressants distort reality in that they tend to portray stereotypically idealized life circumstances, subtly discouraging physicians from exploring the social causes of women's depression such as sexism, poverty, and intimate partner violence (Nikelly, 1995). Ads for psychiatric medications also neglect racism as a source of psychological distress. An ad that appeared in the *Archives of General Psychiatry* in 1974 pictured an African American woman, dressed in professional clothing, looking menacing and raising a fist, with the heading, "Assaultive and belligerent? Cooperation often begins with HALDOL" (Metzl, 2003). This ad, which ran during the heyday of the civil rights movement and the feminist second wave, implied that the remedy for African American women's outrage was medication rather than social change.

Ads for antidepressants are misleading also in that they imply that these medications are a generally effective treatment. A meta-analysis of 35 drug trials submitted to the U.S. Food and Drug Administration (FDA) found that the benefits of antidepressants depended on how severely depressed patients were initially. Antidepressants were significantly effective for treating the most severely depressed patients, but for those with initially low levels of depression, drugs like Paxil and Prozac worked no better than a placebo (Kirsch et al., 2008). Given that clinicians have been led to believe that antidepressants work for most every depressed individual, these drugs are likely overprescribed.

Direct-to-consumer advertising of anti-depressants may also lead to overprescribing, and this may disproportionately affect women, who are both more likely to experience depression and more likely to seek treatment. Individuals diagnosed with depression were more likely to start medication during years where spending on direct-to-consumer advertising was the highest (Donohue & Berndt, 2004). In an interesting experimental study, Richard Kravitz and colleagues (2005) randomly assigned professional actors to portray a patient seeking treatment for either depression or adjustment disorder. Medication is a first-line treatment for depression, but not for adjustment disorder. During their physician visit, the actor-patients either asked for a specific name-brand antidepressant they'd seen in a commercial, a general antidepressant, or did not ask for treatment. Actor-patients with either depression or adjustment disorder who requested a specific antidepressant were prescribed that antidepressant 53 and 55 percent of the time, respectively. When the patient made a request for a general antidepressant, prescribing rates were 76 percent for depressed patients and only 39 percent for the adjustment disorder patients. And when the patient didn't make any request at all, antidepressants were prescribed 31 percent of the time for the depressed patient and only 10 percent for the adjustment disorder patient. Thus, anti-depressants are likely prescribed even when not the first-choice treatment—and patient requests appear to have a strong impact on physician prescribing.

Selling Drugs Directly to Women

In 1985, the FDA lifted its moratorium on direct-to-consumer advertising for prescription drugs. The annual number of direct-to-consumer appeals submitted to the FDA for approval has quadrupled since 1999 (U.S. General Accountability Office, 2008). According to FDA guidelines, drug manufacturers may solicit consumers with three types of advertisements: *product claim ads,* which describe the drug, what it does, and must include information about risks and side effects; *reminder ads,* which mention the drug by name but do not make any claims about what it does, and so do not have to include risk information; and *help-seeking ads,* which describe a disorder or condition without mention of a specific drug, and are not regulated by the FDA (U.S. General Accountability Office, 2002).

In a content analysis of 10 leading U.S. magazines, researchers found that prescription drug advertisements appeared more often in the publications aimed at women than in those geared toward men or general readership (Woloshin et al., 2001). What are women readers to conclude when they routinely encounter antidepressant ads in magazines like *Self* and *Marie Claire* alongside articles about how to be more attractive and how to find love (Metzl, 2003)? Print ads for the antidepressant Paxil have appeared since 1993 and have overwhelmingly featured women—who happen to be young, White, conventionally attractive, thin, well-dressed, and heterosexual (Hanganu-Bresch, 2008). In one of these ads, a woman is standing separated from her helpless looking husband and son, and the text reads, "What's standing between you and your life?" In the "after" picture, she is crouched next to her son, hugging him and gazing happily upward (at her husband?). Her normal life as a mother and wife has been restored.

Because of the gender biases that exist in the use of psychotropic drugs, some psychiatrists and psychologists advocate "feminist psychopharmacology" (e.g., Hamilton & Jensvold, 1995; Marsh, 1995). They argue that a feminist perspective will help counter sexism in psychiatric diagnosis and prescription patterns. In addition, they suggest that a feminist perspective would add social and cultural context to biologically-focused research on gender-related differences in responses to psychotropic drugs and their effectiveness. Especially lacking from outcome research is a consideration of ethnic and racial factors; psychopharmacological treatment for women of color has been studied very little although psychiatrists seem particularly inclined to favor drugs over other forms of therapy for people of color (Jacobsen, 1994). A contemporary feminist approach would consider ethnic and racial factors along with gender.

Traditional Psychotherapy

Critics of traditional psychotherapy are referring not only to psychological treatment before the rise of feminist practice in the 1970s, but also to the work of contemporary clinicians who fail to adopt a non-sexist or feminist approach. The primary criticisms that have been leveled at traditional psychotherapy include the following:

1. The theoretical orientation and/or personal perspective that informs the therapist's appraisal of the client's distress and guides the treatment may be based on gender stereotypes and sexist attitudes.
2. Traditional psychotherapeutic orientations focus on the individual as the source of the psychological distress with little or no consideration of social contextual factors that may contribute to the client's problems, such as sexism and racism.
3. The relationship between the therapist and client is an unequal one in which the therapist is the more powerful expert and the client is in a subordinate and vulnerable position.

The second two criticisms listed apply to pre-feminist psychotherapy in general, whereas the first one applies to individual therapists or primarily to psychoanalysis and its offshoots.

Sexism in Therapy

Most therapists today are *eclectic* in their orientations—they borrow from classic behavioral therapy, cognitive therapy, Freudian and post-Freudian psychodynamic thought, tailoring their approach to the client and the problem. The most popular single approach is *cognitive-behavioral therapy*, in which the therapist and client work on changing not only maladaptive behavioral patterns, but also destructive thought patterns. This approach is not in itself sexist; however, it may be biased if the therapist thinks in gender stereotypical ways. For example, a traditional cognitive-behavioral therapist might respond to a woman client's continual fears about her mothering with the suggestion that she take a parenting class to bolster her skills, instead of critically examining the unrealistic and idealized version of mothering that pervades our popular culture. The cognitive-behavioral approach may be less than optimal for women unless the therapist infuses it with a distinctly feminist orientation (e.g., Cohen, 2008; Hurst & Genest, 1995).

Whatever the therapist's orientation, one who is traditionally schooled and does not employ a feminist approach will tend to ignore how the client's gender, sexual orientation, race, ethnicity, disability, or other social categories may affect her experience. By focusing only on intrapsychic factors, such as personality and counterproductive thought patterns, a traditional therapist will overlook factors outside the individual that may be contributing to her distress. Instead of challenging those factors, perhaps working with the client to change the ones that are under her control and find new ways to deal with those that are not, a traditional therapist would more likely focus on the client's maladaptive response to her situation. The goal of traditional therapy is to adapt the client to the social context, not critically examine the social context itself.

Sexual Misconduct by Therapists

There is an imbalance of power when people seek psychotherapy. Patients are vulnerable, and in a needy position, which automatically makes them less powerful relative to the therapist from whom they desire treatment. They are psychologically distressed and eager to feel better, so they are probably more open and trusting than they might normally be in a new relationship with a stranger. Add to this the therapist's impressive title and academic credentials, and the relationship ends up very unbalanced, indeed. This power differential need not necessarily be a problem—after all there are many circumstances under which people need to make themselves vulnerable to others; however, some therapists have abused their higher status. The most egregious form of abuse is sexual misconduct between the therapist and client, which in the vast majority of cases involves male therapists and female clients.

In national studies, about 7 percent of male therapists report having had sexual relationships with their clients, compared to 1.5 percent of female therapists (Pope, 2001). The therapist-client relationship is an intimate one, and sexual attraction between therapists and clients is not uncommon; however, professional ethical guidelines for therapists in the U.S. prohibit sexual interaction with clients. Every state in the U.S. prohibits therapist–client sexual relationships through licensing regulations; offenders may be sued for malpractice in civil court, and in some states may be charged with criminal conduct (Pope, 2001). Sexual interaction between therapists and their clients is considered unethical precisely because of the power imbalance between them.

Sexual relationships between therapists and clients are potentially psychologically damaging to the clients, and may, of course, have repercussions for the therapist and his family as well. Women who have had sexual relationships with their therapists later report a variety of negative feelings including shame, guilt, anger, helplessness, and powerlessness (Nachmani & Somer, 2007; Somer & Saadon, 1999; Pope, 2001). In a survey of 958 patients who had been sexually involved with their therapists, 90 percent reported having been harmed by the experience, 14 percent attributed suicide attempts to their experience, and 11 percent required hospitalization during their recovery from it (Pope & Vetter, 1991). Sometimes the negative feelings are mixed with an illusory sense of achievement for having been chosen as a sexual partner and having supposedly gained control over the therapist (Nachmani & Somer, 2007) or with a sense of romance that may temporarily shield women against the ultimate negative effects of the abusive relationship (Somer & Nachmani, 2005).

Feminist Therapy

The characteristics that define feminist therapy read like a list of remedies to the problems of traditional therapy described above. The general principles of feminist therapy have been outlined by numerous authors (e.g., Brown, 2010;

Ballou et al., 2008; Enns, 2004; Worell & Remer, 2003). From a feminist therapy perspective,

1. Women's subjective experiences are valid and important to attend to, given the androcentrism that has pervaded psychological theory;
2. Not all problems originate in the individual and "personal" problems are not merely personal but are sometimes social and political.
3. Therapy should be an egalitarian collaboration between therapist and client rather than a hierarchical relationship.
4. The goals of therapy are to help women feel positive about themselves and empowered to make social change, not to educate them about what is wrong with them.
5. The therapist must be aware of the fact that women are diverse and their experiences are affected by social factors such as their age, race, ethnicity, sexual orientation, class, disability, etc.

Feminist therapy is not a theoretical orientation in the same way as cognitive-behaviorism or psychoanalysis; rather, it is a set of values that may be applied in a variety of therapeutic contexts.

Conducting Feminist Therapy

In a survey study of feminist therapists, Hill & Ballou (1998) asked whether the therapists had "adapted a specific therapeutic strategy so that it is feminist." Their respondents explained how they had taken traditional tools, such as cognitive techniques and dream analysis, and revised them so as to incorporate feminist principles. For example, one therapist challenges women to question whether their negative thinking may be a learned response to gender expectations; another teaches self-hypnosis as a skill under the control of the client, instead of using standard hypnosis which can lead to feelings that the therapist is controlling the client.

Studies comparing the practices of therapists who identify as feminist and those who do not suggest that, even when traditional tools are used, feminist therapy is distinctly different than non-feminist therapy. Feminist and non-feminist therapists respond differently to items such as, "I consider my clients' problems through a gender-role perspective" (Worell & Johnson, 2001). In one study, clients who had worked with feminist therapists reported that they felt more respected, validated, and empowered than did those who worked with non-feminist therapists (Piran, 1999). In another study, clients reported feeling that sessions with feminist therapists were more egalitarian than sessions with traditional therapists (Rader & Gilbert, 2005).

Though feminist therapists use mostly traditional techniques that they have adapted to be consistent with the principles of feminist therapy, some are employing novel techniques that may not be well-established in traditional psychotherapy. One such example is exercise therapy. Only since the 1980s has there been much research on the use of exercise in treating mental illness (Rejeski & Thompson, 1993). Some research has shown that exercise is effective in treating anxiety and depression (for a review, see Salmon, 2001), both of which are more common in women than in men. But, it is not merely the antidepressant and anxiety-reducing effects of exercise that make it appealing to some feminist therapists. Women's engagement in exercise can contribute to the goals of feminist therapy because of its empowering effects, and because it can be considered a form of resistance to the oppressive idea that strength and activity are unfeminine (Chrisler & Lamont, 2002).

Although exercise therapy has the potential to benefit women, therapists who use it should be aware of cultural factors that may affect individual women's attitudes toward exercise. For example, exercise may be viewed differently by African American women than by Caucasian American women (e.g., Hall, 1998), or by veiled Muslim women than by women who are accustomed to presenting themselves less modestly. Many other things may also affect a woman's openness to exercise therapy and what form it might take for her: her socioeconomic status (does she have leisure time and access to recreational facilities?), her family situation (if she is a stay-at-home mother of small children, does she have childcare while she exercises?), and her physical condition. Fortunately, because exercise can take so many different forms (walking, swimming, dancing, yoga, or weight-lifting), it can potentially be adapted as a positive form of feminist therapy for almost any woman.

Intersectionality and Feminist Therapy

One of the unifying principles of feminist therapy is sensitivity on the part of the therapist to intersecting characteristics of the individual such as age, race, ethnicity, sexual orientation, class, and disability (see Figure 13.5). Certainly this is not a complete list of the intersections of identities that influence women's experiences, but they are the primary ones addressed in the feminist therapy literature. This

©Lisa F. Young/Alamy RF

FIGURE 13.5   Feminist therapists are sensitive to personal characteristics of the client such as age, ethnicity, sexual orientation, and social class.

section will briefly address just a few of the issues that arise in feminist therapy with three particular populations of women: older women, women of color, and lesbian and bisexual women.

Aging Women

It may seem peculiar to refer to age as a diversity characteristic. Most women (if they are fortunate) will eventually fall into the category of older or elderly. Yet, older women are relatively invisible within the clinical context just as they are in our broader social context. For example, when researchers study body image and eating disorders, they typically focus on young women, even though the physical appearance changes that come with aging are a source of concern for many women (Chrisler & Ghiz, 1993; Hurd, 2000; Midlarsky & Nitzburg, 2008) and eating disorders may be increasing in this group (Gura, 2007). As women in our youth-oriented society reach their 50s and 60s, they may experience what Pearlman (1993) refers to as "late midlife astonishment," a sudden awareness that they in the eyes of the culture they have become stigmatized as unimportant and undesirable, especially because of their perceived loss of physical attractiveness and sexual appeal.

As women mature into the middle and latter stages of their lives, they may have to deal with issues that were not as immediate, or perhaps not even relevant, when they were younger. Thinking back to Chapter 11, can you recall some of these issues? They include retirement, economic stress, loss of a life partner (and diminishing prospects for new partners), loss of peers, physical limitations, caretaking of elderly parents (and perhaps children at the same time), health concerns, living alone, poverty in old age, ageism . . . the list could go on.

Feminist therapists are already well aware of the ways in which gender stereotypes can color perceptions and behaviors; when treating older women they must be equally attuned to the effects of age stereotypes on women's mental health. For example, older women are stereotyped as feeble and less feminine. Feminist therapy can help women redefine what it means to be powerful and worthwhile, disentangling those notions from the dominant cultural emphasis on youth (Dougherty et al., 2016; Mitchell & Bruns, 2010).

Therapists seeking to understand the sources of an older woman's psychological distress may not think to explore certain possibilities if they rely on age stereotypes. For example, just because a woman is older, and is in a relationship with an older partner, does not mean that she is not being physically or emotionally abused (Bonomi et al., 2007). Just because she is someone's grandmother does not mean she isn't struggling with an addiction to alcohol or other drugs (Katz, 2002). She may be well past menopause and living in a nursing home but that does not mean that her sexual functioning is unimportant to her (Aizenberg et al., 2002). The narrow thinking and patronizing attitude sometimes displayed by traditional health care providers working with older women (Feldman, 1999) are potentially minimized when the provider adopts an age-aware, feminist perspective.

Women of Color

Feminist therapists working with women of color must first understand one basic fact: women "of color" often have common experiences, such as being the target of racial or ethnic prejudice, but the experiences of women identified by this label also vary tremendously (Comas-Díaz & Greene, 1994; Sanchez-Hucles, 2016). Issues of central importance to Native American women will likely be different than the concerns of recent Somali immigrant women. African American women come from a very different cultural background than Asian American women. Latina women living in Texas are worlds apart from Hmong women living in Minnesota. And yet, all of these women—and many more—are typically considered "women of color" in the U.S.

Some women of color are more reluctant than White women to seek mental health care. This is sometimes due to cultural norms against seeking help. For example, Asian American women may not seek mental health care because of family and community stigma. Seeking treatment is viewed as a form of weakness, violates familial privacy, and brings shame to one's family (Augsberger et al., 2015). Women of color may also be hesitant to seek therapy because it is very probable that their only option will be to work with a White therapist of European descent. This therapist probably will have little personal experience with racism, will not likely be fluent in any language other than English, will be highly educated and financially comfortable, and will have only limited knowledge of ethnic or religious cultures other than her own. The therapist is likely to have learned stereotypes about the client's nationality, race, culture, and religion.

Of particular relevance in feminist therapy is the potential gap between feminist ideals—originally formulated by mostly White, middle-class women within a Western European tradition—and the ideas about gender that women of color may bring with them from their cultures of origin. Women from Asian and South Asian origins may subscribe to rigid gender roles in which girls are considered property from birth and are prepared throughout childhood for an eventual arranged marriage (Jayakar, 1994). Native American women may be accustomed to a variety of flexible gender roles such as the bold and assertive "manly-hearted" role for post-menopausal women among the Canadian Blackfeet and the *two-spirit* role for gender-benders in many North American Indian cultures that was described in Chapter 5 (LaFramboise et al., 1994). Also relevant are the preconceived notions that the therapist may have regarding gender roles in the client's culture of origin. For example, what is your stereotype of gender relations within Latina/o cultures? Do you think only of dominant *macho* men and submissive, second-class women? Many scholars have characterized Latina/o cultures in this way, yet some studies have suggested that this stereotype is an exaggeration and overgeneralization (Vasquez, 1994). Feminist therapists must be careful not to assume that they know how a woman of color feels about gender. At the same time, a feminist therapist will be more prepared than a non-feminist therapist to deal with the intersections between gender, race, and ethnicity for women of color.

Lesbian and Bisexual Women

Throughout traditional psychological theory and practice, "healthy" sexuality has been very narrowly defined. Assumptions of heterosexuality and homosexuality permeate the literature (Worell & Remer, 2003; Garnets & Peplau, 2001; Peplau & Garnets, 2000). Heterosexuality has been viewed as normal, while homosexuality and bisexuality have been pathologized. Sexual orientation has been presumed stable across the lifetime, casting a suspicious light on deviations later in life. Gender and sexual orientation have been confounded such that lesbian women all have been presumed masculine. Sexual orientation has been conceptualized as an attribute of the individual, rather than a variable pattern of erotic and romantic attractions influenced by the social and cultural context of women's lives (Garnets & Peplau, 2001).

Linda Garnets and Letitia Peplau (2001) recommend that therapists abandon these outdated models of women's sexual orientation. Instead, they favor a model where women's sexual orientation cannot be categorized, nor attributed to a single cause. They suggest that much of the theorizing about sexual orientation has been based on a male norm. As discussed in Chapter 7, women's sexual orientation may be more variable across the lifespan than men's; therefore, therapists should not be surprised if a woman client who felt her sexual identity was well-established ends up confused and distressed when she experiences changes in her sexual attractions. And when a woman does experience such changes, the therapist should not assume that the client's new sexual orientation is her "true" identity.

A Word about Feminist Therapy for Men

Can men benefit from feminist therapy? Several feminist therapists think so, some of whom are men themselves (Remer & Rostosky, 2001a; 2001b). Because feminist therapy is sensitive to sexual orientation, it may have more to offer gay and bisexual men than a traditional approach would. Other feminist therapists have suggested that heterosexual men may benefit from a relationship with a female feminist therapist because it can help illuminate some aspects of their relationships with women that a more traditional therapist might miss (Remer & Rostosky, 2001b). Finally, feminist therapists may be able to help increase male clients' awareness of the costs of rigidly conforming to a traditional masculine gender role (Remer & Rostotsky, 2001a). For example, a feminist therapeutic framework may benefit veterans suffering from PTSD by increasing treatment engagement through an exploration of gender role and military socialization, and fostering a sense of personal empowerment (Carr & McKernan, 2015).

Evaluating Feminist Therapy

In principle, feminist therapists strive to remedy the shortcomings of traditional therapy, but are they successful? At this point we have very little formal data on the effectiveness of the feminist therapeutic approach (Vasquez & Vasquez, 2017; Worell & Johnson, 2001). Anecdotally, feminist clinicians have been very successful at identifying and treating psychological distress specific to women, such as trauma experienced by survivors of sexual assault, incest, and battering—all things that were unnamed and untreated by pre-feminist therapists (Chesler, 2005; Marecek, 1999). Several feminist therapists have published accounts of successful treatment of other kinds of distress as well (Brown, 2006). And, if the international growth of feminist therapy since the 1970s is any indication, there is a substantial demand for woman-friendly, gender-aware, and diversity-sensitive therapy (Chesler, 2005).

It will be increasingly important, however, to generate support for feminist therapy effectiveness that goes beyond mere anecdote. Psychotherapies are typically evaluated by *outcome studies* that measure reductions in personal distress. However, the very nature of feminist therapy makes it hard to isolate its components to study in a controlled experiment (Brown, 2010). Although specific outcome studies on the effectiveness of feminist therapy are lacking, there is evidence that some of the key components of feminist therapy improve outcomes for women (Norcross, 2002). Consciousness raising, social and gender role analysis, and resocialization can all positively impact women (Israeli & Santor, 2000). There is also the question of what the appropriate outcome variable should be when examining the effectiveness of feminist therapy. Although traditional psychotherapy focuses on reducing distress, Judith Worell (2001), a pioneer of feminist therapy (see Box 13.3), suggests that its assessment should also measure empowerment; that is, she considers feminist therapy successful if it not only makes a woman feel better, but also inspires her to work for social change in her community.

In any case, the lack of outcome data regarding feminist therapy raises questions about its viability given that the current trend in healthcare and health insurance is in the direction of evidence-based practice—that is, only providing treatments that have been empirically supported with scientific research (Brown, 2006). If a practitioner

Box 13.3 ∾ Judith Worell: Pioneer in Feminist Therapy

Courtesy of Psychology's Feminist Voices (www.feministvoices.com)

According to the empowerment model, there are ten outcomes associated with women's health and well-being:

- positive self-evaluation
- positive comfort-distress balance
- gender and cultural role awareness
- personal control and self-efficacy
- self-nurturance and self-care
- effective problem solving skills
- assertiveness skills
- access to social economic, and community resources
- gender and cultural flexibility in behavior
- socially constructive activism

Judith Worell was an early and influential contributor to the development of feminist therapy. With her colleague Pam Remer, she developed the empowerment model of feminist therapy. The empowerment model takes a positive view of women's strength and abilities, and the feminist therapist can target these goals to improve women's well-being.

Worell's feminist identity can be traced back to her childhood. She grew up in an Orthodox Jewish family with strict gender roles and rules, and from a young age, questioned the unequal power dynamic she saw in her parents' relationship.

Continued on next page

Box 13.3 ∽ Judith Worell: Pioneer in Feminist Therapy (*Concluded*)

Although her home life was strictly gendered, she grew up in the progressive Greenwich Village area of New York City, and attended an alternative school she described as "radically political." She also attended Encampment for Citizenship, which trained young people to become community leaders. These early life experiences played an important role in the development of her feminism and social activism.

Worrell attended Queen's College in New York and studied psychology. It was there she met her first husband. Together they attended graduate school at Ohio State University, studying clinical psychology. At the time she received her degree, very few women were employed at colleges and universities. While her husband took up faculty positions, Worell worked in a family mental health clinic, private practice, and then did research at a psychiatric hospital. At each of the universities where her husband was employed, Worell was the first female instructor in the department. In 1968, both she and her husband took faculty positions at the University of Kentucky, and she remained there until her retirement in 1999.

The rise of the feminist movement in the 1970s helped catalyze Worell's feminist identity. Her involvement with the Southeastern Psychological Association allowed her to meet other women in psychology, and she realized her experience of being devalued in psychology departments was not unique to her but a form of structural discrimination.

She also began having conversations with colleagues about the prevalence of sexual violence. She helped develop the first sexual harassment code at the University of Kentucky, and established a feminist counseling and referral service.

Worell also served as editor of the journal *Psychology of Women Quarterly*. As editor, she felt it was important that all of the articles in the journal have a feminist component, rather than just being about women. She has served as president of APA Division 35 Society for the Psychology of Women, the Kentucky Psychological Association, and the Southeastern Psychological Association. She has also received lifetime achievement awards for her contribution to the psychology of women, including the Division 35 Carolyn Sherif Award (2001) and the Heritage Award (2004). In 2010, she received the Gold Medal Award for Life Achievement in the Practice of Psychology for the American Psychological Foundation.

Sources: MacKay, J. (2010). Profile of Judith Worell. In A. Rutherford (Ed.), *Psychology's Feminist Voices Multimedia Internet Archive.* Retrieved from http://www.feministvoices.com /judith-worell/

Worell, J. P. (2010). Gold Medal Award for Life Achievement in the Practice of Psychology. *American Psychologist, 65*(5), 373–375.

Worell, J., & Johnson, D. M. (2002). Feminist approaches to psychotherapy. In J. Worell (Ed.) *Encyclopedia of Women and Gender,* pp. 425–438. San Diego, CA: Academic Press.

Contributed by Annie B. Fox

provides an empirically supported treatment, such as cognitive-behavioral therapy, and infuses it with a feminist perspective, this is not a problem; however, if a therapist wants to formally and exclusively identify her (or his) treatment as "feminist therapy," there may be problems with the insurance company (Brown, 2006).

Feminist therapy is not without its critics. Even supporters of the approach have highlighted its limitations. Jane Ussher (1992) points out that as highly educated, professionally credentialed individuals, feminist therapists, like traditional therapists, still represent a privileged group. She warns that feminist theory generated by elite academics and activists may not be applicable or accessible to all women. The academics and clinicians who write about and practice feminist therapy constitute a less diverse group than women in general.

Speaking of women in general, some have warned against the tendency of some feminist therapists to think of all women as sharing characteristics unique to their sex (e.g., Cosgrove, 2003). For example, when researchers interviewed a sample of feminist therapists about their practice, many of them implied a belief in a fundamental feminine or womanly nature—referring to "the essence of being a woman" and "the feminine character" (Marecek & Kravetz, 1998, p. 18). Assuming that all women share a uniquely feminine perspective as women ignores the diversity among women. It can contribute to biased attitudes favoring women as a group with special qualities—a kind of benevolent sexism that has costs as well as benefits for women.

Making a Difference

By now you have a better sense of why this chapter began with the idea that traditional clinical practice may be at odds with women's well-being. Feminist therapy is a step in the right direction toward improving the mental health context for women. Equally important is social change that will challenge the perception of women's madness relative to a male norm, and will lead to a reduction in the external factors that contribute to women's real psychological distress.

Transforming Ourselves: Finding (or Becoming) a Feminist Therapist

Not all feminist therapists are alike. In fact, not all therapists who call themselves feminist are necessarily feminist. Why would a therapist adopt the feminist label if his or her work is not truly informed by feminist therapy principles? Hypothetically, an unscrupulous clinician might do so in order to attract business (Caplan, 1992). But it's also possible that a self-named feminist therapist might *seem* not feminist because of different ideas about what feminism means.

There are many flavors of feminism and potentially as many different varieties of feminist therapy. So, how does one find the right feminist therapist? Besides referrals from family, friends, or other clinicians, an individual in search of a feminist therapist could consult some of the several therapist search engine sites on the Internet, most of which list feminist therapy as a specialty option. Some larger metropolitan areas have woman-centered social services that can direct people to feminist clinicians, such as the Feminist Therapy Referral Project (FTRP) in Berkeley, CA.

If you are a student of psychology who aspires to become a therapist, consider whether the feminist label may be right for your future practice. At this point in time, there is no centralized institute that trains feminist therapists; when such training is available, it tends to be in the form of sporadic opportunities, such as continuing education courses or conference workshops (Brown, 2010). Still, given that nearly all of the founders of feminist therapy practice are still alive today (and are still writing and teaching about feminist therapy), future feminist therapists may yet have the opportunity to learn directly from first generation predecessors (Brown, 2010).

Transforming Social Relations: Challenging the "Crazy Woman" Stereotype

How many times have you heard someone make a wisecrack about women being "nuts" when they are "on the rag"? Have you ever had a guy (or his new girlfriend) tell you with a shudder that all of his ex-girlfriends were "psycho"? Do you and your friends agree that your mothers are all "crazy"? The idea that women as a group are mentally ill permeates our culture. From now on, pay attention to the examples you encounter in everyday conversation, movies and television, crime reports, advice columns, and stand-up comedy routines etc. Take note when women's behavior is pathologized relative to a male standard of rationality and wellness. And then: Challenge it! Challenge yourself and your acquaintances to steer clear of the loony women comments and jokes. Treat women's perspectives and experiences with the respect that they deserve (including your own, if you are a woman). Question the "experts" who would have us believe that women are irrational, illogical, too dependent, and emotionally overwrought.

Another way to challenge the crazy woman stereotype is to become an informed advocate for women who *are* mentally ill. One place to start is the National Alliance on Mental Illness (NAMI), a grassroots organization that has provided more than 30 years of support, education, advocacy, and research to help mentally ill individuals. NAMI's Web site (www.nami.org) offers numerous ways to get involved, such as becoming one of their "stigma-busters," currently more than 20,000 individuals across the world who speak out against inaccurate and harmful representations of mental illness in media in an effort to reduce the prejudice and discrimination commonly faced by mentally ill individuals and their families.

Transforming Society: Promoting Women's Psychological Well-Being

Clearly, women's well-being is intimately tied to their social circumstances. Sexism, racism, poverty, violence—all of these are significant contributors to women's psychological distress. Women have long been told that the remedy for their distress is individual change (or medication or hospitalization), but no amount of therapy for an individual woman is going to alleviate her symptoms if the source of the problem is economic inequality, sexual harassment, or domestic abuse. Feminist therapists encourage their clients to seek relief through social change. By engaging in activism to address the social problems that women face, you, too, can work to promote women's mental health.

Exploring Further

❧

Ballou, M. (2008) (Ed.). *Feminist therapy theory and practice: A contemporary perspective.* New York: Springer.
  Diverse contributors discuss key issues in feminist therapy and how they are played out in the actual practice of therapy.

Chesler, P. (2005). *Women and madness* (Revised and updated for the first time in 30 years). New York: Palgrave Macmillan.
   First published in 1972, this groundbreaking book challenges traditional definitions of madness and critiques the use of psychiatry as a form of social control over women.

Comas-Diaz, L., & Weiner, M. B. (Eds.) *Women psychotherapists: Journeys in healing.* Lanham, MD: The Rowman & Littlefield Publishing Group, 2011. ISBN 978076570787
   The rich, personal narratives of 11 diverse women who describe their journeys becoming feminist psychotherapists and healers.

Mussap, A. J. (2007). The relationship between feminine gender role stress and disordered eating symptomatology in women. *Stress and Health, 23(5)*, 343-348.

Worell, J., & Remer, P. (2003). *Feminist perspectives in therapy: Empowering diverse women.* Hoboken, NJ: Wiley.
   Two pioneering feminist therapists show how feminist therapy is not just about adjustment, it's about empowerment.

Text Credits

∾

p. 415: Caplan, P. J. (1985). *The myth of women's masochism.* New York: E.P. Dutton. **pp. 415–416:** Wylie, P. (1942). *A generation of vipers.* New York: Farrar & Rinehart. **p. 416:** *Diagnostic and Statistical Manual of Mental Disorders,* Fifth Edition. **p. 423:** Contributed by Annie B. Fox. **p. 428:** Freud, S. (1914). *On the history of the Psycho-Analytic movement.* New York: W. W. Norton, Inc., 1966. **p. 430:** Charlotte Perkins Gilman, *The Yellow Wallpaper,* 1892. **p. 431:** All excerpts from Geller, J. L., & Harris, M. (1994). *Women of the asylum: Voices from behind the walls, 1840–1945.* New York: Anchor Books. **pp. 442–443:** Contributed by: Annie B. Fox.

CHAPTER 14

Making a Difference:
Toward a Better Future for Women

*T*hroughout history, women have struggled to have their voices heard and their contributions to society accepted. For over 150 years, the women's movement has provided a powerful force for change.

The first wave of feminist activists included the suffragists who achieved the vote for women in the early 1900s. The second wave, whose activism began in the 1960s, worked on issues such as reproductive rights, workplace equality, sexism in the media, nonsexist child raising, the integration of women into science and politics, and an end to violence against women. Today, third-wave feminists continue the tradition, working on some of the same inequities that second-wave feminism tackled, and adding new ones: the continued objectification of women, reproductive rights in a high-tech era, global trafficking in girls and women, LGBTQ rights, and many more.

Contemporary Feminism

Feminists are a diverse group on dimensions such as nationality, ethnicity, social class, and religion. This diversity is a strength because it encourages people to work for social change in many areas and to use a variety of strategies. Throughout this book, we have seen that the problems faced by working-class women are quite different from those faced by professional women. Older women experience different forms of sexism than younger women. Women who mother run into a different kind of stereotyping and inequality than those who do not. Anyone whose sexual orientation is different from the heterosexual norm may encounter prejudice and discrimination on that basis. People whose bodies are marked by difference are claiming the right to their own dimensions of diversity, as shown by activism for the rights of intersex and transgender people. Women of color have taken their rightful place in feminist leadership and activism, and women from around the globe speak to their own societies' issues. The Nigerian-born writer Chimamanda Ngozi Adichie, recipient of a MacArthur "genius" grant, authored a TED talk, "We Should All Be Feminists," that has been viewed more than 3.2 million times and sampled by Beyoncé (see Figure 14.1).

Respect for differences is a cornerstone of feminist philosophy and activism. Feminists also have other shared values and goals. At the most basic level, a feminist is one who believes in the worth and value of women. As a 1970s bumper sticker proclaimed, "Feminism is the radical notion that women are people." Moreover, feminists recognize that social change is necessary and that no one can create social justice by herself. They believe that people should work together to change society so that women can lead more secure, satisfying, and fulfilling lives. This belief in *collective action,* or group solidarity toward social change, differentiates feminism from just individual women achieving success.

Increasingly, feminism is a global social movement. International conferences like the landmark Beijing Conference of 1995 and Beijing + 15, a 2010 forum, have brought women together to learn from each other about the particular forms that patriarchy takes in each society and to share effective strategies for change. And

FIGURE 14.1   Chimamanda Ngozi Adichie. You can watch her viral TED talk We Should All Be Feminists on YouTube.

international activism is growing, based on the recognition that the unfulfilled promise of human rights for women is one of the biggest issues of the twenty-first century (see Box 14.1).

Imagery and Attitudes

Like other progressive movements for social justice, feminism has met with resistance from those who benefit from inequality. Each time that feminist perspectives have gained power, there has been a *backlash*—attempts to put women, and particularly feminists, back in their place (Faludi, 1991). The backlash has taken different forms at different times in history, but some characteristic patterns emerge repeatedly. One form of backlash is to label feminists and their ideas as crazy. As noted in Chapter 13, women until recently risked being labeled mad if they wanted to think or act independently. Today, the label is more likely to be lesbian or man-hater. Let's look more closely at resistance to feminism.

Images and Stereotypes of Feminists

When first-wave feminists began organizing to win the right to vote, political cartoonists depicted them in ways that seem very familiar today. Figure 14.2 shows suffragists as ugly, cigar-smoking, angry women who foist their babies off on men. Their exposed legs represent their dangerously out-of-control sexuality. They are labeled as brassy, sharp-tongued man-tamers.

Box 14.1 ∾ Half the Sky: Turning Oppression into Opportunity for Women Worldwide

Half the Sky is a call to arms, a call for help, a call for contributions, but also a call for volunteers. It asks us to open our eyes to this enormous humanitarian issue . . . I really do think this is one of the most important books I have ever reviewed.

—*Carolyn See, Washington Post*

Nicholas Kristof and Sheryl WuDunn are journalists, Pulitzer Prize winners, and most importantly, strong advocates for women's rights across the globe. In 2009, they published *Half the Sky: Turning Oppression into Opportunity for Women Worldwide*. The phrase "half the sky" comes from a Chinese proverb, "Women hold up half the sky."

In the book, Kristof and WuDunn tell the stories of courageous women in the developing world. These women have experienced some of the most egregious forms of violence and oppression, from trafficking and forced prostitution to genital cutting and rape. Their book also brings attention to the issue of maternal mortality, as thousands of women die needlessly each year from inadequate access to medical care. Although the stories are anecdotal, they serve as a powerful reminder of the kinds of experiences that women are subjected to on a daily basis in countries hampered by violence and poverty.

Probably the most important contribution that Kristof and WuDunn have made to improving the lives of women is their advocacy for "outsiders" (us!) to get involved in the education and economic empowerment of women. For only a few dollars, someone could sponsor the education of a young girl or provide microcredit to a woman to start her own business. Such small actions can dramatically improve the lives of women across the globe.

In addition to encouraging activism through the book, Kristof and WuDunn also maintain a Web site, www.halftheskymovement.org, which serves as a hub of information for people who are looking to get involved in activism to end poverty and violence against women. The Web site provides links to more than 40 organizations that deal with violence against women, economic empowerment, education, maternal mortality, sex trafficking, and humanitarian relief. They also encourage people to use social media such as Facebook and Twitter to get the message out.

In September 2009, Kristof and WuDunn spoke to government representatives and the media in Washington DC about their book and stressed the need to make improving the lives of women across the globe a top priority. Kristof stated, "There is a tipping point on this issue . . . now, increasingly, the role of women is seen, not only as a good thing to do but as a security issue as well as an economic issue, and all these things are coming together and I think, making it the time to address this truly as the cause of our time."

Sources: Half the Sky Movement. www.halftheskymovement.org "Nick Kristof and Sheryl WuDunn bring their Half the Sky global women's movement to Washington." *White House Correspondents: Insider.* Available at: http://www.whitehouse correspondentsweekendinsider.com/2009/09/12/nick -kristof-and-sheryl-wudunn-bring-their-half-the-sky-global -women%E2%80%99s-movement-to-washington/ Contributed by Annie B. Fox.

In the 1970s, these images and stereotypes resurfaced. The media image of second-wave feminists was negative:

News reports and opinion columnists created a new stereotype, of fanatics, "braless bubbleheads," Amazons, "the angries," and "a band of wild lesbians." The result is that we all know what feminists are. They are shrill, overly aggressive, man-hating, ball-bust-

FIGURE 14.2   Backlash against first-wave feminists.

Source: Library of Congress, Reproduction Number#LC-DIG-pga-05762

ing, selfish, hairy, extremist, deliberately unattractive women with absolutely no sense of humor who see sexism at every turn. They make men's testicles shrivel up to the size of peas, they detest the family and think all children should be deported or drowned. Feminists are relentless, unforgiving, and unwilling to bend or compromise; they are single-handedly responsible for the high divorce rate, the shortage of decent men and the unfortunate proliferation of Birkenstocks in America. (Douglas, 1994, p. 7)

By the 1980s, the media began to declare feminism outdated, claiming that equal rights had been fully achieved, society was now in a "post feminist" era, and women were abandoning feminism because it had terrible costs. In the 1980s version of backlash, everything from infertility to the breakdown of society was blamed on feminism, and its time was declared long past (Faludi, 1991).

Today, the public image of feminists has both positive and negative aspects. Feminists are viewed positively as women working together to achieve goals and negatively as man-hating extremists. Even when people do not hold negative beliefs themselves, they think that others do. In one study, 171 women completed measures of attitudes toward feminism for themselves and also were asked to complete the measures as they thought other people would. Both feminists and non-feminists believed that others have negative views of feminists and consider them more likely to be lesbian than straight (Ramsey et al., 2007). Men's attitudes are mixed, too. Interviews with British male high-school students and adult men revealed that they had "Jekyll and Hyde" views: Feminists are reasonable women who just want equality *and* ugly, man-hating lesbians who go around "banging and shouting" and just want men to "jump in the river." Surprisingly, many men held *both* these contradictory views (Edley & Wetherell, 2001).

A recurring theme in these stereotypes is that feminists are man-haters. Psychologist Kristin Anderson and her colleagues decided to get some empirical evidence on this claim (Anderson et al., 2009). In an ethnically diverse sample of nearly 500 college students, they found that feminists had significantly *less* hostility toward men than non-feminists. In a review of the most recent research, Anderson still found "no empirical evidence whatsoever to support the notion that feminists' attitudes toward men are more negative than non-feminists'" (Anderson, 2015, p. 66).

Conservatives with influence in the media play to all the negative stereotypes. Two days after the 9/11 tragedy, televangelists Jerry Falwell and Pat Robertson famously concurred that "pagans, and the abortionists, and the feminists, and the gays and the lesbians," had contributed to the attacks by undermining moral standards and causing God to stop protecting America. In the news media, conservative commentators try to scare men and turn women away from working together for equality by referring to "feminazis" and characterizing any criticism of the status quo as "male-bashing." A favorite right-wing term is "militant feminist," though what it means is unclear. Personally, I have never met a feminist with an assault weapon or heard of any feminist armies about to march on Congress or the guys' locker room. Feminism, of course, is not about "bashing" or making war on men; it is about working to change the social structural, interactional, and individual levels of the gender system that disadvantage girls and women.

Attitudes toward Feminism

The societal images of feminism and feminists clearly influence individuals' attitudes. On the one hand, studies during the 1980s and 1990s showed that college women described feminists as strong, caring, capable, open-minded, knowledgeable, and intelligent (Berryman-Fink & Verderber, 1985). On the other hand, being labeled a feminist brings a certain stigma. When college women were asked to report their own beliefs and those of a "typical feminist," even those who identified themselves as feminists felt that the typical feminist was more extreme in beliefs than they themselves were (Liss et al., 2000). Many women are reluctant to label themselves feminists. In one survey, 78 percent of college women said they were not feminists, although the majority agreed with some or most of the goals of the women's movement (Liss et al., 2001). And even the feminists reported that they didn't always admit to being feminists in public!

Despite the negative stereotypes, some women do identify themselves as feminists and support collective action for social change on behalf of women. Psychologists Miriam Liss and Mindy Erchull and their colleagues have explored feminist identity and its correlates. For example, they conducted several studies of the factors that predict whether a woman will choose to identify as a feminist. Exposure to feminist ideas, having a generally positive view of feminists, and recognizing that discrimination exists are important (Liss et al., 2001). In a study of 282 women college students, they found that life experiences such as having a feminist mother, taking a women's studies course, and having personal experience with sexism predicted liberal beliefs. In turn, these beliefs led to identifying oneself as a feminist and believing in collective action (Nelson et al., 2008). When a woman says of herself "I am a feminist," she is more likely to engage in activism on behalf of women than are other women who have similar beliefs about gender equality but who do not label themselves as feminists (Yoder, et al., 2011). In other words, feminist identity is linked to feminist activism.

There has been very little systematic research on attitudes toward feminism among women of diverse ethnic groups, and almost none on men's attitudes. Are African-American, Asian-American, and Latina women likely to identify as feminists? What about men from these groups? One study approached these questions by surveying 1,140 students at an urban university (Robnett & Anderson, 2016). Students were asked for their definitions of feminism and their reasons for identifying (or not) as feminists.

Overall, four out of five participants defined feminism in terms of gender equality. For example, a Latino man said that feminism is "a movement that demands equality in women's rights." However, some students in all groups endorsed stereotypes; one European American woman said that feminists are "radical women who believe men are inferior to them and that women should rule the world" (Robnett & Anderson, 2016, pp. 3, 4). European American women were most likely to identify as feminists, followed by Latina, African-American women, and finally Asian-American women. The finding that African- and Asian-American women were much less likely to identify as feminist suggests that the feminist movement needs to do more work on goals relevant to these groups. As for the men, only a small minority in any of the ethnic groups identified as feminist. Moreover, 24% of the men who did not identify as feminists said it was *because they were men*. This result is disheartening, because saying that a man cannot be a feminist is like saying that a White person cannot participate in the Civil Rights movement. Egalitarian men are important and valued allies for women, and have been since the birth of feminism.

I invite you to think critically about the ways that feminists and feminism are portrayed in our society. Contrary to stereotype, feminists are not monsters. In a study of over 650 women who filled in an online questionnaire about their feminist beliefs and identity, those who called themselves feminists acknowledged the existence of sexism, perceived the current gender system as unjust, and believed that women should work together to change it (Liss & Erchull, 2010). In addition, those who call themselves feminists support the goals of the women's movement and tend not to hold conservative beliefs (Liss et al., 2001). They neither hate men nor idealize them (Anderson et al., 2009).

Feminists are more likely than non-feminists to see through and reject unrealistic ideals for women—such as the overemphasis on extreme thinness, appearance, and romantic relationships (Hurt et al., 2007). In a review of research on the relationship between feminist attitudes and psychological well-being, Anderson (2015) found that in virtually all the areas that have been measured, feminist attitudes and feminist identity are linked with positive effects on women, including more satisfying heterosexual relationships, healthier sexual attitudes, greater self-efficacy, feelings of empowerment, and a more positive body image. It is important to remember, however, that research on attitudes and well-being is correlational. We cannot know whether feminism causes positive changes in psychological well-being, whether women with these characteristics are more likely to become feminists, or whether other factors are responsible. We just know that feminists, on average, have better psychological well-being than non-feminists.

©Jim West/Alamy; (right): Courtesy of Dr. Mary Crawford

FIGURE 14.3   On January 21, 2017, millions of people marched in support of women's rights following the inauguration of Donald J. Trump—in the nation's capital (left), in towns and cities across the U.S., such as Santa Cruz, California (right), and in cities around the globe.

Personally, I am proud to call myself a feminist, and I find distorted media portrayals of feminists and feminism disturbing. Consider this question: Whose interests does it serve if a movement to end sexism and the oppression of women is portrayed as crazy, misguided, and totally unnecessary? Yet the women's movement is unstoppable. On January 21, 2017, more than 2½ million people in cities and towns around the world participated in women's rights marches to protest the inauguration of President Donald Trump (Przybyla & Schouten, 2017). In Washington DC, the pink "pussycat" hat became a new symbol of women's resistance to patriarchal control (see Figure 14.3).

Women's rights are human rights. They are so important that, far from holding to an inflexible party line, feminists have always encouraged debate and a plurality of viewpoints. In writing this book, I have tried to present a variety of feminist perspectives with the goal of encouraging you to think critically about them.

Feminist Psychology and Social Change

The second wave of the women's movement had important effects on psychology. One of the most basic changes was the number of women in psychology and their status within the field. Even more important than numbers is the influence of feminist theory and research.

The Changing Face of Psychology

Only a few short years ago, psychologists who happened to be women could not get hired by high-status universities and were rarely taken seriously as scientists (Rutherford et al., 2012). Ethnic minority psychologists, too, were marginalized (Jenkins et al., 2002). Today, women earn the majority of higher degrees in psychology. Psychologists who are women and ethnic minorities lead well-established professional organizations, produce many books and journals, and participate in every aspect of psychological research, education, and practice.

I saw a small example of the changing gender norms within psychology recently. At my university, there are regular lunchtime research talks for faculty and graduate students. At one, the speakers were a married couple (with different last names) who do their research jointly. With them were their two children, a 4-year-old son and a 1-month-old infant. The man started their research presentation, while Mom took the children to play outside. Sexist? Not exactly. Halfway through the talk, she returned, Dad took the kids outside, and she concluded the presentation and discussion of their research. A lunchtime psychology program became an example of collaborative research, shared parenting, and the balancing act of multiple roles for both women and men.

Progress is uneven, however. It will probably be a while before such a scene occurs regularly enough that it is taken for granted. Women in psychology still have trouble making it into the top ranks; on average, they publish less and their work is cited less than the work of their male peers (Eagly & Miller, 2016). It's difficult to determine how much this is due to overt discrimination and how much to the broader sociocultural factors discussed throughout this book, such as stereotype threat, backlash against agentic women, the unequal division of labor at home, and the lack of governmental policies to support working families in the U.S., such as paid parental leave and government-supported childcare.

Imagine a World . . .

Imagine a world that is free of gender-based violence against girls and women. Imagine a world where husbands do half the housework, every child is protected from sexual abuse, and no old woman is forced to end her life in poverty. Imagine a world where half of the CEOs, judges, generals, and members of parliament or congress are women—in every country. What would the world be like if all pregnancies were chosen and all children wanted? If the human capacity for emotion and empathy were considered manly as well as womanly? If all body shapes and sizes were accepted, and no woman felt she had to starve herself to look good?

It's true that none of these visions is close to becoming reality. But nobody expected it would be easy to remedy the patriarchal power imbalances that shape women's lives. The psychology of women and gender has made a huge contribution toward a more just society. Its contribution began with naming androcentrism and sexism in psychological theories and research. It continued with the development of many new research topics and theories. Think back for a moment to the hundreds of research articles described in this book. This research is now being integrated into virtually every subfield of psychology, including social, developmental, biological, personality, and clinical. In the process, it is changing the way psychologists think about women and gender, and helping to build a better, more inclusive science of human behavior.

Feminist psychologists also founded organizations (such as the Society for the Psychology of Women and AWP), started new research journals that have flourished for four decades, and developed feminist approaches to counseling and therapy that have helped many women and men. The work of feminist scholars, clinicians, and organizational activists in psychology illustrates the principle of using feminist values to "do work that matters" (Yoder, 2015, p. 427).

What Can One Student Do?

> Never doubt that a small group of thoughtful, committed people could change the world. Indeed, it's the only thing that ever has.
>
> — *Margaret Mead*

You can make a difference as a student by contributing to research and by using your knowledge of the psychology of women and gender to work for change. When you have a choice of topic, you can write term papers on women or gender in your psychology, history, and literature courses. You can do an independent study or thesis on women and gender. You can ask questions in class when women are excluded or trivialized in readings and lectures. These strategies can help raise awareness for yourself and others.

You can connect with the women's center on your campus. If your campus has no women's center or women's studies program, start asking why. By taking courses that focus on women and gender, and recommending them to others, you can show the administration that there is a demand for this knowledge.

You can join an organization for women's equality, such as the National Organization for Women (www.NOW.org), or the Feminist Majority Foundation (www.feminist.org). Your dues will support activism on behalf of all women, and you will be kept updated on issues of gender equity. Another way to stay and updated and connected is to follow feminist blogs such as Feministing (http://feministing.com) and Everyday Feminism (http://everydayfeminism.com). You can also volunteer your time. Many feminist organizations have internship opportunities for college students—just check their Web sites for information. Become a Big Sister or Big Brother to a girl or boy in need of guidance (www.bbbs.org). Or do an internship or volunteer work at a rape crisis hotline or domestic violence shelter in your community, or help out an elderly woman or single mom who needs assistance.

Your knowledge of the psychology of women and gender can help in your career planning. If you are planning to apply to graduate schools in psychology (or any other area), look carefully at the number of women faculty in the programs you consider, and how many have tenure. Look for courses on women and gender in the catalog, and find out whether there are women's studies and ethnic studies programs and a women's center. When visiting, ask about the level of support for feminist scholarship on campus. Psychology students (both male and female) can find information and support on a variety of gender issues by joining the Association for Women in Psychology (www.awpsych.org) or Division 35 of APA (www .apa.org/about/division/div35.aspx) as student affiliates. These organizations allow students to become part of networks of people with similar concerns. Through organizations like these, you can develop friendships with others who share your values and work together for social change.

If you are seeking employment after graduation, look carefully at the gender-related policies and family sensitivity of the companies you consider. Do they have flex-time, on-site day care, parental leave, and benefits for same-sex partners? Does the health care plan cover women's reproductive needs? What proportion of management are women? How often do women get promoted from inside the company? Is there ethnic and racial diversity? What is the company's record on sexual harassment complaints? Ask questions based on your knowledge of the psychology of women and gender.

One of the most important things you can do is to continue to educate yourself on the issues facing girls and women. Even though you have completed this book and your current course, continue to challenge the androcentrism in your education and the sexism in the world around you. This will help you think critically about what you read and hear in other textbooks, classes, and the media. It also will help you become an equal partner in relationships, an effective employee, and a responsible citizen after graduation.

Psychological research and theory have provided a wealth of evidence and reason on why women want and deserve full human rights. I offer the research and theory in this book as a resource and a gift. This gift can be made meaningful only by the one who receives it. How will you use your knowledge of psychology to make a difference?

Exploring Further

〜

Anderson, Kristin J. (2015). *Modern misogyny: Anti-feminism in a post-feminist era*. New York: Oxford University Press.
Conservative and antifeminist writers fill the media with claims that boys and men are victimized by feminism and that feminists are unhappy, maladjusted women who hate men. Kristin Anderson offers an eye opening look at the misinformation, showing how psychological research refutes these and other antifeminist claims.

Roberts, Tomi-Ann, Curtin, Nicola, Duncan, Lauren E., & Cortina, Lilia M. (eds) (2016). *Feminist Perspectives on Building a Better Psychological Science of Gender*. Switzerland: Springer International.
This collaboration among leading feminist scholars begins with an overview of the latest research on gender, followed by reflections on specific areas. The final section explores innovations in diverse areas such as the study of men and masculinity, weight stigma, objectification, health psychology, and emotion. An excellent guide to feminist psychology and its future paths.

Text Credits

∿

p. 450: Carolyn See, *Washington Post.* **p. 450:** Half the Sky Movement. www.halftheskymovement.org "Nick Kristof and Sheryl WuDunn bring their Half the Sky global women's movement to Washington." White House Correspondents: Insider. Available at: http://www.whitehouse correspondentsweekendinsider.com/2009/09/12/nickkristof-and-sheryl-wudunn-bring-their-half-the-sky-globalwomen%E2%80%99s-movement-to-washington/ Contributed by Annie B. Fox. **p. 451:** Douglas, S. J. (1994). *Where the girls are: Growing up female with the mass media.* New York: Times Books/Random House. **p. 452:** Jerry Falwell and Pat Robertson, 2001. **p. 456:** Margaret Meade.

References

Abbasi, S., Chuang, C. H., Dagher, R., Zhu, J., & Kjerulff, K. (2013). Unintended pregnancy and postpartum depression among first-time mothers. *Journal of Women's Health, 22*(5), 412–416.

Abrams, D., Swift, H. J., & Drury, L. (2016). Old and unemployable? How age-based stereotypes affect willingness to hire job candidates. Journal of Social Issues, 72(1), 105–121.

Abramson, L. Y., & Alloy, L. B. (2006). Cognitive vulnerability to depression: Current status and developmental origins. In T. E. Joiner, J. S. Brown, & J. Kistner (Eds.), *The interpersonal, cognitive, and social nature of depression* (pp. 83–100). Mahwah, NJ: Erlbaum.

Abusharaf, R. M. (1998, March/April). Unmasking tradition. *The Sciences,* 22–27.

Adachi, T. (2013). Occupational gender stereotypes: Is the ratio of women to men a powerful determinant? *Psychological Reports, 112*(2), 640–650. doi:10.2466/17.07.PR0.112.2.640–650

Adams, R. C. (1997). Friendship patterns among older women. In J. M. Coyle (Ed.), *Handbook on women and aging* (pp. 400–417). Westport, CT: Greenwood Press.

Addis, M. E., & Mahalik, J. R. (2003). Men, masculinity, and the contexts of help seeking. *American Psychologist, 58,* 5–14.

Ader, D. N., & Johnson, S. B. (1994). Sample description, reporting and analysis of sex in psychological research: A look at APA and APA division journals in 1990. *American Psychologist, 49,* 216–218.

Affonso, D. D., & Mayberry, L. J. (1989). Common stressors reported by a group of childbearing American women. In P. N. Stern (Ed.), *Pregnancy and parenting* (pp. 41–55). New York: Hemisphere.

Agrawal, A., Jacobson, K. C., Gardner, C. O., Prescott, C. A., & Kendler, K. S. (2004). Population-based twin study of sex differences in depressive symptoms. *Twin Research, 7,* 176–181.

Ahlqvist, S., Halim, M. L., Greulich, F. K., Lurye, L. E., & Ruble, D. (2013). The potential benefits and risks of identifying as a tomboy: A social identity perspective. *Self and Identity, 12*(5), 563–581. doi:10.1080/15298868.2012.717709

Aizenberg, D., Weizman, A., & Barak, Y. (2002). Attitudes toward sexuality among nursing home residents. *Sexuality and Disability, 20,* 185–189.

Algoe, S. B., Buswell, B. N., & DeLamater, J. D. (2000). Gender and job status as contextual cues for the interpretation of facial expression of emotion. *Sex Roles, 42,* 183–208.

Alindogan-Medina, N. (2006). Women's studies: A struggle for a better life. In M. Crawford & R. Unger (Eds.), *In our own words: Writings from women's lives* (2nd ed., pp. 45–57). Long Grove, IL: Waveland Press.

Allen, B. D., Nunley, J. M., & Seals, A. (2011). The effect of joint-child-custody legislation on the child-support receipt of single mothers. *Journal of Family and Economic Issues, 32*(1), 124–139. doi:10.1007/s10834-010-9193-4

Allison, R., & Risman, B. J. (2013). A double standard for "hooking up": How far have we come toward gender equality? *Social Science Research, 42*(5), 1191–1206. doi:10.1016/j.ssresearch.2013.04.006

Alter, J. (2016). The Carters' platinum anniversary. *The New Yorker.* Retrieved from http://www.newyorker.com/magazine/2016/08/01/the-carters-platinum-anniversary

Alvarez, M. J., & Garcia-Marques, L. (2009). Condom inclusion in cognitive representations of sexual encounters. *Journal of Sex Research, 45,* 358–370.

Amanatullah, E. T., & Tinsley, C. H. (2013). Punishing female negotiators for asserting too much . . . or not enough: Exploring why advocacy moderates backlash against assertive female negotiators. *Organizational Behavior and Human Decision Processes, 120*(1), 110–122. doi:10.1016/j.obhdp.2012.03.006

Amaro, H., Raj, A., & Reed, E. (2001). Women's sexual health: The need for feminist analyses in public health in the decade of behavior. *Psychology of Women Quarterly, 25,* 324–334

Amato, P. R., Booth, A., Johnson, D. R., & Rogers, S. J. (2007). *Alone together: How marriage in America is changing.* Cambridge, MA: Harvard University Press.

Amato, P. R., & Previti, D. (2003). People's reasons for divorcing: Gender, social class, the life course, and adjustment. *Journal of Family Issues, 24,* 602–626.

American Association of University Women Educational Foundation. (2001). *Hostile hallways: Bullying, teasing and sexual harassment in school.* Washington, DC: Author.

American Psychiatric Association. (2000). *Diagnostic and statistical manual of psychological disorders* (4th ed., text revision). Washington, DC: Author.

American Psychiatric Association. (2013). *Diagnostic and statistical manual of mental disorders* (5th ed.). Washington, DC: Author.

American Psychological Association. (2009). *Report of the task force on gender identity and gender variance.* Washington, DC: Author.

American Psychological Association, Task force on the Sexualization of Girls. (2007). *Report of the APA Task Force on the Sexualization of Girls.* Retrieved from http://www.apa.org/pi/women/programs/girls/report.aspx

American Psychological Association, Task Force on Trafficking of Women and Girls. (2014). *Report of the Task Force on Trafficking of Women and Girls.* Washington, DC: American Psychological Association.

American Society of Plastic Surgeons. (2015). *2015 Cosmetic plastic surgery statistics.* Retrieved from https://d2wirczt-3b6wjm.cloudfront.net/News/Statistics/2015/cosmetic-procedure-trends-2015.pdf

Anderson, C. A., Berkowitz, L., Donnerstein, E., Huesmann, L. R., Johnson, J. D., Linz, D., . . . Wartella, E. (2003). The influence of media violence on youth. *Psychological Science in the Public Interest, 4,* 81–110.

Anderson, C. A., & Carnagey, N. L. (2009). Causal effects of violent sports video games on aggression: Is it competitiveness or violent content? *Journal of Experimental Social Psychology, 45,* 731–739.

Anderson, C. A., Sakamoto, A., Gentile, D. A., Ihori, N., Shibuya, A., Yukawa, S., . . . Kobayashi, K. (2008). Longitudinal effects of violent video games on aggression in Japan and the United States. *Pediatrics, 122,* 1067–1072.

Anderson, K. A., & Hiersteiner, C. (2008). Recovering from childhood sexual abuse: Is a "storybook ending" possible? *The American Journal of Family Therapy, 36,* 413–424.

Anderson, K. J. (2015). *Modern misogyny: Anti-feminism in a post-feminist era.* New York: Oxford University Press.

Anderson, K. J., Kanner, M., & Elsayegh, N. (2009). Are feminists man haters? Feminists' and nonfeminists' attitudes toward men. *Psychology of Women Quarterly, 33,* 216–224.

Anderson, K. J., & Leaper, C. (1998). Meta-analysis of gender effects on conversational interruptions: Who, what, when, where, and how. *Sex Roles, 39,* 225–252.

Anderson, K. L., & Umberson, D. (2001). Gendering violence: Masculinity and power in men's accounts of domestic violence. *Gender & Society, 15,* 358–380.

Anderson, N. (2014, March 26). The gender factor in college admissions. *The Washington Post.* Retrieved from https://www.washingtonpost.com/local/education/the-gender-factor-in-college-admissions/2014/03/26/4996e988-b4e6-11e3-8020-b2d790b3c9e1_story.html

Andreoletti, C., Leszczynski, J. P., & Disch, W. B. (2015). Gender, race, and age: The content of compound stereotypes across the life span. *The International Journal of Aging & Human Development, 81*(1–2), 27–53. doi:10.1177/0091415015616395

Andrusewicz, M. (2016, July 6). University of Tennessee settles sexual assault law suit. *National Public Radio.* Retrieved from http://www.npr.org/sections/thetwo-way/2016/07/06/484891430/university-of-tennessee-settles-sexual-assault-lawsuit

Ansell, E. B., Grilo, C. M., & White, M. A. (2012). Examining the interpersonal model of binge eating and loss of control over eating in women. *International Journal of Eating Disorders, 45*(1), 43–50.

Anusic, I., & Lucas, R. E. (2014). Do social relationships buffer the effects of widowhood? A prospective study of adaptation to the loss of a spouse. *Journal of Personality, 82*(5), 367–378. doi:10.1111/jopy.12067

Aosved, A. C., & Long, P. J. (2006). Co-occurrence of rape myth acceptance, sexism, racism, homophobia, ageism, classism, and religious intolerance. *Sex Roles, 55,* 481–492.

Appignanesi, L. (2008). *Mad, bad, and sad: A history of women and the mind doctors from 1800 to the present.* London, UK: Virago.

Apuzzo, V. M. (2001). A call to action. In D. C. Kimmel & D. L. Martin (Eds.), *Midlife and aging in gay America: Proceedings of the SAGE conference 2000* (pp. 1–11). New York: Harrington Park Press.

Arbuckle, J., & Williams, B. D. (2003). Students' perceptions of expressiveness: Age and gender effects on teacher evaluations. *Sex Roles, 49,* 507–516.

Arcelus, J., Bouman, W. P., Van, D. N., Claes, L., Witcomb, G., & Fernandez-Aranda, F. (2015). Systematic review and meta-analysis of prevalence studies in transsexualism. *European Psychiatry, 30*(6), 807–815. doi:10.1016/j.eurpsy.2015.04.005\

Archer, D., Iritani, B., Kimes, D. D., & Barrios, M. (1983). Faceism: Five studies of sex differences in facial prominence. *Journal of Personality and Social Psychology, 45,* 725–735.

Archer, J. (2000). Sex differences in physical aggression to partners: A meta-analytic review. *Psychological Bulletin, 126,* 651–680.

Archer, J. (2004). Sex differences in aggression in real-world settings: A meta-analytic review. *Review of General Psychology, 8*(4), 291–322. doi:10.1037/1089-2680.8.4.291

Archer, J. (2006). Cross-cultural differences in physical aggression between partners: A social role analysis. *Personality and Social Psychology Review, 10,* 133–153.

Arendell, T. (1997). A social constructionist approach to parenting. In R. Arendell (Ed.), *Contemporary parenting: Challenges and issues* (pp. 1–44). Thousand Oaks, CA: Sage.

Arima, A. N. (2003). Gender stereotypes in Japanese television advertisements. *Sex Roles, 49,* 81–90.

Armenta, B. E. (2010). Stereotype boost and stereotype threat effects: The moderating role of ethnic identification. *Cultural Diversity and Ethnic Minority Psychology, 16,* 94–99.

Armstrong, E. A., England, P., & Fogarty, A. C. K. (2012). Accounting for women's orgasm and sexual enjoyment in college hookups and relationships. *American Sociological Review, 77*(3), 435–462.

Armstrong, E. A., & Hamilton, L. T. (2013). *Paying for the party: How college maintains inequality.* Cambridge, MA: Harvard University Press.

Arnold, D. H., & Doctoroff, G. L. (2003). The early education of socioeconomically disadvantaged children. In S. T.

Fiske, D. L. Schacter, & C. Zahn-Waxler (Eds.), *Annual review of psychology.* (Vol. 54, pp. 517–545). Palo Alto, CA: Annual Reviews.

Arnold, S. C. (1994). Transforming body image through women's wilderness experiences. In E. Cole, E. Erdman, & E. Rothblum (Eds.), *Wilderness therapy for women: The power of adventure* (pp. 43–54). New York: Hayworth Press.

Aronson, J., Lustina, M. J., Good, C., Keough, K., Steele, C. M., & Brown, J. (1999). When White men can't do math: Necessary and sufficient factors in stereotype threat. *Journal of Experimental Social Psychology, 35,* 29–46.

Ascher-Svanum, H., & Sobel, T. S. (1989). Caregivers of mentally ill adults: A woman's agenda. *Hospital and Community Psychiatry, 40,* 843–845.

Ashburn-Nardo, L. (2017). Parenthood as a moral imperative? Moral outrage and the stigmatization of voluntarily childfree women and men. *Sex Roles, 76*(5–6), 393–401. doi:10.1007/s11199-016-0606-1

Ashcraft, C. (2008). So much more than "Sex Ed": Teen sexuality as vehicle for improving academic success and democratic education for diverse youth. *American Education Research Journal, 45,* 631–667.

Augsberger, A., Yeung, A., Dougher, M., & Hahm, H. C. (2015). Factors influencing the underutilization of mental health services among Asian American women with a history of depression and suicide. *BMC Health Services Research, 15*(1), 542.

Auster, C. J., & Mansbach, C. S. (2012). The gender marketing of toys: An analysis of color and type of toy on the Disney store website. *Sex Roles, 67*(7–8), 375–388. doi:10.1007/s11199-012-0177-8

Avellar, S., & Smock, P. J. (2005). The economic consequences of the dissolution of cohabiting unions. *Journal of Marriage and Family, 67*(2), 315–327.

Averett, P., Yoon, I., & Jenkins, C. L. (2011). Older lesbians: Experiences of aging, discrimination and resilience. *Journal of Women & Aging, 23*(3), 216–232. doi:10.1080/08952841.2011.587742

Averett, P., Yoon, I., & Jenkins, C. L. (2012). Older lesbian sexuality: Identity, sexual behavior, and the impact of aging. *Journal of Sex Research, 49*(5), 495–507.

Avis, N. (2003). Depression during the menopausal transition. *Psychology of Women Quarterly, 27,* 91–100.

Avis, N. E., & McKinlay, S. M. (1991). A longitudinal analysis of women's attitudes toward the menopause: Results from the Massachusetts women's health study. *Maturitas, 13,* 65–79.

Aznar, A., & Tenenbaum, H. R. (2015). Gender and age differences in parent–child emotion talk. *British Journal of Developmental Psychology, 33*(1), 148–155. doi:10.1111/bjdp.12069

Baber, K. M., & Allen, K. R. (1992). *Women and families: Feminist reconstructions.* New York: Guilford.

Bachar, K., & Koss, M. (2001). Rape. In J. Worell (Ed.), *Encyclopedia of women and gender* (pp. 893–903). San Diego, CA: Academic Press.

Bachman, J. G., O'Malley, P. M., Freedman-Doan, P., Trzesniewski, K. H., & Donnellan, M. B. (2011). Adolescent self-esteem: Differences by race/ethnicity, gender, and age. *Self and Identity, 10*(4), 445–473. doi:10.1080/15298861003794538

Bachrach, L. L. (1984). Deinstitutionalization and women: Assessing the consequences of public policy. *American Psychologist, 39,* 1171–1177.

Bagès, C., Verniers, C., & Martinot, D. (2016). Virtues of a hardworking role model to improve girls' mathematics performance. *Psychology of Women Quarterly, 40,* 55–64. doi:10.1177/0361684315608842

Bailey, D., & Jackson, J. (2005). The occupation of household financial management among lesbian couples. *Journal of Occupational Science, 12,* 57–68.

Baker, J. M., & Reiss, A. L. (2016). A meta-analysis of math performance in Turner syndrome. *Developmental Medicine & Child Neurology, 58*(2), 123–130. doi:10.1111/dmcn.12961

Baker, K. (2016, June 6). Here is the powerful letter the Stanford victim read aloud to her attacker. *Buzzfeed.* Retrieved from https://www.buzzfeed.com/katiejmbaker/heres-the-powerful-letter-the-stanford-victim-read-to-her-ra?utm_term=.is232aZK3#.puXxz9YBx

Baker, M. W. (2007). Elder mistreatment: Risk, vulnerability, and early mortality. *Journal of the American Psychiatric Nurses Association, 12,* 313–321.

Ballou, M., Hill, M., & West, C. (Eds.) (2008). *Feminist therapy theory and practice.* New York: Springer.

Balsam, K. F., Molina, Y., Blayney, J. A., Dillworth, T., Zimmerman, L., & Kaysen, D. (2015). Racial/ethnic differences in identity and mental health outcomes among young sexual minority women. *Cultural Diversity and Ethnic Minority Psychology, 21*(3), 380–390. doi:10.1037/a0038680

Bandura, A. (1965). Influence of model's reinforcement contingencies on the acquisition of imitative responses. *Journal of Personality and Social Psychology, 1,* 589–595.

Bandura, A., & Walters, R. H. (1963). *Social learning and personality development.* New York: Holt, Rinehart & Winston.

Banks, D., & Kyckelhahn, T. (2011). Characteristics of suspected human trafficking incidents. Washington, D. C. U.S. Department of Justice, Office of Justice Programs, 2008–2010. Retrieved from https://www.bjs.gov/content/pub/pdf/cshti0810.pdf

Banner, L. (2006). *American beauty: A social history . . . through two centuries of the American idea, ideal, and image of the beautiful woman.* Los Angeles: Figueroa Press.

Bannon, L. (2000, March). More kids' marketers pitch number of single-sex products. *The Wall Street Journal,* pp. B1, 4.

Banyard, V. L., Williams, L. M., Siegel, J. A., & West, C. M. (2002). Childhood sexual abuse in the lives of Black women: Risk and resilience in a longitudinal study. *Women & Therapy, 25,* 45–58.

Barak, A., Feldman, S., & Noy, A. (1991). Traditionality of children's interests as related to their parents' gender stereotypes and traditionality of occupations. *Sex Roles, 24,* 511–524.

Baretto, M., & Ellmers, N. (2005). The burden of benevolent sexism: How it contributes to the maintenance of gender inequalities. *European Journal of Social Psychology, 35,* 633–642.

Bargad, A., & Hyde, J. S. (1991). Women's studies: A study of feminist identity development in women. *Psychology of Women Quarterly, 15,* 181–201.

Barnack-Tevlaris, J. (2015). The medicalization of women's moods: Premenstrual syndrome and premenstrual dysphoric disorder. In M. C. McHugh & J. C. Chrisler (Eds.), *The wrong prescription for women: How medicine and media create a "need" for treatments, drugs, and surgery.* Santa Barbara, CA: ABC-CLIO.

Barnett, R. C., & Hyde, J. S. (2001). Women, men, work, and family: An expansionist theory. *American Psychologist, 56,* 78–96.

Barone, C. (2011). Some things never change: Gender segregation in higher education across eight nations and three decades. *Sociology of Education, 84*(2), 157–176.

Barr, A. B., Simons, R. L., & Simons, L. G. (2015). Nonmarital relationships and changing perceptions of marriage among African American young adults. *Journal of Marriage and Family, 77*(5), 1202–1216.

Barr, J. (2008). Postpartum depression, delayed maternal adaptation, and mechanical infant caring: A phenomenological hermeneutic study. *International Journal of Nursing Studies, 45*(3), 362–369.

Barrett, L. F., Lane, R. D., Sechrest, L., & Schwartz, G. E. (2000). Sex differences in emotional awareness. *Personality and Social Psychology Bulletin, 26,* 1027–1035.

Bart, P. B. (1971). Sexism and social science: From the gilded cage to the iron cage, or, the perils of Pauline. *Journal of Marriage and the Family, 33,* 734–735.

Barth, J., Bermetz, L., Heim, E., Trelle, S., & Tonia, T. (2013). The current prevalence of child sexual abuse worldwide: A systematic review and meta-analysis. *International Journal of Public Health, 58*(3), 469–483.

Barth, S. K., Kimerling, R. E., Pavao, J., McCutcheon, S. J., Batten, S. V., Dursa, E., . . . Schneiderman, A. I. (2016). Military sexual trauma among recent veterans: Correlates of sexual assault and sexual harassment. *American Journal of Preventive Medicine, 50*(1), 77–86. doi:10.1016/j.amepre.2015.06.012

Barto, H. H., Lambert, S. F., & Brott, P. E. (2015). The career development of adolescent mothers: A review of 25 years of professional literature. *Journal of Employment Counseling, 52*(2), 65–76. doi:10.1002/joec.12005

Bartsch, R. A., Burnett, T., Diller, T. R., & Rankin-Williams, E. (2000). Gender representation in television commercials: Updating an update. *Sex Roles, 43,* 735–743.

Baruch, G. K., Barnett, R. C., & Rivers, C. (1983). *Lifeprints: New patterns of love and work for today's women.* New York: New American Library.

Basu, J., & Ray, B. (2001). Friends and lovers: A study of human mate selection in India. *Psychologia: An International Journal of Psychology in the Orient, 44,* 281–291.

Baum, K., Catalano, S., Rand, M., & Rose, K. (2009). Stalking victimization in the United States. U.S. Department of Justice Bureau of Justice Statistics. *NCJ 224527.*

Baumgardner, J., & Richards, A. (2000). *Manifesta: Young women, feminism, and the future.* New York: Farrar, Straus and Giroux.

Baumgardner, J., & Richards, A. (2005). *Grassroots: A field guide for feminist activism.* New York: Farrar, Straus, and Giroux.

Bay-Cheng, L. Y., & Zucker, A. N. (2007). Feminism between the sheets: Sexual attitudes among feminists, nonfeminists, and egalitarians. *Psychology of Women Quarterly, 31,* 157–163.

BBC News. (2016, May 26). *Woman's bid to use deceased daughter's egg continues.* Retrieved from http://www.bbc.com/news/health-36378972

Beals, K. P., & Peplau, L. A. (2001). Social involvement, disclosure of sexual orientation, and the quality of lesbian relationships. *Psychology of Women Quarterly, 25,* 10–19.

Beaman, R., Wheldall, K., & Kemp, C. (2006). Differential teacher attention to boys and girls in the classroom. *Educational Review, 58,* 339–366.

Beaulaurier, R. L., Seff, L. R., & Newman, F. L. (2008). Barriers to help seeking for older women who experience intimate partner violence: A descriptive model. *Journal of Women and Aging, 20*(3/4), 231–248.

Beauvoir, S. (1953). *The second sex* (H. M. Parshley, Trans.). New York: Knopf.

Becker, A. L. (2010, January 18). Man, woman die after apparent murder-suicide in West Haven. *Hartford Courant Online.* Retrieved from http://www.courant.com/news/domestic-violence/hc-murder-suicide-0118.artjan18,0,1640867.story

Becker, D., Kenrick, D., Neuberg, S., Blackwell, K., & Smith, D. (2007). The confounded nature of angry men and happy women. *Journal of Personality and Social Psychology, 92*(2), 179–190. doi:10.1037/0022-3514.92.2.179

Becker, D., & Lamb, S. (1994). Sex bias in the diagnosis of borderline personality disorder and post traumatic stress disorder. *Professional Psychology: Research and Practice, 25,* 55–61.

Becker, J. C., & Wright, S. C. (2011). Yet another dark side of chivalry: Benevolent sexism undermines and hostile sexism motivates collective action for social change. *Journal of Personality and Social Psychology, 101*(1), 62–77. doi:10.1037/a0022615

Beggs, J. M., & Doolittle, D. C. (1993). Perceptions now and then of occupational sex typing: A replication of Shinar's 1975 study. *Journal of Applied Social Psychology, 23,* 1435–1453.

Bekker, M. (1996). Agoraphobia and gender: A review. *Clinical Psychology Review, 16,* 129–146.

Bell, M. E., Goodman, L. A., & Dutton, M. A., (2009). Variations in help-seeking, battered women's relationship course, emotional well-being, and experiences of abuse over time. *Psychology of Women Quarterly, 33,* 149–162.

Belle, D. (2008). Poor women in a wealthy nation. In J. C. Chrisler, C. Golden, & P. D. Rozee (Eds.), *Lectures on the psychology of women* (4th ed., pp. 26–41). New York: McGraw-Hill.

Belle, D., & Doucet, J. (2003). Poverty, inequality, and discrimination as sources of depression among U.S. women. *Psychology of Women Quarterly, 27,* 101–103.

Belser, P. (2005). Forced labour and human trafficking: Estimating the profits. Retrieved from http://digitalcommons.ilr.cornell.edu/cgi/viewcontent.cgi?article=1016&context=forcedlabor

Beltz, A. M., Swanson, J. L., & Berenbaum, S. A. (2011). Gendered occupational interests: Prenatal androgen effects on psychological orientation to things versus people. *Hormones and Behavior, 60*(4), 313–317. doi:10.1016/j.yhbeh.2011.06.002

Bem, S. L. (1981). Gender schema theory: A cognitive account of sex typing. *Psychological Review, 88,* 354–364.

Bem, S. L. (1983). Gender schema theory and its implications for child development: Raising gender-aschematic children in a gender-schematic society. *Signs, 8,* 598–616.

Bem, S. L. (1993). *The lenses of gender.* New Haven, CT: Yale University Press.

Bem, S. L. (1998). *An unconventional family.* New Haven, CT: Yale University Press.

Bemporad, J. R. (1996). Self-starvation through the ages: Reflections on the pre-history of anorexia nervosa. *International Journal of Eating Disorders, 19,* 217–237.

Ben-Ari, A., & Livni, T. (2006). Motherhood is not a given thing: Experiences and constructed meanings of biological and nonbiological lesbian mothers. *Sex Roles, 54*(7–8), 521–531.

Ben-David, S., & Schneider, O. (2005). Rape perceptions, gender role attitudes, and victim-perpetrator acquaintance. *Sex Roles, 53,* 385–399.

Ben Ze'ev, A., & Goussinsky, R. (2008). *In the name of love: Romantic ideology and its victims.* New York: Oxford University Press.

Ben-Zeev, T., Duncan, S., & Forbes, C. (2005). Stereotypes and math performance. In J. I. D. Campbell (Ed.), Handbook of mathematical cognition (pp. 235–249). New York: Psychology Press.

Berenbaum, S. A., & Beltz, A. M. (2011). Sexual differentiation of human behavior: Effects of prenatal and pubertal organizational hormones. *Frontiers in Neuroendocrinology, 32*(2), 183–200. doi:10.1016/j.yfrne.2011.03.001

Berg, R. C., & Denison, E. (2012a). Does female genital mutilation/cutting (FMG/C) affect women's sexual functioning? A systematic review of the sexual consequences of FGM/C. *Sexuality Research & Social Policy: A Journal of the NSRC, 9*(1), 41–56. doi:10.1007/s13178-011-0048-z

Berg, R. C., & Denison, E. (2012b). Effectiveness of interventions designed to prevent female genital mutilation/cutting: A systematic review. *Studies in Family Planning, 43*(2), 135–146. doi:10.1111/j.1728-4465.2012.00311.x

Berg, R. C., & Denison, E. (2013). A tradition in transition: Factors perpetuating and hindering the continuance of female genital mutilation/cutting (FGM/C) summarized in a systematic review. *Health Care for Women International, 34*(10), 837–859. doi:10.1080/07399332.2012.721417

Berger, J. (1972). *Ways of seeing.* London: Penguin Books.

Berger, R. M. (1990). Passing: Impact of the quality of same-sex couple relationships. *Social Work, 35,* 328–332.

Bernard, J. (1974). *The future of motherhood.* New York: Penguin.

Berryman-Fink, C., & Verderber, K. S. (1985). Attributions of the term feminist: A factor analytic development of a measuring instrument. *Psychology of Women Quarterly, 9,* 51–64.

Best, D. L. (2001). Cross-cultural gender roles. In J. Worell (Ed.), *Encyclopedia of women and gender* (pp. 279–290). San Diego, CA: Academic Press.

Biedlingmaier, M. (2007, March 15). CNN's, ABC's beck on Clinton: "[S]he's the stereotypical bitch." *Media Matters for America.* Retrieved from http://mediamatters.org/research/2007/03/15/cnns-abcs-beck-on-clinton-shes-the-stereotypica/138303

Biernat, M., & Kobrynowicz, D. (1999). A shifting standards perspective on the complexity of gender stereotypes and gender stereotyping. In W. B. Swann, Jr., J. H. Langlois, & L. A. Gilbert (Eds.), *Sexism and stereotypes: The gender science of Janet Taylor Spence* (pp. 75–106). Washington, DC: American Psychological Association.

Biernat, M., & Sesko, A. K. (2013). Evaluating the contributions of members of mixed-sex work teams: Race and gender matter. *Journal of Experimental Social Psychology, 49*(3), 471–476.

Biernat, M., Tocci, M. J., & Williams, J. C. (2012). The language of performance evaluations: Gender-based shifts in content and consistency of judgment. *Social Psychological and Personality Science, 3*(2), 186–192. doi:10.1177/1948550611415693

Bihagen, E., & Ohls, M. (2007). Are women over-represented in dead-end jobs? A Swedish study using empirically derived measures of dead-end jobs. *Social Indicators Research, 84,* 159–177.

Bing, V. M., & Reid, P. T. (1996). Unknown women and unknowing research: Consequences of color and class in feminist psychology. In N. R. Goldberger & J. M. Tarule (Eds.), *Knowledge, difference, and power: Essays inspired by "women's ways of knowing"* (pp. 175–202). New York: Basic Books.

Bishop, N. (1989). Abortion: The controversial choice. In J. Freeman (Ed.), *Women: A feminist perspective* (4th ed., pp. 45–56). Mountain View, CA: Mayfield.

Black, K. A., Marola, J. A., Littleman, A. I., Chrisler, J. C., & Neace, W. P. (2009). Gender and form of cereal box characters: Different medium, same disparity. *Sex Roles, 60,* 882–889.

Blair, I. V. (2002). The malleability of automatic stereotypes and prejudice. *Personality and Social Psychology Review, 6,* 242–261.

Blakemore, J. E., & Centers, R. E. (2005). Characteristics of boys' and girls' toys. *Sex Roles, 53,* 619–633.

Blashill, A. J., & Powlishta, K. K. (2009). Gay stereotypes: The use of sexual orientation as a cue for gender-related attributes. *Sex Roles, 61,* 783–793.

Bleier, R. (Ed.). (1986). *Feminist approaches to science.* Elmsford, NY: Pergamon Press.

Blood, R. O., & Wolfe, D. M. (1960). *Husbands and wives.* New York: Free Press.

Blumstein, P., & Schwartz, P. (1983). *American couples.* New York: William Morrow.

Blytheway, B. (2003). Visual representations of late life. In C. A. Faircloth, (Ed.), *Aging bodies: Images and everyday experiences* (pp. 11–49). New York: AltaMira Press.

Boardman, S. K., Harrington, C. C., & Horowitz, S. V. (1987). Successful women: A psychological investigation of family class and education origins. In B. A. Gutek & L. Larwood (Eds.), *Women's career development* (pp. 66–85). Newbury Park, CA: Sage.

Boatwright, K. J., Gilbert, M. S., Forrest, L., & Ketzenberger, K. (1996). Impact of identity development upon career trajectory: Listening to the voices of lesbian women. *Journal of Vocational Behavior, 48,* 210–228.

Bograd, M. (1988). Feminist perspectives on wife abuse: An introduction. In K. Yllo & M. Bograd (Eds.), *Feminist perspectives on wife abuse* (pp. 11–26). Berkeley, CA: Sage.

Bohan, J. S. (1996). *Psychology and sexual orientation: Coming to terms.* New York: Routledge.

Bohn, D. K. (2003). Lifetime physical and sexual abuse, substance abuse, depression, and suicide attempts among Native American women. *Issues in Mental Health Nursing, 24,* 333–352.

Boislard, M. A., van de Bongardt, D., & Blais, M. (2016). Sexuality (and lack thereof) in adolescence and early adulthood: A review of the literature. *Behavioral Science, 6*(8). doi:10.3390/bs6010008

Bolin, A. (1996). Transcending and transgendering: Male-to-female transsexuals, dichotomy, and diversity. In G. Herdt (Ed.), *Third sex, third gender: Beyond sexual dimorphism in culture and history* (pp. 447–485). New York: Zone Books.

Bonomi, A. E., Anderson, M. L., Reid, R. J., Carrell, D., Fishman, P. A., Rivara, F. P., & Thompson, R. S. (2007). Intimate partner violence in older women. *The Gerontologist, 47,* 34–41.

Bordini, G. S., & Sperb, T. M. (2013). Sexual double standards: A review of the literature between 2001 and 2010. *Sexuality & Culture: An Interdisciplinary Quarterly, 17*(4), 686–704. doi:10.1007/s12119–012-9163–0

Bordone, V., & Arpino, B. (2016). Do grandchildren influence how old you feel? *Journal of Aging and Health, 28*(6), 1055–1072.

Boring, A., Ottoboni, K., & Stark, P. B. (2016). Student evaluations of teaching (mostly) do not measure teaching effectiveness. *ScienceOpen Research.* doi:10.14293/S2199–1006.1.SOR-EDU.AETBZC.v1

Bornstein, K. (1994). *Gender outlaw: On men, women, and the rest of us.* New York: Routledge.

Boston Women's Health Book Collective. (1998). *Our bodies, ourselves for the new century.* New York: Simon & Schuster.

Bostwick, W., & Hequembourg, A. (2014). 'Just a little hint': bisexual-specific microaggressions and their connection to epistemic injustices. *Culture, Health & Sexuality, 16*(5), 488–503. doi:10.1080/13691058.2014.889754

Boswell, S. L. (1979). *Nice girls don't study mathematics: The perspective from elementary school.* Paper presented at the meeting of the American Educational Research Association, San Francisco, CA.

Boswell, S. L. (1985). The influence of sex-role stereotyping on women's attitudes and achievement in mathematics. In S. F. Chipman, L. R. Brush, & D. M. Wilson (Eds.), *Women and mathematics: Balancing the equation* (pp. 175–198). Hillsdale, NJ: Erlbaum.

Bourassa, K. J., Sbarra, D. A., & Whisman, M. A. (2015). Women in very low quality marriages gain life satisfaction following divorce. *Journal of Family Psychology, 29*(3), 490–499.

Bourque, P., Pushkar, D., Bonneville, L., & Beland, F. (2005). Contextual effects on life satisfaction of older men and women. *Canadian Journal of Aging, 24,* 31–44.

Boyce, P., & Hickey, A. (2005). Psychosocial risk factors to major depression after childbirth. *Social Psychiatry and Psychiatric Epidemiology, 40*(8), 605–612.

Bradway, K. E., & Beard, R. L. (2015). "Don't be trying to box folks in": Older women's sexuality. *Affilia: Journal of Women & Social Work, 30*(4), 504–518.

Bramlet, M. D., & Mosher, W. D. (2001). *First marriage dissolution, divorce, and remarriage: United States.* Hyattsville, MD: National Center for Health Statistics.

Breiding, M. J., Smith, S. S., Basile, K. C., Walters, M. L., Chen, J., & Merrick, M. T. (2014). Prevalence and characteristics of sexual violence, stalking, and intimate partner violence victimization—National Intimate Partner and Sexual Violence Survey, United States, 2011. *Morbidity and mortality weekly report. Surveillance summaries (Washington, DC: 2002), 63*(8), 1. Retrieved from https://www.cdc.gov/mmwr/preview/mmwrhtml/ss6308a1.htm?s_cid =ss6308a1_e

Brescoll, V. L. (2011). Who takes the floor and why: Gender, power, and volubility in organizations. *Administrative Science Quarterly, 56*(4), 622–641. doi:10.1177/0001839212439994

Breshears, D. (2011). Understanding communication between lesbian parents and their children regarding outsider discourse about family identity. *Journal of GLBT Family Studies, 7*(3), 264–284.

Brett, J. M. (2011). Thirty-five years of studying work and family. *Psychology of Women Quarterly, 35*(3), 500–503. doi:10.1177/0361684311414828

Bridges, J. S. (1993). Pink or blue: Gender-stereotypic perceptions of infants as conveyed by birth congratulations cards. *Psychology of Women Quarterly, 17*(2), 193–205. doi:10.1111/j.1471–6402.1993.tb00444.x

Brimhall, A., Wampler, K., & Kimball, T. (2008). Learning from the past, altering the future: A tentative theory of the effect of past relationships on couples who remarry. *Family Process, 47,* 373–387.

Brodsky, A. E. (2003). *With all our strength: The revolutionary association of the women of Afghanistan.* New York: Routledge.

Brody, E. M. (2004). *Women in the middle: Their parent care years* (2nd ed.). New York: Springer.

Brody, L. R., & Hall, J. A. (2000). Gender, emotion, and expression. In M. Lewis & J. Haviland-Jones (Eds.), *Handbook of emotions* (pp. 338–349). New York: Guilford.

Bronstein, P. (2006). The family environment: When gender role socialization begins. In J. Worrell & C. Goodheart (Eds.), *Handbook of girls' and women's psychological health.* New York: Oxford University Press.

Brooks-Gunn, J. (1988). Antecedents and consequences of variations in girls' maturational timing. *Journal of Adolescent Health Care, 9,* 365–373.

Broverman, I. K., Vogel, S. R., Broverman, D. M., Clarkson, F. E., & Rosenkrantz, P. S. (1972). Sex-role stereotypes: A current appraisal. *Journal of Social Issues, 28,* 59–78.

Brown, L. M. (1998). *Raising their voices: The politics of girls' anger.* Cambridge, MA: Harvard University Press.

Brown, L. M., & Gilligan, C. (1992). *Meeting at the crossroads: Women's psychology and girls' development.* Cambridge, MA: Harvard University Press.

Brown, L. S. (2006). Still subversive after all these years: The relevance of feminist therapy in the age of evidence-based practice. *Psychology of Women Quarterly, 30,* 15–24.

Brown, L. S. (2010). *Feminist therapy.* Washington, DC: American Psychological Association.

Browne, K. (2011). Lesbian separatist feminism at Michigan Womyn's music festival. *Feminism & Psychology, 21*(2), 248–256. doi:10.1177/0959353510370185

Browne, T. K. (2015). Is premenstrual dysphoric disorder really a disorder? *Journal of Bioethical Inquiry, 12*(2), 313–330.

Brownmiller, S. (1975). *Against our will: Men, women and rape.* Newark: Simon & Schuster.

Brownridge, D. A. (2009). *Violence against women: Vulnerable populations.* New York: Routledge/Taylor & Francis Group.

Brumberg, J. J. (2000). *Fasting girls: The history of anorexia nervosa.* New York: Vintage Books.

Bruni, F. (2016, February 28). If Trump changed genders. *New York Times.* Retrieved from http://www.nytimes.com/2016/02/28/opinion/sunday/if-donald-trump-changed-genders.html

Buchholz, A., Henderson, K. A., Hounsell, A., Wagner, A., Norris, M., & Spettigue, W. (2007). Self-silencing in a clinical sample of female adolescents with eating disorders. *Journal of the Canadian Academy of Child and Adolescent Psychiatry/Journal de l'Académie canadienne de psychiatrie de l'enfant et de l'adolescent, 16*(4), 158–163.

Buhle, M. J. (1998). *Feminism and its discontents: A century of struggle with psychoanalysis.* Cambridge, MA: Harvard University Press.

Bulanda, J. R. (2011). Gender, marital power, and marital quality in later life. *Journal of Women & Aging, 23*(1), 3–22. doi:10.1080/08952841.2011.540481

Bullock, H. E., Wyche, K. F., & Williams, W. R. (2001). Media images of the poor. *Journal of Social Issues, 57,* 229–246.

Burgess, M. C. R., Stermer, S. P., & Burgess, S. R. (2007). Sex, lies, and videogames: The portrayal of male and female characters on videogame covers. *Sex Roles, 57,* 419–433.

Burke, R. J. (1997). Alternate family structures: A career advantage? *Psychological Reports, 81,* 812–814.

Burke, R. J., & McKeen, C. A. (1997). Gender effects in mentoring relationships. In R. Crandall (Ed.), *Handbook of gender research* (pp. 91–104). Corte Madera, CA: Select Press.

Burnes, D., Pillemer, K., Caccamise, P. L., Mason, A., Henderson, C. R., Berman, J.,. . . Salamone, A. (2015). Prevalence of and risk factors for elder abuse and neglect in the community: A population-based study. *Journal of the American Geriatrics Society, 63*(9), 1906–1912.

Burt, M. (1980). Cultural myths and supports for rape. *Journal of Personality and Social Psychology, 38,* 217–230.

Buss, D. M. (2011). *Evolutionary psychology: The new science of the mind* (4th ed.). London, England: Allyn & Bacon.

Buss, D. M., Abbott, M., Angleitner, A., & Asherian, A. (1990). International preferences in selecting mates: A study of 37 cultures. *Journal of Cross-Cultural Psychology, 21*(1), 5–47, doi:10.1177/0022022190211001

Bussey, K., & Bandura, A. (2004). Social cognitive theory of gender development and functioning. In A. H. Eagly, A. E. Beall, & R. J. Sternberg (Eds.), *The psychology of gender* (pp. 92–119). New York: Guilford Press.

Cachelin, F. M., Veisel, C., Barzegarnazari, E., & Striegel-Moore, R. H. (2000). Disordered eating, acculturation, and treatment-seeking in a community sample of Hispanic, Asian, Black, and White women. *Psychology of Women Quarterly, 24,* 244–253.

Calasanti, T. M., & Slevin, K. F. (2001). *Gender, social inequalities, and aging.* New York: AltaMira Press.

Callaghan, J. E., Gambo, Y., & Fellin, L. C. (2015). Hearing the silences: Adult Nigerian women's accounts of 'early marriages'. *Feminism & Psychology, 25*(4) 506–552.

Callimachi, R. (2016, March 12). To maintain supply of sex slaves, ISIS pushes birth control. *The New York Times.* Retrieved from http://www.nytimes.com/2016/03/13/world/middleeast/to-maintain-supply-of-sex-slaves-isis-pushes-birth-control.html?_r=0

Calogero, R. M., Pina, A., & Sutton, R. M. (2014). Cutting words: Priming self-objectification increases women's intention to pursue cosmetic surgery. *Psychology of Women Quarterly, 38*(2), 197–207. doi:10.1177/0361684313506881

Calzo, J. P., Antonucci, T. C., Mays, V. M., & Cochran, S. D. (2011). Retrospective recall of sexual orientation identity development among gay, lesbian, and bisexual adults. *Developmental Psychology, 47*(6), 1658–1673. doi:894159778?accountid=14523

Cameron, D. (1996). The language-gender interface: Challenging co-optation. In V. L. Bergvall, J. M. Bing, & A. F. Freed (Eds.), *Rethinking language and gender research: Theory and practice* (pp. 31–53). New York: Addison-Wesley.

Cameron, D. (1997). Performing gender identity: Young men's talk and the construction of heterosexual masculinity. In S. Johnson & U. H. Meinof (Eds.), *Language and masculinity* (pp. 47–64). Cambridge, MA: Blackwell.

Cameron, R. P., Grabill, C. M., Hobfoll, S. E., & Crowther, J. H. (1996). Weight, self-esteem, ethnicity, and depressive symptomatology during pregnancy among inner-city women. *Health Psychology, 15,* 293–297.

Campbell, A. (1992). *Men, women, and aggression.* New York: Basic Books.

Canetto, S. S. (2001). Older adult women: Issues, resources, and challenges. In R. K. Unger (Ed.), *Handbook of the psychology of women and gender* (pp. 183–197). New York: Wiley.

Cantor, D., Fisher, B., Chibnall, S., Townsend, R., Lee, H., Bruce, C., & Thomas, G. (2015). Report on the AAU campus climate survey on sexual assault and sexual misconduct. *Association of American Universities, 21.* Retrieved from https://assets.documentcloud.org/documents/2674806/University-of-Virginia-Climate-Survey.pdf

Cantos, A. L., & O'Leary, K. D. (2014). One size does not fit all in treatment of intimate partner violence. *Partner Abuse, 5*(2), 204–236.

Capaldi, D. M., Knoble, N. B., Shortt, J. W., & Kim, H. K. (2012). A systematic review of risk factors for intimate partner violence. *Partner Abuse, 3*(2), 231–280.

Caplan, P. J. (1985). *The myth of women's masochism.* New York: E.P. Dutton.

Caplan, P. J. (1989). *Don't blame mother.* New York: Harper & Row.

Caplan, P. J. (1992). Driving us crazy: How oppression damages women's mental health and what we can do about it. *Women & Therapy, 12,* 5–28.

Caplan, P. J. (1995). *They say you're crazy: How the world's most powerful psychiatrists decide who's normal.* Reading, MA: Perseus Books.

Caplan, P. J. (2004). The debate about PMDD and Sarafem: Suggestions for therapists. In J. C. Chrisler (Ed.), *From menarche to menopause: The female body in feminist therapy* (pp. 55–67). New York: Haworth Press.

Caplan, P. J. (2008, Summer). Pathologizing your period. *Ms.,* 63–64.

Caplan, P. J., & Hall-McCorquodale, I. (1985). Motherblaming in major clinical journals. *American Journal of Orthopsychiatry, 55,* 345–353.

Carey, R. N., Donaghue, N., & Broderick, P. (2011). 'What you look like is such a big factor': Girls' own reflections about the appearance culture in an all-girls' school. *Feminism & Psychology, 21*(3), 299–316. doi:10.1177/095 9353510369893

Carli, L. L. (2001). Gender and social influence. *Journal of Social Issues, 57,* 735–741.

Carli, L. L., Alawa, L., Lee, Y., Zhao, B., & Kim, E. (2016). Stereotypes about gender and science: Women ≠ scientists. *Psychology of Women Quarterly, 40*(2), 244–260. doi:10.1177/0361684315622645

Carnes, M., Devine, P. G., Isaac, C., Manwell, L. B., Ford, C. E., Byars-Winston, A., . . . Sheridan, J. (2012). Promoting institutional change through bias literacy. *Journal of Diversity in Higher Education, 5*(2), 63–77. doi:10.1037/a0028128

Carp, F. M. (1997). Retirement and women. In J. M. Coyle (Ed.), *Handbook on women and aging* (pp. 112–128). Westport, CT: Greenwood Press.

Carpenter, L. M. (2005). *Virginity lost: An intimate portrait of first sexual experiences.* New York: New York University Press.

Carr, E. R., & McKernan, L. C. (2015). "Keep your chin up": Treating male veterans with posttraumatic stress disorder from an integrative feminist theoretical perspective. *Journal of Psychotherapy Integration, 25*(4), 253–266.

Carreon, D., & Noymer, A. (2011). Health-related quality of life in older adults: Testing the double jeopardy hypothesis. *Journal of Aging Studies, 25*(4), 371–379.

Carter, G. (2010, February 19–21). Mo'Nique talks. USA Weekend, p. 9.

Case, K. A., Hensley, R., & Anderson, A. (2014). Reflecting on heterosexual and male privilege: Interventions to raise awareness. *Journal of Social Issues, 70*(4), 722–740. doi:10.1111/josi.12088

Casini, A. (2016). Glass ceiling and glass elevator. In N. Naples (Ed.), *The Wiley Blackwell Encyclopedia of Gender and Sexuality Studies.* 1–2. Malden, MA: John Wiley & Sons, Ltd. doi:10.1002/9781118663219.wbegss262

Castañeda, D. (2008). Gender issues among Latinas. In J. C. Chrisler, C. Golden, & P. Rozee (Eds.), *Lectures on the psychology of women* (4th ed., pp. 250–267). New York: McGraw Hill.

Catalano, S. M. (2013). Intimate partner violence: Attributes of victimization, 1993–2011. *U.S. Department of Justice, Bureau of Justice Statistics.* Retrieved from https://www.bjs.gov/content/pub/pdf/ipvav9311.pdf

Catalyst w (2016). *Quick take: statistical overview of women in the workplace.* Retrieved from http://www.catalyst.org/knowledge/statistical-overview-women-workforce

Ceballo, R., Graham, E. T., & Hart, J. (2015). Silent and infertile: An intersectional analysis of the experiences of socioeconomically diverse African American women with infertility. *Psychology of Women Quarterly, 39*(4), 497–511. doi:10.1177/0361684315581169

Ceci, S. J., Williams, W. M., & Barnett, S. M. (2009). Women's underrepresentation in science: Sociocultural and biological considerations. *Psychological Bulletin, 135*(2), 218–261. doi:10.1037/a0014412

Center for Disease Control (2013). *Leading Causes of Death by Race/Ethnicity, All Females-United States.* Retrieved from http://www.cdc.gov/women/lcod/2013/womenrace_2013.pdf

Cha, Y. (2013). Overwork and the persistence of gender segregation in occupations. *Gender & Society, 27*(2), 158–184. doi:10.1177/0891243212470510

Chambers, C. (1972). An assessment of drug use in the general population. In J. Sussman (Ed.), *Drug use and social policy,* 50–61.

Chan, C. S. (2008). Asian American women and adolescent girls: Sexuality and sexual expression. In J. C. Chrisler, C. Golden, & P. Rozee (Eds.), *Lectures on the psychology of women* (4th ed., pp. 220–231). New York: McGraw Hill.

Chapleau, K. M., Oswald, D. L., & Russell, B. L. (2007). How ambivalent sexism toward women and men support rape myth acceptance. *Sex Roles, 57,* 131–136.

Chappell, B. (2016, June 8). Stanford has most sexual violence cases under review, U.S. agency says. *National Public Radio.* Retrieved from http://www.npr.org/sections/thetwo-way/2016/06/08/481307558/stanford-tops-federal-agency-s-list-with-5-sexual-violence-investigations

Charlesworth, W. R., & LaFreniere, P. (1983). Dominance, friendship utilization and resource utilization in preschool children's groups. *Ethology and Sociobiology, 4,* 175–186.

Chen, C. (2015). Advertising representations of older people in the United Kingdom and Taiwan: A comparative analysis. *The International Journal of Aging & Human Development, 80*(2), 140–183. doi:10.1177/0091415015590305

Chen, M., & Bargh, J. A. (1997). Nonconscious behavioral confirmation processes: The self-fulfilling nature of automatically-activated stereotypes. *Journal of Experimental Social Psychology, 33,* 541–560.

Chesler, P. (1972). *Women and madness.* New York: Doubleday.

Chesler, P. (2005). *Women and madness* (Revised and updated for the first time in thirty years). New York: Palgrave Macmillan.

Cheung, F. M., & Halpern, D. F. (2010). Women at the top: Powerful leaders define success at work + family in a culture of gender. *American Psychologist, 65,* 182–193.

Chicago, J. (1990, March). *The birth project*. Women's History Month Lecture, Trenton State College, Trenton, NJ.

Choi, P., Henshaw, C., Baker, S., & Tree, J. (2005). Supermom, superwife, supereverything: Performing femininity in the transition to motherhood. *Journal of Reproductive and Infant Psychology, 23*(2), 167–180.

Chonody, J. M. (2015). Addressing ageism in students: A systematic review of the pedagogical intervention literature. *Educational Gerontology, 41*(12), 859–887.

Chopik, W. J. (2016). The benefits of social technology use among older adults are mediated by reduced loneliness. *Cyberpsychology, Behavior, and Social Networking, 19*(9), 551–556.

Chrisler, J. C. (2001). Gendered bodies and physical health. In R. K. Unger (Ed.), *Handbook of the psychology of women and gender* (pp. 289–302). New York: Wiley.

Chrisler, J. C. (2012). PMS as a culture bound syndrome. In J. Chrisler, C. Golden, & P. D. Rozee (Eds.) *Lectures on the Psychology of Women* (4th ed.) Waveland Press: Long Grove, IL.

Chrisler, J. C., Barney, A., & Palatino, B. (2016). Ageism can be hazardous to women's health: Ageism, sexism, and stereotypes of older women in the healthcare system. *Journal of Social Issues, 72*(1), 86-104. doi:10.1111/josi.12157

Chrisler, J. C., & Caplan, P. (2002). The strange case of Dr. Jekyll and Ms. Hyde: How PMS became a cultural phenomenon and a psychiatric disorder. *Annual Review of Sex Research, 13*(1), 274–306.

Chrisler, J. C., de las Fuentes, C., Durvasula, R. S., Esnil, E. M., McHugh, M. C., Miles-Cohen, S., . . . Wisdom, J. P. (2013). The American Psychological Association's Committee on Women in Psychology: 40 years of contributions to the transformation of psychology. *Psychology of Women Quarterly, 37*(4), 444–454. doi:10.1177/0361684313505442

Chrisler, J. C., & Ghiz, L. (1993). Body image issues of older women. *Women & Therapy, 14*, 67–75.

Chrisler, J. C., & Gorman, J. A. (2015). The medicalization of women's moods: Premenstrual syndrome and premenstrual dysphoric disorder. In M. McHugh & J. Chrisler (Eds.), *The wrong prescription for women: how medicine and media create a "need" for treatments, drugs, and surgery* (pp. 77–98). Santa Barbara, CA: Praeger.

Chrisler, J. C., Gorman, J. A., Serra, K. E., & Chapman, K. R. (2012). Facing up to aging: Mid-life women's attitudes toward cosmetic procedures. *Women & Therapy, 35*(3–4), 193–206. doi:10.1080/02703149.2012.684540

Chrisler, J. C., & Lamont, J. M. (2002). Can exercise contribute to the goals of feminist therapy? In R. L. Hall & C. A. Oglesby (Eds.), *Exercise and sport in feminist therapy: Constructing modalities and assessing outcomes* (pp. 9–22). New York: Haworth Press.

Chrisler, J. C., & Palatino, B. (2016). Stronger than you think: Older women and physical activity. *Women & Therapy, 39*(1–2), 157–170. doi:10.1080/02703149.2016.1116328

Chrisler, J. C., Rossini, M., & Newton, J. R. (2015). Older women, power, and the body. In V. Muhlbauer, J. C. Chrisler & Denmark, F. L. (Eds.), *Women and Aging: An International, Intersectional Power Perspective* (pp. 9–30). Switzerland: Springer International.

Christiaens, W., Verhaeghe, M., & Bracke, P. (2008). Childbirth expectation and experiences in Belgian and Dutch models of maternity care. *Journal of Reproductive and Infant Psychology, 26*(4), 309–322.

Christopher, A. N., & Mull, M. S. (2006). Conservative ideology and ambivalent sexism. *Psychology of Women Quarterly, 30*, 223–230.

Christopher, A. N., Zabel, K. L., & Miller, D. E. (2013). Personality, authoritarianism, social dominance, and ambivalent sexism: A mediational model. *Individual Differences Research, 11*(2), 70–80.

Chun, H., & Gupta, M. (2009). Gender discrimination in sex selective abortions and its transition in South Korea. *Women's Studies International Forum, 32*(2), 89–97. doi:10.1016/j.wsif.2009.03.008

Clarke, L. H. (2007). The body natural and body unnatural: beauty work and aging. *Journal of Aging Studies, 21*, 187–201.

Clarke, L. H., & Griffin, M. (2008). Visible and invisible aging: beauty work as a response to ageism. *Aging & Society, 28*, 653–674.

Clarke, V., Burns, M., & Burgoyne, C. (2008). "Who would take whose name?" Accounts of naming practices in same-sex relationships. *Journal of Community & Applied Social Psychology, 18*, 420–439.

Clear, E. R., Coker, A. L., Cook-Craig, P., Bush, H. M., Garcia, L. S., Williams, C. M., . . . Fisher, B. S. (2014). Sexual harassment victimization and perpetration among high school students. *Violence Against Women, 20*(10), 1203–1219. doi:10.1177/1077801214551287

Cohen, J. N. (2008). Using feminist, emotion-focused, and developmental approaches to enhance cognitive-behavioral therapies for posttraumatic stress disorder related to childhood sexual abuse. *Psychotherapy: Theory, Research, Practice, Training, 45*, 227–246.

Cohen, S. A. (2007). New data on abortion incidence, safety illuminate key aspects of worldwide abortion debate. *Guttmacher Policy Review, 10*. Retrieved March 10, 2010, from http://www.guttmacher.org/pubs/gpr/10/4/gpr100402.html

Cole, E. R. (2009). Intersectionality and research in psychology. *American Psychologist, 64*(3), 170–180. doi:10.1037/a0014564

Cole, S. G. (1987). *Pornography and harm*. Toronto: Metro Action Committee on Public Violence Against Women and Children.

Coley, R. J. (2001). *Differences in the gender gap: Comparisons across racial/ethnic groups in education and work*. Princeton: Educational Testing Service.

Collaer, M. L., Brook, C. G. D., Conway, G. S., Hindmarsh, P. C., & Hines, M. (2009). Motor development in individuals with congenital adrenal hyperplasia: Strength, targeting and fine motor skills. *Psychoneuroendocrinology, 34*, 249–258.

College Board. (2015). College-Bound Seniors, 2015: *Total Group Profile Report*. Retrieved from https://secure-media.collegeboard.org/digitalServices/pdf/sat/total-group-2015.pdf

Collins, P. H. (1991). The meaning of motherhood in Black culture and Black mother-daughter relationships. In P. Bell-Scott, B. Guy-Sheftall, J. J. Royster, J. Sims-Wood, M. DiCosta-Willis, & L. P. Fultz (Eds.), *Double stitch: Black women write about mothers and daughters* (pp. 42–60). New York: HarperCollins.

Collins, R. L., Ellickson, P. L., & Klein, D. J. (2006). The role of substance use in young adult divorce. *Addiction, 102,* 786–794.

Coltrane, S., & Adams, M. (1997). Work-family imagery and gender stereotypes: Television and the reproduction of difference. *Journal of Vocational Behavior, 50,* 323–347.

Coltrane, S., & Messineo, M. (2000). The perpetuation of subtle prejudice: Race and gender imagery in 1990s television advertising. *Sex Roles, 42,* 363–389.

Colvin, G. (2009). A CEO masters micro-credit. *Fortune Magazine Online.* Retrieved April 1, 2010, from http://money.cnn.com/2009/01/09/magazines/fortune/colvin_barnevik.fortune/index.htm

Comas-Díaz, L., & Greene, B. (1994). *Women of color: Integrating ethnic and gender identities in psychotherapy.* New York: Guilford Press.

Commuri, S., & Gentry, J. (2005). Resource allocation in households with women as chief wage earners. *Journal of Consumer Research, 32*(2), 185–195.

Condit, C. M. (1996). Media bias for reproductive technologies. In R. L. Parrott & C. M. Condit (Eds.), *Evaluating women's health messages* (pp. 341–355). Thousand Oaks, CA: Sage.

Conley, T. D., & Ramsey, L. R. (2011). Killing us softly? Investigating portrayals of women and men in contemporary magazine advertisements. *Psychology of Women Quarterly, 35*(3), 469–478. doi:10.1177/0361684311413383

Connolly, M. K., Quin, E., & Redding, E. (2011). Dance 4 your life: Exploring the health and well-being implications of a contemporary dance intervention for female adolescents. *Research in Dance Education, 12*(1), 53–66. Doi:10.1080/14647893.2011.561306

Conway, F., Jones, S., & Speakes-Lewis, A. (2011). Emotional strain in caregiving among African American grandmothers raising their grandchildren. *Journal of Women & Aging, 23*(2), 113–128.

Cooper, H. (2016, November 27). What is the color of beauty? *New York Times,* 12–13.

Copen, C. E., Daniels, K., Vespa, J., & Mosher, W. D. (2012). First marriages in the United States: Data from the 2006–2010 National Survey of Family Growth. *National Health Statistics Reports, 49.* Hyattsville, MD: National Center for Health Statistics.

Cosgrove, L. (2003). Resisting essentialism in feminist therapy theory: Some epistemological considerations. *Women & Therapy, 25,* 89–112.

Cosgrove, L., & Krimsky, S. (2012). A comparison of DSM-IV and DSM-5 panel members' financial associations with industry: A pernicious problem persists. *PLoS Med, 9*(3), e1001190.

Cosgrove, L., Krimsky, S., Vijayaraghavan, M., & Schneider, L. (2006). Financial ties between DSM-IV panel members and the pharmaceutical industry. *Psychotherapy and Psychosomatics, 75*(3), 154–160.

Cosgrove, L., & Wheeler, E. E. (2013). Industry's colonization of psychiatry: Ethical and practical implications of financial conflicts of interest in the DSM-5. *Feminism & Psychology, 23*(1), 93-106.

Covan, E. K. (2005). Meaning of aging in women's lives. *Journal of Women & Aging, 17*(3), 3–22.

Covert, J. J., & Dixon, T. L. (2008). A changing view: Representation and effects of the portrayal of women of color in mainstream women's magazines. *Communication Research, 35,* 232–258.

Cox, C. B. (2005). *Community care for an aging society: Issues, policies, and services.* New York: Springer.

Coyne, S. M., Linder, J. R., Rasmussen, E. E., Nelson, D. A., & Collier, K. M. (2014). It's a bird! It's a plane! It's a gender stereotype!: Longitudinal associations between superhero viewing and gender stereotyped play. *Sex Roles, 70*(9–10), 416–430. doi:10.1007/s11199–014-0374–8

Cozzarelli, C., & Major, B. (1998). The impact of antiabortion activities on women seeking abortions. In L. J. Beckman & S. M. Harvey (Eds.), *The new civil war: The psychology, culture, and politics of abortion* (pp. 81–104). Washington, DC: American Psychological Association.

Cramer, E., & MacFarlane, J. (1994). Pornography and abuse of women. *Public Health Nursing, 11,* 268–272.

Crawford, M. (1988). Gender, age, and the social evaluation of assertion. *Behavior Modification, 12,* 549–564.

Crawford, M. (1995). *Talking difference: On gender and language.* London: Sage.

Crawford, M. (2000). Editor's introduction: How to make sex and do gender. *Feminism & Psychology, 10,* 7–10.

Crawford, M. (2001). Gender and language. In R. K. Unger (Ed.), *Handbook of the psychology of women and gender* (pp. 228–244). New York: Wiley.

Crawford, M. (2010). *Sex trafficking in South Asia: Telling Maya's story.* London: Routledge.

Crawford, M. (2016). Sex Trafficking. In N. Naples (Ed.), *The Wiley Blackwell Encyclopedia of Gender and Sexuality Studies* (pp. 1–2). Malden, MA: John Wiley & Sons, Ltd. doi:10.1002/9781118663219.wbegss097

Crawford, M. (2017). International Sex Trafficking. *Women & Therapy, 40*(1–2), 101–122. doi:10.1080/02703149.2016.1206784

Crawford, M., & English, L. (1984). Generic versus specific inclusion of women in language: Effects on recall. *Journal of Psycholinguistic Research, 13,* 373–381.

Crawford, M., Kerwin, G., Gurung, A., Khati, D., Jha, P., & Regmi, A. C. (2008). Globalizing beauty: Attitudes toward beauty pageants among Nepali women. *Feminism & Psychology, 18,* 62–86.

Crawford, M., Lee, I., Portnoy, G., Gurung, A., Khati, D., Jha, P., & Regmi, A. C. (2009). Objectified body consciousness in a developing country: A comparison of mothers and daughters in the US and Nepal. *Sex Roles, 60,* 174–185.

Crawford, M., & Marecek, J. (1989). Psychology reconstructs the female. *Psychology of Women Quarterly, 13,* 147–166.

Crawford, M., & Popp, D. (2003). Sexual double standards: A review and methodological critique of two decades of research. *The Journal of Sex Research, 40,* 13–26.

Crawford, M., Stark, A., & Renner, C. (1998). The meaning of *Ms.*: Social assimilation of a gender concept. *Psychology of Women Quarterly, 22,* 197–208.

Crawford, P. A., & Bhattacharya, S. (2014). Grand images: Exploring images of grandparents in picture books. *Journal of Research in Childhood Education, 28*(1), 128–144. doi: 10.1080/02568543.2013.853004

Crick, N. R., & Rose, A. J. (2000). Toward a gender-balanced approach to the study of social-emotional development: A look at relational aggression. In P. H. Miller & E. K. Scholnick (Eds.), *Toward a feminist developmental psychology* (pp. 153–168). New York: Routledge.

Crittenden, A. (2001). *The price of motherhood.* New York: Metropolitan Books.

Croghan, R. (1991). First-time mothers' accounts of inequality in the division of labour. *Feminism & Psychology, 1,* 221–246.

Crosby, F. J. (1982). *Relative deprivation and working women.* New York: Oxford University Press.

Crosby, F. J. (1991). *Juggling: The unexpected advantages of balancing career and home for women and their families.* New York: Free Press.

Crosby, F. J. (2004). *Affirmative action is dead: Long live affirmative action.* New Haven, CT: Yale University Press.

Crosby, F. J., Clayton, S., Alksnis, O., & Hemker, K. (1986). Cognitive biases in the perception of discrimination: The importance of format. *Sex Roles, 14,* 637–646.

Crosby, F. J., Iyer, A., Clayton, S., & Downing, R. A. (2003). Affirmative action: Psychological data and the policy debates. *American Psychologist, 58,* 93–115.

Crowley, J. E. (2015). Unpacking the power of the mommy wars. *Sociological Inquiry, 85*(2), 217–238.

Crowther, M. R., Huang, C. S., & Allen, R. S. (2015). Rewards and unique challenges faced by African-American custodial grandmothers: The importance of future planning. *Aging & Mental Health, 19*(9), 844–852. doi :10.1080/13607863.2014.967175

Cruikshank, M. (2003). *Learning to be old: Gender, culture, and aging.* Lanham, MD: Rowman & Littlefield.

Cuddy, A. J. C., & Fiske, S. T. (2002). Doddering but dear: Process, content, and function in stereotyping of older persons. In T. D. Nelson (Ed.), *Ageism: Stereotyping and prejudice against older persons* (pp. 3–26). Cambridge, MA: MIT Press.

Cuddy, A., Norton, M., & Fiske, S., (2005). This old stereotype: The pervasiveness and persistence of the elderly stereotype. *Journal of Social Issues, 61,* 267–285.

Cummins, L. H., Simmons, A. M., & Zane, N. W. (2005). Eating disorders in Asian populations: A critique of current approaches to the study of culture, ethnicity, and eating disorders. *American Journal of Orthopsychiatry, 75*(4), 553–574.

Currier, D. M. (2013). Strategic ambiguity: Protecting emphasized femininity and hegemonic masculinity in the hookup culture. *Gender & Society, 27*(5), 704–727. doi:10.1177/0891243213493960

Curry, M. A., Renker, P., Hughes, R. B., Robinson-Whelen, S., Oschwald, M. M., Swank, P., & Powers, L. E. (2009). Development of measures of abuse among women with disabilities and the characteristics of their perpetrators. *Violence Against Women, 15,* 1001–1025.

Cyber Civil Rights Initiative. (2014, January 3). Power in numbers [blog post]. Retrieved from https://www.cyber-civilrights.org/revenge-porn-infographic/

Daigneault, I., Hebert, M., & McDuff, P. (2009). Men's and women's childhood sexual abuse and victimization in adult partner relationships: A study of risk factors. *Child Abuse & Neglect, 33,* 638–647.

Dallos, S., & Dallos, R. (1997). *Couples, sex, and power: The politics of desire.* Philadelphia: Open University Press.

Daniluk, J. C. (1996). When treatment fails: The transition to biological childlessness for infertile women. *Women & Therapy, 19,* 81–98.

Dank, M., Khan, P., Downey, P. M., Kotonias, C., Mayer, D., Owens, C., & Yu, L. (2014). Estimating the size and structure of the underground commercial sex economy in eight major US cities. *Urban Institute Research Report,* March 2014. Retrieved from http://www.urban.org/sites/default/files/publication/22376/413047-estimating-the-size-and-structure-of-the-underground-commercial-sex-economy-in-eight-major-us-cities.pdf

Danowski, J., & Robinson, T. (2012). The portrayal of older characters in popular children's picture books in the US. *Journal of Children and Media, 6*(3), 333–350.

Dansky, B. S., & Kilpatrick, D. G. (1997). Effects of sexual harassment. In W. O'Donohue (Ed.), *Sexual harassment: Theory, research and treatment* (pp. 152–174). Boston: Allyn & Bacon.

Dardenne, B., Dumont, M., & Bollier, T. (2007). Insidious dangers of benevolent sexism: Consequences for women's performance. *Journal of Personality and Social Psychology, 93,* 764–779.

Dar-Nimrod, I., & Heine, S. J. (2011). Genetic essentialism: On the deceptive determinism of DNA. *Psychological Bulletin, 137*(5), 800–818. doi:10.1037/a0021860

Darwin, C. (1872/1998). *The expression of emotions in man and animals.* New York: Oxford University Press.

Das, A. (2007). Masturbation in the United States. *Journal of Sex & Marital Therapy, 33,* 301–317.

Davey, C. L., & Davidson, M. J. (2000). The right of passage? The experiences of female pilots in aviation. *Feminism and Psychology, 10,* 195–225.

Davey, H. L., Tough, S. C., Adair, C. E., & Benzies, K. M. (2011). Risk factors for sub-clinical and major postpartum depression among a community cohort of Canadian women. *Maternal Child Health Journal, 15*(7), 866–875. doi:10.1007/s10995–008-0314–8

Davis, G., Dewey, J. M., & Murphy, E. L. (2016). Giving sex: Deconstructing intersex and trans medicalization practices. *Gender & Society, 30*(3), 490–514. doi:10.1177/0891243215602102

Davis, S. N., Jacobsen, S. K., & Anderson, J. (2012). From the great recession to greater gender equality? Family mobility and the intersection of race, class, and gender. *Marriage & Family Review, 48*(7), 601–620. doi:10.1080/014949 29.2012.691083

Davis, T. L. (1995). Gender differences in masking negative emotions: Ability or motivation? *Developmental Psychology, 31,* 650–667.

Davison, H. K., & Burke, M. J. (2000). Sex discrimination in simulated employment contexts: A meta-analytic investigation. *Journal of Vocational Behavior, 56,* 225–248.

Davison, H. K. (2014). The paradox of the contented female worker: Why are women satisfied with lower pay? *Employee Responsibilities and Rights Journal, 26*(3), 195–216. doi:10.1007/s10672-014-9238-1

Dawson, A. E., Bernstein, B. L., & Bekki, J. M. (2015). Providing the psychosocial benefits of mentoring to women in STEM: CareerWISE as an online solution. *New Directions for Higher Education, 171*, 53–62. doi:10.1002/he.20142

Deaux, K., & Lewis, L. L. (1984). The structure of gender stereotypes: Interrelationships among components and gender labels. *Journal of Personality and Social Psychology, 46*, 991–1004.

Deaux, K., & Major, B. (1987). Putting gender into context: An interactive model of gender-related behavior. *Psychological Review, 94*, 369–389.

Deaux, K., Winton, W., Crowley, M., & Lewis, L. L. (1985). Level of categorization and content of gender stereotypes. *Social Cognition, 3*, 145–167.

DeLamater, J. (2012). Sexual expression in later life: A review and synthesis. *Journal of Sex Research, 49*, 125–141.

DeLamater, J. D., & Sill, M. (2005). Sexual desire in later life. *The Journal of Sex Research, 42*, 138–149.

DeLyser, G. (2012). At midlife, intentionally childfree women and their experiences of regret. *Clinical Social Work Journal, 40*(1), 66–74. doi:10.1007/s10615-011-0337-2

Denmark, F. L., Russo, N. F., Frieze, I. H., & Sechzer, J. A. (1988). Guidelines for avoiding sexism in psychological research: A report of the ad hoc committee on nonsexist research. *American Psychologist, 43*, 582–585.

Desmarais, S., & Curtis, J. (1997). Gender differences in pay histories and view on payment entitlement among university students. *Sex Roles, 37*, 623–642.

De Smet, O., Uzieblo, K., Loeys, T., Buysse, A., & Onraedt, T. (2015). Unwanted pursuit behavior after breakup: Occurrence, risk factors, and gender differences. *Journal of Family Violence, 30*(6), 753–767.

Deutsch, F. (1999). *Halving it all: How equally shared parenting works.* Cambridge, MA: Harvard University Press.

Devine, P. G., & Sharp, L. B. (2009). Automaticity and control in stereotyping and prejudice. In T. D. Nelson (Ed.), *Handbook of prejudice, stereotyping, and discrimination* (pp. 61–87). New York: Psychology Press.

de Vries, D. A., Peter, J., Nikken, P., & de Graaf, H. (2014). The effect of social network site use on appearance investment and desire for cosmetic surgery among adolescent boys and girls. *Sex Roles, 71*, 283–295. doi:10.1007/s11199-014-0412-6

Devries, K., Watts, C., Yoshihama, M., Kiss, L., Schraiber, L. B., Deyessa, N., . . . Berhane, Y. (2011). Violence against women is strongly associated with suicide attempts: Evidence from the WHO multi-country study on women's health and domestic violence against women. *Social Science & Medicine, 73*(1), 79–86.

Dewey, C. (2016). Every 10 seconds someone on Twitter calls a woman a slut or whore. *The Washington Post.* Retrieved from https://www.washingtonpost.com/news/the-intersect/wp/2016/05/26/every-10-seconds-someone-on-twitter-calls-a-woman-a-slut-or-whore/?tid=sm_tw

Dhejne, C., Van Vlerken, R., Heylens, G., & Arcelus, J. (2016). Mental health and gender dysphoria: A review of the literature. *International Review of Psychiatry, 28*(1), 44–57. doi:10.3109/09540261.2015.1115753

Diamond, L. (2008). *Sexual fluidity: Understanding women's love and desire.* Cambridge: Harvard University Press.

Diamond, L. M. (2000). Sexual identity, attractions, and behavior among young sexual-minority women over a 2-year period. *Developmental Psychology, 36*, 241–250.

Diamond, M. (2011). Developmental, sexual and reproductive neuroendocrinology: Historical, clinical and ethical considerations. *Frontiers in Neuroendocrinology, 32*(2), 255–263. doi:10.1016/j.yfrne.2011.02.003

Diamond, M. (2013). Transsexuality among twins: Identity concordance, transition, rearing, and orientation. *International Journal of Transgenderism, 14*(1), 24–38. doi:10.1080/15532739.2013.750222

Diamond, M., & Garland, J. (2014). Evidence regarding cosmetic and medically unnecessary surgery on infants. *Journal of Pediatric Urology, 10*(1), 2–6.

Diamond, M., & Watson, L. A. (2004). Androgen insensitivity syndrome and Klinefelter's syndrome: Sex and gender considerations. *Child and Adolescent Psychiatric Clinics of North America*, 623–640.

Diamond-Smith N., Luke, N., & McGarvey, S. (2008). "Too many girls, too much dowry": Son preference and daughter aversion in rural Tamil Nadu, India. *Culture, Health and Sexuality, 10*(7), 697–708.

Dickerson, B. J. (Ed.). (1995). *African-American single mothers.* Thousand Oaks, CA: Sage.

Dickey, L. M., Ducheny, K. M., & Ehrbar, R. D. (2016). Family creation options for transgender and gender nonconforming people. *Psychology of Sexual Orientation and Gender Diversity, 3*(2), 173–179.

Dickhäuser, O., & Meyer, W. (2006). Gender differences in young children's math ability attributions. *Psychology Science, 48*, 3–16.

Diekman, A. B., & Eagly, A. H. (2000). Stereotypes as dynamic constructs: Women and men of the past, present, and future. *Personality and Social Psychology Bulletin, 26*, 1171–1188.

Diekman, A. B., McDonald, M., & Gardner, W. L. (2000). Love means never having to be careful: The relationship between reading romance novels and safe sex behavior. *Psychology of Women Quarterly, 24*, 179–188.

Di Leonardo, M. (1987). The female world of cards and holidays: Women, families, and the work of kinship. *Signs, 12*, 440–453.

Dill, K. E., Brown, B. P., & Collins, M. A. (2008). Effects of exposure to sex-stereotyped video game characters on tolerance of sexual harassment. *Journal of Experimental Social Psychology, 44*, 1402–1408.

Dill, K. E., & Thill, K. P. (2007). Video game characters and the socialization of gender roles: Young people's perceptions mirror sexist media depictions. *Sex Roles, 57*, 851–865.

Dillon, G., Hussain, R., Loxton, D., & Rahman, S. (2013). Mental and physical health and intimate partner violence against women: A review of the literature. *International Journal of Family Medicine, 2013.* doi:10.1155/2013/313909

Dion, K. L. (1987). What's in a title? The Ms stereotype and images of women's titles of address. *Psychology of Women Quarterly, 11*, 21–36.

DiPalma, L. M. (1994). Patterns of coping and characteristics of high-functioning incest survivors. *Archives of Psychiatric Nursing, 8*, 82–90.

Dittmar, H., Halliwell, E., & Ive, S. (2006). Does Barbie make girls want to be thin? The effect of experimental exposure to images of dolls on the body image of 5- to 8-year old girls. *Developmental Psychology, 42,* 283–292.

Dodson, B. (1987). *Sex for one: The joy of self-loving.* New York: Crown.

Dohm, F. A., & Cummings, W. (2002). Research mentoring and women in clinical psychology. *Psychology of Women Quarterly, 26,* 163–167.

Domínguez-Folgueras, M. (2013). Is cohabitation more egalitarian? The division of household labor in five European countries. *Journal of Family Issues, 34*(12), 1623–1646.

Donnelly, K., Twenge, J. M., Clark, M. A., Shaikh, S. K., Beiler-May, A., & Carter, N. T. (2016). Attitudes toward women's work and family roles in the United States, 1976–2013. *Psychology of Women Quarterly, 40,* 41–54. doi:10.1177/0361684315590774

Donohue, J. M., & Berndt, E. R. (2004). Effects of direct-to-consumer advertising on medication choice: The case of antidepressants. *Journal of Public Policy and Marketing, 23*(2), 115–127.

Dorahy, M. J., Lewis, C. A., & Wolfe, F. A. M. (2007). Psychological distress associated with domestic violence in Northern Ireland. *Current Psychology, 25,* 295–305.

Doress-Worters, P. B., & Siegal, D. L. (1994). *The new ourselves growing older.* New York: Simon & Schuster.

Dorian, L., & Garfinkel, P. E. (2002). Culture and body image in Western society. *Eating and Weight Disorders, 7,* 1–19.

Dougherty, E. N., Dorr, N., & Pulice, R. T. (2016). Assisting older women in combating ageist stereotypes and improving attitudes toward aging. *Women & Therapy, 39* (1–2), 12–34.

Dougherty, T. W., Dreher, G. F., Arunachalam, V., & Wilbanks, J. E. (2013). Mentor status, occupational context, and protégé career outcomes: Differential returns for males and females. *Journal of Vocational Behavior, 83*(3), 514–527.

Douglas, S. J. (1994). *Where the girls are: Growing up female with the mass media.* New York: Times Books/Random House.

Dovidio, J. F., Ellyson, S. L., Keating, C. F., Heltman, K., & Brown, C. E. (1988). The relationship of social power to visual displays of dominance between men and women. *Journal of Personality and Social Psychology, 54,* 233–242.

Drouin, M., Vogel, K. N., Surbey, A., & Stills, J. R. (2013). Let's talk about sexting, baby: Computer-mediated sexual behaviors among young adults. *Computers in Human Behavior, 29*(5), A25–A30.

Drout, C. E. (1997). Professionals' and students' perceptions of abuse among married and unmarried cohabitating couples. *Journal of Social Behavior and Personality, 12,* 965–978.

Dryden, C. (1999). *Being married, doing gender.* New York: Routledge.

Duberley, J., & Carmichael, F. (2016). Career pathways into retirement in the UK: Linking older women's pasts to the present. *Gender, Work and Organization, 23*(6), 582–599.

Duberley, J., Carmichael, F., & Szmigin, I. (2014). Exploring women's retirement: Continuity, context and career transition. *Gender, Work and Organization, 21*(1), 71–90.

Dubourg, D., Richard, F., Leye, E., Ndame, S., Rommens, T., & Maes, S. (2011). Estimating the number of women with female genital mutilation in Belgium. *The European Journal of Contraception and Reproductive Health Care, 16*(4), 248–257. doi:10.3109/13625187.2011.579205

Durik, A., Hyde, J., Marks, A., Roy, A., Anaya, D., & Schultz, G. (2006). Ethnicity and gender stereotypes of emotion. *Sex Roles, 54*(7–8), 429–445. doi:10.1007/s11199-006-9020-4

Dutton, D. G. (1996). Patriarchy and wife assault: The ecological fallacy. In L. K. Hamberger & C. Renzetti (Eds.), *Domestic partner abuse* (pp. 125–151). New York: Springer.

Dutton, Y. C., & Zisook, S. (2005). Adaptation to bereavement. *Death Studies, 29,* 877–903.

Duval, L. L., & Ruscher, J. B. (1994, July). *Men use more detail to explain a gender-neutral task to women.* Poster presented at the annual meeting of the American Psychological Society, Washington, DC.

Dworkin, S. L., & O'Sullivan, L. (2007). "It's less work for us and it shows us she has good taste": Masculinity, sexual initiation, and contemporary sexual scripts. In M. Kimmell (Ed.), *The sexual self: The construction of sexual scripts* (pp. 105–121). Nashville, TN: University of Vanderbilt Press.

Eagly, A. H., & Heilman, M. E. (2016). Gender and leadership: Introduction to the special issue. *The Leadership Quarterly, 27*(3), 349–353. doi:10.1016/j.leaqua.2016.04.002

Eagly, A. H., & Johannesen-Schmidt, M. C. (2001). The leadership styles of women and men. *Journal of Social Issues, 57,* 781–797.

Eagly, A. H., & Johnson, B. T. (1990). Gender and leadership style: A meta-analysis. *Psychological Bulletin, 108,* 233–256.

Eagly, A. H., & Karau, S. J. (2002). Role congruity theory of prejudice toward female leaders. *Psychological Review, 109,* 573–598.

Eagly, A., & Miller, D. I. (2016). Scientific eminence: Where are the women? *Perspectives on Psychological Science, 11*(6), 899–904.

Eagly, A. H., & Mladinic, A. (1993). Are people prejudiced against women? Some answers from research on attitudes, gender stereotypes, and judgments of competence. In W. Strobe & M. Hewstone (Eds.), *European review of social psychology* (pp. 1–35). New York: Wiley.

Eagly, A. H., & Wood, W. (1999). The origins of sex differences in human behavior: Evolved dispositions versus social roles. *American Psychologist, 54,* 408–423.

Eastwick, P. W., & Finkel, E. J. (2008). Sex differences in mate preference revisited: Do people know what they initially desire in a romantic partner? *Journal of Personality and Social Psychology, 94,* 245–264.

Eccles, J. S. (1989). Bringing young women to math and science. In M. Crawford & M. Gentry (Eds.), *Gender and thought: Psychological perspectives* (pp. 36–58). New York: Springer Verlag.

Eccles, J. S. (1994). Understanding women's educational and occupational choices: Applying the Eccles et al. model of achievement-related choices. *Psychology of Women Quarterly, 18,* 585–610.

Eccles, J. S. (2011). Understanding women's achievement choices: Looking back and looking forward. *Psychology of Women Quarterly, 35*(3), 510–516. doi:10.1177/0361684 311414829

Eccles, J. S., Barber, B., Jozefowicz, D., Malenchuk, D., & Vida, M. (2000). Self-evaluations of competence, task values, and self-esteem. In N. G. Johnson, M. C. Roberts, & J. Worell (Eds.), *Beyond appearances: A new look at adolescent girls* (pp. 53–83). Washington, DC: American Psychological Association.

Eccles, J. S., & Wang, M. (2016). What motivates females and males to pursue careers in mathematics and science? *International Journal of Behavioral Development, 40*(2), 100–106.

Edley, N., & Wetherell, M. (2001). Men's construction of feminism and feminists. *Feminism & Psychology, 11*, 439–458.

Edwards, L. M., Haglund, K., Fehring, R. J., & Pruszynski, J. (2011). Religiosity and sexual risk behaviors among Latina adolescents: Trends from 1995 to 2008. *Journal of Women's Health, 20*(6), 871–877. doi:10.1089/jwh. 2010.1949

Ehrenreich, B., & English, D. (1973). *Complaints and disorders: The sexual politics of sickness.* New York: The Feminist Press.

Eicher, V., Settersten, R. A., Penic, S., Glaeser, S., Martenot, A., & Spini, D. (2015). Normative climates of parenthood across Europe: Judging voluntary childlessness and working parents. *European Sociological Review, 32*(1), 135–150. doi:10.1093/esr/jcv083

Eichler, M. (1988). *Nonsexist research methods.* Boston: Allen & Unwin.

Eisenach, J. C., Pan, P. H., Smiley, R., Lavand'homme, P., Landau, R., & Houle, T. T. (2008). Severity of acute pain after childbirth, but not type of delivery, predicts persistent pain and postpartum depression. *Pain, 140*(1), 87–94. doi:10.1016/j.pain.2008.07.011

Eisenstat, S. A., & Bancroft, L. (1999). Domestic violence. *New England Journal of Medicine, 341*, 886–892.

Eisikovits, Z., & Buchbinder, E. (1999). Talking control: Metaphors used by battered women. *Violence Against Women, 5*, 845–868.

Elavsky, S., & McAuley, E. (2005). Physical activity, symptoms, esteem, and life satisfaction during menopause. *Maturitas, 52*, 374–285.

Elfenbein, H. A., & Ambady, N. (2003). Universals and cultural differences in recognizing emotions. *Current Directions in Psychological Science, 12*, 159–164.

Elkind, S. N. (1991, Winter). Letter to the editor. *Psychology of Women, 18*, 3.

Elklit, A., & O'Connor, M. (2005). Post-traumatic stress disorder in a Danish population of elderly bereaved. *Scandinavian Journal of Psychology, 46*, 439–445.

Elliot, P. (2009). Engaging trans debates on gender variance: A feminist analysis. *Sexualities, 12*, 5.

Elliot, R. (1989). *Song of love.* New York: Harlequin.

Ellis, R. (2016, June 19). Former Vanderbilt football player found guilty in sex assault. CNN. Retrieved from http://www.cnn.com/2016/06/18/us/vanderbilt-rape-case/

Ellison, N.B., Hancock, J., & Toma, C.L. (2011). Profile as promise: A framework for conceptualizing veracity in online dating self-presentations. *New Media & Society, 14*(1), 45–62. doi:10.1177/1461444811410395

Ellsberg, M., Heise, L., Pena, R., Agurto, S., & Winkvist, A. (2001). Researching domestic violence against women: Methodological and ethical considerations. *Studies in Family Planning, 32*, 1–16.

Ellsberg, M., Jansen, H. A., Heise, L., Watts, C. H., & Garcia-Moreno, C. (2008). Intimate partner violence and women's physical and mental health in the WHO multi-country study on women's health and domestic violence: An observational study. *The Lancet, 371*(9619), 1165–1172.

Else-Quest, N., & Grabe, S. (2012). The political is personal: Measurement and application of nation-level indicators of gender equity in psychological research. *Psychology of Women Quarterly, 36*(2), 131–144. doi:10.1177/03616 84312441592

Else-Quest, N., Mineo, C. C., & Higgins, A. (2013). Math and science attitudes and achievement at the intersection of gender and ethnicity. *Psychology of Women Quarterly, 37*(3), 293–309.

Emmerink, P. M. J., van, d. E., Vanwesenbeeck, I., & ter Bogt, T. F. M. (2016). The relationship between endorsement of the sexual double standard and sexual cognitions and emotions. *Sex Roles, 75*(7–8), 363–376. doi:10.1007/s11199-016-0616-z

Englander, E. (2014). Bullying and harassment in a digital world. *Bullying, Teen Aggression and Social Media*, December, 1–4.

Englander, E. (2015). Coerced sexting and revenge porn among teens. *Bullying, Teen Aggression & Social Media, 1*(2), 19–21.

Enns, C. Z. (2004). *Feminist theories and feminist psychotherapies: Origins, themes and variations.* Binghampton, NY: Haworth Press.

Erchull, M. J. (2013). Distancing through objectification? Depictions of women's bodies in menstrual product advertisements. *Sex Roles, 68*(32), 32–40. doi:10.1007/s11199-011-0004-7

Erchull, M. J., Liss, M., & Lichiello, S. (2013). Extending the negative consequences of media internalization and self-objectification to dissociation and self-harm. *Sex Roles, 69*, 583–593. doi:10.1007/s11199-013-0326-8

Erickson-Schroth, L. (2013). Update on the biology of transgender identity. *Journal of Gay & Lesbian Mental Health, 17*(2), 150–174. doi:10.1080/19359705.2013.753393

Erkut, S., Fields, J. P., Sing, R., & Marks, F. (1997). Diversity in girls' experiences: Feeling good about who you are. In B. J. R. Leadbeater & N. Way (Eds.), *Urban girls: Resisting stereotypes, creating identities* (pp. 53–64). New York: New York University Press.

Erwin, T. (2007). Two moms and a baby: Counseling lesbian couples choosing motherhood. *Women & Therapy, 30* (1–2), 99–149.

Espeland, M. A., Rapp, S. R., Shumaker, S. A., Brunner, R., Manson, J. E., & Sherwin, B. (2004). Conjugated equine estrogens and global cognitive function in postmenopausal women: Women's health initiative memory study. *Journal of the American Medical Association, 291*, 2959–2968.

Espin, O. M. (1987). Issues of identity in the psychology of Latina lesbians. In Boston Lesbian Psychologies Collective (Ed.), *Lesbian psychologies: Explorations and challenges* (pp. 35–55). Urbana: University of Illinois Press.

Espín, O. M. (2012). "An illness we catch from American women"? The multiple identities of Latina lesbians. *Women & Therapy, 35*(1–2), 45–56. doi:10.1080/02703149.2012.634720

Esteve, A., Garcia-Roman, J., & Permanyer, I. (2012). Gender-gap reversal in education and its effect on union formation: The end of hypergamy? *Population and Development Review, 38*(3): 535–546.

Etaugh, C., & Liss, M. B. (1992). Home, school, and playroom: Training grounds for adult gender roles. *Sex Roles, 26,* 129–147.

Etehad, M. & Lin, J. C. F. (2016, August 13). *The world is getting better at paid maternity leave. The U.S. is not.* Retrieved from https://www.washingtonpost.com/news/worldviews/wp/2016/08/13/the-world-is-getting-better-at-paid-maternity-leave-the-u-s-is-not/?wpisrc=nl_heads-draw6&wpmm=1

European Union Agency for Fundamental Rights (2014). Violence against women: An EU-wide survey: Main results. Retrieved from http://fra.europa.eu/sites/default/files/fra-2014-vaw-survey-main-results-apr14_en.pdf

Evans, G. W. (2004). The environment of childhood poverty. *American Psychologist, 59,* 77–92.

Evans, L., & Davies, K. (2000). No sissy boys here: A content analysis of the representation of masculinity in elementary school reading textbooks. *Sex Roles, 42,* 255–270.

Fabiano, P., Perkins, W., Berkowitz, A., Linkenbach, J., & Stark, C. (2003). Engaging men as social justice allies in ending violence against women: Evidence for a social norms approach. *Journal of American College Health, 52,* 105–112.

Facio, E. (1997). Chicanas and aging: Toward definitions of womanhood. In J. M. Coyle (Ed.), *Handbook on women and aging* (pp. 335–350). Westport, CT: Greenwood Press.

Fägerskiöld, A. (2008). A change in life as experienced by first time fathers. *Scandinavian Journal of Caring Science, 22,* 64–71.

Fagot, B. I., & Leinbach, M. D. (1995). Gender knowledge in egalitarian and traditional families. *Sex Roles, 32,* 513–526.

Faircloth, C. A. (Ed.). (2003). *Aging bodies: Images and everyday experiences.* New York: AltaMira Press.

Falconier, M. K. (2013). Traditional gender role orientation and dyadic coping in immigrant Latino couples: Effects on couple functioning. *Family Relations: An Interdisciplinary Journal of Applied Family Studies, 62*(2), 269–283.

Faludi, S. (1991). *Backlash: The undeclared war against American women.* New York: Doubleday.

Fanti, K. A., Vanman, E., Henrich, C., & Avramides, M. N. (2009). Desensitization to media violence over a short period of time. *Aggressive Behavior, 35,* 179–187.

Fardouly, J., Diedrichs, P. C., Vartanian, L. R., & Halliwell, E. (2015). The mediating role of appearance comparisons in the relationship between media usage and self-objectification in young women. *Psychology of Women Quarterly, 39*(4), 447–457. doi:10.1177/0361684315581841

Farmer, H. S. (Ed.). (1997). *Diversity & women's career development: From adolescence to adulthood.* Thousand Oaks, CA: Sage.

Farr, K. (2005). *Sex trafficking: The global market in women and children.* New York: Worth.

Farrell, B. (2003, August 17). American TV raises the stars and strips: The major US networks are doing the unthinkable—putting porn in their schedules. *The Observer,* p. 8.

Fasula, A. M., Miller, K. S., & Wiener, J. (2007). The sexual double standard in African American adolescent women's sexual risk reduction. *Women & Health, 46,* 3–21.

Fausto-Sterling, A. (2000). *Sexing the body: Gender politics and the construction of sexuality.* New York: Basic Books.

Favreau, O. E. (1997). Sex and gender comparisons: Does null hypothesis testing create a false dichotomy? *Feminism and Psychology, 7,* 63–81.

Feder, L., Wilson, D. B., & Austin, S. (2008). Court-mandated interventions for individuals convicted of domestic violence. *Campbell Systematic Reviews, 12,* 1–46.

Federal Bureau of Investigation (2015). *Crime in the United States.* Retrieved from https://ucr.fbi.gov/crime-in-the-u.s/2015/crime-in-the-u.s.-2015

Federal Glass Ceiling Commission. (1998). Working women face barriers to advancement. In M. E. Williams (Ed.), *Working women: Opposing viewpoints* (pp. 64–72). San Diego, CA: Greenhaven Press.

Feldman, S. (1999). Please don't call me "dear": Older women's narratives of health care. *Nursing Inquiry, 6,* 269–276.

Fidell, L. S. (1970). Empirical verification of sex discrimination in hiring practices in psychology. *American Psychologist, 25,* 1094–1098.

Fikkan, J. L., & Rothblum, E. D. (2012). Is fat a feminist issue? Exploring the gendered nature of weight bias. *Sex Roles, 66*(9–10), 575–592. doi:10.1007/s11199-011-0022-5

Fine, M. (1988). Sexuality, schooling, and adolescent females: The missing discourse of desire. *Harvard Educational Review, 58,* 29–53.

Fine, M., & Asch, A. (1988). *Women with disabilities: Essays in psychology, culture, and politics.* Philadelphia, PA: Temple University Press.

Finkel, E. J., Eastwick, P. W., Karney, B. R., Reis, H. T., & Sprecher, S. (2012). Online dating: A critical analysis from the perspective of psychological science. *Psychological Science in the Public Interest, 13*(1), 3–66. doi:10.1177/1529100612436522

Firestein, B. A. (1998, March 7). Bisexuality: A feminist vision of choice and change. Paper presented at the annual meeting of the Association for Women in Psychology, Baltimore, MD.

Fisher, H. (2014). 'It would help if the teacher helps you a bit more...instead of going to the brainiest who don't need a lot of help': Exploring the perspectives of dissatisfied girls on the periphery of primary classroom life. *British Educational Research Journal, 40*(1), 150–169. doi:10.1002/berj.3034

Fisher, J. D., & Fisher, W. A. (2000). Theoretical approaches to individual-level change in HIV risk behavior. In J. L. Peterson & R. J. DiClemente (Eds.), *Handbook of HIV prevention, AIDS prevention and mental health* (pp. 3–55). New York: Kluwer Academic/Plenum.

Fisher, J. D., Fisher, W. A., Misovich, S. J., Kimble, D. L., & Malloy, T. E. (1996). Changing AIDS risk behavior: Effects of an intervention emphasizing AIDS risk reduction information, motivation, and behavioral skills in a college student population. *Health Psychology, 15,* 114–123.

Fisher, W. A., Williams, S. S., Fisher, J. D., & Malloy, T. E. (1999). Understanding AIDS risk behavior among sexually active urban adolescents: An empirical test of the information-motivation-behavioral skills model. *AIDS and Behavior, 3,* 13–23.

Fiske, A. P., Haslam, N., & Fiske, S. T. (1991). Confusing one person with another: What errors reveal about the elementary forms of social relations. *Journal of Personality and Social Psychology, 60,* 656–674.

Fiske, S. T., Bersoff, D. N., Borgida, E., Deaux, K., & Heilman, M. E. (1991). Social science research on trial: Use of sex stereotyping research in Price Waterhouse v. Hopkins. *American Psychologist, 46,* 1049–1060.

Fitch, R. H., & Denenberg, V. H. (1998). A role for ovarian hormones in sexual differentiation of the brain. *Behavior and Brain Science, 21,* 311–352.

Fitz, C. C., & Zucker, A. N. (2014). Feminist with benefits: College women's feminist beliefs buffer sexual well-being amid hostile (not benevolent) sexism. *Psychology of Women Quarterly, 38*(1), 7–19. doi:10.1177/0361684313504736

Fitzgerald, L. F. (1993). Sexual harassment: Violence against women in the workplace. *American Psychologist, 48,* 1070–1076.

Fitzgerald, L. F., Swan, S., & Magley, V. J. (1997). But was it really sexual harassment? Legal, behavioral, and psychological definitions of the workplace victimization of women. In W. O'Donohue (Ed.), *Sexual harassment: Theory, research, and treatment* (pp. 5–28). Boston, MA: Allyn & Bacon.

Fivush, R. (1989). Exploring sex differences in the emotional content of mother-child conversations about the past. *Sex Roles, 20,* 675–692.

Fivush, R., Brotman, M. A., Buckner, J. P., & Goodman, S. H. (2000). Gender differences in parent-child emotion narratives. *Sex Roles, 42,* 233–253.

Fivush, R., & Buckner, J. P. (2000). Gender, sadness, and depression: The development of emotional focus through gendered discourse. In A. H. Fischer (Ed.), *Gender and emotion: Social psychological perspectives* (pp. 232–254). Cambridge, England: Cambridge University Press.

Fixmer-Oraiz, N. (2013). Speaking of solidarity: Transnational gestational surrogacy and the rhetorics of reproductive (in)justice. *Frontiers: A Journal of Women Studies, 34*(3), 126–163. doi:10.5250/fronjwomestud.34.3.0126

Flynn, M. A., Craig, C. M., Anderson, C. N., & Holody, K. J. (2016). Objectification in popular music lyrics: An examination of gender and genre differences. *Sex Roles, 1*(13). doi:10.1007/s11199-016-0592-3

Forbes, G. B., Adams-Curtis, L. E., Holmgren, K. M., & White, K. B. (2004). Perceptions of the social and personal characteristics of hypermuscular women and of the men who love them. *Journal of Social Psychology, 144,* 487–506.

Ford, A. R. (1986). When women outlive their ovaries. *New Internationalist, 165.*

Ford, M. T., Heinen, B. A., & Langkamer, K. L. (2007). Work and family satisfaction and conflict: A meta-analysis of cross-domain relations. *Journal of Applied Psychology, 92,* 57–80.

Foreit, K. G., Agor, A. T., Byers, J., Larue, J., Lokey, H., Palazzini, M., . . . Smith, L. (1980). Sex bias in the newspaper treatment of male-centered and female-centered news stories. *Sex Roles, 6,* 475–480.

Forste, R., & Tanfer, K. (1996). Sexual exclusivity among dating, cohabiting, and married women. *Journal of Marriage and Family, 58,* 33–47.

Foster, D. G. (2016). Unmet need for abortion and woman-centered contraceptive care. *The Lancet, 388,* 216–217. doi:10.1016/S0140–6736(16)30452–4

Foster, M. D. (2015). Tweeting about sexism: The well-being benefits of a social media collective action. *British Journal of Social Psychology, 54*(4), 629–647. doi:10.1037/t04754–000

Fouquier, K. F. (2011). The concept of motherhood among three generations of African American women. *Journal of Nursing Scholarship, 43*(2), 145–153. doi:10.1111/j.1547-5069.2011.01394.x

Fouts, G., & Burggraf, K. (2000). Television situation comedies, female weight, male negative comments, and audience reactions. *Sex Roles, 42,* 925–932.

Fouts, H. N., Hallam, R. A., & Purandare, S. (2013). Gender segregation in early-childhood social play among the Bofi foragers and Bofi farmers in central Africa. *American Journal of Play, 5*(3), 333–356.

Fox, A. B., & Quinn, D. M. (2015). Pregnant women at work: The role of stigma in predicting women's intended exit from the workforce. *Psychology of Women Quarterly, 39*(2), 226–242. doi:10.1177/0361684314552653

Fox, J., Ahn, S. J., Janssen, J. H., Yeykelis, L., Segovia, K. Y., & Bailenson, J. N. (2015). Avatars versus agents: A meta-analysis quantifying the effect of agency on social influence. *Human-Computer Interaction, 30*(5), 401–432. doi:10.1080/07370024.2014.921494

Franks, M. A. (2016, July 18). It's time for Congress to protect intimate privacy. *Huffington Post: The Blog.* Retrieved from http://www.huffingtonpost.com/mary-anne-franks/revenge-porn-intimate-privacy-protection-act_b_11034998.html

Fraser, L. (2002, December 1). The islands where boys grow up to be girls: In the South Pacific, the fa'fafine men who spend their lives as women—turn gender roles upside down. *Marie Claire, 9,* 72–78.

Fredrickson, B. L., & Roberts, T. (1997). Objectification theory: Toward understanding women's lived experiences and mental health risks. *Psychology of Women Quarterly, 21,* 173–206.

Fredrickson, B. L., Roberts, T., Noll, S. M., Quinn, D. M., & Twenge, J. M. (1998). That swimsuit becomes you: Sex differences in self-objectification, restrained eating, and math performance. *Journal of Personality and Social Psychology, 75,* 269–284.

Friedemann, M., & Buckwalter, K. C. (2014). Family caregiver role and burden related to gender and family relationships. *Journal of Family Nursing, 20*(3), 313–336. doi:10.1177/1074840714532715

Friedlander, L. J., Connolly, J. A., Pepler, D. J., & Craig, W. M. (2013). Extensiveness and persistence of aggressive media exposure as longitudinal risk factors for teen dating violence. *Psychology of Violence, 3*(4), 310.

French, H. W. (2003, June 29). Victims say Japan ignores sex crimes committed by teachers. *The New York Times,* p. A4.

Frenzel, A. C., Pekrun, R., & Goetz, T. (2007). Girls and mathematics—A "hopeless" issue? A control-value approach to gender differences in emotions towards mathematics. *European Journal of Psychology of Education, 22*(4), 497–514.

Freud, S. (1914). *On the history of the Psycho-Analytic movement.* New York: W. W. Norton, Inc., 1966.

Freud, S. (1933). Femininity. In J. Strachey (Ed. & Trans.), *New introductory lectures on psycho-analysis* (pp. 112–135). New York: Norton, 1965.

Friedman, S. D., & Greenhaus, J. H. (2000). *Work and family—Allies or enemies?* New York: Oxford University Press.

Frieze, I. H. (2005). *Hurting the one you love: Violence in relationships.* Belmont, CA: Wadsworth/Thomson Learning.

Frintner, M. P., & Rubinson, L. (1993). Acquaintance rape: The influence of alcohol, fraternity membership, and sports team membership. *Journal of Sex Education and Therapy, 19,* 272–284.

Frisch, R. E. (1983). Fatness, menarche, and fertility. In S. Golub (Ed.), *Menarche: The transition from girl to woman* (pp. 5–20). Lexington, MA: Lexington Books.

Fulcher, M., Sutfin, E. L., Chan, R. W., Scheib, J. E., & Patterson, C. J. (2006). Lesbian mothers and their children. In A. M. Omoto & H. S. Kurtzman (Eds.), *Sexual orientation and mental health: Examining identity and development in lesbian, gay, and bisexual people* (pp. 281–99). Washington, DC: American Psychological Association.

Furdyna, H., Tucker, M., & James, A. (2008). Relative spousal earnings and marital happiness among African American and white women. *Journal of Marriage and Family, 70,* 332–344.

Furnham, A., & Mak, T. (1999). Sex-role stereotyping in television commercials: A review and compendium of fourteen studies done on five continents over twenty-five years. *Sex Roles, 41,* 413–437.

Fuss, J., Auer, M. K., & Briken, P. (2015). Gender dysphoria in children and adolescents: A review of recent research. *Current Opinion in Psychiatry, 28*(6), 430–434. doi:10.1097/YCO.0000000000000203

Gagnon, J. H., & Simon, W. (1973). *Sexual conduct: The social sources of human sexuality.* Chicago: Aldine.

Gaillard, A., Strat, Y. L., Mandelbrot, L., Keita, H., & Dubertret, C. (2014). Predictors of postpartum depression: Prospective study of 264 women followed during pregnancy and postpartum. *Psychiatry Research, 215*(2), 341–346. doi:10.1016/j.psychres.2013.10.003

Galupo, M. P., Bauerband, L. A., Gonzalez, K. A., Hagen, D. B., Hether, S. D., & Krum, T. E. (2014). Transgender friendship experiences: Benefits and barriers of friendships across gender identity and sexual orientation. *Feminism & Psychology, 24*(2), 193–215.

Ganahl, D. J., Prinsen, T. J., & Netzley, S. B. (2003). A content analysis of prime time commercials: A contextual framework of gender representation. *Sex Roles, 49,* 545–551.

Gannon, L. R., Luchetta, T., Rhodes, K., Pardie, L., & Segrist, D. (1992). Sex bias in psychological research: Progress or complacency? *American Psychologist, 47,* 389–396.

Ganong, L., Coleman, M., & Hans, J. (2006). Divorce as a prelude to stepfamily living and the consequences of redivorce. In M. A. Fine & J. H. Harvey (Eds.), *Handbook of divorce and relationship dissolution* (pp. 409–434). Mahwah, NJ: Lawrence Erlbaum Associates.

Ganong, L. H., & Coleman, M. (2000). Remarried families. In C. Hendrick & S. S. Hendrick (Eds.), *Close relationships: A sourcebook* (pp. 155–170). Thousand Oaks, CA: Sage.

Garcia, J. R., Reiber, C., Massey, S. G., & Merriwether, A. M. (2012). Sexual hookup culture: A review. *Review of General Psychology, 16*(2), 161-176. doi:1020055192?accountid=14523

García-Moreno, J. (2005). *WHO multi-country study on women's health and domestic violence against women.* Initial results on prevalence, health outcomes and women's responses, Geneva: WHO.

Garner, J. H., & Maxwell, C. D. (2000). What are the lessons of the police arrest studies? *Journal of Aggression, Maltreatment & Trauma, 4,* 83–114.

Garnets, L. D. (2008). Life as a lesbian: What does gender have to do with it? In J. Chrisler, C. Golden, & P. Rozee (Eds.), *Lectures on the psychology of women* (4th ed., pp. 233–249). New York: McGraw-Hill.

Garnets, L. D., & Peplau, L. A. (2001). A new paradigm for women's sexual orientation: Implications for therapy. *Women & Therapy, 24,* 111–121.

Garofoli, J. (2007, May 13). White men get the lion's share. *San Francisco Chronicle.* Retrieved February 2, 2011, from http://www.sfgate.com/cgi-bin/article.cgi?f=/c/a/2007/05/13/GUESTS.TMP

Gates, G. (2012). Same-sex couples in Census 2010: Race and ethnicity. *Williams Institute.* Retrieved from http://williamsinstitute.law.ucla.edu/wp-content/uploads/Gates-CouplesRaceEthnicity-April-2012.pdf

Gates, G. (2013). LGBT parenting in the United States. *William's Institute: UCLA.* Retrieved from http://williamsinstitute.law.ucla.edu/wp-content/uploads/LGBT-Parenting.pdf

Gauchet, G., Kelly, M., & Wallace, M. (2012). Occupational gender segregation, globalization, and gender earnings inequality in U. S. metropolitan areas. *Gender & Society, 26*(5), 718–747. doi:10.1177/0891243212453647

Gavey, N. (2005). *Just sex: The cultural scaffolding of rape.* New York: Routledge.

Gazmarian, J., Petersen, P., Spitz, A., Goodwin, M., Saltzman, L., & Marks, J. (2000). Violence and reproductive health: Current knowledge and future research directions. *Maternal and Child Health Journal, 4,* 79–84.

Geber, H., & Roughneen, C. (2011). Tinkering, tailoring, and transforming: Retention of scientific excellence of women researchers through WiSER mentoring. *International Journal of Evidence Based Coaching and Mentoring, 9*(1), 59–75.

Ge, X., & Natsuaki, M. N. (2009). In search of explanations for early pubertal timing effects on developmental psychopathology. *Current Directions in Psychological Science, 18,* 327–331.

Geist, C., & Cohen, P. N. (2011). Headed toward equality? Housework change in comparative perspective. *Journal of Marriage and Family, 73*(4), 832–844.

Gelaye, B., Arnold, D., Williams, M. A., Goshu, M., & Berhane, Y. (2009). Depressive symptoms among female college students experiencing gender-based violence in Awassa, Ethiopia. *Journal of Interpersonal Violence, 24,* 464–481.

Geller, J. L., & Harris, M. (1994). *Women of the asylum: Voices from behind the walls, 1840–1945.* New York: Anchor Books.

Gender bias in college admissions tests. (2007). Retrieved February 17, 2010, from www.fairtest.org/gender-bias-college-admissions-tests

Gendron, T. L., & Lydecker, J. (2016). The thin-youth ideal: Should we talk about aging anxiety in relation to body image? *The International Journal of Aging & Human Development, 82*(4), 255–270.

Gentile, D. A., Coyne, S., & Walsh, D. A. (2011). Media violence, physical aggression, and relational aggression in school age children: A short-term longitudinal study. *Aggressive Behavior, 37*(2), 193–206. doi:10.1002/ab.20380

Georgakis, M. K., Thomopoulos, T. P., Diamantaras, A., Kalogirou, E. I., Skalkidou, A., Daskalopoulou, S. S., & Petridou, E. T. (2016). Association of age at menopause and duration of reproductive period with depression after menopause: A systematic review and meta-analysis. *JAMA Psychiatry, 73*(2), 139–149.

George, S. M., & Dickerson, B. J. (1995). The role of the grandmother in poor single-mother families and households. In B. J. Dickerson (Ed.), *African American single mothers* (pp. 146–163). Thousand Oaks, CA: Sage.

Gerstel, N. (1988). Divorce, gender, and social integration. *Gender & Society, 2*, 343–367.

Ghavami, N., & Peplau, L. A. (2013). An intersectional analysis of gender and ethnic stereotypes: Testing three hypotheses. *Psychology of Women Quarterly, 37*(1), 113–127.

Gibb, S. J., Fergusson, D. M., Horwood, L. J., & Boden, J. M. (2015). Early motherhood and long-term economic outcomes: Findings from a 30-year longitudinal study. *Journal of Research in Adolescents, 25*: 163–172. doi:10.1111/jora.12122

Gibson, P. A. (2014). Grandmother caregiver-in-chief continues the tradition of African American families. *Affilia: Journal of Women & Social Work, 29*(3), 298–309.

Giddings, P. (1984). *When and where I enter: The impact of black women on race and sex in America.* New York: Morrow.

Gilbert, L. A. (1993). *Two careers/one family: The promise of gender equality.* London: Sage.

Gilbert, L. A., & Kearney, L. (2006). Sex, gender, and dual-earner families: Implications and applications for career counseling for women. In W. B. Walsh & M. J. Heppner (Eds.), *Handbook of career counseling for women* (2nd ed., pp. 193–217). Mahwah, NJ: Erlbaum.

Gilbert, L. A., & Rossman, K. M. (1992). Gender and the mentoring process for women: Implications for professional development. *Professional Psychology: Research and Practice, 23*, 233–238.

Gilbert, S. C. (2003). Eating disorders in women of color. *Clinical Psychology: Science and Practice, 10*, 444–455.

Gill, A. K., & Brah, A. (2014). Interrogating cultural narratives about 'honour'-based violence. *European Journal of Women's Studies, 21*(1), 72–86.

Gilman, C. P. (1892). The yellow wallpaper. Reprinted in *The Yellow Wallpaper and Other Stories.* Mineola, NY: Dover Publications Incorporated, 1997.

Glick, P., Diebold, J., Bailey-Werner, B., & Zhu, L. (1997). The two faces of Adam: Ambivalent sexism and polarized attitudes toward women. *Personality and Social Psychology Bulletin, 23*, 1323–1334.

Glick, P., & Fiske, S. T. (1996). The ambivalent sexism inventory: Differentiating hostile and benevolent sexism. *Journal of Personality and Social Psychology, 70*, 491–512.

Glick, P., & Fiske, S. T. (2001). An ambivalent alliance: Hostile and benevolent sexism as complementary justifications for gender inequality. *American Psychologist, 56*, 109–118.

Glick, P., Fiske, S. T., Mladinic, A., Saiz, J. L., Abrams, D., Masser, B., . . . López López, W. (2000). Beyond prejudice as simple antipathy: Hostile and benevolent sexism across cultures. *Journal of Personality and Social Psychology, 79*, 763–775. doi:10.1037/0022-3514.79.5.763

Glick, P., Larsen, S., Johnson, C., & Branstiter, H. (2005). Evaluations of sexy women in low- and high-status jobs. *Psychology of Women Quarterly, 29*, 389–395.

Global Network of Women's Shelters (GNWS). (2012). 2012 Global data count. Retrieved from http://gnws.org/docs/GNWS_GlobalDataCount_2012.pdf

Godart, N. T., Perdereau, F., Rein, Z., Berthoz, S., Wallier, J., Jeammet, P., & Flament, M. F. (2007). Comorbidity studies of eating disorders and mood disorders. Critical review of the literature. *Journal of Affective Disorders, 97*, 37–49.

Goffman, E. (1961). *Asylums: Essays on the social situation of mental patients and other inmates.* New York: Doubleday.

Goldberg, A. E. (2013). "Doing" and "undoing" gender: The meaning and division of housework in same-sex couples. *Journal of Family Theory & Review, 5*(2), 85–104.

Goldberg, A. E., Kashy, D. A., & Smith, J. Z. (2012). Gender-typed play behavior in early childhood: Adopted children with lesbian, gay, and heterosexual parents. *Sex Roles, 67*(9–10), 503–515. doi:10.1007/s11199-012-0198-3

Goldberg, P. A. (1968). Are women prejudiced against women? *Transaction, 5*, 28–30.

Goldberg, W. A., & Lucas-Thompson, R. (2014). College women miss the mark when estimating the impact of full-time maternal employment on children's achievement and behavior. *Psychology of Women Quarterly, 38*(4), 490–502. doi:10.1177/0361684314529738

Golden, C. (1987). Diversity and variability in women's sexual identities. In Boston Lesbian Psychologies Collective (Eds.), *Lesbian psychologies* (pp. 18–34). Urbana: University of Illinois Press.

Golden, C. (2008). The intersexed and the transgendered: Rethinking sex/gender. In J. C. Christler, C. Golden, & P. D. Rozee (Eds.), *Lectures on the psychology of women* (4th ed., pp. 136–153). New York: McGraw-Hill.

Golding, J. M. (1999). Intimate partner violence as a risk factor for mental disorders: A meta-analysis. *Journal of Family Violence, 14*, 99–132.

Golombok, S., Perry, B., Burston, A., Murray, C., Mooney-Somers, J., Stevens, M., & Golding, J. (2003). Children with lesbian parents: A community study. *Developmental Psychology, 39*, 20–33.

Gooden, A. M., & Gooden, M. A. (2001). Gender representations in notable children's picture books: 1995–1999. *Sex Roles, 45*, 89–101.

Goodin, S. M., Van Denburg, A., Murnen, S. K., & Smolak, L. (2011). "Putting on" sexiness: A content analysis of the presence of sexualizing characteristics in girls' clothing. *Sex Roles, 65*(1–2), 1–12. doi:10.1007/s11199-011-9966-8

Goodwin, R., & Pillay, U. (2006). Relationships, culture, and social change. In A. L. Vangelsiti & D. Perlman (Eds.), *The Cambridge handbook of personal relationships* (pp. 695–707). New York: Cambridge University Press.

Gooren, L. (2006). The biology of human psychosexual differentiation. *Hormones and Behavior, 50,* 589–601.

Gordon, J. S. (1996). Community services of abused women: A review of perceived usefulness and efficacy. *Journal of Family Violence, 11,* 315–329.

Gordon, K. H., Castro, Y., Sitnikov, L., & Holm-Denoma, J. M. (2010). Cultural body shape ideals and eating disorder symptoms among White, Latina, and Black college women. *Cultural Diversity and Ethnic Minority Psychology, 16,* 135–143.

Gould, S. J. (1980). *The panda's thumb.* New York: Norton.

Gould, S. J. (1981). *The mismeasure of man.* New York: Norton.

Gove, W. R., & Shin, H. C. (1989). The psychological well-being of divorced and widowed men and women: An empirical analysis. *Journal of Family Issues, 10,* 122–144.

Gowen, L. K., Hayward, C., Killen, J. D., Robinson, T. N., & Taylor, C. B. (1999). Acculturation and eating disorder symptoms in adolescent girls. *Journal of Research on Adolescence, 9,* 67–83.

Grabe, S., & Else-Quest, N. (2012). The role of transnational feminism in psychology: Complementary visions. *Psychology of Women Quarterly, 36*(2), 158–161. doi:10.1177/0361684312442164

Grabe, S., & Hyde, J. S. (2006). Ethnicity and body dissatisfaction among women in the United States: A meta-analysis. *Psychological Bulletin, 132,* 622–640.

Grabe, S., Ward, L. M., & Hyde, J. S. (2008). The role of the media in body image concerns among women: A meta-analysis of experimental and correlational studies. *Psychological Bulletin, 134,* 460–476.

Grady, K. E. (1977, April). *The belief in sex differences.* Paper presented at the meeting of the Eastern Psychological Association, Boston.

Grall, T. S. (2009). *Custodial mothers and fathers and their child support: 2007.* Retrieved May 22, 2010, from http://singleparents.about.com/gi/o.htm?zi 5 1/XJ&zTi 5 1&sdn 5 singleparents&cdn 5 parenting&tm 5 101&gps 5 311_67_1259_626&f 5 00&su 5 p284.9.336.ip_p504.3.336 .ip_&tt 5 11&bt 5 0&bts 5 0&zu 5, http%3A//www.census . gov/prod/2009pubs/p60-237.pdf

Grana, S. J. (2002). *Women and (in)justice: The criminal and civil effects of the common law on women's lives.* Boston, MA: Allyn & Bacon.

Grant, B. F., & Weissman, M. M. (2007). Gender and the prevalence of psychiatric disorders. In W. E. Narrow, M. B. First, P. J. Sirovatka, & D. A. Regier (Eds.), *Age and gender considerations in psychiatric diagnosis: A research agenda for DSM-V.* Arlington, VA: American Psychiatric Publishing, Inc.

Gray, H. M., & Phillips, S. (1998). *Real girl real world: Tools for finding your true self.* Seattle, WA: Seal Press.

Grech, V. (2015). Gendercide and femineglect. *Early Human Development, 91*(12), 851–854. doi:10.1016/j.earlhumdev.2015.10.014

Greeff, A. P., & Du Toit, C. (2009). Resilience in remarried families. *The American Journal of Family Therapy, 37,* 114–126.

Green, S. E., Liao, K. Y.-H., Hallengren, J. J., Davids, C. M., Carter, L. P., Kugler, D. W., . . . Jepson, A.J. (2009). Eating disorder behaviors and depression: A minimal relationship beyond social comparison, self-esteem, and body dissatisfaction. *Journal of Clinical Psychology, 65,* 989–999.

Greene, B. A. (1990). Sturdy bridges: The role of African-American mothers in the socialization of African-American children. In J. P. Knowles & E. Cole (Eds.), *Motherhood: A feminist perspective* (pp. 205–225). New York: Haworth.

Greene, K., & Faulkner, S. L. (2005). Gender, belief in the sexual double standard, and sexual talk in heterosexual dating relationships. *Sex Roles, 53,* 239–251.

Greenhouse, S. (2004, November, 17). Abercrombie & Fitch bias case is settled. *The New York Times.* Retrieved from http://www.nytimes.com/2004/11/17/us/abercrombie-fitch-bias-case-is-settled.html?_r=0

Greitemeyer, T., & Mügge, D. O. (2014). Video games do affect social outcomes: A meta-analytic review of the effects of violent and prosocial video game play. *Personality and Social Psychology Bulletin, 40*(5), 578–589. doi:10.1177/0146167213520459

Gremaux, R. (1996). Woman becoming man in the Balkans. In G. Herdt (Ed.), *Third sex, third gender: Beyond sexual dimorphism in culture and history* (pp. 241–281). New York: Zone Books.

Gresky, D., Ten Eyck, L., Lord, C., & McIntyre, R. (2005). Effects of salient multiple identities on women's performance under mathematics stereotype threat. *Sex Roles, 53*(9–10), 703–716. doi:10.1007/s11199-005-7735-2

Groesz, L. M., Levine, M. P., & Murnen, S. K. (2002). The effect of experimental presentation of thin media images on body satisfaction: A meta-analytic review. *International Journal of Eating Disorders, 31,* 1–16.

Gross, J. (2004, February 27). Older women team up to face future together. *The New York Times,* p. A1.

Grossman, A. H., D'Augelli, A. R., & O'Connell, T. S. (2001). Being lesbian, gay, bisexual, and 60 or older in North America. In D. C. Kimmel & D. L. Martin (Eds.), *Midlife and aging in gay America: Proceedings of the SAGE conference, New York City, 2000* (pp. 23–40). New York: Harrington Park Press.

Grossman, A. L., & Tucker, J. S. (1997). Gender differences and sexism in the knowledge and use of slang. *Sex Roles, 37,* 101–110.

Grossman, F. K., Gilbert, L. A., Genero, N. P., Hawes, S. E., Hyde, J. S., & Marecek, J. (1997). Feminist research: Practice and problems. In J. Worell & N. G. Johnson (Eds.), *Shaping the future of feminist psychology: Education, research, and practice* (pp. 73–91). Washington, DC: American Psychological Association.

Grossman, J. B., & Tierney, J. P. (1998). Does mentoring work? An impact study of the Big Brothers Big Sisters program. *Evaluation Review, 22,* 403–426.

Grossman, M., & Wood, W. (1993). Sex differences in intensity of emotional experience: A social role interpretation. *Journal of Personality and Social Psychology, 65,* 1010–1022.

Grubbs, J. B., Exline, J. J., & Twenge, J. M. (2014). Psychological entitlement and ambivalent sexism: Understanding the role of entitlement in predicting two forms of sexism.

Sex Roles, 70(5–6), 209–220. doi:10.1007/s11199-014-0360-1

Grynbaum, M. M. & Koblin, J. (2016, September 6). Fox settles with Gretchen Carlson over Roger Ailes sex harassment claims. *The New York Times.* http://www.nytimes.com/2016/09/07/business/media/fox-news-roger-ailes-gretchen-carlson-sexual-harassment-lawsuit-settlement.html?_r=0

Gubrium, J. F., & Holstein, J. A. (2003). The everyday visibility of the aging body. In C. A. Faircloth (Ed.), *Aging bodies: Images and everyday experiences* (pp. 205–227). New York: AltaMira Press.

Guo, J., Parker, P. D., Marsh, H. W., & Morin, A. J. S. (2015). Achievement, motivation, and educational choices: A longitudinal study of expectancy and value using a multiplicative perspective. *Developmental Psychology, 51*(8), 163–1176. doi:10.1037/a0039440

Gura, T. (2007). *Lying in weight: The hidden epidemic of eating disorders in adult women.* New York: Harper Collins.

Gutek, B. A. (1985). *Sex and the workplace.* San Francisco, CA: Jossey-Bass.

Gutek, B. A. (2001). Women and paid work. *Psychology of Women Quarterly, 25,* 379–393.

Gutek, B. A., & Done, R. S. (2001). Sexual harassment. In R. K. Unger (Ed.), *Handbook of the psychology of women and gender* (pp. 367–387). New York: Wiley.

Gutek, B. A., & Larwood, L. (Eds.). (1987). *Women's career development.* Newbury Park, CA: Sage.

Gutiérrez, C. V., Luque, G. T., Medina, G. M. A., del Castillo, M. J. A., Guisado, I. M., Barrilao, R. G., & Rodrigo, J. R. (2012). Influence of exercise on mood in postmenopausal women. *Journal of Clinical Nursing, 21*(7–8), 923–928.

Guttmacher Institute. (2002). *Facts in brief: Teenagers' sexual and reproductive health.* New York: Author.

Guttmacher Institute (2016a, April). *U.S. teenage pregnancies, births and abortions, 2011: National trends by age, race, and ethnicity.* Retrieved from https://www.guttmacher.org/report/us-teen-pregnancy-trends-2011

Guttmacher Institute (2016b, May.) *Induced abortion worldwide: Global incidence and trends.* Retrieved from https://www.guttmacher.org/fact-sheet/induced-abortion-worldwide

Guttmacher Institute (2016c, July). *Laws affecting reproductive health and rights: State trends at midyear, 2016.* https://www.guttmacher.org/article/2016/07/laws-affecting-reproductive-health-and-rights-state-trends-midyear-2016

Guttmacher Institute (2016d, September). *Induced abortion in the United States.* Retrieved from https://www.guttmacher.org/fact-sheet/induced-abortion-united-states

Guven, C., Senik, C., & Stichnoth, H. (2012). You can't be happier than your wife: Happiness gaps and divorce. *Journal of Economic Behavior & Organization, 82*(1), 110–130.

Guzzo, K. B. (2014). Trends in cohabitation outcomes: Compositional changes and engagement among never-married young adults. *Journal of Marriage and Family, 76*(4), 826–842.

Gygax, P., Gabriel, U., Sarrasin, O., Oakhill, J., & Garnham, A. (2008). Generically intended, but specifically interpreted: When beauticians, musicians and mechanics are all men. *Language and Cognitive Processes, 23,* 464–485.

Ha, T., Berg, J. E. M., Engels, R. C. M. E., & Lichtwarck-Aschoff, A. (2012). Effects of attractiveness and status in dating desire in homosexual and heterosexual men and women. *Archives of Sexual Behavior, 41*(3), 673–682.

Haaken, J., & Yragui, N. (2003). Going underground: Conflicting perspectives on domestic violence shelter practices. *Feminism & Psychology, 13,* 49–71.

Haboush, A., Warren, C. S., & Benuto, L. (2012). Beauty, ethnicity, and age: Does internalization of mainstream media ideals influence attitudes towards older adults? *Sex Roles, 66*(9–10), 668–676.

Hahn, C. S. (2001). Review: Psychosocial well-being of parents and their children born after assisted reproduction. *Journal of Pediatric Psychology, 26,* 525–538.

Haines, B. A., Ajayi, A. A., & Boyd, H. (2014). Making trans parents visible: Intersectionality of trans and parenting identities. *Feminism & Psychology, 24*(2), 238–247.

Haines, E. L., Deaux, K., & Lofaro, N. (2016). The times they are a-changing . . . or are they not? a comparison of gender stereotypes, 1983–2014. *Psychology of Women Quarterly, 40*(3), 1–11. doi:10.1177/0361684316634081

Hald, G. M., Malamuth, N. M., & Yuen, C. (2010). Pornography and attitudes supporting violence against women: Revisiting the relationship in nonexperimental studies. *Aggressive Behavior, 36,* 14–20.

Halford, W. K., & Sweeper, S. (2013). Trajectories of adjustment to couple relationship separation. *Family Process, 52*(2), 228–243.

Halim, M. L., Ruble, D. N., & Amodio, D. M. (2011). From pink frilly dresses to 'one of the boys': A social-cognitive analysis of gender identity development and gender bias. *Social and Personality Psychology Compass, 5*(11), 933–949. doi:10.1111/j.1751-9004.2011.00399.x

Halim, M. L., Ruble, D., Tamis-LeMonda, C., & Shrout, P. E. (2013). Rigidity in gender-typed behaviors in early childhood: A longitudinal study of ethnic minority children. *Child Development, 84*(4), 1269–1284. doi:10.1111/cdev.12057

Hall, J. A. (1996). Touch, status, and gender at professional meetings. *Journal of Nonverbal Behavior, 20,* 23–44.

Hall, J. A. (2006). How big are nonverbal sex differences? The case of smiling and nonverbal sensitivity. In K. Dindia & D. J. Canary (Eds.), *Sex differences and similarities in communication* (2nd ed., pp. 59–81). Mahwah, NJ: Lawrence Erlbaum Associates Publishers.

Hall, J. A., Carter, J. D., & Horgan, T. G. (2000). Gender differences in nonverbal communication of emotion. In A. H. Fischer (Ed.), *Gender and emotion: Social psychological perspectives* (pp. 97–117). New York: Cambridge University Press.

Hall, K. (1995). Lip service on the fantasy lines. In K. Hall & M. Bucholtz (Eds.), *Gender articulated* (pp. 183–216). New York: Routledge.

Hall, L. J., & Donaghue, N. (2013). 'Nice girls don't carry knives': Constructions of ambition in media coverage of Australia's first female prime minister. *British Journal of Social Psychology, 52*(4), 631–647. doi:10.1111/j.2044-8309.2012.02114.x

Hall, R. L. (1998). Softly strong: African American women's use of exercise in therapy. In K. F. Hays (Ed.), *Integrating exercise, sports, movement and mind: Therapeutic unity* (pp. 81–100). Binghamton, NY: The Haworth Press.

Hall, R. L. (2008). Sweating it out: The good news and the bad news about women and sport. In J. C. Chrisler, C. Golden, & P. D. Rozee (Eds.), *Lectures on the psychology of women* (4th ed., pp. 97–115). New York: McGraw-Hill.

Halliwell, E., & Dittmar, H. (2003). A qualitative investigation of women's and men's body image concerns and their attitudes toward aging. *Sex Roles, 49,* 675–684.

Halliwell, E., Malson, H., & Tischner, I. (2011). Are contemporary media images which seem to display women as sexually empowered actually harmful to women? *Psychology of Women Quarterly, 35*(1), 38–45. doi:10.1177/0361684310385217

Halpern, D. F. (1992). *Sex differences in cognitive abilities* (2nd ed.). Hillsdale, NJ: Erlbaum.

Hamilton, J. A., & Jensvold, M. F. (1995). Sex and gender as critical variables in feminist psychopharmacology research and pharmacotherapy. *Women & Therapy, 16,* 9–30.

Hamilton, M. C. (1991). Masculine bias in the attribution of personhood: People = male, male = people. *Psychology of Women Quarterly, 15,* 393–402.

Hamilton, M. C., Anderson, D., Broaddus, M., & Young, K. (2006). Gender stereotyping and under-representation of female characters in 200 popular children's picture books: A twenty-first century update. *Sex Roles, 55,* 757–765.

Hammond, M. D., Sibley, C. G., & Overall, N. C. (2014). The allure of sexism: Psychological entitlement fosters women's endorsement of benevolent sexism over time. *Social Psychological and Personality Science, 5*(4), 422–429. doi:10.1177/1948550613506124

Han, J., & Richardson, V. E. (2015). The relationships among perceived discrimination, self-perceptions of aging, and depressive symptoms: A longitudinal examination of age discrimination. *Aging & Mental Health, 19*(8), 747–755.

Hanganu-Bresch, C. (2008). *Faces of depression: A study of antidepressant advertisements in the American and British journals of psychiatry, 1960–2004.* Unpublished dissertation: University of Minnesota.

Hankin, B. L., & Abramson, L. Y. (2001). Development of gender differences in depression: An elaborated cognitive vulnerability-transactional stress theory. *Psychological Bulletin, 127,* 773–796.

Hansen, F. J., & Osborne, D. (1995). Portrayal of women and elderly patients in psychotropic drug advertisements. *Women & Therapy, 16,* 129–141.

Hanson, R. (2002). Adolescent dating violence: Prevalence and psychological outcomes. *Child Abuse and Neglect, 26,* 449–453.

Harding, R., & Peel E. (2006). "We do"? International perspectives on equality, legality and same sex relationships. *Lesbian & Gay Psychology Review, 7*(2), 123–140.

Harding, S. (1986). *The science question in feminism.* Ithaca, NY: Cornell University Press.

Hare-Mustin, R. T., & Marecek, J. (Eds.). (1990). *Making a difference: Psychology and the construction of gender.* New Haven, CT: Yale University Press.

Harris, B. J. (1984). The power of the past: History and the psychology of women. In M. Lewin (Ed.), *In the shadow of the past* (pp. 1–5). New York: Columbia University Press.

Harrison, K. (2003). Television viewers' ideal body proportions: The case of the curvaceously thin woman. *Sex Roles, 48,* 255–265.

Hartung, C. M., & Widiger, T. A. (1998). Gender differences in the diagnosis of mental disorders: Conclusions and controversies of the DSM-IV. *Psychological Bulletin, 123,* 260–278.

Hartwell, C. E. (1996). The schizophrenogenic mother concept in American psychiatry. *Psychiatry: Interpersonal and Biological Processes, 59,* 274–297.

Harville, M. L., & Rienzi, B. M. (2000). Equal worth and gracious submission: Judeo-Christian attitudes toward employed women. *Psychology of Women Quarterly, 24,* 145–147.

Harwood, K., McLean, N., & Durkin, K. (2007). First-time mothers' expectations of parenthood: What happens when optimistic expectations are not matched by later experiences? *Developmental Psychology, 43,* 1–12.

Hash, K. (2001). Preliminary study of caregiving and post-caregiving experiences of older gay men and lesbians. In D. C. Kimmel & D. L. Martin (Eds.), *Midlife and aging in gay America: Proceedings of the SAGE conference, New York City, 2000* (pp. 87–94). New York: Harrington Park Press.

Hatfield, E. (2016, Spring). What impact will social media sites have on women in the Middle East? *The Feminist Psychologist,* 13–14.

Hawkins, D. (2016, October 14). Flight attendant to black female doctor: 'We're looking for actual physicians'. *The Washington Post.* Retrieved from https://www.washingtonpost.com/news/morning-mix/wp/2016/10/14/blatant-discrimination-black-female-doctor-says-flight-crew-questioned-her-credentials-during-medical-emergency/?utm_term=.fdf76500e91f

Hawkins, J. W., & Aber, C. S. (1993). Women in advertisements in medical journals. *Sex Roles, 28,* 233–242.

Hayes, R. M., Abbott, R. L., & Cook, S. (2016). It's her fault:-Student acceptance of rape myths on two college campuses. *Violence Against Women, 22*(13), 1540–1555.

Hayes, R. M., Lorenz, K., & Bell, K. A. (2013). Victim blaming others: Rape myth acceptance and the just world belief. *Feminist Criminology, 8*(3), 202–220.

Hayfield, N., Clarke, V., & Halliwell, E. (2014). Bisexual women's understandings of social marginalisation: 'The heterosexuals don't understand us but nor do the lesbians'. *Feminism & Psychology, 24*(3), 352–372.

Hazen, A. L., Connelly, C. D., Soriano, F. I., & Landsverk, J. A. (2008). Intimate partner violence and psychological functioning in Latina women. *Health Care for Women International, 29,* 282–299.

Heaphy, B., Yip, A. K. T., & Thompson, D. (2004). Ageing in a non-heterosexual context. *Ageing and Society, 24,* 881–902.

Hebl, M., King, E., Glick, P., Singletary, S., & Kazama, S. (2007). Hostile and benevolent reactions towards pregnant women: Complementary interpersonal punishments and rewards that maintain traditional roles. *Journal of Applied Psychology, 92,* 1499–1511.

Hecht, M. A., & LaFrance, M. (1998). License or obligation to smile: The effect of power and sex on amount and type of smiling. *Personality and Social Psychology Bulletin, 24,* 1332–1342.

Hedges, L. V., & Becker, B. J. (1986). Statistical methods in the meta-analysis of research on gender differences. In J. G. Hyde & M. C. Linn (Eds.), *The psychology of gender: Advances through meta-analysis* (pp. 14–50). Baltimore, MD: Johns Hopkins University Press.

Heflin, C. M., & Iceland, J. (2009). Poverty, material hardship, and depression. *Social Science Quarterly, 90,* 1051–1071.

Heigl, A. (2014). School calls 9-year-old's My Little Pony backpack a 'trigger for bullying'. *People.* Retrieved from http://www.people.com/people/article/0,,20797857,00.html

Hek, K., Demirkan, A., Lahti, J., Terracciano, A., Teumer, A., Cornelis, M. C., . . . Liu, Y. (2013). A genome-wide association study of depressive symptoms. *Biological Psychiatry, 73*(7), 667–678.

Helwig, A. A. (1998). Gender-role stereotyping: Testing theory with a longitudinal sample. *Sex Roles, 38,* 403–424.

Henderson, K., & Roberts, N. (1998). An integrative review of the literature on women in the outdoors. In K. M. Fox, L. H. McAvoy, & M. D. Bialeschki (Eds.), *Coalition for education in the outdoors fourth research symposium proceedings* (pp. 9–21). Bradford Woods, IN: Coalition for Education in the Outdoors.

Henley, N. M. (1973). Status and sex: Some touching observations. *Bulletin of the Psychonomic Society, 2,* 91–93.

Henley, N. M. (1977). *Body politics: Power, sex, and nonverbal communication.* Englewood Cliffs, NJ: Prentice-Hall.

Henley, N. M. (1989). Molehill or mountain? What we do know and don't know about sex bias in language. In M. Crawford & M. Gentry (Eds.), *Gender and thought* (pp. 59–78). New York: Springer-Verlag.

Henley, N. M., Meng, K., O'Brien, D., McCarthy, W. J., & Sockloskie, R. (1998). Developing a scale to measure the diversity of feminist attitudes. *Psychology of Women Quarterly, 22,* 317–348.

Herrera, C., Grossman, J. B., Kauh, T. J., & McMaken, J. (2011). Mentoring in schools: An impact study of big brothers big sisters school-based mentoring. *Child Development, 82*(1), 346–361. doi:10.1111/j.1467–8624.2010.01559.x

Herrett-Skjellum, J., & Allen, M. (1996). Television programming and sex stereotyping: A meta-analysis. In B. Burleson (Ed.), *Communication yearbook 19* (pp. 157–185). Thousand Oaks, CA: Sage.

Herzberg, D. (2009). *Happy pills in America: From Miltown to Prozac.* Baltimore, MD: Johns Hopkins University Press.

Hesketh, T., Lu, L., & Xing, Z. W. (2011). The consequences of son preference and sex-selective abortion in China and other Asian countries. *Canadian Medical Association Journal, 183*(12), 1374–1377. doi:10.1503/cmaj.101368

Heuer, C. A., McClure, K. J., & Puhl, R. M. (2011). Obesity stigma in online news: A visual content analysis. *Journal of Health Communication, 16*(9), 976–987.

Hewlett, S. A., & West, C. (1998). *The war against parents: What we can do for America's beleaguered moms and dads.* Boston, MA: Houghton Mifflin.

Heymann, J. (2010). *If companies really mean business on work and family issues.* Retrieved May 23, 2010, from http://www.huffingtonpost.com/dr-jody-heymann

Hicks, M. H. R., & Li, Z. (2003). Partner violence and major depression in women: A community study of Chinese Americans. *Journal of Nervous and Mental Disease, 191,* 722–729.

Hill, C., Corbett, C., & St. Rose, A. (2010). *Why so few? Women in science, technology, engineering, and mathematics.* Washington, DC: AAUW.

Hill, M. (1987). Child-rearing attitudes of black lesbian mothers. In Boston Lesbian Psychologies Collective (Eds.), *Lesbian psychologies* (pp. 215–225). Urbana: University of Illinois Press.

Hill, M., & Ballou, M. (1998). Making therapy feminist: A practice survey. *Women & Therapy, 21,* 1–16.

Hill, S. A. (2002). Teaching and doing gender in African American families. *Sex Roles, 47,* 493–506.

Hilt, L. M., & Nolen-Hoeksema, S. (2009). The emergence of gender differences in depression in adolescence. In S. Nolen-Hoeksema & L. M. Hilt (Eds.), *Handbook of depression in adolescents* (pp. 111–135). New York: Routledge/Taylor & Francis Group.

Himmelstein, M. S., & Sanchez, D. T. (2014). Masculinity impediments: Internalized masculinity contributes to healthcare avoidance in men and women. *Journal of Health Psychology,* 1–10. doi:10.1177/1359105314551623

Hines, M. (2004). *Brain gender.* Oxford: Oxford University Press.

Hines, M. (2011). Prenatal endocrine influences on sexual orientation and on sexually differentiated childhood behavior. *Frontiers in Neuroendocrinology, 32*(2), 170–182. doi:10.1016/j.yfrne.2011.02.006

Hite, S. (1976). *The Hite report.* New York: Macmillan.

Hitsch, G. J., Hortaçsu, A., & Ariely, D. (2010). What makes you click? Mate preferences in online dating. *Quantitative Marketing and Economics, 8,* 393–427.

Hoburg, R., Konik, J., Williams, M., & Crawford, M. (2004). Bisexuality among self-identified heterosexual college students. *Journal of Bisexuality, 4,* 25–36.

Hochschild, A. R. (1989). *The second shift: Working parents and the revolution at home.* New York: Viking.

Hockett, J. M., Saucier, D. A., Hoffman, B. H., Smith, S. J., & Craig, A. W. (2009). Oppression through acceptance? Predicting rape myth acceptance and attitudes toward rape victims. *Violence Against Women, 15,* 877–897.

Hogue, M., & Yoder, J. D. (2003). The role of status in producing depressed entitlement in women's and men's pay allocations. *Psychology of Women Quarterly, 27,* 330–337.

Holland, E., & Haslam, N. (2016). Cute little things: The objectification of prepubescent girls. *Psychology of Women Quarterly, 40*(1), 108–119. doi:10.1177/0361684315602887

Holm, K. E., Werner-Wilson, R. J., Cook, A. S., & Berger, P. S. (2001). The association between emotion work balance and relationship satisfaction of couples seeking therapy. *American Journal of Family Therapy, 29,* 193–205.

Holman, A., & Sillars, A. (2012). Talk about "hooking up": The influence of college student social networks on non-relationship sex. *Health Communication, 27*(2), 205–216. doi:10.1080/10410236.2011.575540

Holson, L. (2016). Sexy sells, but it doesn't always pay. *New York Times.* Retrieved from http://www.nytimes.com/2016/04/03/business/media/with-romance-novels-booming-beefcake-sells-but-it-doesnt-pay.html

Hoobler, J. M., Wayne, S. J., & Lemmon, G. (2009). Bosses' perceptions of family-work conflict and women's promotability: Glass ceiling effects. *Academy of Management Journal, 52,* 939–957.

hooks, b. (1984). *Feminist theory: From margin to center.* Boston, MA: South End Press.

hooks, b. (1989). *Talking back: Thinking feminist, thinking black.* Boston, MA: South End Press.

Horne, S., & Biss, W. (2009). Equality discrepancy between women in same-sex relationships: The mediating role of attachment in relationship satisfaction. *Sex Roles, 60,* 721–730.

Hornstein, G. A. (2013). Whose account matters? A challenge to feminist psychologists. *Feminism & Psychology, 23(1),* 29–40.

Hrdy, S. B. (1988, April). Daughters or sons. *Natural History,* 64–82.

Huang, K. (2014). Marriage squeeze in China: Past, present, and future. *Journal of Family Issues, 35(12),* 1642–1661. doi:10.1177/0192513X14538027

Huang, Y., Osborne, D., Sibley, C. G., & Davies, P. G. (2014). The precious vessel: Ambivalent sexism and opposition to elective and traumatic abortion. *Sex Roles, 71(11–12),* 436–449.

Huffington Post (2013, May 4). Porn sites get more visitors each month than Netflix, Amazon and Twitter combined. Retrieved from http://www.huffingtonpost.com/2013/05/03/internet-porn-stats_n_3187682.html

Hunter, G. T. (1974). Pediatrician. In R. B. Kundsin (Ed.), *Women and success: The anatomy of achievement* (pp. 58–61). New York: Morrow.

Hurd, L. C. (2000). Older women's body image and embodied experience: An exploration. *Journal of Women and Aging, 12,* 77–97.

Hurst, S. A., & Genest, M. (1995). Cognitive-behavioural therapy with a feminist orientation: A perspective for therapy with depressed women. *Canadian Psychology, 36,* 236–257.

Hurt, M. M., Nelson, J. A., Turner, D. L., Haines, M. E., Ramsey, L. R., Erchull, M. J., & Liss, M. (2007). Feminism: What is it good for? Feminine norms and objectification as the link between feminist identity and clinically relevant outcomes. *Sex Roles, 57,* 355–363.

Hussain, K. M., Leija, S. G., Lewis, F., & Sanchez, B. (2015). Unveiling sexual identity in the face of marianismo. *Journal of Feminist Family Therapy, 27(2),* 72.

Huston, A. C. (2014). Poverty, public policy, and children's wellbeing. In S. H. Landry & C. L. Cooper (Eds.), *Wellbeing in Children & Families: Wellbeing: A Complete Reference Guide, Volume I.* UK: John Wiley & Sons, Ltd. doi:10.1002/9781118539415.wbwell014

Huston, T. L., Caughlin, J. P., Houts, R. M., Smith, S. E., & George, L. J. (2001). The connubial crucible: Newlywed years as predictors of marital delight, distress, and divorce. *Journal of Personality and Social Psychology, 80,* 237–252.

Hutton, F., Griffin, C., Lyons, A., Niland, P., & McCreanor, T. (2016). "Tragic girls" and "crack whores": Alcohol, femininity, and Facebook. *Feminism & Psychology, 26(1),* 73–93. doi:10.1177/0959353515618224

Hyde, J. S. (2014). Gender similarities and differences. *Annual Review of Psychology, 65,* 373–398. doi:10.1146/annurev-psych-010213-115057

Hyde, J. S., & DeLamater, J. D. (2017). *Understanding human sexuality* (13th ed.). New York: McGraw Hill.

Hyde, J. S., Fennema, E., Ryan, M., Frost, L., & Hopp, C. (1990). Gender comparisons of mathematics attitudes and affects: A meta-analysis. *Psychology of Women Quarterly, 14,* 299–324.

Hyde, J. S., & Kling, K. C. (2001). Women, motivation, and achievement. *Psychology of Women Quarterly, 25,* 364–378.

Hyde, J. S., & Linn, M. C. (Eds.). (1986). *The psychology of gender: Advances through meta-analysis.* Baltimore, MD: Johns Hopkins University Press.

Hyde, J. S., Mezulis, A. H., & Abramson, L. Y. (2008). The ABCs of depression: Integrating affective, biological, and cognitive models to explain the emergence of the gender difference in depression. *Psychological Review, 115,* 291–313.

Hymas, L. (2013, August 3). *Time* magazine catches on to the childfree movement, misses the green angle. *Grist.* Retrieved from http://grist.org/living/time-magazine-catches-on-to-the-childfree-movement-misses-the-green-angle/

Ihinger-Tallman, M., & Pasley, K. (1987). *Remarriage.* Beverly Hills, CA: Sage.

Ilies, R., Hauserman, N., Schwochau, S., & Stibal, J. (2003). Reported incidence rates of work-related sexual harassment in the United States: Using meta-analysis to explain reported rate disparities. *Personnel Psychology, 56,* 607–631.

Impett, E. A., Henson, J. M., Breines, J. G., Schooler, D., & Tolman, D. L. (2011). Embodiment feels better: Girls' body objectification and well-being across adolescence. *Psychology of Women Quarterly, 35(1),* 46–58. doi:10.1177/0361684310391641

Impett, E. A., Sorsoli, L., Schooler, D., Henson, J. M., & Tolman, D. L. (2008). Girls' relationship authenticity and self-esteem across adolescence. *Developmental Psychology, 44,* 722–733.

Inesi, M. E., & Cable, D. M. (2015). When accomplishments come back to haunt you: The negative effect of competence signals on women's performance evaluations. *Personnel Psychology, 68(3),* 615–657.

Inzlicht, M., & Ben-Zeev, T. (2000). A threatening intellectual environment: Why females are susceptible to experiencing problem-solving deficits in the presence of males. *Psychological Science, 11,* 365–371.

Irmen, L. (2006). Automatic activation and use of gender subgroups. *Sex Roles, 55,* 435–444.

Isaac, R. J., & Armat, V. C. (1990). *Madness in the streets: How psychiatry and the law abandoned the mentally ill.* New York: Simon & Schuster.

Israeli, A. L., & Santor, D. A. (2000). Reviewing effective components of feminist therapy. *Counselling Psychology Quarterly, 13(3),* 233–247.

Jackson, T. E., & Falmagne, R. J. (2013). Women wearing white: Discourses of menstruation and the experience of menarche. *Feminism & Psychology, 23(3),* 379–398. doi:10.1177/0959353512473812

Jacobsen, F. M. (1994). Psychopharmacology. In L. Comas-Diaz & B. Green (Eds.), *Women of color: Integrating ethnic and gender identities in psychotherapy.* New York: The Guilford Press.

Jacobson, N. S., & Gottman, J. M. (1998). *When men batter women.* New York: Simon & Schuster.

James, D., & Drakich, J. (1993). Understanding gender differences in amount of talk: A critical review of research. In D. Tannen (Ed.), *Gender and conversational interaction* (pp. 281–312). New York: Oxford University Press.

Jamieson, D. (2015, June 2). Supreme Court rules against Abercrombie & Fitch in discrimination case. *The Huffington Post.* Retrieved from http://www.huffingtonpost.com/2015/06/01/supreme-court-abercrombie_n_7464534.html

Jane, J. S., Oltmanns, T. F., South, S. C., & Turkheimer, E. (2007). Gender bias in diagnostic criteria for personality disorders: An item response theory analysis. *Journal of Abnormal Psychology, 116,* 166–175.

Jansen, N. A., & Onge, J. M. S. (2015). An internet forum analysis of stigma power perceptions among women seeking fertility treatment in the United States. *Social Science & Medicine, 147,* 184–189. doi:10.1016/j.socscimed.2015.11.002

Javdani, M. (2015). Glass ceilings or glass doors? The role of firms in male-female wage disparities. *Canadian Journal of Economics, 48*(2), 529–560.

Jayakar, K. (1994). Women of the Indian subcontinent. In L. Comas-Díaz & B. Greene (Eds.), *Women of color: Integrating ethnic and gender identities in psychotherapy* (pp. 161–181). New York: Guilford Press.

Jenkins, A. M., Albee, G. W., Paster, V. S., Sue, S., Baker, D. B., Comas-Diaz, L., . . . Root, M. P. P. (2002). Ethnic minorities. In I. B. Weiner (Series Ed.) & D. K. Freedheim (Vol. Ed.), *Comprehensive handbook of psychology: Vol. 1. The history of psychology* (pp. 483–506). New York: Wiley and Sons.

Jensen, R. (2007). *Getting off: Pornography and the end of masculinity.* Cambridge, MA: South End Press.

Jerman, J. and Jones, R. K. (2014). Secondary measures of access to abortion services in the United States, 2011 and 2012: Gestational age limits, cost, and harassment. *Women's Health Issues, 24*(4), 419–424. doi:10.1016/j.whi.2014.05.002

Jewkes, R., & Abrahams, N. (2002). The epidemiology of rape and sexual coercion in South Africa: An overview. *Social Science and Medicine, 55*(1), 231–244.

John, R., Blanchard, P. H., & Hennessy, C. H. (1997). Hidden lives: Aging and contemporary American Indian women. In J. M. Coyle (Ed.), *Handbook on women and aging* (pp. 290–315). Westport, CT: Greenwood Press.

Johns, M., Schmader, T., & Martens, A. (2005). Knowing is half the battle: Teaching stereotype threat as a means of improving women's math performance. *Psychological Science, 16,* 175–179.

Johnson, M. P. (1995). Patriarchal terrorism and common couple violence: Two forms of violence against women. *Journal of Marriage and the Family, 57,* 283–294.

Johnson, M. P., & Ferraro, K. J. (2000). Research on domestic violence in the 1990's: Making distinctions. *Journal of Marriage and the Family, 62,* 948–963.

Johnston-Robledo, I. (2000). From postpartum depression to the empty nest syndrome: The motherhood mystique revisited. In J. C. Chrisler, C. Golden, & P. D. Rozee (Eds.), *Lectures on the psychology of women* (pp. 129–148). Boston, MA: McGraw-Hill.

Johnston-Robledo, I., Barnack, J., & Wares, S. (2006). "Kiss your period good-bye": Menstrual suppression in the popular press. *Sex Roles, 54,* 353–360.

Jonathan, N. & Knudson-Martin, C. (2012). Building connection: Attunement and gender equality in heterosexual relationships. *Journal of Couple & Relationship Therapy, 11*(2), 95–111. doi:10.1080/15332691.2012.666497

Jones, R. G., Tigas, M., & Ornstein, C. (2016, December 13). We've updated dollars for docs. Here's what's new. ProPublica. Retrieved from https://www.propublica.org/article/updated-dollars-for-docs-heres-whats-new

Jones, R. K. & Jerman, J. (2014). Abortion incidence and service availability in the United States, 2011. *Perspectives on Sexual and Reproductive Health, 46*(1), 3–14. doi:10.1363/46e0414

Jordan, J. V., Kaplan, A. G., Miller, J. B., Stiver, I. P., & Surrey, J. L. (1991). *Women's growth in connection.* New York: Guilford.

Jordan, K. M., & Deluty, R. H. (2000). Social support, coming out, and relationship satisfaction in lesbian couples. *Journal of Lesbian Studies, 4,* 145–164.

Jordan-Young, R. (2012). Hormones, context, and "brain gender": A review of evidence from congenital adrenal hyperplasia. *Social Science & Medicine, 74*(11), 1738–1744. doi:10.1016/j.socscimed.2011.08.026

Jorge, J. C., Echeverri, C., Medina, Y., & Acevedo, P. (2008). Male gender identity in an XX individual with congenital adrenal hyperplasia. *Journal of Sexual Medicine, 5*(1), 122–131. doi:10.1111/j.1743–6109.2007.00558.x

Joseph, D., & Newman, D. (2010). Emotional intelligence: An integrative meta-analysis and cascading model. *Journal of Applied Psychology, 95*(1), 54–78. doi:10.1037/a0017286

Joseph, J. (1997). Woman battering: A comparative analysis of black and white women. In G. Kaufman Kantor & J. L. Jasinski (Eds.), *Out of darkness: Contemporary perspectives on family violence* (pp. 161–169). Thousand Oaks, CA: Sage.

Jost, J. T. (1997). An experimental replication of the depressed entitlement effect among women. *Psychology of Women Quarterly, 21,* 387–393.

Jozkowski, K. N., & Peterson, Z. D. (2013). College students and sexual consent: Unique insights. *Journal of Sex Research, 50*(6), 517–523.

Juniper Research. (2013, September 25). 250 Million to Access Adult Content on their Mobile or Tablet by 2017, Juniper Report Finds." Retrieved from https://www.juniperresearch.com/press-release/mobile-adult-pr1

Jussim, L., Cain, T. R., Crawford, J. T., Harber, K., & Cohen, F. (2009). The unbearable accuracy of stereotypes. In T. D. Nelson (Ed.), *Handbook of prejudice, stereotyping, and discrimination* (pp. 199–227). New York: Psychology Press.

Kaestle, C. E., & Allen, K. R. (2011). The role of masturbation in healthy sexual development: Perceptions of young adults. *Archives of Sexual Behavior, 40*(5), 983–994. doi:10.1007/s10508–010-9722–0

Kahn, A. S., Jackson, J., Kully, C., Badger, K., & Halvorsen, J. (2003). Calling it rape: Differences in experiences of women who do or do not label their sexual assault as rape. *Psychology of Women Quarterly, 27,* 233–242.

Kahn, A. S., & Yoder, J. D. (1989). The psychology of women and conservatism: Rediscovering social change. *Psychology of Women Quarterly, 13,* 417–432.

Kahn, J. R., McGill, B. S., & Bianchi, S. M. (2011). Help to family and friends: Are there gender differences at older ages? *Journal of Marriage and Family, 73*(1), 77–92. doi:10.1111/j.1741-3737.2010.00790.x

Kalichman, S. C., Simbay, L. C., Kaufman, M., Cain, D., Cherry, C., Jooste, S., & Mathiti, V. (2005). Gender attitudes, sexual violence, and HIV/AIDS risks among men and women in Cape Town, South Africa. *Journal of Sex Research, 42,* 299–305.

Kalra, G. (2012). Hijras: The unique transgender culture of India. *International Journal of Culture and Mental Health, 5*(2), 121–126. doi:10.1080/17542863.2011.570915

Kalra, G., & Bhugra, D. (2015). Hijras in Bollywood cinema. *International Journal of Transgenderism, 16*(3), 160–168. doi:10.1080/15532739.2015.1080646

Kanter, R. M. (1977). *Men and women of the corporation.* New York: Basic Books.

Kapidzic, S., & Herring, S. C. (2011). Gender, communication, and self-presentation in teen chatrooms revisited: Have patterns changed? *Journal of Computer-Mediated Communication, 17*(1), 39–59. doi:10.1111/j.1083 -6101.2011.01561.x

Kara, S. (2009). *Sex trafficking: Inside the business of modern slavery.* Columbia University Press.

Karraker, K. H., Vogel, D. A., & Lake, M. A. (1995). Parents' gender stereotyped perceptions of newborns: The eye of the beholder revisited. *Sex Roles, 33,* 687–701.

Katz, B. L. (1991). The psychological impact of stranger versus nonstranger rape on victims' recovery. In A. Parrot & L. Bechhofer, (Eds.), *Acquaintance rape: The hidden crime* (pp. 251–269). New York: Wiley.

Katz, P. A. (1996). Raising feminists. *Psychology of Women Quarterly, 20,* 323–340.

Katz, R. S. (2002). Older women and addictions. In S. L. A. Straussner & S. Brown (Eds.), *The handbook of addiction treatment for women* (pp. 272–297). San Francisco, CA: Jossey-Bass.

Katz-Wise, S., & Hyde, J. S. (2015). Sexual fluidity and related attitudes and beliefs among young adults with a same-gender orientation. *Archives of Sexual Behavior, 44*(5), 1459–1470. doi:10.1007/s10508-014-0420-1

Katz-Wise, S. L., Reisner, S. L., White Hughto, J., & KeoMeier, C. L. (2016) Differences in sexual orientation diversity and sexual fluidity in attractions among gender minority adults in Massachusetts. *The Journal of Sex Research, 53*(1), 74-84. doi:10.1080/00224499.2014 .1003028

Kaufman, G., & White, D. (2016). "For the good of our family": Men's attitudes toward their wives' employment. *Journal of Family Issues, 37*(11), 1585–1610.

Kaufman, M. R. (2010). Testing of the healthy "little" lives project: A training program for big sister mentors. *American Journal of Sexuality Education, 5*(4), 305–327.

Kay, A., & Furnham, A. (2013). Age and sex stereotypes in British television advertisements. *Psychology of Popular Media Culture, 2*(3), 171–186.

Kaysen, S. (1993). *Girl, interrupted.* New York: Turtle Bay Books, a Division of Random House.

Keel, P. K., Mitchell, J. E., Davis, T. L., & Crow, S. J. (2001). Relationship between depression and body dissatisfaction in women diagnosed with bulimia nervosa. *International Journal of Eating Disorders, 30,* 48–56.

Kelle, H. (2000). Gender and territoriality in games played by nine-to-twelve-year-old schoolchildren. *Journal of Contemporary Ethnology, 29,* 164–197.

Keller, J. (2003, September). The H-Bomb. *Boston Magazine,* pp. 70–78.

Keller J. (2007). Stereotype threat in classroom settings: The interactive effect of domain identification, task difficulty and stereotype threat on female students' maths performance. *British Journal of Educational Psychology, 77,* 323–338.

Kelly, K. (2014). The spread of 'Post abortion syndrome' as social diagnosis. *Social Science & Medicine, 102,* 18–25. doi:10.1016/j.socscimed.2013.11.030

Kelly, M. (2010). Regulating the reproduction and mothering of poor women: The controlling image of the welfare mother in television news coverage of welfare reform. *Journal of Poverty, 14,* 76–96. doi:10.1080/108755409 03489447

Kelly, M., & Hauck, E. (2015). Doing housework, redoing gender: Queer couples negotiate the household division of labor. *Journal of GLBT Family Studies, 11*(5), 438–464.

Kelly, S., Martin, S., Kuhn, I., Cowan, A., Brayne, C., & Lafortune, L. (2016). Barriers and facilitators to the uptake and maintenance of healthy behaviours by people at mid-life: A rapid systematic review. *PLoS ONE, 11*(1), 26.

Keltner, D., Capps, L., Kring, A. M., Young, R. C., & Heerey, E. A. (2001). Just teasing: A conceptual analysis and empirical review. *Psychological Bulletin, 127,* 229–248.

Keltner, D., Gruenfeld, D., & Anderson, C. (2003). Power, approach, and inhibition. *Psychological Review, 110,* 265–284.

Kennell, J., Klaus, M., McGrath, S., Robertson, S., & Hinkley, C. (1991). Continuous emotional support during labor in a US hospital. *Journal of the American Medical Association, 265,* 2197–2201.

Kenney-Benson, G., Pomerantz, E., Ryan, A., & Patrick, H. (2006). Sex differences in math performance: The role of children's approach to schoolwork. *Developmental Psychology, 42,* 11–26.

Kessler, E.-M., Rakoczy, K., & Staudinger, U. R. (2004). The portrayal of older people in prime time television series: The match with gerontological evidence. *Aging & Society, 24,* 531–552.

Kessler, R. C. (2003). Epidemiology of women and depression. *Journal of Affective Disorders, 74,* 5–13.

Kessler, R. C., Berglund, P. A., Chiu, W. T., Deitz, A. C., Hudson, J. I., Shahly, V., . . . Bruffaerts, R. (2013). The prevalence and correlates of binge eating disorder in the World Health Organization World Mental Health Surveys. *Biological Psychiatry, 73*(9), 904–914.

Kessler, R. C., Petukhova, M., Sampson, N. A., Zaslavsky, A. M., & Wittchen, H. U. (2012). Twelve-month and lifetime prevalence and lifetime morbid risk of anxiety and mood disorders in the United States. *International Journal of Methods in Psychiatric Research, 21*(3), 169–184.

Kessler, S. J. (1998). *Lessons from the intersexed.* New Brunswick, NJ: Rutgers University Press.

Kessler, S. J. (2002, October). *Intersexuality in the 21st century: Medical emergency or medical invention?* Colloquium presented to the Social Psychology Division, University of Connecticut, Storrs.

Kessler, S. J., & McKenna, W. (1978). *Gender: An ethnomethodological approach.* New York: John Wiley.

Khazan, I., McHale, J., & Decourcey, W. (2008). Violated wishes about division of childcare labor predict early coparenting process during stressful and nonstressful family evaluations. *Infant Mental Health Journal, 29,* 343–361.

Kilbourne, J. (2002). *Killing us softly 3: Advertising's image of women* (Videotape). Northampton, MA: Media Education.

Kim, J. L., Sorsoli, C., Collins, K., Zylbergold, B. A., Schooler, D., & Tolman, D. L. (2007). From sex to sexuality: Exposing the heterosexist script on primetime network television. *Journal of Sex Research, 44,* 145–157.

Kimball, M. M. (1995). *Feminist visions of gender similarities and differences.* New York: Harrington Park Press.

Kimball, M. M. (2001). Gender similarities and differences as feminist contradictions. In R .K. Unger (Ed.), *Handbook of the psychology of women and gender* (pp. 66–83). New York: Wiley.

Kimmel, D. C., & Martin, D. L. (Eds.). (2001). *Midlife and aging in gay America: Proceedings of the SAGE conference, New York City, 2000.* New York: Harrington Park Press.

Kimmel, E., & Crawford, M. (Eds.). (2000). *Innovations in feminist psychological research.* Cambridge: Cambridge University Press.

Kimmell, M. (Ed.). (2007). *The sexual self: The construction of sexual scripts.* Nashville: University of Vanderbilt Press.

King, E. B., Botsford, W. E., & Huffman, A. H. (2009). Work, family, and organizational advancement: Does balance support the perceived advancement of mothers? *Sex Roles, 61,* 879–891.

Kinsey, A. C., Pomeroy, W. B., & Martin, C. E. (1948). *Sexual behavior in the human male.* Philadelphia: Saunders.

Kinsey, A. C., Pomeroy, W. B., Martin, C. E., & Gebhard, P. H. (1953). *Sexual behavior in the human female.* Philadelphia, PA: Saunders.

Kirsch, A. C., & Murnen, S. K. (2015). "Hot" girls and "cool dudes": Examining the prevalence of the heterosexual script in American children's television media. *Psychology of Popular Media Culture, 4*(1), 18–30. doi:10.1037/ppm0000017

Kirsch, I., Deacon, B. J., Huedo-Medina, T. B., Scoboria, A., Moore, T. J., & Johnson, B. T. (2008). Initial severity and antidepressant benefits: A meta-analysis of data submitted to the food and drug administration. *PLoS Medicine, 5*(2). Retrieved January 24, 2011, from http://www.plosmedicine.org/article/info%3Adoi%2F10.1371%2Fjournal.pmed.0050045

Kitayama, S., Markus, H. R., & Kurokawa, M. (2000). Culture, emotion, and well-being: Good feelings in Japan and the United States. *Cognition and Emotion, 14,* 93–124.

Kite, M. E., Stockdale, G. D., Whitley, B. E., Jr, & Johnson, B. T. (2005). Attitudes toward younger and older adults: An updated meta-analytic review. *Journal of Social Issues, 61*(2), 241–266.

Kitzinger, C. (1987). *The social construction of lesbianism.* London: Sage.

Kitzinger, C. (2001). Sexualities. In R. K. Unger (Ed.), *Handbook of the psychology of women and gender* (pp. 272–285). New York: Wiley.

Kling, K. C., Hyde, J. S., Showers, C., & Buswell, B. (1999). Gender differences in self-esteem: A meta-analysis. *Psychological Bulletin, 125,* 470–500.

Klonoff, E. A., & Landrine, H. (1995). The schedule of sexist events: A measure of lifetime and recent sexist discrimination in women's lives. *Psychology of Women Quarterly, 19,* 439–472.

Klonoff, E. A., Landrine, H., & Campbell, R. (2000). Sexist discrimination may account for well-known differences in psychiatric symptoms. *Psychology of Women Quarterly, 24,* 93–99.

Klusmann, V., Evers, A., Schwarzer, R., & Heuser, I. (2012). Views on aging and emotional benefits of physical activity: Effects of an exercise intervention in older women. *Psychology of Sport and Exercise, 13*(2), 236–242.

Knight, J. L., & Giuliano, T. A. (2001). He's a Laker; she's a "Looker": The consequences of gender-stereotypical portrayals of male and female athletes by the print media. *Sex Roles, 45,* 217–229.

Knight, J. L., & Guiliano, T. A. (2003). Blood, sweat, and jeers: The impact of the media's heterosexist portrayals on perceptions of male and female athletes. *Journal of Sport Behavior, 26,* 272–284.

Knoble, N. B., & Linville, D. (2012). Outness and relationship satisfaction in same-gender couples. *Journal of Marital and Family Therapy, 38*(2), 330–339.

Knudson-Martin, C., & Mahoney, A. (1996). Gender dilemmas and myth in the construction of marital bargains: Issues for marital therapy. *Family Process, 35,* 137–153.

Knudson-Martin, C., & Mahoney, A. (2005). Moving beyond gender: Processes that create relationship equality. *Journal of Marital and Family Therapy, 31*(2), 235–246.

Koenig, A. M., Eagly, A. H., Mitchell, A. A., & Ristikari, T. (2011). Are leader stereotypes masculine? A meta-analysis of three research paradigms. *Psychological Bulletin, 137*(4), 616–642. doi:10.1037/a0023557

Koeser, S., Kuhn, E. A., & Sczesny, S. (2015). Just reading? How gender-fair language triggers readers' use of gender-fair forms. *Journal of Language and Social Psychology, 34*(3), 343–357. doi:10.1177/0261927X14561119

Koeser S., & Sczesny S. (2015). Promoting gender-fair language: The impact of arguments on language use, attitudes, and cognitions. *Journal of Language and Social Psychology, 33,* 548–560. doi:10.1177/0261927x14541280

Kohlberg, L. (1966). A cognitive-developmental analysis of children's sex role concepts and attitudes. In E. E. Maccoby (Ed.), *The development of sex differences* (pp. 82–173). Stanford, CA: Stanford University Press.

Konrath, S., Au, J., & Ramsey, L. R. (2012). Cultural differences in faceism: Male politicians have bigger heads in more gender-equal cultures. *Psychology of Women Quarterly, 36*(4), 476–487. doi:10.1177/0361684312455317

Koren, C. (2016). Men's vulnerability–women's resilience: From widowhood to late-life repartnering. *International Psychogeriatrics, 28*(5), 719–731.

Koropeckyj-Cox, T., & Call, V. A. (2007). Characteristics of older childless persons and parents: Cross-national comparisons. *Journal of Family Issues, 28*(10), 1362–1414. doi:10.1177/0192513X07303837

Kosciw, J. G., Palmer, N. A., & Kull, R. M. (2015). Reflecting resiliency: Openness about sexual orientation and/or gender identity and its relationship to well-being and educational outcomes for LGBT students. *American Journal of Community Psychology, 55*(1–2), 167–178. doi:10.1007/s10464–014-9642–6

Koss, M. P., Bailey, J. A., Yuan, N. P., Herrera, V. M., & Lichter, E. L. (2003). Depression and PTSD in survivors of male violence: Research and training initiatives to facilitate recovery. *Psychology of Women Quarterly, 27,* 130–142.

Koss, M. P., & Gaines, J. A. (1993). The prediction of sexual aggression by alcohol use, athletic participation, and fraternity affiliation. *Journal of Interpersonal Violence, 8,* 94–108.

Koss, M. P., & Kilpatrick, D. G. (2001). Rape and sexual assault. In E. Gerrity, T. M. Keane, & T. Garis (Eds.), *The mental health consequences of torture* (pp. 177–193). New York: Plenum.

Krahé, B., Bieneck, S., & Scheinberger-Olwig, R. (2007). Adolescents' sexual scripts: Schematic representations of consensual and nonconsensual heterosexual interactions. *Journal of Sex Research, 44,* 316–327.

Krakauer, J. (2015). *Missoula: Rape and the justice system in a college town.* New York: Doubleday.

Kramarae, C., & Treichler, P. A. (1985). *A feminist dictionary.* Boston: Pandora.

Kravetz, D. (1980). Consciousness-raising and self-help. In M. Brodsky & R. Hare-Mustin (Eds.), *Women and psychotherapy* (pp. 267–283). New York: Guilford.

Kravitz, R. L., Epstein, R. M., Feldman, M. D., Franz, C. E., Azari, R., Wilkes, M. S., . . . Franks, P. (2005). Influence of patients' requests for direct-to-consumer advertised antidepressants: a randomized controlled trial. *JAMA, 293*(16), 1995–2002.

Kreager, D. A., & Staff, J. (2009). The sexual double standard and adolescent peer acceptance. *Social Psychology Quarterly, 72,* 143–164.

Kreager, D. A., Staff, J., Gauthier, R., Lefkowitz, E. S., & Feinberg, M. E. (2016). The double standard at sexual debut: Gender, sexual behavior and adolescent peer acceptance. *Sex Roles (Online First),* doi:10.1007/s11199–016-0618-x

Kreukels, B. P. C., & Guillamon, A. (2016). Neuroimaging studies in people with gender incongruence. *International Review of Psychiatry, 28*(1), 120–128. doi:10.3109/09540261.2015.1113163

Kristoff, N. D., & WuDunn, S. (2009). *Half the sky: Turning oppression into opportunity for women worldwide.* New York: Knopf.

Kroon Van Diest, A. M., Tartakovsky, M., Stachon, C., Pettit, J. W., & Perez, M. (2014). The relationship between acculturative stress and eating disorder symptoms: Is it unique from general life stress? *Journal of Behavioral Medicine, 37*(445). doi:10.1007/s10865–013-9498–5

Krumrei, E., Coit, C., Martin, S., Fogo, W., & Mahoney, A. (2007). Post-divorce adjustment and social relationships: A meta-analytic review. *Journal of Divorce & Remarriage, 46,* 145–166.

Kulik, L. (2011). Developments in spousal power relations: Are we moving toward equality? *Marriage & Family Review, 47*(7), 419–435.

Kuper, L. E., Coleman, B. R., & Mustanski, B. S. (2014). Coping with LGBT and racial–ethnic-related stressors: A mixed-methods study of LGBT youth of color. *Journal of Research on Adolescence, 24*(4), 703–719. doi:10.1111/jora.12079

Kurdek, L. A. (1988). Perceived social support in gays and lesbians in cohabitating couples. *Journal of Personality and Social Psychology, 54,* 504–509.

Kurdek, L. A. (1997). Adjustment to relationship dissolution in gay, lesbian, and heterosexual partners. *Personal Relationships, 4,* 145–161.

Kurdek, L. A. (2007). The allocation of household labor by partners in gay and lesbian couples. *Journal of Family Issues, 28,* 132–148.

Kurtulus, F. A. (2012). Affirmative action and the occupational advancement of minorities and women during 1973–2003. *Industrial Relations: A Journal of Economy & Society, 51*(2), 213–246.

Kurtulus, F. A. (2016). The impact of affirmative action on the employment of minorities and women: A longitudinal analysis using three decades of EEO-1 filings. *Journal of Policy Analysis and Management, 35*(1), 34–66.

LaBrie, J. W., Hummer, J. F., Ghaidarov, T. M., Lac, A., & Kenney, S. R. (2014). Hooking up in the college context: The event-level effects of alcohol use and partner familiarity on hookup behaviors and contentment. *Journal of Sex Research, 51*(1), 62–73. doi:10.1080/00224499.2012.714010

Lachs, M. S., & Pillemer, K. A. (2015). Elder abuse. *New England Journal of Medicine, 373*(20), 1947–1956.

LaFramboise, T. D., Berman, J. S., & Sohi, B. K. (1994). American Indian women. In L. Comas-Díaz & B. Greene (Eds.), *Women of color: Integrating ethnic and gender identities in psychotherapy* (pp. 30–71). New York: Guilford Press.

LaFrance, M. (1992). Gender and interruptions: Individual infraction or violation of the social order? *Psychology of Women Quarterly, 16,* 497–512.

LaFrance, M. (2001). Gender and social interaction. In R. K. Unger (Ed.), *Handbook of the psychology of women and gender* (pp. 245–255). New York: Wiley.

LaFrance, M., Hetcht, M. A., & Paluck, E. (2003). The contingent smile: A meta-analysis of sex differences in smiling. *Psychological Bulletin, 129,* 305–334.

Lai, Y., & Hynie, M. (2011). A tale of two standards: An examination of young adults' endorsement of gendered and ageist sexual double standards. *Sex Roles, 64*(5–6), 360–371. doi:10.1007/s11199–010-9896-x

Laing, R. D. (1970). *The divided self.* New York: Random House.

Lambdin, J. R., Greer, K. M., Jibotian, K. S., Wood, K. R., & Hamilton, M. C. (2003). The animal = male hypothesis: Children's and adult's beliefs about the sex of non-sex specific stuffed animals. *Sex Roles, 48,* 471–483.

Lamont, R. A., Swift, H. J., & Abrams, D. (2015). A review and meta-analysis of age-based stereotype threat: Negative stereotypes, not facts, do the damage. *Psychology and Aging, 30*(1), 180–193.

Landa, A. (1990). No accident: The voices of voluntarily childless women–An essay on the social construction of fertility choices. In J. P. Knowles & E. Cole (Eds.), *Motherhood: A feminist perspective* (pp. 139–158). New York: Haworth.

Landrine, H., Klonoff, E. A., Gibbs, J., Manning, V., & Lund, M. (1995). Physical and psychiatric correlates of gender discrimination: An application of the schedule of sexist events. *Psychology of Women Quarterly, 19,* 473–492.

Lansford, J. E., Skinner, A. T., Sorbring, E., Giunta, L. D., Deater-Deckard, K., Dodge, K. A., . . . Chang, L. (2012). Boys' and girls' relational and physical aggression in nine countries. *Aggressive Behavior, 38*(4), 298–308. doi:10.1002/ab.21433

LaRossa, R., Jaret, C., Gadgil, M., & Wynn, G. R. (2001). Gender disparities in Mother's Day and Father's Day comic strips: A fifty-four year history. *Sex Roles, 44,* 693–718.

Larson, M. S. (2003). Gender, race, and aggression in television commercials that feature children. *Sex Roles, 48,* 67–76.

Latu, I. M., Mast, M. S., & Stewart, T. L. (2015). Gender biases in (inter) action: The role of interviewers' and applicants' implicit and explicit stereotypes in predicting women's job interview outcomes. *Psychology of Women Quarterly, 39*(4), 539–552. doi:10.1177/0361684315577383

Laumann, E. O., Gagnon, J. H., Michael, R. T., & Michaels, S. (1994). *The social organization of sexuality: Sexual practices in the United States.* Chicago: University of Chicago Press.

Laumann, E. O., & Michael, R. T. (Eds.). (2000). *Sex, love, and health in America: Private choices and public policies.* Chicago: University of Chicago Press.

Laumann, E. O., Paik, A., & Rosen, R. C. (1999). Sexual dysfunction in the United States: Prevalence and predictors. *JAMA, 281,* 537–544.

Laurance, J. (2001, August 22). Doctors must refuse to collude in this abusive practice: "Genital mutilation is one of many harmful practices affecting women in traditional societies." *The Independent,* p. 5.

Lauzen, M. M., & Dozier, D. M. (2005). Maintaining the double standard: Portrayals of age and gender in popular films. *Sex Roles, 52,* 437–446.

Lauzen, M. M., Dozier, D. M., & Horan, N. (2008, June). Constructing gender stereotypes through social roles in prime-time television. *Journal of Broadcasting & Electronic Media,* 200–221.

Lavigne, P. (2016, February 2). Baylor faces accusations of ignoring sex assault victims. ESPN. Retrieved from http://www.espn.com/espn/otl/story/_/id/14675790/baylor-officials-accused failing-investigate-sexual-assaults-fully-adequately-providing-support-alleged-victims

Leadbeater, B. J. R., & Way, N. (2001). *Growing up fast: Transitions to early adulthood of inner-city adolescent mothers.* Mahwah, NJ: Erlbaum.

Leaper, C. (2000). The social construction and socialization of gender during development. In P. H. Miller & E. K. Scholnick (Eds.), *Toward a feminist developmental psychology* (pp. 127–152). New York: Routledge.

Leaper, C. (2015). Gender and social-cognitive development. In R. M. Lerner, L. S. Liben, & U. Muller (Eds.), *Handbook of child psychology and developmental science: Vol. 2. Cognitive processes* (7th ed., pp. 806–853). New York: Wiley.

Leaper, C., Anderson, K., & Sanders, P. (1998). Moderators of gender effects on parents' talk to their children: A meta-analysis. *Developmental Psychology, 34,* 3–27.

Leaper, C., Farkas, T., & Brown, C. S. (2012). Adolescent girls' experiences and gender-related beliefs in relation to their motivation in math/science and English. *Journal of Youth and Adolescence, 41*(3), 268–282.

Lee, G. R. (1988). Marital intimacy among older persons: The spouse as confidant. *Journal of Family Issues, 9,* 273–284.

Lee, I., & Crawford, M. (2007). Lesbians and bisexual women in the eyes of scientific psychology. *Feminism & Psychology, 17,* 109–127.

Lee, I., & Crawford, M. (2012). Lesbians in empirical psychological research: A new perspective for the twenty-first century? *Journal of Lesbian Studies, 16*(1), 4–16. doi:10.1080/10894160.2011.557637

Lee, I., Pratto, F., & Johnson, B. T. (2011). Intergroup consensus/disagreement in support of group-based hierarchy: An examination of socio-structural and psycho-cultural factors. *Psychological Bulletin, 137*(6), 1029–1064. doi:10.1037/a0025410

Lee, J. (2003). Menarche and the (hetero)sexualization of the female body. In R. Weitz (Ed.), *The politics of women's bodies* (2nd ed., pp. 82–99). Oxford, England: Oxford University Press.

Lee, K. S., & Ono, H. (2012). Marriage, cohabitation, and happiness: A cross-national analysis of 27 countries. *Journal of Marriage and Family, 74*(5), 953–972.

Lee-Winn, A., Mendelson, T., & Mojtabai, R. (2014). Racial/ethnic disparities in binge eating: Disorder prevalence, symptom presentation, and help-seeking among Asian Americans and Non-Latino Whites. *American Journal of Public Health, 104*(7), 1263–1265.

Legate, N., Ryan, R. M., & Weinstein, N. (2012). Is coming out always a "good thing"? exploring the relations of autonomy support, outness, and wellness for lesbian, gay, and bisexual individuals. *Social Psychological and Personality Science, 3*(2), 145–152. doi:10.1177/1948550611411929

Leibenluft, E. (1996). Women with bipolar illness: Clinical and research issues. *American Journal of Psychiatry, 153,* 163–173.

Leibowitz, S., & de Vries, A. L. C. (2016). Gender dysphoria in adolescence. *International Review of Psychiatry, 28*(1), 21–35. doi:10.3109/09540261.2015.1124844

Lemkau, J. P. (1983). Women in male-dominated professions: Distinguishing personality and background characteristics. *Psychology of Women Quarterly, 8,* 144–165.

Lenhart, A. (2015, April 9). Teens, Social Media, & Technology Overview 2015. *Pew Research Center: Internet, Science, & Tech.* Retrieved from pewinternet.org/2015/04/09

Lenton, A. P., Bruder, M., & Sedekides, C. (2009). A meta-analysis on the malleability of automatic gender stereotypes. *Psychology of Women Quarterly, 33,* 183–196.

Lester, R., & Petrie, T. A. (1995). Personality and physical correlates of bulimic symptomatology among Mexican American female college students. *Journal of Counseling Psychology, 42,* 199–203.

Lester, R., & Petrie, T. A. (1998). Physical, psychological, and societal correlates of bulimic symptomatology among African American college women. *Journal of Counseling Psychology, 45,* 315–321.

Lev, A. I. (2013). Gender dysphoria: Two steps forward, one step back. *Clinical Social Work Journal, 41*(3), 288–296. doi:10.1007/s10615-013-0447-0

Levine, R., Sato, S., Hashimoto, T., & Verma, J. (1995). Love and marriage in eleven cultures. *Journal of Cross-Cultural Psychology, 26,* 554–571.

Levitt, H. M., & Ippolito, M. R. (2014a). Being transgender: Navigating minority stressors and developing authentic self-presentation. *Psychology of Women Quarterly, 38*(1), 46–64. doi:10.1177/0361684313501644

Levitt, H. M., & Ippolito, M. R. (2014b). Being transgender: The experience of transgender identity development. *Journal of Homosexuality, 61*(12), 1727–1758. doi:10.1080/00918369.2014.951262

Lewis, J. (2002). *Playing the human part: Lupe Ontiveros on how not to be a diva.* Retrieved August 25, 2002, from http://www.laweekly.com/ink/02/16/cover-lewis2.php

Lewis, J. M., & Kreider, R. M. (2015). Remarriage in the United States. *U. S. Census.* Retrieved from https://www.census.gov/content/dam/Census/library/publications/2015/acs/acs-30.pdf

Lewis, K. M., Robkin, N., Gaska, K., & Njoki, L. C. (2011). Investigating motivations for women's skin bleaching in Tanzania. *Psychology of Women Quarterly, 35*(1), 29–37. doi:10.1177/0361684310392356

Lewis, M. A., Lee, C. M., Patrick, M. E., & Fossos, N. (2007). Gender-specific normative misperceptions of risky sexual behavior and alcohol-related risky sexual behavior. *Sex Roles, 57,* 81–90.

Lichty, L. F., & Campbell, R. (2012). Targets and witnesses: Middle school students' sexual harassment experiences. *The Journal of Early Adolescence, 32*(3), 414–430. doi:10.1177/0272431610396090

Liles, E. G., & Woods, S. C. (1999). Anorexia nervosa as viable behaviour: Extreme self-deprivation in historical context. *History of Psychiatry, 10,* 205–225.

Lindberg, L. L., Santelli, J., & Desai, S. (2016). Understanding the decline in adolescent fertility in the United States, 2007–2012. *Journal of Adolescent Health, 59*(5), 577–583. doi:10.1016/j.jadohealth.2016.06.024

Lindberg, S. M., Grabe, S., & Hyde, J. S. (2007). Gender, pubertal development, and peer sexual harassment predict objectified body consciousness in early adolescence. *Journal of Research on Adolescence, 17,* 723–742.

Lindsey, E. W., & Mize, J. (2001). Contextual differences in parent-child play: Implications for children's gender role development. *Sex Roles, 44,* 155–176.

Lindsey, E. W., Mize, J., & Pettit, G. (1997). Differential play patterns of mothers and fathers of sons and daughters: Implications for children's gender role development. *Sex Roles, 37,* 643–662.

Linehan, M., & Scullion, H. (2008). The development of female global managers: The role of mentoring and networking. *Journal of Business Ethics, 83,* 29–40.

Linz, D., Donnerstein, E., & Penrod, S. (1987). Sexual violence in the mass media: Social psychological implications. In P. Shaver & C. Hendrick (Eds.), *Review of personality and social psychology: Vol. 7. Sex and gender* (pp. 95–123). Newbury Park, CA: Sage.

Lippman, J. R., Ward, L. M., & Seabrook, R. C. (2014). Isn't it romantic? Differential associations between romantic screen media genres and romantic beliefs. *Psychology of Popular Media Culture, 3*(3), 128–140. doi:10.1037/ppm0000034

Lipman-Blumen, J., & Leavitt, H. J. (1976). Vicarious and direct achievement patterns in adulthood. *The Counseling Psychologist, 6,* 26–31.

Liss, M., & Erchull, M.J. (2010). Everyone feels empowered: Understanding feminist self-labeling. *Psychology of Women Quarterly, 34,* 85–96.

Liss, M., Hoffner, C., & Crawford, M. (2000). What do feminists believe? *Psychology of Women Quarterly, 24,* 279–284.

Liss, M., O'Connor, C., Morosky, E., & Crawford, M. (2001). What makes a feminist? Predictors and correlates of feminist social identity in college women. *Psychology of Women Quarterly, 25*(2), 124–133. doi:10.1111/1471-6402.00014

Litwin, H. (2011). The association between social network relationships and depressive symptoms among older Americans: What matters most? *International Psychogeriatrics, 23*(6), 930–940.

Litwin, H., & Shiovitz-Ezra, S. (2011). Social network type and subjective well-being in a national sample of older Americans. *The Gerontologist, 51*(3), 379–388.

Lloyd, S. A. (1991). The dark side of courtship. *Family Relations, 40,* 14–20.

Lobo, R. A. (2016). Hormone-replacement therapy: Current thinking. *Nature Reviews Endocrinology (Online First).* doi:10.1038/nrendo.2016.164

Locher, P., Unger, R. K., Sociedade, P., & Wahl, J. (1993). At first glance: Accessibility of the physical attractiveness stereotype. *Sex Roles, 28,* 729–743.

Locke, L. M., & Richman, C. L. (1999). Attitudes toward domestic violence: Race and gender issues. *Sex Roles, 40,* 227–247.

Logel, C., Walton, G. M., Spencer, S. J., Iserman, E. C., von Hippel, W., & Bell, A. E. (2009). Interacting with sexist men triggers social identity threat among female engineers. *Journal of Personality and Social Psychology, 96*(6), 1089–1103. doi:10.1037/a0015703

Loiacano, D. K. (1993). Gay identity issues among Black Americans: Racism, homophobia, and the need for validation. In L. D. Garnets & D. C. Kimmel (Eds.), *Psychological perspectives on lesbian and gay male experiences* (pp. 364–375). New York: Columbia University Press.

Longino, H. (1980). What is pornography. In L. Lederere (Ed.), *Take back the night* (p. 44). New York: William Morrow.

Longmore, M. A., Eng., A. L., Giordano, P. C., & Manning, W. D. (2009). Parenting and adolescents' sexual initiation. *Journal of Marriage and Family, 71,* 969–982.

Lonsway, K. A., & Fitzgerald, L. F. (1994). Rape myths: In review. *Psychology of Women Quarterly, 18,* 133–164.

Lonsway, K. A., & Fitzgerald, L. F. (1995). Attitudinal antecedents of rape myth acceptance: A theoretical and empirical reexamination. *Journal of Personality and Social Psychology, 68,* 704–711.

Lopez, S. R. (1989). Patient variable biases in clinical judgment: Conceptual overview and methodological considerations. *Psychological Bulletin, 106,* 184–203.

LoPiccolo, J., & Stock, W. E. (1986). Treatment of sexual dysfunction. *Journal of Consulting and Clinical Psychology, 54,* 158–167.

Lorber, J. (1993). *Paradoxes of gender.* New Haven, CT: Yale University Press.

Lott, B. (1987). Sexist discrimination as distancing behavior: I. A laboratory demonstration. *Psychology of Women Quarterly, 11,* 47–58.

Ludden, J. (2016). Should we be having kids in the age of climate change? National Public Radio: *All Things Considered.* Retrieved from http://www.npr.org/2016/08/18/479349760/should-we-be-having-kids-in-the-age-of-climate-change

Ludermir, A. B., Schraiber, L., D'Oliveira, A. F. P. L., Franca-Junior, I., & Jansen, H. A. (2008). Violence against women by their intimate partner and common mental disorders. *Social Science & Medicine, 66,* 1008–1018.

Lueptow, L. B., Garovich, L., & Lueptow, M. B. (1995). The persistence of gender stereotypes in the face of changing sex roles: Evidence contrary to the sociocultural model. *Ethology & Sociobiology, 16,* 509–530.

Lunau, T., Bambra, C., Eikemo, T. A., van der Wel, K. A., & Dragano, N. (2014). A balancing act? Work–life balance, health and well-being in European welfare states. *European Journal of Public Health, 24*(3), 422–427.

Luo, B., Zhou, K., Jin, E. J., Newman, A., & Liang, J. (2013). Ageism among college students: A comparative study between U.S. and China. *Journal of Cross-Cultural Gerontology, 28*(1), 49–63.

Lyndon, A. E., Sinclair, H. C., MacArthur, J., Fay, B., Ratajack, E., & Collier, K. E. (2012). An introduction to issues of gender in stalking research. *Sex Roles, 66*(5–6), 299–310.

Lyons, H., Giordano, P. C., Manning, W. D., & Longmore, M. A. (2011). Identity, peer relationships, and adolescent girls' sexual behavior: An exploration of the contemporary double standard. *Journal of Sex Research, 48*(5), 437–449. doi:10.1080/00224499.2010.506679

Lytton, H., & Romney, D. M. (1991). Parents' differential socialization of boys and girls: A meta-analysis. *Psychological Bulletin, 109,* 267–296.

Maccoby, E. E. (1998). *The two sexes: Growing up apart, coming together.* Cambridge, MA: Belknap Press of Harvard University Press.

Maccoby, E. E., & Jacklin, C. (1974). *The psychology of sex differences.* Stanford, CA: Stanford University Press.

MacFarlane, A. (1977). *The psychology of childbirth.* Cambridge, MA: Harvard University Press.

MacKinnon, C. A. (1994). Sexuality. In A. C. Herrmann & A. J. Stewart (Eds.), *Theorizing feminism: Parallel trends in the humanities and social sciences* (pp. 257–287). Boulder, CO: Westview Press.

MacNeil, S., & Byers, E.S. (2009). Role of sexual self-disclosure in the sexual satisfaction of long-term heterosexual couples. *Journal of Sex Research, 46,* 3–14.

Mahalingam, R. (2003). Essentialism, culture, and beliefs about gender among the Aravanis of Tamil Nadu, India. *Sex Roles, 49,* 489–496.

Mahalingam, R., Haritatos, J., & Jackson, B. (2007). Essentialism and the cultural psychology of gender in extreme son preference communities in India. *American Journal of Orthopsychiatry, 77*(4), 598–609.

Mahay, J. W., Laumann, E. O., & Michaels, S. (2001). Race, gender, and class in sexual scripts. In E. O. Laumann & R. T. Michael (Eds.), *Sex, love, and health: Private choices and public policies* (pp. 197–238). Chicago: University of Chicago Press.

Major, B. (1994). From social inequality to personal entitlement: The role of social comparisons, legitimacy appraisals, and group membership. In M. P. Zanna (Ed.), *Advances in experimental social psychology* (Vol. 26, pp. 293–355). New York: Academic Press.

Major, B., Appelbaum, M., Beckman, L., Dutton, M., Russo, N., & West, C. (2009). Abortion and Mental Health: Evaluating the Evidence. *American Psychologist, 64*(9), 863–890.

Major, B., Barr, L., Zubek, J., & Babey, S. H. (1999). Gender and self-esteem: A meta-analysis. In W. B. Swann Jr., J. H. Langlois, & L. A. Gilbert (Eds.), *Sexism and stereotypes in modern society: The gender science of Janet Taylor Spence* (pp. 223–253). Washington, DC: American Psychological Association.

Major, B., Gramzow, R. H., McCoy, S. K., Levin, S., Schmader, T., & Sidanius, J. (2002). Perceiving personal discrimination: The role of group status and legitimizing ideology. *Journal of Personality & Social Psychology, 82,* 269–282.

Makepeace, J. M. (1986). Gender differences in courtship violence victimization. *Family Relations: Journal of Applied Family and Child Studies, 35,* 383–388.

Malacrida, C., & Boulton, T. (2012). Women's perceptions of childbirth "choices": Competing discourses of motherhood, sexuality, and selflessness. *Gender & Society, 26*(5), 748–772.

Malcolmson, K. A., & Sinclair, L. (2007). The Ms. Stereotype revisited: Implicit and explicit facets. *Psychology of Women Quarterly, 31,* 305–310.

Malfatto, E. & Prtoric, J. (2014). Last of the burrnesha: Balkan women who pledged celibacy to live as men. *The Guardian.* Retrieved from http://www.theguardian.com/world/2014/aug/05/women-celibacy-oath-men-rights-albania

Malmquist, A. (2015). Women in lesbian relations: Construing equal or unequal parental roles? *Psychology of Women Quarterly, 39*(2), 256–267.

Mangiolio, R. (2009). The impact of child sexual abuse on health: A systematic review of reviews. *Clinical Psychology Review, 29,* 647–657.

Manley, M. H., Diamond, L. M., & van Anders, S. M. (2015). Polyamory, monoamory, and sexual fluidity: A longitudinal study of identity and sexual trajectories. *Psychology of Sexual Orientation and Gender Diversity, 2*(2), 168–180. doi:10.1037/sgd0000098

Manning, W. D., & Cohen, J. A. (2012). Premarital cohabitation and marital dissolution: An examination of recent marriages. *Journal of Marriage and Family, 74*(2), 377–387.

Manning, W. D., & Landale, N. S. (1996). Racial and ethnic differences in the role of cohabitation in premarital child-bearing. *Journal of Marriage and the Family, 58,* 63–77.

Mannino, C., & Deutsch, F. (2007). Changing the division of household labor: A negotiated process between partners. *Sex Roles, 56*(5–6), 309–324.

Marcuccio, E., Loving, N., Bennett, S. K., & Hayes, S. N. (2003). A survey of attitudes and experiences of women with heart disease. *Women's Health Issues, 13,* 23–31.

Marecek, J. (1999). Trauma talk in feminist clinical practice. In S. Lamb (Ed.), *New versions of victims: Feminists struggle with the concept* (pp. 158–182). New York: New York University Press.

Marecek, J., Crawford, M., & Popp, D. (2004). On the construction of gender, sex, and sexualities. In A. H. Eagly, A. E. Beall, & R. J. Sternberg (Eds.), *The psychology of gender* (2nd ed., pp. 192–216). New York: Guilford.

Marecek, J., & Gavey, N. (2013). DSM-5 and beyond: A critical feminist engagement with psychodiagnosis. *Feminism & Psychology, 23*, 3–9.

Marecek, J., Kimmel, E. B., Crawford, M., & Hare-Mustin, R. T. (2002). Psychology of women and gender. In I. B. Weiner (Series Ed.) & D. K. Freedheim (Vol. Ed.), *Comprehensive handbook of psychology: Vol 1. The history of psychology* (pp. 249–268). New York: Wiley and Sons.

Marecek, J., & Kravetz, D. (1998). Power and agency in feminist therapy. In I. B. Seu & M. C. Heenan (Eds.), *Feminism and psychotherapy: Reflections on contemporary theories and practices* (pp. 13–29). Thousand Oaks, CA: Sage Publications.

Mark, K. P., Garcia, J. R., & Fisher, H. E. (2015). Perceived emotional and sexual satisfaction across sexual relationship contexts: Gender and sexual orientation differences and similarities. *Canadian Journal of Human Sexuality, 24*(2), 120–130. doi:10.3138/cjhs.242-A8

Markson, E. W. (2003). The female aging body through film. In C. A. Faircloth (Ed.), *Aging bodies: Images and everyday experiences* (pp. 77–102). New York: AltaMira Press.

Markus, H. R., & Kitayama, S. (1991). Culture and the self: Implications for cognition, emotion, and motivation. *Psychological Review, 98*, 224–253.

Marsh, M. (1995). Feminist psychopharmacology: An aspect of feminist psychiatry. *Women & Therapy, 16*, 73–84.

Martens, A., Johns, M., Greenberg, J., & Schimel, J. (2006). Combating stereotype threat: The effect of self-affirmation on women's intellectual performance. *Journal of Experimental Social Psychology, 42*(2), 236–243. doi:10.1016/j.jesp.2005.04.010

Martin, C. L., DiDonato, M. D., Clary, L., Fabes, R. A., Kreiger, T., Palermo, F., & Hanish, L. (2012). Preschool children with gender normative and gender non-normative peer preferences: *Psychosocial and environmental correlates. Archives of Sexual Behavior, 41*(4), 831–847. doi:10.1007/s10508-012-9950-6

Martin, C. L., & Fabes, R. A. (2001). The stability and consequences of young children's same sex peer interactions. *Developmental Psychology, 37*, 431–446.

Martin, C. L., & Halverson, C. F. (1983). The effects of sex-typing schemas on young children's memory. *Child Development, 54*, 563–574.

Martin, C. L., & Ruble, D. (2004). Children's search for gender cues. *Current Directions in Psychological Science, 13*, 67–70.

Martin, J. A., Hamilton, B. E., & Osterman, M. (2014, December). Births in the United States, 2013. *National Center for Health Statistics.* Retrieved from https://www.cdc.gov/nchs/data/databriefs/db175.pdf

Martin, K., Verduzco Baker, L., Torres, J., & Luke, K. (2011). Privates, pee-pees, and coochies: Gender and genital labeling for/with young children. *Feminism & Psychology, 21*(3), 420–430. doi:10.1177/0959353510384832

Martin-Uzzi, M., & Duval-Tsioles, D. (2013). The experience of remarried couples in blended families. *Journal of Divorce & Remarriage, 54*(1), 43–57.

Martire, L. M., & Stephens, M. A. P. (2003). Juggling parent care and employment responsibilities: The dilemmas of adult daughter caregivers in the workforce. *Sex Roles, 48*, 167–173.

Marvan, M. L., Ramiriz-Esparza, D., Cortes-Iniestra, S., & Chrisler, J. C., (2006). Development of a new scale to measure beliefs about and attitudes toward menstruation (BATM): Data from Mexico and the United States. *Health Care for Women International, 27*, 453–473.

Masser, B., Viki, G. T., & Power, C. (2006). Hostile sexism and rape procilivity amongst men. *Sex Roles, 54*, 565–574.

Masson, J. M. (1984). *The assault on truth: Freud's suppression of the seduction theory.* New York: Harper Perennial.

Mather, S. (2008). Women and coronary heart disease. In A. L. Clouse & K. Sherif (Eds.), *Women's health in clinical practice: A handbook for primary care* (pp. 71–96). New York: Humana Press.

Matthews, G. A., Fane, B. A., Conway, G. S., Brook, C. G. D., & Hines, M. (2009). Personality and congenital adrenal hyperplasia: Possible effects of prenatal androgen exposure. *Hormones and Behavior, 55*, 285–291.

Mauthner, N. S. (1998). "It's a woman's cry for help": A relational perspective on postnatal depression. *Feminism & Psychology, 8*, 325–355.

Maybury, K. (2015). Peer rejection: An interview with a teen and some tips for coping. *The Feminist Psychologist, 42*, 11–14.

Mayer, A. P., Blair, J. E., Ko, M. G., Patel, S. I., & Files, J. A. (2014). Long-term follow-up of a facilitated peer mentoring program. *Medical Teacher, 36*(3), 260–266.

Mazur, T. (2005). Gender dysphoria and gender change in androgen insensitivity or micropenis. *Archives of Sexual Behavior, 34*(4), 411–421.

Mazzocco, M. M. M. (2009). Mathematical learning disability in girls with Turner Syndrome: A challenge to defining mild and its subtypes. *Developmental Disabilities Research Reviews, 15*, 35–44.

McCabe, K. A., & Manian, S. (2010). *Sex trafficking: A global perspective.* Lanham, MD: Lexington Books.

McCarthy, M. M., & Arnold, A. P. (2011). Reframing sexual differentiation of the brain. *Nature Neuroscience, 14*(6), 677–683. doi:10.1038/nn.2834

McClelland, D. C., Atkinson, J. W., Clark, R. A., & Lowell, E. L. (1953). *The achievement motive.* Englewood Cliffs, NJ: Prentice Hall.

McClure, K. J., Puhl, R. M., & Heuer, C. A. (2011). Obesity in the news: Do photographic images of obese persons influence anti-fat attitudes? *Journal of Health Communication, 16*(4), 359-371.

McCormick, M. J. (2002). The search for the ideal heterosexual role play. In L. Diamant & J. A. Lee (Eds.), *The psychology of sex, gender, and jobs: Issues and resolutions* (pp. 155–170). Westport, CT: Praeger.

McCreary, D. R., & Rhodes, N. D. (2001). On the gender typed nature of dominant and submissive acts. *Sex Roles, 44*, 339–350.

McDonald, P. (2012). Workplace sexual harassment 30 years on: A review of the literature. *International Journal of Management Reviews, 14*(1), 1–17.

McDonald, S. (2011). What's in the "old boys" network? Accessing social capital in gendered and racialized networks. *Social Networks, 33*(4), 317–330. doi:10.1016/j.socnet.2011.10.002

McGlone, M., & Aronson, J. (2007). Forewarning and forearming stereotype-threatened students. *Communication Education, 56*(2), 119–133. doi:10.1080/03634520601158681

McHugh, M. C., & Interligi, C. (2015). Older women, economic power, and consumerism. In Muhlbauer, V., Chrisler, J. C., & Denmark, F.L. (Eds.), *women and aging: An international, intersectional power perspective* (pp. 81–116). Switzerland: Springer International.

McHugh, M. D., Koeske, R. D., & Frieze, I. H. (1986). Issues to consider in conducting nonsexist psychological research: A guide for researchers. *American Psychologist, 41,* 879–890.

McKelvey, M. W., & McKenry, P. C. (2000). The psychosocial well-being of Black and White mothers following marital dissolution. *Psychology of Women Quarterly, 24,* 4–14.

McKenney, S. J., & Bigler, R. S. (2014). High heels, low grades: Internalized sexualization and academic orientation among adolescent girls. *Journal of Research on Adolescence, 26*(1), 30–36. doi:10.1111/jora.12179

McKenney, S. J., & Bigler, R. S. (2016). Internalized sexualization and its relation to sexualized appearance, body surveillance, and body shame among early adolescent girls. *The Journal of Early Adolescence, 36*(2), 171–197. doi:0272431614556889

McKinley, N. M., & Hyde, J. S. (1996). The objectified body consciousness scale: Development and validation. *Psychology of Women Quarterly, 20,* 181–215.

McMahon, M. (1995). *Engendering motherhood.* New York: Guilford.

McMahon, S., & Farmer, G. L. (2009). The bystander approach: Strengths-based sexual assault prevention with at-risk groups. *Journal of Human Behavior in the Social Environment, 19,* 1042–1065.

Meier, E. (2000). Legislative efforts to combat sexual trafficking and slavery of women and children. *Pediatric Nursing, 26,* 216–211.

Ménard, A. D., & Kleinplatz, P. J. (2008). Twenty-one moves guaranteed to make his thighs go up in flames: Depictions of "great sex" in popular magazines. *Sexuality & Culture, 12,* 1–20.

Mennino, S. F., & Brayfield, A. (2002). Job-family trade-offs: The multidimensional effects of gender. *Work and Occupations, 29,* 226–256.

Merchant, C. (1995). *Earthcare: Women and the environment.* New York: Routledge.

Merritt, R. D., & Kok, C. J. (1995). Attribution of gender to a gender-unspecified individual: An evaluation of the people = male hypothesis. *Sex Roles, 33,* 145–157.

Messias, D., & DeJoseph, J. (2007). The personal work of a first pregnancy: Transforming identities, relationships, and women's work. *Women and Health, 45*(4), 41–64.

Messner, M. A., Duncan, M. C., & Jensen, K. (1993). Separating the men from the girls: The gendered language of televised sports. *Gender & Society, 7,* 121–137.

Meston, C. M., Trapnell, P. D., & Gorzalka, B. B. (1996). Ethnic and gender differences in sexuality: Variations in sexual behavior between Asian and non-Asian university students. *Archives of Sexual Behavior, 25,* 33–72.

Metzl, J. (2003). *Prozac on the couch: Prescribing gender in the era of wonder drugs.* Durham: Duke University Press.

Meyer, D. R., Cancian, M., & Chen, Y. (2015). Why are child support orders becoming less likely after divorce? *Social Service Review, 89*(2), 301–334.

Michael, R. T., Gagnon, J. H., Laumann, E. O., & Kolata, G. (1994). *Sex in America: A definitive survey.* Boston: Little Brown.

Midlarsky, E., & Nitzburg, G. (2008). Eating disorders in middle-aged women. *Journal of General Psychology, 135,* 393–407.

Milbank, D. (2016, February 15). The sexist double standards hurting Hillary Clinton. *Santa Cruz Sentinel.* Retrieved from http://www.santacruzsentinel.com/article/NE/20160214/LOCAL1/160219825

Milkie, M. A., Nomaguchi, K. M., & Denny, K. E. (2015). Does the amount of time mothers spend with children or adolescents matter? *Journal of Marriage and Family, 77*(2), 355–372. doi:10.1111/jomf.12170

Milkman, K. L., Akinola, M., & Chugh, D. (2015). What happens before? A field experiment exploring how pay and representation differentially shape bias on the pathway into organizations. *Journal of Applied Psychology, 100*(6), 1678–1712.

Millegan, J., Milburn, E. K., LeardMann, C. A., Street, A. E., Williams, D., Trone, D. W., & Crum-Cianflone, N. F. (2015). Recent sexual trauma and adverse health and occupational outcomes among U.S. service women. *Journal of Traumatic Stress, 28*(4), 298–306.

Miller, A. B., Esposito-Smythers, C., Weismoore, J. T., & Renshaw, K. D. (2013). The relation between child maltreatment and adolescent suicidal behavior: A systematic review and critical examination of the literature. *Clinical Child and Family Psychology Review, 16*(2), 146–172.

Miller, A. J., & Carlson, D. L. (2016). Great expectations? Working- and middle-class cohabitors' expected and actual divisions of housework. *Journal of Marriage and Family, 78*(2), 346–363.

Miller, B. C., Benson, B., & Galbraith, K. A. (2001). Family relationships and adolescent pregnancy risk: A research synthesis. *Developmental Review, 21,* 1–38.

Miller, B. C., Norton, M. C., Curtis, T., Hill, E. J., Schvaneveldt, P., & Young, M. H. (1997). The timing of sexual intercourse among adolescents. *Youth & Society, 29,* 54–83.

Miller, B. D. (2001). Female-selective abortion in Asia: Patterns, policies, and debates. *American Anthropologist, 103,* 1083–1095.

Miller, M. K., & Summers, A. (2007). Gender differences in video game characters' roles, appearances, and attire as portrayed in video game magazines. *Sex Roles, 57,* 733–742.

Milne, M., Divine, A., Hall, C., Gregg, M., & Hardy, J. (2014). Non-participation: How age influences inactive women's views of exercise. *Journal of Applied Biobehavioral Research, 19*(3), 171–191.

Mischel, W. (1966). A social learning view of sex differences in behavior. In E. Maccoby (Ed.), *The development of sex differences* (pp. 56–81). Stanford, CA: Stanford University Press.

Mischel, W. (1970). Sex-typing and socialization. In P. H. Mussen (Ed.), *Carmichael's manual of child psychology* (pp. 3–72). New York: Wiley.

Mitchell, K. J., Ybarra, M. L., & Korchmaros, J. D. (2014). Sexual harassment among adolescents of different sexual orientations and gender identities. *Child Abuse & Neglect, 38*(2), 280–295. doi:10.1037/t29280–000

Mitchell, V., & Bruns, C. M. (2010). Writing one's own story: Women, aging, and the social narrative. *Women & Therapy, 34*(1–2), 114–128.

Mitchell, V., & Helson, R. (1990). Women's prime in life: Is it the 50's? *Psychology of Women Quarterly, 14*, 451–470.

Moayedi, R. (1999). Mentoring a diverse population. In S. Davis, M. Crawford, & J. Sebrechts (Eds.), *Coming into her own: Educational success in girls and women* (pp. 229–243). San Francisco: Jossey-Bass.

Mock, S. E. (2001). Retirement intentions of same-sex couples. *Journal of Gay & Lesbian Social Services, 13*, 81–86.

Moffat, M. (1989). *Coming of age in New Jersey.* New Brunswick, NJ: Rutgers University Press.

Mollen, D. (2014). Reproductive rights and informed consent: Toward a more inclusive discourse. *Analyses of Social Issues and Public Policy, 14*(1), 162–182. doi:10.1111/asap.12027

Moller, L. C., & Serbin, L. A. (1996). Antecedents of toddler gender segregation: Cognitive consonance, gender-typed toy preferences, and behavioral compatibility. *Sex Roles, 35*, 445–460.

Monteith, M. J., & Czopp, A. M. (2003, October). *Confronting prejudice: Making social and personal norms against prejudice salient by meeting prejudice head-on.* Symposium conducted at the conference of the Society of Experimental Social Psychology, Boston.

Montemurro, B. (2014). Getting married, breaking up, and making up for lost time: Relationship transitions as turning points in women's sexuality. *Journal of Contemporary Ethnography, 43*(1), 64–93.

Montemurro, B., & Siefken, J. M. (2014). Cougars on the prowl? New perceptions of older women's sexuality. *Journal of Aging Studies, 28*, 35–43.

Montgomery, H. (2001). *Modern Babylon: Prostituting children in Thailand.* New York: Berghahn.

Monto, M. A., & Carey, A. G. (2014). A new standard of sexual behavior? Are claims associated with the "hookup culture" supported by General Social Survey data? *Journal of Sex Research, 51*(6), 605–615. doi:10.1080/00224499.2014.906031

Moradi, B., Dirks, D., & Matteson, A. V. (2005). Roles of sexual objectification experiences and internalization of standards of beauty in eating disorder symptomatology: A test and extension of objectification theory. *Journal of Counseling Psychology, 52*(3), 420–428.

Moradi, B., & Huang, Y.-P. (2008). Objectification theory and psychology of women: A decade of advances and future directions. *Psychology of Women Quarterly, 32*, 377–398.

Moran, L. (2016). The media are saying and doing a bunch of sexist stuff during the Olympics. *The Huffington Post.* Retrieved from http://www.huffingtonpost.com/entry/rio-2016-sexism-media_us_57a840dbe4b056bad215f03c

Morell, C. (2000). Saying no: Women's experiences with reproductive refusal. *Feminism and Psychology, 10*, 313–322.

Morgan, B. L. (1998). A three generational study of tomboy behavior. *Sex Roles, 39*, 787–800.

Morgan, K. P. (1996). Describing the emperor's new clothes: Three myths of educational (in) equity. In A. Diller, B. Houston, K. P. Morgan, & M. Ayim (Eds.), *The gender questions in education: Theory, pedagogy, and politics* (pp. 105–122). Boulder, CO: Westview.

Morgan, S. W., & Stevens, P. E. (2008). Transgender identity development as represented by a group of femaleto-male transgendered adults. *Issues in Mental Health Nursing, 29*, 585–599.

Morier, D., & Seroy, C. (1994). The effect of interpersonal expectancies on men's self-presentation of gender role attitudes to women. *Sex Roles, 31*, 493–504.

Morison, T., Macleod, C., Lynch, I., Mijas, M., & Shivakumar, S. T. (2016). Stigma resistance in online childfree communities: The limitations of choice rhetoric. *Psychology of Women Quarterly, 40*(2), 184–198. doi:10.1177/0361684315603657

Morris, C. G. (2010). Changes in psychological science: Perspectives from textbook authors. *APS Observer, 23*, 18–24.

Morris, J. (1974). *Conundrum.* New York: Harcourt Brace Jovanovich.

Morris, J. F., Waldo, C. R., & Rothblum, E. D. (2001). A model of predictors and outcomes of outness among lesbian and bisexual women. *American Journal of Orthopsychiatry, 71*, 61–71.

Morris, W. (2016, May 1). Moving on up. *The New York Times Magazine*, 76–79.

Mosca, L., Barrett-Connor, E., & Wenger, N. K. (2011). Sex/gender differences in cardiovascular disease prevention: What a difference a decade makes. *Circulation, 124*(19), 2145–2154. doi:10.1161/CIRCULATIONAHA.110.968792

Moss-Racusin, C., Dovidio, J. F., Brescoll, V. L., Graham, M. J., & Handelsman, J. (2012). Science faculty's subtle gender biases favor male students. *PNAS Proceedings of the National Academy of Sciences of the United States of America, 109*(41), 16474–16479.

Moss-Racusin, C., Molenda, A. K., & Cramer, C. R. (2015). Can evidence impact attitudes? Public reactions to evidence of gender bias in STEM fields. *Psychology of Women Quarterly, 39*(2), 194–209. doi:10.1177/0361684314565777

Moya, M., Glick, P., Expósito, F., De Lemus, S., & Hart, J. (2007). It's for your own good: Benevolent sexism and women's reactions to protectively justified restrictions. *Personality and Social Psychology Bulletin, 33*, 1421–1434.

Mrug, S., Elliott, M. N., Davies, S., Tortolero, S. R., Cuccaro, P., & Schuster, M. A. (2014). Early puberty, negative peer influence, and problem behaviors in adolescent girls. *Pediatrics, 133*(1), 7–14. doi:10.1542/peds.2013–0628

Muehlenkamp, J. J., & Saris-Baglama, R. (2002). Self-objectification and its psychological outcomes for college women. *Psychology of Women Quarterly, 26,* 371–379.

Mulac, A., Jansma, L. L., & Linz, D. G. (2002). Men's behavior toward women after viewing sexually-explicit films: Degradation makes a difference. *Communication Monographs, 69,* 311–329.

Mulongo, P., Martin, C. H., & McAndrew, S. (2014). The psychological impact of female genital mutilation/cutting (FGM/C) on girls/women's mental health: A narrative literature review. *Journal of Reproductive and Infant Psychology, 32*(5), 469–485. doi:10.1080/02646838.2014.949641.

Murdoch, M., Pryor, J. B., Polusny, M., & Gackstetter, G. G. (2007). Functioning and psychiatric symptoms among military men and women exposed to sexual stressors. *Military Medicine, 172,* 718–725.

Murnen, S. K. (2000). Gender and the use of sexually degrading language. *Psychology of Women Quarterly, 24,* 319–327.

Murnen, S. K., Smolak, L., Mills, J. A., & Good, L. (2003). Thin, sexy women and strong, muscular men: Grade-school children's responses to objectified images of women and men. *Sex Roles, 49,* 427–437.

Murphy, A. O., Sutton, R. M., Douglas, K. M., & McClellan, L. M. (2011). Ambivalent sexism and the "do's and "don'ts" of pregnancy: Examining attitudes toward pro-scriptions and the women who flout them. *Personality and Individual Differences, 51*(7), 812–816. doi:10.1016/j.paid.2011.06.031

Murphy, E. M. (2003). Being born female is dangerous for your health. *American Psychologist, 58,* 205–210.

Murphy-Geiss, G. (2011). Married to the minister: The status of the clergy spouse as part of a two-person single career. *Journal of Family Issues, 32*(7), 932–955.

Murray, G., Judd, F., Jackson, H., Fraser, C., Komiti, A., Pattison, P., . . . Robins, G. (2008). Big boys don't cry: An investigation of stoicism and its mental health outcomes. *Personality and Individual Differences, 44*(6), 1369–1381. doi:10.1016/j.paid.2007.12.005

Murray-Johnson, L., Witte, K., Liu, W. Y., Hubbell, A. P., Sampson, J., & Morrison, K. (2001). Addressing cultural orientation in fear appeals: Promoting AIDS-protective behaviors among Mexican immigrant and African American adolescents and American and Taiwanese college students. *Journal of Health Communication, 6,* 335–358.

Murry-McBride, V. (1996). An ecological analysis of coital timing among middle-class African American adolescent females. *Journal of Adolescent Research, 11,* 261–279.

Musaiger, A. O., & Al-Mannai, M. (2014). Association between exposure to media and body weight concern among female university students in five Arab countries: A preliminary cross-cultural study. *Journal of Biosocial Science, 46*(2), 240–247. doi:10.1017/S0021932013000278

Mussap, A. J. (2007). The relationship between feminine gender role stress and disordered eating symptomatology in women. *Stress and Health, 23*(5), 343–348.

Muzzatti, B., & Agnoli, F. (2007). Gender and mathematics: Attitudes and stereotype threat susceptibility in Italian children. *Developmental Psychology, 43*(3), 747–759. doi:10.1037/0012–1649.43.3.747

Mwangi, M. W. (1996). Gender roles portrayed in Kenyan television commercials. *Sex Roles, 34,* 205–214.

Nachmani, I., & Somer, E. (2007). Women sexually victimized in psychotherapy speak out: The dynamics and outcome of therapist-client sex. *Women & Therapy, 30,* 1–17.

Nadal, K. L., Davidoff, K. C., Davis, L. S., Wong, Y., Marshall, D., & McKenzie, V. (2015). A qualitative approach to intersectional microaggressions: Understanding influences of race, ethnicity, gender, sexuality, and religion. *Qualitative Psychology, 2*(2), 147–163. doi:10.1037/qup0000026

Nadal, K. L., Mazzula, S. L., Rivera, D. P., & Fujii-Doe, W. (2014). Microaggressions and Latina/o Americans: An analysis of nativity, gender, and ethnicity. *Journal of Latina/o Psychology, 2*(2), 67–78. doi:10.1037/lat0000013

Nankervis, B. (2013). Gender Inequity in the National Merit Scholarship Program. *Journal of College Admission.* Retrieved from http://files.eric.ed.gov/fulltext/EJ1011761.pdf

Naples, N. A. (1992). Activist mothering: Cross-generational continuity in the community work of women from low-income urban neighborhoods. Special issue: Race, class, and gender. *Gender & Society, 6,* 441–463.

Narayan, C. (2008). Is there a double standard of aging? Older men and women and ageism. *Educational Gerontology, 34,* 782–787.

Nasrullah, M., Haqqi, S., & Cummings, K. J. (2009). Epidemiological patterns of honour killing of women in Pakistan. *European Journal of Public Health, 19,* 193–197.

Nassif, A., & Gunter, B. (2008). Gender representation in television advertisements in Britain and Saudi Arabia. *Sex Roles, 58,* 752–760.

National Center for Health Statistics (NCHS). (2009). *National vital statistics reports: Births final data for 2006. Volume 57, Number 7, January 7, 2009.* Retrieved May 22, 2010, from http://www.cdc.gov/nchs/data/nvsr/nvsr57/nvsr57_07.pdf

National Center for Health Statistics (2012). Anthropometric reference data for children and adults: United States, 2007–2010. Data from the National Health and Nutrition Examination Survey. Retrieved from https://www.cdc.gov/nchs/data/series/sr_11/sr11_252.pdf

National Public Radio. (2016). *Michelle Obama's Speech on Donald Trump's alleged treatment of women.* Retrieved from http://www.npr.org/2016/10/13/497846667/transcript-michelle-obamas-speech-on-donald-trumps-alleged-treatment-of-women

Nelson, A. (2000). The pink dragon is female: Halloween costumes and gender markers. *Psychology of Women Quarterly, 24,* 137–144.

Nelson, A. (2005). Children's toy collections in Sweden—A less gender-typed country? *Sex Roles, 52,* 93–102.

Nelson, E. J. (1996). The American experience of childbirth. In R. L. Parrott & C. M. Condit (Eds.), *Evaluating women's health messages* (pp. 109–123). Thousand Oaks, CA: Sage.

Nelson, J. A., Liss, M., Erchull, M. J., Hurt, M. M., Ramsey, L. R., Turner, D. L., & Haines, M. E. (2008). Identity in action: Predictors of feminist self-identification and collective action. *Sex Roles, 58,* 721–728.

Nelson, M. R., & Paek, H.-J. (2005). Predicting cross-cultural differences in sexual advertising content in a transnational women's magazine. *Sex Roles, 53,* 371–383.

Nelson, M. R., & Paek, H.-J. (2008). Nudity of female and male models in primetime TV advertising across seven countries. *International Journal of Advertising, 27,* 715–744.

Nelson, T. D. (2009). Ageism. In T. D. Nelson (Ed.), *Handbook of prejudice, stereotyping, and discrimination* (pp. 431–440). New York: Taylor & Francis.

Nerøien, A. I., & Schei, B. (2008). Partner violence and health: Results from the first national study on violence against women in Norway. *Scandinavian Journal of Public Health, 36,* 161–168.

Neto, F., & Pinto, I. (1998). Gender stereotypes in Portuguese television advertisements. *Sex Roles, 39,* 153–164.

Nettles, S. M., & Scott-Jones, D. (1987). The role of sexuality and sex equity in the education of minority adolescents. *Peabody Journal of Education, 64,* 183–197.

Neuville, E., & Croizet, J. (2007). Can salience of gender identity impair math performance among 7–8 year old girls? The moderating role of task difficulty. *European Journal of Psychology of Education, 22*(3), 307–316. doi:10.1007/BF03173428

Nevid, J. S. (1984). Sex differences in factors of romantic attraction. *Sex Roles, 11,* 401–411.

New York Times (2002). Press 1 if you're steamed. Retrieved from http://www.nytimes.com/2002/07/07/opinion/press-1-if-you-re-steamed.html

Newman, H. D., & Henderson, A. C. (2014). The modern mystique: Institutional mediation of hegemonic motherhood. *Sociological Inquiry, 84*(3), 472–491. doi:10.1111/soin.12037

Newport, F. (2011). Americans prefer boys to girls, just as they did in 1941. *Gallup.* Retrieved from http://www.gallup.com/poll/148187/americans-prefer-boys-girls-1941.aspx

Newton, N. (1970). The effect of psychological environment on childbirth: Combined cross cultural and experimental approach. *Journal of Cross-Cultural Psychology, 1,* 85–90.

Newton, N., Torges, C., & Stewart, A. (2012). Women's regrets about their lives: Cohort differences in correlates and contents. *Sex Roles, 66*(7–8), 530–543.

Ng, R., Allore, H. G., Monin, J. K., & Levy, B. R. (2016). Retirement as meaningful: Positive retirement stereotypes associated with longevity. *Journal of Social Issues, 72*(1), 69–85. doi:10.1111/josi.12156

Nguyen, H., & Ryan, A. (2008). Does stereotype threat affect test performance of minorities and women? A meta-analysis of experimental evidence. *Journal of Applied Psychology, 93*(6), 1314–1334. doi:10.1037/a0012702

Niedlich, C., & Steffens, M. C. (2015). On the interplay of (positive) stereotypes and prejudice: Impressions of lesbian and gay applicants for leadership positions. *Sensoria: A Journal of Mind, Brain & Culture, 11*(1), 70–80. doi:10.7790/sa.v11i1.408

Niedlich, C., Steffens, M. C., Krause, J., Settke, E., & Ebert, I. D. (2015). Ironic effects of sexual minority group membership: Are lesbians less susceptible to invoking negative female stereotypes than heterosexual women? *Archives of Sexual Behavior, 44*(5), 1439–1447. doi:10.1007/s10508-014-0412-1

Nielsen (2015). *Kids' audience behavior across platforms.* Retrieved from http://www.nielsen.com/us/en/insights/reports/2015/kids-audience-behavior-across-platforms.html

Nieva, V. F., & Gutek, B. A. (1981). *Women and work: A psychological perspective.* New York: Praeger.

NIH Fact Sheet (2015). *Genome-wide association studies.* Retrieved from https://www.genome.gov/20019523/

Nikelly, A. G. (1995). Drug advertisements and the medicalization of unipolar depression in women. *Health Care for Women International, 16,* 229–242.

Nolen-Hoeksema, S. (2012). Emotion regulation and psychopathology: The role of gender. *Annual Review of Clinical Psychology, 8,* 161–187.

Nolen-Hoeksema, S., & Jackson, B. (2001). Mediators of the gender difference in rumination. *Psychology of Women Quarterly, 25,* 37–47.

Nolen-Hoeksema, S., Larson, J., & Grayson, C. (1999). Explaining the gender difference in depressive symptoms. *Journal of Personality and Social Psychology, 77,* 1061–1072.

Nolen-Hoeksema, S., Wisco, B. E., & Lyubomirsky, S. (2009). Rethinking rumination. *Perspectives on Psychological Science, 3,* 400–424.

Noller, P. (2006). Marital relationships. In P. Noller & J. A. Feeney (Eds.), *Close relationships: Functions, forms and processes* (pp. 67–88). Hove England: Psychology Press/Taylor & Francis (UK).

Norcross, J. C. (2002). *Psychotherapy relationships that work: Therapist contributions and responsiveness to patients.* Oxford University Press.

Nordberg, J. (2014). *The underground girls of Kabul: In search of a hidden resistance in Afghanistan.* New York: Broadway.

Norton, K. I., Olds, T. S., Olive, S., & Dank, S. (1996). Ken and Barbie at life size. *Sex Roles, 34,* 287–294.

Oakhill, J., Garnham, A., & Reynolds, D. (2005). Immediate activation of stereotypical gender information. *Memory & Cognition, 33,* 972–983.

Öberg, P. (2003). Images versus experience of the aging body. In C. A. Faircloth (Ed.), *Aging bodies: Images and everyday experiences* (pp. 103–139). New York: AltaMira Press.

Odeku, K., Rembe, S., & Anwo, J. (2009). Female genital mutilation: A human rights perspective. *Journal of psychology in Africa, 19,* 55–62.

Ogas, O., & Gaddam, S. (2011). *A billion wicked thoughts: What the Internet tells us about sexual relationships.* Penguin.

Okimoto, T. G., & Heilman, M. E. (2012). The "bad parent" assumption: How gender stereotypes affect reactions to working mothers. *Journal of Social Issues, 68*(4), 704–724. doi:10.1111/j.1540-4560.2012.01772.x

O'Leary, D., & Sprigg, P. (2015). Understanding and responding to the transgender movement. *Family Research Council.* Retrieved from http://www.frc.org/transgender

Oliver, M. I., Pearson, N., Coe, N., & Gunnell, D. (2005). Help-seeking behaviour in men and women with common mental health problems: Cross-sectional study. *British Journal of Psychiatry, 186*, 297–301.

Olson, L., & Lloyd, S. A. (2005). It depends on what you mean by starting: An exploration of women's initiation of aggression. *Sex Roles, 53*, 603–617.

Opperman, E., Braun, V., Clarke, V., & Rogers, C. (2014). "It feels so good it almost hurts": Young adults' experiences of orgasm and sexual pleasure. *Journal of Sex Research, 51*(5), 503–515. doi:10.1080/00224499.2012.753982

Oransky, M., & Marecek, J. (2002). *Doing boy.* Unpublished manuscript, Swarthmore College.

Orbuch, T. L., & Brown, E. (2006). Divorce in the context of being African American. In M. A. Fine & J. H. Harvey (Eds.), *Handbook of divorce and relationship dissolution* (pp. 481–496). Mahwah, NJ: Erlbaum.

Ortman, J. M., & Velkoff, V. A. (2014). *An aging nation: The older population in the United States.* Retrieved from https://www.census.gov/prod/2014pubs/p25-1140.pdf

O'Shaughnessy, S., & Krogman, N. T. (2012). A revolution reconsidered? Examining the practice of qualitative research in feminist scholarship. *Signs, 37*(2), 493–520. doi:10.1086/66172

O'Sullivan, L. F., Graber, J. A., & Brooks-Gunn, J. (2001). Adolescent gender development. In J. Worell (Ed.). *Encyclopedia of women and gender* (pp. 55–67). San Diego, CA: Academic Press.

Ottati, V., & Lee, Y. (1995). Accuracy: A neglected component of stereotype research. In Y. Lee, L. J. Jussim, & C. R. McCauley (Eds.), *Stereotype accuracy: Toward appreciating group differences* (pp. 29–63). Washington DC: American Psychological Association.

Owen, P. R., & Laurel-Seller, E. (2000). Weight and shape ideals: Thin is dangerously in. *Journal of Applied Social Psychology, 30*, 979–990.

Oyserman, D., Mowbray, C. T., Mears, P. A., & Firminger, K. B. (2000). Parenting among mothers with serious mental illness. *American Journal of Orthopsychiatry, 70*, 296–315.

Palmore, E. (2001). The ageism survey: First findings. *Gerontologist, 41*, 572–575.

Paludi, M. A., & Bauer, W. D. (1983). Goldberg revisited: What's in an author's name? *Sex Roles, 9*, 387–390.

Paludi, M. A., & Strayer, L. A. (1985). What's in an author's name? Differential evaluations of performance as a function of author's name. *Sex Roles, 10*, 353–361.

Papaharitou, S., Nakopoulou, E., Kirana, P., Giaglis, G., Moraitou, M., & Hatzichristou, D. (2008). Factors associated with sexuality in later life: An exploratory study in a group of Greek married older adults. *Archives of Gerontology and Geriatrics, 46*, 191–201.

Papanek, H. (1973). Men, women, and work: Reflections on the two-person career. *American Journal of Sociology, 78*, 852–870.

Papp, L., Cummings, E., & Goeke-Morey, M. (2009). For richer, for poorer: Money as a topic of marital conflict in the home. *Family Relations, 58*, 91–103.

Park, K. (2005). Choosing childlessness: Weber's typology of action and motives of the voluntary childless. *Sociological Inquiry, 75*(3), 372–402.

Parker, M. G., & Yau, M. K. (2012). Sexuality, identity and women with spinal cord injury. *Sexuality and Disability, 30*(1), 15–27. doi:10.1007/s11195-011-9222-8

Parks-Stamm, E., & Grey, C. (2016). Evaluating engagement online: Penalties for low-participating female instructors in gender-balanced academic domains. *Social Psychology, 47*(5), 281–287. doi:10.1027/1864-9335/a000277

Parlee, M. B. (1985). Psychology of women in the 80s: Promising problems. *International Journal of Women's Studies, 8*, 193–204.

Parmley, M., & Cunningham, J. G. (2014). She looks sad, but he looks mad: The effects of age, gender, and ambiguity on emotion perception. *The Journal of Social Psychology, 154*(4), 323–338. doi:10.1080/00224545.2014.901287

Parrot, A., & Bechhofer, L. (Eds.). (1991). *Acquaintance rape: The hidden crime.* New York: Wiley.

Parrot A., & Cummings, N. (2006). *Forsaken females: The Global brutalization of women.* New York: Rowman & Littlefield.

Parrott, S., & Parrott, C. T. (2015). US television's "mean world" for White women: The portrayal of gender and race on fictional crime dramas. *Sex Roles, 73*(1–2), 70–82.

Parsons, T., & Bales, R. F. (1955). *Family, socialization, and interaction process.* Glencoe, IL: Free Press.

Paustian-Underdahl, S., Walker, L. S., & Woehr, D. J. (2014). Gender and perceptions of leadership effectiveness: A meta-analysis of contextual moderators. *Journal of Applied Psychology, 99*(6), 1129–1145.

Pauwels, A. (1998). *Women changing language.* New York: Addison-Wesley Longman.

Payne, D. L., Lonsway, K. A., & Fitzgerald, L. F. (1999). Rape myth acceptance: Exploration of its structure and its measurement using the Illinois rape myth acceptance scale. *Journal of Research in Personality, 33*(1), 27–68.

Pearlman, S. F. (1993). Late mid-life astonishment: Disruptions to identity and self-esteeem. *Women and Therapy, 14*, 1–12.

Pearlstein, T. (2010). Premenstrual dysphoric disorder: Out of the appendix. *Archives of Women's Mental Health, 13*, 21–23.

Pelak, C. F. (2008). The relationship between sexist naming practices and athletic opportunities at colleges and universities in the southern United States. *Sociology of Education, 81*, 189–210.

Peplau, L. A., & Conrad, E. (1989). Beyond nonsexist research: The perils of feminist methods in psychology. *Psychology of Women Quarterly, 13*(4), 379–400. doi:10.1111/j.1471-6402.1989.tb01009.x

Peplau, L. A., & Garnets, P. D. (2000). A new paradigm for understanding women's sexuality and sexual orientation. *Journal of Social Issues, 56*, 329–350.

Peplau, L. A., & Gordon, S. L. (1985). Women and men in love: Gender differences in close heterosexual relationships. In V. E. O'Leary, R. K. Unger, & B. S. Wallston (Eds.), *Women, gender, and social psychology* (pp. 257–292). Hillsdale, NJ: Erlbaum.

Peplau, L. A., & Spalding, L. R. (2000). The close relationships of lesbians, gay men, and bisexuals. In C. Hendrick & S. S. Hendrick (Eds.), *Close relationships: A sourcebook* (pp. 111–124). Thousand Oaks, CA: Sage.

Perry, M. G. (1999). Animated gerontophobia: Ageism, sexism, and the Disney villainess. In S. M. Deats & L. T.

Lender (Eds.), *Aging and identity: A humanities perspective* (pp. 201–212). Westport, CT: Praeger.

Petersen, J. L., & Hyde, J. S. (2009). A longitudinal investigation of peer sexual harassment victimization in adolescence. *Journal of Adolescence, 32,* 1173–1188.

Petersen, J. L., & Hyde, J. S. (2010). A meta-analytic review of research on gender differences in sexuality, 1993–2007. *Psychological Bulletin, 136*(1), 21–38. doi:10.1037/a0017504

Peterson, H. (2015). Fifty shades of freedom: Voluntary childlessness as women's ultimate liberation. *Women's Studies International Forum, 53,* 182–191. doi:10.1016/j.wsif.2014.10.017

Pew Research Center (2010). *Childlessness up among all women; down among women with advanced degrees.* Retrieved from http://www.pewsocialtrends.org/2010/06/25/childlessness-up-among-all-women-down-among-women-with-advanced-degrees/

Pew Research Center (2014). After decades of decline a rise in stay at home mothers. *Pew Social Trends.* Retrieved from http://www.pewsocialtrends.org/2014/04/08/after-decades-of-decline-a-rise-in-stay-at-home-mothers/#fn-18853-1

Phillips, J., & Sweeney, M. (2005). Premarital cohabitation and marital disruption among White, Black, and Mexican American women. *Journal of Marriage and Family, 67,* 296–314.

Phillips, L. (1998). *The girls report: What we know and need to know about growing up female.* New York: National Council for Research on Women.

Phoenix, A., Woollett, A., & Lloyd, E. (Eds.). (1991). *Motherhood: Meanings, practices, and ideologies.* London: Sage.

Pierce, R. L., & Kite, M. E. (1999). Creating expectations in adolescent girls. In S. N. Davis, M. Crawford, & J. Sebrechts (Eds.), *Coming into her own: Educational success in girls and women* (pp. 175–192). San Francisco: Jossey-Bass.

Pilver, C. E., Kasl, S., Desai, R., & Levy, B. R. (2011). Exposure to American culture is associated with premenstrual dysphoric disorder among ethnic minority women. *Journal of Affective Disorders, 130*(1), 334–341.

Pimental, S., Pandjiarjian, V., & Belloque, J. (2006). The "legitimate defence of honour", or murder with impunity? A critical study of legislation and case law in Latin America. In L. Welchman & S. Hossain (Eds.), *"Honour": Crimes, paradigms, and violence against women* (pp. 245–262). New York: Zed Books Ltd.

Pina, A., & Gannon, T. A. (2012). An overview of the literature on antecedents, perceptions and behavioural consequences of sexual harassment. *Journal of Sexual Aggression, 18*(2), 209–232.

Pina, A., Gannon, T. A., & Saunders, B. (2009). An overview of the literature on sexual harassment: Perpetrator, theory, and treatment issues. *Aggression and Violent Behavior, 14,* 126–138.

Piña-Watson, B., Castillo, L. G., Jung, E., Ojeda, L., & Castillo-Reyes, R. (2014). The marianismo beliefs scale: Validation with Mexican American adolescent girls and boys. *Journal of Latina/o Psychology, 2*(2), 113–130. doi:10.1037/lat0000017

Pipher, M. (1994). *Reviving Ophelia: Saving the selves of adolescent girls.* New York: Putnam.

Piran, N. (1999). *The feminist frame scale.* Paper presented at the annual meeting of the American Psychological Association as part of a symposium entitled: Measuring process and outcomes in short- and long-term feminist therapy. J. Worell (Chair), Boston.

Plant, E. A., Baylor, A. L., Doerr, C. E., & Rosenberg-Kima, R. B. (2009). Changing middle-school students' attitudes and performance regarding engineering with computer-based social models. *Computers & Education, 53*(2), 209–215.

Plant, E. A., Hyde, J. S., Keltner, D., & Devine, P. G. (2000). The gender stereotyping of emotions. *Psychology of Women Quarterly, 24,* 81–92.

Poh, H. L., Koh, S. S. L., & He, H. (2014). An integrative review of fathers' experiences during pregnancy and childbirth. *International Nursing Review, 61*(4), 543–554.

Pomerleau, A., Bloduc, D., Malcuit, G., & Cossette, L. (1990). Pink or blue: Environmental gender stereotypes in the first two years of life. *Sex Roles, 22,* 359–367.

Pope, K. (2001). Sex between therapist and client. In J. Worell (Ed.), *Encyclopedia of women and gender* (pp. 955–962). New York: Academic Press.

Pope, K., & Vetter, V. (1991). Prior therapist-patient sexual involvement among patients seen by psychologists. *Psychotherapy, 28,* 429–438.

Pope, M., Corona, R., & Belgrave, F. Z. (2014). Nobody's perfect: A qualitative examination of African American maternal caregivers' and their adolescent girls' perceptions of body image. *Body Image, 11*(3), 307–317. doi:10.1016/j.bodyim.2014.04.005

Potts, M. K., Burnam, M. A., & Wells, K. B. (1991). Gender differences in depression detection: A comparison of clinician diagnosis and standardized assessment. *Psychological Assessment, 3,* 609–615.

Powlishta, K. K., Sen, M. G., Serbin, L. A., Poulin-Dubois, D., & Eichstedt, J. A. (2001). From infancy through middle childhood: The role of cognitive and social factors in becoming gendered. In R. K. Unger (Ed.), *Handbook of the psychology of women and gender* (pp. 116–132). New York: Wiley.

Prairie, B. A., Wisniewski, S. R., Luther, J., Hess, R., Thurston, R. C., Wisner, K. L., & Bromberger, J. T. (2015). Symptoms of depressed mood, disturbed sleep, and sexual problems in midlife women: Cross-sectional data from the study of women's health across the nation. *Journal of Women's Health, 24*(2), 119–126.

Price, S. J., & McKenry, P. C. (1988). *Divorce.* Beverly Hills, CA: Sage.

Prickett, S.N. (2016, Feb. 11). The new power dressing. *The New York Times Style Magazine.* Retrieved from http://www.nytimes.com/2016/02/11/t-magazine/fashion/the-new-dress-code.html

Prieler, M., Kohlbacher, F., Hagiwara, S., & Arima, A. (2011). Gender representation of older people in Japanese television advertisements. *Sex Roles, 64*(5–6), 405–415.

Priess, H. A., Lindberg, S. M., & Hyde, J. S. (2009). Adolescent gender-role identity and mental health: Gender intensification revisited. *Child Development, 80,* 1531–1544.

Prime, J. L., Carter, N., & Welbourne, T. M. (2009). Women "take care," men "take charge": Managers' stereotypic perceptions of women and men leaders. *The Psychologist-Manager Journal, 12,* 25–49.

Propsner, D. (2015, Sept. 2). All-girls STEM camps to keep in mind for next summer. *Huffington Post.* Retrieved from http://www.huffingtonpost.com/diane-propsner/allgirls -stem-camps-to-ke_b_8041664.html

Przybyla, H. M., & Schouten, F. (2017, January 21). At 2.6 million strong, women's marches crush expectations. *USA Today.* Retrieved from http://www.usatoday.com/story /news/politics/2017/01/21/womens-march-aims-start -movement-trump-inauguration/96864158/

Puhl, R. M., Peterson, J. L., DePierre, J. A., & Luedicke, J. (2013). Headless, hungry, and unhealthy: A video content analysis of obese persons portrayed in online news. *Journal of Health Communication, 18*(6), 686–702.

Pullin, Z. (2014). *Two Spirit: The story of a movement unfolds.* Retrieved from http://www.nativepeoples.com /Native-Peoples/May-June-2014/Two-Spirit-The-Story-of- a-Movement-Unfolds/

Puri, J. (1997). Reading romance novels in postcolonial India. *Gender & Society, 11,* 434–452.

Puri, S., Adams, V., Ivey, S., & Nachtigall, R. D. (2011). "There is such a thing as too many daughters, but not too many sons": A qualitative study of son preference and fetal sex selection among Indian immigrants in the United States. *Social Science & Medicine, 72*(7), 1169–1176. doi:10.1016/j.socscimed.2011.01.027

Quek, K., & Knudson-Martin, C. (2006). A push toward equality: Processes among dual-career newlywed couples in collectivist culture. *Journal of Marriage and Family, 68*(1), 56–69.

Quéniart, A., & Charpentier, M. (2012). Older women and their representations of old age: A qualitative analysis. *Ageing & Society, 32*(6), 983–1007.

Quinn, D. M., & Spencer, S. J. (2001). The interference of stereotype threat with women's generation of math problem-solving strategies. *Journal of Social Issues, 57,* 55–72.

Quirouette, C. C., & Pushkar, D. (1999). Views of future aging among middle-aged, university-educated women. *Canadian Journal of Aging, 18,* 236–258.

Raag, T., & Rackliff, C. L. (1998). Preschoolers' awareness of social expectations of gender relationships to toy choices. *Sex Roles, 38,* 685–700.

Rader, J., & Gilbert, L. A. (2005). The egalitarian relationship in feminist therapy. *Psychology of Women Quarterly, 29,* 427–435.

Radway, J. A. (1984). *Reading the romance: Women, patriarchy, and popular literature.* Chapel Hill, NC: University of North Carolina Press.

Raffaelli, M., & Ontai, L. L. (2004). Gender socialization in Latino/a families: Results from two retrospective studies. *Sex Roles, 50,* 287–299.

Ragsdale, J. D. (1996). Gender, satisfaction level and the use of relational maintenance strategies in marriage. *Communication Monographs, 63,* 354–369.

Ralston, P. A. (1997). Midlife and older black women. In J. M. Coyle (Ed.), *Handbook on women and aging* (pp. 273–289). Westport, CT: Greenwood Press.

Ramaswami, A., Dreher, G. F., Bretz, R., & Wiethoff, C. (2010). Gender, mentoring, and career success: The importance of organizational context. *Personnel Psychology, 63*(2), 385–405. doi:10.1111/j.1744-6570.2010.01174.x

Ramirez-Valles, J., Zimmerman, M. A., & Juarez, L. (2002). Gender differences of neighborhood and social control processes: A study of the timing of first intercourse among low-achieving, urban, African American youth. *Youth and Society, 33,* 418–441.

Ramsey, L. R., Haines, M. E., Hurt, M. M., Nelson, J. A., Turner, D. L., Liss, M., & Erchull, M. (2007). Thinking of others: Feminist identification and the perceptions of others' beliefs. *Sex Roles, 56,* 611–616.

Randolph, S. M. (1995). African American children in single-mother families. In B. J. Dickerson (Ed.), *African American single mothers* (pp. 117–145). Thousand Oaks, CA: Sage.

Rashotte, L. S., & Webster, M. (2005). Gender status beliefs. *Social Science Research, 34,* 618–633.

Raymond, J. G. (1993). *Women as wombs: Reproductive technologies and the battle over women's freedom.* New York: HarperCollins.

Re, L., & Birkhoff, J. M. (2015). The 47, XYY syndrome, 50 years of certainties and doubts: A systematic review. *Aggression and Violent Behavior, 22,* 9–17. doi:10.1016/j. avb.2015.02.003

Reagan, B. (2016, October 28). Baylor Regents Found Alleged Sexual Assaults by Football Players 'Horrifying.' *Wall Street Journal.* Retrieved from http://www.wsj.com/ articles/baylor details-horrifying-alleged-sexual- assaults-by-football-players-1477681988

Reame, N. K. (2001). Menstruation. In J. Worell (Ed.). *Encyclopedia of women and gender* (pp. 739–742). San Diego, CA: Academic Press.

Reed, J. (2006). Not crossing the "extra line": How cohabitors with children view their unions. *Journal of Marriage and Family, 68,* 1117–1131.

Reed, M. D. (1994). Pornography addiction and compulsive sexual behavior. In D. Zillmann & J. Bryant (Eds.), *Media, children, and the family: Social scientific, psychodynamic, and clinical perspectives* (pp. 249–269). Hillsdale, NJ: Erlbaum.

Regan, P. C., Medina, R., & Joshi, A. (2001). Partner preferences among homosexual men and women: What is desirable in a sex partner is not necessarily desirable in a romantic partner. *Social Behavior and Personality, 29,* 625–633.

Régner, I., Steele, J. R., Ambady, N., Thinus-Blanc, C., & Huguet, P. (2014). Our future scientists: A review of stereotype threat in girls from early elementary school to middle school. *Revue Internationale de psychologie sociale, 27*(3–4), 13–51.

Reid, A. E., Rosenthal, L., Earnshaw, V. A., Lewis, T. T., Lewis, J. B., Stasko, E. C., . . . Ickovics, J. R. (2016). Discrimination and excessive weight gain during pregnancy among Black and Latina young women. *Social Science & Medicine, 156,* 134–141. doi:10.1016/j.socscimed.2016.03.012

Reid, P. T. (1993). Poor women in psychological research: Shut up and shut out. *Psychology of Women Quarterly, 17,* 133–150.

Reid, P. T. (2011). Revisiting "Poor women: Shut up and shut out." *Psychology of Women Quarterly, 35*(1), 189–192. doi:10.1177/0361684310395917

Reid, P. T., & Kelly, E. (1994). Research on women of color: From ignorance to awareness. *Psychology of Women Quarterly, 18,* 477–486.

Reiger, K., & Dempsey, R. (2006). Performing birth in a culture of fear: An embedded crisis of late modernity. *Health Sociology Review, 15*(4), 364–373.

Reiss, F. (2013). Socioeconomic inequalities and mental health problems in children and adolescents: A systematic review. *Social Science & Medicine, 90,* 24–31. doi:10.1016/j.socscimed.2013.04.026

Reitz, R. R. (1999). Batterers' experiences of being violent: A phenomenological study. *Psychology of Women Quarterly, 23,* 143–166.

Rejeski, W. J., & Thompson, A. (1993). Historical and conceptual roots of exercise psychology. In P. Seraganian (Ed.), *Exercise psychology: The influence of physical exercise on psychological processes* (pp. 3–35). New York: Wiley.

Remer, P., & Rostosky, S. (2001a). Gender role consciousness raising for male clients. *The Feminist Psychologist, Spring,* 29–30.

Remer, P., & Rostosky, S. (2001b). Building feminist therapeutic relationships with male clients. *The Feminist Psychologist, Summer,* 22, 25.

Renaud, M. (2007). We are mothers too: Childbearing experiences of lesbian families. *Journal of Obstetric, Gynecologic, & Neonatal Nursing: Clinical Scholarship for the Care of Women, Childbearing Families, & Newborns, 36*(2), 190–199.

Reyns, B. W., Henson, B., & Fisher, B. S. (2012). Stalking in the twilight zone: Extent of cyberstalking victimization and offending among college students. *Deviant Behavior, 33*(1), 1–25.

Rheingold, H. L., & Cook, K. V. (1975). The contents of boys' and girls' rooms as an index of parents' behavior. *Child Development, 46,* 459–463.

Rhoades, G., Stanley, S., & Markman, H. (2006). Pre-engagement cohabitation and gender asymmetry in marital commitment. *Journal of Family Psychology, 20*(4), 553–560.

Rich, A. (1976). *Of woman born: Motherhood as experience and institution.* New York: Norton.

Richard-Davis, G., & Wellons, M. (2013). Racial and ethnic differences in the physiology and clinical symptoms of menopause. *Seminar in Reproductive Medicine, 31,* 380–386.

Richardson, B. K., & Taylor, J. (2009). Sexual harassment at the intersection of race and gender: A theoretical model of the sexual harassment experiences of women of color. *Western Journal of Communication, 73,* 248–272.

Richman, E. L., & Shaffer, D. R. (2000). "If you let me play sports": How might sports participation influence the self-esteem of adolescent females? *Psychology of Women Quarterly, 24,* 189–199.

Riecher-Rössler, A. (2010). Prospects for the classification of mental disorders in women. *European Psychiatry, 25,* 189–196.

Riggle, E. D. B., Wickham, R. E., Rostosky, S. S., Rothblum, E. D., & Balsam, K. F. (2017). Impact of civil marriage recognition for long-term same-sex couples. *Sexuality Research & Social Policy: A Journal of the NSRC, (In press).* doi:10.1007/s13178-016-0243-z

Ring, T. (2015, April 21). This year's Michigan Womyn's Music Festival will be the last. *The Advocate.* Retrieved from http://www.advocate.com/michfest/2015/04/21/years-michigan-womyns-music-festival-will-be-last

Rintala, D. H., Howland, C. A., Nosek, M. A., Bennett, J. L., Young, M. E., Foley, C. C., . . . Chanpong, G. (1997). Dating issues for women with physical disabilities. *Sexuality and Disability, 15,* 219–242.

Ripa, Y. (1990). *Women and madness: The incarceration of women in nineteenth-century France.* Minneapolis, MN: University of Minnesota Press.

Ripke, S., Wray, N. R., Lewis, C. M., Hamilton, S. P., Weissman, M. M., Breen, G., . . . Heath, A. C. (2013). Major Depressive Disorder Working Group of the Psychiatric GWAS Consortium: A mega-analysis of genome-wide association studies for major depressive disorder. *Molecular Psychiatry, 18*(4), 497–511.

Risman, B. J., & Johnson-Sumerford, D. (1998). Doing it fairly: A study of postgender marriages. *Journal of Marriage and the Family, 60,* 23–40.

Ristori, J., & Steensma, T. D. (2016). Gender dysphoria in childhood. *International Review of Psychiatry, 28*(1), 13–20. doi:10.3109/09540261.2015.1115754

Rivadeneyra, R. (2011). Gender and race portrayals on Spanish-language television. *Sex Roles, 65*(3–4), 208–222. doi:10.1007/s11199-011-0010-9

Roberts, A. R. (1996). Police responses to battered women: Past, present, and future. In A. R. Roberts (Ed.), *Helping battered women* (pp. 85–95). New York: Oxford University Press.

Roberts, D. E. (1998). The future of reproductive choice for poor women and women of color. In R. Weitz (Ed.), *The politics of women's bodies: Sexuality, appearance, and behavior* (pp. 270–277). New York: Oxford University Press.

Roberts, T-A. (2016). Objectification theory model of eating disorders. *Encyclopedia of Feeding and Eating Disorders,* pp. 1–3. doi:10.1007/978-981-287-087-2_34–1

Roberts, T. A., Goldenberg, J. L., Power, C., & Pyszczysnski, T. (2002). "Feminine protection": The effects of menstruation on attitudes toward women. *Psychology of Women Quarterly, 26,* 131–139.

Robinson, D. A., & Worell, J. (2002). Issues in clinical assessment with women. In J. Butcher (Ed.), *Clinical personality assessment: Practical approaches* (2nd ed., pp. 190–207). New York: Oxford University Press.

Robnett, R. D., & Anderson, K. J. (2017). Feminist identity among women and men from four ethnic groups. *Cultural Diversity and Ethnic Minority Psychology, 23*(1), 134–142. doi:10.1037/cdp0000095

Robnett, R. D., & Leaper, C. (2013). "Girls don't propose! ew.": A mixed-methods examination of marriage tradition preferences and benevolent sexism in emerging adults. *Journal of Adolescent Research, 28*(1), 96–121. doi:10.1177/0743558412447871

Rogers, K. (2016). Sure, these women are winning Olympic medals, but are they single? *The New York Times.* Retrieved from http://www.nytimes.com/2016/08/19/sports/olympics/sexism-olympics-women.html?_r=0

Rohner, R. P., & Veneziano, R. A. (2001). The importance of father love: History and contemporary evidence. *Review of General Psychology, 5,* 382–405.

Rojas-García, A., Ruíz-Pérez, I., Gonçalves, D. C., Rodríguez-Barranco, M., & Ricci-Cabello, I. (2014). Healthcare interventions for perinatal depression in socially disadvantaged women: A systematic review and meta-analysis. *Clinical Psychology: Science and Practice, 21*(4), 363–384.

Rosario, M., Meyer-Bahlburg, H. F. L., Hunter, J., & Exner, T. M. (1996). The psychosexual development of urban lesbian, gay, and bisexual youths. *The Journal of Sex Research, 33,* 113–126.

Roscoe, W. (1996). How to become a berdache: Toward a unified analysis of gender diversity. In G. Herdt (Ed.), *Third sex, third gender: Beyond sexual dimorphism in culture and history* (pp. 329–372). New York: Zone Books.

Rose, J. G., Chrisler, J. C., & Couture, S. (2008). Young women's attitudes toward continuous use of oral contraceptives: The effect of priming position attitudes toward menstruation on women's willingness to suppress menstruation. *Health Care for Women International, 29,* 688–701.

Rose, S., & Frieze, I. H. (1989). Young singles' scripts for a first date. *Gender & Society, 3,* 258–268.

Rose, S. M., & Hospital, M. M. (2015). Lesbians over 60: Newer every day. In V. Muhlbauer, J. C. Chrisler, & F. L. Denmark (Eds.), *Women and Aging: An International, Intersectional Power Perspective* (pp. 117–146). Switzerland: Springer International.

Rosenberg, R. (1982). *Beyond separate spheres: Intellectual roots of modern feminism.* New Haven, CT: Yale University Press.

Rosenbluth, S. C., Steil, J. M., & Whitcomb, J. H. (1998). Marital equality: What does it mean? *Journal of Family Issues, 19,* 227–244.

Rosenfield, S. (2000). Gender and dimensions of the self: Implications for internalizing and externalizing behavior. In E. Frank (Ed.), *Gender and its effects on psychopathology* (pp, 23–36). Washington, DC: American Psychiatric Publishing, Inc.

Rosenthal, R., & Jacobson, L. (1968). *Pygmalion in the classroom.* New York: Holt, Rinehart, and Winston.

Rosenthal, L., & Lobel, M. (2016). Stereotypes of Black American women related to sexuality and motherhood. *Psychology of Women Quarterly, 40*(3), 414–427. doi:10.1177/0361684315627459

Rosenthal, L., (2016). Incorporating intersectionality into psychology: An opportunity to promote social justice and equity. *American Psychologist, 71*(6), 474–485. doi:10.1037/a0040323

Rosenthal, M. N., Smidt, A. M., & Freyd, J. J. (2016). Still second class: Sexual harassment of graduate students. *Psychology of Women Quarterly, 40*(3), 364–377. doi:10.1177/0361684316644838

Rothblum, E. D. (2000). Sexual orientation and sex in women's lives: Conceptual and methodological issues. *Journal of Social Issues, 56,* 193–204.

Rouselle, R. (2001). "If it is a girl, cast it out": Infanticide/exposure in ancient Greece. *Journal of Psychohistory, 28,* 303–333.

Rousso, H. (1988). Daughters with disabilities: Defective women or minority women? In M. Fine & A. Asch (Eds.), *Women with disabilities: Essays in psychology, culture, and politics* (pp. 139–171). Philadelphia: Temple University Press.

Roy, A. (1998). Images of domesticity and motherhood in Indian television commercials: A critical study. *Journal of Popular Culture, 32,* 117–134.

Ruble, D. N., Fleming, A. S., Hackel, L. S., & Stangor, C. (1988). Changes in the marital relationship during the transition to first time motherhood: Effects of violated expectations concerning division of household labor. *Journal of Personality and Social Psychology, 85,* 78–87.

Rudman, L. A., & Borgida, E. (1995). The afterglow of construct accessibility: The behavioral consequences of priming men to view women as sexual objects. *Journal of Experimental Social Psychology, 31,* 493–517.

Rudman, L. A., & Glick, P. (1999). Feminized management and backlash against agentic women: The hidden costs to women of a kinder, gentler image of middle managers. *Journal of Personality and Social Psychology, 77,* 1004–1010.

Rudman, L. A., & Glick, P. (2008). *The social psychology of gender: How power and intimacy shape gender relations.* New York: Guilford.

Ruscher, J. B. (2001). *Prejudiced communication: A social psychological perspective.* New York: Guilford.

Ruscher, J. B., & Duval, L. L. (1998). Multiple communicators with unique target information transmit less stereotypical impressions. *Journal of Personality and Social Psychology, 74,* 329–344.

Russell, D. (1995). *Women, madness, & medicine.* Cambridge, UK: Polity Press.

Russell, D. E. H. (1993). *Against pornography: The evidence of harm.* Berkeley, CA: Russell Publications.

Russett, C. E. (1989). *Sexual science: The Victorian construction of womanhood.* Cambridge, MA: Harvard University Press.

Russo, N. F. (1979). Overview: Sex roles, fertility, and the motherhood mandate. *Psychology of Women Quarterly, 4,* 7–15.

Russo, N. F. (2008). Understanding emotional responses after abortion. In J. C. Chrisler, C. Golden, & P. D. Rozee (Eds.), *Lectures on the psychology of women* (4th ed., pp. 172–189). New York: McGraw-Hill.

Russo, N. F., & Dumont, B. A. (1997). A history of division 35 (psychology of women): Origins, issues, activities, future. In D. A. Dewsbury (Ed.), *Unification through division: Histories of the divisions of the american psychological association* (Vol. 2) Washington, DC: American Psychological Association.

Rust, P. C. (2000). Bisexuality: A contemporary paradox for women. *Journal of Social Issues, 56,* 205–222.

Rutherford, A. (2011). From the ground up: Feminist approaches, methods, and critiques. *Psychology of Women Quarterly, 35*(1), 175–179. doi:10.1177/0361684310395912

Rutherford, A., Marecek, J., & Sheese, K. (2012). Psychology of women and gender. In D. K. Freedheim & I. B. Weiner (Eds.), *Handbook of psychology, Volume 1: History of Psychology,* (2nd ed., pp. 279–301). New York: Wiley.

Rutherford, A., & Yoder, J. D. (2011). Thirty-five years and counting: Feminist psychology in PWQ, a job for the long haul. *Psychology of Women Quarterly, 35*(1), 171–174. doi:10.1177/0361684310395915

Ryan, C., Huebner, D., Diaz, R.M., & Sanchez, J. (2009). Family rejection as a predictor of negative health outcomes in White and Latino lesbian, gay, and bisexual young adults. *Pediatrics, 123,* 346–352. Retrieved May 10, 2010, from http://pediatrics.aappublications.org/cgi/content/full/123/1/346

Rydell, R., McConnell, A., & Beilock, S. (2009). Multiple social identities and stereotype threat: Imbalance, accessibility, and working memory. *Journal of Personality and Social Psychology, 96*(5), 949–966. doi:10.1037/a0014846

Sadker, M., & Sadker, D. (1994). *Failing at fairness: How America's schools cheat girls.* New York: Scribner.

Safdar, S., Friedlmeier, W., Matsumoto, D., Yoo, S., Kwantes, C., Kakai, H., & Shigemasu, E. (2009). Variations of emotional display rules within and across cultures: A comparison between Canada, USA, and Japan. *Canadian Journal of Behavioural Science/Revue canadienne des sciences du comportement, 41*(1), 1–10. doi:10.1037/a0014387

Sakraida, T. (2005). Divorce transition differences of midlife women. *Issues in Mental Health Nursing, 26,* 225–249.

Salmon, P. (2001). Effects of physical exercise on anxiety, depression, and sensitivity to stress: A unifying theory. *Clinical Psychology Review, 21,* 33–61.

Sampselle, C. M., Harris, V., Harlow, S. D., & Sowers, M. (2002). Midlife development and menopause in African American and Caucasian women. *Health Care for Women International, 23,* 351–363.

Samuel, D. B., & Widiger, T. A. (2009). Comparative gender biases in models of personality disorder. *Personality and Mental Health 3,* 12–25.

Sanchez, F., & Vilain, E. (2009). Collective self-esteem as a coping resource for male-to-female transsexuals. *Journal of Counseling Psychology, 56,* 202–209.

Sanchez, L., & Thomson, E. (1997). Becoming mothers and fathers: Parenthood, gender, and the division of labor. *Gender & Society, 11,* 747–772.

Sanchez-Hucles, J. V., & Davis, D. D. (2010). Women and women of color in leadership: Complexity, identity, and intersectionality. *American Psychologist, 65,* 171–181.

Sanchez-Hucles, J. (2016). Womanist therapy with Black women. In T. Bryant-Davis & L. Comas-Díaz (Eds.). *Womanist and mujerista psychologies: Voices of fire, acts of courage* (pp. 69–92). Washington, DC: American Psychological Association.

Sanday, P. (1981). *Female power and male dominance: On the origins of sexual inequality.* Cambridge: Cambridge University Press.

Sanders, A. R., Martin, E. R., Beecham, G. W., Guo, S., Dawood, K., Rieger, G., . . . Bailey, J. M. (2015). Genome-wide scan demonstrates significant linkage for male sexual orientation. *Psychological Medicine, 45*(7), 1379–1388. doi:10.1017/S0033291714002451

Sassler, S., Miller, A., & Favinger, S. (2009). Planned parenthood? Fertility intentions and experiences among cohabiting couples. *Journal of Family Issues, 30,* 206–232.

Sassler, S., & Miller, A. J. (2011). Waiting to be asked: Gender, power, and relationship progression among cohabiting couples. *Journal of Family Issues, 32*(4), 482–506.

Sayer, L. C. (2006). Economic aspects of divorce and relationship dissolution. In M. A. Fine & J. H. Harvey (Eds.), *Handbook of divorce and relationship dissolution* (pp. 385–406). Mahwah, NJ: Erlbaum.

Scarborough, E., & Furumoto, L. (1987). *Untold lives: The first generation of American women psychologists.* New York: Columbia University Press.

Schein, A. J. & Haruni, N. (2015). Older women, economic power, and consumerism. In V. Muhlbauer, J. C. Chrisler, & F. L. Denmark (Eds.), *Women and Aging: An International, Intersectional Power Perspective* (pp. 31–49). Switzerland: Springer International.

Scheuble, L. K., & Johnson, D. R. (2005). Married women's situational use of last names: An empirical study. *Sex Roles, 53,* 143–151.

Schick, V. R., Zucker, A. N., & Bay-Cheng, L. Y. (2008). Safer, better sex through feminism: The role of feminist ideology in women's sexual well-being. *Psychology of Women Quarterly, 32,* 225–232.

Schmader, T., Johns, M., & Forbes, C. (2008). An integrated process model of stereotype threat effects on performance. *Psychological Review, 115*(2), 336–356. doi:10.1037/0033-295X.115.2.336

Schmalz, D. L., Deane, G. D., Birch, L. L., & Davison, K. K. (2007). A longitudinal assessment of the links between physical activity and self-esteem in early adolescent non-Hispanic females. *Journal of Adolescent Health, 41*(6), 559–565.

Schultz, M. R. (1975). The semantic derogation of women. In B. Thorne & N. Henley (Eds.), *Language and sex: Difference and dominance* (pp. 64–73). Rowley, MA: Newbury House.

Schwartz, P. (1994). *Peer marriage.* New York: Free Press.

Scott, B. A. (2008). Women and pornography: What we don't know can hurt us. In J. Chrisler, C. Golden, & P. D. Rozee (Eds.), *Lectures on the psychology of women* (4th ed., pp. 339–355). New York: McGraw-Hill.

Scott, J. P. (1997). Family relationships of midlife and older women. In J. M. Coyle (Ed.), *Handbook on women and aging* (pp. 367–384). Westport, CT: Greenwood Press.

Seal, D. W., Smith, M., Coley, B., Perry, J., & Gamez, M. (2008). Urban heterosexual couples' sexual scripts for three shared sexual experiences. *Sex Roles, 58,* 626–638.

Sears, D. O. (1986). College sophomores in the laboratory: Influences of a narrow data base on social psychology's view of human nature. *Journal of Personality and Social Psychology, 51,* 515–530.

Sebastian, C., & Mortensen, A. (2017, February 7). "Putin signs law reducing punishment for domestic battery." *CNN.* Cable News Network. http://www.cnn.com/2017/02/07/europe/russia-domestic-violence-bill-putin/

Sedgh, G., Finer, L. B., Bankole, A., Eilers, M. A., & Singh, S. (2015). Adolescent pregnancy, birth, and abortion rates across countries: Levels and recent trends. *Journal of Adolescent Health, 56*(2), 223–230.

Seepersad, S., Choi, M., & Shin, N. (2008). How does culture influence the degree of romantic loneliness and closeness? *The Journal of Psychology, 142,* 209–216.

Seidah, A., & Bouffard, T. (2007). Being proud of oneself as a person or being proud of one's physical appearance:

What matters for feeling well in adolescence? *Social Behavior and Personality, 35,* 255–268.

Sendén, M. G., Bäck, E. A., & Lindqvist, A. (2015). Introducing a gender-neutral pronoun in a natural gender language: The influence of time on attitudes and behavior. *Frontiers in Psychology, 6*(12).

Senn, C. Y., Eliasziw, M., Barata, P. C., Thurston, W. E., Newby-Clark, I. R., Radtke, H. L., & Hobden, K. L. (2015). Efficacy of a sexual assault resistance program for university women. *New England Journal of Medicine, 372*(24), 2326–2335.

Seto, M. C., Maric, A., & Barbaree, H. E. (2001). The role of pornography in the etiology of sexual aggression. *Aggression and Violence Behavior, 6,* 35–53.

Sevón, E. (2012). 'My life has changed, but his life hasn't': Making sense of the gendering of parenthood during the transition to motherhood. *Feminism & Psychology, 22*(1), 60–80.

Shafer, K., & Jensen, T. M. (2013). Remarital chances, choices, and economic consequences: Issues of social and personal welfare. *Journal of Sociology and Social Welfare, 40*(2), 77–101.

Shaffer, E. S., Marx, D. M., & Prislin, R. (2013). Mind the gap: Framing of women's success and representation in STEM affects women's math performance under threat. *Sex Roles, 68*(7–8), 454–463. doi:10.1007/s11199-012-0252-1

Shapiro, A. F., Gottman, J. M., & Carrere, S. (2000). The baby and the marriage: Identifying factors that buffer against decline in marital satisfaction after the first baby arrives. *Journal of Family Psychology, 14,* 59–70.

Sharma, D. C. (2014). Changing landscape for sexual minorities in India. *The Lancet, 383*(9936), 2199–2200.

Shepard, M. F., Falk, D. R., & Elliott, B. A. (2002). Enhancing coordinated community responses to reduce recidivism in cases of domestic violence. *Journal of Interpersonal Violence, 17,* 551–569.

Sherif, C. W. (1979). Bias in psychology. In J. A. Sherman & E. T. Beck (Eds.), *The prisms of sex: Essays in the sociology of knowledge* (pp. 93–133). Madison: University of Wisconsin Press.

Sherif, C. W. (1983). Carolyn Wood Sherif (autobiography). In A. O'Connell & N. F. Russo (Eds.), *Models of achievement* (pp. 279–293). New York: Columbia University Press.

Sherman, J. A., & Fennema, E. (1978). Distribution of spatial visualization and mathematical problem solving scores: A test of Stafford's X-linked hypothesis. *Psychology of Women Quarterly, 3,* 157–167.

Sherman, A. M., & Zurbriggen, E. L. (2014). "Boys can be anything": Effect of Barbie play on girls' career cognitions. *Sex Roles, 70*(5–6), 195–208. doi:10.1007/s11199-014-0347-y

Shields, S. A. (1975). Functionalism, Darwinism, and the psychology of women: A study in social myth. *American Psychologist, 30,* 739–754.

Shields, S. A. (1982). The variability hypothesis: The history of a biological model of sex difference in intelligence. *Signs, 7,* 769–797.

Shields, S. A., (2002). *Speaking from the heart: Gender and the social meaning of emotion.* Cambridge, MA: Cambridge University Press.

Shifrer, D., Pearson, J., Muller, C., & Wilkinson, L. (2015). College-going benefits of high school sports participation: Race and gender differences over three decades. *Youth & Society, 47*(3), 295–318. doi:10.1177/0044118X12461656

Shih, M., Pittinsky, T. L., & Ambady, N. (1999). Stereotype susceptibility: Identity salience and shifts in quantitative performance. *Psychological Science, 10,* 80–83.

Shisana, O., & Simbayi, L. (2002). *Nelson Mandela/HSRC study of HIV/AIDS: South African national HIV prevalence, behavioral risks and mass media, household survey 2002.* Cape Town, South Africa: Human Sciences Research Council.

Short, L. (2007). Lesbian mothers living well in the context of heterosexism and discrimination: Resources, strategies, and legislative change. *Feminism & Psychology, 17*(1), 57–74.

Showalter, E. (1986). *The female malady: Women, madness, and English culture, 1830–1980.* New York: Pantheon Books.

Shumaker, S. A. (2004). Conjugated equine estrogens and incidence of probable dementia and mild cognitive impairment in postmenopausal women: Women's health initiative memory study. *Journal of the American Medical Association, 291,* 2947–2958.

Shute, R., Owens, L., & Slee, P. (2008). Everyday victimization of adolescent girls by boys: Sexual harassment, bullying, or aggression? *Sex Roles, 58,* 477–489.

Sibley, C. G., Overall, N. C., Duckitt, J., Perry, R., Milfont, T. L., Khan, S. S., . . . Robertson, A. (2009). Your sexism predicts my sexism: Perceptions of men's (but not women's) sexism affects one's own sexism over time. *Sex Roles, 60*(9–10), 682–693. doi:10.1007/s11199-008-9554-8

Sibley, C. G., & Overall, N. C. (2011). A dual process motivational model of ambivalent sexism and gender differences in romantic partner preferences. *Psychology of Women Quarterly, 35*(2), 303–317. doi:10.1177/036168431 1401838

Sidanius, J., & Pratto, F. (1999). *Social dominance: An intergroup theory of social hierarchy and oppression.* New York: Cambridge University Press.

Sieg, E. (2000). "So tell me what you want, what you really want . . .": New women on old footings? *Feminism & Psychology, 10,* 498–503.

Sierminska, E. (2016). Occupational segregation. In N. Naples (Ed.), *The Wiley Blackwell encyclopedia of gender and sexuality studies.* 1–3. Malden, MA: John Wiley & Sons, Ltd. doi:10.1002/9781118663219.wbegss207

Signorella, M. L., & Frieze, I. R. (2008). Interrelations of gender schemas in children and adolescents: Attitudes, preferences, and self-perceptions. *Social Behavior and Personality, 36,* 941–954.

Silveira, J. (1980). Generic masculine words and thinking. In C. Kramarae (Ed.), *The voices and words of women and men* (pp. 165–178). Oxford, England: Pergamon.

Silverman, J. G., Raj, A., Mucci, L. A., & Hathaway, J. E. (2001). Dating violence against adolescent girls and associated substance use, unhealthy weight control, sexual risk behavior, pregnancy, and suicidality. *Journal of the American Medical Association, 286,* 572–579.

Silverstein, L. B. (1996). Fathering is a feminist issue. *Psychology of Women Quarterly, 20,* 3–37.

Silverstein, L. B. (2002). Fathers and families. In J. P. McHale & W. S. Grolnick (Eds.), *Retrospect and prospect in the psychological study of families* (pp. 35–64). Mahwah, NJ: Erlbaum.

Silverstein, L. B., & Auerbach, C. F. (1999). Deconstructing the essential father. *American Psychologist, 54,* 397–407.

Simpson, G. (1996). Factors influencing the choice of law as a career by black women. *Journal of Career Development, 22,* 197–209.

Simon, C. C. (2015, Oct. 28). The test-optional surge. *The New York Times.* Retrieved from http://www.nytimes.com/2015/11/01/education/edlife/the-test-optional-surge.html

Sims, T., Reed, A. E., & Carr, D. C. (2016). Information and communication technology use is related to higher well-being among the oldest-old. *Journals of Gerontology: Psychological Science (online first).* doi:10.1093/geronb/gbw130

Sinclair, A. H., Berta, P., Palmer, M. S., Hawkins, J. R., Griffiths, B. L., Smith, M. J., . . . Goodfellow, P. N. (1990). A gene from the human sex-determining region encodes a protein with homology to a conserved DNA binding motif. *Nature, 346,* 240–244.

Sinno, S. M., & Killen, M. (2011). Social reasoning about 'second-shift' parenting. *British Journal of Developmental Psychology, 29*(2), 313–329.

Skinner, S. R., Smith, J., Fenwick, J., Fyfe, S., & Hendrik, J. (2008). Perceptions and experiences of first sexual intercourse in Australian adolescent females. *Journal of Adolescent Health, 43*(6), 593–599. doi:10.1016/j.jadohealth.2008.04.017

Skodol, A. E., & Bender, D. S. (2003). Why are women diagnosed borderline more than men? *Psychiatric Quarterly, 74,* 349–360.

Slater, A., & Tiggemann, M. (2012). Time since menarche and sport participation as predictors of self-objectification: A longitudinal study of adolescent girls. *Sex Roles, 67*(9–10), 571–581. doi:10.1007/s11199-012-0200-0

Slater, A., Tiggemann, M., Firth, B., & Hawkins, K. (2012). Reality check: An experimental investigation of the addition of warning labels to fashion magazine images on women's mood and body dissatisfaction. *Journal of Social and Clinical Psychology, 31*(2), 105–122. doi:10.1037/t00880-000

Smith, E. A. (1989). A biosocial model of adolescent sexual behavior. In G. R. Adams, R. Montemayor, & T. P. Gullotta (Eds.), *Advances in adolescent development* (pp. 143–167). Newbury Park, CA: Sage.

Smith, J. (1991). Conceiving selves: A case study of changing identities during the transition to motherhood. *Journal of Language and Social Psychology, 10,* 225–243.

Smith, J. S., LaFrance, M., Knol, K. H., Tellinghuisen, D. J., & Moes, P. (2015). Surprising smiles and unanticipated frowns: How emotion and status influence gender categorization. *Journal of Nonverbal Behavior, 39*(2), 115–130. doi:10.1007/s10919-014-0202-4

Smith, J. L. & Huntoon, M. (2014). Women's bragging rights: Overcoming modesty norms to facilitate women's self-promotion. *Psychology of Women Quarterly, 38*(4), 447-459.

Smith, M. (1997). Psychology's undervaluation of single motherhood. *Feminism & Psychology, 7,* 529–532.

Smith, P. H., Smith, J. B., & Earp, J. A. (1999). Beyond the measurement trap: A reconstructed conceptualization and measurement of woman battering. *Psychology of Women Quarterly, 23,* 177–193.

Smith, T., Berg, C., Florsheim, P., Uchino, B., Pearce, G., Hawkins, M., et al. (2009). Conflict and collaboration in middle-aged and older couples: I. Age differences in agency and communion during marital interaction. *Psychology and Aging, 24,* 259–273.

Smolak, L., & Striegel-Moore, R. (2001). Body image concerns. In J. Worell (Ed.), *Encyclopedia of sex and gender* (pp. 201–210). New York: Academic Press.

Snapp, S. Ryu, E., & Kerr, J. (2015). The upside to hooking up: College students' positive hookup experiences. *International Journal of Sexual Health, 27*(1), 43–56. doi:10.1080/19317611.2014.939247

Snyder, M., & Klein, O. (2005). Construing and constructing others: On the reality and the generality of the behavioral confirmation scenario. *Interaction Studies: Social Behaviour and Communication in Biological and Artificial Systems, 6,* 53–67.

Snyder, M., Tanke, E. D., & Berscheid, E. (1977). Social perception and interpersonal behavior: On the self-fulfilling nature of social stereotypes. *Journal of Personality and Social Psychology, 35,* 656–666.

Solberg, K. E. (2009). Killed in the name of honour. *The Lancet, 373,* 1933–1934.

Sojo, V.E., Wood, R.E., & Genat, A.E. (2016). Harmful workplace experiences and women's occupational well-being: A meta-analysis. *Psychology of Women Quarterly, 40*(1), 10–40.

Solinger, R. (2005). *Pregnancy and power: A short history of reproductive politics in America.* New York: NYU Press.

Solomon, M. B., & Herman, J. P. (2009). Sex differences in psychopathology: Of gonads, adrenals and mental illness. *Physiology & Behavior, 97,* 250–258.

Somer, E., & Nachmani, I. (2005). Constructions of therapist-client sex: A comparative analysis of retrospective victim reports. *Sexual Abuse: Journal of Research and Treatment, 17,* 47–62.

Somer, E., & Saadon, M. (1999). Therapist-client sex: Clients' retrospective reports. *Professional Psychology: Research and Practice, 30,* 504–509.

Sommer, B., Avis, N., Meyer, P., Ory, M., Madden, T., Kagawa-Singer, M., et al. (1999). Attitudes toward menopause and aging across ethnic/racial groups. *Psychosomatic Medicine, 61,* 868–875.

Sommers, E. K., & Check, J. V. (1987). An empirical investigation of the role of pornography in the verbal and physical abuse of women. *Violence and Victims, 2,* 189–209.

Spence, J. T., & Buckner, C. E. (2000). Instrumental and expressive traits, trait stereotypes, and sexist attitudes. *Psychology of Women Quarterly, 24,* 44–62.

Spencer, S. J., Steele, C. M., & Quinn, D. M. (1999). Stereotype threat and women's math performance. *Journal of Experimental Social Psychology, 35,* 4–28.

Spitzberg, B. H., & Cupach, W. R. (2007). The state of the art of stalking: Taking stock of the emerging literature. *Aggression and Violent Behavior, 12*(1), 64–86.

Spitzberg, B. H., & Cupach, W. R. (2014). *The dark side of relationship pursuit: From attraction to obsession and stalking*. New York: Routledge.

Spitzberg, B. H., Cupach, W. R., & Ciceraro, L. D. (2010). Sex differences in stalking and obsessive relational intrusion: Two meta-analyses. *Partner Abuse, 1*(3), 259–285.

Spitzer, B. L., Henderson, K. A., & Zivian, M. T. (1999). Gender differences in population versus media body sizes: A comparison over four decades. *Sex Roles, 40,* 545–565.

Sprecher, S., Barbee, A., & Schwartz, P. (1995). "Was it good for you, too?": Gender differences in first sexual intercourse experiences. *The Journal of Sex Research, 32,* 3–15.

Sprecher, S., & Regan, P. C. (2000). Sexuality in relational context. In C. Hendrick & S. S. Hendrick (Eds.), *Close relationships: A sourcebook* (pp. 217–228). Thousand Oaks, CA: Sage Publications, Inc.

Sprock, J., Blashfield, R. K., & Smith, B. (1990). Gender weighting of *DSM-III-R* personality disorder criteria. *American Journal of Psychiatry, 147,* 586–590.

Sprock, J., & Yoder, C. Y. (1997). Women and depression: An update on the report of the APA task force. *Sex Roles, 36,* 269–303.

Staglin, D. (2017, January 27). "Russia Parliament votes 380-3 to decriminalize domestic violence." *USA Today.* https://www.usatoday.com/story/news/2017/01/27/russian-parliament-decrimiinalizes-domestic-violence/97129912/

Stamm, M., & Buddeberg-Fischer, B. (2011). The impact of mentoring during postgraduate training on doctors' career success. *Medical Education, 45*(5), 488–496.

Stanik, C. E., & Bryant, C. M. (2012). Marital quality of newlywed African American couples: Implications of egalitarian gender role dynamics. *Sex Roles, 66*(3–4), 256–267.

Stangor, C. (1995). Content and application inaccuracy in social stereotyping. In Y. Lee, L. J. Jussim, & C. R. McCauley (Eds.), *Stereotype accuracy: Toward appreciating group differences* (pp. 275–293). Washington, DC: American Psychological Association.

Starr, C. R. & Ferguson, G. M. (2012). Sexy dolls, sexy grade-schoolers? Media & maternal influences on young girls' self-sexualization. *Sex Roles, 67*(7–8), 463–476. doi:10.1007/s11199-012-0183-x

Starr, C. R., & Zurbriggen, E. L. (2014, October). Pouty Princesses and Skeletons in Fishnets: A Content Analysis of Sexualization and Stereotypes in Children's Fashion Dolls. Poster presented at Gender Development Conference, San Francisco, California.

Starr, C. R., & Zurbriggen, E. L. (2016). Sandra Bem's gender schema theory after 34 years: A review of its reach and impact. *Sex Roles (Online First)*, doi:10.1007/s11199-016-0591-4

Stavrova, O., Fetchenhauer, D., & Schlösser, T. (2012). Cohabitation, gender, and happiness: A cross-cultural study in thirty countries. *Journal of Cross-Cultural Psychology, 43*(7), 1063–1081.

Steele, J., James, J. B., & Barnett, R. C. (2002). Learning in a man's world: Examining the perceptions of undergraduate women in male-dominated academic areas. *Psychology of Women Quarterly, 26,* 46–50.

Steiger, J. (1981). The influence of the feminist subculture in changing sex-role attitudes. *Sex Roles, 7,* 627–634.

Steil, J. M. (1997). *Marital equality: Its relationship to the well-being of husbands and wives.* Thousand Oaks, CA: Sage.

Steil, J. M. (2001). Family forms and member well-being: A research agenda for the decade of behavior. *Psychology of Women Quarterly, 25,* 344–363.

Steil, J. M., & Hoffman, L. (2006). Gender conflict and the family. In M. Deutsch, P. Coleman, & E. Marcus, (Eds.), *Handbook of conflict resolution: Theory and practice* (2nd ed., pp. 223–241). San Francisco: Jossey-Bass.

Steil, J. M., McGann, V. L., & Kahn, A. S. (2001). Entitlement. In J. Worell (Ed.), *Encyclopedia of women and gender* (pp. 403–410). San Diego, CA: Academic Press.

Steil, J. M., & Turetsky, B. A. (1987). Is equal better? The relationship between marital equality and psychological symptomatology. In S. Oskamp (Ed.), *Family processes and problems: Social psychological aspects* (pp. 73–97). Beverly Hills, CA: Sage.

Steil, J. M., & Weltman, K. (1991). Marital inequality: The importance of resources, personal attributes, and social norms on career valuing and the allocation of domestic responsibilities. *Sex Roles, 24,* 161–179.

Stein, M. B., & Kennedy, C. (2001). Major depressive and post-traumatic stress disorder comorbidity in female victims of intimate partner violence. *Journal of Affective Disorders, 66,* 133–138.

Steinem, G. (1980). Erotica and pornography: A clear and present difference. In L. Lederer (Ed.), *Take back the night* (pp. 35–39). New York: William Morrow.

Steinem, G. (1983). *Outrageous acts and everyday rebellions.* New York: New American Library.

Stevens, D., Kiger, G., & Riley, P. J. (2001). Working hard and hardly working: Domestic labor and marital satisfaction among dual-earner couples. *Journal of Marriage and Family, 63,* 514–526.

Stewart, A. J., Copeland, A. P., Chester, N. L., Malley, J. E., & Barenbaum, N. B. (1997). *Separating together: How divorce transforms families.* New York: Guilford.

Stice, E., & Whitenton, K. (2002). Risk factors for body dissatisfaction in adolescent girls: A longitudinal investigation. *Developmental Psychology, 38,* 669–678.

Stinson, R. D., Levy, L. B., & Alt, M. (2014). "They're just a good time and move on": Fraternity men reflect on their hookup experiences. *Journal of College Student Psychotherapy, 28*(1), 59–73. doi:10.1080/87568225.2014.854683

Stone, L., & McKee, N. P. (2000). Gendered futures: Student visions of career and family on a college campus. *Anthropology and Education Quarterly, 31,* 67–89.

Stout, J. G., & Dasgupta, N. (2011). When he doesn't mean you: Gender-exclusive language as ostracism. *Personality and Social Psychology Bulletin, 37*(6), 757–769. doi:10.1177/0146167211406434

Strassberg, D. S., McKinnon, R. K., Sustaíta, M. A., & Rullo, J. (2013). Sexting by high school students: An exploratory and descriptive study. *Archives of Sexual Behavior, 42*(1), 15–21.

Straus, M. A. (1999). The controversy over domestic violence by women: A methodological, theoretical, and sociology of science analysis. In X. B. Arriaga & S. Oskamp (Eds.), *Violence in intimate relationships* (pp. 12–44). Thousand Oaks, CA: Sage.

Striegel-Moore, R. H., Goldman, S. L., Garvin, V., & Rodin, J. (1996). Within-subjects design: Pregnancy changes both body and mind. In F. E. Donelson (Ed.), *Women's experiences: A psychological perspective* (pp. 430–437). Mountain View, CA: Mayfield.

Stroebe, M., Stroebe, W., & Schut, H. (2001). Gender differences in adjustment to bereavement: An empirical and theoretical review. *Review of General Psychology, 5,* 62–83.

Strober, M., Freeman, R., Lampert, C., & Diamond, J. (2007). The association of anxiety disorders and obsessive compulsive personality disorder with anorexia nervosa: Evidence from a family study with discussion of nosological and neurodevelopmental implications. *International Journal of Eating Disorders, 40* (Suppl), S46–S51.

Sugar, J. A. (2007). Work and retirement: Challenges and opportunities for women over 50. In V. Muhlbauer & J. C. Chrisler (Eds.), *Women over 50: Psychological perspectives* (pp. 164–181). New York: Springer.

Sugarman, D. B., & Hotaling, G. T. (1989). Dating violence: Prevalence, context, and risk markers. In M. A. Pirog-Good & J. E. Stets (Eds.), *Violence in dating relationships* (pp. 3–32). New York: Praeger.

Sullivan, T. P., Meese, K. J., & Swan, S. C. (2005). Precursors and correlates of women's violence: Child abuse, traumatization, victimization of women, avoidance coping, and psychological symptoms. *Psychology of Women Quarterly, 29,* 290–301.

Sun, C., Bridges, A., Wosnitzer, R., Scharrer, E., & Liberman, R. (2008). A comparison of male and female directors in popular pornography: What happens when women are at the helm?. *Psychology of Women Quarterly, 32*(3), 312–325. doi:10.1111/j.1471-6402.2008.00439.x.

Sung, C. C. M. (2012). Exploring the interplay of gender, discourse, and (im)politeness. *Journal of Gender Studies, 21*(3), 285–300. doi:10.1080/09589236.2012.681179

Sung, M. R., Szymanski, D. M., & Henrichs-Beck, C. (2015). Challenges, coping, and benefits of being an Asian American lesbian or bisexual woman. *Psychology of Sexual Orientation and Gender Diversity, 2*(1), 52–64. doi:10.1037/sgd0000085

Sutfin, E. L., Fulcher, M., Bowles, R., & Patterson, C. J. (2008). How lesbian and heterosexual parents convey attitudes about gender to their children: The role of gendered environments. *Sex Roles, 58,* 501–513.

Sutton, R. M., Douglas, K. M., & McClellan, L. M. (2011). Benevolent sexism, perceived health risks, and the inclination to restrict pregnant women's freedoms. *Sex Roles, 65*(7–8), 596–605.

Suyemoto, K. L., & Donovan, R. A. (2015). Exploring intersections of privilege and oppression for Black and Asian immigrant and US born women: Reaching across the imposed divide. In O. M. Espin & A. L. Dottolo A. L. (Eds.), *Gendered Journeys: Women, Migration, and Feminist Psychology,* (54–77). UK: Palgrave Macmillan.

Suzuki, M. F. (1995). Women and television: Portrayal of women in the mass media. In K. Fujimura-Fanselow & A. Kameda (Eds.), *Japanese women: New feminist perspectives on the past, present and future* (pp. 75–90). New York: Feminist Press.

Swim, J. K., Hyers, L. L., Cohen, L. L., & Ferguson, M. J. (2001). Everyday sexism: Evidence for its incidence, nature and psychological impact from three daily diary studies. *Journal of Social Issues, 57,* 31–54.

Swim, J. K., Johnston K., & Pearson, N. (2009). Daily experiences with heterosexism: Relations between hetersexist hassles and psychological well-being. *Journal of Social and Clinical Psychology, 28,* 597–629.

Swinbourne, J. M., & Touyz, S. W. (2007). The co-morbidity of eating disorders and anxiety disorders: A review. *European Eating Disorders Review, 15,* 253–274.

Szasz, T. (1970). *The manufacture of madness: A comparative study of the inquisition and the mental health movement.* New York: Harper & Row.

Szasz, T. (Ed.). (1973). *The age of madness: The history of involuntary mental hospitalization, presented in selected texts.* Garden City, NY: Anchor Books.

Szymanski, D. M. & Feltman, C. E. (2015). Linking sexually objectifying work environments among waitresses to psychological and job-related outcomes. *Psychology of Women Quarterly, 39*(3), 390–404.

Talbot, M. (2016a, December 5). Taking trolls to court. *The New Yorker.* Retrieved from http://www.newyorker.com/magazine/2016/12/05/the-attorney-fighting-revenge-porn

Talbot, M. (2016b, October 24). That's what he said: 2016's Manifest Misogyny. *The New Yorker.* Retrieved from http://www.newyorker.com/magazine/2016/10/24/2016s-manifest-misogyny

Tanaka, K., & Johnson, N. E. (2016). Childlessness and mental well-being in a global context. *Journal of Family Issues, 37*(8), 1027–1045. doi:10.1177/0192513X14526393

Tang, S., & Zuo, J. (2000). Dating attitudes and behaviors of American and Chinese students. *Social Science Journal, 37,* 67–78.

Tangri, S., & Hayes, S. (1997). Theories of sexual harassment. In W. O'Donohue (Ed.), *Sexual harassment: Theory, research, and treatment* (pp. 112–128). Boston: Allyn & Bacon.

Taşdemir, N., & Sakallı-Uğurlu, N. (2010). The relationships between ambivalent sexism and religiosity among Turkish university students. *Sex Roles, 62*(7–8), 420–426. doi:10.1007/s11199-009-9693-6

Tashiro, T., Frazier, P., & Berman, M. (2006). Stress-related growth following divorce and relationship dissolution. M. A. Fine & J. H. Harvey (Eds.), *Handbook of divorce and relationship dissolution* (pp. 361–384). Mahwah, NJ: Lawrence Erlbaum Associates.

Tasker, F. (2005). Lesbian mothers, gay fathers, and their children: A review. *Journal of Developmental & Behavioral Pediatrics, 26*(3), 224–240.

Tasker, F. L., & Golombok, S. (1997). *Growing up in a lesbian family.* New York: Guilford.

Tate, C. C. (2012). Considering lesbian identity from a social–psychological perspective: Two different models of "being a lesbian." *Journal of Lesbian Studies, 16*(1), 17–29. doi:10.1080/10894160.2011.557639

Tate, C. C., & Pearson, M. D. (2016). Toward an inclusive model of lesbian identity development: Outlining a common and nuanced model for cis and trans women. *Journal of Lesbian Studies, 20*(1), 97–115.

Tavris, C. (1992). *The mismeasure of woman: Why women are not the better sex, the inferior sex, or the opposite sex.* New York: Simon & Schuster.

Taylor, J. (2007). Transgender identities and public policy in the United States: The relevance for public administration. *Administration & Society, 39,* 833.

Taylor, J., Gilligan, C., & Sullivan, A. (1995). *Between voice and silence: Women and girls, race and relationship.* Cambridge, MA: Harvard University Press.

Teachman, J., Tedrow, L., & Hall, M. (2006). The demographic future of divorce and dissolution. In M. A. Fine & J. H. Harvey (Eds.), *Handbook of divorce and relationship dissolution* (pp. 59–82). Mahwah, NJ: Lawrence Erlbaum Associates.

Teitelbaum, P. (1989). Feminist theory and standardized testing. In A. M. Jaggar & S. Bordo (Eds.), *Gender/body/knowledge* (pp. 324–335). New Brunswick, NJ: Rutgers University Press.

Tenenbaum, H. R., & Leaper, C. (2002). Are parents' gender schema related to their children's gender-related cognitions? A meta-analysis. *Developmental Psychology, 38,* 615–630.

The Economist Newspaper Limited. (2015, October 24). Plastic surgery in Iran: Under the knife. *The Economist.* Retrieved from http://www.economist.com/news/middle-east-and-africa/21676799-why-one-particular-operation-so-popular-under-knife

Thibault, J. W., & Kelley, H. H. (1959). *The social psychology of groups.* New York: Wiley.

Thomas, A. J., Hacker, J. D., & Hoxha, D. (2011). Gendered racial identity of black young women. *Sex Roles, 64*(7–8), 530–542. doi:10.1007/s11199-011-9939-y

Thomeer, M. B., Reczek, C., & Umberson, D. (2015). Gendered emotion work around physical health problems in mid- and later-life marriages. *Journal of Aging Studies, 32,* 12–22. doi:10.1016/j.jaging.2014.12.001

Thorne, B. (1993). *Gender play: Girls and boys in school.* New Brunswick, NJ: Rutgers University Press.

Thorne, B., & Luria, Z. (1986). Sexuality and gender in children's daily worlds. *Social Problems, 33,* 176–190.

Thurer, S. L. (1983). Deinstitutionalization and women: Where the buck stops. *Hospital and Community Psychiatry, 34,* 1162–1163.

Tiedemann, J. (2000). Parents' gender stereotypes and teachers' beliefs as predictors of children's concept of their mathematical ability in elementary school. *Journal of Educational Psychology, 92,* 144–151.

Tiedens, L. Z., Ellsworth, P. C., & Mesquita, B. (2000). Stereotypes about sentiments and status: Expectations about high- and low-status group members. *Personality & Social Psychology Bulletin, 26,* 560–574.

Tiefer, L. (1989, August). Feminist transformations of sexology. In M. Crawford (Chair), *Feminist psychological science: Frameworks, strengths, visions, and a few examples.* Symposium conducted at the meeting of the American Psychological Association, New Orleans, LA.

Tiefer, L. (1995). *Sex is not a natural act & other essays.* San Francisco: Westview.

Tiggemann, M., & Kuring, J. K. (2004). The role of body objectification in disordered eating and depressed mood. *British Journal of Clinical Psychology, 43,* 299–311.

Tiggemann, M., & Williams, E. (2012). The role of self-objectification in disordered eating, depressed mood, and sexual functioning among women: A comprehensive test of objectification theory. *Psychology of Women Quarterly, 36*(1), 66–75. doi:10.1177/0361684311420250

Tiggemann, M., & Slater, A. (2014). Contemporary girlhood: Maternal reports on sexualized behaviour and appearance concern in 4–10 year-old girls. *Body Image, 11*(4), 396–403. doi:10.1016/j.bodyim.2014.06.007

Tiggemann, M., & Slater, A. (2015). The role of self-objectification in the mental health of early adolescent girls: Predictors and consequences. *Journal of Pediatric Psychology, 40*(7), 704–711. doi:10.1093/jpepsy/jsv021

Tiggemann, M., Slater, A., Bury, B., Hawkins, K., & Firth, B. (2013). Disclaimer labels on fashion magazine advertisements: Effects on social comparison and body dissatisfaction. *Body Image, 10*(1), 45–53. doi:10.1016/j.bodyim.2012.08.001

Tighe, C. A. (2001). "Working at disability": A qualitative study of the meaning of health and disability for women with physical impairments. *Disability and Society, 16,* 511–529.

Timmerman, G. (2003). Sexual harassment of adolescents perpetrated by teachers and by peers: An exploration of the dynamics of power, culture, and gender in secondary schools. *Sex Roles, 48,* 231–244.

Tine, M., & Gotlieb, R. (2013). Gender-, race-, and income-based stereotype threat: The effects of multiple stigmatized aspects of identity on math performance and working memory function. *Social Psychology of Education, 16*(3), 353–376. doi:10.1007/s11218-013-9224-8

Tolman, D. L., & Brown, L. M. (2001). Adolescent girls' voices: Resonating resistance in body and soul. In R. K. Unger (Ed.), *Handbook of the psychology of women and gender* (pp. 133–155). New York: Wiley.

Trahan, D. P., Jr., & Goodrich, K. M. (2015). "You think you know me, but you have no idea": Dynamics in African American families following a son's or daughter's disclosure as LGBT. *The Family Journal, 23*(2), 147–157. doi:10.1177/1066480715573423

Traies, J. (2015). Old lesbians in the UK: Community and friendship. *Journal of Lesbian Studies, 19*(1), 35–49.

Travis, C. B. (2005). 2004 Carolyn Sherif award address: Heart disease and gender inequity. *Psychology of Women Quarterly, 29,* 15–23.

Travis, C. B., & Compton, J. D. (2001). Feminism and health in the decade of behavior. *Psychology of Women Quarterly, 25,* 312–323.

Treadway, C. R., Kane, F. J., Jarrahi-Zadeh, A., & Lipton, M. A. (1969). A psycho-endocrine study of pregnancy and puerperium. *American Journal of Psychiatry, 125,* 1380–1386.

Trinh, S. L., Ward, L. M., Day, K., Thomas, K., & Levin, D. (2014). Contributions of divergent peer and parent sexual messages to Asian American college students' sexual behaviors. *Journal of Sex Research, 51*(2), 208–220. doi:10.1080/00224499.2012.721099

Tsui, L. (1998). The effects of gender, education, and personal skills self-confidence on income in business management. *Sex Roles, 38*, 363–373.

Turk, J. L., & Bell, N. W. (1972). Measuring power in families. *Journal of Marriage and the Family, 34*, 215–223.

Turner, C. S. V., González, J. C., & Wong (Lau), K. (2011). Faculty women of color: The critical nexus of race and gender. *Journal of Diversity in Higher Education, 4*(4), 199–211.

Tylka, T. L., & Hill, M. S. (2004). Objectification theory as it relates to disordered eating among college women. *Sex Roles, 51*, 719–730.

Udry, J. R., Talbert, L., & Morris, N. M. (1986). Biosocial foundations for adolescent female sexuality. *Demography, 23*, 217–230.

Ulrich, M., & Weatherall, A. (2000). Motherhood and infertility: Viewing motherhood through the lens of infertility. *Feminism and Psychology, 10*, 323–336.

UNESCO. (2016). *50th Anniversary of international literacy day: Literacy rates are on the rise but millions remain illiterate.* Retrieved from http://www.uis.unesco.org/literacy/Documents/fs38-literacy-en.pdf

Unger, R. K. (1979). Toward a redefinition of sex and gender. *American Psychologist, 34*, 1085–1094.

UNIFEM. (2007). *Violence against women–facts and figures.* Retrieved May 10, 2010, from http://www.unifem.org/attachments/gender_issues/violence_against_women/

United Nations. (2000). *World marriage patterns.* Retrieved from http://www.un.org/esa/population/publications/worldmarriage/worldmarriagepatterns2000.pdf

United Nations. (2010). *The world's women 2010: Trends and statistics.* Retrieved from http://unstats.un.org/unsd/demographic/products/Worldswomen/wwwork2010.htm

United Nations. (2015). The World's Women 2015: Trends and Statistics. New York: United Nations, Department of Economic and Social Affairs, Statistics Division. Retrieved from http://unstats.un.org/unsd/gender/downloads/WorldsWomen2015_report.pdf

United Nations Children's Fund. (2000, May). Domestic violence against women and girls. *Innocenti Digest* (No. 6). Florence, Italy: Innocenti Research Centre.

United Nations Development Program (2014). *Global status report on violence prevention 2014.* Geneva: World Health Organization. Retrieved from http://www.undp.org/content/dam/undp/library/corporate/Reports/UNDP-GVA-violence-2014.pdf

United Nations Division for the Advancement of Women. (2001). *Women 2000: Widowhood: Invisible women, secluded, or excluded.* Retrieved from http://www.un.org/womenwatch/daw/public/wom_Dec%2001%20single%20pg.pdf

United Nations Population Fund (UNFPA). (2000). *The state of the world population.* Retrieved from http://www.unfpa.org/swp/2000/english/

UN News. (2016. March 22). *UN welcomes ICC's first conviction for rape as war crime.* Retrieved from http://www.un.org/apps/news/story.asp?NewsID=53523#.WJn7wza7odU

UN Women. (2013, June 23). *International Widows' Day: Message from Lakshmi Puri, Acting Head of UN Women.* Retrieved from http://www.unwomen.org/en/news/stories/2013/6/statement-by-lakshmi-puri-for-international-widows-day-2013#sthash.HdWj84TS.dpuf

UN Women. (2016). *Facts and figures: Economic empowerment.* Retrieved from http://www.unwomen.org/en/what-we-do/economic-empowerment/facts-and-figures

Unson, C., Flynn, D., Haymes, E., Sancho, D., & Glendon, M. A. (2016). Predictors of types of caregiver burden. *Social Work in Mental Health, 14*(1), 82–101.

U.S. Bureau of Labor Statistics. (2015, December). *Women in the labor force: A databook.* Retrieved from https://www.bls.gov/opub/reports/womens-databook/archive/women-in-the-labor-force-a-databook-2015.pdf

U.S. Census Bureau. (2010). *American community survey.* Retrieved from http://www.census.gov/acs/www/

U.S. Census Bureau. (2011). *Net worth and asset ownership of households.* Retrieved from https://www.census.gov/people/wealth/

U.S. Census Bureau. (2014). *National population projections.* Retrieved from https://www.census.gov/population/projections/data/national/np-d1.html.

U.S. Department of Justice, Department of Health and Human Services, Connolly, M.T., Brandl, B., & Breckman, R. (2014). *The elder justice roadmap: A stakeholder initiative to respond to an emerging health, justice, financial and social crisis.* Retrieved from https://www.justice.gov/elderjustice/file/829266/download

U.S. Department of Defense. (2009). *Annual report on sexual harassment and violence at U.S. Military service academies: Academic program year 2008–2009.* Retrieved May 10, 2010, from http://www.sapr.mil/media/pdf/reports/2009_msa_report.pdf

U.S. Department of State. (2016). *Trafficking in persons report 2014.* Washington, DC: U.S. Government Printing Office. https://www.state.gov/j/tip/rls/tiprpt/2016/

U.S. General Accountability Office. (2002). *Prescription drugs: FDA oversight of direct-to-consumer advertising has limitations.* Retrieved May, 2004, from http://www.gao.gov/new.items/d03177.pdf

U.S. General Accountability Office. (2008). *Prescription drugs: Trends in FDA's oversight of direct-to-consumer advertising.* Retrieved June, 2010, from http://www.gao.gov/new.items/d08758t.pdf

U.S. Merit Systems Protection Board. (1981). *Sexual harassment in the federal workplace: Is it a problem?* Washington, DC: Office of Merit Systems Review and Studies/Government Printing Office.

U.S. Merit Systems Protection Board. (1987). *Sexual harassment in the federal workplace: An update.* Washington, DC: Office of Merit Systems Review and Studies/Government Printing Office.

U.S. Merit Systems Protection Board. (1995). *Sexual harassment in the federal workplace: Trends, progress, continuing challenges.* Washington, DC: U.S. Government Printing Office.

U.S. v. Commonwealth of Virginia, U.S. 1941 (1994).

Ussher, J. (1992). *Women's madness: Misogyny or mental illness?* Amherst, MA: University of Massachusetts Press.

Ussher, J. M. (1989). *The psychology of the female body.* London: Routledge.

Ussher, J., Perz, J., & Parton, C. (2015). Sex and the menopausal woman: A critical review and analysis. *Feminism & Psychology, 25*(4), 449–468.

Valentine, J. C., Blankenship, V., Cooper, H., & Sullins, E. S. (2001). Interpersonal expectancy effects and the preference for consistency. *Representative Research in Social Psychology, 25,* 26–33.

Valenza, A. (2015). Equality marriage survey: Support for same-sex marriage above all in countries which already have it. *International Lesbian, Gay, Bisexual, Trans and Intersex Association.* Retrieved from http://ilga.org/immediate-release-equality-marriage-survey-support-sex-marriage-countries-already

Valian, V. (1998). *Why so slow? The advancement of women.* Cambridge, MA: MIT Press.

Valiente, C., & Rasmusson, X. (2015). Bucking the stereotypes: My little pony and challenges to traditional gender roles. *Journal of Psychological Issues in Organizational Culture, 5*(4), 88–97. doi:10.1002/jpoc.21162

Vallois, T. (1998). La Salpêtrière. *Paris Kiosque, 5.* Retreived December, 2003, from www.paris.org/Kiosque/

van de Bongardt, D., Reitz, E., Sandfort, T., & Deković, M. (2015). A meta-analysis of the relations between three types of peer norms and adolescent sexual behavior. *Personality and Social Psychology Review, 19*(3), 203–234.

van der Pol, L. D., Groeneveld, M. G., van Berkel, S. R., Endendijk, J. J., Hallers-Haalboom, E., Bakermans-Kranenburg, M., & Mesman, J. (2015). Fathers' and mothers' emotion talk with their girls and boys from toddlerhood to preschool age. *Emotion, 15*(6), 854–864. doi:10.1037/emo0000085

Vanassche, S., Swicegood, G., & Matthijs, K. (2013). Marriage and children as a key to happiness? Cross-national differences in the effects of marital status and children on well-being. *Journal of Happiness Studies, 14*(2), 501–524.

Vance, C. S. (1984). Pleasure and danger: Toward a politics of sexuality. In C. S. Vance (Ed.), *Pleasure and danger: Exploring female sexuality* (pp. 1–27). Boston: Routledge and Kegan Paul.

Vance, E. B., & Wagner, N. N. (1976). Written descriptions of orgasm: A study of sex differences. *Archives of Sexual Behavior, 5,* 87–98.

Vandello, J. A., & Cohen, D. (2006). Male honor and female fidelity: Implicit cultural scripts that perpetuate cultural violence. *Journal of Personality and Social Psychology, 84,* 997–1010.

Vandenbosch, L., Driemans, K., Trekels, J., & Eggermont, S. (2016). Sexualized video game avatars and self-objectification in adolescents: The role of gender congruency and activation frequency. *Media Psychology (Online First).* doi: 10.1080/15213269.2016.1142380

Vandenbosch, L., & Eggermont, S. (2012). Understanding sexual objectification: A comprehensive approach toward media exposure and girls' internalization of beauty ideals, self-objectification and body surveillance. *Journal of Communication, 62,* 69–887.doi:10.1111/j.1460-2466.2012.01667.x

Vasey, P., & Bartlett, N. (2007). What can the Samoan "Fa'afafine" teach us about the western concept of gender identity disorder in childhood? *Perspectives in Biology and Medicine, 50,* 481–490.

Vasey, P., & VanderLaan, D. (2009). Materteral and avuncular tendencies in Samoa: A comparative study of women, men, and fa'afafine. *Humam Nature, 20,* 269–281.

Vasilenko, S. A., Kugler, K. C., & Rice, C. E. (2016). Timing of first sexual intercourse and young adult health outcomes. *Journal of Adolescent Health, 59*(3), 291–297. doi:10.1016/j.jadohealth.2016.04.019

Vasquez, M. J. T. (1994). Latinas. In L. Comas-Díaz & B. Greene (Eds.), *Women of color: Integrating ethnic and gender identities in psychotherapy* (pp. 114–138). New York: Guilford Press.

Vasquez, M. J., & Vasquez, E. (2017). Psychotherapy with women: Theory and practice of feminist therapy. In A. J. Xonsoli, L. E. Beutler, & B. Bongar (Eds.), *Comprehensive Textbook of Psychotherapy: Theory and Practice* (pp. 299–314). New York: Oxford University Press.

Vatican angers many with "grave crimes" list. (2010). Retrieved July 17, 2010, from http://www.aolnews.com/world/article/vatican-puts-ordaining-women-priests-on-par-with-child-sex-abuse/19556837

Vauclair, C., Hanke, K., Huang, L., & Abrams, D. (2016). Are Asian cultures really less ageist than western ones? It depends on the questions asked. *International Journal of Psychology.* doi:10.1002/ijop.12292

Vaughan, E. B., Van Hulle, C. A., Beasley, W. H., Rodgers, J. L., & D'Onofrio, B. M. (2015). Clarifying the associations between age at menarche and adolescent emotional and behavioral problems. *Journal of Youth and Adolescence, 44*(4), 922–939. doi:10.1007/s10964-015-0255-7

Vencill, J. A., Tebbe, E. A., & Garos, S. (2015). It's not the size of the boat or the motion of the ocean: The role of self-objectification, appearance anxiety, and depression in female sexual functioning. *Psychology of Women Quarterly, 39*(4), 471–483. doi:10.1177/0361684315587703

Venkatesh, K. K., Phipps, M. G., Triche, E. W., & Zlotnick, C. (2014). The relationship between parental stress and postpartum depression among adolescent mothers enrolled in a randomized controlled prevention trial. *Maternal and Child Health Journal, 18*(6), 1532–1539.

Veroff, J., Wilcox, S., & Atkinson, J. W. (1953). The achievement motive in high school and college age women. *Journal of Abnormal and Social Psychology, 43,* 108–119.

Versey, H. S., Stewart, A. J., & Duncan, L. E. (2013). Successful aging in late midlife: The role of personality among college-educated women. *Journal of Adult Development, 20*(2), 63–75.

Vespa, J. (2014). Historical trends in the marital intentions of one-time and serial cohabitors. *Journal of Marriage and Family, 76*(1), 207–217.

Vespa J., Lewis, J. M., & Kreider, R. M. (2013). America's families and living arrangements: 2012. *U. S. Department of Commerce.* Retrieved from https://www.census.gov/prod/2013pubs/p20-570.pdf

Vierthaler, K. (2008). Best practices for working with rape crisis centers to address elder sexual abuse. *Journal of Elder Abuse & Neglect, 20,* 306–322.

Vigorito, A. J., & Curry, T. J. (1998). Marketing masculinity: Gender identity and popular magazines. *Sex Roles, 38,* 135–152.

Vilain, E. (2006). Genetics of intersexuality. *Journal of Gay & Lesbian Psychotherapy, 10,* 9–26.

Vobejda, B. (1994, June 16). Abortion rate slowing in U.S., study concludes. *The Washington Post,* p. A13.

von Baeyer, C. L., Sherk, D. L., & Zanna, M. P. (1981). Impression management in the job interview: When the female applicant meets the male (chauvinist) interviewer. *Personality and Social Psychology Bulletin, 7,* 45–51.

von Hippel, W., Sekaquaptewa, D., & Vargas, P. (1995). On the role of encoding processes in stereotype maintenance. In M. P. Zanna (Ed.), *Advances in experimental social psychology* (Vol. 27, pp. 177–254). New York: Academic Press.

von Pfetten, V. (2010). Sultry Katie Couric dishes on dating a younger man. Retrieved February 2, 2011, from http://tv.yahoo.com/blog/sultry-katie-couric-dishes-on-dating-a-younger-man--969

Wadsworth, T. (2016). Marriage and subjective well-being: How and why context matters. *Social Indicators Research, 126*(3), 1025–1048.

Waite, L. J., & Joyner, K. (2001). Emotional satisfaction and physical pleasure in sexual unions: Time horizon, sexual behavior, and sexual exclusivity. *Journal of Marriage and the Family, 63,* 247–264.

Wajcman, J. (1998). *Managing like a man: Women and men in corporate management.* Cambridge, England: Polity Press.

Wakabayashi, C., & Donato, K. M. (2006). Does caregiving increase poverty among women in later life? Evidence from the health and retirement survey. *Journal of Health and Social Behavior, 47,* 258–274.

Walker, E. C., Holman, T. B., & Busby, D. M. (2009). Childhood sexual abuse, other childhood factors, and pathways to survivor's adult relationship quality. *Journal of Family Violence, 24*(6), 397–407.

Walker, J. J. & Longmire-Avital, B. (2012). The impact of religious faith and internalized homonegativity on resiliency for Black lesbian, gay, and bisexual emerging adults. *Developmental Psychology, 49*(9) 1723–1731. doi:10.1037/a0031059

Walker, L. E. A. (2000). *The battered woman syndrome* (2nd ed.). New York: Springer.

Walker, L., Timmerman, G. M., Kim, M., & Sterling, B. (2002). Relationships between body image and depressive symptoms during postpartum in ethnically diverse, low income women. *Women and Health, 36,* 101–121.

Walker, N. A. (Ed.). (1998). *Women's magazines 1940–1960: Gender roles and the popular press.* Boston: Bedford/St. Martin's.

Wallace, J. E. (2001). The benefits of mentoring for female lawyers. *Journal of Vocational Behavior, 58,* 366–391.

Wallston, B. S., & Grady, K. E. (1985). Integrating the feminist critique and the crisis in social psychology: Another look at research methods. In V. E. O'Leary, R. K. Unger, & B. S. Wallston (Eds.), *Women, gender and social psychology* (pp. 7–34). Hillsdale, NJ: Erlbaum.

Walsh, J. L., Ward, L. M., Caruthers, A., & Merriwether, A. (2011). Awkward or amazing: Gender and age trends in first intercourse experiences. *Psychology of Women Quarterly, 35*(1), 59–71. doi:10.1177/0361684310387781

Walter, J. L., & LaFreniere, P. J. (2000). A naturalistic study of affective expression, gender competence, and sociometric status in preschoolers. *Early Education & Development, 1,* 109–122.

Walzer, A. S., & Czopp, A. M. (2011). Mother knows best so mother fails most: Benevolent stereotypes and the punishment of parenting mistakes. *Current Research in Social Psychology, 16*(9).

Walzer, S. (1998). *Thinking about the baby.* Philadelphia: Temple University Press.

Wandrey, R. L., Mosack, K. E., & Moore, E. M. (2015). Coming out to family and friends as bisexually identified young adult women: A discussion of homophobia, biphobia, and heteronormativity. *Journal of Bisexuality, 15*(2), 204–229. doi:10.1080/15299716.2015.1018657

Want, S. C. (2009). Meta-analytic moderators of experimental exposure to media portrayals of women on female appearance satisfaction: Social comparisons as automatic processes. *Body Image, 6,* 257–269.

Ward, L. M., Seabrook, R. C., Manago, A., & Reed, L. (2015). Contributions of diverse media to self-sexualization among undergraduate women and men. *Sex Roles, 74*(1), 12–23. doi:1007/s11199-015-0548-z

Warner, D. F., & Brown, T. H. (2011). Understanding how race/ethnicity and gender define age-trajectories of disability: An intersectionality approach. *Social Science & Medicine, 72*(8), 1236–1248.

Warren, M. P. (1983). Physical and biological aspects of puberty. In J. Brooks-Gunn & A. C. Petersen (Eds.), *Girls at puberty* (pp. 3–28). New York: Plenum.

Warshaw, C. (2001). Women and violence. In N. L. Stotland & D. E. Stewart (Eds.), *Psychological aspects of women's health care* (2nd ed., pp. 477–548). Washington, DC: American Psychiatric Press.

Wassersug, R., Gray, R. E., Barbara, A., Trosztmer, C., Raj, R., & Sinding, C. (2007). Experiences of transwomen with hormone therapy. *Sexualities, 10,* 101–122.

Watson, L. B., Ancis, J. R., White, D. N., & Nazari, N. (2013). Racial identity buffers African American women from body image problems and disordered eating. *Psychology of Women Quarterly, 37*(3), 337–350. doi:10.1177/036168 4312474799

Watson, L. B., Robinson, D., Dispenza, F., & Nazari, N. (2012). African American women's sexual objectification experiences: A qualitative study. *Psychology of Women Quarterly, 36*(4), 458–475. doi:10.1177/036168431 2454724

Watts, B. (1996). Legal issues. In M. A. Paludi (Ed.), *Sexual harassment on college campuses: Abusing the ivory power* (pp. 9–24). Albany, NY: State University of New York Press.

Weatherall, A., & Walton, M. (1999). The metaphorical construction of sexual experience in a speech community of New Zealand university students. *British Journal of Social Psychology, 38,* 479–498.

Webb, J. (2016, March 31). *Women are still paid less than men, even in the same job. Forbes.* Retrieved from http://www.forbes.com/sites/jwebb/2016/03/31/women-are-still-paid-less-than-men-even-in-the-same-job/#1f1554e716ee

Weber, J. C. (1996). Social class as a correlate of gender identity among lesbian women. *Sex Roles, 35,* 271–280.

Weisgram, E. S., Dinella, L. M., & Fulcher, M. (2011). The role of masculinity/femininity, values, and occupational value affordances in shaping young men's and women's occupational choices. *Sex Roles, 65*(3–4), 243–258.

Weisgram, E. S., Fulcher, M., & Dinella, L. M. (2014). Pink gives girls permission: Exploring the roles of explicit gender labels and gender-typed colors on preschool children's toy preferences. *Journal of Applied Developmental Psychology, 35*(5), 401–409. doi:10.1016/j.appdev.2014.06.004

Weiss, K. G. (2009). "Boys will be boys" and other gendered accounts: An exploration of victims' excuses and justifications for unwanted sexual contact and coercion. *Violence Against Women, 15,* 810–834.

Weisstein, N. (1968). *Kinder, Kirche, Kuche as scientific law: Psychology constructs the female.* Boston: New England Free Press.

Weitz, R., & Gordon, L. (1993). Images of black women among Anglo students. *Sex Roles, 28,* 19–34.

Weitzman, L. J. (1979). *Sex role socialization.* Palo Alto, CA: Mayfield.

Welter, B. (1966). The cult of True Womanhood: 1820–1860. *American Quarterly, 18,* 151–174.

Wendorf, C. A., Lucas, T., Imamoğlu, E. O., Weisfeld, C. C., & Weisfeld, G. E. (2011). Marital satisfaction across three cultures: Does the number of children have an impact after accounting for other marital demographics? *Journal of Cross-Cultural Psychology, 42*(3), 340–354. doi:10.1177/0022022110362637

Wentland, J. J., & Reissing, E. (2014). Casual sexual relationships: Identifying definitions for one night stands, booty calls, fuck buddies, and friends with benefits. *Canadian Journal of Human Sexuality, 23*(3), 167–177. doi:10.3138/cjhs.2744

Werner, P. D., & LaRussa, G. W. (1985). Persistence and change in sex-role stereotypes. *Sex Roles, 12,* 1089–1100.

West, C. M. (2008). Mammy, Jezebel, and Sapphire: Developing an "oppositional gaze" toward the images of black women. In J. C. Chrisler, C. Golden, & P. D. Rozee (Eds.), *Lectures on the psychology of women* (4th ed., pp. 236–252). Boston: McGraw-Hill.

West, C., & Zimmerman, D. H. (1987). Doing gender. *Gender & Society, 1,* 125–151.

Weston, R., Temple, J. R., & Marshall, L. L. (2005). Gender symmetry and asymmetry in violent relationships: Patterns of mutuality among racially diverse women. *Sex Roles, 52,* 553–571.

Whitam, F., Diamond, M., & Martin, J. (1993). Homosexual orientation in twins: A report on 61 pairs and three triplet sets. *Archives of Sexual Behavior, 22,* 187–206.

Whitbourne, S. (1986). *The me I know: A study of adult identity.* New York: Springer-Verlag.

White, J. W., Bondurant, B., & Donat, P. L. N. (2004). Violence against women. In M. Crawford & R. Unger (Eds.), *Women and gender: A feminist psychology* (pp. 439–475). New York: McGraw-Hill.

White, J. W., Bondurant, B., & Travis, C. B. (2000). Social constructions of sexuality. In C. B. Travis & J. W. White (Eds.), *Sexuality, society and feminism: Psychological perspectives on women* (pp. 11–33). Washington, DC: American Psychological Association.

White, J. W., Donat, P. L. N., & Bondurant, B. (2001). A developmental examination of violence against girls and women. In R. K. Unger (Ed.), *Handbook of the psychology of women and gender* (pp. 343–357). New York: Wiley.

White, J. W., & Koss, M. P. (1993). Adolescent sexual aggression within heterosexual relationships: Prevalence, characteristics, and causes. In H. E. Barbarbee, W. L. Marshall, & D. R. Laws (Eds.), *The juvenile sexual offender* (pp. 182–202). New York: Guilford.

White Hughto, J. M., Biello, K. B., Reisner, S. L., Perez-Brumer, A., Helfin, K. J., & Mimiaga, M. J. (2016). Health risk behaviors in a representative sample of bisexual and heterosexual female high school students in Massachusetts. *Journal of School Health, 86*(1). doi:10.1111/josh.12353

Whitman, T. L., Borkowski, J. G., Keogh, D. A., & Weed, K. (2001). *Interwoven lives: Adolescent mothers and their children.* Mahwah, NJ: Erlbaum.

Widiger, T. A., & Anderson, K. G. (2003). Personality and depression in women. *Journal of Affective Disorders, 74,* 59–66.

Wieczner, J. (2013, June 5). Drug companies look to profit from DSM-5. *Market Watch.* Retrieved from http://www.marketwatch.com/story/new-psych-manual-could-create-drug-windfalls-2013-06-05

Wight, R. G., LeBlanc, A. J., & Badgett, M. V. L. (2013). Same-sex legal marriage and psychological well-being: Findings from the California health interview survey. *American Journal of Public Health, 103*(2), 339–346.

Wiik, K. A., Keizer, R., & Lappegård, T. (2012). Relationship quality in marital and cohabiting unions across Europe. *Journal of Marriage and Family, 74*(3), 389–398.

Willoughby, T., Adachi, P. J. C., & Good, M. (2012). A longitudinal study of the association between violent video game play and aggression among adolescents. *Developmental Psychology, 48*(4), 1044–1057. doi:10.1037/a0026046

Wilkens, J. (2015). Loneliness and belongingness in older lesbians: The role of social groups as "community." *Journal of Lesbian Studies, 19*(1), 90–101.

Wilkinson, S. (1997). Feminist psychology. In D. Fox & I. Prilleltensky (Eds.), *Critical psychology: An introduction* (pp. 247–264). London: Sage.

Williams, B. R., Sawyer, P., & Allman, R. M. (2012). Wearing the garment of widowhood: Variations in time since spousal loss among community-dwelling older adults. *Journal of Women & Aging, 24*(2), 126–139.

Williams, C. (2014). Transgender. *TSQ: Transgender Studies Quarterly, 1*(1–2): 232–234; doi:10.1215/23289252-2400136

Williams, C. L. (2013). The glass escalator, revisited: Gender inequality in neoliberal times, SWS feminist lecturer. *Gender & Society, 27*(5), 609–629. doi:10.1177/089124 3213490232

Williams, J. E., & Best, D. L. (1990). *Measuring sex stereotypes: A multination study.* Newbury Park, CA: Sage.

Williams, L. S. (1992). Biology or society? Parenthood motivation in a sample of Canadian women seeking in vitro fertilization. In H. B. Holmes (Ed.), *Issues in reproductive technology* (pp. 261–274). New York: Garland.

Williams, M. J., & Tiedens, L. Z. (2016). The subtle suspension of backlash: A meta-analysis of penalties for women's implicit and explicit dominance behavior. *Psychological Bulletin, 142*(2), 165–197.

Williams, W. L. (1987). Women, men, and others: Beyond ethnocentrism in gender theory. *American Behavioral Scientist, 31*, 135–141.

Willoughby, B. J., & Carroll, J. S. (2012). Correlates of attitudes toward cohabitation: Looking at the associations with demographics, relational attitudes, and dating behavior. *Journal of Family Issues, 33*(11), 1450–1476. doi:10.1177/0192513X11429666

Winston, A. (Ed.). (2003). *Defining difference: Race and racism in the history of psychology.* Washington, DC: American Psychological Association.

Witkin, H. A., Mednick, S. A., Schulsinger, F., Bakke-Strom, E., Christiansen, K. O., Goodenough, D. R., . . . Stocking, M. (1976). Criminality in XXY and XYY men. *Science, 193,* 547–555.

Wizemann, T. M., & Pardue, M. (Eds.). (2001). *Exploring the biological contribution to human health: Does sex matter?* Washington, DC: National Academy Press.

Wolff, G. E., Crosby, R. D., Roberts, J. A., & Wittrock, D. A. (2000). Differences in daily stress, mood, coping, and eating behavior in binge eating and nonbinge eating college women. *Addictive Behaviors, 25,* 205–216. doi:10.1016/s0306-4603(99)00049-0

Woloshin, S., Schwartz, L. M., Tremmel, J., & Welch, H. G. (2001). Direct-to-consumer advertisements for prescription drugs: What are Americans being sold? *The Lancet, 358,* 1141–1146.

Women's Health Initiative Steering Committee. (2004). Effects of conjugated equine estrogen in postmenopausal women with hysterectomy: The women's health initiative randomized controlled trial. *Journal of the American Medical Association, 291,* 1701–1712.

Women's Media Center (2015). *The status of women in the U.S. media.* Retrieved from womensmediacenter.com.

Wong, W. I., & Hines, M. (2015a). Effects of gender color-coding on toddlers' gender-typical toy play. *Archives of Sexual Behavior, 44*(5), 1233–1242. doi:10.1007/s10508-014-0400-5

Wong, W. I., & Hines, M. (2015b). Preferences for pink and blue: The development of color preferences as a distinct gender-typed behavior in toddlers. *Archives of Sexual Behavior, 44*(5), 1243–1254. doi:10.1007/s10508-015-0489-1

Woodhams, C., Lupton, B., & Cowling, M. (2015). The presence of ethnic minority and disabled men in feminised work: Intersectionality, vertical segregation and the glass escalator. *Sex Roles, 72*(7–8), 277–293.

Wooldredge, J., & Thistlewaite, A. (2002). Reconsidering domestic violence recidivism: Conditioned effects of legal controls by individual and aggregate levels of stake in conformity. *Journal of Quantitative Criminology, 18,* 45–70.

Wooley, H. T. (1910). Psychological literature: A review of the recent literature on the psychology of sex. *Psychological Bulletin, 7,* 335–342.

Worell, J., & Johnson, D. (2001). Therapy with women: Feminist frameworks. In R. K. Unger (Ed.), *Handbook of the psychology of women and gender* (pp. 317–329). New York: John Wiley & Sons.

Worell, J., & Remer, P. (2003). *Feminist perspectives in therapy: Empowering diverse women* (2nd ed.). New York: John Wiley & Sons.

Wylie, P. (1942). *A generation of vipers.* New York: Farrar & Rinehart.

Worell, J. (2001). Feminist interventions: Accountability beyond symptom reduction. *Psychology of Women Quarterly, 25,* 335–343.

World Economic Forum. (2015). *The global gender gap report.* Retrieved from www.weforum.org

World Health Organization. (2012). Understanding and addressing violence against women: Intimate Partner Violence. Retrieved from http://apps.who.int/iris/bitstream/10665/77432/1/WHO_RHR_12.36_eng.pdf

World Health Organization. (2013). *Global and regional estimates of violence against women: Prevalence and health effects of intimate partner violence and non-partner sexual violence.* Geneva: World Health Organization. Retrieved from http://apps.who.int/iris/bitstream/10665/85239/1/9789241564625_eng.pdf

Wright, P. J., & Tokunaga, R. S. (2016). Men's objectifying media consumption, objectification of women, and attitudes supportive of violence against women. *Archives of Sexual Behavior, 45*(4), 955–964.

Wright, P. J., Tokunaga, R. S., & Kraus, A. (2016). A meta-analysis of pornography consumption and actual acts of sexual aggression in general population studies. *Journal of Communication, 66*(1), 183–205. doi:10.1111/jcom.12201

Wurtele, S. K. (2002). School-based child sexual abuse prevention. In P. A. Schewe (Ed.), *Preventing violence in relationships: Interventions across the life span* (pp. 9–25). Washington, DC: American Psychological Association.

Xu, X., & Lai, S. C. (2002). Resources, gender ideologies, and marital power: The case of Taiwan. *Journal of Family Issues, 23,* 209–245.

Yoder, J. D. (2002). Context matters: Understanding tokenism processes and their impact on women's work. *Psychology of Women Quarterly, 26,* 1–8.

Yoder, J. D. (2015). Looking backward and moving forward: Our feminist imperative to do work that matters. *Psychology of Women Quarterly, 39*(4), 427–431. doi:10.1177/0361684315601861

Yoder, J. D., Adams, J., Grove, S., & Priest, R. F. (1985). To teach is to learn: Overcoming tokenism with mentors. *Psychology of Women Quarterly, 9,* 119–132.

Yoder, J. D., Schleicher, T. L., & McDonald, T. W. (1998). Empowering token women leaders: The importance of organizationally legitimated credibility. *Psychology of Women Quarterly, 22,* 209–222.

Yoder, J. D., Tobias, A., & Snell, A. F. (2011). When declaring "I am a feminist" matters: Labeling is linked to activism. *Sex Roles, 64*(1–2), 9–18. doi:10.1007/s11199-010-9890-3

Youngquist, J. (2008). The effect of gender and interruptions on perceptions of interpersonal dominance. *Dissertation abstracts international section A: Humanities and social sciences, Vol 68*(8-A), 3217.

Yousafzai, M., & Lamb, C. (2013). *I am Malala: The girl who stood up for education and was shot by the Taliban.* Boston: Little, Brown and Company.

Zanna, M. P., & Pack, S. J. (1975). On the self-fulfilling nature of apparent sex differences in behavior. *Journal of Experimental Social Psychology, 11,* 583–591.

Zell, E., Krizan, Z., & Teeter, S. R. (2015). Evaluating gender similarities and differences using metasynthesis. *American Psychologist, 70*(1), 10–20. doi:10.1037/a0038208

Zelnik, M., Kanter, J. F., & Ford, K. (1981). *Sex and pregnancy in adolescence.* Beverly Hills, CA: Sage.

Zentner, M., & Eagly, A. H. (2015). A sociocultural framework for understanding partner preferences of women and men: Integration of concepts and evidence. *European Review of Social Psychology, 26*(1), 328–373.

Zentner, M., & Mitura, K. (2012). Stepping out of the caveman's shadow: Nations' gender gap predicts degree of sex differentiation in mate preferences. *Psychological Science, 23*(10), 1176–1185.

Zernike, K. (1999, March 21). MIT women win a fight against bias. *The Boston Globe,* pp. F1, F4.

Zimmerman, D. H., & West, C. (1975). Sex roles, interruptions, and silences in conversation. In B. Thorne & N. Henley (Eds.), *Language and sex: Difference and dominance* (pp. 105–129). Rowley, MA: Newbury House.

Zosuls, K. M., Martin, C. L., Ruble, D. N., Miller, C. F., Gaertner, B. M., England, D. E., & Hill, A. P. (2011). 'It's not that we hate you': Understanding children's gender attitudes and expectancies about peer relationships.

British Journal of Developmental Psychology, 29(2), 288–304. doi:10.1111/j.2044–835X.2010.02023.x

Zosuls, K. M., Ruble, D. N., Tamis-LeMonda, C. S., Shrout, P. E., Bornstein, M. H., & Greulich, F. K. (2009). The acquisition of gender labels in infancy: Implications for gender-typed play. *Developmental Psychology, 45*(3), 688–701. doi:10.1037/a0014053

Zucker, A. N., Ostrove, J. M., & Stewart, A. J. (2002). College-educated women's personality development in adulthood: Perceptions and age differences. *Psychology and Aging, 17,* 236–244.

Zucker, K. (2001). Biological influences on psychosexual differentiation. In R. K. Unger (Ed.), *Handbook of the psychology of women and gender* (pp. 101–115), New York: Wiley.

Zuckerman, M., & Kieffer, S. C. (1994). Race differences in faceism: Does facial prominence imply dominance? *Journal of Personality and Social Psychology, 66,* 86–92.

Zurbriggen, E. L., & Morgan, E. M. (2006). Who wants to marry a millionaire? Reality dating television programs, attitudes toward sex, and sexual behaviors. *Sex Roles, 54,* 1–17.

Name Index

Subject Index

❦